"A stunning achievement. Lawrence Feingold's up-to-date study of the Eucharist is truly comprehensive, taking the reader from the book of Genesis through the Upper Room and all the way to Pope Francis. The result is a biblical, patristic, medieval, modern, and thoroughly Catholic study of the sacrament that is the 'source and summit of the Christian life.' And all this in clear and accessible prose! This work will be essential reading for anyone interested in Eucharistic theology for decades to come."

—BRANT PITRE
Professor of Sacred Scripture, Notre Dame Seminary

"Dr. Feingold has written a masterful summary of the Catholic theology of the Eucharist that integrates scriptural and patristic foundations with scholastic and magisterial teachings on Eucharistic presence, the Mass as sacrifice, the participation of the faithful in the sacrifice of the Mass, the fruits of the Eucharist, adoration of the Eucharist, and contemporary canonical–pastoral questions regarding the worthy reception of Holy Communion. Drawing upon St. Thomas Aquinas and other eminent theologians, Dr. Feingold provides a treatment of the Holy Eucharist that is ideal for Catholic university and seminary classes on 'the most august sacrament.'"

—ROBERT L. FASTIGGI
Professor of Systematic Theology, Sacred Heart Major Seminary

"In addition to being a Catholic theologian of the highest rank, Professor Lawrence Feingold is also one of the very finest teachers in the Catholic academy today. Like his intellectual and spiritual master, St. Thomas Aquinas, Feingold not only sees deeply into Catholic truth, he also unlocks for his students the wise order by which the faith is most fully intelligible. This book on the Eucharist showcases Professor Feingold at the height of his theological *and* pedagogical powers. Professors of sacramental theology now have a resource that is sure to enrich their courses—and the spiritual lives of their students."

—ROGER W. NUTT
Associate Professor of Theology and Director of the
MA Program in Theology, Ave Maria University

— THE —
EUCHARIST

— THE —
EUCHARIST

Mystery of Presence, Sacrifice, and Communion

LAWRENCE FEINGOLD

EMMAUS
ACADEMIC

www.emmausacademic.com
Steubenville, Ohio

EMMAUS
A C A D E M I C

Steubenville, Ohio
www.emmausacademic.com
A Division of The St. Paul Center for Biblical Theology
Editor-in-Chief: Scott Hahn
1468 Parkview Circle
Steubenville, Ohio 43952

Library of Congress Cataloging-in-Publication Data
Names: Feingold, Lawrence, author.
Title: The Eucharist : mystery of presence, sacrifice, and communion /
  Lawrence Feingold.
Description: Steubenville : Emmaus Academic, 2018. | Includes bibliographical
  references.
Identifiers: LCCN 2017037498 (print) | LCCN 2017039059 (ebook) | ISBN
  9781945125744 (ebook) | ISBN 9781945125720 (hardcover) | ISBN
  9781945125737 (pbk.)
Subjects: LCSH: Lord's Supper--Catholic Church.
Classification: LCC BX2215.3 (ebook) | LCC BX2215.3 .F45 2017 (print) | DDC
  234/.163--dc23
LC record available at https://lccn.loc.gov/2017037498

Imprimatur: In accordance with CIC 827, permission to publish has been granted on October 18, 2017, by the Most Reverend Mark S. Rivituso, Auxiliary Bishop, Archdiocese of St. Louis. Permission to publish is an indication that nothing contrary to Church teaching is contained in this work. It does not imply any endorsement of the opinions expressed in the publication; nor is any liability assumed by this permission.

Cover image: *The Last Supper* (1481–1482), Cosimo Rosselli, Sistine Chapel, Vatican City

Cover design and layout by Margaret Ryland

Contents

Abbreviations xxiii

Introduction xxvii

Structure of the Work xxx

Part I: Foundations 1

Chapter One: Why Did Christ Institute the Eucharist? 3

Reasons of Fittingness for the Eucharist 3

Sacrament of Spiritual Nourishment 3

Sacrament of Charity 5

Presence 6

Sacrificial Love 7

Intimate Union 8

Three Ends of the Eucharist 8

Christ Instituted the Eucharist for the Same Reasons That He Became Man 10

1. Presence 12

Divine Condescension Wishing to Dwell with Us 12

Teaching Perfect Virtue 14

The Merit of Faith 16

2. Sacrifice 18

Expiatory Sacrifice of Atonement 18

Full Revelation of the Divine Love 19

3. Communion 20

Divinization of Man 20

The Eucharist Is the Principal Means of Divinization 23

Dignity of Man 26

The Eucharist Is the Nuptials of the Lamb with His Church 27

The Eucharist and the Giving of the Holy Spirit 28

Mary and the Eucharist 29

The Eucharist Was Instituted to Be
   the Summit of the Sacramental Economy 31

Uniqueness of the Eucharist Compared with
   the Other Sacraments 34

The Eucharist and the New Covenant 36

The Eucharist and the Mysteries of Christ 36

Study Questions 38

Suggestions for Further Reading 38

Chapter Two: The Eucharist Prefigured
in the Old Testament 39

Figure of the Real Presence of
   Christ in the Eucharist: The SHEKHINAH 40

Figures of the Sacrifice of the Eucharist 45

Priesthood and Sacrifice before the Mosaic Law 46

Priesthood and Sacrifice in the Law of Moses 49

Different Kinds of Old Testament Sacrifice 49

Solemnity and Quantity of Sacrifice in the Temple 52

The Passover 55

Sealing of the Old Covenant 57

Figures of the Eucharist as Spiritual Nourishment
   under the Sacramental Signs of Bread and Wine 58

Manna 58

The Offering of Melchizedek 62

The Bread of the Presence 63

Unleavened Bread of the Passover
   and the Four Cups of Wine 66

The Tree of Life 67

Yearning of the Prophets for Union with God 68

Unity of Presence, Sacrifice, and Spiritual Nourishment 68

Study Questions 69

Suggestions for Further Reading 69

Chapter Three: The Eucharist
in the New Testament 71

The Bread of Life Discourse in John 6 71

Four Accounts of the Institution of the Eucharist 81

Synopsis of the Accounts of the Last Supper	83
Preparation for the Last Supper	83
Betrayal of Judas Announced	84
Announcement That Jesus Would Not Eat Another Passover	85
The Institution Narrative	85
The Setting: Preparing the Passover	86
Why Did Christ Choose the Last Supper as the Time to Institute the Eucharist?	89
The Date of the Last Supper according to John	90
Four Positions on the Date of the Last Supper in John and the Synoptics	93
Synoptic Hypothesis	93
Johannine Hypothesis	94
Essene Calendar Hypothesis	96
Passover Hypothesis	99
Significance of the Passover as the Setting for the Last Supper	103
The Passover Seder Described in Luke's Account	104
SACRIFICIAL CONNOTATIONS OF THE WORDS OF INSTITUTION	106
"My Body Given for You"	107
"Do This in Remembrance of Me"	108
Blood Poured Out for the Forgiveness of Sins	111
Blood of the Covenant / New Covenant in My Blood	114
Christ's Knowledge of His Sacrifice	117
OTHER REFERENCES TO THE EUCHARIST IN THE NEW TESTAMENT	117
1 Corinthians 11:23–32	117
1 Corinthians 5:6–8 and 10:16–21	118
The Eucharist in Luke 24 and the Acts of the Apostles	120
Hebrews	122
Revelation	123
STUDY QUESTIONS	127
SUGGESTIONS FOR FURTHER READING	128

CHAPTER FOUR: THE EUCHARIST ACCORDING
TO THE FATHERS OF THE CHURCH — 129

THE *DIDACHE* — 129

ST. IGNATIUS OF ANTIOCH — 133
  The Real Presence — 133
  Sacrament of Ecclesial Unity — 134

ST. JUSTIN MARTYR — 135
  Description of the Liturgy of the Eucharist — 135
  The Real Presence — 137
  Substantial Conversion — 138
  The Mass Is a Sacrifice — 139

ST. IRENAEUS — 140
  Real Presence and Eucharistic Conversion — 140
  Spiritual Nourishment — 141
  New Oblation of the New Covenant — 143

THE EUCHARISTIC PRAYER OF THE *APOSTOLIC TRADITION* — 144

ST. CYPRIAN — 147

ST. ATHANASIUS — 149

ST. CYRIL OF JERUSALEM — 150

ST. HILARY OF POITIERS — 152

ST. AMBROSE — 153
  The Real Presence and the Eucharistic Conversion — 153
  The Eucharistic Sacrifice — 156
  Description of the Canon — 156

ST. AUGUSTINE — 157

ST. GREGORY NAZIANZEN AND ST. GREGORY OF NYSSA — 162

ST. JOHN CHRYSOSTOM — 163

THEODORE OF MOPSUESTIA — 168

ST. CYRIL OF ALEXANDRIA — 170

ST. LEO THE GREAT — 172

ST. GREGORY THE GREAT — 173

ST. JOHN DAMASCENE — 174

CONCLUSION — 175

Study Questions 176

Suggestions for Further Reading 177

Chapter Five: Essential Elements of the Eucharist 179

Three Levels in the Eucharist:
Outward Sign, Inward Reality and Sign,
and the Reality of Grace 179

Sacramental Signs as Instruments of Christ 184

The Sacraments Are Instrumental Causes 184

External and Conjoined Instruments 188

Matter of the Eucharist 190

Matter and Form in the Sacraments 190

Fittingness of Bread and Wine 192

Wheat Bread 194

Bread Is Unleavened in the Latin Rite 195

Wine of the Grape 196

Mixture of Water with the Wine 196

The Eucharist Must Be Consecrated under Both Species 198

The Essential Form of the Eucharist 199

Patristic Witness on the Words of Consecration 201

St. Thomas on the Form of the Eucharist 203

Magisterial Teaching on the Essential
Form of the Eucharist 205

The Epiclesis and the Words of the Institution Narrative 208

The Anaphora of Addai and Mari 212

How Can a Eucharistic Prayer Be Valid
without the Words of Institution? 217

Did the Anaphora of Addai and Mari
Ever Have an Institution Narrative? 219

Hypothesis That the Institution Narrative
Is a Later Development 222

Minister of the Eucharist 225

Luther on the Minister of the Eucharist 225

Study Questions 228

Suggestions for Further Reading 228

Part II: The Real Presence and Transubstantiation   231

Chapter Six: The Berengarian Controversy and Development of Eucharistic Theology   233

St. Paschasius Radbertus   233

Berengarius of Tours   238

Consequences of the Berengarian Controversy for Eucharistic Theology   243

Substantial Conversion   244

Arguments for Substantial Conversion from Scripture and Tradition   245

Distinction of Substance and Accidents   246

Miraculous and Unique Conversion   247

Transubstantiation   249

Christ Remains Whole and Entire   250

Concomitance   252

Res et Sacramentum: Three Levels in the Eucharist   254

Fruits of the Controversy   257

Study Questions   257

Suggestions for Further Reading   258

Chapter Seven: The Doctrine of Transubstantiation according to St. Thomas   259

The Distinction between Substance and Accidents   259

The Eucharistic Conversion: Transubstantiation   261

Presence through Conversion or Local Movement?   261

Transubstantiation Is Not Annihilation   267

The Substantial Conversion Is Instantaneous   268

The Appearances of Bread and Wine Remain   268

Transubstantiation Is above Reason but Not against Reason   273

Comparison between Transubstantiation, Natural Change, and Creation   276

Sacramental Mode of Christ's Presence   278

The Whole Christ Is Present under Each Part of the Sacred Species   279

Christ Is Not Present in the Mode of Quantity   281

Concomitance   282

The Accidents of Christ's Body Are
Made Present by Concomitance   285

The Cessation of Christ's Presence When
the Sacred Species Are Corrupted   288

Transubstantiation Does Not Imply
Any Change in Christ   290

STUDY QUESTIONS   291

SUGGESTIONS FOR FURTHER READING   292

CHAPTER EIGHT: TRANSUBSTANTIATION IN DISPUTE:
THE REFORMATION AND ITS LEGACY   293

PROTESTANT VIEWS ON THE PRESENCE OF
CHRIST IN THE EUCHARIST   293

Martin Luther's Position on the Real Presence   293

Huldrych Zwingli   300

John Calvin   303

Anglican View   306

THE COUNCIL OF TRENT ON CHRIST'S PRESENCE
IN THE EUCHARIST   308

Summary of the Principal Truths on the
Real Presence Defined by the Council of Trent   312

JANSENISM   313

TWENTIETH-CENTURY CHALLENGE TO
TRANSUBSTANTIATION: "TRANSSIGNIFICATION"   314

STUDY QUESTIONS   319

SUGGESTIONS FOR FURTHER READING   320

PART III: SACRIFICE   321

CHAPTER NINE: THE SACRIFICE OF THE MASS   323

SACRIFICE IS A FUNDAMENTAL ACT OF RELIGION   323

Sacrifice and Oblation   327

The Offering of Sacrifice to God Belongs to Natural Law   329

The Priesthood, Mediation, and Sacrifice   331

THE SACRIFICE OF CALVARY   332

THE SACRIFICE OF THE CHURCH   335

   Trinitarian Dimension of the Sacrifice
      of Calvary and the Mass   337

THEOLOGICAL REFLECTION ON
   THE SACRIFICE OF THE MASS   339

   The Fathers and Medieval Theologians
      on the Sacrifice of the Mass   339

   St. Thomas on the Sacrifice of the Mass   343

      The Mass Is the "Representative Image" of the Passion   343

      The Sacrifice of the Mass Applies the Effects of the Passion   348

   Cardinal Cajetan on the Sacrifice of the Mass   351

   The Council of Trent on the Sacrifice of the Mass   353

   Post-Tridentine Catholic Theories on
      What Constitutes the Sacrifice of the Mass   355

   Mediator Dei on the Sacrifice of the Mass   361

   Three Levels of the Eucharistic Sacrifice   364

   Christ's Sacrifice Transcends Time   366

   The Mass Makes Present the Whole of the
      Paschal Mystery: Death, Resurrection, and Ascension   370

   STUDY QUESTIONS   372

   SUGGESTIONS FOR FURTHER READING   373

CHAPTER TEN: OBJECTIONS TO THE
SACRIFICIAL NATURE OF THE MASS   375

   OBJECTIONS OF LUTHER AND CALVIN TO
   THE SACRIFICE OF THE MASS   376

   Argument from the Definition of a
      Sacrament and the Rejection of "Works"   376

   Argument from the Eucharist as Christ's Testament   381

   Objection That the Eucharist Is a Banquet
      Rather Than a Sacrifice   383

   Argument That the Mass as Sacrifice
      Implies an Angry God in Need of Appeasement   387

   Objection That the Sacrifice of the Mass Implies
      That Christ Would Be Killed Again in Every Mass   388

   Objection That the Sacrifice of the Mass
      Would Detract from Calvary   390

Reactions against the Sacrificial Nature
of the Mass in Theology of the Last Century   393

Is the Mass a Banquet Rather Than a Sacrifice?   393

Has Christ Done Away with Cultic Sacrifice?   395

Is the Sacrificial Aspect of the Mass a
Later Development?   399

Study Questions   403

Suggestions for Further Reading   404

Chapter Eleven: The Participation of the
Faithful in Offering the Sacrifice of the Mass   405

The Common Priesthood of the Faithful   405

Communal Nature of Sacrifice   405

The Common Priesthood of the Faithful in Israel   407

The Common Priesthood of the
Faithful in the New Covenant   408

Spiritual Sacrifices of the Common Priesthood   409

*The Common and the Ministerial
Priesthood according to* Lumen Gentium   414

The Common Priesthood in the Prayers
of the Eucharistic Liturgy   415

*The Sacrifices of the Faithful Are Offered on the Altar
of the Body of Christ*   420

Magisterial Texts on the Common Priesthood
and Active Participation in the Mass   423

Pius XII's *Mediator Dei* on the Participation
of the Faithful in the Mass   423

Active Participation in the Mass according to Vatican II   425

*Active Participation in the Mass and
the New Evangelization*   430

Ars Celebrandi *and Active Participation*   432

Sunday Mass: Obligation and Glory   434

Participation of the Faithful and
Church Architecture   437

The *Domus Ecclesiae*   437

Symbolic Significance of "Orientation" in the Liturgy   438

Study Questions   448

Suggestions for Further Reading   449

CHAPTER TWELVE: FRUITS OF THE SACRIFICE OF THE MASS 451

THE MERITS OF THE SACRIFICE OF CALVARY
ARE APPLIED BY THE MASS   451

FOUR ENDS OF THE SACRIFICE OF THE MASS   454

Sacrifice of Praise   454

Sacrifice of Thanksgiving   455

Sacrifice of Impetration   456

The Mass Is a Propitiatory Sacrifice
Benefitting the Living and the Dead   456

PARTICULAR FRUITS OF THE SACRIFICE OF THE MASS   462

Why Does the Church Celebrate Many Masses
If Every Mass Has Infinite Value?   465

The Logic of Superabundance   469

Martin Luther's Rejection of the Fruits of the Mass   469

The Value of "Private" Masses   470

EUCHARISTIC CONCELEBRATION   472

Concelebration and the Fruits of the Mass   474

Vatican II and Post-Conciliar Magisterial
Texts on Concelebration   481

STUDY QUESTIONS   482

SUGGESTIONS FOR FURTHER READING   483

PART IV: COMMUNION   485

CHAPTER THIRTEEN: EFFECTS OF HOLY COMMUNION   487

COMMUNION AND SACRIFICE   487

EFFECTS OF HOLY COMMUNION   490

Witness of Eucharistic Prayers on
the Graces of Communion   490

Sacramental Grace   491

Sacramental Grace and Docility to God's Inspirations   495

Connection between Sacramental Grace
and the "Inward Reality and Sign"   497

St. Thomas on the Effects of Communion   498

The Eucharist Sanctifies by Substantially
Containing Christ   498

The Eucharist Makes Present Christ's Passion   500

The Eucharist Sanctifies by Way of Spiritual Nourishment 500

The Eucharist Is the Sacrament of Ecclesial Charity 501

Increase of Sanctifying Grace 502

Increase of Charity 503

Increase of Faith, Hope, the Infused Moral Virtues,
and Gifts of the Holy Spirit 505

Communion and the Forgiveness of Sins 506

Holy Communion and Spiritual Consolation 509

Indwelling of the Trinity and Holy Communion 510

Sacrament of Ecclesial Unity 516

Corpus Mysticum *and* Corpus Verum 520

The State of Glory as an Effect of Communion 522

SPIRITUAL COMMUNION 526

Is Spiritual Communion Possible for a
Person in a State of Mortal Sin? 530

STUDY QUESTIONS 532

SUGGESTIONS FOR FURTHER READING 532

CHAPTER FOURTEEN: HOLY COMMUNION PRESUPPOSES
ECCLESIAL COMMUNION, INVISIBLE AND VISIBLE 533

HOLY COMMUNION PRESUPPOSES ECCLESIAL COMMUNION 533

WHY BEING IN A STATE OF GRACE IS A NECESSARY
CONDITION FOR RECEIVING COMMUNION 534

Judas as an Example of Unworthy Communion 537

RECIPIENTS OF HOLY COMMUNION AND UNWORTHY
COMMUNION: CANONS 916 AND 915 OF *THE CODE
OF CANON LAW* 540

Canon 916 540

Canon 915 542

POST-CONCILIAR MAGISTERIUM ON COMMUNION
FOR THE DIVORCED AND CIVILLY REMARRIED 544

John Paul II, *Familiaris Consortio*, §84 544

Pastoral Solicitude for the Divorced and Civilly Remarried 547

Pope Benedict XVI, *Sacramentum Caritatis*, §29 550

Pope Francis, *Amoris Laetitia* 551

INTERCOMMUNION (*COMMUNICATIO IN SACRIS*) 555

STUDY QUESTIONS 558

Suggestions for Further Reading ... 559

Chapter Fifteen: Reception of Holy Communion ... 561

Frequency of Communion ... 561
Early Church ... 561
Medieval Period ... 563
The Sixteenth Century and the Council of Trent ... 565
St. Pius X ... 567
Communion for Children ... 569
Viaticum ... 573
The Reception of Communion ... 574
Communion under Both Species ... 574
Communion in the Hand according to the
Instruction *Memoriale Domini* ... 578
*Reception of Communion according to the
General Instruction of the Roman Missal* ... 581
Extraordinary Ministers of Holy Communion ... 582
Thanksgiving after Communion ... 583
Study Questions ... 585
Suggestions for Further Reading ... 585

Chapter Sixteen: Eucharistic Adoration ... 587

Eucharistic Adoration and the Three
Ends of the Eucharist ... 587
Objections to Eucharistic Adoration and
a Response by Joseph Ratzinger ... 589
Magisterial Texts on Eucharistic Adoration ... 592
Paul VI ... 592
St. John Paul II ... 593
Benedict XVI, *Sacramentum Caritatis* ... 597
Pope Francis on Adoration ... 598
The Tabernacle ... 599
Study Questions ... 601
Suggestions for Further Reading ... 602

Conclusion ... 603

The Eucharist and the Sacred Heart   603

Bibliography   609

    Magisterial Texts   609

    Patristic Sources   612

    Medieval Sources   614

    Reformation and Renaissance Sources   616

    Secondary Sources   617

Index of Subjects and Names   645

Scripture Index   667

✠

To Mary, Mother of the Eucharist,
and to Marsha, my wife, who spent countless hours
editing and improving the text

*O God, who in this wonderful Sacrament
have left us a memorial of your Passion,
grant us, we pray,
so to revere the sacred mysteries of your Body and Blood
that we may always experience in ourselves
the fruits of your redemption.*

—Collect, Feast of Corpus Christi

✠

✷

Abbreviations

MAGISTERIAL SOURCES

AAS   *Acta Apostolicae Sedis*

CCC   *Catechism of the Catholic Church.* 2nd ed. Washington, DC: United States Catholic Conference, 2000.

CCT   *The Roman Catechism.* Translated by Robert I. Bradley and Eugene Kevane. Boston: St. Paul Editions, 1985. This work is also known as the *Catechism of the Council of Trent.*

CIC   *Codex Iuris Canonici: Code of Canon Law.* Latin-English Edition. Washington, DC: Canon Law Society of America, 1998.

DS   Denzinger, Heinrich. *Enchiridion Symbolorum: Compendium of Creeds, Definitions, and Declarations on Matters of Faith and Morals.* 43rd edition. Edited by Peter Hünermann. English edition edited by Robert Fastiggi and Anne Englund Nash. San Francisco: Ignatius Press, 2012.

EE   John Paul II. Encyclical Letter on the Eucharist in Its Relationship to the Church, *Ecclesia de Eucharistia.* April 17, 2003.

RM   *The Roman Missal.* 3rd typical edition. Washington, DC: United States Conference of Catholic Bishops, 2011.

GIRM   *General Instruction of the Roman Missal.* Washington, DC: USCCB, 2011.

English quotations from magisterial documents are taken from the Vatican website (http://w2.vatican.va/content/vatican/en.html) unless otherwise indicated.

Patristic, Medieval, and Reformation Sources

ACW	Ancient Christian Writers series. Westminster, MD: Newman Press, 1946–.
ANF	*The Ante-Nicene Fathers.* Reprinted: Peabody, MA: Hendrickson, 1994.
CCCM	*Corpus Christianorum, Continuatio Mediaevalis.* Turnhout: Brepols, 1966–.
CSEL	*Corpus Scriptorum Ecclesiasticorum Latinorum.* Vienna, Prague, and Leipzig: Tempsky, 1865–.
FC	Fathers of the Church series. New York: CIMA Publishing; Washington, DC: Catholic University of America Press, 1947–.
FCMC	Fathers of the Church, Mediaeval Continuation. Washington, DC: Catholic University of America Press.
LW	*Luther's Works.* Edited by Jaroslav Pelikan. 55 vols. Philadelphia, PA, and St. Louis, MO: Fortress Press and Concordia, 1955–1986.
*NPNF*1	*Nicene and Post-Nicene Fathers*, 1st series. Reprint, Peabody, MA: Hendrickson Publishers, 1994.
*NPNF*2	*Nicene and Post-Nicene Fathers*, 2nd series. Reprint, Peabody, MA: Hendrickson Publishers, 1994.
PEER	*Prayers of the Eucharist: Early and Reformed.* Edited by R. C. D. Jasper and G. J. Cuming. 3rd ed. Collegeville, MN: Liturgical Press, 1987.
PG	*Patrologiae Cursus Completus: Series Graeca.* Edited by J. P. Migne. Paris, 1856–1867.
PL	*Patrologiae Cursus Completus: Series Latina.* Edited by J. P. Migne. Paris, 1844–1865.
Sentences IV	Peter Lombard. *The Sentences. Book 4: On the Doctrine of Signs.* Translated by Giulio Silano. Mediaeval Sources in Translation 48. Toronto, CN: Pontifical Institute of Mediaeval Studies, 2010.
ST	*Summa Theologica of St. Thomas Aquinas.* 2nd ed. Translated by Fathers of the English Dominican Province. London: Burns, Oates, & Washbourne, 1920–1932.
SCG	*Summa Contra Gentiles.* Translated by Anton Pegis, James Anderson, Vernon Bourke, and Charles O'Neil. 4 vols. Notre Dame, IN: University of Notre Dame Press, 1975.

In [I–IV] *Sent.* Thomas Aquinas. *Scriptum super libros Sententiarum Magistri Petri Lombardi Episcopi Parisiensis.* Edited by M. F. Moos Mandonnet. 4 vols. Paris: P. Lethielleux, 1929–1947.

WSA The Works of Saint Augustine: A Translation for the 21st Century series.

a.:	article
ad:	response to an objection
bk.:	book or *liber*
ch.:	chapter or *capitulum*
d.:	distinction
lec.:	*lectio* (a section in a commentary)
no.:	paragraph number
obj.:	objection
q.:	question
qla.:	*quaestiuncula* (little question; used in St. Thomas's commentary on the *Sentences*)
§:	Section number in magisterial documents, such as papal encyclicals and *CCC*
sc	*sed contra* ("but on the contrary," a section within articles of *ST*)

Translations of texts from Latin editions are mine unless otherwise noted, with the exception of those from works in the abbreviations list above, which will be from the English translation editions stated there unless other sources are given.

OTHER ABBREVIATIONS

TL Ratzinger, Joseph. *Theology of the Liturgy: The Sacramental Foundation of Christian Existence.* Collected Works, vol. 11. Edited by Michael Miller. Translated by John Saward, Kenneth Baker, Henry Taylor, et al. San Francisco: Ignatius Press, 2014.

✠

Introduction

What is the Eucharist? After the Incarnation and Paschal mystery—which indeed are made present in the Eucharist—it is the greatest conceivable gift of God to man in this state of exile. It is literally heaven on earth. At the beginning of his papacy, in *Dominicae Cenae* of 1980, St. John Paul II wrote:

> We cannot, even for a moment, forget that the Eucharist is a special possession belonging to the whole Church. It is the greatest gift in the order of grace and of sacrament that the divine Spouse has offered and unceasingly offers to His spouse. . . . We should remain faithful in every detail to what it expresses in itself and to what it asks of us, namely, thanksgiving.[1]

Twenty-three years later, in his encyclical *Ecclesia de Eucharistia* (2003), he wrote:

> Today I take up anew the thread of that argument [from *Dominicae Cenae*], with even greater emotion and gratitude in my heart, echoing as it were the word of the Psalmist: "What shall I render to the Lord for all his bounty to me? I will lift up the cup of salvation and call on the name of the Lord" (Ps 116:12–13).[2]

---

[1] John Paul II, Apostolic Letter on the Mystery and Worship of the Eucharist, *Dominicae Cenae* (1980), §12.

[2] John Paul II, *EE*, §9.

He also said: "Holy Mass is the absolute center of my life and of every day of my life."[3] After his election to the pontificate, Benedict XVI quoted this and made it his own in his address to the clergy of Rome on May 13, 2005 in the Basilica of St. John Lateran.

In *Ecclesia de Eucharistia*, §9, St. John Paul II goes even further, writing: "The Eucharist, as Christ's saving presence in the community of the faithful and its spiritual food, is the most precious possession which the Church *can* have in her journey through history."[4] This is a very strong statement. St. John Paul does not say only that the Eucharist *is* the greatest gift that Christ has in fact given us. He says that it is the greatest gift that He *can* give the Church in this period of her earthly pilgrimage.

God can always make better gifts of nature and creation, giving us better bodies and a better physical world. No matter what He gives us in created gifts, His wisdom and omnipotence could always make something better. But His omnipotence and wisdom *cannot* give us a greater gift than the Eucharist. Why not? Because in the Eucharist Christ is giving us *Himself*, whole and entire, as a gift, and God has nothing better to give than Himself. The Eucharist is Christ's complete gift of self to His Church, His Bride. It is the "greatest gift" of God to man because, in this sacrament, Christ the Word Incarnate becomes present in His full personal reality throughout the life of the Church. Furthermore, He makes Himself present as the Victim of Calvary, offered by Himself as High Priest, mystically immolated through the ministry of His ordained priests, and given to us to be consumed as our spiritual nourishment.

The Second Vatican Council teaches that "The most holy Eucharist contains the Church's entire spiritual wealth: Christ himself, our Passover and living bread. Through his own flesh, now made living and life-giving by the Holy Spirit, he offers life to men."[5] In *Ecclesia de*

---

[3] John Paul II, Address at a Symposium in Honor of the Thirtieth Anniversary of the Decree *Presbyterorum Ordinis*, Oct. 27, 1995, §4 (*L'Osservatore Romano*, November 15, 1995, English edition, 7).

[4] My italics.

[5] Second Vatican Council, Decree on the Ministry and Life of Priests, *Presbyterorum Ordinis* (1965), §5. See also Leo XIII, Encyclical Letter on the Holy Eucharist, *Mirae Caritatis* (1902), §15:

   In a word this Sacrament is, as it were, the very soul of the Church; and to it the grace of the priesthood is ordered and directed in all its fulness and in each of its successive grades. From the same source the Church

Eucharistia, St. John Paul formulates this idea using his characteristic theme of "gift of self":

> The Church has received the Eucharist from Christ her Lord not as one gift—however precious—among so many others, but as *the gift par excellence*, for it is the gift of himself, of his person in his sacred humanity, as well as the gift of his saving work. Nor does it remain confined to the past, since "all that Christ is—all that he did and suffered for all men—participates in the divine eternity, and so transcends all times."[6]

Since Christ has fully given Himself for us, John Paul II asks: "What more could Jesus have done for us? Truly, in the Eucharist, he shows us a love which goes 'to the end,' a love which knows no measure." Here, John Paul II is referring to John 13:1, in which John introduces his account of the Last Supper, in which Jesus instituted the Eucharist: "When Jesus knew that his hour had come to depart out of this world to the Father, having loved his own who were in the world, he *loved them to the end*."

Benedict XVI begins his apostolic exhortation on the Eucharist, *Sacramentum Caritatis*, with the same theme of Jesus's gift of self "to the end":

> The sacrament of charity, the Holy Eucharist is the gift that Jesus Christ makes of himself, thus revealing to us God's infinite love for every man and woman. This wondrous sacrament makes manifest that "greater" love which led him to "lay down his life for his friends" (*Jn* 15:13). Jesus did indeed love them "to the end."[7]

---

draws and has all her strength, all her glory, her every supernatural endowment and adornment, every good thing that is here; wherefore she makes it the chiefest of all her cares to prepare the hearts of the faithful for an intimate union with Christ through the Sacrament of His Body and Blood, and to draw them thereto.

[6] John Paul II, *EE*, §11 (italics original). The quotation is from *CCC*, §1085.

[7] Benedict XVI, Post-Synodal Apostolic Exhortation, *Sacramentum Caritatis* (2007), §1. See also §7: "In the Eucharist Jesus does not give us a 'thing,' but himself; he offers his own body and pours out his own blood. He thus gives us the totality of his life and reveals the ultimate origin of this love."

STRUCTURE OF THE WORK

This book, conceived as a textbook for a course on the Eucharist, is structured around the three principal ends of the Eucharist. As the sacrament of love to the end, the Eucharist manifests three aspects of a supreme love of friendship: dwelling *with* the beloved, giving oneself in sacrifice *for* the beloved, and the most intimate gift of self *to* the beloved. Spousal love is built on these three aspects of complete self-giving. The Eucharist is the embodiment of Christ's spousal love for His Bride, and so it makes the Bridegroom present to dwell with His Bride with a love that is at once infinitely sacrificial and unitive. The three principal themes of this book, therefore, are the Eucharist as the mystery of Christ's real presence, His sacrificial offering of Himself to the Father on our behalf, and His gift of Himself to us in Holy Communion, by which He nourishes our spiritual life with His life.

The book is divided into four parts. The first part examines the foundations of the doctrine on the Eucharist, whereas the second, third, and fourth parts discuss, respectively, these three ends of the Eucharist: Presence, Sacrifice, and Communion.

The first part begins, in chapter 1, by posing the question: Why did Jesus institute the Eucharist? As will be seen there, the three fundamental ends of the Eucharist correspond to the purposes for the Incarnation. The second and third chapters examine the biblical sources for the theology of the Eucharist. The Old Testament provides an abundance of figures for all three of these aspects of the Eucharist, such as the Manna, the *Shekhinah*, the Temple sacrifices of bread and wine, the bread of the Presence, the Passover, and so on. In the New Testament these figures become reality in the Last Supper. In His Bread of Life Discourse in John 6, Jesus Himself alludes to how the Old Testament figures point to the reality. Chapter 4 examines the witness of the Fathers of the Church on the real presence, the substantial conversion of the elements, the sacrifice of the Mass, and Communion. Chapter 5 treats the essential aspects of the outward sacramental sign that is seen and heard, which are the matter and form of the Eucharist, and the minister.

The second part of the book, on the real presence and transubstantiation as the first aspect of the Eucharist, is organized historically. The Berengarian controversy in the eleventh century, the subject of chapter 6, was a great stimulus to the development of Catholic doctrine on transubstantiation. Using St. Thomas Aquinas as a guide, chapter 7 examines how Christ becomes present through transubstantiation, a doctrine rejected in different ways by the Protestant Reformers (chapter 8).

Christ's real presence makes possible the two other principal ends of the Eucharist, which are intimately connected. The first of these is the sacrifice, which is made present through the real presence of Christ's Body and Blood offered by the priest acting in the person of Christ. This is the subject of part III, chapters 9–12. We shall examine how the Eucharist is one with Christ's sacrifice on Calvary (chapter 9), answering Protestant objections that the sacrifice of the Mass is injurious to Calvary (chapter 10). The participation of the faithful in the sacrifice is examined in chapter 11, followed by a consideration of the fruits of the Mass (chapter 12).

The real presence also makes possible the third principal end of the Eucharist, spiritual nourishment, which is the subject of part IV. Chapter 13 looks at the effects of Communion. When the faithful receive and consume the sacrificial victim, they receive grace and charity, through which the Church is built up until Christ's Second Coming. Since the reception of Communion presupposes visible and invisible ecclesial communion, the conditions for worthy and fruitful Communion and norms for its reception are examined in chapters 14 and 15. Chapter 16 treats Eucharistic adoration, which is ordered to increasing our hunger and thirst for the Eucharist, to contemplation of the Victim of Calvary present in the Blessed Sacrament, and to an expression of our thanksgiving for this threefold gift.

PART I

FOUNDATIONS

CHAPTER ONE

✣

Why Did Christ Institute the Eucharist?

REASONS OF FITTINGNESS FOR THE EUCHARIST

Why did Christ institute the Eucharist? In asking this simple question, we are seeking reasons of fittingness for one of God's greatest marvels. Asking such questions is a key part of theology, for theology is "faith seeking understanding." When we know through faith that God has done something, we naturally desire to understand why He has done that, how it reveals His love for us, and how it fits in with everything else we know about Him and His plans. Arguments from fittingness cannot demonstrate revealed truth, but, presupposing faith, seek to understand its reasons so that we can come to love God's plan more deeply.[1]

Sacrament of Spiritual Nourishment

When St. Thomas treats the mystery of the Eucharist in the *Summa of Theology*, he begins by posing this question of why it was fitting for Jesus to institute the Eucharist. He answers by making an analogy between what is necessary for our bodily life and what is necessary for our supernatural life of grace. In our bodily life, we need birth, growth, and nourishment. Likewise in our spiritual life we need birth, growth to maturity, and nourishment. Spiritual birth is given by Baptism,

---

[1] On arguments from fittingness, see Lawrence Feingold, *Faith Comes from What Is Heard: Fundamental Theology* (Steubenville, OH: Emmaus Academic, 2016), 162–68.

3

growth to spiritual maturity is given by Confirmation, and spiritual nourishment is given by the Eucharist:

> The Church's sacraments are ordained for helping man in the spiritual life. But the spiritual life is analogous to the corporeal, since corporeal things bear a resemblance to spiritual. Now it is clear that just as generation is required for corporeal life, since thereby man receives life; and growth, whereby man is brought to maturity: so likewise food is required for the preservation of life. Consequently, just as for the spiritual life there had to be Baptism, which is spiritual generation; and Confirmation, which is spiritual growth: so there needed to be the sacrament of the Eucharist, which is spiritual food.[2]

The sacraments give us supernatural life analogously with the way nature provides for the basic needs of our natural life. In this consideration, the Eucharist corresponds, supernaturally, with man's need for nourishment. As we need to eat and drink daily to nourish our bodies, replenish our strength, and to grow, so we need the Eucharist to nourish, replenish, and increase our supernatural life, which is the life of Christ in us. This life consists above all in sanctifying grace and charity. Christ instituted the Eucharist, therefore, to be the food of eternal life. Thus the sacrament produces the spiritual nourishment that it symbolically represents by feeding us with grace and strength-

---

[2] *ST* III, q. 73, a. 1. See also *ST* III, q. 65, a. 1:

> For spiritual life has a certain conformity with the life of the body: just as other corporeal things have a certain likeness to things spiritual.... With regard to himself man is perfected in the life of the body, in two ways; first, directly [*per se*], i.e. by acquiring some vital perfection; secondly, indirectly [*per accidens*], i.e. by the removal of hindrances to life, such as ailments, or the like. Now the life of the body is perfected directly in three ways. First, by generation whereby a man begins to be and to live, and corresponding to this in the spiritual life there is Baptism, which is a spiritual regeneration, according to Titus 3:5: "By the laver of regeneration," etc. Secondly, by growth whereby a man is brought to perfect size and strength. Corresponding to this in the spiritual life there is Confirmation, in which the Holy Spirit is given to strengthen us.... Thirdly, by nourishment, whereby life and strength are preserved to man, and corresponding to this in the spiritual life there is the Eucharist. Wherefore it is said (John 6:54): "Except you eat of the flesh of the Son of Man, and drink His blood, you shall not have life in you."

ening our intimate union with Christ, whom we literally take into ourselves.[3]

When food and drink are taken into our bodies, they are converted into the very substance of our bodies to strengthen and conserve it. Thus an intimate union is created between the food and ourselves: it becomes one with us. This union is another aspect of the sacramental sign of the Eucharist, for the Eucharist is a sacrament of communion: it creates an intimate union between us and Christ, whom we receive. However, Christ does not become transformed into us, as our food is; rather, the Eucharist transforms us spiritually into a closer image of Christ. As St. Augustine relates in his *Confessions*, he heard the voice of Christ saying to him: "I am the food of strong men; grow, and you shall feed upon me; nor shall you convert me, like the food of your flesh, into you, but you shall be converted into me."[4]

Sacrament of Charity

The analogy of spiritual nourishment, however, does not exhaust the richness of the Eucharist. To further bring out the fittingness of the seven sacraments, St. Thomas also compares them with the seven principal virtues: the four cardinal and the three theological. The Eucharist is paired with the theological virtue of charity,[5] which

---

[3] See Council of Florence, Decree for the Armenians, *Exsultate Deo* (1439): "All the effects that material food and drink have on the life of the body—maintaining and increasing life, restoring health, and giving joy—all these effects this sacrament produces for the spiritual life" (DS, 1322).

[4] Augustine, *Confessions* 7.10.16, trans. J. G. Pilkington, *NPNF*1, 1:109 (translation slightly modified). See Ratzinger, *TL*, 287: "In the normal process of eating, man is the stronger being. He takes things in, and they are assimilated into him, so that they become part of his own substance. They are transformed within him and go to build up his bodily life. But in the mutual relation with Christ it is the other way around; he is the heart, the truly existent being. When we truly communicate, this means that we are taken out of ourselves, that we are assimilated into him, that we become one with him and, through him, with the fellowship of our brethren."

[5] See *ST* III, q. 65, a. 1: "Some, again, gather the number of sacraments from a certain adaptation to the virtues and to the defects and penal effects resulting from sin. They say that Baptism corresponds to Faith, and is ordained as a remedy against original sin; Extreme Unction, to Hope, being ordained against venial sin; the Eucharist, to Charity, being ordained against the penal effect which is malice; Order, to Prudence, being ordained against ignorance; Penance to Justice, being ordained against mortal sin; Matrimony, to Temperance, being

is supernatural love of friendship with God, a friendship both filial and spousal. The Eucharist is the sacrament of charity because it was instituted to nourish us with love for God and neighbor, binding the Church together in her vertical and horizontal dimensions. In this way it is the sacrament of ecclesial unity.

Presence

We can gain further insight into the purpose and fittingness of the Eucharist by considering three ways in which the Eucharist is the sacrament of charity, or gift of self. First of all, it is proper to the love of spousal friendship to seek to dwell intimately with the beloved. Christ wished to remain close to His disciples not only as God but also as man, as He was about to leave them to go to His Passion. So He instituted the Eucharist to be the sacrament by which He would continue to dwell with His disciples on earth in His sacred humanity, even as His body would ascend into heaven.

When men die, they leave a testament to their loved ones. They may leave certain reminders of their presence, such as letters, photographs, heirlooms, or their estate. On the night before His Passion, Christ also wished to leave a testament to His loved ones; as God, however, He was not limited in His choices. He left a testament that would not be outdone by any other, for He elected to leave to His bride, the Church, *nothing less than Himself*.

And not only did He devise a way in the Eucharist to remain present as man with His Church, but He is present in it in a far better way than He was during His earthly life. For when Christ took on our human nature, He became subject to the limitations of space and time, and therefore was physically present in only a certain circumscribed geographical region, and for only a few years: the thirty years of His hidden life and the three years of His public ministry, prolonged briefly by the forty days from His Resurrection to His Ascension into heaven. Yet, as the Word Incarnate, He is the Savior and Bridegroom in whom all men find fulfillment and salvation. He would not leave

---

ordained against concupiscence; Confirmation, to Fortitude, being ordained against infirmity." On the Eucharist as the sacrament of charity according to Aquinas, see Daria Spezzano, *The Glory of God's Grace: Deification According to St. Thomas Aquinas* (Ave Maria, FL: Sapientia Press of Ave Maria University, 2015), 317–26.

all of those born in the centuries after His death and living in other regions deprived of contact with His sacred humanity. In order to overcome the limitations of space and time, He devised a way to continue to be present not just in one place, but in all the churches of the world, through all the ages, for everyone who was to come into the world, despite the fact that He has ascended definitively into heaven.

Sacrificial Love

It is proper to spousal love that there be a mutual and total self-giving[2] of the partners to each other, as St. Paul says in Ephesians 5:25–27: "Husbands, love your wives, as Christ loved the church and gave himself up for her, that he might sanctify her, having cleansed her by the washing of water with the word, that he might present the church to himself in splendor, without spot or wrinkle or any such thing, that she might be holy and without blemish."

In the Eucharist, Christ gives to His Bride the very act by which He poured out His life for her to cleanse and sanctify her by meriting the remission of sins. That sacrifice of infinite love is also the act most pleasing to the Father that is conceivable.

In other words, Christ willed to give a testament to His Bride that would be not only His own living presence but also the continued presence of the very act by which He showed Himself as the Supreme Lover of our souls. Of course, His whole life was a continual manifestation of love for us: He became flesh for love of us. However, the full extent of that love was revealed only in His suffering and death on the Cross, offered for our redemption. And so, He left to His loved ones a perfect token of His love, giving to us, sacramentally, the very act by which He died for our sins. This is the Eucharist.

In the Mass, Christ offers Himself, Victim of Love, in the very act of pouring Himself out in sacrifice for us. In the words of Pope Benedict XVI, Jesus left us the Eucharist so that we could forever enter into "His hour":[6] "The Eucharist draws us into Jesus's act of self-oblation. More than just statically receiving the incarnate *Logos*, we enter into the very dynamic of his self-giving."[7]

Through the Eucharist, therefore, Christ not only nourishes His Bride with affective love through Communion but also teaches

---

[6] Benedict XVI, *Sacramentum Caritatis* (2007), §11.
[7] Benedict XVI, Encyclical Letter, *Deus Caritas Est* (2005), §13.

effective love by giving us His supreme sacrifice of His love to be our sacrifice. In the Eucharist, we are given the incomprehensible gift of being able to give God the Son to God the Father for the forgiveness of sins and for every blessing.[8]

Intimate Union

Finally, spousal love seeks not only to dwell with the beloved and sacrifice oneself for the beloved, but, through self-sacrifice, to enter into the most intimate union with the beloved. The Eucharist makes possible this most intimate union through Holy Communion. Furthermore, this spousal union in the Eucharist is realized in a way fitting for human beings, for it is both physical and spiritual, like spousal love. Receiving Communion enables us to take Christ bodily into ourselves, to join with Him in a close physical way. He can then remain with us for about ten minutes, until the sacred species are corrupted by the digestive process. However, the more important union is the enduring spiritual effect of the Eucharist by which sanctifying grace, charity, and the Indwelling of the Trinity is nourished and increased.

As a necessary consequence of our union with Christ, the Eucharist also deepens our communion with one another in the Mystical Body in fraternal charity, and thus it is the sacrament of ecclesial unity.[9] St. Paul states this in 1 Corinthians 10:17: "For we, being many, are one bread, one body, all that partake of one bread." The Eucharist binds us into one Body by strengthening our unity with Christ and with one another.

Three Ends of the Eucharist

In summary, there are three principal reasons for which Christ instituted the Eucharist:

1) to *perpetuate His human presence* among men as our Redeemer and the divine Victim for our souls;

---

[8] See Eugène Masure, *The Sacrifice of the Mystical Body* (London: Burns & Oates, 1954), 158: "God has taken such pity on us that He permits us to give Him His beloved Son that we might realize at last the immensity of the love with which we also have been loved."

[9] Hence, St. Thomas refers to the Eucharist as the "Sacrament of Church unity" (*ST* III, q. 82, a. 2, ad 3).

2) to *perpetuate His redemptive sacrifice*, the supreme act of His burning charity, and allow us to join with Him in offering it to the Father;

3) and to unite Himself in intimate *communion* with us so as to be our spiritual food and drink.[10]

All three of these aspects are sacramentally represented through the signs of bread and wine that become Christ's Body and Blood. The wonderful symbolism of spiritual nourishment and spiritual union is combined with a sacramental presentation of Christ's sacrificial act. His sacrifice is sacramentally presented in the separate consecration of the Body and Blood under the species of bread and wine, mystically making present the real separation of His Body and Blood in His death on the Cross. This significance is clearly shown in Jesus's words of consecration: "This cup which is poured out for you is the new covenant in my blood" (Luke 22:20).[11]

A good summary of these reasons of fittingness for the institution of the Eucharist are given in the Second Vatican Council's Constitution on the Liturgy, *Sacrosanctum Concilium*, §47:

> At the Last Supper, on the night when He was betrayed, our Saviour instituted the eucharistic sacrifice of His Body and Blood. He did this in order to perpetuate the sacrifice of the Cross throughout the centuries until He should come again, and so to entrust to His beloved spouse, the Church, a memorial of His death and resurrection: a sacrament of love, a sign of unity, a bond of charity, a paschal banquet in which Christ is eaten, the mind is filled with grace, and a pledge of future glory is given to us.

This text highlights the principal reasons for which Jesus instituted the Eucharist. He becomes present to remain among us for a twofold end. He comes to perpetuate His sacrifice and to entrust it to His Bride. Then through that very sacrifice He nourishes us with His

---

[10] These three principal reasons for the institution of the Eucharist are mentioned by Emmanuel Doronzo in his *Tractatus Dogmaticus de Eucharistia* (Milwaukee, WI: Bruce, 1948), 2:782.

[11] See Matt 26:28: "This is my blood of the covenant, which is poured out for many for the forgiveness of sins."

Body and Blood in the paschal banquet of Holy Communion, feeding us with charity, by which it becomes the efficacious sign of unity of the whole Church.

CHRIST INSTITUTED THE EUCHARIST FOR THE SAME REASONS THAT HE BECAME MAN

Let us return to our initial question: Why did Christ institute the Eucharist? We can expand our answer and say that Christ instituted the Eucharist for the same reasons that He became incarnate. The motives for the Incarnation are the same as the motives for His Passion and for instituting the Eucharist.[12] This shows us that the Eucharist is not an afterthought, not something secondary, not a mere external rite, but inextricably tied up with the Incarnation and the Passion of the Son of God. It lies at the very center and heart of the Catholic faith. The Eucharist obeys the same divine logic as the Incarnation and the Passion, for it is their sacramental *prolongation* throughout the life of the Church until Christ comes again in glory.[13]

So what are the ends of the Incarnation? Why did the Second Person of the Blessed Trinity wish to take on a human nature in the

---

[12] See *ST* III, q. 79, a. 1: "The effect of this sacrament ought to be considered, first of all and principally, from what is contained in this sacrament, which is Christ; Who, just as by coming into the world, He visibly bestowed the life of grace upon the world, according to John 1:17: 'Grace and truth came by Jesus Christ,' so also, by coming sacramentally into man, causes the life of grace."

[13] Matthias Joseph Scheeben develops at length the intimate connection between the mystery of the Trinity, the Incarnation, and the Eucharist in *The Mysteries of Christianity*, trans. Cyril Vollert (St. Louis, MO: B. Herder, 1951), 469–97. For the idea of the prolongation of the Incarnation, see 485–86:

> We may say with profound truth that the Eucharist is a real and universal prolongation and extension of the mystery of the Incarnation. The Eucharistic presence of Christ is in itself a reflection and extension of His Incarnation, as the Fathers so often observe. The changing of the bread into the body of Christ by the power of the Holy Spirit is a renewal of the wonderful act by which, in the power of the same Holy Spirit, He originally formed His body in the womb of the Virgin and took it to His person. As He effected His first entrance into the world by this act, so by that other act He multiplies His substantial presence over and over again in space and time. But this presence is multiplied only that the body of Christ may grow and spread throughout the members which He attaches to Himself and fuses with Himself.

womb of the Blessed Virgin?[14] Some of the principal reasons are the following:

1) to dwell among us and speak to us as man, so as to establish intimate friendship with us;
2) to teach us perfect virtue by his example, especially love, humility, obedience, religion, magnanimity, and fortitude;
3) to give us the possibility of supreme merit through the exercise of faith;
4) to offer an expiatory sacrifice to satisfy for all human sin in perfect justice and so to nourish our hope of redemption;
5) to show the divine love for man and give us a supreme motive for charity;
6) to give us a participation in His divinity through sanctifying grace and, thus, to found the Church to be His Mystical Body and His Bride;
7) to show man the immense dignity to which he has been elevated by Christ: the dignity of entering into communion with the Blessed Trinity;
8) to enter into a nuptial union with us.

---

[14] St. Thomas gives ten reasons of fittingness for the Incarnation in *ST* III, q. 1, a. 2:

> Now this may be viewed with respect to our *furtherance in good*. First, with regard to faith, which is made more certain by believing God Himself Who speaks. . . . Secondly, with regard to hope, which is thereby greatly strengthened. . . . Thirdly, with regard to charity, which is greatly enkindled by this; . . . Fourthly, with regard to well-doing, in which He set us an example. . . . Fifthly, with regard to the full participation of the Divinity, which is the true bliss of man and end of human life; and this is bestowed upon us by Christ's humanity. So also was this useful for our *withdrawal from evil*. First, because man is taught by it not to prefer the devil to himself, nor to honor him who is the author of sin. . . . Secondly, because we are thereby taught how great is man's dignity, lest we should sully it with sin. . . . Thirdly, because, "in order to do away with man's presumption, the grace of God is commended in Jesus Christ, though no merits of ours went before." . . . Fourthly, because "man's pride, which is the greatest stumbling-block to our clinging to God, can be convinced and cured by humility so great." . . . Fifthly, in order to free man from the thraldom of sin. . . . And there are very many other advantages which accrued, above man's apprehension.

All of these ends serve both the glorification of God and the sanctification of man. Indeed, the sanctification of man is ultimately ordered to the glorification of God.

These reasons for the Incarnation (and thus for the Eucharist) can be grouped under the three headings of presence, sacrifice, and union. God became man to dwell among us on our level, to sacrifice Himself for us to win the forgiveness of sins and merit every grace, and to bring us into intimate union with Himself by giving us a share in His divine life. As we have said above, all three are proper to love, for love seeks to dwell with the beloved, sacrifice for the beloved, and unite oneself with the beloved as intimately as possible.

1. Presence

Divine Condescension Wishing to Dwell with Us

God became man to dwell among us in a way proper to us, as a man among men, taking our nature, so that we could encounter Him sensibly in our world and in our time. This supreme divine condescension was progressively prepared for by God in His revelation to Israel. God chose a particular people to be "His own possession" from all the peoples on the face of the earth (see Deut 7:6), and so He called Abraham out of Mesopotamia and out of his father's house (Gen 12:1). He revealed Himself progressively to the descendants of Abraham, Isaac, and Jacob, said that He will betroth them as His bride (Hos 2:19–20), and dwelt among them by establishing His glory in the Temple and by hearing their prayers. The condescension of God shown in the election of Israel is beautifully described by a Jewish author, Michael Wyschogrod:

> ✴ If Hashem[15] does not find his dignity impaired by being known as the creator of the world, the elector of Abraham, and the redeemer of Abraham's seed from the land of Egypt, then it is not the task of man to protect Hashem's dignity more than he wishes it protected. We must learn from the word of God which attributions constitute the proper praise of God and which do not.[16]

---

[15] Hebrew for "the Name," as a circumlocution for God.
[16] Michael Wyschogrod, *The Body of Faith: Judaism as Corporeal Election* (New York: Seabury Press, 1983), 95.

The Incarnation takes the logic of the election of Israel to its end. If God has first chosen to "impair His dignity" by taking on the children of Israel to be His people, united to Him by a unique covenant, and dwelling with them, why could He not condescend further to assume the human nature of a descendant of Abraham and of David in the womb of a chosen daughter of Zion?[17] Indeed, St. Paul presents the Incarnation in Philippians 2:4–8 as the archetype of condescension: "Christ Jesus, who, though he was in the form of God, did not count equality with God a thing to be grasped, but emptied himself, taking the form of a servant, being born in the likeness of men." If the divine condescension is the characteristic way God reveals Himself in the Old Testament, then the Incarnation of God is in some way the most radically Jewish element of the Christian faith! His self-emptying reveals the incomprehensible depth of the love and mercy that undertakes an infinite humiliation.

The Eucharist takes the divine condescension that culminates in the Incarnation one step further. The love that leads the Word to take on flesh is what leads Him to wish to remain with us forever during our earthly pilgrimage, present with us wherever there is a priest and tabernacle. He completely veils His majesty, hiding behind the appearances of bread and wine, so that we may not be afraid to approach Him whenever we wish. St. Thomas states this admirably in an article on the real presence of Christ in the Eucharist. This presence is fitting because:

> this belongs to Christ's love, out of which for our salvation He assumed a true body of our nature. And because it is the special feature of friendship to live together with friends, as the Philosopher says (*Ethic.* 9), He promises us His bodily presence as a reward, saying (Matt 24:28): "Where the body is, there shall the eagles be gathered together." Yet meanwhile in our pilgrimage He does not deprive us of His bodily presence; but unites us with Himself in this sacrament through the truth of His body and blood. Hence (John 6:57) he says: "He that eateth My flesh, and drinketh My blood, abideth in Me, and I in him." Hence this sacrament is the sign of supreme

---

[17] See the discussion of the divine condescension in Jewish and Christian theology in Christoph Cardinal Schönborn, *God Sent His Son: A Contemporary Christology*, trans. Henry Taylor (San Francisco: Ignatius Press, 2010), 110–16.

charity, and the uplifter of our hope, from such familiar union of Christ with us.[18]

Teaching Perfect Virtue

By becoming man, the Second Person of the Blessed Trinity was able to teach us perfect virtue not only through a law but also through the example of His human words and actions, especially in His Paschal mystery.

Does this continue in the Eucharist? As in all the mysteries of His human life, Christ's Eucharistic presence is also a model of virtue, especially of charity, humility, and obedience.[19] First of all, charity is the gift of self for the sake of the loved one, and the Eucharist is precisely that. It is Christ who performs an incomprehensible miracle, every day, in every locality where there is a Catholic priest and a church, in order to give Himself to us as the Bridegroom of our souls.

Charity seeks not its own. The Eucharist adds nothing to Jesus, but is entirely for our benefit. Christ present in the Eucharist is absolutely disinterested, for He is there entirely for us, for our welfare. Christ's Eucharistic presence on our altars and in our tabernacles, day and night, adds nothing to Him, but everything to us. He is the divine "prisoner of the tabernacle" in order to be able to be with us whenever we wish it, to be available to give us the consolation of His presence whenever we need it, desire it, and seek it, whenever we thirst for the face of God when all other consolations have run dry in this place of exile, this valley of tears.

Charity seeks no price. The Eucharist gives us the greatest treasure of the universe, free for the taking. Charity is patient. Jesus in the Blessed Sacrament endures all abuse, all irreverence, all sacrilege, with the utmost meekness, for the sake of being perpetually present as divine Victim in our midst. Charity is delicate and discreet. Christ in the Blessed Sacrament does not impose Himself on anyone, but He is always there when we wish to pour out our hearts to Him.

Charity condescends to the level of the person loved so that the beloved feels no humiliation or intimidation. Could there be a greater

---

[18] *ST* III, q. 75, a. 1.

[19] This truth has been admirably expounded by St. Peter Julian Eymard, a saint of the nineteenth century who dedicated his life to Eucharistic adoration, founding an order for that mission. See Eymard, *The Real Presence: Eucharistic Meditations* (Cleveland, OH: Emmanuel, 1938).

example of the kindness of condescension than the Blessed Sacrament? Christ puts a veil on all of His divine and human greatness and appears under the humble and common species of bread and wine. If He appeared in all His glory, as on Mount Tabor, we would be overawed and afraid. This condescension of Christ in the Eucharist thus serves to arouse us to respond to His charity with the greatest of confidence.

Finally, charity bears all things. In the Blessed Sacrament, Jesus allows Himself to be received by those who have lost their faith in His presence and His divinity, by those in a state of mortal sin, by those who could not care less about Him, by those who knowingly commit sacrilege. He permits this because He maximally respects our free response to His love and because He remains faithful even when we are unfaithful.

The Blessed Sacrament is the perfect model of humility, self-abnegation, and poverty. Christ, being God, is humbled even more by His sacramental state in the Eucharist than He was in Bethlehem or Calvary. In Bethlehem and Calvary, He veiled His divinity so that only His weak and vulnerable humanity would be seen by men, and seen in an attitude of humiliation. However, in the Blessed Sacrament, even His sacred humanity is veiled under the species of ordinary bread and wine. He foregoes not only the appearance of the omnipotent power which He possesses as God; He also foregoes the beauty of His sacred humanity. This is the utmost extreme of poverty as well. He has divested Himself not only of all possessions, as on Calvary, but even of the appearance of His human nature.

Humility entails hiding our talents and gifts if we can do so without loss to our neighbor. What better model of this than the Holy Eucharist, where the King of glory, the Creator of the world, appears as if He were but a piece of bread or a bit of wine! This divine self-abnegation is greater than that revealed in Bethlehem, or even on Calvary, where the centurion or the good thief could see the ineffable nobility of the suffering of the Son of God.

Finally, Christ in the Blessed Sacrament is the most perfect model of obedience. As He was obedient in Nazareth to St. Joseph and Mary and on Calvary to His executioners, so likewise in the Eucharist He is perfectly and perpetually obedient, submitting to His priests until the end of the world. Christ obeys His priests absolutely and unconditionally in the Blessed Sacrament. He comes when they validly consecrate, and He stays present until the sacred species of the bread and wine are digested or corrupted. He comes regardless of whether the ceremony is solemn or simple (as long as it is valid). He comes whether or not the priest or the communicant is in a state of grace. His obedience and humility is such that He remains present even in the face of great and willful sacrilege.

The Merit of Faith

The Incarnation makes possible the greatest merit of faith, because, of all God's works, the Incarnation is the most arduous to believe and the mystery that most transcends reason. St. Thomas remarks: "Indeed, among divine works, this most especially exceeds reason: for nothing can be thought of which is more marvelous than this divine accomplishment: that the true God, the Son of God, should become true man."[20]

All faith involves a conversion from what is seen to what is unseen, for faith is of things unseen, according to Hebrews 11:1: "Faith is the substance of things to be hoped for, the evidence of things that are not seen." Nothing could be more arduous than to see a man and to believe that He is God, whom we cannot see.

Yet, at the same time, the Incarnation not only makes possible the greatest merit and difficulty of faith; it also makes possible its greatest certainty, for nothing could be more certain than the words of the Word Incarnate. St. Augustine expresses this beautifully:

> In order to give man's mind greater confidence in its journey towards the truth along the way of faith, God the Son of God, who is himself the truth, took manhood without abandoning his godhead, and thus established and founded this faith, so that man might have a path to man's God through the man who was God.[21]

The Eucharist is related to the Incarnation in that both establish the merit of faith by presenting to us a divine reality whose divinity is completely *veiled*. The Eucharist continues the logic of the Incarnation and goes further, increasing both the difficulty and the corresponding

---

[20] *SCG* IV, ch. 27, no. 1.
[21] Augustine, *City of God* 11.2, trans. Henry Bettenson (New York: Penguin Books, 1972), 430–31.

merit of the act of faith.[22] On the Cross, the humanity was visible but the divinity veiled. In the consecrated host, both the divinity and the humanity are veiled. He is *doubly veiled*, for neither of Christ's two natures are visible, and yet we believe that Christ is present in His glorious humanity.[23] We believe this most veiled truth only because it is affirmed by Christ's word.[24]

St. Thomas admirably expresses this truth in his great hymn on the Eucharist, *Adoro Te Devote*. He writes:

Sight, touch, and taste in Thee are each deceived;
the ear alone most safely is believed:
I believe all the Son of God has spoken
than Truth's own word there is no truer token.

The Eucharist perfects in us the merit of faith. St. Thomas continues:

God only on the cross lay hid from view;
but here lies hid at once the Manhood too;
and I, in both professing my belief,
make the same prayer as the repentant thief.

---

[22] See *ST* III, q. 75, a. 1: "And since faith is of things unseen, as Christ shows us His Godhead invisibly, so also in this sacrament He shows us His flesh in an invisible manner."

[23] See Scheeben, *The Mysteries of Christianity*, 477–78:

Thus the mystery of the Eucharist is ontologically joined to the mystery of the Incarnation, just as the mystery of the Incarnation is joined to the Trinity. The Incarnation is the presupposition and explanation of the Eucharist, just as the eternal generation from the bosom of the Father is the presupposition and explanation of the Incarnation, regarded as the stepping forth of God's Son into the world.... All three show us the same Son of God: the first in the bosom of the eternal Father, whence He receives His being; the second in the womb of the Virgin, through which He enters the world; the third in the heart of the Church, where He sojourns by an enduring, universal presence among men and unites Himself to them. Yet He remains ever hidden from the natural eye of body and soul. In all of God's visible creation we cannot find the generation of His Son; nor in the humanity of the Son can we discern His hypostatic union with the divinity; nor under the Eucharistic species can we discover the body of Christ spiritually present.

[24] See *ST* III, q. 75, a. 1: "The presence of Christ's true body and blood in this sacrament cannot be detected by sense, nor understanding, but by faith alone, which rests upon Divine authority."

Thy wounds, as Thomas saw, I do not see;
yet Thee confess my Lord and God to be:
make me believe Thee ever more and more;
in Thee my hope, in Thee my love to store.[25]

2. Sacrifice

Expiatory Sacrifice of Atonement

Christ became man in order to be able to offer an expiatory sacrifice to satisfy for all human sins in perfect justice. This was necessary because of the gravity of sin and the impossibility for man to offer fitting reparation. Every mortal sin involves a rejection of the Law of God and, hence, a rejection of God, who is the author of that law. And God is infinite Good. Therefore, every mortal sin involves an infinite evil, a denial of our infinite Benefactor to whom we owe all honor and reverence. The gravity of sin is proportionate to the honor of the offended party.

The value of satisfaction, however, is determined by the dignity of the party who makes reparation. How could a mere man make satisfaction for an infinite evil, being both finite and rendered ignoble by sin? God therefore chose to make satisfaction Himself in our place by taking on a human nature in order to suffer and die in it to expiate the sins of all men. Other men are born to live, but Christ was born in order to die for us.

St. Thomas speaks of Christ's work of redemption as offering to God something more excellent than all human sin is offensive.[26] The life of the Word Incarnate, offered in His Passion with infinite charity

---

[25] Thomas Aquinas, *Adoro Te Devote*, trans. E. Caswall, in Raniero Cantalamessa, *This Is My Body: Eucharistic Reflections Inspired by* Adoro Te Devote *and* Ave Verum (Boston: Pauline Books & Media, 2005), 13.

[26] *ST* III, q. 48, a. 2:

He properly atones for an offence who offers something which the offended one loves equally, or even more than he detested the offence. But by suffering out of love and obedience, Christ gave more to God than was required to compensate for the offence of the whole human race. First of all, because of the exceeding charity from which He suffered; secondly, on account of the dignity of His life which He laid down in atonement, for it was the life of One Who was God and man; thirdly, on account of the extent of the Passion, and the greatness of the grief endured.

for all men, atones for sin by being more pleasing to God than *all* human sin together—both that of Adam and that of all his descendants—is displeasing.[27]

Christ, however, as mentioned above, wished to mysteriously "perpetuate" that supreme moment of His life and make it sacramentally present every day on every Catholic altar. The Eucharist "contains" the expiatory sacrifice of our redemption. It is mystically that very sacrifice because Christ Himself is the immolated Victim who becomes present on the altar through the ministry of His priests who act in His Person and His Blood is sacramentally poured out for the living and the dead. In the Eucharist, Christ's sacrifice has been given to the Church to be her perpetual sacrifice.[28] We can see this in the very words with which Christ instituted the Eucharist during the Last Supper, calling it "my blood of the covenant, which is poured out for many for the forgiveness of sins" (Matt 26:28). This means that the offering of Christ in every Eucharist glorifies the Father more than all the combined sin of history offends God's goodness.

Full Revelation of the Divine Love

God became man to fully reveal the infinite extent of the divine love for man so that we would have the supreme motive to love God in return. This is summarized in John 3:16: "For God so loved the world that he gave his only-begotten Son, that whoever believes in him should not perish but have eternal life." Nothing could induce us to love God more powerfully than to know that God has become man for love of mankind and has loved us to the point of shedding all His blood in torment for sinners.

See also q. 49, a. 4: "It is the proper effect of sacrifice to appease God; just as man likewise overlooks an offence committed against him on account of some pleasing act of homage shown him. . . . And in like fashion Christ's voluntary suffering was such a good act that, because of its being found in human nature, God was appeased for every offence of the human race with regard to those who are made one with the crucified Christ." See Roger Nutt, *General Principles of Sacramental Theology* (Washington, DC: Catholic University of America Press, 2017), 33–34.

[27] See Proclus, Homily 1.6, in *Proclus, Bishop of Constantinople: Homilies on the Life of Christ*, trans. Jan Harm Barkhuizen (Brisbane, AU: Centre for Early Christian Studies, Australian Catholic University, 2001), 67: "He not only has the value which counterbalances the weight of debt of those liable, but one which also outweighs all accounts!"

[28] See Scheeben, *The Mysteries of Christianity*, 494–95.

The Eucharist continues the logic of divine love that prompted the Incarnation. The same love by which God became man and died on the Cross to save mankind is that by which He wills to remain on the altars and in the tabernacles of the world, sacramentally pouring out His precious Blood and giving us His Body. John 13:1 highlights this by introducing the Last Supper, at which the Eucharist was instituted, as the culmination of Christ's love: "Now before the feast of the Passover, when Jesus knew that his hour had come to depart out of this world to the Father, having loved his own who were in the world, *he loved them to the end.*" The *Catechism of the Catholic Church*, §1380, speaks of the Eucharist as "the memorial of the love with which he loved us 'to the end,' even to the giving of his life."

Furthermore, He willed that this sacrament be the means by which the Church is nourished in that very love by which He became man and died for us. This brings us to the aspect of communion.

3. Communion

Divinization of Man

The principal end of the Incarnation is to give us an incomparable, inconceivable gift, which is to share in God's own divine nature through incorporation into Christ's Mystical Body. The Fathers of the Church frequently formulate this in the startling statement that God became man so that man could be divinized and come to share in the divine nature.[29] This divinization of man does not mean that man takes the place of God. God cannot lose His throne or His divine majesty. On the contrary, the divinization of man is the transformation of man into the full image and likeness of God through the gift of sanctifying grace and supernatural charity.

Through grace we are given a participation in the divine nature, as St. Peter states in his second letter, 1:4: "that you may be made partakers of the divine nature." Through sanctifying grace and charity, we are given a share in the inner life of God Himself. God became

---

[29] For the theme of divinization, see David Meconi and Carl Olson, eds., *Called to Be the Children of God: The Catholic Theology of Human Deification* (San Francisco: Ignatius Press, 2016); Meconi, *The One Christ: St. Augustine's Theology of Deification* (Washington, DC: Catholic University of America Press, 2013); Spezzano, *The Glory of God's Grace*; Daniel Keating, *Deification and Grace* (Naples, FL: Sapientia Press of Ave Maria University, 2007).

man so as to give us a sharing in His divinity. God could have given us grace without becoming man, if He had wished, but the divine wisdom determined that all grace after Adam's fall should come to us through the Incarnation. Grace was given to the Jews and the other righteous men before Christ through Christ's future Incarnation and merits. Thus John says, with reference to the Incarnation, that "from his fullness have we all received, grace upon grace" (John 1:16).[30]

The Fathers of the Church love to describe this divinization of man through the Incarnation of the Son of God as a kind of divine interchange or "commerce" by which the God of majesty takes on the condition of frail mortal man in order to clothe man in the divine garments of sanctifying grace and supernatural charity and bring him to the beatific vision of God in heaven.[31] This interchange is explained in a homily of St. Augustine:

> It was not enough for our God to promise us divinity in himself, unless he also took on our infirmity, as though to say, "Do you want to know how much I love you, how certain you ought to be that I am going to give you my divine reality? I took to myself your mortal reality." . . . The Son of God became a son of man, in order to make sons of men into sons of God. . . . For the maker of man was made man, so that man might be made a receiver of God.[32]

---

[30] See *ST* III, q. 8, a 1.

[31] See Irenaeus, *Against Heresies* 3.19.1:

> For it was for this end that the Word of God was made man, and He who was the Son of God became the Son of man, that man, having been taken into the Word, and receiving the adoption, might become the son of God. For by no other means could we have attained to incorruptibility and immortality, unless we had been united to incorruptibility and immortality. But how could we be joined to incorruptibility and immortality, unless, first, incorruptibility and immortality had become that which we also are, so that the corruptible might be swallowed up by incorruptibility, and the mortal by immortality, that we might receive the adoption of sons? (*ANF*, 1:448–49)

> See also Thomas Aquinas, *Opusculum 57, In Festo Corporis Christi*, lec. 1: "The only-begotten Son of God, wishing to enable us to share in his divinity, assumed our nature, so that becoming man he might make men gods" (*Liturgy of the Hours*, feast of Corpus Christi, Office of Readings, 2nd Reading).

[32] Augustine, Sermon 23B.1, in *Newly Discovered Sermons*, trans. Edmund Hill, WSA, pt. III (Homilies), vol. 11 (Hyde Park, NY: New City Press, 1997), 37.

The Son of God takes on weakness so that we may be clothed with the glory of the resurrection; He takes on humiliation and ignominy so that we may be crowned with the glory of redemption; He takes on excruciating suffering so that we may be freed from the pains of hell; He takes on death so that we may be clothed in immortality; He suffers "abandonment" by His Father on the Cross so that fallen man may be released from his exile and united to God.

The Greek Fathers spoke of this divine interchange as the center of the "divine economy" or the "economy of salvation."[33] This divine interchange or commerce initiates a matrimonial bond. In the Incarnation, God betroths Himself to us in His Church. He is the divine Bridegroom and we, the Church, are the Bride. Through this mysterious betrothal, the unworthy Bride is adorned with the dignity of her Bridegroom; although of lowly origin, she is elevated to His level. This betrothal is announced in the Old Testament prophets. For example, in Hosea 2:19–20, God promises: "And I will betroth you to me for ever; I will betroth you to me in righteousness and in justice, in steadfast love, and in mercy. I will betroth you to me in faithfulness; and you shall know the Lord."[34] Seven centuries later, St. John the Baptist proclaimed that the promised Bridegroom was come at last, saying to his disciples: "He who has the bride is the bridegroom. The friend of the bridegroom, who stands and hears him, rejoices greatly at the bridegroom's voice. For this reason my joy has been fulfilled" (John 3:29).

Jesus Christ Himself then taught the same truth in various parables. For example, He explained that His disciples did not fast as the

---

See the commentary on this text by Meconi, *The One Christ*, 89–94. The same point is made in the *exordium*, which may be by St. Augustine, of Sermon 191, in *Sermons on the Liturgical Seasons*, trans. Mary Sarah Muldowney, FC 38 (Washington, DC: Catholic University of America Press, 1959), 27–28: "God became man so that man might become God. The Lord took the form of a servant so that man might be turned to God. The Founder and Inhabitant of heaven dwelt upon earth so that man might rise from earth to heaven." See also Sermon 192.1 (ibid., 32).

[33] See Daniel Keating, "Deification in the Greek Fathers," in Meconi and Olson, eds., *Called to Be the Children of God*, 40–58.

[34] See also Ezek 16:8–14: "I pledged myself to you and entered into a covenant with you, says the Lord GOD, and you became mine. Then I bathed you with water and washed off your blood from you, and anointed you with oil. I clothed you also with embroidered cloth and shod you with leather, I wrapped you in fine linen and covered you with silk. . . . And your renown went forth among the nations because of your beauty, for it was perfect through the splendor which I had bestowed upon you, says the Lord GOD."

Pharisees did because "the wedding guests cannot mourn as long as the bridegroom is with them. . . . The days will come when the bridegroom is taken away from them, and then they will fast" (Matt 9:15). The most solemn of these parables concerns the wedding of the king's son, to which those invited did not come, and so the King said: "The wedding is ready, but those invited were not worthy. Go therefore to the thoroughfares, and invite to the marriage feast as many as you find" (Matt 22:8–9). Obviously, the wedding feast signifies the wedding of the divine Bridegroom, the Messiah, with His Church, His Bride. The realization of these sacred nuptials was the end and purpose of the Incarnation of the Son of God.

This lesson was not lost on the Apostles. St. Paul understood his apostolic ministry as working to extend the realization of this promise, espousing men to God through incorporation into the Church. In 2 Corinthians 11:2, he writes: "I feel a divine jealousy for you, for I promised you in marriage to one husband, to present you as a chaste virgin to Christ." In Revelation 21:2, John sees "the holy city, the new Jerusalem, coming down out of heaven from God, prepared as a bride adorned for her husband . . . the bride, the wife of the Lamb."

The Eucharist Is the Principal Means of Divinization

The Eucharist is intimately connected with this primary end of the Incarnation—the divinization of man and the giving of sanctifying grace by incorporating us in His Mystical Body. St. Augustine links the divine interchange worked by the Incarnation with the Eucharist: "In order that man might eat the Bread of angels, the Lord of the angels became Man."[35]

While it is true that Baptism opens the door to this new life as children of God and sharers of His nature, the Eucharist was instituted to be the celestial nourishment and content of that spiritual life, bringing what was born in Baptism to perfection by feeding us in grace through giving us sacramentally the very Author of all grace, Christ Himself. The Eucharist is a fountain of grace for all those who are rightly disposed to receive it. It is that fountain of living waters that Christ promised to the Samaritan woman at the well (John 4:10–14). The Eucharist is not the only channel by which God gives us sanctify-

---

[35] Augustine, Sermon 225.2, in *Sermons on the Liturgical Seasons*, 191 (Latin: PL, 38:1097).

ing grace and charity. After they are given through Baptism, they are increased through our good works and prayers performed in a state of grace, as well as by the worthy reception of the other sacraments. The Eucharist, however, is the principal channel for the increase and nourishing of grace and charity, for that is its reason for being. The Eucharist was instituted precisely for this end. It is the sacrament of love and sanctification or "divinization."

In the Incarnation Christ became a partaker of our manhood, assuming a human nature to His divine Person. In the Eucharist, Christ gives us His humanity to be our nourishment so that our humanity, receiving His, may be nourished by His divinity. Christ's humanity, made substantially present in the Eucharist, is the perfect bridge by which to give us a progressive share in His divinity. In other words, the Eucharist is the divine means to realize and perfect the divine interchange by which He who took on our humanity gives us a mysterious share in His divine Life.[36] St. Gregory of Nyssa expresses this central role of the Eucharist in our divinization:

> Since the God who was manifested infused himself into perishable humanity for this purpose, that by this communion with Deity mankind might at the same time be deified, for this end it is that, by dispensation of his grace, he disseminates himself in every believer through that flesh, whose substance comes from bread and wine, <u>blending himself with the bodies of believers,</u> to secure that, by this union with the immortal, man, too, may be a sharer in incorruption.[37]

St. Cyril of Jerusalem, addressing the neophytes in his *Mystagogic Catecheses*, explains that Holy Communion is ordered to our diviniza-

---

[36] See Scheeben, *The Mysteries of Christianity*, 488: "If the Fathers indicate the deification of man as the goal of the incarnation of God's Son, this must be true in fullest measure with regard to the Eucharist as the continuation of the Incarnation."

[37] Gregory of Nyssa, *Catechetical Oration* 37, in *NPNF2*, 5:506. See also John Damascene, *An Exact Exposition of the Orthodox Faith* 4.13, in *Writings: Saint John of Damascus*, trans. F. H. Chase, Jr., FC 37 (Washington, DC: Catholic University of America Press, 1958), 359: "Let us approach it with burning desire. . . . With eyes, lips, and faces turned toward it let us receive the divine burning coal, so that the fire of the coal may be added to the desire within us to consume our sins and enlighten our hearts, and so that by this communion of the divine fire we may be set afire and deified."

tion so that "By partaking of the Body and Blood of Christ you may become of one body and blood with Him. For when His Body and Blood become the tissue of our members, we become Christ-bearers and as the blessed Peter said, 'partakers of the divine nature.'"[38]

This end of the Eucharist is admirably expressed in the prayer of the Offertory of the Mass: "By the mystery of this water and wine may we come to share in the divinity of Christ, who humbled himself to share in our humanity."[39] In the Offertory prayers, we ask God to grant the proper effect of the Eucharist, which is nothing less than that we may come to share in His divinity. The same image is given in the collect for Christmas Mass: "O God, who wonderfully created the dignity of human nature and still more wonderfully restored it, grant, we pray, that we may share in the divinity of Christ, who humbled himself to share in our humanity."[40]

One of the earliest surviving Eucharistic Prayers, the Anaphora[41] of Addai and Mari, begins its thanksgiving section by highlighting this divine interchange: "We give thanks to you, O Lord, even we your lowly, weak and wretched servants, because you have effected in us a great grace which cannot be repaid, in that you put on our humanity so as to quicken us by your divinity."[42] The Incarnation is for the sake of man's divinization, and the Eucharist is the means by which we are progressively being nourished in Christ's divinity, through receiving His humanity.[43]

---

[38] Cyril of Jerusalem, *Mystagogic Catechesis* 4.3 in *The Works of Saint Cyril of Jerusalem*, vol. 2, trans. Leo McCauley, FC 64 (Washington, DC: Catholic University of America Press, 1970), 182.

[39] *RM*, 529.

[40] *RM*, 175.

[41] *Anaphora* is the Greek term for Eucharistic Prayer.

[42] Sarhad Jammo, "The Mesopotamian Anaphora of Addai & Mari: The Organic Dialectic between Its Apostolic Core and Euchological Growth," in *The Anaphoral Genesis of the Institution Narrative in Light of the Anaphora of Addai and Mari: Acts of the International Liturgy Congress, Rome 25–26 October 2011*, ed. Cesare Giraudo (Rome: Edizioni Orientalia Christiana, 2013), 421.

[43] See Scheeben, *The Mysteries of Christianity*, 501:

> That Christ might become a member and the head of our race, it was not enough for Him to assume a human nature like ours; He had to take His nature from the very midst of the race. Similarly, to perfect the organic bond which is to bind us to Him, He wills not merely to bring the substance of His body into contact with us, but to implant Himself in us, or rather us in Him; He wishes us to strike root in Him, just as

Dignity of Man

Another end of the Incarnation is to show man his immense dignity as made in God's image and elevated to share in the divine life. The Incarnation is the most fitting means to show us the dignity of man, for God has assumed a true human nature and, with it, all ordinary human realities. Pope St. Leo the Great says in a sermon on the Nativity: "Realize, O Christian, your dignity. Once made a 'partaker in the divine nature,'[44] do not return to your former baseness by a life unworthy [of that dignity]. Remember whose head it is and whose body of which you constitute a member."[45]

Vatican II also took up this theme in *Gaudium et Spes* (1965), §22, a text quoted again and again by St. John Paul II:

> The truth is that only in the mystery of the incarnate Word does the mystery of man take on light. For Adam, the first man, was a figure of Him Who was to come, namely Christ the Lord. Christ, the final Adam, by the revelation of the mystery of the Father and His love, fully reveals man to man himself and makes his supreme calling clear. . . . Since human nature as He assumed it was not annulled, by that very fact it has been raised up to a divine dignity in our respect too. For by His incarnation the Son of God has united Himself in some fashion with every man. He worked with human hands, He thought with a human mind, acted by human choice and loved with a human heart.

If the Incarnation reveals man's dignity because "the Son of God has united Himself in some fashion with every man," how much more true that is by the institution of the Eucharist! For in Holy Communion we receive His very Self into ourselves so that we may be assimilated into Him.

He took root in our race at the Incarnation. This He does by changing into His body the food that nourishes our body; in this food and by means of it He inserts our body in Himself as a branch is engrafted on a vine.

[44] 2 Peter 1:4.

[45] Leo the Great, Sermon 21 (on the Nativity), in *Sermons*, trans. Jane Patricia Freeland and Agnes Josephine Conway, FC 93 (Washington, DC: Catholic University of America Press, 1996), 79.

The Eucharist continues the logic of the Incarnation. What more could God do to show us our dignity than give us the frequent opportunity to receive the Incarnate Word to be our spiritual nourishment and to offer our lives together with His in sacrifice? Furthermore, all the upright aspects of our daily life are given infinite dignity by the Eucharist, for we can unite them in the Mass with Christ's own sacrifice so as to offer them to the Father together.

The Eucharist Is the Nuptials of the Lamb with His Church

We have said that the Incarnation was ordered to accomplishing a mystical marriage between the Church, the Mystical Body of Christ, and the head of that Body, the Lamb of God. This nuptial union is the heart of the New Covenant. We have seen that Christ spoke of this mystical wedding in parables. How is the wedding to be realized?

We can say that the realization of this marriage has two moments. Its perfect culmination is in the heavenly Jerusalem, in the beatific vision in which we shall see the glory of the Lamb and be united to Him forever in an eternal celestial embrace. This is the goal of all of our hope, described enigmatically in the last chapters of Revelation.

However, that heavenly embrace was not to be entirely deferred for heaven. Our divine Spouse chose to consummate His nuptials with His Church even in the course of this life so that we would not faint from longing and weakness. But how was He to accomplish this mystical union with frail sinning men in this valley of tears, in which we walk by faith and not by vision? He did not wish to consummate His nuptials with us in such a way that would take away the merit of faith or remove the essential conditions of our exile in a world in which we must fight the good fight of faith. How can this wedding be consummated with a Bride in exile, who must remain in exile until the appointed time for the Second Coming of the Lord? The wisdom of God devised a wedding feast fit for His exiled Bride that would not be inappropriate to her state of trial. And that feast, of course, is the Eucharist.[46]

---

[46] For the nuptial dimension of the Eucharist, see John Paul II, *Mulieris Dignitatem* (1988), §26; italics original:

> We find ourselves at the very heart of the Paschal Mystery, which completely reveals the spousal love of God. Christ is the Bridegroom because "he has given himself": his body has been "given", his blood

In the Eucharist we receive the divine Bridegroom of our souls in the most intimate union, for we take Him into us as our spiritual nourishment and repast. However, instead of changing our divine food into ourselves, as we do with other food, here we become gradually transformed into the likeness of our Spouse.

The Eucharist is a consummation of union with our divine Bridegroom perfectly fitting to our present state of trial, for it is a union that we recognize entirely by faith, a union that we cannot grasp with our external senses, conceive with our intellect, or demonstrate by any empirical means. It is a union with Christ that we believe because it was taught to us and enjoined on us by the Word of Truth.

A rich analogy can be drawn between the Eucharist as the consummation of the New Covenant and the act proper to the marital covenant by which the spouses unite themselves in one body. As the conjugal act is both unitive and procreative, so the Eucharist can be said to have these two meanings. It unites us with the Bridegroom in the most intimate way, and it nourishes us with an infusion of charity to enable us to exercise spiritual maternity/paternity in the world.

The Eucharist and the Giving of the Holy Spirit

One of the reasons Christ became man was to communicate His own Spirit—the Holy Spirit—to the members of His Body. Although Confirmation is the special sacrament for the communication of the Spirit, the Eucharist most eminently fulfills this mission of the Incarnate Word through repeatedly nourishing the life of the Spirit in us through frequent reception of the One in whom the Spirit dwells in fullness.

In *Ecclesia de Eucharistia*, §17, St. John Paul II quotes a powerful text of St. Ephrem on the communication of the Spirit through

---

has been "poured out" (cf. Lk 22:19-20). In this way "he loved them to the end" (Jn 13:1). The "sincere gift" contained in the Sacrifice of the Cross gives definitive prominence to the spousal meaning of God's love. As the Redeemer of the world, Christ is the Bridegroom of the Church. *The Eucharist is the Sacrament of our Redemption.* It is *the Sacrament of the Bridegroom and of the Bride.* The Eucharist makes present and realizes anew in a sacramental manner the redemptive act of Christ, who "creates" the Church, his body. Christ is united with this "body" as the bridegroom with the bride.

Benedict XVI also treats this theme in *Sacramentum Caritatis*, §27.

the Eucharist: "He called the bread his living body and he filled it with himself and his Spirit. . . . He who eats it with faith, eats Fire and Spirit. . . . Take and eat this, all of you, and eat with it the Holy Spirit. For it is truly my body and whoever eats it will have eternal life."[47]

Mary and the Eucharist

Because of its intimate relationship with the Incarnation, the Eucharist also has a profoundly Marian dimension.[48] The three finalities of the Eucharist—presence, sacrifice, and communion—can be seen in Mary's relationship to Jesus.

St. John Paul II brings out this Marian dimension in *Ecclesia de Eucharistia*, §§55–58. He begins by relating what Mary received at the Annunciation to what the faithful receive in Communion: "At the Annunciation Mary conceived the Son of God in the physical reality of his body and blood, thus anticipating within herself what to some degree happens sacramentally in every believer who receives, under the signs of bread and wine, the Lord's body and blood."[49] Through Holy Communion the faithful receive in their bodies the same humanity of the Word that Mary received in her womb.[50] In order to acknowledge this presence fittingly, the faithful must participate in the supreme act of faith by which Mary gave her fiat and believed that the Creator of the universe would condescend to become man in her body. The faithful, similarly, must believe the glorious truth that the Creator of the universe, having become man, wishes to dwell in them bodily as well, which we express in our "Amen."[51]

---

[47] Ephrem, *Sermo IV in Hebdomadam Sanctam*, Corpus Scriptorum Christianorum Orientalium 413 (CSCO, Scriptores Syri 182) (Leuven, BE: Peeters, 1979), 55.

[48] See John Paul II, *EE*, §55: "The Eucharist, while commemorating the passion and resurrection, is also in continuity with the incarnation." See also Arthur Burton Calkins, "Mary's Presence in the Mass: The Teaching of Pope John Paul II," *Antiphon* 10, no. 2 (2006): 132–58.

[49] John Paul II, *EE*, §55.

[50] See David W. Fagerberg, "Liturgy and Divinization," in Meconi and Olson, eds., *Called to Be the Children of God*, 283: "Mary is the prototype of liturgical person, for the true end of liturgy is to arrive where Mary did. She gave birth to Christ in body; we must give birth to Christ spiritually."

[51] See John Paul II, *EE*, §55:

"Blessed is she who believed" (Luke 1:45). Mary also anticipated, in the mystery of the incarnation, the Church's Eucharistic faith. When, at

The sacrificial dimension of the Eucharist is also exemplified by Mary as she offered her Son standing by the foot of the Cross on Calvary and, in preparation for that event, throughout the thirty-three years of His earthly life.[52] John Paul II writes:

> Mary, throughout her life at Christ's side and not only on Calvary, made her own *the sacrificial dimension of the Eucharist*. When she brought the child Jesus to the Temple in Jerusalem "to present him to the Lord" (Lk 2:22), she heard the aged Simeon announce that the child would be a "sign of contradiction" and that a sword would also pierce her own heart (cf. Lk 2:34–35). The tragedy of her Son's crucifixion was thus foretold, and in some sense Mary's *Stabat Mater* at the foot of the Cross was foreshadowed. In her daily preparation

---

the Visitation, she bore in her womb the Word made flesh, she became in some way a "tabernacle"—the first "tabernacle" in history—in which the Son of God, still invisible to our human gaze, allowed himself to be adored by Elizabeth, radiating his light as it were through the eyes and the voice of Mary. And is not the enraptured gaze of Mary as she contemplated the face of the newborn Christ and cradled him in her arms that unparalleled model of love which should inspire us every time we receive Eucharistic communion?

[52] See Second Vatican Council, Dogmatic Constitution on the Church, *Lumen Gentium* (1964), §58: "The Blessed Virgin advanced in her pilgrimage of faith, and faithfully persevered in her union with her Son unto the cross, where she stood, in keeping with the divine plan, grieving exceedingly with her only begotten Son, uniting herself with a maternal heart with His sacrifice, and lovingly consenting to the immolation of this Victim which she herself had brought forth." See also Pius X, Encyclical on the Immaculate Conception, *Ad Diem Illum* (1904), §12:

> Moreover it was not only the prerogative of the Most Holy Mother to have furnished the material of His flesh to the Only Son of God, Who was to be born with human members, of which material should be prepared the Victim for the salvation of men; but hers was also the office of tending and nourishing that Victim, and at the appointed time presenting Him for the sacrifice. Hence that uninterrupted community of life and labors of the Son and the Mother, so that of both might have been uttered the words of the Psalmist, "My life is consumed in sorrow and my years in groans" [Ps 31:10]. When the supreme hour of the Son came, beside the Cross of Jesus there stood Mary His Mother, not merely occupied in contemplating the cruel spectacle, but rejoicing that her Only Son was offered for the salvation of mankind, and so entirely participating in His Passion, that if it had been possible she would have gladly borne all the torments that her Son bore.

for Calvary, Mary experienced a kind of "anticipated Eucharist"—one might say a "spiritual communion"—of desire and of oblation, which would culminate in her union with her Son in his passion, and then find expression after Easter by her partaking in the Eucharist which the Apostles celebrated as the memorial of that passion.[53]

What Mary offered at the foot of the Cross—her Son as the divine Victim to atone for the sins of the world—is offered by the Church in every Mass.

Finally, the aspect of spiritual nourishment of the Eucharist is exemplified in Mary as the person in whom the life-giving power of the Eucharist reached its apex because she never put any obstacle to grace and because of the perfection of her disposition of love and yearning for the fullest union with her Son. Mary would have grown in grace through every Holy Communion in an unparalleled way, as she received the Son whom she had nurtured in her womb and accompanied to Calvary. John Paul II helps us to imagine her reception of Communion:

> The body given up for us and made present under sacramental signs was the same body which she had conceived in her womb! For Mary, receiving the Eucharist must have somehow meant welcoming once more into her womb that heart which had beat in unison with hers and reliving what she had experienced at the foot of the Cross.[54]

The Eucharist Was Instituted to Be the Summit of the Sacramental Economy

In all the works of God, where there is multiplicity there is order and hierarchy. Thus there must also be hierarchy in the seven sacraments. Baptism is first in terms of the necessity of grace, and Holy Orders is necessary for the government of the Church and the administration of the sacraments, but the Eucharist is by far the first in dignity. We

---

[53] John Paul II, *EE*, §56 (italics original).
[54] Ibid.

can see this in various ways. First of all, the Eucharist contains the real and substantial presence of Jesus Christ, whereas the other sacraments only contain His power.[55] Secondly, the Eucharist is the sacrament of charity. As charity is the queen of the virtues and of the spiritual life, so the Eucharist is the queen of the sacraments. As charity already attains to the life of heaven, so the Eucharist already begins the nuptial union we will have with God in heaven. Thirdly, while the other sacraments apply the merits of the sacrifice of Christ, the Eucharist does so while also making present and offering His sacrifice.

The *Catechism of the Council of Trent* explains:

> Although all the sacraments have a divine efficacy, it is nevertheless very important to note that they are quite unequal in terms of necessity and dignity. This inequality is based, of course, on the differences in their respective significations. Three of the sacraments are clearly more necessary than the others; but even among these three the nature of their necessity varies. The only sacrament which is universally and uniquely necessary is Baptism.... Secondly, there is a necessity for the sacrament of Penance, but only in a relative sense.... Thirdly, the sacrament of Holy Orders, although not for each one of the faithful, is absolutely necessary for the Church as a whole. If, on the other hand, we compare the sacraments in terms of dignity, we immediately recognize the Holy Eucharist as far and away superior to all the others. This is because of its substantial holiness, and the number and greatness of its mysteries.[56]

To explore this question, St. Thomas has an article in which he asks whether the Eucharist is the greatest of the sacraments. The answer, of course, is affirmative. Since the Eucharist alone contains the substantial presence of Christ and His sacrifice, the other sacraments are all ordered to the Eucharist as to their source and end. This

---

[55] See Lombard, *Sentences* IV, d. 8, ch. 1, p. 41: "And so it is excellently called 'Eucharist,' that is, good grace, because in this sacrament not only is there an increase of virtue and grace, but he who is the fount and origin of all grace is wholly received."

[56] *CCT*, pt. II, intro., §22 (pp. 156–57).

is manifested liturgically in the fact that the celebration of the other sacraments naturally terminates in the Eucharist:

> Absolutely speaking, the sacrament of the Eucharist is the greatest of all the sacraments: and this may be shown in three ways. First of all because it contains Christ Himself substantially: whereas the other sacraments contain a certain instrumental power which is a share of Christ's power, as we have shown above (q. 62, a. 4, ad 3, 5). Now that which is essentially such is always of more account than that which is such by participation.
>
> Secondly, this is made clear by considering the relation of the sacraments to one another. For all the other sacraments seem to be ordained to this one as to their end. For it is manifest that the sacrament of Order is ordained to the consecration of the Eucharist: and the sacrament of Baptism to the reception of the Eucharist: while a man is perfected by Confirmation, so as not to fear to abstain from this sacrament. By Penance and Extreme Unction man is prepared to receive the Body of Christ worthily. And Matrimony at least in its signification, touches this sacrament; in so far as it signifies the union of Christ with the Church, of which union the Eucharist is a figure: hence the Apostle says (Ephesians 5:32): "This is a great sacrament: but I speak in Christ and in the Church."
>
> Thirdly, this is made clear by considering the rites of the sacraments. For nearly all the sacraments terminate in the Eucharist, as Dionysius says;[57] thus those who have been ordained receive Holy Communion, as also do those who have been baptized, if they be adults.
>
> The remaining sacraments may be compared to one another in several ways. For on the ground of necessity, Baptism is the greatest of the sacraments; while from the point of view of perfection, Order comes first; while Confirmation holds a middle place. The sacraments of Penance and Extreme Unction are on a degree inferior to those mentioned above; because, as stated above (a. 2), they are ordained to the Christian life, not directly, but accidentally, as it were,

---

[57] Pseudo-Dionysius, *Ecclesiastical Hierarchy* 3.1.

that is to say, as remedies against supervening defects. And among these, Extreme Unction is compared to Penance, as Confirmation to Baptism; in such a way, that Penance is more necessary, whereas Extreme Unction is more perfect.[58]

The Second Vatican Council speaks of the ordering of the other sacraments to the Eucharist in *Presbyterorum Ordinis* (1965), §5:

> The other sacraments, as well as with every ministry of the Church and every work of the apostolate, are tied together with the Eucharist and are directed toward it. The Most Blessed Eucharist contains the entire spiritual boon of the Church, that is, Christ himself, our Pasch and Living Bread, by the action of the Holy Spirit through his very flesh vital and vitalizing, giving life to men who are thus invited and encouraged to offer themselves, their labors and all created things, together with him. In this light, the Eucharist shows itself as the source and summit of the whole work of preaching the Gospel.

Uniqueness of the Eucharist Compared with the Other Sacraments

The Eucharist is unique among the sacraments in three ways. First, the other sacraments only apply Christ's power and confer the grace He merited on Calvary. The Eucharist alone contains Christ Himself in all His personal reality and makes His humanity present in our midst. In other sacraments, material elements, such as water and oil, are consecrated for use in the sacrament, but they are not substantially changed by that consecration.[59] In the Eucharistic consecration, on

---

[58] *ST* III, q. 65, a. 3. See also q. 63, a. 6, in which St. Thomas, citing Dionysius's *Ecclesial Hierarchy* 3, refers to the Eucharist as "the end and consummation of all the sacraments." He explains here that the Eucharist does not imprint character because "it contains within itself Christ, in Whom there is not the character, but the very plenitude of the Priesthood."

[59] See *ST* III, q. 73, a. 1, ad 3:

> The difference between the Eucharist and other sacraments having sensible matter, is that whereas the Eucharist contains something which is sacred absolutely, namely, Christ's own body; the baptismal water contains something which is sacred in relation to something else, namely,

the contrary, the elements are not just blessed by Christ's word; they become Christ Himself.

Second, the Eucharist alone, in addition to being a sacrament, is also the Christian sacrifice. St. Thomas writes:

> This sacrament is both a sacrifice and a sacrament; it has the nature of a sacrifice inasmuch as it is offered up; and it has the nature of a sacrament inasmuch as it is received. And therefore it has the effect of a sacrament in the recipient, and the effect of a sacrifice in the offerer, or in them for whom it is offered.[60]

Third, the Eucharist alone among the sacraments enables us to receive His entire humanity into our bodies so as to nourish us progressively with a share in His divinity.

In summary, the Eucharist is the sacrament of all sacraments because through it Christ in the fullness of His glorious reality

---

the sanctifying power: and the same holds good of chrism and suchlike. Consequently, the sacrament of the Eucharist is completed in the very consecration of the matter, whereas the other sacraments are completed in the application of the matter for the sanctifying of the individual. And from this follows another difference. For, in the sacrament of the Eucharist, what is both reality and sacrament is in the matter itself; but what is reality only, namely, the grace bestowed, is in the recipient; whereas in Baptism both are in the recipient, namely, the character, which is both reality and sacrament, and the grace of pardon of sins, which is reality only. And the same holds good of the other sacraments.

See also *CCT*, part 2, ch. 3, §9 (p. 214):

It is easier to see now how this sacrament differs from all the others. The formal existence of the other six sacraments consists in the actual use made of the materials composing them, i.e., by their being confected (or administered) and received. Baptism, for instance, becomes a sacrament when the ablution is performed. The Eucharist, on the other hand, is constituted a sacrament solely by the consecration of the elements. And when it is preserved in a pyx or another sacred vessel, it does not cease to be a sacrament. A second point of difference is that in the material elements of which the other sacraments are composed, no change takes place. In Baptism the water or in Confirmation the chrism do not lose their nature of water or oil when they are confected. In the Eucharist, however, that which before consecration was bread and wine becomes after its consecration really and substantially the Body and the Blood of our Lord.

[60] *ST* III, q. 79, a. 5.

becomes present in our midst so that we can adore Him and receive Him in Communion. It is the sacrifice of all sacrifices because Christ, joined by His Church, sacramentally offers to the Father the price of our redemption, Jesus Himself, whom we then are given to receive as the consummation of the sacrifice.

The Eucharist and the New Covenant

Just as the Eucharist builds up the Church and constitutes her supernatural life, so it is the essential content of the New Covenant, which is life in Christ. The sacraments should be understood as the mysterious privileged instruments of the New Covenant for sanctification and worship. Each sacrament realizes a fundamental aspect of the Covenant. We enter the Covenant as children of God in Baptism and are brought to be mature members of the Covenant through Confirmation. Sins against the Covenant are forgiven through Penance and the effects of sin are further purified in Anointing of the Sick. Marriage is the privileged sign of the Covenant, which is essentially spousal, as indicated in Ephesians 5:32. The New Covenant has the glory of an eternal priesthood in which men are given the power to act in the person of Christ in administering the sacraments and to teach and govern the Mystical Body.

The Eucharist, however, does not merely realize an aspect of the New Covenant or symbolize it, as marriage does. Jesus says that the Eucharist *is* "the New Covenant in my blood" (Luke 22:20). By giving us Communion, the Eucharist brings us into the most intimate union with Jesus and causes our divinization, and it also makes it possible for us to offer the most perfect worship of God by giving us the means to offer ourselves to the Father in union with Christ's own sacrifice. The Eucharist therefore is the heart of the New Covenant.

The Eucharist and the Mysteries of Christ

The Eucharist contains the entire mystery of Christ. First of all, it contains Christ Himself in His full substantial presence: Body, Blood, Soul, and Divinity. There is no mystery of Christ's life that is not somehow contained in the Eucharist. Christ is present in the Eucharist with the very same humanity that He received from the virginal womb of His Blessed Mother on the day of the Annunciation, which was born in Bethlehem, which shone in resplendent glory in the

Transfiguration on Mount Tabor, and which, scourged, mocked, and bloody, hung on the Cross on Calvary and expired.

The Eucharist contains Christ's glorious body as He now exists in heaven at the right hand of the Father, but at the same time it mysteriously makes Christ present as the Victim of Calvary who offers the sacrifice of His human life and pierced Heart to the Father for the forgiveness of sins. In this way the Eucharist brings together and makes present the two poles of the Paschal mystery: the Passion and the Resurrection.[61] St. John Paul II emphasizes this dual aspect of the Eucharist in *Ecclesia de Eucharistia*, §14:

> The Eucharistic Sacrifice makes present not only the mystery of the Saviour's passion and death, but also the mystery of the resurrection which crowned his sacrifice. It is as the living and risen One that Christ can become in the Eucharist the "bread of life" (*John* 6:35, 48), the "living bread" (*John* 6:51).

The Eucharist works a miracle like that of the Incarnation, for it introduces the bodily presence of God Incarnate into our midst, on the altar as once in the womb of the Virgin. And it works the redemption of mankind gained for us on the Cross, whose efficacy it "prolongs" through the centuries and "applies" for the salvation of our souls,[62] giving us the pledge of our future resurrection and feeding us with the Risen Lord who has conquered death.

The Eucharist thus suspends, as it were, the natural limitations of space and time, making the adorable person of Christ and His redemptive sacrifice and glorious Resurrection present to all men in all places and succeeding times so as to enrich His Mystical Body with His sacrifice and nourish us spiritually with His Body and Blood. This is the glory of the New Covenant.

---

[61] On the presence of the resurrected Christ in the Eucharist, see Gustave Martelet, *The Risen Christ and the Eucharistic World*, trans. René Hague (New York: Seabury Press, 1976); Dominic M. Langevin, O.P., *From Passion to Paschal Mystery: A Recent Magisterial Development concerning the Christological Foundation of the Sacraments* (Fribourg, CH: Academic Press, 2015).

[62] See Council of Trent, Doctrine Concerning the Sacrifice of the Mass (session 22, September 17, 1562), ch. 2 (DS, 1744); Pius XII, Encyclical on the Sacred Liturgy, *Mediator Dei* (1947), §§77–79.

Study Questions

1. What are the three principal reasons for which Christ instituted the Eucharist?
2. Why can it be said that Christ instituted the Eucharist for the same reasons that He became man? Explain several reasons for the Incarnation and the Eucharist (different from the previous question).
3. In what sense is the Eucharist a model for every virtue?
4. The Fathers frequently teach that God become man so that man could be divinized. How does this reason for the Incarnation relate to the Eucharist?
5. Explain the Marian dimension of the Eucharist.
6. How does the Eucharist contain the whole of the Paschal mystery?
7. How is the Eucharist the greatest of the sacraments and the summit of the sacramental system?
8. What is the relationship between the Eucharist and the New Covenant?

Suggestions for Further Reading

Summa theologiae III, q. 73, aa. 1–5.

John Paul II. Encyclical Letter *Ecclesia de Eucharistia*. April 17, 2003, §§1–33.

Scheeben, Matthias Joseph. *The Mysteries of Christianity*. Translated by Cyril Vollert. St. Louis, MO: B. Herder, 1951. Pp. 469–97.

✠

CHAPTER TWO

The Eucharist Prefigured in the Old Testament

The Eucharist, as the great sacrament of the New Covenant and the masterwork of God, is abundantly prefigured in the Old Testament and in the religions of mankind. All the sacrifices and offerings of the patriarchs and of Israel, and even those offered by pagan cults, were figures of the Eucharist.

The figures of the Eucharist can be conveniently divided according to the three fundamental aspects of the Eucharist presented in the previous chapter: the sacrament of God's intimate dwelling with us in the real presence; the sacrifice for our redemption; and the sacrament of spiritual nourishment and communion.[1] All three of these aspects were prefigured in manifold ways.

---

[1] St. Thomas Aquinas categorizes the Old Testament types of the Eucharist according to a different threefold division in which the sacraments are considered as *sacramentum tantum*, *res et sacramentum*, and *res tantum*. See *ST* III, q. 73, a. 6:

> We can consider three things in this sacrament: namely, that which is sacrament only, and this is the bread and wine; that which is both reality and sacrament, to wit, Christ's true body; and lastly that which is reality only, namely, the effect of this sacrament. Consequently, in relation to what is sacrament only, the chief figure of this sacrament was the oblation of Melchizedek, who offered up bread and wine. In relation to Christ crucified, Who is contained in this sacrament, its figures were all the sacrifices of the Old Testament, especially the sacrifice of expiation, which was the most solemn of all. While with regard to its effect, the chief figure was the Manna, "having in it the sweetness of every taste" (Wisdom 16:20), just as the grace of this sacrament refreshes the soul in all respects.

FIGURE OF THE REAL PRESENCE OF CHRIST
IN THE EUCHARIST: THE *SHEKHINAH*

The mystery of the Incarnation and the substantial presence of Christ in the Eucharist—Body, Blood, Soul, and Divinity—were prefigured in the Old Covenant in a special presence of God manifested at certain times by a visible glory overshadowing the holy place. This overshadowing presence of God is referred to by Jews as the *shekhinah*, which is derived from the Hebrew verb *shachan*: "to dwell or abide." The *shekhinah* was manifested first on Mount Sinai in a cloud of glory and a devouring fire, out of which God spoke to Moses.[2] The cloud of glory marking God's "dwelling" with Israel later covered the Tent of Meeting that housed the Ark of the Covenant and finally came to rest over the Holy of Holies in the Temple.[3] The dwelling of God with His people in the Temple can be understood as the reestablishment, after original sin, of a place of intimacy with God, like the garden of Eden that was lost.[4]

---

[2] See Exod 24:16–17: "The glory of the LORD settled on Mount Sinai, and the cloud covered it six days; and on the seventh day he called to Moses out of the midst of the cloud. Now the appearance of the glory of the LORD was like a devouring fire on the top of the mountain in the sight of the sons of Israel."

[3] See 1 Kings 8:10–13. For the *shekhinah* in rabbinical thought, see Joseph Sievers, "'Where Two or Three …': The Rabbinic Concept of Shekhinah and Matthew 18:20," in *The Jewish Roots of Christian Liturgy*, ed. Eugene J. Fisher (New York: Paulist Press, 1990), 47–64; Solomon Schechter, *Aspects of Rabbinic Theology: Major Concepts of the Talmud* (New York: Schocken Books, 1961), 48–49, 223–34, 238; Martin McNamara, *Targum and Testament Revisited: Aramaic Paraphrases of the Hebrew Bible: A Light on the New Testament*, 2nd ed. (Grand Rapids, MI: Eerdmans, 2010), 148–52.

[4] See Joshua Berman, *The Temple: Its Symbolism and Meaning Then and Now* (Northvale, NJ: Jason Aronson, 1995), 26:

> If the laws concerning life in the land of Israel are designed to create an environment in which the children of Israel can encounter God, the Temple represents this environment at its apex. Within the land of Israel as a whole, the entire nation lives a collective, Eden-like existence in God's presence. The Temple, however, represents the spiritual center of the country. Here, at the site where God's presence is most immanent, the representatives of the Jewish people execute commandments and rites that symbolize the service of the nation as a whole. Here, too, the garden of Eden serves as a paradigm for the parameters of this encounter. Throughout the Bible, the Sanctuary is described via language and terms that are borrowed from the Eden narrative of Genesis, chapters 2 and 3.

The liturgy of the Old Covenant centered on the Ark of the Covenant, which was a magnificent type (foreshadowing likeness) of Christ and His presence in the Eucharist, for it contained the two tablets of the Ten Commandments, a jar of manna, and the rod of Aaron that had blossomed as a sign of Aaron's election to the high priesthood. The tablets of the Law prefigure Christ as the living Torah who reveals the will of God not just in commandments, but in every aspect of His life, and particularly in His Passion. The manna prefigures Christ as the true Bread from heaven who gives life to the world. The rod of Aaron prefigures Christ as the eternal High Priest.

Hebrews 9:2–7 gives a description of the Tabernacle housing the Ark:

> For a tent was prepared, the outer one, in which were the lampstand and the table and the bread of offering; it is called the Holy Place. Behind the second curtain stood a tent called the Holy of Holies, having the golden altar of incense and the ark of the covenant covered on all sides with gold, which contained a golden urn holding the manna, and Aaron's rod that budded, and the tables of the covenant; above it were the cherubim of glory overshadowing the mercy seat. Of these things we cannot now speak in detail. These preparations having thus been made, the priests go continually into the outer tent, performing their ritual duties; but into the second only the high priest goes, and he but once a year, and not without taking blood which he offers for himself and for the errors of the people.

The privileged place in which God dwelt with His people was in the Tabernacle housing the Ark of the Covenant, also called the Sanctuary or Tent of Meeting. In Exodus 25:8, God says to Moses: "And let them make me a sanctuary, that I may dwell in their midst. According to all that I show you concerning the pattern of the tabernacle, and of all its furniture, so you shall make it."

On top of the Ark there was the mercy seat, where Israel was to encounter the mercy of God. Moses himself was to seek out counsel from the Lord before the mercy seat: "And you shall put the mercy seat on the top of the ark. . . . There I will meet with you, and from above the mercy seat, from between the two cherubim that are upon the ark of the testimony, I will speak with you of all that I will give you in commandment for the people of Israel" (Exod 25:21–22).

Exodus 29:42–46 speaks of the Tent of Meeting as the place of encounter of all Israel with the personal presence of God dwelling among them:

> [The lamb] shall be a continual burnt offering throughout your generations at the door of the tent of meeting before the LORD, where I will meet with you, to speak there to you. There I will meet with the sons of Israel, and it shall be sanctified by my glory; I will consecrate the tent of meeting and the altar; Aaron also and his sons I will consecrate, to serve me as priests. And I will dwell among the sons of Israel, and will be their God. And they shall know that I am the LORD their God, who brought them forth out of the land of Egypt that I might dwell among them; I am the LORD their God.

When the Tent of Meeting was finished and consecrated, Exodus 40:34–38 describes how the glory of the Lord visibly descended on it and remained there, except when they were to travel:

> Then the cloud covered the tent of meeting, and the glory of the LORD filled the tabernacle. And Moses was not able to enter the tent of meeting, because the cloud abode upon it, and the glory of the LORD filled the tabernacle. Throughout all their journeys, whenever the cloud was taken up from over the tabernacle, the sons of Israel would go onward; but if the cloud was not taken up, then they did not go onward till the day that it was taken up. For throughout all their journeys the cloud of the LORD was upon the tabernacle by day, and fire was in it by night, in the sight of all the house of Israel.

Because of God's presence in the sanctuary, the whole of Israel was sanctified. In Numbers 35:34, God says: "You shall not defile the land in which you live, in the midst of which I dwell; for I the LORD dwell in the midst of the sons of Israel."

During the time of Eli, the high priest, the Ark of the Covenant was captured by the Philistines. The special presence of the Lord was no longer seen in its visible glory, but rather in the destruction of the Philistine idols and in a plague on the Philistines.

The Temple in Jerusalem was constructed by Solomon in about 1000 BC to take the place of the Tent of Meeting and house the Ark of the Covenant. When Solomon dedicated the Temple, the glory of God filled it:

> When Solomon had ended his prayer, fire came down from heaven and consumed the burnt offering and the sacrifices, and the glory of the LORD filled the temple. And the priests could not enter the house of the LORD, because the glory of the LORD filled the LORD's house. (2 Chr 7:1–2)[5]

The visible manifestation of God's presence in the *shekhinah* was one of the glories of Israel, showing the nearness of God to Israel. As Moses said to Israel: "What great nation is there that has a god so near to it as the LORD our God is to us, whenever we call upon Him?" (Deut 4:7).

God's mysterious indwelling in the Tent of Meeting and in the Holy of Holies in the Temple was a figure of the supreme indwelling of God that occurred when "the Word became flesh and dwelt among us" (John 1:14). John chose the word "dwell" (ἐσκήνωσεν, from the root *skhnh*), which literally means to "dwell as in a tent," to recall the dwelling of God with His people through the *shekhinah* in the Tabernacle that housed the Ark.[6]

Joseph Ratzinger, in *Jesus of Nazareth: The Infancy Narratives*, comments on John 1:14:

> The man Jesus is the dwelling-place of the Word, the eternal divine Word, in this world. Jesus' "flesh," his human existence, is the "dwelling" or "tent" of the Word: the reference to the sacred tent of Israel in the wilderness is unmistakable. Jesus is,

---

[5] See also the parallel text, 1 Kings 8:10–13, which describes the installation of the Ark of the Covenant in Solomon's Temple: "And when the priests came out of the holy place, a cloud filled the house of the LORD, so that the priests could not stand to minister because of the cloud; for the glory of the LORD filled the house of the LORD. Then Solomon said, 'The LORD has set the sun in the heavens, but has said that he would dwell in thick darkness. I have built you an exalted house, a place for you to dwell in for ever.'"

[6] John 1:14 also recalls Sir 24:8: "Then the Creator of all things gave me a commandment, and the one who created me assigned a place for my tent. And he said, 'Make your dwelling in Jacob, and in Israel receive your inheritance.'"

so to speak, the tent of meeting—he is the reality for which the tent and the later Temple could only serve as signs.[7]

And, since the humanity of Jesus is truly and substantially contained in the Blessed Sacrament, the Tent of Meeting and the Temple are signs prefiguring not only the Incarnation, but also the Eucharist and every church housing the Blessed Sacrament, through which Christ "dwells" with His Church.

Jesus demonstrates that the Temple is a type of Him in John 2:19–21 when He is asked for a sign for chasing out the money-changers from the Temple and answers: "Destroy this temple, and in three days I will raise it up." John clarifies that "he spoke of the temple of his body." Through the Eucharist, this Temple of Christ's Body is made present in every tabernacle containing a consecrated host. Every church with the Blessed Sacrament is infinitely holier than the Temple in Jerusalem, for that was but a type or figure of the real presence of the Word Incarnate.

The Temple is also the type of the Christian who receives Christ in Holy Communion and of the souls of the just who have the divine Indwelling of the Blessed Trinity. St. Paul speaks of the Temple with reference to the Christian in 1 Corinthians 6:13–20:

> The body is not meant for immorality, but for the Lord, and the Lord for the body. . . . Do you not know that your bodies are members of Christ? Shall I therefore take the members of Christ and make them members of a prostitute? Never! Do you not know that he who joins himself to a prostitute becomes one body with her? For, as it is written, "The two shall become one." But he who is united to the Lord becomes one spirit with him. . . . Do you not know that your body is a temple of the Holy Spirit within you, which you have from God? You are not your own; you were bought with a price. So glorify God in your body.

The Temple, finally, is a type of the unity of the Church and her worship, as will be seen below.

---

[7] Joseph Ratzinger, *Jesus of Nazareth: The Infancy Narratives*, trans. Philip J. Whitmore (New York: Image, 2012), 11.

FIGURES OF THE SACRIFICE OF THE EUCHARIST

The sacrificial rites of the Old Testament are figures of the sacrifice of Calvary and of the Eucharistic sacrifice. These rites begin with those of the patriarchs—Adam, Abel, Noah, Abraham, Isaac, and Jacob—and continue in the Mosaic Covenant, which offers figures of Christ's sacrifice that are richer and more explicit. The paschal lamb is a type of the sacrifice of Christ, and therefore also of His sacrifice made present in the Eucharist. The same is true of all the holocausts of Israel, the scapegoat offered on the Day of Atonement, the morning and evening sacrifice, the peace offerings, the communion offerings, the thanksgiving offerings, the memorial offerings, the offerings of wheat, and the offering of bread and wine by the priest Melchizedek. All of these are figures pointing to the reality of Christ's sacrifice, which is sacramentally contained and offered in the Eucharist. St. Thomas writes:

> Now of all the gifts which God vouchsafed to mankind after they had fallen away by sin, the chief is that He gave His Son; wherefore it is written (John 3:16): "God so loved the world, as to give His only-begotten Son." . . . Consequently the chief sacrifice is that whereby Christ Himself "delivered Himself . . . to God for an odor of sweetness" (Eph 5:2). And for this reason all the other sacrifices of the Old Law were offered up in order to foreshadow this one individual and paramount sacrifice—the imperfect forecasting the perfect.[8]

The typology of the sacrifice of the paschal lamb and other Old Testament events is beautifully explained in an ancient Easter homily from the second century by St. Melito, bishop of Sardis:

> For he who was led away as a lamb and who was sacrificed as a sheep, by himself delivered us from servitude to the world as from the land of Egypt, and released us from bondage to the devil as from the hand of Pharaoh, and sealed our souls by his own spirit and the members of our bodies by his own blood. . . . This is he who is the Passover of our salvation.[9] He is the

---

[8]   *ST* I-II, q. 102, a. 3.
[9]   See Exod 12:1–14.

silent lamb,[10] the lamb that was slaughtered, the lamb born of Mary, the fair ewe; he was taken from the flock, dragged off to be slaughtered, slain during the evening,[11] and buried at night. No bone of his was broken; his body in the earth knew no corruption; he rose from the dead and raised up humankind from the depths of the tomb.[12]

Christ's sacrifice that is sacramentally made present and offered in the Mass recapitulates the entire history and liturgy of the Chosen People. St. Leo the Great also makes this point in a sermon given in Holy Week:

> You have drawn all things to yourself, Lord, so that what was done in the one temple of Judea with concealed meanings, the devotion of all nations everywhere celebrates in a clear and open mystery. Now, when the variety of animal sacrifices has ceased, the one oblation of your body and blood fulfills all the many kinds of offering. You are the true "Lamb of God that takes away the sins of the world," and thus you perfect all mysteries in yourself. As one sacrifice is made on behalf of all victims, so there will be one kingdom for all nations.[13]

Priesthood and Sacrifice before the Mosaic Law

Before God revealed Himself to Abraham, Genesis shows us the patriarchs fulfilling a priestly function. We first encounter sacrifice offered to God right after the Fall, offered by Cain and Abel in Genesis 4:3–5: "In the course of time Cain brought to the LORD an offering of the fruit of the ground, and Abel brought of the firstlings of his flock and of their fat portions. And the LORD had regard for Abel and his offering, but for Cain and his offering he had no regard."

---

[10] See Isa 53:7: "He was oppressed, and he was afflicted, yet he opened not his mouth; like a lamb that is led to the slaughter, and like a sheep that before its shearers is silent, so he opened not his mouth."

[11] See Exod 12:1–14.

[12] Melito, "Homily on the Passion," nos. 65–71, in *Worship in the Early Church: An Anthology of Historical Sources*, ed. Lawrence J. Johnson (Collegeville, MN: Liturgical Press, 2009), 98–99. This text is included in the Office of Readings on Holy Thursday.

[13] Leo the Great, Sermon 59.7 (Freeland and Conway, 258).

After the flood, Noah offered sacrifice, as we see in Genesis 8:20–21:

> Then Noah built an altar to the LORD, and took of every clean animal and of every clean bird, and offered burnt offerings on the altar. And when the LORD smelled the pleasing odor, the LORD said in his heart, "I will never again curse the ground because of man, for the imagination of man's heart is evil from his youth; neither will I ever again destroy every living creature as I have done."

Noah here performed the priestly function of mediation between God and man. On behalf of mankind saved from the flood, he offers up to God the burnt offerings of animals regarded as "clean" for sacrifice. This sacrifice propitiates God and calls down His favor on the family of Noah, from whom all mankind descends. Noah's priestly activity thus has an ascending and descending dimension: the sacrifice ascends to God, expressing acts of thanksgiving, praise, petition, and satisfaction directed to God and reconciliation with Him, and this merits God's blessing descending on the people.[14]

Abraham likewise served the priestly function of mediation between man and God. The greatest example was his preparation to offer the sacrifice of Isaac, through whom and in whose seed God had designated the promised blessing.[15] In this event, only the interior sacrifice was accepted, whereas its exterior realization was transferred to a ram. This ascending mediation of sacrifice was followed by a descending mediation of grace. On account of Abraham's extraordinary faith and fidelity, God renewed His promise to make of Isaac a people as numerous as the sands of the sea and a blessing for all the nations of the earth.[16] Abraham's readiness to offer his son Isaac is a figure of Christ's immolation on Calvary in obedience to the salvific will

---

[14] See *ST* III, q. 22, a. 1: "The office proper to a priest is to be a mediator between God and the people. This occurs inasmuch as he bestows divine things on the people, wherefore *sacerdos* [priest] means a giver of sacred things [*sacra dans*], . . . and again, insofar as he offers up the people's prayers to God, and, in a manner, makes satisfaction to God for their sins."

[15] On the sacrifice of Isaac and its typological relation to the Eucharist, see Matthew Levering, *Sacrifice and Community: Jewish Offering and Christian Eucharist* (Malden, MA: Blackwell, 2005), 29–49.

[16] See Gen 22:16–18.

of His heavenly Father. Thus it is fitting that Abraham's sacrifice be remembered in the Roman Canon, together with that of Abel and Melchizedek.[17]

In this event, Isaac is clearly a figure of Christ, the beloved only-begotten Son of God the Father in whom all the promises to the human race are contained. The promises were contained in Isaac as forefather of the Messiah. As Abraham was ordered to sacrifice Isaac, so God the Father, in His eternal providence, had determined the sacrifice of His only-begotten Son for the redemption of the human race. As Isaac is a figure of Christ, the sacrificed Son, so Abraham, in this episode, corresponds to God the Father, a father who sacrifices the object of his greatest love.

This figure, however, magnificent as it is, falls far short of the reality of the sacrifice of the New Covenant that is its fulfillment. Isaac was spared, whereas Christ was not. It seems that St. Paul makes reference to this difference between the sacrifice of Isaac and Christ in Romans 8:32: "He who did not spare his own Son but gave him up for us all, will he not also give us all things with him?" Furthermore, Isaac was not the promise itself, but only the forefather of the Promise that was Christ, in whom all nations are truly blessed.

Finally, a type of the sacrifice of Christ is present in Abraham's answer to Isaac's question about the sacrificial animal. Abraham replies: "God will provide himself the lamb for a burnt offering, my son" (Gen 22:8). The significance of this phrase is reinforced in Genesis 22:14, as Abraham calls the name of that place "The Lord will provide." In the literal sense, the Lord provided the sacrifice in the ram found in the thicket. But typologically, the Father provides the sacrifice through the Incarnation of His Son. What no mere man could accomplish—a sacrifice to redeem the world—the Lord provided in His Incarnation and Passion.[18]

---

[17] Eucharistic Prayer I: "Be pleased to look upon these offerings with a serene and kindly countenance, and to accept them, as once you were pleased to accept the gifts of your servant Abel the just, the sacrifice of Abraham, our father in faith, and the offering of your high priest Melchizedek, a holy sacrifice, a spotless victim" (RM, 641).

[18] See Joseph Ratzinger, "The Theology of the Liturgy," in TL, 549: "The vision of the lamb that appears in the story of Isaac—the lamb that gets entangled in the undergrowth and ransoms the son—has come true: the Lord became Lamb; He allows Himself to be bound and sacrificed in order to set us free."

Priesthood and Sacrifice in the Law of Moses

The Law of Moses gave a new, divinely established form to the priesthood. The Mosaic Law put the priesthood and the offering of sacrifice at the heart of the worship of Israel. These sacrifices were offered first in the Tent of Meeting and then in the Temple in Jerusalem.

The principal task of the Old Testament priests was offering sacrifice. They offered up sacrifice to God and brought down blessings and teaching from God to man.[19] There were daily morning and evening offerings, and there were special sacrifices, especially in the principal feasts of Passover, Pentecost, Yom Kippur (the Day of Atonement), and the feast of Tabernacles (Sukkoth). The principal part of these sacrifices involved the shedding of the blood of domestic animals as a sign of vicarious atonement, as stated in Leviticus 17:11: "For the life of the flesh is in the blood; and I have given it for you upon the altar to make atonement for your souls; for it is the blood that makes atonement, by reason of the life."

Different Kinds of Old Testament Sacrifice

The first seven chapters of the Book of Leviticus give the prescriptions for the various kinds of sacrifices that the Israelites were to offer to the Lord.[20] The fundamental categories are: burnt offerings,[21] sin offerings for inadvertent sins, guilt offerings to atone for deliberate sin,[22] cereal offerings, and peace offerings.[23]

---

[19] See Deut 33:10: "They shall teach Jacob your ordinances, and Israel your law; they shall put incense before you, and whole burnt offering upon your altar." See also Ezek 44:15, 23.

[20] On the different kinds of Levitical sacrifices, see Philip P. Jenson, "The Levitical Sacrificial System," in *Sacrifice in the Bible*, ed. Roger T. Beckwith and Martin J. Selman (Grand Rapids, MI: Baker Book House, 1995), 25–40; Royden Keith Yerkes, *Sacrifice in Greek and Roman Religions and Early Judaism* (London: Adam and Charles Black, 1953); Bruce Chilton, *The Temple of Jesus: His Sacrificial Program Within a Cultural History of Sacrifice* (University Park: Pennsylvania State University Press, 1992), 54–67; Berman, *The Temple*, 120–33; Alfred Edersheim, *The Temple: Its Ministry and Services* (Peabody, MA: Hendrickson, 1994), 90–104.

[21] See Berman, *The Temple*, 123–24.

[22] Ibid., 120–23.

[23] Ibid., 126–33, especially 126: "The *korban shelamim* [peace offering] is a votive or voluntary offering, and it is never alluded to within the context of trans-

In animal sacrifices, the person offering the sacrifice put his hand on the head of the animal to express solidarity with it.[24] Then the animal was killed before the Lord, present in the Tent of Meeting, and later in the Temple. The blood was poured out on the altar as the portion for the Lord, for the blood represents the soul.[25] Burnt offerings were entirely consumed by fire. In the other sacrifices, the fat was reserved for the Lord, and the meat was eaten by the priests. The cereal offerings of unleavened bread were partly burnt for the Lord and partly consumed by the priests. In peace offerings or votive offerings, the meat was consumed also by those who offered it as a sign of communion with God.[26]

All of these sacrifices are figures of the sacrifice of Calvary, which is made present in the Mass. For Christ gave Himself entirely, holding absolutely nothing back, and in this He is a whole burnt offering or holocaust. He offers Himself under the sacramental sign of (unleavened) bread, and in this the Mass is like the cereal offerings. Christ offers Himself to atone for the sins of the world, and this fulfills the types of the sin and guilt offerings that were offered in propitiation for sin. Finally, Christ's sacrifice establishes peace between God and man and between men, and thus it fulfills the types of the peace offerings. Furthermore, the immolated victim is given to all the faithful in communion, and this is also represented by the peace offerings.[27]

---

gression or expiation. . . . While the owner never partakes of the meat of the expiatory *korbanot*, he is required to do so in abundance when offering a *korban shelamim*."

[24] See ibid., 117–20.

[25] See Lev 3:2. For an insightful Jewish perspective on the meaning of the blood poured out for the Lord, see Berman, *The Temple*, 124–26.

[26] See Lev 7:15–16: "And the flesh of the sacrifice of his peace offerings for thanksgiving shall be eaten on the day of his offering; he shall not leave any of it until the morning. But if the sacrifice of his offering is a votive offering or a freewill offering, it shall be eaten on the day that he offers his sacrifice, and the next day what remains of it shall be eaten." See also Deut 12:26–27: "But the holy things which are due from you, and your votive offerings, you shall take, and you shall go to the place which the LORD will choose, and offer your burnt offerings, the flesh and the blood, on the altar of the LORD your God; the blood of your sacrifices shall be poured out on the altar of the LORD your God, but the flesh you may eat."

[27] See *ST* III, q. 22, a. 2:

Now man is required to offer sacrifice for three reasons: First, for the remission of sin, by which he is turned away from God. Hence the Apostle says (Heb. 5:1) that it appertains to the priest "to offer gifts

In addition to the general offerings described in Leviticus 1–7, Leviticus 23 and Numbers 28–29 mandate special sacrifices for each day, for the Sabbath, for the beginning of each month, for Passover, Pentecost (offering of the First Fruits; Feast of Weeks), Rosh Hashanah (Feast of Trumpets), Yom Kippur (the Day of Atonement), and for Sukkoth (the Feast of Booths).

Each day a year-old unblemished male lamb was offered morning and evening in the Temple as a burnt offering, together with the offering of wine and unleavened bread. On the Sabbath, the offering was doubled.[28] At the beginning of each month (the new moon), these burnt offerings were further multiplied: "two young bulls, one ram, seven male lambs a year old without blemish" (Num 28:11), accompanied by an increase of the unleavened bread and wine and the sin offering of a goat.

The most numerous offerings occurred on the day of Passover, as each household offered its own one-year-old unblemished male whose blood was to be poured out in the Temple court. In addition to the paschal lamb for each family, additional burnt offerings—two young bulls, one ram, and seven male lambs a year old—were offered in the Temple for the seven days of the feast.[29] Similar offerings were made on each of the days of the other feasts. At Pentecost, each family also offered a cereal offering from the first fruits of their harvest.

The most solemn and dramatic form of sacrifice took place on Yom Kippur.[30] In addition to burnt offerings as on the other feasts, this day was also marked by a unique offering of atonement for the sins of the priests and for all of Israel. On this day alone the High Priest entered the Holy of Holies behind the veil and prostrated himself before the mercy seat, uttering the most holy name of God, and "not without taking blood" of a bull, ram, and goat, "which he offers for himself and

---

and sacrifices for sins." Secondly, that man may be preserved in a state of grace, by ever adhering to God, in Whom his peace and salvation consist. Wherefore under the Old Law the sacrifice of peace-offerings was offered up for the salvation of the offerers, as is prescribed in the third chapter of Leviticus. Thirdly, in order that the spirit of man be perfectly united to God: which will be most perfectly realized in glory. Hence, under the Old Law, the holocaust was offered up, so called because the victim was wholly burnt up, as we read in the first chapter of Leviticus.

[28] Num 28:9.

[29] Num 28:19–24.

[30] See Lev 16.

for the errors of the people" (Heb 9:7). The blood was sprinkled by the High Priest upon the mercy seat that covered the Ark of the Covenant, between the sculpted cherubim. The blood of the bull atoned for the sins of the High Priest and his house, whereas the blood of the goat was for the sins of the people.

In addition to the goat's blood sprinkled in the Holy of Holies for the people, this day also included the sending out of the scapegoat bearing their sins. Leviticus 16:21–22 describes the strange ritual:

> Aaron shall lay both his hands upon the head of the live goat, and confess over him all the iniquities of the sons of Israel, and all their transgressions, all their sins; and he shall put them upon the head of the goat, and send him away into the wilderness by the hand of a man who is in readiness. The goat shall bear all their iniquities upon him to a solitary land; and he shall let the goat go in the wilderness.

The scapegoat most clearly represents vicarious atonement. What is implicit in other sacrifices is here made explicit. The scapegoat is laden with the sins of Israel and is exiled from the camp to atone for those who remain inside. The scapegoat is therefore a magnificent type of Christ, who is rejected by His people while bearing the sins of the whole world.

Solemnity and Quantity of Sacrifice in the Temple

When King Solomon consecrated the first Temple in Jerusalem (2 Chr 7:5), 22,000 oxen and 120,000 sheep were sacrificed. Every Passover, on the afternoon of the fourteenth day of Nisan between the ninth and eleventh hours, perhaps tens of thousands of paschal lambs were sacrificed in the court of the Temple at the hands of hundreds of priests, in rapid succession.[31] The blood poured out in such quantity must have made an indelible impression on the mind.

The Mosaic Law stipulated that all sacrifice was to be done in the place that God would appoint, which, after its consecration

---

[31] See the description by Josephus in *Wars of the Jews* 6.9.3.423–25 and *Antiquities* 17.9.3.213.

by Solomon, was the Temple in Jerusalem.[32] This commandment, however, was also a great difficulty for the Jewish people, requiring them to travel to Jerusalem three times a year.

Why did God command that all sacrifice be offered in the Temple? First of all, the Temple was a visible symbol of the unity that God wanted in His liturgy. Secondly, it helped preserve the unity of faith and worship in Israel, since all sacrifice was offered in one place under the High Priest. Beyond these reasons, however, the precept that all sacrifice had to be offered in the Temple was a great symbol prefiguring the unity of worship in the New Covenant.

Although sacrifice is offered everywhere in the Catholic world, from the rising of the sun to its setting,[33] the worship of the Church is even more unified than that of Israel. Everywhere in the Catholic Church, *one and the same sacrifice*—the sacrifice of Calvary—is offered until the end of time in the Holy Mass. In Israel, many animal sacrifices were offered in only one place, whereas in the Church, one and the same sacrifice is offered in every place under the sun.

Furthermore, the fact that all sacrifice had to be offered and consumed at the Temple where God dwelt in a mysterious presence (the *shekhinah*) also served to unite the types or figures of the three different aspects of the Eucharist as the sacrament of the real presence, of spiritual nourishment, and of sacrifice. In the Eucharist, the real

---

[32] See Deut 12:10–14:

> When you go over the Jordan, and live in the land which the LORD your God gives you to inherit, and when he gives you rest from all your enemies round about, so that you live in safety, then to the place which the LORD your God will choose, to make his name dwell there, there you shall bring all that I command you: your burnt offerings and your sacrifices, your tithes and the offering that you present, and all your votive offerings which you vow to the LORD. . . . Take heed that you do not offer your burnt offerings at every place that you see; but at the place which the LORD will choose in one of your tribes, there you shall offer your burnt offerings, and there you shall do all that I am commanding you.

> See also Deut 16:5–6: "You may not offer the Passover sacrifice within any of your towns which the LORD your God gives you; but at the place which the LORD your God will choose, to make his name dwell in it, there you shall offer the Passover sacrifice."

[33] See Mal 1:11: "For from the rising of the sun to its setting my name is great among the nations, and in every place incense is offered to my name, and a pure offering; for my name is great among the nations, says the LORD of hosts."

presence is one with the sacrifice and with the spiritual nourishment received in Communion. In Israel, the sacrifice, the spiritual nourishment, and the Indwelling were distinct, but they were united in that they occurred in the same place: the Temple and the precincts of Jerusalem where the Passover had to be eaten.

After the destruction of the Temple in AD 70 and the impossibility of rebuilding it, this commandment linking all sacrifice with the Temple meant that the entire sacrificial system of Mosaic Judaism could no longer be observed.[34] The Jews mourn that destruction in an annual fast on the ninth day of the month of Av. With the loss of the offering of sacrifice, the Old Testament priesthood lost its principal function.[35]

The visual spectacle of the great quantities of animal sacrifices, day after day and year after year, must have impressed on the Jewish mind the reality of sin, the need for atonement through reparation and the spilling of the blood of an innocent victim, and the inefficacy of the sacrificial blood that was poured out. For if it was efficacious, why did it need to be replaced by new sacrifices every day? Thus the Temple sacrifices would have reinforced the hope that redemption would be fully and finally accomplished in the messianic age. Indeed, some of the ancient rabbis held that the only sacrifice that would continue in the messianic age would be the sacrifice of thanksgiving or praise (*zebach tôdâ*),[36] which is the meaning of the Greek term "Eucharist."[37]

---

[34] On the impact of the destruction of the Second Temple for Jewish life, see Berman, *The Temple*, 185–87.

[35] The name "Cohen" is the direct transliteration of the Hebrew word for "priest" (כֹּהֵן). The priestly line is preserved in those whose Aaronic lineage is indicated in the last name Cohen (or derivatives such as Kahn, Cohn, Kogan, Kagan, or Kahanowitz). Descendants of the priestly line still have the duty of giving the priestly blessing from Num 6:24–27: "'The LORD bless you and keep you: The LORD make his face to shine upon you, and be gracious to you: The LORD lift up his countenance upon you, and give you peace.' 'So shall they put my name upon the sons of Israel, and I will bless them.'"

[36] See *Midrash Rabbah Leviticus* 9.7, in *Midrash Rabbah*, ed. Harry Freedman, 10 vols. (London: Soncino Press, 1961), 4:114: "In the Time to Come all sacrifices will be annulled, but that of thanksgiving will not be annulled." See also *Pesikta* 79a. In addition, see Emil G. Hirsh, et. al., "Sacrifice," in *The Jewish Encyclopedia*, ed. Isidore Singer (New York: Ktav, 1964), 10:622a.

[37] On the connection between the Old Testament sacrifice of thanksgiving (*tôdâ*) and the Eucharist, see Joseph Ratzinger, *The Feast of Faith: Approaches to a Theology of the Liturgy*, trans. Graham Harrison (San Francisco: Ignatius Press, 1986), 51–60 (reproduced in *TL*, 312–18).

The animal sacrifices of the Old Testament, mandated by God Himself through Moses, were the center of the religious rites of Judaism, but they were always insufficient. This is clearly taught both in the Old[38] and the New Testaments, especially in Hebrews 10:1–7:

> For since the law has but a shadow of the good things to come instead of the true form of these realities, it can never, by the same sacrifices which are continually offered year after year, make perfect those who draw near. Otherwise, would they not have ceased to be offered? . . . But in these sacrifices there is a reminder of sin year after year. For it is impossible that the blood of bulls and goats should take away sins.

> Consequently, when Christ came into the world, he said,
> "Sacrifices and offerings you have not desired,
>   but a body you have prepared for me;
> in burnt offerings and sin offerings you have
>   taken no pleasure.
> Then I said, 'Lo, I have come to do your
>   will, O God,'
> as it is written of me."

Another key difference is that, in the sacrifices of the Old Covenant, the victim and the priest were always distinct, even though the victim represented the priest and those for whom he offered sacrifice. In the New Covenant, on the contrary, Priest and Victim are one and the same. The spotless Lamb of God offers not another, but Himself, to the Father on behalf of all mankind, and especially for His Bride, the Church.

The Passover

Of all the sacrifices of Israel, the immolation of the paschal lamb during the feast of Passover most perfectly prefigures the Eucharist in all three aspects: sacrifice, communion, and the effect of grace.[39] A

---

[38] See Ps 40:4–6; Ps 50; 1 Sam 15:22; Ps 51:17; Isa 1:11; Amos 5:21.

[39] *ST* III, q. 73, a. 6:

> The Paschal Lamb foreshadowed this sacrament in these three ways [*sacramentum tantum*, *res et sacramentum*, and *res tantum*]. First of all,

lamb was immolated on behalf of each household and was entirely consumed by them, protecting them in the first Passover from the angel of death. In the first Passover in Egypt, the blood of the sacrificial lamb was applied to the doorposts and lintels of the houses of the Israelites to save them from the angel of death. In the Eucharist, the blood of the true Lamb of God offered in sacrifice is not applied to doorposts but consumed and applied to our interior being to save us from the dominion of Satan and communicate the grace of supernatural life.[40]

Like the other rites of Israel, the Passover was not only a memorial of the past deliverance from Egypt but also a prefiguring of the future messianic deliverance. Pope Benedict XVI comments on how the Eucharist fulfills the typology of the sacrifice of the paschal lamb:

> This ritual meal, which called for the sacrifice of lambs (cf. Ex 12:1–28, 43–51), was a remembrance of the past, but at the same time a prophetic remembrance, the proclamation of a deliverance yet to come. The people had come to realize that their earlier liberation was not definitive, for their history continued to be marked by slavery and sin. The remembrance of their ancient liberation thus expanded to the invocation and expectation of a yet more profound, radical, universal and definitive salvation. This is the context in which Jesus introduces the newness of his gift. In the prayer of praise, the *Berakah*, he does not simply thank the Father for the great events of past history, but also for his own "exaltation." In instituting the sacrament of the Eucharist, Jesus anticipates

---

because it was eaten with unleavened loaves, according to Exodus 12:8: "They shall eat flesh ... and unleavened bread." As to the second because it was immolated by the entire multitude of the children of Israel on the fourteenth day of the moon; and this was a figure of the Passion of Christ, Who is called the Lamb on account of His innocence. As to the effect, because by the blood of the Paschal Lamb the children of Israel were preserved from the destroying Angel, and brought from the Egyptian captivity; and in this respect the Paschal Lamb is the chief figure of this sacrament, because it represents it in every respect.

See Thomas J. White's commentary on Exod 12, in *Exodus* (Grand Rapids, MI: Brazos Press, 2016), 100–5.

[40] See John Chrysostom, *Baptismal Instructions* 3.13–19, trans. Paul Harkins (Westminster, MD: Newman Press, 1963), 60–62, included in the *Liturgy of the Hours*, Good Friday, Office of Readings, 2nd Reading.

and makes present the sacrifice of the Cross and the victory of the resurrection. At the same time, he reveals that he himself is the *true* sacrificial lamb, destined in the Father's plan from the foundation of the world, as we read in The First Letter of Peter (cf. 1:18–20). By placing his gift in this context, Jesus shows the salvific meaning of his death and resurrection, a mystery which renews history and the whole cosmos. . . . Jesus thus brings his own radical *novum* to the ancient Hebrew sacrificial meal. For us Christians, that meal no longer need be repeated. As the Church Fathers rightly say, *figura transit in veritatem*: the foreshadowing has given way to the truth itself. The ancient rite has been brought to fulfilment and definitively surpassed by the loving gift of the incarnate Son of God. The food of truth, Christ sacrificed for our sake, *dat figuris terminum*.[41]

Sealing of the Old Covenant

Another key figure of the Eucharistic sacrifice was the solemn sealing of the Mosaic covenant on Sinai with the blood of many oxen.[42] Burnt offerings and peace offerings of oxen were offered, and the blood was gathered in basins. Half of the blood was poured out on the altar, and the other half "poured out" or sprinkled on the people after they promised to be faithful to the covenant: "And Moses took the blood and threw it upon the people, and said, 'Behold the blood of the covenant which the LORD has made with you in accordance with all these words'" (Exod 24:8).

Normally the blood was reserved exclusively for God as His portion. Only on two occasions was blood also sprinkled on the people or their doorposts: the first Passover and the sealing of the Covenant at Sinai. Why? Both were covenantal events prefiguring the Eucharist. At the Passover, the blood signified the propitiation worked by the Blood of Christ. At Sinai it represented the mysterious fellowship between God and His people, which is achieved through our being adopted to receive a share in His divine life. This was represented on Sinai but fully realized only in the Eucharist, in which the Blood—which is not only God's portion, but God's own Blood—is not merely sprinkled on

---

[41] Benedict XVI, *Sacramentum Caritatis*, §§10–11.

[42] See Exod 24:5–8.

us, but given to all the Christian faithful as our spiritual nourishment. Just as the Old Covenant was sealed with sacrificial blood poured out and sprinkled on the people, so too the New Covenant is sealed with Blood, which is then given to the faithful. The difference lies in the victim whose blood is poured out. The Victim in the New Covenant is not a multitude of irrational beasts, but the Messiah, the Son of God made man, "who loved me and gave himself for me" (Gal 2:20).

Figures of the Eucharist as Spiritual Nourishment under the Sacramental Signs of Bread and Wine

Manna

The manna that nourished the Israelites for forty years as they wandered in the desert is a magnificent figure of the Eucharist as a sacrament of spiritual nourishment. The event is described in Exodus 16:4–35. After the people blamed Moses for taking them out of Egypt, where they "sat by the fleshpots and ate bread to the full," the Lord said to Moses:

> "Behold, I will rain bread from heaven for you; and the people shall go out and gather a day's portion every day, that I may test them, whether they will walk in my law or not. On the sixth day, when they prepare what they bring in, it will be twice as much as they gather daily." So Moses and Aaron said to all the sons of Israel, "At evening you shall know that it was the LORD who brought you out of the land of Egypt, and in the morning you shall see the glory of the LORD."

> . . . In the morning dew lay round about the camp. And when the dew had gone up, there was on the face of the wilderness a fine, flake-like thing, fine as hoarfrost on the ground. When the people of Israel saw it, they said to one another, "What is it?" For they did not know what it was. And Moses said to them, "It is the bread which the LORD has given you to eat. This is what the LORD has commanded: 'Gather of it, every man of you, as much as he can eat; you shall take an omer apiece, according to the number of the persons whom each of

you has in his tent.'" And the sons of Israel did so; they gathered, some more, some less. But when they measured it with an omer, he that gathered much had nothing over, and he that gathered little had no lack; each gathered according to what he could eat. And Moses said to them, "Let no man leave any of it till the morning." But they did not listen to Moses; some left part of it till the morning, and it bred worms and became foul; and Moses was angry with them. Morning by morning they gathered it, each as much as he could eat; but when the sun grew hot, it melted.

. . . Now the house of Israel called its name manna; it was like coriander seed, white, and the taste of it was like wafers made with honey. And Moses said, "This is what the LORD has commanded: 'Let an omer of it be kept throughout your generations, that they may see the bread with which I fed you in the wilderness, when I brought you out of the land of Egypt.'" . . . And the sons of Israel ate the manna forty years, till they came to a habitable land; they ate the manna, till they came to the border of the land of Canaan.

The manna is a figure of the Eucharist in various respects. First, it is "bread from heaven." Normal bread comes from the earth, in that it is made from grains of wheat. This bread was rained down on Israel from above. Thus it is an apt symbol of the fact that the Eucharist nourishes us with a reality that is not from this earth, nor even from the natural order, but supremely from above. It is in fact the Word Incarnate. Jesus brings out this figure in John 6:48–51:

I am the bread of life. Your fathers ate the manna in the wilderness, and they died. This is the bread which comes down from heaven, that a man may eat of it and not die. I am the living bread which came down from heaven.

The manna also was not the product of human toil like normal bread, since it came down from above as the dewfall. This prefigures the fact that the Eucharist, in its interior reality, is not the fruit of human technology or accomplishment, but rather the supremely gratuitous gift of God.

The manna is a figure of the Eucharist also because it was something utterly *unknown* to the Israelites. This is indicated by the name "manna," which means "what is it?" This prefigures the Eucharist because it is the reality of the New Covenant most veiled in mystery. Transubstantiation, the sacrifice of the Mass, and Holy Communion utterly transcend everything that pertains to our ordinary experience. The mysteriousness of the manna as a figure of the supernatural mystery of the Eucharist is also indicated in Deuteronomy 8:3: "And he humbled you and let you hunger and fed you with manna, which you did not know, nor did your fathers know; that he might make you know that man does not live by bread alone, but that man lives by everything that proceeds out of the mouth of the LORD."[43]

Furthermore, the manna is a figure of the effects of grace of the Eucharist in that God gave each one only so much as was needed each day. Those who gathered a greater physical quantity did not receive more, and those who gathered a lesser physical amount did not receive less than they needed. This is a figure of two aspects of the Eucharist. First, the tiniest particle of the consecrated bread and wine contains the whole Christ just as much as the largest quantity. Second, the Eucharist nourishes the recipient with grace according to the level of his own spiritual state and fervor, not according to the quantity received.

Another aspect of the symbolism of the manna with regard to the effects of the Eucharist is that it was "suited to every taste," according to Wisdom 16:20–21:

> Instead of these things you gave your people
>   the food of angels,
> and without their toil you supplied them from
>   heaven with bread ready to eat,
> providing every pleasure and suited to every
>   taste.
> For your sustenance manifested your sweetness
>   toward your children;
> and the bread, ministering to the desire of the
>   one who took it,
> was changed to suit every one's liking.

---

[43] See also Deut 8:16, in which Moses told the people that God "fed you in the wilderness with manna which your fathers did not know, that he might humble you and test you, to do you good in the end."

As the manna was suited to every sensible taste, so the Eucharist is suited to every spiritual taste, for it gives us the supreme reality of Christ's life and charity. The grace of God communicated in the Eucharist is always perfectly adapted to our personal spiritual needs. This is also expressed in Psalm 34:8: "O taste and see that the LORD is good!" This symbolism of the sweetness of the manna has been incorporated into the office of Corpus Christi written by St. Thomas and the rite of Eucharistic Benediction: P./ "Thou hast given them bread from heaven. R./ Having within it all sweetness."

The manna is described in Psalm 78:25 as the "bread of angels." This was not literally true of the manna, for it was a material food in which angels cannot partake. It was angelic only in its supernatural origin. The Eucharist, however, is indeed "bread of angels" in its interior effect, for by it we are nourished in sanctifying grace, which is a participation in the divine nature.[44] Like us, the holy angels have been given a participation in the divine nature through grace and glory, and thus they too partake of this "bread."[45]

Finally, the manna prefigures the Eucharist in that it was food only for the pilgrimage in the desert. After the Israelites entered into the Chosen Land, the manna ceased. Similarly, the Eucharist is spiritual nourishment only for this present life. Once the faithful enter into the true promised land, the heavenly Jerusalem, the Eucharistic nourishment will cease together with the other sacraments because God will be seen face to face.[46]

In addition, Eucharistic adoration was prefigured by the jar of manna being conserved in the Ark of the Covenant in the Holy of Holies, in which God's presence was adored. The manna itself, however,

---

[44] See 2 Pet 1:4.

[45] See Paschasius Radbertus (785–865), *De Corpore et Sanguine Domini: Cum Appendice Epistola ad Fredugardum* 5.33–34: "Thus by what the angels live, man also lives, for there is a totally spiritual and divine reality in that which man receives [i.e., the Eucharist]" (ed. Beda Paulus, CCCM, 16:32).

[46] See Lombard, *Sentences* IV, d. 8, ch. 2, no. 2:

> That manna was given to the people of old after the crossing of the Red Sea, where the Hebrews were freed by the drowning of the Egyptians; in the same way, this heavenly manna is not to be given to anyone, except the reborn. That bodily bread led the people of old through the desert to the promised land; this heavenly food brings the faithful to heaven as they cross through the desert of this world. And so it is rightly called a viaticum, or bread for the journey, because it sustains us on the way and brings us to our fatherland. (*Sentences* IV, p. 41)

was not properly the object of adoration, for it was a purely material reality, although of supernatural origin. Its placement in the Holy of Holies was a type of the Eucharist in the tabernacle, which alone is the proper object of adoration.[47]

The Offering of Melchizedek

The sacramental sign of the Eucharist, through which we receive spiritual nourishment, is prefigured also by the offering of bread and wine by Melchizedek related in Genesis 14:17–20:

> After his return from the defeat of Chedorlaomer and the kings who were with him, the king of Sodom went out to meet him at the Valley of Shaveh (that is, the King's Valley). And Melchizedek king of Salem brought out bread and wine; he was priest of God Most High. And he blessed him and said,

> "Blessed be Abram by God Most High,
>   maker of heaven and earth;
> and blessed be God Most High,
>   who has delivered your enemies into your hand!"

The name "Melchizedek" means "king of righteousness," and the city of which he was king, "Salem," means "peace." The significance of this text might have been missed if it had not been taken up later by the psalmist in Psalm 110:4, which says of the Messiah: "The LORD has sworn and will not change his mind, 'You are a priest for ever according to the order of Melchizedek.'" The Messiah thus is foretold to possess a priesthood prefigured by Melchizedek. One clear aspect of this prefigurement is the fact that Melchizedek offered bread and wine to God. Chapter 7 of the Letter to the Hebrews further develops this figure.

---

[47] With regard to the symbolism of the manna in relation to the Eucharist, see Brant Pitre, *Jesus and the Jewish Roots of the Eucharist: Unlocking the Secrets of the Last Supper* (New York: Doubleday Religion, 2011), 77–115; and *Jesus and the Last Supper* (Grand Rapids, MI: Eerdmans, 2015), 148–250. Pitre argues that there were expectations in the Jewish tradition that the Messiah would feed the Israelites with manna from heaven in the Messianic age.

The Bread of the Presence

The Tent of Meeting (and later the Holy Place in the Temple) held another figure of the Eucharist: the "bread of the Presence"[48] and libations of wine. God commanded Moses to place in the tabernacle a table plated with gold on which the Israelites were to "set the bread of the Presence on the table before me always" (Exod 25:30) and pour libations into flagons of pure gold.

Further details of the offering of the "bread of the Presence" are given in Leviticus and Numbers. In Leviticus 24:5–9 the Lord describes the offering of bread to be made every Sabbath:

> And you shall take fine flour, and bake twelve cakes of it; two tenths of an ephah shall be in each cake. And you shall set them in two rows, six in a row, upon the table of pure gold. And you shall put pure frankincense with each row, that it may go with the bread as a memorial portion to be offered by fire to the LORD. Every Sabbath day Aaron shall set it in order before the LORD continually on behalf of the sons of Israel as a covenant for ever. And it shall be for Aaron and his sons, and they shall eat it in a holy place, since it is for him a most holy portion out of the offerings by fire to the LORD, a perpetual debt.

Exodus 29:40[49] and Numbers 28:4–7 describe a daily offering of bread and wine and specify that it is to accompany the daily offering of two unblemished one-year-old male lambs, one in the morning and the other in the evening:

> The one lamb you shall offer in the morning, and the other lamb you shall offer in the evening; also a tenth of an ephah of fine flour for a cereal offering, mixed with a fourth of a hin of beaten oil. It is a continual burnt offering, which was ordained at Mount Sinai for a pleasing odor, an offering by fire to the

---

[48] The Hebrew expression is *lechem haPanim*, which literally means "bread of the face [of God]." See the treatment of this figure in Pitre, *Jesus and the Jewish Roots of the Eucharist*, 116–46, and *Jesus and the Last Supper*, 121–47, to which I am indebted.

[49] "With the first lamb [you shall offer] a tenth measure of fine flour mingled with a fourth of a hin of beaten oil and a fourth of a hin of wine for a libation."

LORD. Its drink offering shall be a fourth of a hin for each lamb; in the holy place you shall pour out a drink offering of strong drink to the LORD.[50]

The "bread of the Presence" comes up in 1 Samuel 21:4–6 when David and his men were fleeing from the persecution of Saul. David asks Ahimelech, the High Priest, for bread, and the priest responds that the only bread he has is the "holy bread" that had been set before the Lord. Ahimelech gives it to David and his men, since they fulfilled at least the one condition that they be pure from sexual intercourse, although the Mosaic law stipulates that it is the priest who partakes of this bread. Jesus refers to this episode in the following passage from Matthew 12:1–6:

> At that time Jesus went through the grainfields on the sabbath; his disciples were hungry, and they began to pluck heads of grain and to eat. But when the Pharisees saw it, they said to him, "Look, your disciples are doing what is not lawful to do on the sabbath." He said to them, "Have you not read what David did, when he was hungry, and those who were with him: how he entered the house of God and ate the showbread, which it was not lawful for him to eat nor for those who were with him, but only for the priests? Or have you not read in the law how on the sabbath the priests in the temple profane the sabbath,[51] and are guiltless? I tell you, something greater than the temple is here."[52]

The showbread, or bread of the Presence, was consecrated to the Lord and thus normally could be eaten only by the sons of Aaron, consecrated through priestly ordination. The story prefigures that all the faithful of the New Israel would partake of the bread. What in the Old Covenant had been reserved for the sons of Aaron is extended in the Church to all who have been consecrated by Baptism.

This "bread of the Presence" and the libations of wine in the

---

[50] Num 28:4–7. See also Num 15:5–7, which prescribes offerings of bread and wine to accompany the sacrifices of lambs, rams, and bulls.

[51] The priests worked on the Sabbath by preparing and offering the bread of the Presence and the other sacrifices.

[52] The parallel texts are Mark 2:25–26 and Luke 6:1–5.

tabernacle prefigure the Eucharist in four fundamental ways. First, they prefigure the sacramental sign of the Eucharist in their matter of bread and wine that was consecrated and set aside from ordinary use. Second, they prefigure Holy Communion in that they were consumed by the priests as a sign of communion with God. Third, they are sacrificial offerings that accompanied the daily sacrifice of the unblemished lamb, which is also a figure of Christ's sacrifice, and so they also prefigure the sacrificial aspect of the Eucharist. Finally, they prefigure the adoration of the Eucharist, in that they were placed with the Ark of the Covenant in the tabernacle.

Brant Pitre has shown that there was even a tradition of blessing the people of Israel who came to the Temple on the pilgrimage feasts with the bread of the Presence.[53] The Babylonian Talmud records that the priests "used to lift it [the golden Table] up and exhibit the Bread of the Presence on it to those who came up for the festivals, saying to them, 'Behold, God's love for you!'"[54] This was probably understood in the sense that the oblation of the consecrated bread was a sign of the covenant, which is a manifestation of God's love for man.

Although a marvelous figure, it must be remembered that the bread of the Presence and the libations of wine were but bread and wine. They prefigured something infinitely greater than their own reality. St. Cyril of Jerusalem brings out the figure in his catechetical lecture on the Eucharist:

> Even in the Old Testament there were "Loaves of the Presence," but since they belonged to the old dispensation they have come to fulfillment. But in the New Testament the bread is of heaven and the chalice brings salvation, and they sanctify the soul and the body. . . . Do not, then, regard the bread and wine as nothing but bread and wine, for they are the body and blood of Christ as the master himself has proclaimed.[55]

---

[53] Pitre, *Jesus and the Jewish Roots of the Eucharist*, 130–33.

[54] Babylonian Talmud, Menahot 29a, quoted in Pitre, *Jesus and the Jewish Roots of the Eucharist*, 130–31.

[55] Cyril of Jerusalem, *Mystagogic Catecheses* 4.5–6, in Edward Yarnold, S.J., *The Awe-Inspiring Rites of Initiation: The Origins of the RCIA* (Collegeville, MN: Liturgical Press, 1994), 87.

Unleavened Bread of the Passover and the Four Cups of Wine

Although not offered as an oblation, unleavened bread (*matzah*) and wine play an important role in the Jewish Passover. The Israelites were commanded to remove all leaven from their houses and to eat only unleavened bread for the seven days of Passover. This was a memorial of the first Passover, when they ate unleavened bread because they left Egypt in haste. In the Jewish Passover seder, there is the custom (perhaps of later date than the time of Jesus) of having the youngest child in the family ask why unleavened bread is eaten during Passover. The father responds: "This is the bread of affliction that our fathers ate in Egypt. He who is hungry, come and eat."[56] *Matzah* is also a sign of purity of heart, for unleavened bread is the simplest possible form of bread and leaven puffs up, and thus serves as a natural symbol of pride and hypocrisy.[57]

The unleavened bread of Passover is a figure of the Eucharist in these two respects. First, as a memorial of the food of the Exodus and the crossing of the Red Sea, *matzah* is a fitting figure of the Eucharist, the spiritual food for those who are renewed by the new Exodus, which is insertion into Christ's Paschal mystery by the waters of Baptism. Secondly, the unleavened bread symbolizes the purity of heart produced by worthy reception of the Eucharist.

The Passover seder also combines wine with the unleavened bread, stipulating the drinking of four cups of wine that represent redemption from slavery while saying Psalm 116:13: "I lift up the cup of salvation."[58]

---

[56] Quoted in Roch Kereszty, *Wedding Feast of the Lamb: Eucharistic Theology from a Historical, Biblical, and Systematic Perspective* (Chicago: Hillenbrand Books, 2004), 25.

[57] See Luke 12:1, where Jesus says to His disciples, "Beware of the leaven of the Pharisees, which is hypocrisy," and 1 Cor 5:6–8: "Your boasting is not good. Do you not know that a little leaven leavens all the dough? Cleanse out the old leaven that you may be new dough, as you really are unleavened. For Christ, our Paschal Lamb, has been sacrificed. Let us, therefore, celebrate the festival, not with the old leaven, the leaven of malice and evil, but with the unleavened bread of sincerity and truth."

[58] See Lawrence A. Hoffman and David Arnow, eds., *My People's Passover Haggadah: Traditional Texts, Modern Commentaries*, vol.1 (Woodstock, VT: Jewish Lights, 2008), 136.

The Tree of Life

The Old Testament contains figures not only of the sacramental signs of bread and wine in the Eucharist but also of the supernatural life communicated by Holy Communion. The most important figure of the spiritual effects of the Eucharist is the tree of life. After the original sin, God expelled man from the Garden of Eden (see Gen 3:22–24) so that man could no longer eat from the tree of life, for man had deserved to experience death by his sin:

> Then the LORD God said, "Behold, the man has become like one of us, knowing good and evil; and now, lest he put forth his hand and take also of the tree of life, and eat, and live forever"—therefore the LORD God sent him forth from the garden of Eden, to till the ground from which he was taken. He drove out the man; and at the east of the garden of Eden he placed the cherubim, and a flaming sword which turned every way, to guard the way to the tree of life.

The tree of life indicates the gift of physical immortality, given in Eden as a preternatural gift and lost by original sin. It also represents the sharing in the divine life made possible by sanctifying grace, which will be perfected in glory.

In both respects, the tree of life prefigures the Eucharist, which is a pledge of the future resurrection and a present provider of the nourishment of sanctifying grace. The access to the tree of life that was lost after the original sin is restored through the Eucharist—the bread of life. Christ brings out this aspect of the Eucharist in the Bread of Life Discourse in John 6:50–51:

> This is the bread which comes down from heaven, that a man may eat of it and not die. I am the living bread which came down from heaven; if any one eats of this bread, he will live for ever; and the bread which I shall give for the life of the world is my flesh.[59]

---

[59] See also Rev 2:7 and 22:2, which speak of Jesus giving to eat of the tree of life.

St. Ignatius of Antioch, in one of the first post-biblical reflections on the Eucharist, brings out the parallel of the Eucharist with the tree of life, speaking of it as a "medicine of immortality, the antidote we take in order not to die but to live forever in Jesus Christ."[60]

Yearning of the Prophets for Union with God

Another figure of the interior effect of the Eucharist is the aspiration of the prophets and saints of the Old Covenant for union with God. The Psalmist speaks for Israel when he says: "As a deer longs for flowing streams, so longs my soul for you, O God. My soul thirsts for God, for the living God. When shall I come and behold the face of God?" (Ps 42:1–2). Although we cannot yet behold the face of God on this side of death, we can receive Him in the Eucharist under the veils of the Eucharistic species. This yearning is perhaps most poignantly expressed in Isaiah 64:1: "O that you would tear the heavens and come down." This yearning finds its realization in the Incarnation and the Eucharist. Isaiah is referring to the Eucharist when he prophesies, "everyone who thirsts, come to the waters; and he who has no money, come, buy wine and milk without money and without price . . . and I will make with you an everlasting covenant, my steadfast, merciful love for David" (Isa 55:1–3). Prophetically foreseeing the fulfillment of this yearning, the Psalmist exclaims: "Taste and see that the LORD is good!" (Ps 34:8).

Unity of Presence, Sacrifice, and Spiritual Nourishment

As we have seen, the three ends of the Eucharist—divine presence, sacrifice, and spiritual nourishment—are prepared for in different Old

---

[60] Ignatius of Antioch, *Letter to the Ephesians* 20, in M. Holmes, trans., *The Apostolic Fathers: Greek Texts and English Translations*, 3rd ed. (Grand Rapids, MI: Baker Academic, 2007), 199. This analogy between the tree of life and the Eucharist is found, for example, in Justin Martyr, *Dialogue with Trypho* 86.1, and in the ninth century in Paschasius, *De Corpore et Sanguine Domini* 1.150–53 (Paulus, CCCM, 16:19) and 7.35–45: "Christ is now the tree of life in the Church, whose image in paradise was that tree. . . . Therefore it [the Eucharist] is rightly said to be the tree of life, for as that would have given immortality of the body to those receiving it, this in a more perfect way gives eternal life for those who observe the commandments of God" (Paulus, CCCM, 16:39); see also 9.65–78 (Paulus, CCCM, 16:54–55).

Testament figures. However, these figures also point to the unification of these three ends. First of all, the Temple was the site in which all three of these ends were accomplished. God was present in the Temple; all sacrifice had to be offered in the Temple; and it was in Jerusalem that one had to partake of the Passover. The jar of manna was preserved in the Ark of the Covenant in the Temple of Jerusalem, and the bread of the Presence was likewise offered before the face of the Lord in the sanctuary of the Temple.

Furthermore, sacrifice and spiritual nourishment are intrinsically linked by the fact that partaking of the sacrificial victim was generally a part of the whole rite of sacrifice.[61] This would be the case in all the sacrifices that involved a communion in the sacrifice, whether by priest or people, of which the Passover is the most prominent example.

STUDY QUESTIONS

1. How is the presence of God in the Temple (*shekhinah*) a figure of the Eucharist?
2. How are the sacrifices of the Mosaic Law and of the religions of the world a figure of the Eucharist?
3. In what ways is the Passover a figure of the Eucharist?
4. In what ways does the manna in the desert serve as a figure of the Eucharist?
5. How is the offering of Melchizedek a figure of the Eucharist?
6. How is the bread of the Presence (showbread) a figure of the Eucharist?
7. How is the tree of life a figure of the Eucharist?

SUGGESTIONS FOR FURTHER READING

Berman, Joshua. *The Temple: Its Symbolism and Meaning Then and Now.* Northvale, NJ: Jason Aronson, 1995. Pp. 1–56, 111–57.
Daniélou, Jean. *The Bible and the Liturgy.* Notre Dame, IN: University of Notre Dame Press, 1956. Pp. 127–176.

---

[61] See Maurice de la Taille, S.J. *The Mystery of Faith*, vol. 1, *The Sacrifice of Our Lord* (New York: Sheed & Ward, 1940), 17–20.

Levering, Matthew. *Sacrifice and Community: Jewish Offering and Christian Eucharist*. Malden, MA: Blackwell Publishing, 2005. Pp. 29–114.

Nash, Thomas J. *The Biblical Roots of the Mass*. Manchester, NH: Sophia Institute Press, 2015.

Pitre, Brant. *Jesus and the Jewish Roots of the Eucharist: Unlocking the Secrets of the Last Supper*. New York: Doubleday Religion, 2011.

———. *Jesus and the Last Supper*. Grand Rapids, MI: Eerdmans, 2015. Pp. 53–250, 374–443.

White, O.P., Thomas J. *Exodus*. Grand Rapids, MI: Brazos Press, 2016. Pp. 97–105.

✠

CHAPTER THREE

The Eucharist in the New Testament

THE BREAD OF LIFE DISCOURSE IN JOHN 6

In the first chapter of the present book we saw that the Eucharist is not something marginal in Christ's work or in the life of the Church, but rather it stands at the very center of the mission of the Word Incarnate and of the Kingdom He founded. The Word became flesh for the same reasons that He instituted the Eucharist. This centrality of the Eucharist is borne out by the New Testament, especially in John 6, in which we find Jesus's clearest explanation of the Eucharist as a sacrament of spiritual nourishment.

Jesus prepares for His teaching on the Eucharist in the Bread of Life Discourse by feeding the five thousand the day before. We are also told in John 6:4 that this occurred just before the feast of Passover, a feast with strong messianic significance. To understand both the event of the multiplication of the loaves and the Bread of Life Discourse, we must remember that Jews were expecting the Messiah to recapitulate the miracles of the Exodus.[1] One of those miracles was

---

[1] See Jean Daniélou, *From Shadows to Reality: Studies in the Biblical Typology of the Fathers*, trans. Dom Wulstan Hibberd (Westminster, MD: Newman Press, 1960), 153–54:

> The Old Testament is both a memory and a prophecy. We can go further, and say that it is the prophecy which makes it a memory: the mighty works of the past are recalled only as the foundation of future hope. For it is very noticeable that the Prophets foretell events to come as the recovery of what has passed. When we turn to the theme in hand we find that Isaiah and Jeremiah hold up to the Jews of the Captivity

Moses's providing food from heaven for the Israelites as they wandered in the desert for forty years. The Messiah, understood as a new Moses,[2] would likewise provide abundance of bread for the messianic kingdom of Israel.[3]

After Jesus performed the multiplication of the loaves, the people said, "This is indeed the prophet who is to come into the world!" and they were "about to come and take him by force to make him king" (John 6:14–15). They rightly interpreted His act as a messianic sign, but they failed to understand the sign as a figure of spiritual nourishment rather than as physical food.

On the following day, the crowds were looking for Him, and Jesus said they were seeking Him for the wrong reason. They were looking for a free lunch: "Truly, truly, I say to you, you seek me, not because you saw signs, but because you ate your fill of the loaves. Do not labor for the food which perishes, but for the food which endures to eternal life, which the Son of man will give to you; for on him has God the Father set his seal" (John 6:26–27).

This passage contains four themes that are essential to the discourse as a whole: Jesus's messianic mission of giving eternal and divine life; His Body and Blood as spiritual nourishment and the medicine of immortality; His identity from above; and the necessity of faith to receive these three things. First we see the contrast between physical and spiritual nourishment. The people are expecting messianic provisions so that they will not have to work, but Jesus comes to give something infinitely better. Hence, He says: "Do not labor for the

---

the future which God has in store for them as a new Exodus, of which the earlier one was the type.

See Feingold, *Faith Comes from What Is Heard*, 517–22.

[2] See Deut 18:15–19:

The Lord your God will raise up for you a prophet like me from among you, from your brethren—him you shall heed—just as you desired of the Lord your God at Horeb on the day of the assembly, when you said, "Let me not hear again the voice of the Lord my God, or see this great fire any more, lest I die." And the Lord said to me, "They have rightly said all that they have spoken. I will raise up for them a prophet like you from among their brethren; and I will put my words in his mouth, and he shall speak to them all that I command him. And whoever will not give heed to my words which he shall speak in my name, I myself will require it of him."

[3] See Brant Pitre, *Jesus and the Jewish Roots of the Eucharist*, 77–115; Pitre, *Jesus and the Last Supper*, 53–250.

food which perishes, but for the food which endures to eternal life." Second, Jesus promises that He will give the food of eternal life. Third, He indicates His mysterious identity in saying that the Father has set His seal on Him. Finally, it is implied that they must believe in Him to receive the life that He wishes to give them. The necessity of faith comes to the fore in John 6:28–29. The people asked Him: "What must we do, to be doing the works of God?" Jesus tells them to have faith in Him because He is sent from the Father: "This is the work of God, that you believe in him whom he has sent."

At this point, the crowd asks for a sign like the manna so that they can believe in Him. This is a classic "teachable moment." This question provided a perfect opening for the teaching on the Eucharist that He was about to give. The crowd said: "Our fathers ate the manna in the wilderness; as it is written, 'He gave them bread from heaven to eat'" (John 6:31), and Jesus responded:

> "Truly, truly, I say to you, it was not Moses who gave you the bread from heaven; my Father gives you the true bread from heaven. For the bread of God is that which comes down from heaven, and gives life to the world." They said to him, "Lord, give us this bread always." Jesus said to them, "I am the bread of life; he who comes to me shall not hunger, and he who believes in me shall never thirst." (John 6:32–35)

We can see that the crowd was still thinking of the bread that Jesus would give them in too material a sense, such that the messianic bread would simply be a recovery of the kind of nourishment they received in the forty years in the desert. The dialogue is parallel to what happens in Jesus's conversations with Nicodemus and the Samaritan woman in John 3 and 4. In both cases, Jesus was speaking to them about a spiritual birth and spiritual water, but He was understood at first as referring to carnal birth and physical drink. The crowd in Capernaum, like the Samaritan woman in John 4:15, apparently asked for Christ's gift to save themselves from toil, but Jesus went on to explain that He Himself is the bread from heaven that He was promising them.

In the desert, Israel was fed by a bread that, although mysterious, was merely a created reality whose purpose was to nourish the body. The new bread from heaven that Jesus is promising is something utterly different in kind. Jesus proposes to feed His disciples with His own life from above. This nourishment differs, furthermore, from physical nourishment in that the latter is always insufficient. Just as no food can satisfy us for long, no finite gift, no matter how great, can actually satisfy the human heart such that we will never desire anything else. In saying that He will satisfy us so that we will never hunger or thirst for more, Jesus is making an implicit divine claim. Only union with God can fully satisfy our hunger, for God has made us for Himself. Jesus therefore is promising that He will feed us with Himself and that this will completely fill our restless heart as only God can.

There is also a divine claim in His saying that this bread comes down from heaven, implying that He existed in heaven prior to His coming as man. As man, Christ comes from heaven not physically, but through the supreme mystery of the hypostatic union by which the Word of God, existing from eternity, took flesh in the womb of the Virgin Mary: "No one has ascended into heaven but he who descended from heaven, the Son of man" (John 3:13). In the Eucharist, this Body continues to come to us "from heaven" through transubstantiation, by which He who sits now in heaven at the right hand of the Father is truly and substantially present on our altars under the appearances of bread and wine.

Up to this point, however, one could think that Jesus was speaking of Himself as the bread of life in a figurative and symbolic sense, using bread as a metaphor for His mysterious divine identity that is life-giving. He proceeded to clarify that He is the "bread from heaven" and the "bread of life" not only because He is from above but also because He has become man so that He can nourish us with His own divine and eternal life and so give us a share in that life that is incompatible with death, raising us up on the last day:

> This is the will of him who sent me, that I should lose nothing of all that he has given me, but raise it up at the last day. For this is the will of my Father, that every one who sees the Son and believes in him should have eternal life; and I will raise him up at the last day. (John 6:39–40)

Once again there is an implicit divine claim, for no one can give what he does not possess. If Jesus promised to give eternal life, it can only be because He possesses that life. The crowd thus murmurs about this claim: "How does he now say, 'I have come down from heaven'?" (John 6:42).

Jesus responded to the murmuring by speaking about His identity from the Father and His immediate knowledge of the Father: "Not that any one has seen the Father except him who is from God; he has seen the Father" (John 6:46). In other words, Jesus should be believed here because He spoke not by hearsay, but through vision: He has seen the Father. In other words, He possesses the beatific vision that is the very life of heaven.[4]

Jesus then insisted still more on the power of the bread of life to give eternal life:

> "I am the bread of life. Your fathers ate the manna in the wilderness, and they died. This is the bread which comes down from heaven, that a man may eat of it and not die. I am the living bread which came down from heaven; if any one eats of this bread, he will live forever." (John 6:48–51)

Jesus here presents Himself as the bread of life that will have the same effect as the tree of life lost to man through original sin. Jesus is thus presenting the manna of the New Covenant as a "medicine of immortality," a means of restoration to the original blessed state in which our first parents were created. In other words, Jesus is promising a return to the beginning, which is an eschatological restoration spoken of by the prophets in various texts. In Isaiah 25:6–8, God says:

> On this mountain the LORD of hosts will make for all peoples a feast of fat things, a feast of choice wines—of fat things full of marrow, of choice wines well refined. And he will destroy on this mountain the covering that is cast over all peoples, the veil that is spread over all nations. He will swallow up death for ever, and the Lord God will wipe away tears from all faces, and the reproach of his people he will take away from all the earth.

In this prophecy, a mysterious feast of "fat things" and wine is combined with the destroying of the power of death. This is exactly Jesus's claim

---

[4] See Lawrence Feingold, "The Vision of God in Christ: 'Who Loved Me and Gave Himself for Me,'" in *Love and Friendship: Maritain and the Tradition*, ed. Montague Brown (Washington, DC: Catholic University of America Press, 2013), 218–32.

in the Bread of Life Discourse: He is giving a sumptuous banquet that destroys the power of eternal death.[5]

The disciples might also have thought of the prophecy of Ezekiel 37 about the resurrection of the dead bones of the house of Israel. In Ezekiel 37:12–14, God promises:

> "Behold, I will open your graves, and raise you from your graves, O my people; and I will bring you home into the land of Israel. And you shall know that I am the LORD, when I open your graves, and raise you from your graves, O my people. And I will put my Spirit within you, and you shall live."

After promising that those who receive Him as the bread of life will live forever, Jesus went one step further, connecting this "bread of life" with His own flesh: "The bread which I shall give for the life of the world is my flesh" (John 6:51). This verse is doubly shocking, for it contains first the proclamation that He will give His life in sacrifice for the salvation of the world and then states that this very life given for the life of the world will be communicated by giving us His flesh. In other words, Jesus is presenting Himself as a kind of sin offering or peace offering to God, a sacrifice that is consumed by those who offer the sacrifice. The difference, of course, is that no animal sacrifice of Israel was given for the "life of the world." Not surprisingly, the crowd murmurs in a new way after this verse, asking, "How can this man give us his flesh to eat?"

If Jesus meant to speak in a purely figurative manner, this would have been the time to clarify. Instead, He emphasizes still more the literal meaning of His words, explaining that He will give His flesh to be consumed as "living bread":

---

[5] See the interpretation of Isaiah 25:6–7 by Guitmund of Aversa, an eleventh-century adversary of Berengarius, in his *On the Truth of the Body and Blood of Christ in the Eucharist* 1.12:

> What does he mean when he says, "on this mountain," except the one on which Christ was crucified? And what is meant by saying: "He will provide a feast for all peoples," save only that all people will eat what hangs there? And what is meant by: "those juicy, rich foods," except that flesh made most rich by the grace of the Holy Spirit, "in which the fullness of the divinity dwells bodily"? And what is signified by "refined wine," if not the holy blood which is drunk in the species of wine? And what will happen for us in this banquet? "He will destroy death," he says, "forever." (trans. Mark Vaillancourt, FCMC, 10:101)

So Jesus said to them, "Truly, truly, I say to you, unless you eat the flesh of the Son of man and drink his blood, you have no life in you; he who eats my flesh and drinks my blood has eternal life, and I will raise him up at the last day. For my flesh is food indeed, and my blood is drink indeed. He who eats my flesh and drinks my blood abides in me, and I in him. As the living Father sent me, and I live because of the Father, so he who eats me will live because of me. (John 6:53–57)

In John 6:54, Jesus introduces a different verb for eating that emphasizes the physical chewing or gnawing: τρώγω.[6] Even rationalist scholars recognize the implications of this verb. Rudolf Bultmann writes:

> The offence is heightened in v. 54 by the substitution of the stronger *trogein* for *phagein*. It is a matter of real eating and not simply of some sort of spiritual participation. Thus there is every indication that v. 55 should also be taken in this way. It is really so! Jesus' flesh is real food and his blood is real drink![7]

Jesus heightens the realism and shock of this consumption by adding the drinking of His blood, which would have seemed especially abhorrent to His listeners, for the blood of animal sacrifice was reserved by the Law of Moses to God alone.[8] Imagine how disturbing this teaching must have been to people who had never heard of the Eucharist! Only at the Last Supper could the Apostles understand that Christ was giving His Body and His Blood to them to be consumed, not in their ordinary and "raw" state so as to be divided up as in a meat market, but under the Eucharistic species of bread and wine to accommodate the sensibilities of human nature.

---

[6] Ceslas Spicq, "*Trogein*. Est-il synonyme de *phagein* et d'*esthiein* dans le Nouveau Testament?" *New Testament Studies* 26 (1979–1980): 414–19; "τρώγω," in *A Greek-English Lexicon of the New Testament and Other Early Christian Literature*, 3rd ed., revised by Frederick William Danker (Chicago: University of Chicago Press, 2000), 1019.

[7] Rudolf Bultmann, *The Gospel of John: A Commentary*, trans. G. R. Beasley-Murray (Oxford: Basil Blackwell, 1971), 236, quoted in Pitre, *Jesus and the Last Supper*, 210.

[8] See Lev 7:26–27: "Moreover you shall eat no blood whatever, whether of fowl or of animal, in any of your dwellings. Whoever eats any blood, that person shall be cut off from his people." See also Lev 3:17.

It is no surprise that John then tells us that many of Christ's disciples found His teaching to be a "hard saying" and left Him. Surprisingly, however, Jesus let them leave. This was the opportunity for clarification, as He had done with Nicodemus and the Samaritan woman. If the disciples who found it a hard saying were misinterpreting Him, He should have clarified that He did not really mean that they were to eat His flesh and drink His blood. Instead He said: "Then what if you were to see the Son of man ascending where he was before? It is the Spirit that gives life, the flesh is of no avail. The words which I have spoken to you are Spirit and life" (John 6:62–63).

Some interpreters, especially in the Protestant tradition (such as Huldrych Zwingli),[9] see these words, "the flesh is of no avail," as retreating from the realism of the previous verses. In reality, Jesus is explaining that the "bread of life" of which He speaks—His flesh—is infinitely higher than the manna in the desert. This is a bread that gives eternal life from the Spirit. One cannot give what one does not possess. Jesus is identifying Himself as the one who gives the Spirit and who is able to give life through the Spirit. His future ascension is put forward as a sign that He can send the Spirit and give the life of the eschatological Kingdom. John 6:63 also reinforces the parallel with the prophecy of Ezekiel 37, in which the Spirit breathes on the dead bones of Israel and raises them up. Jesus is claiming to fulfill Israel's hope through words of "Spirit and life."

Jesus's reference to His ascension into heaven reinforces this idea. The disciples are scandalized because they are thinking that Christ's flesh is to be eaten like other flesh that perishes in the eating of it. Christ is calling attention to the incorruptibility of His Body and its

---

[9] See Huldrych Zwingli, *On the Lord's Supper*, art. 1, in *Zwingli and Bullinger: Selected Translations*, trans. G. W. Bromiley, Library of Christian Classics 24 (Philadelphia, PA: Westminster Press, 1953), 206:

> Moreover, when you see me ascend up to heaven, you will see clearly that you have not eaten me literally and that I cannot be eaten literally. . . . For how could the physical flesh either nourish or give life to the soul? To partake of the flesh does not profit anything if you do it as something necessary to the life of the soul. But the words which I have spoken to you . . . should all be interpreted in this sense, that I am the nourishment and consolation of the soul as I was put to death for the world, not as I am eaten with the mouth: for only then do we interpret them spiritually.

See also Paul Althaus, *The Theology of Martin Luther*, trans. Robert Schultz (Philadelphia, PA: Fortress Press, 1966), 395.

life-giving power: He will rise from the dead and ascend into heaven as a sign of this vivifying power. St. Augustine, in his *Treatises on the Gospel of John*, writes:

> Of course this scandalizes you. "What then if you should see the Son of man ascending where he was before?" What does this mean? By this did he resolve what had disturbed them? By this did he make clear why they had been scandalized? Clearly he did this, if they understood. For they thought that he was going to disburse his body; but he said that he was going to ascend to heaven, whole, of course. "When you see the Son of man ascending where he was before," surely then, at least, you will see that he does not disburse his body in the way in which you think; surely then, at least, you will understand that his grace is not consumed in bite-sized pieces.[10]

John 6:63 further clarifies John 6:54 by eliminating a potential misinterpretation according to which Jesus's flesh would be present in the Eucharist in the same way as a chunk of meat, with "parts outside of parts"[11] to be cut up and dissected (an error sometimes referred to as "Capernaism"). It is instead through consuming the flesh of the Son of man, made present in the Eucharist through the power of the Spirit in a unique sacramental mode that is proper to spiritual beings who exist whole and entire wherever they are present,[12] that His divine life is communicated to us, again through the power of the Spirit. St. Augustine interprets Jesus's words in John 6:63 eloquently:

> It [the flesh] profits nothing, but as they understood it; for, of course, they so understood flesh as [something that] is torn to pieces in a carcass or sold in a meat market, not as [something

---

[10] Augustine, *In Ioannis Evangelium* 27.5, in *Tractates on the Gospel of John, 11–27*, trans. J. W. Rettig, FC 79 (Washington, DC: Catholic University of America Press, 1988), 278–79.

[11] According to Aristotelian philosophy, all material things have dimensive quantity by which they have parts of their extension outside of their other parts such that they can be divided indefinitely. As will be seen below (chapter 7), Christ is not present in the Eucharist in this way proper to dimensive quantity, but in the mode of substance or essence, which is whole and entire under every part of the quantity of a thing.

[12] See Scheeben, *The Mysteries of Christianity*, 473, 517.

that] is enlivened by a spirit. . . . Let spirit be added to flesh, as love is added to knowledge, and it profits very much. For if flesh profited nothing, the Word would not have become flesh to dwell among us. . . . The flesh was a vessel; observe what it had, not what it was.[13]

St. Cyril of Alexandria also has a marvelous commentary on John 6:63:

It was not completely without reason, he says, that you have attributed to the flesh no ability to give life. When the nature of the flesh is considered alone and in itself, it will clearly not be life-giving. . . . However, ... since it has been united to the life-giving Word, it has risen to the power of the better nature and has become life-giving in its entirety. . . . The body belongs, after all, to him who is life by nature. . . . He now fills his whole body with the life-giving activity of the Spirit since he calls his flesh "spirit" without overturning the fact that it is flesh.[14]

Finally Jesus asks the Apostles if they also would leave Him. This highlights once again the theme of faith in Christ's words, as Peter answers: "Lord, to whom shall we go? You have the words of eternal life" (John 6:68).

In summary, Christ wished to give us a share in His divine life of

---

[13] Augustine, *In Ioannis Evangelium* 27.5 (p. 280).

[14] Cyril of Alexandria, *Commentary on John*, trans. David R. Maxwell, ed. Joel C. Elowsky, 2 vols., Ancient Christian Texts (Downers Grove, IL: InterVarsity Press, 2013), 1:246–47. See Thomas J. Nash, *The Biblical Roots of the Mass* (Manchester, NH: Sophia Institute Press, 2015), 139: "I also suggest that Jesus is simply saying that his flesh, that is his human nature *by itself*, has no power to give life, eternal or otherwise. However, when united to his divine Person by the Holy Spirit at his Incarnation . . . it becomes a participant in wondrous divine blessing. St. Cyril of Alexandria argues similarly, equating 'the spirit that quickeneth' with Christ's divinity, and 'the flesh that profiteth nothing' with Christ's mere human nature on its own." See also Scheeben, *The Mysteries of Christianity*, 517, with reference to those who were scandalized by the discourse: "But the ultimate reason why they held fast to this idea and could not rise to a loftier notion was that the Jews did not believe at all in the divinity of the Savior, and the faltering disciples believed only faintly. Had they believed firmly and unshakably like Peter, they too, like him, could have perceived with the aid of grace that the flesh and blood of Christ had their nourishing strength not from His fleshly nature, but from the Godhead dwelling in that nature, and hence that there could be no question of a cannibalistic repast."

glory. What better way to accomplish this than to nourish us with His very Body and Blood, thus communicating to us a frequent increase in sanctifying grace (as long as we do not reject it through mortal sin). In this discourse, Jesus indicated that the manna that fed the Israelites in the wilderness for forty years was a figure of the spiritual nourishment He would give the world through the sacrament of His Body and Blood. Furthermore, He clearly states that the type falls immeasurably short of the antitype, which is the Eucharist. Only the Eucharist is the "*true* bread from heaven." The type was a great sign, for it was literally bread that came physically down from heaven like dew to give bodily nourishment to the Israelites in their pilgrimage in the desert. Christ's Body and Blood is spiritual bread and drink by which Christ gives Himself to nourish us not physically, but through an increase of His divine life in us. Hence in John 6:63, Jesus says: "It is the Spirit that gives life, the flesh is of no avail. The words that I have spoken to you are Spirit and life." The Eucharist communicates to those who worthily receive it the life not of the flesh but of the Spirit. Jesus's words in John 6:63 are emphasizing that the nourishment that Jesus is speaking about is supernatural.

As we have seen, Jesus also refers to the sacrificial aspect of the Mass in the Bread of Life Discourse. When He says, "The bread which I shall give for the life of the world is my flesh," He is speaking of the sacrifice of His life for the redemption of the world also in terms of the Mass.[15]

Four Accounts of the Institution of the Eucharist

In the Bread of Life Discourse, Jesus did not make it clear that He would give us His flesh to eat and His blood to drink *under sacramental signs* of bread and wine by which it would not be repugnant to human nature. He explained the purpose and substance of the Eucharist with only an allusion to the fact that it would be realized under sacramental signs. He explained the "what" but not the "how." Jesus clearly wanted them to believe in His words without at first being able to understand how they were to be realized, which would be revealed to them at the

---

[15] See *CCC*, §1355; Nash, *Biblical Roots of the Mass*, 136–37.

proper time.[16] This time was a subsequent Passover, the last night of His earthly life—the Last Supper.

The institution of the Eucharist at the Last Supper is given to us in four parallel accounts that can be grouped into two pairs, which are Matthew and Mark, on the one hand, and Luke and St. Paul in 1 Corinthians 11, on the other. John does not give us an account of the institution of the Eucharist but gives us instead the Bread of Life Discourse and the washing of the feet at the Last Supper, both of which shed light on the Eucharist.

Why does John not give an account of the institution of the Eucharist? The most reasonable explanation is that he is interested in supplementing the synoptic gospels by giving accounts of things they omitted. Hence, he adds the Bread of Life Discourse and the washing of the feet but omits the institution narrative already transmitted in four accounts. A second possible complementary reason is that John was writing later, at which time it was considered prudent to maintain a veil of secrecy over the most sacred heart of Christian worship. This practice, known as the *disciplina arcani*, was common in the early Church. Joachim Jeremias writes: "All difficulties disappear, however, with the realization that the fourth evangelist consciously omitted the account of the Lord's Supper *because he did not want to reveal the sacred formula to the general public*."[17] The tendency to cover the most sacred of things behind an allusive veil may have led St. John to speak about the Eucharist through the image of the washing of the feet of the disciples rather than giving a direct account of the institution of the

---

[16] See Cyril of Alexandria, *Commentary on John*, 1:236. In his commentary on John 6:53, Cyril explains why Jesus did not make it clear in the Bread of Life Discourse how He would give them His Flesh to eat but reserved that explanation for the following year at the Last Supper:

> Therefore, after faith is first rooted in them, the understanding of what they do not know should be brought in next, but inquiry should not precede faith. That is why, I think, the Lord has good reason for not telling them in what manner he will give his flesh to eat, and he calls them to the duty of believing before investigating. For those who had already believed, he broke the bread and gave it to them saying, "Take, eat, This is My Body." ... Do you see how to those who are still ignorant and who refuse to believe without investigation, he does not explain the manner of the mystery, but to those who have already believed he is found to declare it most clearly?

[17] Joachim Jeremias, *The Eucharistic Words of Jesus*, trans. Norman Perrin from the 3rd German ed. (Philadelphia, PA: Fortress Press, 1977), 125 (italics original).

Eucharist. All that is said about the washing of the feet could also be said about the Eucharist.[18]

The account in 1 Corinthians 11 can be dated to about AD 53–57, and in it, Paul recounts what he passed on to the Corinthians when he first evangelized them around the year AD 51.[19] He also mentions that what he passed on to them is what he himself received, presumably before he arrived in Antioch in AD 40–42, as recounted in Acts 11, if not some years before. The origin of his account therefore goes back to the first decade after the Crucifixion.

Although they differ in some details, the essential nucleus is the same in all four accounts. The liturgical practice of the Church has been to consider the various accounts as forming a whole and present together the different aspects each sacred writer has highlighted.

Synopsis of the Accounts of the Last Supper

Preparation for the Last Supper

Matthew 26	Mark 14
17 Now on the first day of Unleavened Bread the disciples came to Jesus, saying, "Where will you have us prepare for you to eat the Passover?" 18 He said, "Go into the city to such a one, and say to him, 'The Teacher says, My time is at hand; I will keep the Passover at your house with my disciples.'" 19 And the disciples did as Jesus had directed them, and they prepared the Passover.	12 And on the first day of Unleavened Bread, when they sacrificed the Passover lamb, his disciples said to him, "Where will you have us go and prepare for you to eat the Passover?" 13 And he sent two of his disciples, and said to them, "Go into the city, and a man carrying a jar of water will meet you; follow him, 14 and wherever he enters, say to the householder, 'The Teacher says, Where is my guest room, where I am to eat the Passover with my disciples?' 15And he will show you a large upper room furnished and ready; there prepare for us." 16 And the disciples set out and went to the city, and found it as he had told them; and they prepared the Passover.

---

[18] See Anthony A. La Femina, *Eucharist and Covenant in John's Last Supper Account* (New Hope, KY: New Hope Publications, 2011).

[19] See *Ignatius Catholic Study Bible: New Testament* (San Francisco: Ignatius Press, 2010), 283.

Luke 22

7 Then came the day of Unleavened Bread, on which the Passover lamb had to be sacrificed. 8 So Jesus sent Peter and John, saying, "Go and prepare the Passover for us, that we may eat it." 9 They said to him, "Where will you have us prepare it?" 10 He said to them, "Behold, when you have entered the city, a man carrying a jar of water will meet you; follow him into the house which he enters, 11 and tell the householder, 'The Teacher says to you, Where is the guest room, where I am to eat the Passover with my disciples?' 12 And he will show you a large upper room furnished; there make ready." 13 And they went, and found it as he had told them; and they prepared the Passover.

John 13

1 Now before the feast of the Passover, when Jesus knew that his hour had come to depart out of this world to the Father, having loved his own who were in the world, he loved them to the end.

Betrayal of Judas Announced

Matthew 26

20 When it was evening, he sat at table with the twelve disciples; . . . 23 He answered, "He who has dipped his hand in the dish with me, will betray me.

Mark 14

17 And when it was evening he came with the Twelve.

Luke 22

21 But behold the hand of him who betrays me is with me on the table. 22 For the Son of man goes as it has been determined; but woe to that man by whom he is betrayed!" 23 And they began to question one another, which of them it was that would do this.

John 13

"Truly, truly, I say to you, one of you will betray me.". . . 23 One of his disciples, whom Jesus loved, was lying close to the breast of Jesus; . . . 25 So lying thus, close to the breast of Jesus, he said to him, "Lord, who is it?" 26 Jesus answered, "It is he to whom I shall give this morsel when I have dipped it." So when he had dipped the morsel, he gave it to Judas, the son of Simon Iscariot. . . . 30 So, after receiving the morsel, he immediately went out; and it was night.

Announcement That Jesus Would
Not Eat Another Passover

Matthew 26

29 "I tell you I shall not drink again of this fruit of the vine until that day when I drink it new with you in my Father's kingdom."

Mark 14

25 "Truly, I say to you, I shall not drink again of the fruit of the vine until that day when I drink it new in the kingdom of God."

Luke 22

14 And when the hour came, he sat at table, and the apostles with him. 15 And he said to them, "I have earnestly desired to eat this Passover with you before I suffer; 16 for I tell you I shall not eat it until it is fulfilled in the kingdom of God." 17 And he took a chalice, and when he had given thanks he said, "Take this, and divide it among yourselves; 18 for I tell you that from now on I shall not drink of the fruit of the vine until the kingdom of God comes."

The Institution Narrative

Matthew 26

26 Now as they were eating, Jesus took bread, and blessed, and broke it, and gave it to the disciples and said, "Take, eat; this is my body."

27 And he took a chalice, and when he had given thanks he gave it to them, saying, "Drink of it, all of you; 28 for this is my blood of the covenant, which is poured out for many for the forgiveness of sins."

30 . . . And when they had sung a hymn, they went out to the Mount of Olives.

Mark 14

22 And as they were eating, he took bread, and blessed, and broke it, and gave it to them, and said, "Take; this is my body."

23 And he took a chalice, and when he had given thanks he gave it to them, and they all drank of it. 24 And he said to them, "This is my blood of the covenant, which is poured out for many."

26 And when they had sung a hymn, they went out to the Mount of Olives.

Luke 22	1 Corinthians 11
19 And he took bread, and when he had given thanks he broke it and gave it to them, saying, "This is my body which is given for you. Do this in remembrance of me."	23 For I received from the Lord what I also delivered to you, that the Lord Jesus on the night when he was betrayed took bread, 24 and when he had given thanks, he broke it, and said,
20 And likewise the chalice after supper, saying, "This chalice which is poured out for you is the new covenant in my blood."	"This is my body which is for you. Do this in remembrance of me." 25 In the same way also the chalice, after supper, saying, "This chalice is the new covenant in my blood. Do this, as often as you drink it, in remembrance of me."
39 And he came out, and went, as was his custom, to the Mount of Olives; and the disciples followed him.	

The Setting: Preparing the Passover

The three synoptic gospels situate the institution of the Eucharist in a Passover supper,[20] and all three accounts begin with the disciples asking Jesus where He wishes them to prepare the Passover. In the Gospel of Mark, this day is said to be "the first day of Unleavened Bread, when they sacrificed the Passover lamb" (Mark 14:12).[21]

To understand the chronology of the Last Supper, it should be kept in mind that in the Jewish reckoning of time each new calendar day begins at sunset (as in Genesis 1). While the Temple stood, the proximate preparation for the Passover began on the 14th of the Jewish month of Nisan in the afternoon, at which time the lambs were sacrificed in the Temple, where their blood was poured out or sprinkled on the altar.[22] They were then roasted with fire for the evening meal, which had to be in Jerusalem.[23] This was the begin-

---

[20] The synoptics state that the Last Supper is a Passover meal in Matt 26:17–19; Mark 14:12, 14, 16; Luke 22:7, 8, 11, 13, 15. See Pitre, *Jesus and the Last Supper*, 315–16; Jeremias, *The Eucharistic Words of Jesus*, 41–62; Mary Healy, *The Gospel of Mark* (Grand Rapids, MI: Baker Academic, 2008), 281–82.

[21] Luke 22:7 likewise says that this occurred on "the day of Unleavened Bread, on which the Passover lamb had to be sacrificed." Matthew simply says that this occurred on the "first day of Unleavened Bread" (Matt 26:17).

[22] See Deut 12:26–27.

[23] See Deut 16:5–7: "You may not offer the Passover sacrifice within any of your towns which the LORD your God gives you; but at the place which the LORD your God will choose, to make his name dwell in it, there you shall offer the Passover sacrifice, in the evening at the going down of the sun, at the time you

ning of the seven-day period in which only unleavened bread could be eaten in commemoration of the flight from Egypt. This evening meal was celebrated after sunset at the beginning of the 15th of Nisan and it centered on the consumption of the paschal lamb, preceded by the sharing of unleavened bread and accompanied by the ceremonial drinking of wine before and after the meal.

Exodus 12:3–15 gives the essential ritual:

> Tell all the congregation of Israel that on the tenth day of this month [Nisan] they shall take every man a lamb according to their fathers' houses, a lamb for a household; . . . and you shall keep it until the fourteenth day of this month, when the whole assembly of the congregation of Israel shall kill their lambs in the evening. Then they shall take some of the blood, and put it on the two doorposts and the lintel of the houses in which they eat them. They shall eat the flesh that night, roasted; with unleavened bread. . . . And you shall let none of it remain until the morning, anything that remains until the morning you shall burn. . . . It is the LORD's Passover. . . . This day shall be for you a memorial, and you shall keep it as a feast to the Lord. . . . Seven days you shall eat unleavened bread.

It is interesting to note that the lamb was solemnly taken four days earlier on the 10th of Nisan. It seems that it is not by accident that Jesus made a solemn entrance to Jerusalem some days before the Passover on Palm Sunday, which could well have been the 10th of Nisan.

It follows therefore that the synoptic gospels situate the preparation for the Last Supper as taking place in the afternoon of the 14th of Nisan and the Last Supper as taking place at the beginning of the 15th of Nisan after sunset.

When the disciples ask Jesus where He wishes them to prepare the Passover, He answers cryptically by telling Peter and John that they are to go into the city where they will meet a man carrying a jug:

> And he sent two of his disciples, and said to them, "Go into the city, and a man carrying a jar of water will meet you;

---

came out of Egypt. And you shall boil it and eat it at the place which the LORD your God will choose; and in the morning you shall turn and go to your tents."

follow him, and wherever he enters, say to the householder,
'The Teacher says, Where is my guest room, where I am to eat
the Passover with my disciples?' And he will show you a large
upper room furnished and ready; there prepare for us." And
the disciples set out and went to the city, and found it as he
had told them; and they prepared the Passover. And when it
was evening he came with the twelve. (Mark 14:13–17)

It seems from this account that Jesus had not revealed to His
disciples the place He intended to celebrate the Passover meal, pre-
arranging it without their knowledge.[24] Even Peter and John are told
only that they were to meet a man who would take them there. It
is not hard to discover a significant motive for this unusual secrecy.
Jesus did not want to be disturbed and captured before He had instituted the Eucharist in the Last Supper.[25] He had a most momentous
work to accomplish and He did not want Judas to be able to betray
Him until after the Eucharist was instituted and the Last Supper
concluded.

It should also be noticed that in the preceding days Jesus had
been teaching at the Temple but returning to Bethany. The Passover, however, could not be eaten in Bethany, but only within the holy
city of Jerusalem. Hence, He needed a room within the city, but such
rooms would have been in great demand, for Jerusalem would have
been full of a great number of pilgrims from Israel and the diaspora.[26]

---

[24] See Pitre, *Jesus and the Last Supper*, 392: "It seems best to conclude that what
is in view is a meeting that has been prepared in advance by Jesus, in some
unknown manner."

[25] See ibid.: "Why does Jesus celebrate Passover in this somewhat secretive
fashion? The most plausible suggestion is that Jesus is taking the necessary
precautions because he is aware that he has already been marked out by the
Jerusalem authorities for arrest.... Jesus has one final prophetic sign to perform,
and he cannot have Judas handing him over to the authorities before the Last
Supper is complete." See also Healy, *The Gospel of Mark*, 281–82.

[26] See Josephus's testimony about the immense number of pilgrims in Jerusalem
for the Passover shortly before the destruction of Jerusalem in *Wars of the Jews*
6.9.3.423–25 and *Antiquities* 17.9.3.213–14.

Why Did Christ Choose the Last Supper as the Time to Institute the Eucharist?

It was fitting that Christ institute this sacrament of His presence and sacrifice on the Passover the night before He died. In this way He left it as His last testament, thus impressing it more deeply in the hearts and minds of His Apostles. Furthermore, since it is the sacrament of His bloody sacrifice, He wished to institute it as close to His Crucifixion as possible. He also wished to institute the Eucharist in the context of the Passover to show the continuity and passage between the great sacraments of the Old and the New Covenants. St. Thomas explains the fittingness of the institution of the Eucharist on the last night of Christ's earthly life as follows:

> This sacrament was appropriately instituted at the supper, when Christ conversed with His disciples for the last time. First of all, because of what is contained in the sacrament: for Christ is Himself contained in the Eucharist sacramentally. Consequently, when Christ was going to leave His disciples in His proper species, He left Himself with them under the sacramental species; as the Emperor's image is set up to be reverenced in his absence. . . .
>
> Secondly, because without faith in the Passion there could never be any salvation . . . it was necessary accordingly that there should be at all times among men something to show forth our Lord's Passion; the chief sacrament of which in the old Law was the Paschal Lamb. . . . But its successor under the New Testament is the sacrament of the Eucharist, which is a remembrance of the Passion now past, just as the other was figurative of the Passion to come. And so it was fitting that when the hour of the Passion was come, Christ should institute a new Sacrament after celebrating the old, as Pope Leo I says.[27]
>
> Thirdly, because last words, chiefly such as are spoken by departing friends, are committed most deeply to memory; since then especially affection for friends is more enkindled, and the things which affect us most are impressed the deepest in the soul. Consequently, since, as Pope Alexander I says,

---

[27] Leo the Great, Sermon 58.1 (Freeland and Conway, 249).

"among sacrifices there can be none greater than the body and blood of Christ, nor any more powerful oblation"; our Lord instituted this sacrament at His last parting with His disciples, in order that it might be held in the greater veneration.[28]

The Date of the Last Supper According to John

Was the Last Supper a true Passover celebration? There is a long-standing debate over whether the chronology of the Passion in John's Gospel is compatible or has contradictions with the account of the synoptic gospels, which portray the Last Supper as the first night of Passover.[29] Although John does not give an account of the institution

---

[28] *ST* III, q. 73, a. 5. See also Thomas Aquinas, *Opusculum 57, In Festo Corporis Christi*, lec. 4: "It was to impress the vastness of this love more firmly upon the hearts of the faithful that our Lord instituted this sacrament at the Last Supper. As he was on the point of leaving the world to go to the Father, after celebrating the Passover with his disciples, he left it as a perpetual memorial of his passion. It was the fulfillment of ancient figures and the greatest of all his miracles, while for those who were to experience the sorrow of his departure, it was destined to be a unique and abiding consolation" (*Liturgy of the Hours*, feast of Corpus Christi, Office of Readings, 2nd Reading).

[29] See the summary account of the modern arguments on either side in Craig S. Keener, *The Gospel of John: A Commentary* (Peabody, MA: Hendrickson, 2003), 2:1100–3. St. Thomas alludes to this controversy in his commentary on John 13:1, lec. 1, nos. 1729–30, in *Commentary on the Gospel of John: Chapters 13–21*, trans. Fabian Larcher and James A. Weisheipl (Washington, DC: Catholic University of America Press, 2010), 2:

> A problem arises as to why he says here, *before the feast of the Passover*, for the feast of the Passover is when the lamb was sacrificed, that is, on the fourteenth day of the month. So since he says, *before the feast of the Passover*, it seems that this was taking place on the thirteenth day, the day before the fourteenth. And indeed, the Greeks accept this, and say that our Lord suffered on the fourteenth, when the Jews were supposed to celebrate the Passover, and that our Lord, knowing that his passion was near, anticipated the celebration of the Passover and celebrated his own Passover on the day before the Passover feast of the Jews. And because it is commanded in Exodus (12:18) that from the evening of the fourteenth day to the twenty-first day the Hebrews should not have any leavened bread, they further say that the Lord celebrated not with unleavened bread, but with leavened bread, because Hebrews did have leavened bread on the thirteenth day, that is, before the Passover. But the other three Evangelists do not agree with this, for they say the time was the first day of Unleavened Bread, when the lamb was to be sacrificed (Matt 26:17; Mark 14:12; Luke 22:7). It follows from this that our Lord's Supper

of the Eucharist, the meal described in John 13 has clear marks of a Passover meal,[30] as can be seen from various details. In addition to the solemnity of the meal, proper to a feast such as Passover, there is the fact that the participants reclined, as we can see from the detail that the beloved disciple had his head close to Jesus's breast (John 13:23, 25). Jews reclined during the Passover meal as a ritual duty, reminding the participants of the freedom won by the Exodus.[31] Furthermore, John mentions that Jesus dipped a morsel and gave it to Judas (John 13:26, in harmony with Mark 14:20 and Matt 26:23), which probably refers to the custom at the Passover seder to dip the bitter herbs into a mixture of nuts, apples, and wine called *haroseth*.[32] Finally, John emphasizes that, when Judas exited after taking the morsel, it was night. This would be necessary for a Passover supper, the one Jewish festal meal held at night, for it was stipulated that it had to be celebrated after sundown and extend late into the night.[33]

Despite these elements that strongly suggest a Passover meal,[34] John's account has other features that have led many to think that John implies that the Last Supper could not properly be a Passover meal but must be situated one evening earlier, after sunset at the beginning

---

took place on the very day that the Jews sacrificed the lamb. The Greeks respond to this that the other Evangelists did not report this truly; and so John, who wrote the last of the Gospels, corrected them. But it is heresy to say that there is anything false not only in the Gospels but anywhere in the canonical scriptures. Consequently, we have to say that all the Evangelists state the same thing and do not disagree.

[30] See Jeremias, *The Eucharistic Words of Jesus*, 42–55.

[31] See ibid., 49: "At the passover meal it was a *ritual duty* to recline at table as a symbol of freedom" (italics original).

[32] See Pierre Benoit, *Jesus and the Gospel*, trans. Benet Weatherhead (New York: Herder and Herder, 1973), 1:100: "The morsel which Jesus moistens and gives to the traitor (John 13:21–30) was probably those bitter herbs which they dipped in the vinegar sauce." See also Pitre, *Jesus and the Last Supper*, 346–47; Pitre, *Jesus and the Jewish Roots of the Eucharist*, 155; C. K. Barrett, *The Gospel according to St. John*, 2nd ed. (Philadelphia, PA: Westminster, 1978), 447; *The Ignatius Bible*, commentary on John 13 (p. 188); Cesare Giraudo, *Eucaristia per la chiesa: prospettive teologiche sull'eucaristia a partire dalla "lex orandi"* (Rome: Gregorian University Press, 1989), 172–74.

[33] See Jeremias, *The Eucharistic Words of Jesus*, 46; Giraudo, *Eucaristia per la chiesa*, 169.

[34] See, for example, Raymond Brown, *The Gospel according to John*, 2 vols. (Garden City, NY: Doubleday, 1970), 2:556: "That there are Passover characteristics in the meal, even in John, is undeniable.... Yet this fact does not settle the chronological question."

of the 14th of Nisan, before the Passover lambs would have been sacrificed on the following afternoon. <u>According to this hypothesis, Jesus's</u>
<u>death would have occurred at roughly the same time as the sacrifice of</u>
<u>the paschal lambs in the Temple on the afternoon of the 14th of Nisan.</u>
There are several reasons for holding this position.

First, John 13:1 seems to situate the Last Supper before the Passover, for he says: "Now before the feast of the Passover, when Jesus
knew that his hour had come to depart out of this world to the Father,
having loved his own who were in the world, he loved them to the
end." This is a weak argument, however, because this chronological
indication may well refer directly to Jesus's awareness that His hour
had come, not to the date of the Last Supper itself.[35]

Secondly, John 18:28 suggests that the Jewish authorities were
going to celebrate the Passover on the evening after the Crucifixion
(Friday evening), for it states: "Then they led Jesus from the house
of Caiaphas to the praetorium. It was early. They themselves did not
enter the praetorium, so that they might not be defiled, but *might eat
the Passover.*" Entering a Gentile house was regarded as an act that
would make one ritually unclean for seven days.[36] It could be inferred
from this that Jesus's trial occurred on the morning of the 14th of
Nisan before the beginning of Passover. A third reason for thinking
that John's account is incompatible with the Last Supper being a Passover meal is suggested by John 19:14, which says that the time of
the Crucifixion was the sixth hour on the "day of Preparation of the
Passover."[37] This phrase would seem to imply that Christ was crucified
on the day of preparation before the beginning of the Passover, which
would be the 14th of Nisan. A fourth argument, which also applies to
the synoptic accounts, is that it seems that it would be impossible for
the Sanhedrin to convene for Jesus's trial if the feast of Passover had
already begun.[38]

---

[35] See Jeremias, *The Eucharistic Words of Jesus*, 80: "John 13:1, 'before the feast of
the Passover' cannot be used in support of this chronology, because the time
reference here clearly belongs to 'knew' and simply asserts that Jesus already
knew before the Passover that his death was imminent." See also Bultmann, *The
Gospel of John*, 463; Brown, *The Gospel according to John*, 2:549.

[36] See Rudolf Schnackenburg, *The Gospel According to St. John*, trans. David Smith
and G. A. Kon (New York: Crossroad, 1982), 3:244; Brown, *The Gospel according to John*, 2:846.

[37] See, for example, Schnackenburg, *The Gospel According to St. John*, 3:264–65.

[38] See Brown, *The Gospel according to John*, 2:556: "Jeremias, in *The Eucharistic
Words of Jesus*, 75–79, who follows the synoptic chronology, has made a heroic

Four Positions on the Date of the Last Supper in John and the Synoptics

Brant Pitre, in his detailed study of this question, outlines four principal ways of dealing with the apparent conflict in the Gospels over the date of the Last Supper and whether or not it was a proper Passover meal.[39] One way holds that only the synoptic gospels have the right chronology, and Pitre calls this the "Synoptic hypothesis." The opposing view defends the accuracy of John's chronology, and is called the "Johannine hypothesis." A third, more recent view seeks to reconcile John and the synoptics by holding that Jesus was following the Essene calendar, and so Pitre calls this the "Essene calendar hypothesis." The fourth, and most traditional, hypothesis holds that the Last Supper was truly a Passover meal as presented in the synoptic gospels and seeks to explain the apparently divergent elements of John's account as not incompatible with the Last Supper being a true Passover meal.[40] Pitre refers to this as the "Passover hypothesis," which seems to me to be the most probable position.

Synoptic Hypothesis

The synoptic hypothesis favors the chronology of the synoptic gospels while holding that John departed from the actual historical chronology for a symbolic purpose.[41] According to this view, John chose to portray Jesus's death as coinciding with the time of the sacrifice of the paschal lambs in the Temple on the 14th of Nisan, even though He was crucified on the following day in historical reality.[42] In a homily

---

attempt to show that all the individual actions that the Gospels report on Friday (trials, flogging, carrying a cross, men coming from the fields, crucifixion, purchasing spices, opening a tomb, and burial) could have taken place on Passover without violation of the Jewish Law. However, so much activity on a feast remains a difficulty; and it seems more plausible to accept John's chronology whereby such activity was taking place on an ordinary day."

[39] Pitre, *Jesus and the Last Supper*, 258–59. See also Jeremias, *The Eucharistic Words of Jesus*, 20–26; Keener, *The Gospel of John*, 2:1100–1103; Benoit, *Jesus and the Gospel*, 97–98.

[40] See Jeremias, *The Eucharistic Words of Jesus*, 20–21.

[41] This view is vigorously defended by Jeremias, *The Eucharistic Words of Jesus*, 20–23, 62–84.

[42] See Pitre's summary and criticism of this position in *Jesus and the Last Supper*, 314–30.

for Holy Thursday, Pope Benedict XVI gives a good description of the logic of this position, although he ends up siding with the Essene hypothesis:

> There is an apparent discrepancy in the Evangelists' accounts, between John's Gospel on the one hand, and what on the other Mathew, Mark and Luke tell us. According to John, Jesus died on the Cross at the very moment when the Passover lambs were being sacrificed in the temple. The death of Jesus and the sacrifice of the lambs coincided. However, this means that he must have died the day before Easter [Passover] and could not, therefore, have celebrated the Passover meal in person—this, at any rate, is how it appears. According to the three synoptic gospels, the Last Supper of Jesus was instead a Passover meal into whose traditional form he integrated the innovation of the gift of his Body and Blood. This contradiction seemed unsolvable until a few years ago. The majority of exegetes were of the opinion that John was reluctant to tell us the true historical date of Jesus' death, but rather chose a symbolic date to highlight the deeper truth: Jesus is the new, true Lamb who poured out his Blood for us all.[43]

This position agrees with the Passover hypothesis on the point of principal importance for understanding the Eucharist, which is that Jesus Himself chose the first night of Passover as the fitting time for its institution, even though this view holds that John did not portray it that way.[44] The major problem with this position is that it denies the historical accuracy of certain elements of John's account.

Johannine Hypothesis

Another way to interpret the date of the Last Supper is to hold that only John's account is historically accurate and that the Last Supper was held after sunset on the evening that marks the beginning of the 14th of Nisan, the night before the sacrifice of the paschal lambs

---

[43] Benedict XVI, Homily of Holy Thursday, Mass of the Lord's Supper, April 5, 2007, accessed June 25, 2017, http://w2.vatican.va/content/benedict-xvi/en/homilies/2007/documents/hf_ben-xvi_hom_20070405_coena-domini.html.

[44] See the rich analysis of Giraudo, *Eucaristia per la chiesa*, 162–86.

that would occur in the afternoon of the 14th of Nisan.[45] This would mean either that the Last Supper was not a true Passover or that Jesus celebrated the Passover one day early.[46] The great difficulty here is how to reconcile this with the clear words of the synoptic gospels that say that the Last Supper was on the feast of the Passover.[47] Why should the ambiguous and indirect indications of John be given more historical weight than the clear testimony of the synoptics? On historical grounds, a difficulty is that it fails to account for several details of John's narration of the Last Supper that strongly suggest a Passover meal, as seen above.

In terms of typology, this position has the advantage of making the sacrifice of Jesus on Calvary and the sacrifice of the paschal lambs

---

[45] This view is defended, among others, by Brown, *The Gospel according to John*, 2:555–58, 787–802. He summarizes his position on 556: "We suggest then that, for unknown reasons, on Thursday evening, the 14th of Nisan by the official calendar, the day before Passover, Jesus ate with his disciples a meal that had Passover characteristics. The Synoptists or their tradition, influenced by these Passover characteristics, too quickly made the assumption that the day was actually Passover; John, on the other hand, preserved the correct chronological information." This view is also defended by: John P. Meier, *A Marginal Jew: Rethinking the Historical Jesus*, vol. 1, *The Roots of the Problem and the Person* (New York: Doubleday, 1991), 395–401; William Oscar Emil Oesterley, *The Jewish Background of the Christian Liturgy* (Gloucester, MA: P. Smith, 1965), 158–67; Joseph Blinzler, *The Trial of Jesus*, trans. Isabel and Florence McHugh (Westminister, MD: Newman Press, 1959), 75–77. See the discussion of this hypothesis in Pitre, *Jesus and the Last Supper*, 281–313, and Jeremias, *The Eucharistic Words of Jesus*, 21.

[46] St. John Chrysostom gives this interpretation as one of two possible solutions, the other being the Passover hypothesis; see *In John*, homily 83, on John 18:28: "But what is the meaning of 'that they might eat the Passover?' Christ Himself, to be sure, had kept the Passover on the first day of the azymes. Therefore, the Evangelist meant the whole festival by the word 'passover'; or else he meant that they were then observing the Passover, while Christ had done so a day ahead, keeping His own actual immolation for the Day of Preparation, the day when the Passover really took place in olden times" (*Commentary on Saint John the Apostle and Evangelist: Homilies 48–88*, trans. T. A. Goggin, FC 41 [Washington, DC: Catholic University of America Press, 1959], 409–10).

[47] See Second Vatican Council, Dogmatic Constitution on Divine Revelation, *Dei Verbum* (1965), §19: "Holy Mother Church has firmly and with absolute constancy held, and continues to hold, that the four Gospels just named, whose historical character the Church unhesitatingly asserts, faithfully hand on what Jesus Christ, while living among men, really did and taught for their eternal salvation until the day He was taken up into heaven." See also Pontifical Biblical Commission, Instruction on the Historical Truth of the Gospels, *Sancta Mater Ecclesia* (1964), and Feingold, *Faith Comes from What Is Heard*, 451–468.

coincide: the afternoon of the 14th of Nisan, thus highlighting Jesus as the true Lamb of God. The typological disadvantage of this position is that it would somewhat weaken the connection between the Passovers of the Old and the New Covenants, since the Last Supper, according to this view, would not have been a proper Passover meal.[48]

Essene Calendar Hypothesis

One way of reconciling John and the synoptics is the hypothesis that Jesus celebrated a true Passover but according to a different calendar than the one used by the Temple authorities. Thus the sacrifice of the paschal lambs would have coincided with Jesus's death on the Cross and the official Passover meal would have taken place on Friday evening, after Jesus's death. This hypothesis has been proposed in three different forms.

One version of this hypothesis supposes a difference between the calendar of the Sadducees and the Pharisees. According to this proposal, Jesus would have celebrated the Passover according to the calendar of the Pharisees, on Thursday evening, together with the majority of the people. The Sadducees, however, would have celebrated the feast a day later, on Friday evening. This would explain the difficulty posed by John 18:28, according to which those who led Jesus to the Praetorium did not enter, "so that they might not be defiled, but might eat the Passover." The High Priest and his family belonged to the sect of the Sadducees. There is no evidence, however, to support this view, which remains "wholly conjectural."[49]

A second proposal is that the Passover was celebrated on two successive evenings due to the logistical difficulty of sacrificing the great number of lambs that needed to be sacrificed in the afternoon of the 14th of Nisan. It has been proposed that the pilgrims from Galilee

---

[48] See Keener, *The Gospel of John*, 2:1100: "Both traditions—a paschal Last Supper and a paschal crucifixion—are theologically pregnant, but we suspect that Jesus, followed by the earliest tradition, may have intended the symbolism for the Last Supper whereas John has applied the symbolism more directly to the referent to which the Last Supper itself symbolically pointed."

[49] Jeremias, *The Eucharistic Words of Jesus*, 23–24. He summarizes this position and comments: "This theory has been so thoroughly and carefully argued, especially by Billerbeck, that its possibility has to be admitted. Its weakness is that it is wholly conjectural; there is no evidence that the Passover lambs were ever slaughtered on two consecutive days in the Temple."

were assigned the preceding day (the 13th of Nisan) for the sacrifice.[50]

Another more recent and more plausible proposal is that the divergence of calendar was between the Essenes and the Temple cult. We know that the Essenes maintained a different liturgical calendar, regulated by a solar rather than a lunar year. In this solar calendar, feast days always occurred on the same day of the week, and thus the Essene Passover was on a Tuesday evening. Annie Jaubert proposes that Jesus celebrated the Passover according to the Essene calendar.[51] According to this hypothesis, Jesus was captured and imprisoned on Tuesday night at Gethsemane. The various trials recounted in the Gospels, according to Jaubert's thesis, would have been spread out over the following two days, ending finally on Friday with Pilate's order to crucify Him.[52]

By celebrating the Passover before the official date, it would have been possible for Jesus to combine two crucial aspects of symbolism: He could institute the Eucharist in the context of a Passover meal, and He could be sacrificed when the paschal lambs were being sacrificed, which would more clearly show Him to be the true Lamb of God, represented typologically by all the paschal lambs.

Pope Benedict speaks about this problem in his homily for Holy Thursday in 2007. He says there is "a possible and convincing solution which, although it is not yet accepted by everyone, is a highly plausible hypothesis,"[53] that Jesus celebrated the Passover according to the Essene calendar, in which it fell at least one day earlier, which could have been Thursday. This hypothesis would enable one to affirm the accuracy of both the chronology of John[54] and that of the synoptics without losing the symbolism proper to each account. Thus Jesus would have celebrated the Last Supper on the Essene Passover, in which He Himself was the Temple and the Lamb that was offered,

---

[50] See J. Pickl, *Messiaskönig Jesus in der Auffassung seiner Zeitgenossen* (Munich: J. Kösel & F. Pustet, 1935), 247–48, and Jeremias's comment on Pickl in *The Eucharistic Words of Jesus*, 24: "There is therefore no evidence for Pickl's thesis; it, too, remains pure conjecture."

[51] Annie Jaubert, *The Date of the Last Supper* (Staten Island, NY: Alba House, 1965).

[52] Ibid., 103–17.

[53] Benedict XVI, 2007 Holy Thursday Homily for the Mass of the Lord's Supper. From this summary assessment we can see that Benedict does not intend this homily to be a definitive solution to the problem.

[54] Ibid.: "We can now say that John's account is historically precise."

and He would be crucified on Friday, the official "day of preparation" in which the paschal lambs were sacrificed in the Temple.

> Jesus truly shed his blood on the eve of Easter at the time of the immolation of the lambs. In all likelihood, however, he celebrated the Passover with his disciples in accordance with the Qumran calendar, hence, at least one day earlier; he celebrated it without a lamb, like the Qumran community which did not recognize Herod's temple and was waiting for the new temple.
>
> Consequently, Jesus celebrated the Passover without a lamb—no, not without a lamb: instead of the lamb he gave himself, his Body and his Blood. . . . He himself was the awaited Lamb, the true Lamb, just as John the Baptist had foretold at the beginning of Jesus' public ministry: "Behold, the Lamb of God, who takes away the sin of the world!" (John 1:29). And he himself was the true Temple, the living Temple where God dwells and where we can encounter God and worship him.[55]

The Essene hypothesis, however, although attractive, remains largely unsubstantiated and hypothetical.[56] The biggest problem with it is that it contradicts the clear statements of Mark 14:12 and Luke 22:7–8 that the Last Supper took place in the evening after the paschal lambs were sacrificed. Supporters of the Essene hypothesis have to discount these texts as later interpolations.[57] A second problem is that the Essene hypothesis requires a period of three days between the Last Supper and the Crucifixion but the four Gospels all present the Crucifixion as occurring the day after the Last Supper.[58] Third, there is no evidence that Jesus ever deviated from the Temple calendar in any other instance.[59] If He did not do it on other occasions, it is very

---

[55] Ibid. See also the treatment of this theme in Joseph Ratzinger, *Jesus of Nazareth: Holy Week from the Entrance into Jerusalem to the Resurrection* (San Francisco: Ignatius Press, 2011), 106–16.

[56] See the explanation of the problems associated with the Essene hypothesis by Brant Pitre in *Jesus and the Last Supper*, 268–80. See also Benoit, *Jesus and the Gospel*, 1:87–93; Keener, *The Gospel of John*, 2:1102; Jeremias, *The Eucharistic Words of Jesus*, 24–25; Blinzler, *The Trial of Jesus*, 78–80.

[57] See Jaubert, *The Date of the Last Supper*, 97–98.

[58] See Pitre, *Jesus and the Last Supper*, 272–73.

[59] See Meier, *A Marginal Jew*, 1:393; Pitre, *Jesus and the Last Supper*, 270–71.

unlikely that He would have deviated in this instance, in which the typology of the Passover was absolutely critical for the institution of the Eucharist. Here more than ever, it seems, Jesus would have been attentive to observing the Old Law as it was publicly observed by those who sat in the chair of Moses. These three problems, it seems to me, render this hypothesis less probable than the Passover hypothesis.

Passover Hypothesis

The synoptic, Johannine, and Essene calendar hypotheses all start with the same first step, which is to show the incompatibility between the account of the synoptics and that of John. In addition to this, defenders of the Johannine and Essene hypotheses then have to demonstrate a reasonable probability that Jesus departed from the Temple calendar in this key event. Adherents of the Passover hypothesis, on the contrary, need to show that the supposed contradictions between the synoptic account and that of John can be reconciled.

A notable defender of the Passover hypothesis and the possibility of reconciling the chronology of John and the synoptics is St. Thomas. He holds that the phrase "eat the Passover" in John 18:28 need not necessarily refer to the eating of the lamb (which was done only on the first night of Passover), but could also refer to the eating of the unleavened bread, which is done throughout the eight-day celebration and also requires ritual purity. In his commentary on John 18:28, he writes:

> A problem arises about the first point: that they would not enter the praetorium so as not to be defiled. The other Evangelists say that Christ was seized in the evening, on the day of the supper; and this would be the Passover meal: "I have earnestly desired to eat this Passover with you" (Lk 22:15). And then in the morning of the next day he was brought to the praetorium. Why then do we read so that they might eat the Passover, since it was the day after the Passover? Some of the modern Greeks say that we are now on the fourteenth lunar day of the month, and that Christ was crucified on the day the Jews celebrated the Passover, but that Christ anticipated the Passover by one day, since he knew he would be killed on the day of the Jewish Passover. Thus, he celebrated the Passover on the thirteenth lunar day, in the evening. And since the law commanded that the Jews should not have leavened bread

from the fourteenth day of the first month to the twenty-first day, they say that Christ consecrated leavened bread.

This is not acceptable for two reasons. First, the Old Testament has no instance where anyone was permitted to anticipate the celebration of the Passover. But if one was prevented, he could postpone it to the next month: "If any man of you or of your descendants is unclean . . . he shall still keep the Passover to the Lord. In the second month on the fourteenth day in the evening they shall keep it" (Num 9:10). And since Christ never omitted any observance of the law, it is not true to say that he anticipated the Passover. Secondly, Mark (14:12) states explicitly that Christ came on the first day of Unleavened Bread, when they sacrificed the Passover lamb; and Matthew says that "on the first day of Unleavened Bread the disciples came to Jesus saying, 'Where will you have us prepare for you to eat the Passover?'" (Matt 26:17). So, we should not say that Christ anticipated the Passover. . . .

Therefore we should say with Jerome, Augustine[60] and other Latin Fathers,[61] that the fourteenth day is the beginning of the feast; but the Passover refers not just to that evening, but to the entire time of the seven days during which they ate unleavened bread, which was to be eaten by those who were clean. And because the Jews would have contracted uncleanness by entering the residence of a foreign judge, they did not enter so that they might not be defiled, but might eat the Passover, that is, the unleavened bread.[62]

---

[60] Augustine, *In Ioannis Evangelium* 114.2: "But explaining the reason why they went not into the praetorium, 'that they might not be defiled,' [the Evangelist] says, 'but that they might eat the passover.' For they had begun to celebrate the days of unleavened bread, and on these days it was a defilement for them to enter the dwelling of a foreigner" (Rettig, trans., *Tractates on the Gospel of John, 112–24*; [and] *Tractates on the First Epistle of John*, 17).

[61] See Alcuin's commentary on John 18:28, *Commentaria in S. Joannis Evangelium* 7.40 (PL, 100:974), cited in Thomas Aquinas, *Catena Aurea*, trans. John Henry Newman, 4 vols. (Oxford: John Henry Parker, 1841–1845; repr. with an introduction by Aidan Nichols, London: Saint Austin Press, 1997), on John 18:28.

[62] Thomas Aquinas, commentary on John 18:28, lec. 5, nos. 2331–34, in *Commentary on the Gospel of St. John*, 215–16. See also the parallel text in *ST* III, q. 46, a. 9, ad 1.

The idea, maintained by St. Thomas and others,[63] that "eating the Passover" refers not only to the banquet on the first night of the feast but also to all seven days of the Passover, is supported by Deuteronomy 16:2–3, which commands the Israelites to "eat the Passover" for *seven* days:

> And you shall offer the Passover sacrifice to the Lord your God, from the flock or the herd, at the place which the Lord will choose, to make his name dwell there. You shall eat no leavened bread with it; *seven days you shall eat it* with unleavened bread.

Another reason that the Jewish leaders of the priestly class did not want to enter the praetorium is that peace offerings were sacrificed and consumed each night of the week of Passover, as we see in Leviticus 23:8: "You shall present an offering by fire to the LORD seven days." To offer and consume the sacrifices required ritual purity. Rabbinical sources speak of the eating of these peace offerings during the seven days of the feast as "eating the Passover."[64] John 18:28, therefore, does not seem to pose any significant obstacle to the thesis that the Last Supper was a proper Passover meal.

The difficulty with regard to John 19:14, which states that the day of the Crucifixion (Good Friday) "was the day of preparation of the Passover,"[65] seems to have a simple solution. The term "day of preparation" can be understood in two ways. It is often understood to mean the day before the feast of Passover, which is the 14th of Nisan. If it is interpreted in this way, then the synoptic gospels and John are in contradiction with one another. "Day of preparation," however, is the normal Jewish way of referring to Friday, the day of preparation for the Sabbath that begins after sundown on Friday.[66] Thus the "day

---

[63] See John Chrysostom, *In John*, homily 83, on John 18:28: "But what is the meaning of 'that they might eat the Passover?' Christ Himself, to be sure, had kept the Passover on the first day of the azymes. Therefore, the Evangelist meant the whole festival by the word 'passover'" (in *Commentary on Saint John the Apostle*, 409–10).

[64] See Pitre, *Jesus and the Last Supper*, 352–56.

[65] παρασκευὴ τοῦ πάσχα.

[66] See Pitre, *Jesus and the Last Supper*, 357: "In the first-century AD, the Greek word 'preparation (*paraskeuē*) is simply the Jewish name for 'Friday,' because that was the day of the week on which one would 'prepare' (*paraskeuazō*) for the

of preparation of the Passover" would normally designate the Friday within Passover week, even if that evening were not the beginning of Passover.[67] This interpretation is favored by the use of the same term (*paraskeuē*) to refer to Friday (as the preparation for the Sabbath) in John 19:31[68] and 19:42. If John 19:14 is also using the term in this way, which would be a natural assumption, then there is no contradiction between John and the synoptics. Obviously, an interpretation that avoids placing the Gospels in contradiction with each other should be preferred.

With regard to the argument that a trial and execution could not occur during the feast of the Passover, it should be pointed out that Jewish law, as later recorded in the Tosefta, required false prophets to be executed precisely during a pilgrim feast such as Passover so that the many pilgrims to Jerusalem would witness it:

> A rebellious and incorrigible son, a defiant elder, one who leads people astray to worship idols, one who leads a town to apostasy, a false prophet, and perjured witnesses—they do not kill them immediately. But they bring them up to the court in Jerusalem and keep them until the festival, and then they put them to death on the festival, as it is said, "And all the peoples

---

Sabbath." See the commentary on John by Theodore of Mopsuestia, in *Ancient Christian Commentary on Scripture*, vol. 14/b, *John 11–21*, ed. Joel Elowsky (Downers Grove, IL: InterVarsity Press, 2007), 304: "It was the day of preparation, that is, the sixth holy day of the week."

[67] See Pitre, *Jesus and the Last Supper*, 357–59. See also Thomas Aquinas's commentary on John 19:14, lec. 3, no. 2404: "Among the Jews the Sabbath was in some respects more solemn than any other feast, insofar as out of reverence for that day no food was prepared on the Sabbath; it was prepared on the preceding Friday. Thus this Friday was called the day of Preparation of the Passover" (*Commentary on the Gospel of John*, 233).

[68] See Schnackenburg, *The Gospel According to St. John*, 3:287–88. With regard to John 19:31, he explains that "the 'day of Preparation' (without more) could refer back to the 'day of preparation of the Passover' in 19:14; but the following ἵνα-clause which reminds about the sabbath, does not leave any room for doubt that the day of preparation for the sabbath (that is Friday) is intended—the normal Jewish usage." Schnackenburg thus thinks that the term "preparation day" has two different meanings in John 19:14 and 19:31. I think that it is better to understand both uses of the word as signifying Friday, the day of preparation before the Sabbath, which is the normal usage. As Schnackenburg notes, the term "preparation day" is used to refer to Friday by, for example, Josephus, *Antiquities of the Jews*, 16.6.2.163.

shall hear and fear, and no more do presumptuously" (Deut 17:13). The words of Rabbi Aquiba.[69]

This seems to be an exact description of the motivation for choosing the first day of Passover (15th of Nisan), on which there would be the maximum presence of pilgrims in Jerusalem, for the execution of Jesus.

This solution, it seems, is preferable because it is the most in conformity with all the Gospel texts, despite the difficulties, which, as we have seen, are not insuperable.[70] According to the clear witness of the synoptic gospels, Jesus celebrated the Last Supper on the night on which all Israel ate the Passover lamb.

Significance of the Passover as the Setting for the Last Supper

However one decides the chronological question of the date of the Last Supper, it is undeniable that Jesus chose a paschal setting according to all four Gospels and that this context is emphasized as having great theological significance for interpreting the event.[71] The paschal setting helps us to see the profound continuity between the Old and the New Covenants, which are related to one another as figure and fulfillment. It is supremely fitting that "Jesus prays his new prayer within the Jewish liturgy."[72] The *Catechism of the Catholic Church*, §1340 highlights the importance of this Passover setting:

> By celebrating the Last Supper with his apostles in the course of the Passover meal, Jesus gave the Jewish Passover its definitive meaning. Jesus' passing over to his father by his death and Resurrection, the new Passover, is anticipated in the Supper and celebrated in the Eucharist, which fulfills the Jewish

---

[69] Tosefta, Sanhedrin 11:7, trans. Jacob Neusner, *The Tosefta* (Peabody, MA: Hendrickson, 2002), cited in Pitre, *Jesus and the Last Supper*, 303.

[70] This is the conclusion of Pitre in *Jesus and the Last Supper*, 331–73.

[71] See Benoit, *Jesus and the Gospel*, 98–99: "Whether it was celebrated at the usual time or anticipated, there is hardly a doubt in actual fact that the last meal taken by Jesus was held in the atmosphere of the feast of the Pasch, that the Master intended them to coincide, and made use of this for the institution of his new rite." See also Healy, *The Gospel of Mark*, 281.

[72] Ratzinger, *The Feast of Faith*, 41 (in *TL*, 304).

Passover and anticipates the final Passover of the Church in the glory of the kingdom.

Charles Journet gives a good explanation of the typological fittingness of the institution of the Eucharist on the Passover:

> There is nothing fortuitous in the coincidence of the Last Supper with the Jewish Feast of Passover. It means that the Jewish Passover must give way to a more mysterious Passover that it was prefiguring. The Jewish Passover was the sacrificial offering of a lamb to which one united himself by eating it, in recognition of God's goodness in delivering his people from the captivity of Egypt so as to enable them to enter the Promised Land.[73]

Jesus is the true Lamb of God of the new Passover of the New Covenant. The lambs of the Old Covenant had to be sacrificed before the beginning of the feast of Passover[74] so that they could be received in communion at the feast, which was the culmination of the ritual. Christ, however, could reverse the order. At the Last Supper, on the first night of Passover, He offered Himself as the new Lamb of the New Covenant and gave Himself in communion to His Apostles as such, though He would not be physically immolated before the supper, as were the paschal lambs of the Old Covenant, but after the Supper, on Friday, which was still the first day of Passover (15th of Nisan). The Lamb of God was immolated in a bloody way a day after the lambs in the Temple, but he was sacramentally immolated and consumed on the first evening of Passover, together with the paschal lambs of the Old Covenant.

The Passover Seder Described in Luke's Account

Luke begins his account of the Supper with the words of Jesus: "I have earnestly desired to eat this Passover with you before I suffer" (Luke 22:15). The expression to "eat the Passover" normally implies the eating

---

[73] Charles Journet, "Transubstantiation," *The Thomist* 38 (1974): 735.

[74] Nevertheless, Exodus 12:6 says that the paschal lambs were to be immolated "in the evening" just before the beginning of the feast. At the time of Jesus this was done earlier, in the afternoon of the 14th of Nisan, presumably because of the great quantity of lambs to be sacrificed.

of the Passover lamb, which is referred to by the same word, πάσχα.[75] We should understand Jesus's great desire for *this* Passover as directed not merely to His participation in the Mosaic rite, but rather to the institution of the Eucharist—the Passover of the New Covenant—in the midst of the Passover meal in which He makes Himself present as the new paschal Victim to be sacrificed and consumed by the faithful.

St. Luke gives us more details than the other Gospels about the Last Supper, and these enable us to situate the institution of the Eucharist within the structure of the Passover *seder*. While the other Evangelists mention only one chalice, St. Luke mentions two: one before the institution of the Eucharist, at the beginning of the meal, and another after the supper, in which He says the Eucharistic words: "This cup is the new covenant in my blood. Do this, as often as you drink it, in remembrance of me."[76] This detail, which may seem confusing at first sight, corresponds to the structure of the seder, at which four cups of red wine are drunk.[77]

The general form of the seder as practiced today is quite ancient and seems to go back to the time before the destruction of the Temple.[78] The first cup (*kiddush*) is drunk at the beginning of the seder, after the blessing: "Blessed are you, O Lord our God, King of the universe, who creates the fruit of the vine."[79] The second cup is then mixed with water but not yet drunk. The youngest child asks his father why this night is different from all other nights. The father explains by telling the story of Exodus and interpreting it, which would include the explanation of the paschal lamb and why unleavened bread and bitter herbs are eaten. Afterward, the second cup is drunk. Then there is a blessing over the *matzah*, it is broken and distributed to all by the host, and a piece of it is consumed. Presumably it would have been at the moment that Jesus "took bread, and when he had given thanks, . . . broke it and gave

---

[75] Luke 22:6 and Luke 22:15. See also Mark 14:12 and Pitre, *Jesus and the Last Supper*, 291.

[76] Luke 22:20. There is an important text-critical variance in the manuscript tradition of Luke that contains a longer and a shorter variant of 22:19–20, of which only the longer includes the words of institution over the second chalice. See the discussion in Jeremias, *The Eucharistic Words of Jesus*, 139–59, in which he defends the genuineness of the longer text.

[77] See ibid., 52; Marie-Joseph Nicolas, *What Is the Eucharist?* Twentieth Century Encyclopedia of Catholicism 52 (New York: Hawthorn Books, 1960), 18.

[78] See the discussion in Frédéric Manns, *Jewish Prayer in the Time of Jesus* (Jerusalem: Franciscan Printing Press, 1994), 184–211.

[79] See Pitre, *Jesus and the Jewish Roots of the Eucharist*, 152.

it to them, saying, 'This is my body which is given for you. Do this in remembrance of me'" (Luke 22:19).

There follows the dinner, at the end of which a third cup of wine is drunk while reciting the blessing of thanksgiving after the meal. This cup is known as the cup of blessing (*berakah*).[80] Then Psalms 115–18 (*Hallel*) are recited,[81] after which the fourth cup of wine is drunk. Psalms 116 and 118 are messianic psalms, and Psalm 116:12–17 is particularly appropriate to the occasion of the institution of the Eucharist:

> What shall I render to the Lord for all his bounty to me?
> I will lift up the cup of salvation and call on the name of the
>   Lord,
> I will pay my vows to the Lord in the presence of all his
>   people.
> Precious in the sight of the Lord is the death of his saints.
> I will offer to thee the sacrifice of thanksgiving and call on
>   the name of the Lord.

The first chalice mentioned by Luke corresponds to either the first or second cup of the seder. The cup that Jesus used to become His Blood is most probably the third cup, the cup of blessing and thanksgiving, after the *matzah* and the meal, as Luke specifies.[82]

SACRIFICIAL CONNOTATIONS OF THE WORDS OF INSTITUTION

The words of institution, in all four accounts, are steeped in sacrificial connotations.[83] We know that the Eucharist makes present the sacri-

---

[80] See ibid., 155.

[81] Matt 26:30 and Mark 14:26 probably allude to the recitation of the *Hallel* psalms (see Jeremias, *The Eucharistic Words of Jesus*, 55).

[82] See Josef Jungmann, *The Mass: An Historical, Theological, and Pastoral Survey*, trans. Julian Fernandes, ed. Mary E. Evans (Collegeville, MN: Liturgical Press, 1976), 8; Jungmann, *The Early Liturgy to the Time of Gregory the Great*, trans. Francis A. Brunner (Notre Dame, IN: University of Notre Dame Press, 1959), 32; Christoph Cardinal Schönborn, *The Source of Life*, trans. Brian McNeil, ed. Hubert Philipp Weber (New York: Crossroad Publishing Co., 2007), 22–32.

[83] See, among others, Jeremias, *The Eucharistic Words of Jesus*, 220–55, and Raymond Moloney, *The Eucharist* (Collegeville, MN: Liturgical Press, 1995), 40–46.

fice of Calvary above all from what Christ says in all four accounts of the institution of the Eucharist at the Last Supper. His words establish an identity between His presence in the Eucharist, the sacrifice of Calvary, and the sacrifices of the Temple that prefigured it. Jesus makes Himself present and gives Himself to us as the Victim of a sacrifice in which the body is given and the blood poured out. As witnesses of this event, the Apostles would have been struck forcefully not only by the affirmation of the presence of His Body and Blood under the appearances of bread and wine but also by the fact that the Body and Blood of their beloved master were being presented and offered in sacrifice![84]

"My Body Given for You"

In Luke's account, Christ took bread and said: "This is my body *which is given for you*. Do this in remembrance of me" (Luke 22:19). The expression "given for you" implies a sacrifice of expiation offered on our behalf.[85] Jesus does not say that His Body is given *to* the disciples, but that it is given *for* them. The sacrificial Victim is "given" or "offered" for the forgiveness of the sins of the people.[86] In Isaiah 53:10, the suffering servant "makes himself an offering for sin." In Matthew 20:28, Jesus says that He has come to "give His life as a ransom for many."

---

[84] See Masure, *The Sacrifice of the Mystical Body*, 126–27; Joseph Ratzinger, *God Is Near Us: The Eucharist, The Heart of Life*, trans. Henry Taylor, ed. Stephan Ott Horn and Vinzenz Pfnür (San Francisco: Ignatius Press, 2003), 43; and Benoit, *Jesus and the Gospel*, 1:101: "The first lesson which stands out in the words of Christ, a lesson concerning which the disciples could not have made a mistake, is that he is going to die and give his life for them. . . . Then he puts this imminent death, in a sense, before their eyes, by showing them under the bread and the wine his body and blood. . . . The separation of the bread and the wine expresses the separation of the body and the blood, that is to say, death."

[85] The Greek preposition ὑπέρ means "on behalf of." See Jeremias, *The Eucharistic Words of Jesus*, 226: "'Which will be shed for many,' continues the comparison with the sacrifices. . . . It makes clear *for whom the atoning and redeeming power of Jesus is effective*. It is linked with an Old Testament passage: Isa. 53:12." For a study of the words of institution, see Jean Galot, "Le parole eucaristiche di Gesù," *Civiltà Cattolica* 144, no. 2 (1993): 16–28. See also Benoit, *Jesus and the Gospel*, 1:100–105.

[86] See Galot, "Le parole eucaristiche di Gesù," 28; Ángel García Ibáñez, *L'Eucaristia, Dono e Mistero: Trattato storico-dogmatico sul mistero eucaristico* (Rome: Edizioni Università della Santa Croce, 2008), 70.

In order to be given *to* the disciples to consume, Christ's Body must first be given *for* them in sacrifice. A victim must be immolated before it can be ritually consumed. The Old Testament uses the expression "to give" to refer both to the portion offered to the Lord in sacrifice, as in Numbers 18:12, and to the portion given to the priests and Levites to consume, as in Leviticus 10:14.[87]

These words of institution said over the bread are very close to Jesus's words in John 6:51: "The bread which I shall give for the life of the world is my flesh." This text from the Bread of Life Discourse indicates the full extension of the "given for you." Instead of being offered just for the disciples, Jesus makes it clear that His flesh is given on behalf of the world to restore its life.

We can say that His body is doubly given. It is given to the Father in sacrifice on behalf of the disciples and of the life of the world.[88] And then it is given *to* the disciples that they may share in the life of the One who, in the discourse after the supper, affirmed that He *is* the Life. In other words, Christ's body offered in sacrifice expiates sin so that the world may receive life through His life-giving flesh. Because of the hypostatic union, Christ's flesh communicates a share in the divine life that it has won for us.

"Do This in Remembrance of Me"

Christ then says to "do this in remembrance of me" (Luke 22:19; 1 Cor 11:24), which follows the pattern of the memorial offerings of the Old Testament. By this Christ is commanding that the sacramental

---

[87] Lev 10:12–14: "And Moses said to Aaron and to Eleazar and Ithamar, his sons who were left.... 'But the breast that is waved and the thigh that is offered you shall eat in any clean place, you and your sons and your daughters with you; for they are given as your due and your sons' due, from the sacrifices of the peace offerings of the people of Israel.'"

[88] See John Paul II, *EE*, §13: "The Eucharist is *a sacrifice in the strict sense*, and not only in a general way, as if it were simply a matter of Christ's offering himself to the faithful as their spiritual food. The gift of his love and obedience to the point of giving his life (cf. John 10:17–18) is in the first place a gift to his Father. Certainly it is a gift given for our sake, and indeed that of all humanity (cf. Matt 26:28; Mark 14:24; Luke 22:20; John 10:15), yet it is *first and foremost a gift to the Father*" (italics original). See also CIC, can. 899, §1: "In it Christ the Lord, by the ministry of a priest, offers Himself, substantially present under the forms of bread and wine, to God the Father and gives Himself as spiritual food to the faithful who are associated with His offering."

re-presentation of His sacrifice on Calvary, which He celebrated at the Last Supper, be repeated until the end of the world. This command has two parts: first, it tells the Apostles to "do this," and then it explains how it is to be done, which is "in remembrance." Both parts indicate that Christ is offering a sacrifice and commanding His Apostles to do likewise, thus ordaining them as priests of the New Covenant.

The Old Testament frequently uses the verb "to do" (עָשָׂה) to refer to the offering of a sacrifice.[89] For example, in Exodus 10:25 Moses says to Pharaoh, "You must also let us have sacrifices and burnt offerings, that we may sacrifice to the LORD our God." The Hebrew word for "that we may sacrifice" is literally "that we may do" (וְעָשִׂינוּ). Exodus 29:35–41 also uses the verb "do" repeatedly in this sense. Leviticus 16:24 describes the offering of the High Priest on the Day of Atonement: "He shall bathe his body in water in a holy place, and put on his garments, and come forth, and offer [literally, "do"] his burnt offering and the burnt offering of the people, and make atonement for himself and for the people."

The reference to "remembrance" or "memorial" is also a sacrificial term frequently used in the Old Testament.[90] Some sacrifices are said to be memorials of the great works of God.[91] Leviticus 23:25 speaks of the feast of Rosh Hashanah as a *memorial* (*zikaron*) (זִכָּרוֹן) in which "you shall present an offering by fire to the LORD." The most important reference to "memorial" sacrifice is in the institution of the Passover: "This day shall be for you a memorial [*zikaron*] day, and you shall keep it as a feast to the LORD" (Exod 12:14). The sacrifice of the Passover lamb was a "memorial" of the liberation of Israel from Egypt so that Israel's foundational event would be liturgically reenacted every year and stay alive in the minds and hearts of the people. Furthermore, each liturgical re-presentation of the event of the Exodus was itself a sacrifice in which the paschal lamb was offered in memory of and in continuity with the institutional sac-

---

[89] Other examples include Num 15:11–14; Judg 13:16; 2 Kings 5:17; Lev 9:22; Ezek 43:25.

[90] See Moloney, *The Eucharist*, 45–46: "For Israel, 'memory' is a sacrificial word. Already in the book of Leviticus the portion of the victim burnt on the altar is called a 'reminder' or a 'memorial,' and it is clear that it is a question of God's remembering the sacrifice. God's remembering, therefore, is an intrinsic part of all worship in the Bible."

[91] See, among others, Exod 20:24 and Lev 2:2 and 24:7, which speak of a memorial offering of fine flour, oil, and frankincense.

rifice. The Eucharist is likewise a memorial of the event of Good Friday, on which Israel and the entire world was liberated from the dominion of sin and death. And as the event of Good Friday was itself a sacrifice—the sacrifice of all sacrifices—so is its sacramental re-presentation.

Since the liturgical "memorials" of Israel celebrate the mighty works of God establishing His covenant, there is a sense in which they ask not only Israel to remember, but also God, in that Israel's sacrifices are put before the Lord as a memorial of His covenant and a pledge of His fidelity.[92] We see this sense of the word "memorial" in Acts 10:4, in which the centurion is told that his "prayers and . . . alms have ascended as a memorial before God." Similarly, Ben Sira speaks of Aaron as ordained to "offer sacrifice to the Lord . . . as a memorial portion, to make atonement for the people" (Sir 45:16).[93]

Applying this liturgical sense of "memorial" to the Eucharist, we should understand Christ's command to "do this in remembrance of me" to mean that He is giving His Church His sacrifice of Calvary to remember this event and to place it forever before God the Father, that He might remember His promised covenantal graces merited by that sacrifice.[94] Furthermore, as the "memorial portions" offered by Aaron were propitiatory sacrifices to "make atonement for the people," Christ's reference to the Eucharist as a memorial should lead us to understand it also as a propitiatory sacrifice.

---

[92] See Max Thurian, *The One Bread*, trans. Theodore DuBois (New York: Sheed and Ward, 1969), 15–23; Jeremias, *The Eucharistic Words of Jesus*, 246–55; Moloney, *The Eucharist*, 45–46. Against this interpretation, see Giraudo, *Eucaristia per la chiesa*, 240–41.

[93] For other Old Testament sacrifices spoken of as a "memorial" put before the Lord, see Lev 2:2, 9, 16; 5:12; Sir 35:6–7; 38:11. See Danker, *A Greek-English Lexicon of the New Testament and Other Early Christian Literature*, 656.

[94] This double sense of the notion of "memorial"—that the Church remember Christ's Paschal mystery and that God remember it for the sake of His Church—is manifested in the early Eucharistic prayer the Anaphora of Addai and Mari: "Lord, through your unspeakable mercies make a gracious *remembrance* of all the upright and just fathers who have pleased you, in the *commemoration* of the body and blood of your Christ, which we offer to you upon the pure and holy altar as you have taught us" (Jammo, "The Mesopotamian Anaphora of Addai & Mari," 416, 421).

Blood Poured Out for the Forgiveness of Sins

The words of the institution of the chalice have much clearer sacrificial connotations.[95] Although the verbal construction of the consecration of the wine differs in the accounts of Matthew and Mark, on the one hand, and that of Luke and Paul on the other, their essential content is the same.[96] Luke and Paul speak of the chalice as a common metaphor for its contents,[97] which is said to be "the new covenant in my blood," whereas Matthew and Mark affirm that it is "the blood of the covenant."[98]

All three synoptic gospels speak of the blood as "poured out." The blood of the sacrificial victims offered in the Temple, such as the paschal lambs, is said to be "poured out" at the foot of the altar (or sprinkled) in order to win God's favor and the forgiveness of sins.[99] Jesus's use of this expression is the clearest indication of the sacrificial nature of the rite that He instituted at the Last Supper. He is in effect saying that He is the true Passover lamb of the New Covenant, whose blood is to be poured out in sacrifice and whose flesh (and blood) is to be consumed by the faithful in a new Passover rite of the New Covenant.[100]

It is true that Christ's Body was "given for" us on Calvary, and there His Blood was "poured out for many for the forgiveness of sins." However, Christ spoke of His Body as given and His Blood as poured out in the Last Supper, *before* the sacrifice of Calvary. Thus He was speaking of His Body and Blood in the Eucharist as making present

---

[95] See Thomas Aquinas, *Commentary on 1 Corinthians 11*, lec. 6, Marietti no. 682, in *Commentary on the Letters of Saint Paul to the Corinthians*, trans. Fabian R. Larcher (Lander, WY: Aquinas Institute for the Study of Sacred Doctrine, 2012).

[96] See Jeremias, *The Eucharistic Words of Jesus*, 169: "The great disparity in the common words . . . is only superficial."

[97] Luke 22:20: "This chalice which is poured out for you is the new covenant in my blood"; 1 Cor 11:25: "This chalice is the new covenant in my blood. Do this, as often as you drink it, in remembrance of me."

[98] Matt 26:27–28: "Drink of it, all of you; for this is my blood of the covenant, which is poured out for many for the forgiveness of sins"; Mark 14:24: "This is my blood of the covenant, which is poured out for many."

[99] See Exod 29:12; Lev 4:7, 18, 25, 30, 34; 9:9; Deut 12:26–27.

[100] Pitre, *Jesus and the Last Supper*, 414: "He is also saying to His disciples: 'I am the eschatological Passover lamb, whose blood will be poured out as a sacrifice for others.'" See also Healy, *The Gospel of Mark*, 285.

the same sacrifice of Calvary that was to be enacted on the following afternoon. The Mass of the Church makes the sacrifice of Calvary present again—the Body being given and the Blood poured out sacramentally—in all succeeding days and ages so that all believers can participate in it.

When Christ says that His blood "is *poured out for many* for the forgiveness of sins" (Matt 26:28), there is an allusion to the prophecy of the Suffering Servant in Isaiah 53:11–12, who shall "make *many* to be accounted righteous; and . . . shall bear their iniquities . . . because he *poured out his soul* to death, and was numbered with the transgressors; yet . . . bore the sin of *many*."[101] Christ's Blood is poured out in

---

[101] The word "many" here—indicating a great multitude—does not exclude the meaning of "all." Compare Rom 5:12 and 15. See the Congregation for Divine Worship and the Discipline of the Sacraments, Letter on Amending the Translation of "Pro Multis" (October 17, 2006):

> Indeed, the formula "for all" would undoubtedly correspond to a correct interpretation of the Lord's intention expressed in the text. It is a dogma of faith that Christ died on the Cross for all men and women (cf. John 11:52; 2 Corinthians 5:14–15; Titus 2:11; 1 John 2:2). There are, however, many arguments in favor of a more precise rendering of the traditional formula *pro multis*:
>
> a) The synoptic gospels (Matt 26:28; Mark 14:24) make specific reference to "many" for whom the Lord is offering the Sacrifice, and this wording has been emphasized by some biblical scholars in connection with the words of the prophet Isaiah (53:11–12). It would have been entirely possible in the Gospel texts to have said "for all" (for example, cf. Luke 12:41); instead, the formula given in the institution narrative is "for many," and the words have been faithfully translated thus in most modern biblical versions.
>
> b) The Roman Rite in Latin has always said *pro multis* and never *pro omnibus* in the consecration of the chalice.
>
> c) The anaphoras of the various Oriental Rites, whether in Greek, Syriac, Armenian, the Slavic languages, etc., contain the verbal equivalent of the Latin *pro multis* in their respective languages.
>
> d) "For many" is a faithful translation of *pro multis*, whereas "for all" is rather an explanation of the sort that belongs properly to catechesis.
>
> e) The expression "for many," while remaining open to the inclusion of each human person, is reflective also of the fact that this salvation is not brought about in some mechanistic way, without one's own willing or participation; rather, the believer is invited to accept in faith the gift that is being offered and to receive the supernatural life that is given to those who participate in this mystery, living it out in their lives as well so as to be numbered among the "many" to whom the text refers.

the Eucharist for *many*, an innumerable multitude, for the forgiveness of the sins of the world. The "many" should be seen as referring to both Israel and all peoples, for all are called to enter the Church.[102] That the "many" should be connected with the Church is supported by the fact that, in Luke 22:20, Jesus says that the cup "is poured out for you"—the community of disciples—instead of "for many."[103] The Roman Canon puts both phrases together: "poured out for you and for many."[104] The words of Christ in the institution of the Eucharist make it clear that Isaiah 53 is fulfilled in the Blood of Christ poured out on Calvary—and sacramentally in every Mass—for *many*, for the great multitude called to enter His Church.

For the inclusive sense of "many" in Hebrew (*rabbim*) and Aramaic, see also Jeremias, *The Eucharistic Words of Jesus*, 179–82; Galot, "Le parole eucaristiche di Gesù," 19. For more recent studies of this question contesting the view of Jeremias, see Manfred Hauke, "Shed for Many: An Accurate Rendering of the *Pro Multis* in the Formula of Consecration," *Antiphon* 14, no. 2 (2010): 169–229; Franz Prosinger, *Das Blut des Bundes vergossen für viele? Zur Übersetzung und Interpretation des hyper pollôn in Mk 14,24* (Siegburg, DE: Franz Schmitt, 2007). See also Healy, *The Gospel of Mark*, 286: "'Many' does not mean a limited number, but is a Semitic way of expressing a vast multitude."

[102] Jeremias, in *The Eucharistic Words of Jesus*, 229, translates the sense of Matt 26:28 as: "which will be shed for the peoples of the world." See his discussion on 227–31.

[103] See Hauke, "Shed for Many," 175–76. See also his analysis of the early Eucharistic prayers (pp. 192–97).

[104] *RM*, 639. See Aquinas's commentary on these words of the Roman Canon in his commentary on 1 Cor 11, lec. 6, Marietti no. 682:

> The blood was indeed shed for the remission of sins, not only for many but for all. . . . But because some make themselves unworthy to receive such an effect, as far as its efficacy is concerned, it is said to have been shed for many, in which the passion of Christ has an effect. But he expressly says, "for you and for many," because this sacrament can produce remission of sin for those who receive it after the manner of a sacrament, which is clearly signified when it is said: "for you," to whom he had said "take." Or it also avails after the manner of sacrifice for many not receiving, for whom it is offered; which is signified when it is said: "and for many." (Larcher, *Commentary on Corinthians*, 254–55; I have corrected the translation of the last sentence.)

See also the explanation of the *Roman Catechism* (*CCT*), 223–24: "The next phrase, 'for you and for many' . . . is meant to designate the actual effectiveness of the Passion. If we consider its potential efficacy, we would have to say that the Blood of the Savior was shed for all men. But if we look to what it actually achieves in terms of mankind's acceptance of it, we see that it does not extend to the whole, but only to a large part of the human race."

Blood of the Covenant / New Covenant in My Blood

When Christ speaks of the Eucharistic chalice as the cup of "the new covenant in my blood" (Luke 22:20; 1 Cor 11:25), or directly of "my blood of the covenant" (Matt 26:28; Mark 14:24), He is making a clear connection with the sacrificial offering at Mount Sinai that sealed the Mosaic covenant. Covenants between Israel and God were always sealed by the blood of sacrificial animals.[105] The Mosaic covenant was sealed at the foot of Sinai with the blood of many oxen.[106] The oxen were offered as burnt offerings and peace offerings, and the blood was gathered in basins. Half of the blood was poured out on the altar, and the other half was "poured out" or sprinkled on the people after they promised to be faithful to the covenant: "And Moses took the blood and threw it upon the people, and said, 'Behold the blood of the covenant which the LORD has made with you in accordance with all these words'" (Exod 24:8). Just as the Old Covenant was sealed with sacrificial blood poured out and sprinkled on the people, so too the New Covenant is sealed with Blood. The difference lies in the victim whose blood is poured out. The Victim in the New Covenant is not a multitude of irrational beasts, but the Messiah, the Son of God made man, "who loved me and gave himself for me" (Gal 2:20).

On Mount Sinai, the blood of oxen was merely a sign of the covenant, of a communion between God and man. The glory of the New Covenant is that the Blood that seals the covenant is not only a sign of this communion, but its very life, being the Blood of Him who is the *Life*. For this reason, Jesus's Blood is said to be not only the "blood of the covenant," but also the "new testament in my blood" (Luke 22:20; 1 Cor 11:25). That is, Jesus's Blood is not just the price of the covenant, but its essential content, which is a communion of life with the Word

---

[105] See Marie-Joseph Lagrange, *The Gospel of Jesus Christ* (London: Burns, Oates & Washbourne, 1947), 206: "That blood serves like the blood that was used in the ritual of making a covenant, according to which those entering into the covenant were sprinkled with the blood of a sacrificial victim; in this case the victim was Jesus, whose Blood was in the cup. Thus He was inaugurating a new covenant." See also Benoit, *Jesus and the Gospel*, 102: "A covenant, according to the Semitic idea, must be made 'in blood,' that is to say by the immolation of victims (cf. Gen 15:17), of which the blood is henceforth called 'blood of the covenant.'"

[106] See Exod 24:5–8.

Incarnate.[107] Jesus's Blood is the "lifeblood" of the New Covenant.

Jesus's words over the chalice, "the new covenant in my blood" (Luke 22:20; 1 Cor 11:25), make reference to the prophecy of Jeremiah 31:31–33,[108] which speaks of a New Covenant:

> Behold, the days are coming, says the LORD, when I will make a new covenant with the house of Israel and the house of Judah, not like the covenant which I made with their fathers when I took them by the hand to bring them out of the land of Egypt, my covenant which they broke, and I showed myself their Master, says the LORD. But this is the covenant which I will make with the house of Israel after those days, says the LORD: I will put my law within them, and I will write it upon their hearts; and I will be their God, and they shall be my people. . . . I will forgive their iniquity, and I will remember their sin no more.

Since the expression "New Covenant" occurs in the Old Testament only in this prophecy of Jeremiah, it is reasonable to think that Jesus had this text in mind and was fulfilling the ancient prophecy in the institution of the Eucharist and on Calvary.

Although Matthew and Mark do not use the term "new" with regard to the "blood of the covenant," their versions of the words over the chalice add a key aspect that is also present in Jeremiah 31:31–33: the forgiveness of sins. The blood of the covenant is poured out precisely to gain the forgiveness of sins for many. It is this that Jeremiah puts forth as a principal purpose of the New Covenant.

Another prophecy that is alluded to by Jesus's words over the chalice, especially in the version of Matthew and Mark, is Zechariah 9:9–12:

> Behold, your king comes to you;
>   triumphant and victorious is he,
> humble and riding on a donkey,
>   on a colt the foal of a donkey.
>   . . . He shall command peace to the nations;

---

[107] See Galot, "Le parole eucaristiche di Gesù," 26–27.

[108] See also Isa 42:6, in which the Suffering Servant is said to be "given to you as a covenant to the people."

his dominion shall be from sea to sea,
> and from the River to the ends of the earth.
As for you also, because of the blood of my
> covenant with you,
I will set your captives free from the
> waterless pit.
Return to your stronghold, O prisoners of hope.

Zechariah speaks about a covenant that will be worked by a Messiah king with a universal dominion who triumphantly enters Jerusalem and, through the *blood of the covenant*, sets free those who are captives of death. Jesus proclaims that the Eucharist is the fulfillment of this prophecy of the sealing of a covenant in blood that will free the captives of death. Since Jesus's Blood is poured out for the forgiveness of sins, it has the power to free the people of God from the consequences of sin, which are death and separation from God. Thus it has the power to set free the "prisoners of hope." This text of Zechariah is also in harmony with the Bread of Life Discourse, in which Jesus promises that one who eats His Flesh and drinks His Blood "has eternal life" and that He "will raise him up at the last day" (John 6:54).

Jesus's words also recall the Suffering Servant canticles in Isaiah. In Isaiah 42:6, God says: "I have given you as a covenant to the people, a light to the nations." This is further developed in Isaiah 49:8–9: "I have kept you and given you as a covenant to the people, to establish the land, to apportion the desolate heritages; saying to the prisoners, 'Come forth,' to those who are in darkness, 'Appear.' They shall feed along the ways, on all bare heights shall be their pasture." By saying that His Blood is that of the covenant, Jesus is identifying Himself as the Suffering Servant and the mediator of the New Covenant. His life, offered on Calvary and communicated by His Body and Blood, is the price of the covenant and its essential content and promise. As in Zechariah, the covenant is connected in Isaiah 49 with the conquering of the power of death and the liberation of those in the darkness of *sheol*.

The blood of the New Covenant is shown to be superior to that of Sinai because its effects are interior. It has the power to give sanctifying grace, to write the Law of God on our hearts and give us the inner strength to keep it, and it has the power to forgive all sin and iniquity.

Christ's Knowledge of His Sacrifice

The words of Jesus in instituting the Eucharist show not only that He had a clear awareness of His impending sacrifice, but also that He was celebrating that future sacrifice in a sacramental way. For here He has offered Himself to the sacrifice as something already present in His Father's eyes. Thus the Blood that would be poured out the following day is sacramentally poured out in atonement. Unlike the earlier prophecies He had made of His impending death, this is more than a prophecy; it is the sacramental offering of His Passion as something already mysteriously present. In fact, it makes that still future event something that will be mysteriously relived throughout the time of His Church.

Furthermore, Christ's institution of the Eucharist, like the discourse in John 6, implies an awareness not only of His impending death, but also of His Resurrection. For the offering of Christ's Body and Blood on the part of the Church cannot be the offering of dead things, but of the living Lord, whose sacrifice is life-giving because it contains Him who is the life.

Other References to the Eucharist in the New Testament

1 Corinthians 11:23–32

The most important text on the Eucharist outside the Gospels is 1 Corinthians 11:23–32. St. Paul is speaking in this letter, written circa AD 53–57, about various problems in the infant church in Corinth, and one of these problems concerns the celebration of the Eucharist. He begins the section by giving the words of institution, which he introduces in a solemn way by emphasizing that he has delivered to them a most sacred deposit that had been entrusted to him: "For I received from the Lord what I also delivered to you, that the Lord Jesus on the night when he was betrayed took bread, and when he had given thanks, he broke it, and said, 'This is my body which is for you'" (1 Cor 11:23–24). The institution of the Eucharist is presented as a crucial part of the Church's Tradition through the solemn use of the verbs "received" and "delivered." What St. Paul received from the other Apostles, he delivered to the Church in Corinth. Not surprisingly, since St. Luke was a disciple of Paul, Luke's account is close to that of his master.

After the institution narrative, St. Paul also adds the phrase: "For as often as you eat this bread and drink the cup, you proclaim the Lord's death until he comes" (1 Cor 11:26). The reception of Holy Communion is presented not simply as a sacred banquet, but as a participation in Jesus's sacrifice and a commemoration of the Passion and death of the Lord who will return in glory. The Eucharist unites the sorrowful and glorious mysteries.

St. Paul adds to the institution narrative a very important warning about unworthy reception of the Eucharist, which will be discussed below in chapter 14. This text also clearly implies the doctrine of the real presence:

> Whoever, therefore, eats the bread or drinks the cup of the Lord in an unworthy manner will be guilty of profaning the body and blood of the Lord. Let a man examine himself, and so eat of the bread and drink of the cup. For anyone who eats and drinks without discerning the body eats and drinks judgment upon himself. That is why many of you are weak and ill, and some have died. But if we judged ourselves truly, we should not be judged. (1 Cor 11:27–31)

1 Corinthians 5:6–8 and 10:16–21

Although 1 Corinthians 11 is St. Paul's principal text on the Eucharist, he also alludes to it in two other texts of the same epistle. In 1 Corinthians 5:6–8, he is speaking of the scandal caused by a man guilty of incest:

> Do you not know that a little leaven leavens the whole lump? Cleanse out the old leaven that you may be a new lump, as you really are unleavened. For Christ, our paschal lamb, has been sacrificed. Let us, therefore, celebrate the festival, not with the old leaven, the leaven of malice and evil, but with the unleavened bread of sincerity and truth.

This text identifies Christ with the paschal lamb and the Christian life with the celebration of the festival of the Christian Passover, which is the Eucharist. The unleavened bread is the sign that the Christian is ready to receive new leaven—a new life to become "a new lump," a new creation—by the sacrifice of the Paschal Lamb.

Another Eucharistic text is 1 Corinthians 10:16–21, in which St. Paul addresses the issue of eating meat sacrificed to idols. He writes:

> The cup of blessing which we bless, is it not a participation in the blood of Christ? The bread which we break, is it not a participation in the body of Christ? Because there is one bread, we who are many are one body, for we all partake of the one bread. Consider the people of Israel; are not those who eat the sacrifices partners in the altar? What do I imply then? That food offered to idols is anything, or that an idol is anything? No, I imply that what pagans sacrifice they offer to demons and not to God. I do not want you to be partners with demons. You cannot drink the cup of the Lord and the cup of demons. You cannot partake of the table of the Lord and the table of demons.

The expression "cup of blessing" clearly refers to the Eucharist. As mentioned above, it also was the term used by Jews for the third cup of the Passover seder, which seems to be the cup used by Jesus to become the chalice of His Blood.

This text implies four fundamental truths about the Eucharist. First, it is the sacrament of the unity of the Church, for all the faithful partake of the "one bread." It is one bread not in the appearances, but in the fact that every host contains one and the same Christ. It causes the unity of the Church by uniting those who partake of it with Christ and in Christ. Second, Holy Communion is said (by way of a rhetorical question) to be a partaking of the Blood and Body of Christ, which presupposes the doctrine of the real presence. Third, partaking in the Eucharist is compared analogously to partaking in the sacrifices offered to demons. As partaking of sacrifice offered to demons creates a union with the demons, so partaking of the Eucharist creates a union with Christ. Fourth, the comparison of the Eucharist with participation in a sacrifice to demons implies that the Eucharist is likewise a sacrifice in which the faithful participate.[109]

---

[109] See Ibáñez, *L'Eucaristia, Dono e Mistero*, 102–3.

The Eucharist in Luke 24 and the
Acts of the Apostles

The Acts of the Apostles shows us the Eucharist in the life of the early Church. It is referred to as the "breaking of the bread." The first occurrence of this expression is in the account of the two disciples on the way to Emmaus on Easter Sunday: "When he was at table with them, he took the bread and blessed, and broke it, and gave it to them. And their eyes were opened and they recognized him; and he vanished out of their sight" (Luke 24:30–31). They then returned to Jerusalem and recounted their experience to the Apostles: "Then they told what had happened on the road, and how he was known to them in the breaking of the bread" (Luke 24:35).

It is interesting that the experience of the disciples on the road to Emmaus also shows the larger form of the liturgy. While they were walking, Jesus opened the Scriptures to them, showing how the Old Testament points to the event of the Passion, and this corresponds to the liturgy of the Word. He then blessed and broke the bread and distributed it to those present, which is the Eucharistic liturgy. The reactions of the disciples are also emblematic: their hearts burned at the explanation of the Word, and their eyes were opened in the "breaking of the bread."

It is significant that Jesus was induced to have supper with the disciples at Emmaus, even though He seemed to intend to travel further, because they implored Him: "Stay with us" (Luke 24:29). The Eucharist is Christ's presence with His disciples until He comes again in His visible presence at the end of history. It is also significant that Jesus disappeared with His visible appearance right after they recognized Him in faith in the breaking of the bread. In the Eucharist Jesus stays with us, as the disciples implored, but to be seen only by the eyes of faith.[110]

The expression "breaking of the bread" is consistently used to refer to the Eucharist throughout the book of Acts. We first encounter it in Acts 2:42–46, right after Pentecost: "[The three thousand neophytes] held steadfastly to the apostles' teaching and fellowship, to the breaking of the bread and to the prayers. . . . And day by day, attending the temple together and breaking bread in their homes, they partook of food with glad and generous hearts." In this text, the breaking of bread must be understood as the Eucharist, rather than simply eating together,

---

[110] See Pitre, *Jesus and the Jewish Roots of the Eucharist*, 200–2.

because the community held to it "steadfastly," which would be an odd description of mere eating, and because it caused profound joy, like that experienced by the two disciples at Emmaus. This is not the natural joy of nourishing the body, but the joy of the Spirit through the Eucharist. Furthermore, the breaking of the bread is connected in Acts 2:42 with the preaching of the Apostles, prayer, and fellowship, all of which would have taken place in the context of the Eucharistic liturgy.[111]

We see from this text that the first Christians continued to attend the Jewish liturgy in the Temple while celebrating the Eucharist "in their homes."[112] Because of persecution (first by the synagogue and then by the empire) and because it was restricted to the baptized faithful, the Eucharist was first celebrated in the secrecy of house churches.

The prototype of these house churches was the upper room in which Jesus celebrated the Last Supper and where the Apostles continued to gather, as on Pentecost. Another house church in Jerusalem was the house of Mary, the mother of John Mark, where Peter went after his miraculous liberation from Herod's prison in Acts 12:12. There he found many who "were gathered together and were praying."

We encounter the "breaking of bread" again in Acts 20:7–8, in which St. Paul is celebrating the Eucharist with the faithful in Troas: "On the first day of the week, when we were gathered together to break bread, Paul talked with them, intending to depart on the morrow; and he prolonged his speech until midnight. There were many lights in the upper chamber where we were gathered." The first day of the week refers to Sunday, the first day of the Jewish week. This is our first indication of Sunday as the day of special solemnity in the celebration of the Eucharist. We also see that the Eucharist was celebrated by preference in an upper room (considered more suitable for liturgy and prayer) and illuminated by many lights.

Another indirect reference to Eucharistic celebrations on Sunday is in 1 Corinthians 16:1–2, in which St. Paul is speaking about a collection for the poor Christians in Jerusalem. He tells the Corinthians: "Now concerning the contribution for the saints: as I directed the churches of Galatia, so you also are to do. On the first day of every week, each of you is to put something aside and store it up, as he

---

[111] See Ibáñez, *L'Eucaristia, Dono e Mistero*, 98.

[112] See John D. Zizioulas, *Eucharist, Bishop, Church: The Unity of the Church in the Divine Eucharist and the Bishop During the First Three Centuries*, trans. Elizabeth Theokritoff (Brookline, MA: Holy Cross Orthodox Press, 2001), 51.

may prosper, so that contributions need not be made when I come." It seems the first day of the week was the day of Eucharistic gatherings in which an offering for the poor could be made.

Hebrews

An indirect reference to the Eucharistic liturgy is found in Hebrews 12:18–28, which compares the theophany of Mount Sinai, in which the Old Covenant was sealed, with the encounter with God characteristic of the New Covenant:

> For you have not come to what may be touched, a blazing fire, and darkness, and gloom, and a tempest, and the sound of a trumpet, and a voice whose words made the hearers entreat that no further messages be spoken to them. For they could not endure the order that was given, "If even a beast touches the mountain, it shall be stoned." Indeed, so terrifying was the sight that Moses said, "I tremble with fear." But you have come to Mount Zion and to the city of the living God, the heavenly Jerusalem, and to innumerable angels in festal gathering, and to the assembly of the first-born who are enrolled in heaven, and to a judge who is God of all, and to the spirits of just men made perfect, and to Jesus, the mediator of a new covenant, and to the sprinkled blood that speaks more graciously than the blood of Abel. . . . Therefore let us be grateful for receiving a kingdom that cannot be shaken, and thus let us offer to God acceptable worship, with reverence and awe.

The theophany of the New Covenant is very different from the terrifying spectacle of Sinai. The Eucharist is associated with another mountain, Zion, which is in Jerusalem, the city of peace, and is the place of the upper room of the Last Supper. Everywhere the Eucharist is celebrated, the heavenly Jerusalem is made present, in which the faithful worship God in a festal gathering together with innumerable angels and with the saints in heaven. In this "acceptable worship, with reverence and awe," Jesus is made present through His sacramentally "sprinkled blood that speaks more graciously than the blood of Abel." This "acceptable worship" should be understood as referring to the Eucharist.

The Letter to the Hebrews also contains various allusions to Jesus's words of consecration of the chalice. Hebrews 10:29 and 13:20 use the expression "blood of the covenant," which was used by Matthew 26:28 and Mark 14:24. Another echo of words of institution is in Hebrews 9:28: "So Christ, having been offered once to bear the sins of many."[113] This recalls Matthew 26:28: "poured out for many for the forgiveness of sins."

Hebrews 13:7–21 also seems to make reference to the Eucharistic sacrifice.[114] After 13:10 speaks of an altar proper to the New Covenant, of which the Levitical priesthood of the Old Testament has no right to partake, Hebrews 13:15 says: "Through him [Jesus] then let us continually offer up a sacrifice of praise to God, that is, the fruit of lips that acknowledge his name." The expression "sacrifice of praise" corresponds to a category of Old Testament sacrifice called *zebach tôdâ*, sacrifice of thanksgiving or praise,[115] which is also the meaning of the word "Eucharist." As mentioned above, there is a rabbinic saying that this category of sacrifice would be the only one that would continue in the messianic age.[116] Hebrews 13:15 connects this Old Testament type of sacrifice with the worship of the New Covenant. It is interesting that this expression also appears in the Roman Canon: "For them we offer you this *sacrifice of praise* or they offer it for themselves."[117]

Revelation

The book of Revelation is also full of liturgical and Eucharistic references.[118] Revelation 4–5 describes a heavenly liturgy. If we are attentive,

---

[113] See also Heb 10:10 and 9:20, both of which seem to show familiarity with the institution account as it would have been experienced in the liturgy.

[114] See James Swetnam, S.J., *Hebrews: An Interpretation* (Rome: Gregorian and Biblical Press, 2016); Swetnam, "A Liturgical Approach to Hebrews 13," *Letter & Spirit* 2 (2006): 159–73.

[115] See Lev 7:12–15.

[116] *Midrash Rabbah Leviticus* 9.7, in H. Freedman, ed., *Midrash Rabbah*, 4:114: "In the Time to Come all sacrifices will be annulled, but that of thanksgiving will not be annulled."

[117] *RM*, 636.

[118] See Scott Hahn, *The Lamb's Supper: The Mass as Heaven on Earth* (New York: Doubleday, 1999), in which he shows that many aspects of the book of Revelation can best be understood with reference to the Mass. See also John Paul II, *EE*, §19; Peter Williamson, *Revelation* (Grand Rapids, MI: Baker Academic, 2015); Michael Barber, *Coming Soon: Unlocking the Book of Revelation and Applying Its Lessons Today* (Steubenville, OH: Emmaus Road, 2005), 23–32.

we can discern various elements from the Mass. Revelation 4 begins by saying:

> After this I looked, and lo, in heaven an open door! And the first voice, which I had heard speaking to me like a trumpet, said, "*Come up hither*, and I will show you what must take place after this." At once I was in the Spirit, and lo, a throne stood in heaven, with one seated on the throne! (Rev 4:1–2)[119]

The Eucharist is a door open to men of every place and time so that we can join with the angels in the heavenly liturgy. The invitation to "come up hither" is also reminiscent of the invitatory dialogue at the beginning of every Eucharistic Prayer: *Sursum corda*—"Lift up your hearts"—so as to join in the celebration of the sacrifice of the Lamb with the angels in heaven before the throne of God.

The Second Vatican Council, in §8 of its Constitution on the Sacred Liturgy, *Sacrosanctum Concilium*, speaks about the Mass in these same terms, as a foretaste of heavenly worship:

> In the earthly liturgy we take part in a foretaste of that heavenly liturgy which is celebrated in the holy city of Jerusalem toward which we journey as pilgrims, where Christ is sitting at the right hand of God, a minister of the holies and of the true tabernacle; we sing a hymn to the Lord's glory with all the warriors of the heavenly army; venerating the memory of the saints, we hope for some part and fellowship with them; we eagerly await the Savior, Our Lord Jesus Christ, until He, our life, shall appear and we too will appear with Him in glory.

Revelation 4 describes the elders around the throne of God and the four creatures symbolizing the four evangelists who are singing the Sanctus. This seems to correspond to the Eucharistic liturgy up to the consecration:

> And round the throne, on each side of the throne, are four living creatures, full of eyes in front and behind: the first living creature like a lion, the second living creature like an ox, the

---

[119] My italics.

third living creature with the face of a man, and the fourth living creature like a flying eagle. And the four living creatures, each of them with six wings, are full of eyes all round and within, and day and night they never cease to sing, "Holy, holy, holy, is the Lord God Almighty, who was and is and is to come!"

And whenever the living creatures give glory and honor and thanks to him who is seated on the throne, who lives for ever and ever, the twenty-four elders fall down before him who is seated on the throne and worship him who lives for ever and ever; they cast their crowns before the throne, singing,

"Worthy are you, our Lord and God,
to receive glory and honor and power,
for you created all things,
and by your will they existed and were created."
(Rev 4:6–11)

The acclamation "Worthy . . ." is similar to the beginning of several early Eucharistic Prayers, such as that of St. Mark[120] or St. James[121] or the Chaldean Anaphora of Addai and Mari, in which God is praised and thanked for His work of creation: "Worthy of glory from every mouth and thanksgiving from every tongue is the adorable and glorious name of the Father and of the Son and of the Holy Spirit. He created the world through his grace and its inhabitants in his compassion."[122]

Up to this point we have not yet encountered the protagonist of the earthly and heavenly liturgy, who is the Lamb who was slain. He is introduced in Revelation 5:6–14:

And between the throne and the four living creatures and among the elders, I saw a Lamb standing, as though it had

---

[120] Liturgy of St. Mark (the liturgy of Alexandria): "It is truly fitting and right, holy and suitable, and profitable to our souls, Master, Lord, God, Father Almighty, to praise you, . . . you who have made heaven and what is in heaven, the earth and what is on earth" (*PEER*, 59).

[121] Liturgy of St. James (the liturgy of Jerusalem): "It is truly fitting and right, suitable and profitable, to praise you . . . [and] to give thanks to you, the creator of all creation, visible and invisible" (*PEER*, 90).

[122] Anaphora of Addai and Mari (*PEER*, 42).

been slain, with seven horns and with seven eyes, which are the seven spirits of God sent out into all the earth; and he went and took the scroll from the right hand of him who was seated on the throne. And when he had taken the scroll, the four living creatures and the twenty-four elders fell down before the Lamb, each holding a harp, and with golden bowls full of incense, which are the prayers of the saints; and they sang a new song, saying,

> "Worthy are you to take the scroll and to open its seals,
>   for you were slain and by your blood you ransomed men
>   for God
>   from every tribe and tongue and people and nation,
>   and have made them a kingdom and priests to our God,
>   and they shall reign on earth." (Rev 5:6–10)

As does Hebrews 12, this text shows that Christian worship unites the faithful with the heavenly worship given by the angels and saints. The center of the liturgy is the Lamb who was slain, ransomed the faithful for God from "every tribe and tongue and people and nation," and made them a kingdom of "priests to our God." The Catholic faithful, assembled in worship, exercise their royal priesthood by offering "the Lamb who was slain."

There follows a final doxology ending with a solemn Amen:

> Then I looked, and I heard around the throne and the living creatures and the elders the voice of many angels, numbering myriads of myriads and thousands of thousands, saying with a loud voice, "Worthy is the Lamb who was slain, to receive power and wealth and wisdom and might and honor and glory and blessing!" And I heard every creature in heaven and on earth and under the earth and in the sea, and all therein, saying, "To him who sits upon the throne and to the Lamb be blessing and honor and glory and might for ever and ever!" And the four living creatures said, "Amen!" and the elders fell down and worshiped. (Rev 5:11–14)

Another magnificent liturgical image is in Revelation 19:1–9:

After this I heard what seemed to be the loud voice of a great
multitude in heaven, crying,

"Hallelujah! Salvation and glory and power belong to our
God,"

. . . And the twenty-four elders and the four living creatures
fell down and worshiped God who is seated on the throne,
saying, "Amen. Hallelujah!" And from the throne came a voice
crying,

"Praise our God, all you his servants,
you who fear him, small and great."

Then I heard what seemed to be the voice of a great multitude,
like the sound of many waters and like the sound of mighty
thunderpeals, crying,

"Hallelujah! For the Lord our God the Almighty reigns.
Let us rejoice and exult and give him the glory,
for the marriage of the Lamb has come,
and his Bride has made herself ready;
it was granted her to be clothed with fine linen, bright
and pure"—
for the fine linen is the righteous deeds of the saints.

And the angel said to me, "Write this: Blessed are those
who are invited to the marriage supper of the Lamb."

What is the marriage supper of the Lamb? In addition to the feast of
heaven, it also refers to the foretaste of heavenly communion realized
in the Holy Mass. At every Mass, each of the faithful individually is
the Bride who makes herself ready to encounter the Lamb sacramentally sacrificed on the altar and given to each one who is clothed in
grace in the nuptial embrace of Holy Communion.

STUDY QUESTIONS

1. Why did Jesus choose to give the Bread of Life Discourse the day
   after the miracle of the multiplication of loaves? How does Jesus
   clarify the people's messianic expectation of a renewal of the miracles of the Exodus?

2. What themes does Jesus present in the Bread of Life Discourse?
   What is their connection and how do they relate to the Eucharist?

3. Why can Jesus's words in John 6 about eating His flesh and drinking His blood not be taken in a merely symbolic sense?
4. Why was it fitting for Christ to choose the Last Supper as the time to institute the Eucharist?
5. What are the reasons for thinking that the Last Supper was a Passover meal? Why is this important for understanding the Eucharist?
6. What are two ways of reconciling the accounts of the synoptic gospels with that of John with regard to the date of the Passover?
7. How does the fact that the institution of the Eucharist is given by four accounts that differ in details corroborate the historicity of the institution narrative?
8. How do the words of institution at the Last Supper express the sacrificial nature of the Mass?
9. Besides John 6 and the accounts of the Last Supper, what are other important references to the Eucharist in the New Testament?

Suggestions for Further Reading

Hahn, Scott. *The Lamb's Supper: The Mass as Heaven on Earth*. New York: Doubleday, 1999.

Healy, Mary. *The Gospel of Mark*. Grand Rapids, MI: Baker Academic, 2008. Pp. 281–87.

Jeremias, Joachim. *The Eucharistic Words of Jesus*. Translated by Norman Perrin from the 3rd German edition. Philadelphia, PA: Fortress Press, 1977.

Jungmann, Josef, S.J. *The Mass: An Historical, Theological, and Pastoral Survey*. Translated by Julian Fernandes. Edited by Mary E. Evans. Collegeville, MN: Liturgical Press, 1976. Pp. 5–19.

Martin, Francis, and William M. Wright IV. *The Gospel of John*. Grand Rapids, MI: Baker Academic, 2015. Pp. 120–34.

Pitre, Brant. *Jesus and the Last Supper*. Grand Rapids, MI: Eerdmans, 2015. Pp. 193–373.

Ratzinger, Joseph. "Is the Eucharist a Sacrifice?" In *TL*. Pp. 210–217.

Schönborn, Christoph Cardinal. *The Source of Life*. Translated by Brian McNeil. Edited by Humbert Philipp Weber. New York: Crossroad, 2007. Pp. 1–63.

✢

CHAPTER FOUR

The Eucharist according to the Fathers of the Church

The Fathers of the Church give a united testimony regarding the Eucharist, although expressed in differing ways. They emphasize above all the reality of Christ's Body and Blood, that it is the sacrifice of Christ, and that it is a sacrament that brings about interior unity in the Mystical Body of Christ and thus must be celebrated in union with the bishop. The substantial conversion of the bread and the wine into the Body and Blood of Christ was strongly affirmed hundreds of years before the term "transubstantiation" was developed. We shall look briefly at these early sources in which this doctrine unfolds and develops as the Church reflects on that deposit of faith, making it clearer and generating a more perfect terminology.

THE *DIDACHE*

Perhaps the earliest description of the celebration of the Eucharist outside the New Testament is from *Didache* 14, which is dated either to the second half of the first century or to the first half of the second century.[1]

On the Lord's own day gather together and break bread and give thanks, having first confessed your sins so that your sac-

---

[1] Jean-Paul Audet dates the *Didache* to roughly AD 50–80 (*La Didachè: Instruction des Apôtres* [Paris: J. Lecoffre, 1958], 187–210). See also Kurt Niederwimmer, *The Didache: A Commentary*, trans. Linda Maloney, ed. Harold W. Attridge (Minneapolis, MN: Fortress Press, 1998), 53, where it is dated to AD 110 or 120.

rifice may be pure. But let no one who has a quarrel with a companion join you until they have been reconciled, so that your sacrifice may not be defiled.[2] For this is the sacrifice concerning which the Lord said, "In every place and time offer me a pure sacrifice, for I am a great king, says the Lord, and my name is marvelous among the nations."[3]

Although brief, the text is important, first of all, for associating the solemn celebration of the Eucharist with the "Lord's Day," meaning Sunday, also referred to as the "first day of the week" by St. Justin (see below). Second, the text repeatedly refers to the Eucharist as a sacrifice.[4] Third, the text connects the ability to offer a clean sacrifice with interior purity, which requires reconciliation with one's neighbors and confession of sins. In support of the sacrificial aspect of the Eucharist and its connection with interior purity, the *Didache* quotes the prophecy of Malachi 1:11, which will be quoted extensively by the Fathers with regard to the Eucharistic sacrifice. Malachi 1:10–14 says:

> I have no pleasure in you, says the Lord of hosts, and I will not accept an offering from your hand. For from the rising of the sun to its setting my name is great among the nations, and in every place incense is offered to my name, and a pure offering; for my name is great among the nations, says the Lord of hosts. . . . For I am a great King, says the Lord of hosts, and my name is feared among the nations.

Prayers for what is called the "Eucharist" are given in *Didache* 9–10, but the text seems to refer to an agape meal of Christian fraternity[5] that

---

2   See Matt 5:23–24.

3   *Didache* 14, in Holmes, trans., *The Apostolic Fathers: Greek Texts and English Translations*, 365–67.

4   See Joseph A. Jungmann, *The Eucharistic Prayer: A Study of the Canon Missae*, trans. Robert Batley (Notre Dame, IN: Fides, 1963), 14: "Even in the *Didache* the Mass was called θυσια; even then this almost solid, ancient word is used for sacrifice. And the same work sees the prophecy of Malachi concerning the pure sacrifice fulfilled in the Eucharist."

5   A blessing over the wine (not Eucharistic consecration) is given first, as was the Jewish custom, and as we see in the Last Supper in Luke 22:17. The term "Eucharist," meaning thanksgiving, is perhaps not yet being used as a technical term for the Mass. Interpreters are divided over whether *Didache* 9–10 should be regarded as a primitive Eucharistic liturgy or an agape meal. See Nieder-

is either joined to a Eucharistic celebration, as we see was the case in the Corinthian community when St. Paul reproved them in 1 Corinthians 11 for their lack of fraternal charity in their agape, or distinct from it.[6] It seems that *Didache* 9 gives the prayers for the blessing over the food in the agape. It is possible that there is a transition in *Didache* 10 to properly Eucharistic Prayers,[7] although there is no institution narrative, epiclesis, or mention of sacrifice (as there is repeatedly in *Didache* 14), which strongly suggests that this is an agape distinct from the Eucharist in which the faithful perhaps received the presanctified Eucharist[8] or

---

wimmer, *The Didache: A Commentary*, 140–142, for a brief survey of positions, and 143:

> If we allow the text to stand as it has been handed down we have scarcely any other choice but to suppose that 10.6 is the invitation to the Lord's Supper which follows immediately thereafter. In that case, however, the meal envisioned in *Did.* 10.1 cannot be a Eucharist in the sacramental sense, but only a community meal. . . . In that case the difficulty otherwise produced by the "reversed" sequence of wine and bread in 9.2–4 disappears. If we are to suppose that the sacramental meal follows after *Did.* 10.6 it seems plausible (with Rordorf) to understand the prayer of thanksgiving in 10.2–6 as also a kind of "preface" preceding the sacrament to follow.

[6] See Joseph A. Jungmann, *The Mass of the Roman Rite: Its Origins and Development*, trans. Francis Brunner (New York: Benziger Brothers, 1951), 1:12–13: "We have table prayers in the setting of a Christian meal: Blessing of wine and bread, and grace at the end. That the meal included the sacramental Eucharist is hardly likely. The call at the end of the final grace may perhaps relate to the Eucharist. But again it is not clear how it is connected here. At a much later time, after the close of the second century, we learn more about the agapes which the Christian community conducted. . . . But these agapes are absolutely separate from the Eucharist."

[7] See Klaus Gamber, "Die 'Eucharistia' der Didache," *Ephemerides Liturgicae* 101 (1987): 3–32. See also Louis Bouyer, *Eucharist: Theology and Spirituality of the Eucharistic Prayer*, trans. Charles Underhill Quinn (Notre Dame, IN: University of Notre Dame Press, 1968), 117: "In their final state, they obviously apply to a sacred meal of a Christian community that is still very close to Judaism, and it could only be its eucharist."

[8] For the hypothesis that these prayers concern presanctified hosts consecrated at the Sunday Mass, see Ansgar Santogrossi, "Anaphoras without Institution Narrative: Historical and Dogmatic Considerations," *Nova et Vetera* (English) 10, no. 1 (2012): 49–50:

> It is natural to take *Didache* 9 as referring to the weekday communion of the reserved consecrated bread at the communal meal, taken with a formula of thanksgiving and preceded by thanksgiving for a fresh cup which recalled the cup (naturally not conserved) of Sunday. Thus

simply blessed bread.[9] In the prayers of thanksgiving, which are clearly related to Jewish thanksgiving after meals,[10] God is praised because He has given food and drink for all men to enjoy, but much more because "to us you have graciously given spiritual food and drink, and eternal life through your servant."[11]

These prayers of thanksgiving contain a beautiful prayer that asks that the Church may be gathered from the four winds and made perfect in love.[12] The prayer concludes with the plea that the Lord return and "the world pass away,"[13] followed by what seems to be an invitation to Communion for those who are rightly disposed: "If anyone is holy, let him come; if anyone is not, let him repent."[14]

---

the *Didache* churches celebrated what is essential to the later liturgies of the "pre-sanctified": a liturgy which by certain actions and words closely resembled the liturgy properly so called of Sunday, but which comprised communion of previously consecrated bread and non-consecrated wine. Thus *Didache* 9–10 witnesses to the mysterious presence of Christ's true body in the Eucharist, while not undermining the necessity of the words of the Lord for a valid consecration.

See also Jungmann, *The Mass of the Roman Rite*, 1:12–13, 13n28, which cites Theodore Schermann, *Die allgemeine Kirchenordnung, frühchristliche Liturgien und kirchliche Überlieferung* (Paderborn: Schöningh, 1915), 2:282ff.

[9] In Burton Scott Easton, trans., *The Apostolic Tradition of Hippolytus* 26.32 (Ann Arbor, MI: Archon Books, 1962), 59, prayers are given for an agape evening meal, distinct from the Eucharistic sacrifice, in which the faithful receive bread blessed by the bishop: "Then, when the Psalm is completed, he [the bishop] shall give thanks over the bread, and shall give the fragments to all the believers."

[10] See Bouyer, *Eucharist*, 115–19, esp. 117: "The whole is in continuity, and follows the traditional succession of the [Jewish] meal *berakoth* (blessing over the initial cup, blessing over the broken bread, threefold blessing over the last cup)."

[11] *Didache* 10.3 (Holmes, *The Apostolic Fathers*, 359). The reference to Jesus as "servant" (as in the "Suffering Servant" canticles in Isaiah) is a sign of the primitive Jewish-Christian nature of this text. See Niederwimmer, *The Didache: A Commentary*, 147. See also Matthieu Smyth, "The Anaphora of the So-Called 'Apostolic Tradition' and the Roman Eucharistic Prayer," in *Issues in Eucharistic Praying in East and West: Essays in Liturgical and Theological Analysis*, ed. Maxwell Johnson (Collegeville, MN: Liturgical Press, 2010), 79, who speaks of this as "a title already outdated by the time of the redaction of the New Testament, where it is only witnessed in the early records of Acts 3:13–26 and 4:27–30."

[12] *Didache* 10.5 (Holmes, *The Apostolic Fathers*, 361).

[13] See Bouyer, *Eucharist*, 118–19: "*Maran atha*, the expression of the expectation of the parousia, which St. Paul has preserved for us, confirms what he himself has allowed us to see of the eschatological orientation of these first Christian eucharists, where they 'proclaimed' the death of the Lord, 'until he comes.'"

[14] *Didache* 10.6 (Holmes, *The Apostolic Fathers*, 361).

St. Ignatius of Antioch

The Eucharistic faith of the age of the Apostolic Fathers is given in an extraordinarily clear way by St. Ignatius of Antioch in his seven letters written on his way to be fed to the wild beasts in the Coliseum around the year AD 107.

The Real Presence

In his letters, St. Ignatius was combatting the Docetist heresy, which denies the true humanity of Jesus, holding that He was a man only in appearance and not in reality. In order to refute this error, Ignatius brings in the doctrine of the real presence of Christ in the Eucharist as evidence against it. For if Christ did not have a true humanity, then the realism of the Eucharistic conversion would make no sense. If Christ were not true man, then the consecrated host could not be His true human body. St. Ignatius is relying for proof of Christ's humanity on what he puts forth as a very solid and popular belief in the real presence of Christ in the Eucharist. Since we truly receive Christ's flesh in the Eucharist, Christ is true man and not a mere apparition of the divinity. The Docetists were thus the first heretics to deny the real presence of Christ's humanity in the Eucharist. St. Ignatius speaks against this Eucharistic consequence of Docetism in the *Letter to the Smyrnaeans*:

> They abstain from Eucharist and prayer because they refuse to acknowledge that the Eucharist is the flesh of our savior Jesus Christ, which suffered for our sins and which the Father by his goodness raised up.[15]

This is a very strong witness. The Docetists are condemned by Ignatius for refusing to believe that the Eucharist *is the very "flesh of our Savior Jesus Christ,"* that same flesh that suffered and died on Calvary and was raised from the dead on Easter and that same blood that was poured out for our sins.

In *Letter to the Romans* 7, Ignatius speaks still more passionately of the realism of the presence of Christ's Body and Blood under the species of bread and wine:

---

[15] Ignatius of Antioch, *Letter to the Smyrnaeans* 6 (Holmes, *The Apostolic Fathers*, 255).

My passionate love has been crucified. . . . I take no pleasure in corruptible food or the pleasures of this life. I want the bread of God, which is the flesh of Christ who is of the seed of David; and for drink I want his blood, which is incorruptible love.[16]

Drawing on John 6 and alluding to the tree of life in the Garden of Eden, St. Ignatius refers to the Eucharist as the "medicine of immortality" in his *Letter to the Ephesians*:

At these meetings you should heed the bishop and presbytery attentively, and break one loaf, which is the medicine of immortality, and the antidote which wards off death but yields continuous life in union with Jesus Christ.[17]

The Eucharist is the antidote to death precisely because it gives "continuous life," that is, eternal life, by feeding us with "union with Jesus Christ."

Sacrament of Ecclesial Unity

Another aspect of Ignatius's Eucharistic teaching is his emphasis on the ecclesial dimension of the Eucharist. The Eucharist unites us with Christ's physical Body and Blood in order to unite us more closely with His Mystical Body, the Church. Every Eucharistic celebration pertains to the entire Church and is part of her public worship. The liturgy, and the Eucharist in particular, is therefore the act of worship of the *whole Christ*: Head and members *hierarchically ordered*. The liturgy is a prolongation or continuation of the priestly worship of Christ.

Because the Eucharist is the sacrament of Christian unity, St. Ignatius stresses the role of the bishop in the Eucharistic celebration. In the *Letter to the Philadelphians* 4, his reference to the Eucharist emphasizes the obligation of celebrating it in union with the bishop. The Eucharist is presented as the source of Christian unity by giving the faithful communion with the one Flesh and Blood of Christ. This

---

[16] Ignatius, *Letter to the Romans* 7 (Holmes, *The Apostolic Fathers*, 233).
[17] Ignatius, *Letter to the Ephesians* 20 (Holmes, *The Apostolic Fathers*, 199).

unity must be liturgically represented and preserved through communion with the bishop:

> Take care, therefore, to participate in one Eucharist (for there is one flesh of our Lord Jesus Christ, and one cup that leads to unity through his blood; there is one altar, just as there is one bishop, together with the council of presbyters and the deacons, my fellow servants), in order that whatever you do, you do in accordance with God.[18]

The connection between the Eucharist and the bishop is stressed again in the *Letter to the Smyrnaeans* 8:

> Only that Eucharist which is under the authority of the bishop (or whomever he himself designates) is to be considered valid. Wherever the bishop appears, there let the congregation be; just as wherever Jesus Christ is, there is the catholic church.[19]

In his *Letter to the Ephesians* 5, Ignatius writes: "Let no one be misled: if anyone is not within the sanctuary, he lacks the bread of God. For if the prayer of one or two has such power, how much more that of the bishop together with the whole church!"[20]

St. Justin Martyr

Description of the Liturgy of the Eucharist

A brief account of the liturgy of the Eucharist is offered by St. Justin in his work, *First Apology*, written about AD 150. After describing the rite of Baptism, Justin states that the neophytes are brought to the Eucharistic celebration, in which prayers are made for them and for all men everywhere, and after the prayers, "we greet one another with

---

[18] Ignatius, *Letter to the Philadelphians* 4 (Holmes, *The Apostolic Fathers*, 239).

[19] Ignatius, *Letter to the Smyrnaeans* 8 (Holmes, *The Apostolic Fathers*, 255). This is perhaps the first use that has come down to us of the expression "Catholic Church." Catholic means universal. Here it signifies the one Church that is present throughout the world.

[20] Ignatius, *Letter to the Ephesians* 5 (Holmes, *The Apostolic Fathers*, 187).

a kiss."[21] Justin then describes the parts of the Mass that follow, which are the Offertory, the Eucharistic Prayer, and the distribution of Communion through the deacons:

> Then there is brought to the Ruler[22] of the Brethren bread and a cup of water and of wine mixed with water,[23] and he taking them sends up praise and glory to the Father of the Universe through the name of the Son and of the Holy Spirit, and offers thanksgiving at some length for our being accounted worthy to receive these things from Him. When he has concluded the prayers and the thanksgiving, all the people present assent by saying, Amen. Amen in the Hebrew language signifies "so be it." And when the Ruler has given thanks and all the people have assented, those who are called by us deacons give to each of those present a portion of the eucharistized bread and wine and water, and they carry it away to those who are absent.[24]

Justin concludes his account of Christian worship with a fuller description of the liturgy of the Mass celebrated every Sunday with all the faithful:

> And on the day called Sunday all who live in cities or in the country gather together in one place, and the memoirs of the Apostles or the writings of the prophets are read, as long as time permits. Then when the reader has finished, the Ruler in a discourse instructs and exhorts to the imitation of these good things. Then we all stand up together and offer prayers; and, as we said before, when we have finished the prayer, bread is brought and wine and water, and the Ruler likewise offers

[21] Justin Martyr, *First Apology* 65, in *St. Justin Martyr: The First and Second Apologies*, trans. Leslie William Barnard (New York: Paulist Press, 1997), 70.

[22] See Barnard, *St. Justin Martyr*, 18 and 178n398, for discussion of the translation of this term, which is often translated as "he who presides" or "president." Justin is most probably referring to the bishop and using a generic title rather than the technical term, *episkopos*.

[23] This rather puzzling expression is translated more simply as "a cup of wine mixed with water" by Denis Minns and Paul Parvis, in *Justin, Philosopher and Martyr: Apologies* (Oxford: Oxford University Press, 2009), 253.

[24] Justin Martyr, *First Apology* 65 (Barnard, *St. Justin Martyr*, 70).

up prayers and thanksgivings to the best of his ability,[25] and the people assent, saying the Amen; and the distribution and the partaking of the eucharistized elements is to each, and to those who are absent a portion is sent by the deacons. And those who prosper, and so wish, contribute what each thinks fit; and what is collected is deposited with the Ruler, who takes care of the orphans and widows, and those who, on account of sickness or any other cause, are in want, and those who are in bonds, and the strangers who are sojourners among us, and in a word [he] is the guardian of all those in need. But we all hold this common gathering on Sunday, since it is the first day, on which God transforming darkness and matter made the Universe, and Jesus Christ our Savior on the same day rose from the dead. For they crucified Him on the day before Saturday, and on the day after Saturday, He appeared to His Apostles.[26]

The Real Presence

Justin mentions that three conditions are necessary for receiving Communion because of Christ's real presence in the Eucharist:

And this food is called among us the *Eucharist*, of which no one is allowed to partake except one who believes that the things

---

[25] This expression can be interpreted in two different ways. According to the more common and probable interpretation, it would indicate that the Eucharistic Prayer was not yet fixed and that the celebrant had a certain liberty to elaborate, presumably within a fixed structure. Another possibility, however, is that this text means that the celebrant prayed according to his ability to "put his heart and soul into it." See James T. O'Connor, *The Hidden Manna: A Theology of the Eucharist* (San Francisco: Ignatius Press, 1988), 20; Eques de Otto, *Iustini philosophi et martyris Opera quae feruntur omnia* (Wiesbaden, DE: Sändig, 1969), 1:187.

[26] Justin Martyr, *First Apology* 67 (Barnard, *St. Justin Martyr*, 71). It is interesting to note that St. Justin connects the celebration of Sunday as the Lord's Day not only with the Resurrection, but also with the creation. There is a beautiful typology here. The Jewish Law sanctified the seventh day of the week, on which day God rested. The Christian dispensation celebrates the eighth day, which is also the first day of the week, to symbolize that the Passion and Resurrection of Christ effect a "new creation," opening the way to the supernatural order. The change of holy day from the seventh to the eighth day also shows symbolically that Judaism was instituted to prepare for the Christian dispensation, and thus its sabbaths give way to the Lord's Day.

which we teach are true, and has received the washing that is for the remission of sins and for rebirth, and who so lives as Christ has handed down. For we do not receive these things as common bread nor common drink; but in like manner as Jesus Christ our Savior having been incarnate by God's logos took both flesh and blood for our salvation, so also we have been taught that the food eucharistized through the word of prayer that is from Him, from which our blood and flesh are nourished by transformation, is the flesh and blood of that Jesus who became incarnate. For the Apostles in the memoirs composed by them, which are called Gospels, thus handed down what was commanded them: that Jesus took bread and having given thanks, said: "Do this for my memorial, this is my body"; and likewise He took the chalice and having given thanks said: "This is my blood;" and gave it to them alone. Which also the wicked demons have imitated in the mysteries of Mithra, and handed down to be done.[27]

The realism with which St. Justin speaks of the Eucharistic conversion is absolutely clear. Just as Jesus Christ took on true flesh and blood for our salvation, so the Eucharist contains "the flesh and blood of that Jesus who became incarnate." St. Justin establishes an interesting threefold parallelism here. First he refers to the flesh and blood assumed by Christ in the Incarnation; then he refers to our flesh and blood that will be nourished by the Eucharist; and finally he refers to the Flesh and Blood of Christ present in the Eucharist, through which our flesh will be nourished. Christ took on flesh and blood so that our flesh and blood may be spiritually nourished with His through the Eucharist.

Substantial Conversion

There is also a parallelism in the same sentence between the Word of God that took on flesh and blood and the "prayer of His word" by which the food (i.e., the bread and the wine) is converted into the Flesh and Blood of Christ. St. Justin's point is that the same divine power that realized the Incarnation is at work in the "prayer of His word" uttered in the words of consecration, which should be identified with the words of the institution narrative that Justin goes on to

---

[27] Justin Martyr, *First Apology* 66 (Barnard, *St. Justin Martyr*, 70–71).

cite.[28] That is, the conversion of bread and wine into Christ's Flesh and Blood is a work of divine power effected by the words of Christ (later to be called transubstantiation), just as the Incarnation was a work of divine power effected by the divine Word.[29]

The Mass Is a Sacrifice

In his *Dialogue with Trypho*, St. Justin defends the sacrificial nature of the Eucharist by affirming, like the *Didache*,[30] that the Eucharist is the fulfillment of the prophecy of Malachi 1:11:

> "For from the rising of the sun even to the going down, My name is great among the Gentiles, and in every place incense is offered to My name, and a clean oblation; for My name is great among the Gentiles, saith the Lord, but you profane it." By making reference to the sacrifices which we Gentiles offer to Him everywhere, the Eucharistic Bread and the Eucharistic Chalice, He predicted that we should glorify His name.[31]

Later in the same work, Justin returns to the theme of the Eucharist as the Church's pure sacrifice that commemorates the Passion:

> Now, I also admit that prayers and thanksgivings, offered by worthy persons, are the only perfect and acceptable sacrifices to God. For Christians were instructed to offer only such prayers, even at their thanksgiving for their food, both liquid and solid, whereby the Passion which the Son of God endured for us is commemorated.[32]

---

[28] See Kereszty, *Wedding Feast of the Lamb*, 96.

[29] Although the Incarnation is the work of the Blessed Trinity, we normally appropriate it to the Holy Spirit, since it maximally reveals the divine love. St. Justin here appropriates the Incarnation to the Logos. His purpose seems to be to create a parallelism between the consecration of the Eucharistic species through the words of Jesus and the Incarnation of the Word through the divine power of the Word.

[30] *Didache* 14.3 (Holmes, *The Apostolic Fathers*, 365).

[31] Justin Martyr, *Dialogue with Trypho* 41, trans. Thomas Falls, in *The First Apology, The Second Apology, Dialogue with Trypho, Exhortation to the Greeks, Discourse to the Greeks, The Monarchy or The Rule of God*, FC 6 (Washington, DC: Catholic University of America Press, 1948), 210.

[32] Ibid., 117.3 (Falls, 328).

In the middle of the second century, therefore, the Eucharist was understood by St. Justin to be the offering of a true and pure sacrifice "in every place" through the offering of the "eucharistized" elements of the consecrated host and chalice, which make present "the flesh and blood of that Jesus who became incarnate"[33] and serve as a memorial of His Passion.

St. Irenaeus

St. Irenaeus, writing some seventy years after St. Ignatius and thirty years after St. Justin, develops the same themes with regard to the Eucharist. This should not be surprising, for St. Irenaeus was a disciple of St. Polycarp, who was a disciple of St. John the Apostle and an associate of and fellow bishop with St. Ignatius. In his great work, *Against Heresies*, written about AD 180, St. Irenaeus develops the theme of the Eucharist as the medicine of immortality. Like St. Ignatius and St. Justin, Irenaeus understands the Eucharistic conversion in a completely realist sense, and the doctrine of transubstantiation is implicit.

Real Presence and Eucharistic Conversion

The Gnostics whom St. Irenaeus is combating, like the Docetists mentioned by St. Ignatius, rejected the goodness of the body, for they saw matter as the source of all evil. Thus they also denied the resurrection of the body and the true humanity of Christ, which forced them to deny the true presence of that human nature in the Eucharist. St. Irenaeus combats all these errors through the doctrine of the real presence:

> But vain in every respect are they who despise the entire dispensation of God, and disallow the salvation of the flesh, and treat with contempt its regeneration, maintaining that it is not capable of immortality. If the body be not saved, then, in fact, neither did the Lord redeem us with His Blood; and neither is the cup of the Eucharist the partaking [communion] of His Blood nor is the Bread which we break the partaking of His Body. For blood can only come from veins and flesh, and

---

[33] Justin Martyr, *First Apology* 66 (Barnard, *St. Justin Martyr*, 71).

whatsoever else makes up the substance of man, such as the Word of God was actually made.[34]

Interestingly, like St. Ignatius, St. Irenaeus argues *from* the real presence of Christ in the Eucharist *to* the truth of His humanity. This argumentation shows that the faith of the early Christians in the true Body and Blood of Christ in the Eucharist was no less vigorous than their faith in the true humanity of Christ. The fact that Ignatius and Irenaeus could argue in this way also shows that for the ordinary Christian the faith of the Church is most palpable in the liturgy, for the principal contact of the faithful with the Church is through the liturgy. Thus there is the Patristic axiom that "the rule of prayer is the rule of faith."

As St. Irenaeus develops this argument against the Gnostics, he also briefly mentions what later came to be called "transubstantiation," the miraculous conversion of the bread and wine into the true Body and Blood of Christ through the omnipotent power of the words of consecration spoken by the priest *in the person of Christ*. St. Irenaeus writes: "When, therefore, the mingled cup and the manufactured bread receives the Word of God, . . . [it] becomes the Eucharist, the body and blood of Christ."[35] The "Word of God" here probably refers to the words of institution that form the center of the Eucharistic liturgy.[36]

Spiritual Nourishment

St. Irenaeus then speaks of how the Body and Blood of Christ in the Eucharist is our spiritual nourishment, which prepares us for the future gift of our participation in the glory of Christ's risen Body:

> How can they affirm that the flesh is incapable of receiving the gift of God, which is life eternal, which [flesh] is nourished from the body and blood of the Lord, and is a member of Him?—even as the blessed Paul declares in his Epistle to the Ephesians, that "we are members of His body, of His flesh, and of His bones." He does not speak these words of

---

[34] Irenaeus, *Against Heresies* 5.2.2 (*ANF*, 1:528).

[35] Ibid., 5.2.3 (*ANF*, 1:528).

[36] See O'Connor, *The Hidden Manna*, 25, who interprets these words as applying to the epiclesis.

some spiritual and invisible man, for a spirit has not bones nor flesh; but [he refers to] that dispensation [by which the Lord became] an actual man, consisting of flesh, and nerves, and bones,—that [flesh] which is nourished by the cup which is His blood, and receives increase from the bread which is His body. And just as a cutting from the vine planted in the ground fructifies in its season, or as a corn of wheat falling into the earth and becoming decomposed, rises with manifold increase by the Spirit of God, who contains all things, and then, through the wisdom of God, serves for the use of men, and having received the Word of God, becomes the Eucharist, which is the body and blood of Christ; so also our bodies, being nourished by it, and deposited in the earth, and suffering decomposition there, shall rise at their appointed time, the Word of God granting them resurrection to the glory of God, even the Father, who freely gives to this mortal immortality, and to this corruptible incorruption, because the strength of God is made perfect in weakness, in order that we may never become puffed up, as if we had life from ourselves.[37]

St. Irenaeus thus makes a parallelism between the Eucharist and our bodies. As the bread and wine are transformed by the Word of God in the consecration to become the Body and Blood of Christ, so the bodies of the faithful who have been nourished by the Eucharist will be transformed to share in the glory of the Body of Christ.[38]

This parallel is given also in *Against Heresies* 4.18.5:

Then, again, how can they say that the flesh, which is nourished with the body of the Lord and with His blood, goes to corruption, and does not partake of life? Let them, therefore, either alter their opinion, or cease from offering the things just mentioned. But our opinion is in accordance with the Eucharist, and the *Eucharist in turn establishes our opinion*. For we offer to Him His own, announcing consistently the fellowship and union of the flesh and Spirit. For as the bread, which is produced from the earth, *when it receives the invocation of*

---

[37] Irenaeus, *Against Heresies* 5.2.3 (*ANF*, 1:528).

[38] St. Irenaeus stresses the resurrection of the body because the Gnostics denied it, since they viewed the material world as the source of evil.

God, is no longer common bread, but the Eucharist, consisting of
two realities, earthly and heavenly; so also our bodies, when
they receive the Eucharist, are no longer corruptible, having
the hope of the resurrection to eternity.[39]

New Oblation of the New Covenant

Like the *Didache* and St. Justin, St. Irenaeus also affirms that the
correct interpretation of the prophecy of Malachi is that the Eucharist is the acceptable sacrifice among the Gentiles: "The oblation of
the Church, therefore, which the Lord gave instructions to be offered
throughout all the world, is accounted with God a pure sacrifice, and
is acceptable to Him."[40] Indeed, he speaks of the Eucharist as the "new
oblation of the New Covenant":

> He took that created thing, bread, and gave thanks, and said,
> "This is my Body." And the cup likewise, which is part of that
> creation to which we belong, He confessed to be His blood,
> and taught the *new oblation of the New Covenant*; which the
> Church receiving from the Apostles, offers to God through-
> out all the world . . . concerning which Malachi, among the
> twelve prophets, thus spoke beforehand: ". . . From the rising
> of the sun, unto the going down, My name is glorified among
> the Gentiles, and in every place incense is offered to My name,
> and a pure sacrifice . . ."—indicating in the plainest manner,
> by these words, that the former people shall indeed cease to
> make offerings to God, but that in every place sacrifice shall
> be offered to Him, and that a pure one; and His name is glo-
> rified among the Gentiles.[41]

As the Old Covenant was sealed by sacrifice, which it commanded
to be offered continuously, so the New Covenant has a new sacrifice, a
new oblation, that is proper to it, which is the Eucharist. The bloody
animal sacrifices of the Old Testament ceased with the destruction of
the Temple in AD 70. In their place, the Eucharistic sacrifice is now

---

[39] Irenaeus, *Against Heresies* 4.18.5 (*ANF*, 1:486; my italics).
[40] Ibid., 4.18.1 (*ANF*, 1:484).
[41] Ibid., 4.17.5 (*ANF*, 1:484). See also 4.18, in which the discussion of sacrifice in
the New Covenant continues.

offered in every part of the world. As the mystical offering of the true Blood of Christ poured out on Calvary, it is infinitely more noble than the blood of slain animals.

The Eucharistic Prayer of the Apostolic Tradition

One of the earliest complete Eucharistic Prayers that has come down to us is in the work often attributed to St. Hippolytus called the *Apostolic Tradition*, which is commonly dated to the first part of the third century. Some recent scholars, however, no longer connect it with either Hippolytus or the church in Rome.[42] Whatever its precise origin, it is of great interest because of its early date, its brevity, and its archaic nature.[43] It contains six parts: the invitatory dialogue, the preface of thanksgiving, the institution narrative, the anamnesis, the epiclesis, and

---

[42] This work has been the subject of much scholarly debate concerning its date, attribution, and sources. See, among others, Smyth, "The Anaphora of the So-Called 'Apostolic Tradition' and the Roman Eucharistic Prayer," 71–98, who, to my mind, convincingly shows that the anaphora cannot be associated with Rome, for the only Eucharistic Prayer witnessed to by authentic Roman sources is the Roman Canon in different stages of development: "As far as we can go back in the assuredly Roman sources, and as far as we can go in the sources influenced by the Roman liturgy, always and without exception we encounter as a Roman prayer the only and unique tradition of the Roman Canon" (75). See also Bryan Spinks, *Do This in Remembrance of Me: The Eucharist from the Early Church to the Present Day* (London: SCM Press, 2013), 62–66; Paul F. Bradshaw, Maxwell E. Johnson, and L. Edward Phillips, *The Apostolic Tradition: A Commentary* (Minneapolis, MN: Augsburg Fortress, 2002); Hippolytus, *On the Apostolic Tradition*, trans. Alistair Stewart-Sykes (Crestwood, NY: St. Vladimir's Seminary Press, 2001); Allen Brent, *Hippolytus and the Roman Church in the Third Century: Communities in Tension before the Emergence of a Monarch-Bishop* (Leiden: Brill, 1995); Gregory Dix, *Apostolike Paradosis: The Treatise on the Apostolic Tradition of St. Hippolytus of Rome*, 2nd ed. (London: SPCK, 1968); Bernard Botte, *Hippolyte de Rome: La Tradition apostolique*, 2nd ed. (Paris: Cerf, 1968); Botte, *La Tradition apostolique de saint Hippolyte: Essai de reconstitution*, 5th ed. (Münster, DE: Aschendorff, 1989).

[43] For dating, see Spinks, *Do This in Remembrance of Me*, 64: "Although the prayer has archaic features—Jesus is described as a child and the angel of God's will— it also has features that suggest a fourth-century date, particularly the inclusion of the Words of Institution within the prayer. . . . Whatever else may be said of the anaphora, it is not the universal Eucharistic Prayer of Rome in 215." I would strongly challenge, however, the idea that the presence of the words of institution ought to suggest a fourth-century date.

the doxology, followed by the "amen" of the faithful.[44] The Eucharistic Prayer II of the *Novus Ordo* is based on this ancient anaphora.

The invitatory dialogue is that to which we are accustomed from later forms of the liturgy:

> The Lord be with you. *And with thy spirit.*
> Lift up your hearts. *We lift them up unto the Lord.*
> Let us give thanks to the Lord. *It is meet and right.*[45]

The invitation to the faithful to lift up their hearts, present in all Eucharistic Prayers, manifests the ascending movement of the sacrificial offering, in which the hearts of the faithful are to ascend from the altar in the church to God's altar on high.[46]

There follows a preface in which God is thanked for sending His Son "at the end of time":

> We give thee thanks, O God, through thy beloved Servant Jesus Christ, whom at the end of time thou didst send to us a Saviour and Redeemer and the Messenger of thy counsel. Who is thy Word, inseparable from thee; through whom thou didst make all things and in whom thou art well pleased. Whom thou didst send from heaven into the womb of the

---

[44] Another early Eucharistic Prayer to which one can compare that of the *Apostolic Tradition* is that found in the Barcelona Papyrus, also dated, in its original form, to the third century (although the manuscript in which it is found is from the mid-fourth century) by Michael Zheltov, "The Anaphora and the Thanksgiving Prayer from the Barcelona Papyrus: An Underestimated Testimony to the Anaphoral History in the Fourth Century," *Vigiliae Christianae* 62 (2008): 467–504 (see 498 for the dating and 493 for its structure). It has eight parts: invitatory dialogue, the preface of thanksgiving, Sanctus, oblation and epiclesis over the elements, the institution narrative, the anamnesis, a second epiclesis for sanctification of the faithful, and the doxology. A ninth part of most Eucharistic Prayers is the intercessions for the living and the dead that generally follow the epiclesis for the sanctification of the faithful.

[45] Easton, *The Apostolic Tradition of Hippolytus*, 35.

[46] The Roman Canon makes this idea explicit in the petition: "Command that these gifts be borne by the hands of your holy Angel to your altar on high in the sight of your divine majesty" (*RM*, 641). It is interesting to note that, in the invitatory dialogue before the ceremony of lighting the lamps later in the *The Apostolic Tradition* (ch. 26 [Easton, *Apostolic Tradition of Hippolytus*, 59]), it specifies that "they shall not say 'lift up your hearts,' for that belongs to the oblation."

Virgin, and who, dwelling within her, was made flesh, and was manifested as thy Son, being born of the Holy Spirit and the Virgin. Who, fulfilling thy will, and winning for himself a holy people, spread out his hands when he came to suffer, that by his death he might set free them that believed on thee.[47]

The anaphora from the *Apostolic Tradition* lacks the Sanctus, which is the normal culmination of this movement of praise and thanksgiving. There then follows the institution narrative, at the center of the Eucharistic Prayer:

Who, when he was betrayed to his willing death, that he might bring to nought death, and break the bonds of the devil, and tread hell under foot, and give light to the righteous, and set up a boundary post, and manifest his resurrection, taking bread and giving thanks to thee said: Take, eat: this is my body, which is broken for you. And likewise also the cup, saying, This is my blood, which is shed for you. As often as ye perform this, perform my memorial.[48]

After quoting the command of Jesus to the Apostles to do what He had done as His memorial, the Eucharistic Prayer proceeds to offer His sacrifice to the Father in remembrance of the whole Paschal mystery of His death and Resurrection. This is called the "anamnesis":[49]

Having in memory, therefore, his death and resurrection, we offer to thee the bread and the cup, yielding thee thanks, because thou hast counted us worthy to stand before thee and minister to thee.[50]

After the anamnesis there follows the epiclesis, or invocation of the Holy Spirit, which here, as in other Eucharistic Prayers, is directed to two ends. The Spirit is invoked to realize both the consecration of the bread and wine and the sanctification of the faithful

---

[47] Easton, *The Apostolic Tradition of Hippolytus*, 35.
[48] Ibid., 35–36.
[49] *Anamnesis* comes from the Greek word for "remember." See *CCC*, §1103.
[50] Easton, *The Apostolic Tradition of Hippolytus*, 36.

so as to build up the Church.[51] In the anaphora from the *Apostolic Tradition*, as in other early Eucharistic Prayers, the emphasis is on the second aspect:[52]

> And we pray that thou wouldst send thy Holy Spirit upon the offerings of thy holy Church; that thou, gathering them into one, wouldst grant to all thy saints who partake to be filled with the Holy Spirit, that their faith may be confirmed in truth, that we may praise and glorify thee.[53]

The Eucharistic Prayer concludes with the final doxology, followed by the Amen of the faithful: "Through thy Servant Jesus Christ, through whom be to thee glory and honor, with the Holy Spirit in the holy church, both now and always and world without end. Amen."[54]

St. Cyprian

St. Cyprian of Carthage treats the Eucharist in a letter written around AD 253 to a fellow bishop named Cecil. The occasion for the letter is the report that some were celebrating the Eucharist without wine, with only water in the chalice. St. Cyprian first stresses that this is contrary to the Tradition that Christ gave to the Apostles and then that it is necessary that the wine become Christ's Blood so that His

---

[51] The two ends for which the Holy Spirit is invoked in the epiclesis of a Eucharistic Prayer correspond, in the terminology of Latin scholasticism, to the *res et sacramentum*, which is the real presence of the Body and Blood, and the *res tantum*, the effects of grace that build up the unity and holiness of the Church. On the purposes of the epiclesis in early Eucharistic Prayers, and especially in the Anaphora of Addai and Mari, see Thomas Elavanal, "The Pneumatology of the Anaphora of Addai and Mari Especially in Its Epiclesis," in *Studies on the Anaphora of Addai and Mari*, ed. Bosco Puthur (Kochi, India: L.R.C. Publications, 2004), 146–67.

[52] See the epiclesis of the Anaphora of Addai and Mari, which dates roughly to the same period: "May your Holy Spirit, Lord, come and rest on this offering of your servants, and bless and sanctify it, that it may be to us, Lord, for remission of debts, forgiveness of sins, and the great hope of resurrection from the dead, and new life in the kingdom of heaven, with all who have been pleasing in your sight" (*PEER*, 43).

[53] Easton, *The Apostolic Tradition of Hippolytus*, 36.

[54] Ibid.

sacrifice can be made present.[55] St. Cyprian repeatedly manifests the conviction that the Mass is a "true and full sacrifice" in which the priest acts "in the place of Christ":

> But if it is not allowed to break the least of the command-ments of the Lord, how much more important is it not to infringe upon matters which are so great, so tremendous, so closely connected to the very Sacrament of the Passion of the Lord and of our Redemption, or in any way to change for human tradition what has been divinely instituted? For, if Christ Jesus, our Lord and God, is Himself the High Priest of God the Father and first offered Himself as a Sacrifice to His Father and commanded this to be done in commemoration of Himself, certainly the priest who imitates that which Christ did and then offers the true and full Sacrifice in the Church of God the Father, if he thus begins to offer according to what he sees Christ Himself offered, performs truly in the place of Christ. [56]

He also states that what is offered in the Mass is the sacrifice of Calvary: "And since we make mention of His Passion in all Sacrifices, for the Passion of the Lord is, indeed, the Sacrifice which we offer, we ought to do nothing other than what He did."[57] In order for the Mass to make present Christ's sacrifice, offering what He offered, it needs to contain Christ's Blood, according to the pattern of what Christ did at the Last Supper. Speaking of the words of institution, Cyprian says:

> We find that the Chalice which the Lord offered was mixed and that He called Blood what had been wine. Whence it appears that the Blood of Christ is not offered if wine is lacking in the Chalice and that the Sacrifice of the Lord is not celebrated with lawful sanctification unless the Oblation and our Sacrifice correspond to the Passion.[58]

---

[55] See Johannes Quasten, *Patrology*, 4 vols., vol. 2, *The Ante-Nicene Literature after Irenaeus* (Westminster, MD: Newman Press, 1953), 381: "The entire letter is dominated by the idea of sacrifice."

[56] Cyprian, Letter 63.14, in *Saint Cyprian: Letters (1–81)*, trans. R. B. Donna, FC 51 (Washington, DC: Catholic University of America Press, 1964), 212–13.

[57] Ibid., 63.17 (Donna, *Letters*, 213–14).

[58] Ibid., 63.9 (Donna, *Letters*, 208).

St. Cyprian is concerned above all about the sacrificial aspect of the Mass, rather than the real presence, but the true sacrifice requires that there be wine that truly becomes Christ's Blood according to the word of the Lord so that "our Sacrifice corresponds to the Passion." Without Christ's Blood there would be no sacramental representation of the sacrifice of Calvary.

St. Cyprian also touches on the effects of the Eucharist in this letter when he explains the symbolism of the mixing of the water with the wine in the chalice to represent the union of the faithful with Christ:

> Because Christ, who bore our sins, also bore us all, we see that people are signified in the water, but in the wine the Blood of Christ is shown. But when water is mixed with wine in the Chalice, the people are united to Christ, and the multitude of the believers is bound and joined to Him in whom they believe. This association and mingling of water and wine are so mixed in the Chalice of the Lord that the mixture cannot mutually be separated. Whence nothing can separate the Church, that is, the multitude established faithfully and firmly in the Church, persevering in that which it has believed, from Christ as long as it clings and remains in undivided love.[59]

St. Athanasius

One of our primary sources of knowledge about the faith of the early Church in the Eucharist can be found in homilies given to the newly baptized to catechize them on the Church's faith regarding the sacraments of Christian initiation. A fragment of a homily of St. Athanasius to the neophytes has been preserved in which St. Athanasius emphasizes the realism of the Eucharistic conversion:

> You shall see the Levites bringing loaves and a cup of wine, and placing them on the table. So long as the prayers of supplication and entreaties have not been made, there is only bread and wine. But after the great and wonderful prayers have been completed, then the bread has become the Body, and the wine

---

[59] Ibid., 63.13 (Donna, *Letters*, 211).

the Blood, of our Lord Jesus. . . . Let us approach the celebration of the mysteries. This bread and this wine, so long as the prayers and supplications have not taken place, remain simply what they are. But after the great prayers and holy supplications have been sent forth, the Word comes down into the bread and wine—and thus is His Body confected.[60]

St. Cyril of Jerusalem

St. Cyril of Jerusalem's *Mystagogic Catecheses*, which are the sermons he gave in the Basilica of the Resurrection in Jerusalem to the newly baptized sometime before his death in AD 387,[61] conclude with a robust affirmation of faith in the mystery of the real presence:

> You have now been taught and fully instructed that what seems to be bread is not bread, though it appear to be such to the sense of taste, but the body of Christ; and that what seems to be wine is not wine, though the taste would have it so, but the blood of Christ. . . . So strengthen your heart by partaking of that spiritual bread.[62]

Similarly, he says:

> Since, then, Christ himself clearly described the bread to us in the words "This is my body," who will dare henceforward to dispute it? And since he has emphatically said, "This is my blood," who will waver in the slightest and say it is not his blood?
> By his own power on a previous occasion he turned the water into wine at Cana in Galilee; so it is surely credible that

---

[60] Athanasius, *Fragmentum apud Eutychium*, in M. J. Rouët de Journel, *Enchiridion Patristicum*, 25th ed., no. 802 (Barcelona/Rome: Herder, 1981), 294; in Dennis Billy, *The Beauty of the Eucharist: Voices from the Church Fathers* (Hyde Park, NY: New City Press, 2010), 250.

[61] For the attribution of the *Mystagogic Catecheses* to St. Cyril of Jerusalem, see the thorough study by Alexis James Doval, *Cyril of Jerusalem, Mystagogue: The Authorship of the Mystagogic Catecheses* (Washington, DC: Catholic University of America Press, 2001); see also Yarnold, *Awe-Inspiring Rites*, 69.

[62] Cyril of Jerusalem, *Mystagogic Catecheses* 4.9 (Yarnold, *Awe-Inspiring Rites*, 89).

he has changed wine into blood. If he performed that wonderful miracle just because he had been invited to a human marriage, we shall certainly be much more willing to admit that he has conferred on the wedding guests[63] the savouring of his body and blood.[64]

St. Cyril then explains that the purpose of the Eucharistic conversion of the bread and wine into Christ's Body and Blood is so that by receiving His Body and Blood we may receive a share in His divinity:

> So let us partake with the fullest confidence that it is the body and blood of Christ. For his body has been bestowed on you in the form [τύπος][65] of bread, and his blood in the form of wine, so that by partaking Christ's body and blood you may share with him the same body and blood. This is how we become bearers of Christ, since his body and blood spreads throughout our limbs; this is how, in the blessed Peter's words, "we become partakers of the divine nature" (2 Peter 1:4).[66]

St. Cyril speaks of the Eucharistic conversion as the work of the Holy Spirit: We "call upon the merciful God to send the Holy Spirit on our offerings, so that he may make the bread Christ's body, and the wine Christ's blood; for clearly whatever the Holy Spirit touches is sanctified and transformed."[67]

St. Cyril is also an important witness to the sacrificial nature of the Mass and its propitiatory effect on behalf of the living and the dead. He says that "we offer Christ who has been slain for our sins, and so we appease the merciful God both on their behalf [the faithful

---

[63] See Mark 2:19.

[64] Cyril of Jerusalem, *Mystagogic Catecheses* 4.1–2 (Yarnold, *Awe-Inspiring Rites*, 86).

[65] The species of bread and wine are not infrequently said to be the "type" or "antitype" of Christ's Body and Blood in early liturgical texts. This is the case, for example, in the Anaphora of Addai and Mari and the liturgy of St. Basil.

[66] Cyril of Jerusalem, *Mystagogic Catecheses* 4.3 (Yarnold, *Awe-Inspiring Rites*, 86–87).

[67] Ibid., 5.7 (Yarnold, *Awe-Inspiring Rites*, 92). This text is quoted in Benedict XVI, *Sacramentum Caritatis*, §13. See also Cyril of Jerusalem, *Mystagogic Catecheses* 1.7: "The bread and wine of the Eucharist is merely bread and wine before the invocation of the sacred and adorable Trinity, but after the invocation the bread becomes the body of Christ and the wine his blood" (Yarnold, *Awe-Inspiring Rites*, 71).

departed] and on ours."[68] The Mass has a propitiatory effect because it is the sacramental offering of the real presence of Christ, "slain for our sins," and makes present the fruits of His sacrifice.

St. Hilary of Poitiers

St. Hilary, great fourth-century bishop of Poitiers, France, affirms the real presence, explaining that the Eucharist has the power to sanctify or divinize us because the true Body of Christ, present in the Eucharist, is united to His soul and the divine nature of the Son. By reverently receiving Christ's Eucharistic Body and Blood, we come to partake more deeply in His Spirit and divine life, which is the foundation of the unity of the Church.[69] This Eucharistic text is situated in the context of a polemic against the Arian heresy, according to which Christ is not one with the Father in nature, but only by a union of wills, in that Christ's will is always in conformity with that of the Father. To refute this, Hilary compares the unity of Christ and the Father to the unity that the faithful have with Christ in the Eucharist. This unity is not merely a union of wills, but a real reception of the human nature of Christ, and through receiving His humanity, we receive a participation in His divine nature:

> I now ask those who introduce a unity of will between the Father and the Son, whether Christ is in us by the truth of His nature or by the harmony of the will? If the Word has indeed become flesh, and we indeed receive the Word as flesh in the Lord's food [cibo dominico], how are we not to believe that He dwells in us by His nature, He who, when He was born as man, has assumed the nature of our flesh that is bound inseparably with Himself, and has mingled the nature of His flesh to His eternal nature in the mystery of the flesh that was to be communicated to us? . . . If, therefore, Christ has truly taken the flesh of our body, and that man who was born from Mary is truly Christ, and we truly receive the flesh of

---

[68] Ibid., 5.10 (Yarnold, *Awe-Inspiring Rites*, 94).

[69] For a brief summary of St. Hilary's Eucharistic teaching, see Edward J. Kilmartin, *The Eucharist in the West: History and Theology*, ed. Robert J. Daly (Collegeville, MN: Liturgical Press, 1998), 11–14.

His body in the mystery (and we are one, therefore, because
the Father is in Him and He is in us), how can you assert that
there is a unity of will, since the attribute of the nature in the
sacrament is the mystery of the perfect unity?

... He Himself declares: "For my flesh is food indeed, and
my blood is drink indeed. He who eats my flesh and drinks
my blood abides in me and I in him" [John 6:55–56]. It is
no longer permitted us to raise doubts about the true nature
of the body and the blood, for, according to the statement of
the Lord Himself as well as our faith, this is indeed flesh and
blood. And these things that we receive bring it about that we
are in Christ and Christ is in us. Is not this the truth?[70]

In a way similar to St. Ignatius of Antioch and St. Irenaeus, St.
Hilary seeks to combat a Christological and Trinitarian heresy by
starting from faith in the presence of Christ's true Body and Blood in
the Eucharist and its divinizing power. Receiving His Body could not
sanctify us if His humanity were not inseparably united to His true
divinity through what will later be called the "hypostatic union."

St. Ambrose

The Real Presence and the
Eucharistic Conversion

In his *De Sacramentis*, which is a collection of homilies given to the
neophytes in Easter week, St. Ambrose speaks very clearly about the
conversion of the bread and wine into the Body and Blood of Christ
through the power of the words of institution said at the consecration.[71]
This forms one of the main themes of his discourse to the neophytes
in his fourth Sermon on the Sacraments. He writes:

Perhaps you say: "The bread I have here is ordinary bread."
Yes, before the sacramental words are uttered this bread is

---

[70] Hilary of Poitiers, *On the Trinity* 8.13–14, in S. McKenna, *Hilary of Poitiers: The
Trinity*, FC 25 (Washington, DC: Catholic University of America Press, 1954),
285–86.
[71] For a summary of St. Ambrose's Eucharistic teaching, see Kilmartin, *The
Eucharist in the West*, 14–23.

nothing but bread. But at the consecration this bread becomes the body of Christ. Let us reason this out. How can something which is bread be the body of Christ? Well, by what words is the consecration effected, and whose words are they? The words of the Lord Jesus. All that is said before are the words of the priest: praise is offered to God, the prayer is offered up, petitions are made for the people, for kings, for all others. But when the moment comes for bringing the most holy sacrament into being, the priest does not use his own words any longer: he uses the words of Christ. Therefore, it is Christ's word that brings this sacrament into being.

What is this word of Christ? It is the word by which all things were made. The Lord commanded and the heavens were made, the Lord commanded and the earth was made, the Lord commanded and the seas were made, the Lord commanded and all creatures came into being. See, then, how efficacious the word of Christ is. If, then, there is such power in the word of the Lord Jesus that things begin to exist which did not exist before, how much more powerful it is for changing what already existed into something else.

To answer your question, then, before the consecration it was not the body of Christ, but after the consecration I tell you that it is now the body of Christ. He spoke and it was made, he commanded and it was created. You yourself were in existence, but you were a creature of the old order; after your consecration, you began to exist as a new creature.[72]

You see from all this, surely, the power that is contained in the heavenly word. If it is effective in the earthly spring,[73] if the heavenly word is effective in the other cases, why should it not be so in the heavenly sacraments? So now you have learnt that the bread becomes the body of Christ, and that, though wine and water are poured into the chalice, through the consecration effected by the heavenly word it becomes his blood.[74]

---

[72] Ambrose, *De Sacramentis* 4.14–16 (Yarnold, *Awe-Inspiring Rites*, 132–33).
[73] This is a reference to the words of Moses that brought water from the rock in Exod 15:23–25.
[74] Ambrose, *De Sacramentis* 4.19 (Yarnold, *Awe-Inspiring Rites*, 134–35).

. . . The day before he suffered, it says, he took bread in his
holy hands. Before it is consecrated, it is bread; but when the
words of Christ have been uttered over it, it is the body of
Christ. Listen to what he says then: "Take and eat of this, all
of you, for this is my body." And the chalice, before the words
of Christ, is full of wine and water. But when the words of
Christ have done their work, it becomes the blood of Christ
which has redeemed the people. So you can see the ways in
which the word of Christ is powerful enough to change all
things. Besides, the Lord Jesus himself is our witness that we
received his body and blood. Should we doubt his authority
and testimony?[75]

In this text it is clear that St. Ambrose teaches a substantial conversion of the bread and wine into Christ's Body and Blood, that this
substantial conversion is caused by the words of Christ, and that the
conversion takes place when these words are uttered.

A parallel text of equal power is in St. Ambrose's *De Mysteriis*. He
strengthens faith in the miracle of the Eucharist by comparing it to
the miracles of Moses, Elijah, the Incarnation, and the virgin birth. It
is also interesting that he draws in some philosophy, speaking of the
Eucharistic consecration as a change in nature:

But if the benediction of man had such power as to change
nature, what do we say of divine consecration itself, in which
the very words of our Lord and Saviour function? For that sacrament, which you receive, is effected by the words of Christ.
But if the words of Elias had such power as to call down fire
from heaven, will not the words of Christ have power enough
to change the nature of the elements? You have read about the
works of the world: "that He spoke and they were done; He
commanded and they were created" (Ps 148:5). So, cannot the
words of Christ, which were able to make what was not out
of nothing, change those things that are into the things that
were not? For it is not of less importance to give things new
natures than to change natures.

. . . It is clear then that the Virgin conceived contrary to
the course of nature. And this body which we make is from

---

[75] Ibid., 4.23 (Yarnold, *Awe-Inspiring Rites*, 137).

the Virgin. Why do you seek here the course of nature in the body of Christ, when the Lord Jesus himself was born of the Virgin contrary to nature? Surely it is the true flesh of Christ which was crucified, which was buried; therefore it is truly the sacrament of that flesh.

The Lord Jesus himself declares: "This is my body." Before the benediction of the heavenly words another species is mentioned; after the consecration the body is signified. He Himself speaks of His blood. Before the consecration it is mentioned as something else; after the consecration it is called blood. And you say "Amen," that is, "It is true." What the mouth speaks, let the mind within confess; what words utter, let the heart feel.[76]

The Eucharistic Sacrifice

St. Ambrose also regards the separate consecration of the Body and Blood as sacramentally realizing the sacrifice of Christ, thus "showing the Lord's death":

"My flesh is meat indeed, and My Blood is drink" (John 6:56). You hear Him speak of His Flesh and of His Blood, you perceive the sacred pledges (conveying to us the merits and power) of the Lord's death. . . . Now we, as often as we receive the Sacramental Elements, which by the mysterious efficacy of holy prayer are transformed into the Flesh and the Blood, "do show the Lord's Death" (1 Cor 11:26).[77]

Description of the Canon

St. Ambrose also gives some precious information on the Eucharistic Prayer as it was celebrated in Milan in the late fourth century and quotes a part of it. This sheds light on the development of the Roman Canon at this time:

---

[76] Ambrose, *De Mysteriis* 9.52–54, trans. Roy Deferrari, in *Saint Ambrose: Theological and Dogmatic Works* (Washington, DC: Catholic University of America Press, 1963, FC 44), 25–26.

[77] Ambrose, *Exposition of the Christian Faith* 4.10.125 (PL, 16:641), trans. H. de Romestin, in *NPNF2*, 10:278.

Do you wish to know how it is consecrated with heavenly words? Accept what the words are. The priest speaks. He says: "Perform for us this oblation written, reasonable, acceptable, which is a figure of the body and blood of our Lord Jesus Christ. On the day before He suffered He took bread in His holy hands, looked toward heaven, toward you, holy Father omnipotent, eternal God, giving thanks, blessed, broke, and having broken it gave it to the Apostles and His disciples, saying: 'Take and eat of this, all of you; for this is my body, which shall be broken for many.' . . . Similarly also, on the day before He suffered, after they had dined, He took the chalice, looked toward heaven, toward thee, holy Father omnipotent, eternal God and giving thanks He blessed it, and gave it to the Apostles and His disciples, saying: 'Take and drink of this, all of you; for this is my blood.' . . .

Next, realize how great a sacrament it is. See what He says: "As often as you shall do this, so often will you do a commemoration of me, until I come again." And the priest says: "Therefore, mindful of His most glorious passion and resurrection from the dead and ascension into heaven, we offer you this immaculate victim, a reasonable sacrifice, an unbloody victim, this holy bread, and chalice of eternal life. And we ask and pray that you accept this offering upon your sublime altar through the hands of your angels, just as you deigned to accept the gifts of your just son Abel and the sacrifice of our patriarch Abraham and what the highest priest Melchisedech offered you."[78]

St. Augustine

St. Augustine's theology of the Eucharist stresses its proper effect, which is the unity of the Mystical Body.[79] It has this effect of binding together the Mystical Body of Christ precisely because the members of the Church receive the real Body and Blood of Christ. In other words, the charity that binds the Church together is the proper effect

---

[78] Ambrose, *De Sacramentis* 4.21–22, 26–27 (Deferrari, *Saint Ambrose*, 304–6).

[79] For St. Augustine's theology of the Eucharist, see Joseph T. Lienhard, S.J., "*Sacramentum* and the Eucharist in St. Augustine," *The Thomist* 77 (2013): 173–92.

of receiving the Body and Blood of Christ. The Eucharist can build up the Body of Christ in charity (later to be called the *res tantum*) only because it is itself the Body of Christ sacramentally present (*res et sacramentum*). In this way St. Augustine is also stressing the realism of Christ's Body and Blood in the Eucharist, present under the sacramental species.

In Sermon 227 to the neophytes on Easter, St. Augustine says that the visible bread and wine on the altar, "sanctified by the word of God," is His Body and Blood. Through devoutly receiving that Body and that Blood that was shed for us, we become that Body, which means that we are joined in the close union of the Mystical Body:

> You ought to know what you have received, what you are about to receive, and what you ought to receive every day. That bread which you can see on the altar, sanctified by the word of God, is the body of Christ. That cup, or rather what the cup contains, sanctified by the word of God, is the blood of Christ. It was by means of these things that the Lord Christ wished to present us with his body and blood, which he shed for our sake for the forgiveness of sins. If you receive them well, you are yourselves what you receive.[80]

He makes this same point in Sermon 229 to the neophytes on the Eucharistic liturgy, in which he also stresses the conversion of the elements through the power of the word by which the communicants are made into the Body of Christ:

> What you can see here, dearly beloved, on the table of the Lord, is bread and wine; but this bread and wine, when the word is applied to it, becomes the body and blood of the Word. ... Because, yes, the very Word took to himself a man, that is the soul and flesh of a man, and became man, while remaining God. For that reason, because he also suffered for us, he also presented us in this sacrament with his body and blood and this is what he even made us ourselves into as well.[81]

---

[80] Augustine, Sermon 227, preached to the neophytes on Easter in AD 414–415, trans. Edmund Hill, in *Sermons (184–229Z) on the Liturgical Seasons*, WSA, pt. III (Homilies), vol. 6 (New Rochelle, NY: New City Press, 1993), 254.

[81] Augustine, Sermon 229.1, preached to the neophytes on Easter (AD 405–411), in Hill, *Sermons (184–229Z)*, 265.

Later in the same sermon, St. Augustine again emphasizes the substantial conversion of the elements through the word of Christ:

> And from there we come now to what is done in the holy prayers which you are going to hear, that with the application of the word we may have the body and blood of Christ. Take away the word, I mean, it's just bread and wine; add the word, and it's now something else. And what is that something else? The body of Christ, and the blood of Christ. So take away the word, it's bread and wine; add the word and it will become the sacrament. To this you say, *Amen*.[82]

St. Augustine's Eucharistic realism can be seen in his affirmation that what we receive in Communion is the same Body of Christ that hung on the Cross, from which we are fed.[83] In a sermon to the neophytes, he says: "Recognize in the bread what hung on the cross, and in the cup what flowed from his side."[84]

In his commentary on Psalm 99 [98], he interprets verse 5, which says "worship [at] his footstool," with regard to Christ's humanity present in the Eucharist:

> In my uncertainty I turn to Christ, for he it is whom I am seeking in this psalm; and then I discover how . . . God's footstool may be adored without impiety. . . . He received his flesh from the flesh of Mary. He walked here below in that flesh, and even gave us that same flesh to eat for our salvation. But *since no one eats it without first worshipping it*, we plainly see how the Lord's footstool is rightly worshiped. *Not only do we commit no sin in worshipping it; we should sin if we did not.*[85]

---

[82] Augustine, Sermon 229.3, in Hill, *Sermons (184–229Z)*, 266.

[83] See Augustine, Exposition of Psalm 100, no. 9: "We too are fed from the Lord's cross . . . when we eat his body"; see *Exposition of the Psalms 99–120*, trans. Maria Boulding, WSA, pt. III (Homilies), vol. 19 (Hyde Park, NY: New City Press, 2003), 40.

[84] Augustine, Sermon 228B.1–3, in Hill, *Sermons (184–229Z)*, 262.

[85] Augustine, *Ennarationes in Psalmos* 98.9, trans. Maria Boulding, in *Expositions of the Psalms 73–98*, WSA, pt. III (Homilies), vol. 18 (Hyde Park, NY: New City Press, 2002), 474–75 (my italics).

St. Augustine's insistence on worship of the Eucharist before receiving Communion shows that he clearly acknowledges the substantial presence of Christ's Body and Blood in the Eucharist. The Eucharist is worthy of worship only because it contains the substantial presence of the humanity of the Word. This is a good example of how liturgical practice—in this case, the adoration of the consecrated host in the Eucharistic liturgy—manifests doctrine.

St. Augustine stresses the identity of the Priest and the Victim in the Eucharist at the Last Supper. In a commentary on Psalm 33, he speaks of Christ holding His own Body in His hands at the Last Supper: "Christ was being carried in his own hands when he handed over his body, saying, 'This is my body'; for he was holding that very body in his hands as he spoke."[86] In *De Trinitate*, he speaks similarly of the Mass as a sacrifice in which Christ is Priest and Victim: "And what could be so acceptably offered and received, as the flesh of our sacrifice, made the body of our priest?[87]

St. Augustine also emphasizes the sacrificial nature of the Eucharist in his sermons to the neophytes on Easter day. In Sermon 228, he speaks of the Eucharist as the true sacrificial offering of Christ's Body and Blood that was prefigured in all the sacrifices of the Old Covenant. The Eucharist alone is the sacrifice of the "body and blood of the priest himself":

> You have all just now been born again of water and the Spirit, and can see that food and drink upon this table of the Lord's in a new light, and receive it with a fresh love and piety. So I am obliged . . . to remind you infants of what the meaning is of such a great and divine sacrament, such a splendid and noble medicine, such a pure and simple sacrifice, which is not offered now just in the one earthly city of Jerusalem, nor in that tabernacle which was constructed by Moses, nor in the temple built by Solomon. These were just "shadows of things to come" (Col 2:17; Heb 10:1). But "from the rising of the sun to its setting" (Mal 1:11) it is offered as the prophets foretold,

---

[86] Augustine, *Ennarationes in Psalmos* 33.10, trans. Maria Boulding, in *Expositions of the Psalms 33–50*, WSA, pt. III (Homilies), vol. 16 (Hyde Park, NY: New City Press, 2000), 21.

[87] Augustine, *The Trinity* 4.14, trans. S. McKenna, FC 45 (Washington, DC: Catholic University of America Press, 1963), 155.

and as a sacrifice of praise to God, according to the grace of the New Testament.

No longer is a victim sought from the flocks for a blood sacrifice, nor is a sheep or a goat any more led to the divine altars, but *now the sacrifice of our time is the body and blood of the priest himself. . . .*

So Christ our Lord, who offered by suffering for us what by being born he had received from us, has become our high priest for ever, and has given us the *order of sacrifice which you can see, of his body that is to say, and his blood. . . . Recognize in the bread what hung on the cross, and in the cup what flowed from his side.*

You see, *those old sacrifices of the people of God also represented in a variety of ways this single one that was to come. . . .* And therefore receive and eat the body of Christ, yes, you that have become members of Christ in the body of Christ; receive and drink the blood of Christ. In order not to be scattered and separated, eat what binds you together; in order not to seem cheap in your own estimation, *drink the price that was paid for you. . . .* You are then, after all, receiving that flesh about which Life itself says, "The bread which I shall give is my flesh for the life of the world" (John 6:51).[88]

This magnificent homily brings together the themes of the real presence of the Body crucified on Calvary and the Blood poured out there, the sacrificial nature of the Mass making present the sacrifice of Calvary, and the Eucharist's effect of binding the Church together in charity.

St. Augustine also stresses that the sacrifice of the Mass involves, together with the sacrifice of Christ, the sacrifice of the faithful of themselves. In Sermon 227 for the neophytes on Easter, he says:

Then, after the consecration of the Holy Sacrifice of God, because he wished us also to be his sacrifice, a fact which was made clear when the Holy Sacrifice was first instituted, and because that Sacrifice is a sign of what we are, behold, when the Sacrifice is finished, we say the Lord's Prayer.[89]

---

[88] Augustine, Sermon 228B.1–3, in Hill, *Sermons (184–229Z)*, 261–62; my italics.
[89] Augustine, Sermon 227, trans. Mary Sarah Muldowney, *Sermons on the Liturgical Seasons*, FC 38 (p. 197).

St. Augustine so strongly identifies the Eucharistic Body of Christ and the ecclesial Body of Christ that, if the one is offered, so must be the other. The sacrifice of the Head, made present on the altar, demands the interior self-sacrifice of the members who gather to offer the Holy Mass.

St. Gregory Nazianzen and St. Gregory of Nyssa

Gregory of Nazianzen (AD 329–390) likens the words of the consecration to a mystical knife that sacramentally immolates the Lamb of God. He writes to Amphilochius, bishop of Iconium:

> Scarcely yet delivered from the pains of my illness, I hasten to you, the guardian of my cure. For the tongue of a priest meditating on the Lord raises the sick. Do then the greater thing in your priestly ministration, and loose the great mass of my sins when you lay hold of the Sacrifice of Resurrection. . . . Most reverend friend, cease not both to pray and to plead for me when you draw down the Word by your word, when with a bloodless cutting you sever the Body and Blood of the Lord, using your voice for the sacrificial knife.[90]

Gregory of Nyssa (AD 335–395) likewise speaks with great realism of the Eucharistic conversion effected by the power of the words of institution:

> Rightly, then, do we believe that now also the bread which is consecrated by the Word of God is changed into the Body of God the Word. . . . It is at once changed into the body by means of the Word, as the Word itself said, "This is My Body."[91]

---

[90] Gregory Nazianzen, Letter 171 to Amphilochius, trans. Charles Browne and James Swallow, in *NPNF2*, 7:469.

[91] Gregory of Nyssa, *Great Catechism* [*Catechetical Oration*] 37.105–7, trans. William Moore and Henry Wilson, in *NPNF2*, 5:505–6.

In a homily on the Resurrection, Gregory of Nyssa speaks of the sacrificial nature of the Last Supper. The same reasoning applies to every Mass:

> He who arranges all things by His power does not await the necessity that is imminent from the betrayal by Judas ... but of His own accord He forestalls them and by a hidden kind of sacrifice, which cannot be discerned by men, He offers Himself as a sacrifice and immolates Himself as a victim— He who is at once Priest and Lamb of God, who takes away the sin of the world. When did He do this? When He gave to His assembled disciples His body to eat and His blood to drink, He then clearly showed that the Sacrifice of the Lamb was already completed, for the body of a victim would not be suitable to eat if it were living. Hence, when He presented to His disciples His body to eat and His blood to drink, His body was already immolated in an unspeakable and invisible manner, in accordance with the freedom and power of Him who performed the mystery.[92]

St. John Chrysostom

St. John Chrysostom (AD 347–407), patriarch of Constantinople, Doctor of the Church, and one of the most famous preachers of the Patristic period, has some extraordinary texts on the real presence of Christ in the Eucharist, the Eucharistic conversion, and the sacrificial aspect of the Mass.[93] In his commentary on 1 Corinthians 11, he says:

> "The cup of blessing which we bless, is it not a communion of the Blood of Christ?" (1 Cor 10:16). Very persuasively spoke he, and with awe. For what he says is this: *"This which is in the cup is that which flowed from His side*, and of that do we partake." But he called it a cup of blessing, because holding it in our hands, we so exalt Him in our hymn, wondering, aston-

---

[92] Gregory of Nyssa, *In Sanctum Pascha Sive in Christi Resurrectionem*, oratio 1 (PG, 46:612), dated to AD 382 (Quasten, *Patrology*, 3:277), in Michael D. Forrest, *The Clean Oblation* (St. Paul, MN: Radio Replies Press, 1945), 33.

[93] For a brief summary, see Quasten, *Patrology*, 3:479–481.

ished at His unspeakable gift, blessing Him, among other
things, . . . for the pouring it out, but also for the imparting
thereof to us all. "Wherefore if you desire blood," says He,
"redden not the altar of idols with the slaughter of brute beasts,
but My altar with My blood." Tell me, what can be more tre-
mendous than this? What more tenderly kind?[94]

In other words, what we receive in the Eucharist is the very same
Blood that was poured forth on Calvary, the same Body that was
pierced to make us partakers in the fruit of His sacrifice. What greater
gift could God give than His very self, immolated for us and made
present in such a way that we can receive Him through the aid of sensible realities, under the veils of bread and wine?

Chrysostom again movingly affirms the real presence of Christ
in comparing the Eucharistic sacrifice with the sacrifices of the Old
Covenant:

And in the old covenant, because they were in an imperfect
state, the blood which they used to offer to idols He Himself
submitted to receive, that He might separate them from those
idols; which very thing again was a proof of His unspeakable
affection: but here He transferred the service to that which is
far more awful and glorious, changing the very sacrifice itself,
and instead of the slaughter of irrational creatures, commanding to offer up Himself.[95]

Later in the same homily, he stresses the momentousness of
Christ's real presence in the Eucharist, and says that it is the supreme
manifestation of the divine Love:

When you see [the Body of Christ] set before you, say to yourself: Because of this Body I am no longer earth and ashes, no
longer a prisoner, but free: because of this I hope for heaven,
and to receive the good things therein, immortal life, the
portion of angels, converse with Christ; this Body, nailed and
scourged, was more than death could stand against; this Body

---

[94] John Chrysostom, *Homilies on First Corinthians* 24.1 (PG, 61:199; *NPNF*1,
12:139).
[95] Ibid.

the very sun saw sacrificed, and turned aside his beams; for this both the veil was rent in that moment, and rocks were burst asunder, and all the earth was shaken. This is even that Body, the bloodstained, the pierced, and that out of which gushed the saving fountains, the one of blood, the other of water, for all the world. This Body He has given to us both to hold and to eat; a thing appropriate to intense love.[96]

In his commentary on Hebrews 9:24–26, St. John Chrysostom stresses that every sacrifice of the Mass is one sacrifice, the sacrifice of Calvary:

> He is Himself then both victim and Priest and sacrifice. . . . For we always offer the same Lamb, not one now and another tomorrow, but always the same one, so that the sacrifice is one. And yet by this reasoning, since the offering is made in many places, are there many Christs? But Christ is one everywhere, being complete here and complete there also, one Body. As then while offered in many places, He is one body and not many bodies; so also [He is] one sacrifice. He is our High Priest, who offered the sacrifice that cleanses us. We now offer that victim which was then offered, which cannot be exhausted.[97]

Chrysostom explains that the sacrificial aspect of the Eucharist does not add a new sacrifice to that of Calvary, as if such an addition would be desirable, or multiply sacrifices as in the Old Covenant. No, the sacrifice of the Mass is one, throughout all the centuries and on all the altars on which a valid Mass is celebrated. The sacrifice of the Mass is the same as the sacrifice of Calvary, because the words of consecration make Christ's Body and Blood truly present on the altar, that same Body and Blood immolated for us at Calvary, which is made present on the altar as the "new oblation of the new Covenant," in the words of St. Irenaeus.

In his *On the Priesthood*, Chrysostom extols the office of the priest by speaking of the Eucharist as the sacrifice of the Lord who, through

---

[96] Ibid., 24.7 (*NPNF*1, 12:142).
[97] John Chrysostom, *In Epistolam ad Hebraeos Homiliae* 17 (*NPNF*1, 14:447, 449; I have slightly modified the translation), quoted in John Paul II, *EE*, §12.

the priest, is mystically immolated on the altar. He who sits at the right hand of the Father is continually touched and held by the priest and offered to the faithful:

> When you see the Lord sacrificed and lying before you, and the High Priest standing over the sacrifice and praying, and all who partake being tinctured with that precious blood, can you think that you are still among men and still standing on earth? Are you not at once transported to heaven? . . . Oh, the loving-kindness of God to men! He who sits above with the Father is at that moment held in our hands, and gives himself to those who wish to clasp and embrace him—which they do, all of them, with their eyes.[98]

He continues later:

> But when he invokes the Holy Spirit and offers that awful sacrifice and keeps on touching the common Master of us all, tell me, where shall we rank him? What purity and what piety shall we demand of him? . . . At that moment angels attend the priest, and the whole dais and the sanctuary are thronged with heavenly powers in honor of Him who lies there.[99]

The ministerial priest can perform the great sacrifice because Christ works sacramentally through the priest's words offered in the name of Christ, as Chrysostom emphasizes in his second homily on 2 Timothy:

> The Offering is the same, whether a common man, or Paul or Peter offer it. It is the same which Christ gave to His disciples, and which the Priests now minister. This is nowise inferior to that, because it is not men that sanctify even this, but the Same who sanctified the one sanctifies the other also. For as the words which God spoke are the same which the Priest now utters, so is the Offering the same.[100]

---

[98] John Chrysostom, *Six Books on the Priesthood* 3.4, trans. Graham Neville (Crestwood, NY: St. Vladimir's Seminary Press, 1964), 70–71.

[99] Ibid., 6.4, p. 140.

[100] John Chrysostom, Homily 2 on 2 Timothy (*NPNF*1, 13:483). See also Homily 50 on Matthew, no. 3 (PG, 58:507): "Believe that there takes place now the

That Christ works through the words of consecration uttered by the priest is again eloquently explained in a homily on Maundy Thursday, *On the Betrayal of Judas*:

> It is not man who causes what is present to become the Body and Blood of Christ, but Christ Himself who was crucified for us. The priest is the representative when he pronounces those words, but the power and the grace are those of the Lord. "This is my Body," he says. This word changes the things that lie before us; and as that sentence "increase and multiply," once spoken, extends through all time and gives to our nature the power to reproduce itself; even so that saying "This is my Body," once uttered, does at every table in the Churches from that time to the present day, and even till Christ's coming, make the sacrifice complete.[101]

This text is also of great importance because it affirms a substantial conversion of the Eucharistic elements and attributes this conversion to the omnipotent power of Christ's words of institution: "This is my Body." He also acknowledges that these words realize the sacrifice.

Although he attributes the Eucharistic conversion (transubstantiation) here to the words of institution, he also attributes great importance to the prayer of the epiclesis in calling down the Holy Spirit to work the transformation of human hearts through the Eucharistic sacrifice and Holy Communion. In *On the Priesthood*, he compares the descent of the Holy Spirit in the Eucharistic sacrifice to the sacrifice performed by Elijah in which the fire of God came down from heaven to consume the offering:

> Would you like to be shown the excellence of this sacred office by another miracle? Imagine in your mind's eye, if you will, Elijah and the vast crowd standing around him and the sacri-

---

same banquet as that in which Christ sat at table, and that this banquet is in no way different from that. For it is not true that this banquet is prepared by a man while that was prepared by Himself" (Quasten, *Patrology*, 3:481).

[101] John Chrysostom, *De Proditione Judae* [On the Betrayal of Judas], homily 1 and an almost identical homily 2 (PG, 49:380, 389), trans. Quasten, *Patrology*, 3:481. See also John H. McKenna, *The Eucharistic Epiclesis: A Detailed History from the Patristic to the Modern Era*, 2nd ed. (Chicago: Hillenbrand Books, 2009), 54.

fice lying upon the stone altar. All the rest are still, hushed in deep silence. The prophet alone is praying. Suddenly fire falls from the skies on to the offering. It is marvelous; it is charged with bewilderment. Turn, then, from that scene to our present rites, and you will see not only marvelous things, but things that transcend all terror. The priest stands bringing down, not fire, but the Holy Spirit. And he offers prayer at length, not that some flame lit from above may consume the offerings, but that grace may fall on the sacrifice through that prayer, set alight the souls of all, and make them appear brighter than silver refined in the fire.[102]

THEODORE OF MOPSUESTIA

Theodore of Mopsuestia († AD 428), who, like St. John Chrysostom, was from the school of Antioch, speaks unambiguously in his instructions to neophytes about the real presence. In his *Baptismal Homilies*, he writes:

> When he gave his apostles the bread he did not say, "This is the symbol of my body," but, "This is my body." So too with the chalice he did not say, "This is the symbol of my blood," but, "This is my blood"—and with good reason. For he wanted us to turn our attention from the nature of the bread and the chalice once they received the grace and the presence of the Lord. . . . But if the life-giving Spirit gave our Lord's body [in the Resurrection] a nature it did not possess before, we too, who have received the grace of the Holy Spirit by sacramental symbols should not regard the offering as bread and chalice any longer, but as the body and blood of Christ. It is the descent of the grace of the Holy Spirit that transforms them, obtaining for those who receive them the gift which we believe the faithful obtain by means of our Lord's body and blood.[103]

---

[102] John Chrysostom, *Six Books on the Priesthood* 3.4 (Neville, *Six Books*, 71).

[103] Theodore of Mopsuestia, Baptismal Homily 4.10–11 (Yarnold, *Awe-Inspiring Rites*, 205–6). For a summary of Theodore's Eucharistic doctrine, see Quasten, *Patrology*, 3:420–421. See also Theodore's commentary on Matthew here: "He [Christ] did not say: 'This is a symbol of My body and this of My blood,' but: 'This is My body and My blood,' teaching us not to consider the nature of the

Theodore also explains that the communicants receive not a portion of Christ, but the whole of Him, whatever the size of the host:

> Eventually, then, all the bread is broken, so that all of us who are present can receive a share. When we receive one little mouthful, we believe that in this mouthful we each receive Christ whole. [104]

Theodore also speaks about how the Mass is a sacrifice that makes present both Calvary and the celestial liturgy:

> But it is evident also that what we perform in the liturgy is a kind of sacrifice. The duty of the High Priest of the New Covenant is to offer this sacrifice which revealed the nature of the New Covenant. It is clearly a sacrifice, although it is not something that is new or accomplished by the efforts of the bishop: it is a recalling of this true offering. Since the bishop performs in symbol signs of the heavenly realities, the sacrifice must manifest them, so that he presents, as it were, an image of the heavenly liturgy. [105]

Theodore says that it is a true sacrifice, for it makes present the one sacrifice of Calvary that is the heart of the celestial liturgy. Theodore is applying to the Mass the teaching of Hebrews 8–10, which speaks of the liturgy of the New Covenant as the icon or image of the heavenly liturgy, whereas the liturgy of the Old Covenant was only its "shadow."[106] Theodore stresses that every Mass offered in every time and place equally makes present the one sacrifice of Christ:

> For we believe that what Christ our Lord performed in reality, and will continue to perform, is performed through the sacraments by those whom divine grace has called to be priests of the New Covenant. . . . This is why they do not offer new sac-

---

laid-out things, but through the accomplished thanksgiving they have been changed into the flesh and blood" (Quasten, *Patrology*, 3:420).

[104] Ibid., 5.19 (Yarnold, *Awe-Inspiring Rites*, 237).

[105] Ibid., 4.15 (Yarnold, *Awe-Inspiring Rites*, 209).

[106] See Heb 10:1: "For since the law has but a shadow of the good things to come instead of the true form [εἰκών] of these realities, it can never, by the same sacrifices which are continually offered year after year, make perfect those who draw near."

rifices, like the repeated immolations prescribed by the Law.
. . . They offered a succession of new victims; when one lot
had been offered, killed and completely destroyed, others were
offered in their place. But with priests of the New Covenant
it is just the reverse: they continue to offer the same sacrifice
in every place and at every time. For there is only one sacrifice
which was offered for us all, the sacrifice of Christ our Lord,
who underwent death for our sake.[107]

St. Cyril of Alexandria

St. Cyril of Alexandria (AD 376–444) affirms the reality of Christ's
life-giving humanity in the Eucharist in the context of his Christological thought and his refutation of the Nestorian heresy. His emphasis
is on the divinizing power of Christ's Flesh and Blood in the Eucharist on account of the hypostatic union. Because Christ's Flesh is that
of a divine Person, it is life-giving, capable of giving us a share in the
divine life and glory. This argument, of course, presupposes the real
and substantial presence of Christ's humanity in the Eucharist. In his
Third Letter against Nestorius, included in the Acts of the Council of
Ephesus, he writes:

> Proclaiming the death according to the flesh of the only
> begotten Son of God, that is, of Jesus Christ, and confess-
> ing his Resurrection from the dead and his Ascension into
> heaven, we celebrate the unbloody sacrifice in the churches,
> and we thus approach the spiritual blessings and are made
> holy, becoming partakers of the holy flesh and of the precious
> blood of Christ, the Savior of us all. And we do this, not as
> men receiving common flesh, far from it, nor truly the flesh
> of a man sanctified and conjoined to the Word according to
> a unity of dignity, or as one having had a divine indwelling,
> but as the truly life-giving and very own flesh of the Word
> himself. For, being life according to nature as God, when he
> was made one with his own flesh, He proclaimed it life-giv-
> ing. Wherefore even if he may say to us, "Amen, I say to you:
> Except you eat the flesh of the Son of Man, and drink his

---

[107] Theodore, Baptismal Homily 4.19 (Yarnold, *Awe-Inspiring Rites*, 212–13).

blood" [John 6:53], we shall not conclude that his flesh is of some one as of a man who is one of us (for how will the flesh of a man be life-giving according to its own nature?), but as being truly the very flesh of the Son who was both made man and named man for us.[108]

Although the emphasis here is on the underlying Christology, St. Cyril brings out its importance for the Eucharist, in which we offer in sacrifice the very Flesh and Blood of the Word Incarnate and receive it in Communion. Three of the canons of the Council of Ephesus (from the twelve anathemas that St. Cyril sent to Nestorius in AD 430) concern the Eucharist. Canon 10 speaks of the priesthood of the Word Incarnate and canon 12 condemns those who do not confess that the Word of God was crucified and died in the flesh, which is life-giving by being the flesh of God. Canon 11 speaks most directly of the Eucharist:

> If anyone does not confess that the flesh of the Lord is life-giving and that it is the flesh of the Word of God himself who is from the Father, but [regards it] as the flesh of someone other than him, united with him in dignity or possessing only divine indwelling, and if he does not confess that it is life-giving, as we have said, because it has become the flesh of the Word himself, who has the power to enliven all things, let him be anathema.[109]

In his commentary on John 6:51, written before the Nestorian controversy, St. Cyril likewise emphasizes the life-giving power of Christ's flesh:

> Therefore, Christ has given his own body for the life of all, and through it he makes life dwell in us again. How he does this I will explain as I am able. Since the life-giving Word of God has taken up residence in the flesh, he has transformed it so that it has his own good attribute, that is, life. And since, in an ineffable mode of union, he has completely come together

---

[108] Cyril of Alexandria, Third Letter Against Nestorius (Letter 17.12), in *Letters, 1–50*, trans. J. I. McEnerney, FC 76 (Washington, DC: Catholic University of America Press, 1987), 86–87.

[109] Anathemas of Cyril of Alexandria (DS, 262).

with it, he has rendered it life-giving, just as he himself is by
nature. For this reason, the body of Christ gives life to those
who participate in it. His body drives out death when that
body enters those who are dying, and it removes decay since it
is fully pregnant with the Word who destroys decay.[110]

The same emphasis is found in his commentary on the words of institution in Luke 22:19–20:

He transforms them [the bread and wine] into the effectiveness of his flesh, that we may have them for a life-giving
participation, that the body of life thus might be found in us
as a life-producing seed. Do not doubt that this is true. Christ
plainly says, "This is my body. This is my blood."[111]

Cyril's belief in a substantial conversion of the elements into
Christ's flesh and blood can also be seen in his commentary on the
words of institution in Matthew 26:27:

But he said quite plainly "This is my body," and "This is my
blood," so that you may not suppose that the things you see
are a type; rather, in some ineffable way they are changed
[μεταποιεσθαι] by God, into the body and blood of Christ
truly offered. Partaking of them, we take into us the life-giving and sanctifying power of Christ.[112]

St. Leo the Great

In the middle of the fifth century, St. Leo affirmed the real presence:

Since the Lord said, "If you do not eat the flesh of the Son of
Man and drink his blood, you will not have life in you," you

---

[110] Cyril of Alexandria, *Commentary on John*, 1:232.

[111] Cyril of Alexandria, *Commentary on Luke*, homily 142, in Arthur Just Jr., *Luke*,
Ancient Christian Commentary on Scripture, New Testament, vol. 3 (Downers
Grove, IL: InterVarsity Press, 2003), 333.

[112] Cyril of Alexandria, *Commentary on Matthew*, 26:27 (PG, 72:512CD), trans.
Lawrence Welch in *Christology and Eucharist in the Early Thought of Cyril of
Alexandria* (San Francisco: Catholic Scholars Press, 1994), 124.

ought to participate in the holy table in such a way that you do not doubt henceforth of the truth of the body and blood of Christ. Faith believes in what the mouth is receiving.[113]

St. Leo also affirms that the Mass is a sacrifice fulfilling the figure of the sacrifice of the Passover lamb with a new and perfect Victim, replacing the blood of the lamb with that of Christ:

In fact, all of those things which had been divinely established through Moses concerning the immolation of the lamb had foretold Christ and had openly announced the killing of Christ. Consequently, that the shadow might yield to the body, and images cease in the presence of truth, the ancient ritual has been replaced by a new mystery, victims pass into the Victim, blood is removed by blood, and the feast held according to the law, in being transformed, was actually being fulfilled. . . . While in the atrium of Caiaphas the manner of killing Christ was being discussed,[114] he himself, establishing the Sacrament of his Body and Blood, taught them what kind of victim ought to be offered to God.[115]

ST. GREGORY THE GREAT

St. Gregory eloquently manifests faith in the sacrificial aspect of the Eucharist in his *Dialogues*, written in AD 593:

We should, therefore, . . . offer our sacrifice of tears to God each day as we immolate His sacred Flesh and Blood. This Sacrifice alone has the power of saving the soul from eternal death, for it presents to us mystically the death of the only-begotten Son. Though He is now risen from the dead and dies no more, and "death has no more power over him," yet, living in Himself immortal and incorruptible, He is again immolated for us in the mystery of the holy Sacrifice. Where His Body is eaten, there His Flesh is distributed among the people

---

[113] Leo the Great, Sermon 91.3 (Freeland and Conway, 384).
[114] See John 11:47–53.
[115] Leo the Great, Sermon 58.2–3 (Freeland and Conway, 249–50).

for their salvation. His Blood no longer stains the hands of the godless, but flows into the hearts of His faithful followers. See, then, how august the Sacrifice that is offered for us, ever reproducing in itself the passion of the only-begotten Son for the remission of our sins. For, who of the faithful can have any doubt that at the moment of the immolation, at the sound of the priest's voice, the heavens stand open and choirs of angels are present at the mystery of Jesus Christ. There at the altar the lowliest is united with the most sublime, earth is joined to heaven, the visible and invisible somehow merge into one.[116]

St. Gregory also stresses the identity of the sacrifice with that of Calvary, for Christ has risen and can die no more. Although he says that Christ "is again immolated for us in the mystery of the holy Sacrifice," the aspect of repetition clearly refers only to the sacramental celebration, "ever reproducing in itself the passion." St. Gregory also highlights the unity of the Church militant and triumphant in the celebration of the sacrifice.

St. John Damascene

St. John Damascene (ca. AD 676–749) is often regarded as the last of the Fathers of the Church and is noted for his synthesis of the previous tradition. He summarizes the thought of the Greek Fathers on the Eucharistic conversion in an admirable way, pointing out how the power of the Word of God manifested in creation and in the Incarnation can also work through the words of Jesus—"This is my body" and "This is my blood"—so as to realize what is signified. This power is attributed to the overshadowing of the Holy Spirit:

If, then, "the word of the Lord is living and effectual" [Heb 4:12], and if "whatsoever the Lord pleased he hath done" [Ps 134:6]; if He said: "Be light made, and it was made"; . . . if by His will God the Word Himself became man and without seed caused the pure and undefiled blood of the blessed Ever-Virgin to form a body for Himself;—if all this, then

---

[116] Gregory the Great, *Dialogues* 4.60, trans. O. J. Zimmerman, FC 39 (Washington, DC: Catholic University of America Press, 1959), 272–73.

can He not make the bread His body and the wine and water His blood? In the beginning He said: "Let the earth bring forth the green herb" [Gen 1:11], and even until now, when the rain falls, the earth brings forth its own shoots under the influence and power of the divine command. God said: "This is my body," and, "This is my blood," and, "This do in commemoration of me," and by His almighty command it is done, until He shall come, for what He said was "until he come." And through the invocation the overshadowing power of the Holy Ghost becomes a rainfall for this new cultivation. For, just as all things whatsoever God made He made by the operation of the Holy Ghost, so also it is by the operation of the Spirit that these things are done which surpass nature and cannot be discerned except by faith alone. "How shall this be done to me," asked the blessed Virgin, "because I know not man?" The archangel Gabriel answered, "The Holy Ghost shall come upon thee and the power of the Most High shall overshadow thee" [Luke 1:34–35]. And now you ask how the bread becomes the body of Christ and the wine and water the blood of Christ. And I tell you that the Holy Ghost comes down and works these things which are beyond description and understanding.[117]

It is interesting that the conversion of the bread and wine into Christ's Body and Blood is attributed both to the power of Christ's words at the Last Supper and to the power of the invocation to the Holy Spirit, who overshadows the gifts as He overshadowed the Blessed Virgin at the Annunciation to realize the Incarnation.

CONCLUSION

The Church Fathers offer clear and eloquent testimony to the Catholic understanding of the Eucharist. They explain that the Eucharist is a sacrament tied to the power of the bishop who has the fullness of the priesthood, that it is the one sacrifice of Christ on Calvary, and that therefore it is indeed His true Body and Blood, His true Flesh given

---

[117] John Damascene, *An Exact Exposition of the Orthodox Faith* 4.13 (Chase, 356–57).

for the life of the world. The continuity and clarity of this teaching throughout the early history of the Church is a luminous revelation of the faith of the Church. As Blessed John Henry Newman famously claimed in the introduction to his great work, *The Development of Doctrine*: "To be deep in history is to cease to be a Protestant."[118]

Study Questions

1. How do some of the Fathers use the Eucharistic faith of the Church to combat Gnosticism or other Christological heresies?
2. In what ways do the Fathers assert the real presence of Christ in the Eucharist?
3. In what ways do the Fathers highlight the sacrificial dimension of the Eucharist?
4. What does the *Didache* say about the Eucharist?
5. What does St. Ignatius of Antioch say about the Eucharist with regard to the presence of Christ, its ecclesial dimension, and its effects?
6. St. Justin Martyr
    a. How does St. Justin describe the Sunday Eucharistic celebration?
    b. What does he say about the presence of Christ in the Eucharist? What effects the Eucharistic conversion according to St. Justin?
    c. What does he say about the Eucharist as a sacrifice?
7. St. Irenaeus
    a. What does St. Irenaeus say about the presence of Christ in the Eucharist?
    b. How does he use the Eucharist in his argument against the Gnostics?
    c. What does he say about the effects of the Eucharist?
8. What are the principal parts of the Eucharistic Prayer given in the *Apostolic Tradition*?
9. What does St. Hilary say about the presence of Christ in the Eucharist? How does he use the Eucharist to combat a Christological heresy?

---

[118] John Henry Cardinal Newman, *An Essay on the Development of Christian Doctrine* (London: Basil Montagu Pickering, 1878), 8.

10. What does St. Cyril of Jerusalem say about the presence of Christ in the Eucharist?
11. What does St. Ambrose say about the presence of Christ in the Eucharist and the Eucharistic conversion?
12. According to St. Augustine, what is the connection between the ecclesial effect of the Eucharist and the real presence of Christ in His Body and Blood?
13. What do St. Gregory Nazianzen and St. Gregory of Nyssa say about the presence of Christ in the Eucharist?
14. What does St. John Chrysostom say about the presence of Christ in the Eucharist?
15. What does St. Cyril of Alexandria say about the presence of Christ in the Eucharist?
16. What does St. Gregory say about the sacrifice of the Mass?

Suggestions for Further Reading

Aquilina, Mike. *The Mass of the Early Christians*. 2nd edition. Huntington, IN: Our Sunday Visitor, 2007.

Billy, Dennis Joseph. *The Beauty of the Eucharist: Voices from the Church Fathers*. Hyde Park, NY: New City Press, 2010.

Lienhard, Joseph T., S.J. "*Sacramentum* and the Eucharist in St. Augustine." *The Thomist* 77 (2013): 173–92.

O'Connor, James T. *The Hidden Manna*. San Francisco: Ignatius, 1988. Pp. 1–85.

Yarnold, Edward. *The Awe-Inspiring Rites of Initiation: The Origins of the RCIA*. Collegeville, MN: The Liturgical Press, 1994.

✠

CHAPTER FIVE

Essential Elements of the Eucharist

THREE LEVELS IN THE EUCHARIST: OUTWARD SIGN, INWARD REALITY AND SIGN, AND THE REALITY OF GRACE

As will be seen below, one of the fruits of the Eucharistic contro-versy in the eleventh century was the distinction between three "levels" in the sacraments.[1] A sacrament is a sacred sign that accom-plishes what it signifies.[2] Being a sensible sign (*sacramentum tantum*) is the first or most sensible level of its reality.[3] The other two levels of a sacrament—the inward reality and sign (*res et sacramentum*) and the reality of grace (*res tantum*)—constitute the hidden realization of the mystery that the outward sign signifies.

St. Augustine explicitly distinguished only two levels of a sacra-ment: the sacramental sign and the reality of grace communicated by it. In explaining why some people do not seem to benefit from receiv-ing the sacraments, he stresses the importance of the disposition of the recipient, who can pose an obstacle to the power of the sacrament, for "the sacrament is one thing, the efficacy of the sacrament another."[4]

---

[1] On the historical development of this threefold distinction, see R. F. King, "The Origin and Evolution of a Sacramental Formula: *Sacramentum Tantum, Res et Sacramentum, Res Tantum,*" *The Thomist* 31 (1967): 21– 82.

[2] For the definition of sacrament, see *ST* III, q. 60, a. 2; Peter Lombard, *Sentences* IV, d. 1, ch. 4, no. 2 (p. 4): "It is a sign of God's grace and a form of invisible grace in such manner that it bears its image and is its cause. And so the sacra-ments were not instituted only for the sake of signifying, but also to sanctify."

[3] See *ST* III, q. 60, a. 1.

[4] Augustine, *In Ioannis Evangelium* 26.10, in *Tractates on the Gospel of John, 11–27* (Rettig, 268).

With regard to the Eucharist, he wrote that the reason the species of bread and wine "are called sacraments is that in them one thing is seen, another is to be understood. What can be seen has a bodily appearance, what is to be understood provides spiritual fruit."[5] Often this distinction is formulated as between the *sacramentum* and the *res sacramenti*.[6] Literally, the latter term means "the thing (or reality) of the sacrament," which refers to the reality imparted by the sacrament, which is the infusion of grace and charity. The two levels that Augustine has discerned can thus be called *sacramentum* and *res*.

As we shall see, this distinction, although certainly true, is inadequate for the Eucharist. Between the sacramental sign and the grace communicated there is another hidden reality: (a) the presence of the Body and Blood of Christ, (b) that is offered in sacrifice, and (c) received in Communion as spiritual nourishment. This invisible reality is signified and realized by the outward sacramental sign, but it is also itself a sign of the grace that is communicated by the offering of the sacrifice and the reception of Holy Communion.

Thus the three levels are: (1) the outward sacramental sign, (2) the reality of the Body and Blood offered in sacrifice, and (3) the grace, charity, and other effects communicated by the sacrifice and the fruitful reception of the Body and Blood[7] that work to build up the ecclesial Body of the Church. The first is an efficacious sign of the second level, which in turn is an efficacious sign of the third level of grace and the unity of the Church. The second and third of these levels correspond to the three fundamental ends of the Eucharist: abiding presence, sacrifice, and intimate union in charity.

Hugh of St. Victor (AD 1096–1141) was among the first to clearly distinguish these three levels:

---

5   Augustine, Sermon 272, in *Sermons (230–272B) on the Liturgical Seasons*, trans. Edmund Hill, WSA, pt. III (Homilies), vol. 7 (New Rochelle, NY: New City Press, 1993), 300.

6   See, for example, *ST* III, q. 80, a. 1, ad 1.

7   St. Jerome alludes to the distinction between the second and third levels—the real presence of the Body and Blood and the Eucharistic grace of spiritual nourishment sanctifying the faithful—but does not develop the insight. In his commentary on Ephesians 1:7 he writes: "Indeed the blood of Christ and body are understood in a twofold sense, either that spiritual and divine, about which he himself said: 'My flesh is truly food . . .' [John 6:55]; and 'Unless you eat my flesh and drink my blood . . .' [John 6:53]; or the flesh and blood which was crucified, and which was shed by the lance of the soldier [John 19:34]" (Kilmartin, *The Eucharist in the West*, 6–7).

For although the sacrament is one, three distinct things are set forth there, namely, visible appearance, truth of body, and virtue of spiritual grace. For the visible species which is perceived visibly is one thing, the truth of body and blood which under visible appearance is believed invisibly another thing, and the spiritual grace which with body and blood is received invisibly and spiritually another.[8]

In Latin, the technical terms to designate these three levels are, respectively: *sacramentum tantum*, *res et sacramentum*, and *res tantum*. These terms were popularized by appearing in the *Sentences* of Peter Lombard (ca. AD 1100–1160), which became the standard scholastic textbook for the following centuries, commented on by most other important scholastic theologians. Peter Lombard writes:

The thing [*res*] of this sacrament is twofold: namely one contained and signified, the other signified and not contained. The thing contained and signified is the flesh of Christ, which he derived from the Virgin, and the blood, which he shed for us. . . . But the thing signified and not contained is "the unity of the Church in those who are predestined, called, justified, and glorified."[9]

And so there are three things to distinguish here: one, which is the sacrament alone [*sacramentum tantum*]; another, which is sacrament and thing [*res et sacramentum*]; a third, which is thing and not sacrament [*res et non sacramentum*]. The sacrament and not thing [*sacramentum et non res*] is the visible species of bread and wine; the sacrament and thing [*res et sacramentum*] is Christ's own flesh and blood; the thing and not sacrament [*res et non sacramentum*] is his mystical flesh.[10]

---

[8] Hugh of St. Victor, *On the Sacraments of the Christian Faith* 2.8.7, trans. Roy J. Deferrari (Cambridge, MA: Mediaeval Academy of America, 1951), 308–9.

[9] Lombard is quoting St. Augustine, *In Joannem* 26.15.

[10] Lombard, *Sentences* IV, d. 8, ch. 7, nos. 1–2 (pp. 44–45). For an appreciation of the achievement of Lombard in working out the doctrine of *sacramentum et res*, see Ludwig Hödl, "Sacramentum und res: Zeichen und Bezeichnetes. Eine begriffsgeschichtliche Arbeit zum frühscholastischen Eucharistietraktat," *Scholastik* 38 (1963): 161–82, esp. 173. It seems that Lombard drew this threefold distinction from Hugh of St. Victor.

By the expression, "mystical flesh," Lombard is referring to the unity of Christ's Mystical Body, which is the ultimate effect of the Eucharist. The following diagram shows the three levels of the Eucharist:

(sensible) sacramental sign (*sacramentum tantum*)	bread and wine
(invisible) reality and sign (*res et sacramentum*)	Body and Blood
(invisible) reality alone (*res tantum*)	grace and charity; unity of the Church

Referring to the Eucharist, Pope Innocent III speaks of these three levels as follows:

> We must, however, distinguish accurately between three [elements] that in this sacrament are distinct; namely, the visible form, the reality of the body, and the spiritual power. The form is of bread and wine; the reality is the flesh and blood; the power is for unity and of charity. The first is "sacrament and not reality"; the second is "sacrament and reality"; the third is "reality and not the sacrament." But, the first is the sacrament of a twofold reality; the second is the sacrament of one [element] and the reality of the other; the third is the reality of a twofold sacrament.[11]

The second and third of these Latin terms are difficult to render into English in such a way that their meaning is understandable. The first term is easily translated as the (outward) sacramental sign. The third term refers to the reality of grace communicated by the sacrament (sacramental grace) that is not a sign of anything else. The difficulty is particularly with the second term, *res et sacramentum*, which signifies a hidden reality (of Christ or Christian identity) that is *also* an efficacious sign of grace, or a hidden mystery that is the sign and cause of grace. "Sacrament" can be used both of the outward sign and of the

---

[11] Innocent III, *Cum Marthae*, Letter of November 29, 1202, to Archbishop John of Lyon (DS, 783).

invisible sign, but "mystery" always refers to the hidden reality. Thus "mystery" better captures the sense of *res et sacramentum*.[12]

A memorable formulation of these three levels is given in the collect for the feast of Corpus Christi (and the rite of benediction), which was composed by St. Thomas Aquinas: "O God, who [1] in this wonderful Sacrament have left us a memorial of your Passion, grant us, we pray, so to revere [2] the sacred mysteries of your Body and Blood [3] that we may always experience in ourselves the fruits of your redemption."[13] The sacrament is wonderful because it contains a twofold mystery—Christ's Body and Blood and His Passion—and grants us the fruits of that Passion in a sharing of His divine life.

A simpler and clearer formulation of these three levels is given in John 6:51: "The bread which I shall give for the life of the world is my flesh." The bread is the outward sacramental sign; the grace-giving mystery is Christ's flesh truly present under the form of bread, and the grace communicated is the "life of the world."

These three levels of the Eucharist will be examined in this and the following chapters. In this chapter we shall look at the first level, the sacramental sign in the Eucharist. In chapters 6–8 we shall examine the *res et sacramentum*, which is the real presence of the Body and Blood of Christ, which becomes present through transubstantiation. Christ's real presence, the first end of the Eucharist, makes possible the two other principal ends of the Eucharist. The first of these is the sacrifice, made present through the substantial conversion of the bread and wine into Christ's Body and Blood on the altar and offered by the priest acting in the person of Christ. This will be the subject of chapters 9–12. The sacrifice can be seen as a second dimension of the *res et sacramentum*, for it is a hidden reality represented by the visible species and words of the Eucharistic Prayer, and at the same time it is

---

[12] Alger of Liège, in his treatise on the Eucharist against Berengarius makes this distinction between the Latin *sacramentum* and *mysterium* (*De Sacramentis Corporis et Sanguinis Dominici* 1.4: "It should be understood that sacrament and mystery differ in this, that sacrament is a visible sign that signifies something, whereas mystery refers to that hidden thing signified by it" (PL, 180:751).

[13] *RM*, 499. For the Latin original, see *Missale Romanum: Ex Decreto SS. Concilii Tridentini Restitutum Summorum Pontificum Cura Recognitum* (Vatican City: Typis Polyglottis Vaticanis, 1962), 1:375: "Deus, qui nobis [1] sub *sacramento* mirabili, passionis tuae memoriam reliquisti, tribue, quæsumus, [2] ita nos Córporis et Sánguinis tui sacra mystéria venerári; [3] ut redemptiónis tuæ fructum in nobis iúgiter sentiámus."

a sign of the bloody sacrifice of Calvary, of the interior oblation of the faithful, and of the fruits of the sacrifice.[14]

The third level of the Eucharist corresponds with its third end, which is intimate communion with Christ in His Mystical Body. This is brought about by receiving the substantial presence of the sacrificial Victim in Holy Communion, through which grace and charity are imparted and the Church is thereby built up in unity and supernatural life. This reality of grace (*res tantum*) thus has both a personal and a social or ecclesial dimension. Grace is received by each person individually, and the unity of the Church is thereby brought about and deepened. In chapter 13 we shall look at Holy Communion and its effects.

SACRAMENTAL SIGNS AS INSTRUMENTS OF CHRIST

The Sacraments Are Instrumental Causes

The Word became flesh so that His humanity would be the instrument for the salvation of all men of all times. However, since Jesus lived as a man on this earth for a short time in a tiny part of the world, He desired some way to make Himself present as man to succeeding ages. While leaving us in the darkness of faith, with the corresponding possibility of merit, He still wishes that we truly encounter His humanity and its salvific power. The sacraments are the divinely appointed means for this encounter in faith. They offer this encounter with Christ by functioning as instruments of His humanity. They sanctify us by providing a mysterious contact with Christ's humanity even after He has physically ascended into heaven.

The seven sacraments have a capacity to efficiently cause the grace they signify. But how can sensible signs cause grace? Since sanctifying grace is a participation in the divine nature (see 2 Pet 1:4), grace can be produced in a creature only through the omnipotence of God. How then are the sacraments true causes of grace? The problem would be insoluble without the notion of instrumental causality.[15]

---

[14] For the sacrifice of the Mass as *res et sacramentum*, see below, chapter 9, pp. 364–66. See also Masure, *The Sacrifice of the Mystical Body*, 23–25.

[15] For the historical development of the Thomistic doctrine of sacramental causality as instrumental efficient causality, see Reginald Lynch, O.P, "The Sac-

Philosophers speak of instrumental causality when a cause produces its effect by means of a subordinate agent. This subordinate agent is called an instrument or instrumental cause, which is an efficient cause that produces an effect higher than itself by executing a design that does not originate in itself but in a higher cause, referred to as the principal cause, which moves the instrument directly or indirectly. The artist's paintbrush, for example, is an instrumental cause that executes an intention that originates in the artist's mind, which is the principal cause of the artwork.

In living things, the organs are instruments of the soul to achieve its vital functions. Our senses, hands, feet, voice, and so on are all instruments of our soul. All human technology makes use of instruments and instrumental causality. All our tools are instruments to enhance the capacity of our natural instruments, which are our hands, eyes, ears, and other organs. The paintbrush is the instrument of the painter's hand, which is the instrument of his imagination, intellect, and will. The telescope is an instrument of the eye, which is the instrument of the mind.

What is the relationship between the instrumental and the principal causes? The instrumental cause *serves* the principal cause, and the effect is produced through the cooperation of the instrumental cause with the principal cause that is directing it. The canvas is painted by the paintbrush under the direction of the hand, eye, mind, and will of the artist. In this way, the paintbrush produces an effect that it could never have achieved without this superior direction and impulse stemming from the artist's mind. The instrument thus produces an effect that surpasses the capacity of its own form taken by itself.

How can a thing be a true cause of an effect that is higher than itself? The instrument seems to violate a first principle of reason: nothing can give what it does not have. The paintbrush produces something it does not have: an intelligible and beautiful design. The violation, however, is only apparent, and instrumental causality provides an explanation for it. The instrument gives what it does not have, but only insofar as it is moved by a superior cause that *does* have what is communicated to the effect. The effect transcends the power of the instrumental cause taken alone and manifests the power of the principal cause that moved and directed the instrumental cause. Therefore,

raments as Causes of Sanctification," *Nova et Vetera* (English) 12, no. 3 (2014): 791–836; Lynch, "Cajetan's Harp: Sacraments and the Life of Grace in Light of Perfective Instrumentality," *The Thomist* 78 (2014): 65–106.

the effect is attributed most properly to the principal cause, which is the artist, and only secondarily to the paintbrush, chisel, pen, violin, or orchestra.[16] Aquinas writes:

> An efficient cause is twofold: principal and instrumental. The principal cause works by the power of its form, to which form the effect is likened; just as fire by its own heat makes something hot. In this way none but God can cause grace. . . . But the instrumental cause works not by the power of its form, but only by the motion whereby it is moved by the principal agent: so that the effect is not likened to the instrument but to the principal agent: for instance, the couch is not like the axe, but like the art which is in the craftsman's mind. [17]

In other words, instrumental causality is present when, through the impulse and direction of a superior cause, an inferior cause is elevated above its own level, and made capable of producing an effect that transcends its proper capacity taken alone.[18] Instrumental causes are moved movers, which can create effects only insofar as they are moved themselves by a higher cause, as the paintbrush is moved by the artist's hand and mind.[19]

There are many examples of instrumental causality in theology, for it occurs whenever anything acts as an instrument of God and of His plan. The sacred writers of the books of Scripture wrote as instrumental causes inspired by the Holy Spirit. Ultimately all creatures and their operations are instruments, each in their own way, of God's providence, which directs all things to their ends for the realization of God's plan in the universe. Even the humanity of Christ works as an instrumental cause[20] moved by the divinity, and the sacraments also are clearly instrumental causes, serving as "extensions" of the humanity of Christ so that He can touch us today with the

---

[16] See *ST* I-II, q. 16, a. 1: "An action is not properly attributed to the instrument, but to the principal agent." See also *In IV Sent.*, d. 47, q. 2, a. 1, qla. 3, ad 2.

[17] *ST* III, q. 62, a. 1.

[18] See the discussion of instrumental causality in Feingold, *Faith Comes from What Is Heard*, 289–90.

[19] See Thomas Aquinas, *De Veritate*, q. 27, a. 4: "It is the nature of an instrument as instrument to move something else when moved itself" (*Truth*, trans. Robert W. Schmidt, S.J. [Chicago: Henry Regnery, 1954], 3:332).

[20] See *ST* III q. 2, a. 6, ad 4.

salvific power that He merited for us in His Passion.

During His public ministry Christ spoke with authority, and devils were expelled, winds were calmed, lepers healed, the blind were given sight, the sick healed, the dead were raised, and sinners were forgiven and reconciled. Theologians refer to these actions as "theandric," which means divine-human. It is a term applied to certain actions of Christ in which we see the complementary operation of both natures, divine and human, at the same time, each acting in the way proper to it. We see this, for example, when Christ worked miracles. He spoke with His human voice and touched with His hands, but the power that caused the miracle came from His divine omnipotence. His human words and gestures were the instrument for the exercise of His divine power.

As the divine omnipotence alone can work miracles above the power of all creatures, so God alone is the principal cause of the infusion of grace in the soul that produces justification and sanctification. However, there is nothing to prevent God from producing this effect by means of instruments situated in the created and sensible order, as long as they are moved by Him, as were Jesus's words and gestures when He worked miracles and when He instituted the Eucharist at the Last Supper. As the mind of the artist produces beauty in a statue by means of his hands and chisels, so God worked miracles through Christ's words and gestures, and in like manner, He produces grace in the soul by means of Christ's humanity (through which all grace was merited), and through the sacraments, as if they were chisels or paintbrushes in the hands of Christ.

Without using the terminology of "instrumental cause," Peter Lombard, writing in the middle of the twelfth century, made use of the concept of instrumentality in his explanation of how the words uttered by a merely human minister can work the forgiveness of sins in Baptism or Penance:

> To which it may be said that he was able to give them the power to remit sins: not the same power by which he himself is powerful, but a created power, by which a servant may be able to remit sins, and yet not as the author of the remission, but as its minister, and yet not without God as author: just as the minister has it as part of his ministry that he sanctify outwardly, so he might have it in his ministry to cleanse inwardly; and just as he does the former with God as author, who with him and in him works that outwardly, so he might cleanse

interiorly, with God as author, who would make use of his word as if of some ministry.[21]

As an instrumental power to remit sins has been given to the words of absolution and Baptism, so the power to transubstantiate is given to the words Christ used at the Last Supper, when spoken by a rightly ordained priestly minister.

External and Conjoined Instruments

There are actually two levels of instrumental causes in play in all human arts, as well as in the sacraments. The hands, eyes, ears, and voice of an artist are instruments of the mind of the artist, who is the principal cause. We can call these organs "conjoined instruments" because they are intrinsically joined to the person of the artist. However, the chisels, paintbrushes, trumpets, flutes, spoken words, and so on are *external* and *separated* instruments. Normally, we make use of separated instruments by means of the conjoined instruments of our hands.

If we apply this distinction to the sacraments, it is clear that the sacramental signs are *separated* and *extrinsic* instruments of God the Son, whereas His sacred humanity is an instrument most intimately *conjoined* to His divinity in the unity of His one divine Person through the hypostatic union. Thus the sacramental signs are separated instruments wielded, through the mediation of a minister, by the humanity of Christ, who merited their efficacy and instituted them. St. Thomas explains:

> A sacrament works to cause grace in the manner of an instrument, of which there are two kinds. One kind is separate, as in the case of a stick; the other is united, as a hand. Now the separate instrument is moved by means of the united instrument, as a stick by the hand. The principal efficient cause of grace is God Himself, in comparison with whom Christ's humanity is a united instrument, whereas the sacrament is a separate instrument. It is necessary, therefore, that the saving power in the sacraments be derived from Christ's divinity through His humanity.[22]

---

[21] Lombard, *Sentences* IV, d. 5, ch. 3, no. 3 (p. 31).

[22] *ST* III, q. 62, a. 5 (my translation from the Latin of the Leonine edition).

The sacraments function as separated instruments in the hand of Christ (through the mediation of a sacred minister) that extend the reach of His sacred humanity to all men throughout the world and throughout the time from His Ascension to the Second Coming. For this reason, they could be instituted only directly by Him.

Because the Word Incarnate merited all grace for mankind in His Passion, God does not will to bypass the humanity of Christ when He infuses that grace into our souls. The infusion of grace makes use of Christ's humanity as the great conjoined instrument who works through the sacraments as His extrinsic instruments. The Church is created by contact with Christ's humanity through the instruments by which His humanity touches us—the chisels and paintbrushes, so to speak—which are the sacraments.

There are actually two kinds of extrinsic instruments in the sacraments. The minister who acts intentionally in the person of Christ is a living instrument of Christ, as are the words, gestures, and things (matter and form of the sacraments) that the minister makes use of. Thus the divine power makes use of Christ's humanity, which makes use of a human minister as a living but separated instrument, who makes use of words, gestures, and things.

The sacrament of Holy Orders enables the ordained priest or bishop to act as a living instrument of the humanity of Christ so as to administer the sacraments *in persona Christi capitis* (in the person of Christ, the head of the Church). It follows from this that the sacrament of Holy Orders is crucial to the sacramental economy, because the priest is the sacramental link between the conjoined instrument—the humanity of Christ—and the other extrinsic instruments of the Godhead in the application of grace to souls. The priest, as one who acts in the person of Christ, enables Christ to realize the other sacraments through the ordained minister and apply them to souls.[23] As Jesus spoke words of power in His public ministry, so through His sacramental ministers He continues to speak efficacious words of power in every valid celebration of the sacraments.

The Eucharist is unique among the sacraments because it does not

---

[23] There are two exceptions to this. Because of the necessity of Baptism, Christ willed that, in extraordinary circumstances such as danger of death, any person can serve as the minister that makes Christ's voice present. Nevertheless, the ordinary minister is the bishop, priest, or deacon, as prescribed in CIC, can. 861. The other exception is matrimony in which the ministers are the spouses.

function merely as a separated instrument wielded by Christ through the ministry of His priests, but on account of the substantial presence of Christ's humanity in the sacrament, the Eucharist *alone* functions as a *conjoined* instrument. Receiving Christ in the Eucharist, we receive the humanity of the Redeemer who merited all grace on Calvary, which humanity is hypostatically joined to the divinity, the Author of grace.

✳ The sacramental sign of the Eucharist—composed of the bread and wine and the words of Christ at the Last Supper pronounced by the priestly minister—is the *separated* instrumental cause for bringing about the real presence of Christ's Body and Blood, the *res et sacramentum*, which is the second level of the Eucharist. The Body and Blood of Christ then serves as the *conjoined* instrumental cause for bringing about the third level of the Eucharist, the *res tantum*, which is the infusion of grace and charity as the spiritual nourishment of the soul with supernatural life. By receiving His humanity, we are given a share in His divinity.

Matter of the Eucharist

Matter and Form in the Sacraments

The sacramental sign itself is composed of two parts, which theologians, beginning in the twelfth century, speak of in terms of "matter" and "form," by analogy with the hylomorphic composition of all bodies. The "matter" is comprised of sensible things (such as water, bread, and wine) and gestures (such as pouring). However, since sensible objects and gestures can signify many different things, words are necessary to specify the exact symbolism that is being both represented and realized. This formula of words that specifies the meaning of the sign more precisely is called the "form" of the sacrament. It "signifies what is effected in the sacrament."[24] As the form determines the indeterminate matter of physical bodies and makes a thing to be what it is, so likewise in the sacraments, the formula of words determines the sensible sign consisting of a material element or gesture to a particular meaning.[25] The

---

[24] *CCT*, part 2, ch. 3, §19 (p. 220). On matter and form in the sacraments, see Roger Nutt, *General Principles of Sacramental Theology*, 67–73.

[25] See Leo XIII, Encyclical on the Nullity of Anglican Orders, *Apostolicae Curae* (1896), §24: "In the examination of any rite for the effecting and administering of Sacraments, distinction is rightly made between the part which is ceremonial

sensible conjunction of the matter and form (together with the proper minister and subject) realizes the sacramental sign.

The classical expression of this understanding of matter and form as, respectively, "potency" and "act" in the sacraments comes from St. Augustine, who, speaking of Baptism, says:

> Take away the word, and what is the water except water? The word is added to the elemental substance, and it becomes a sacrament, also itself, as it were, a visible word. . . . Whence is this power of water of such magnitude that it touches the body and yet washes clean the heart, except from the word's effecting it, not because it is said, but because it is believed? For also in the word itself the passing sound is one thing, the abiding power another.[26]

An example of this distinction of matter and form is implied by St. Paul in Ephesians 5:26 when he says that Christ gave himself up for the Church, His bride, "that he might sanctify her, having cleansed her by the washing of water with the word." The washing of water is the matter of the sacrament, and the form is the word. This word would be the baptismal formula given by Christ in Matthew 28:19.

This idea is also present in St. Irenaeus, who speaks of the Eucharist being made when "the mingled cup and the manufactured bread receives the Word of God."[27] The bread and wine are the matter, and the "Word of God" presumably refers to the prayer of consecration (institution narrative), which is the form. The distinction of matter and form is evident in five sacraments, but is less clear in the Sacraments of Matrimony and Penance, in which there is no external physical element or gesture that functions as the matter.[28]

This distinction between matter and form is taught by the Council

---

and that which is essential, the latter being usually called the 'matter and form.' . . . Although the signification ought to be found in the whole essential rite, that is to say, in the 'matter and form,' it still pertains chiefly to the 'form'; since the 'matter' is the part which is not determined by itself, but which is determined by the 'form.'"

[26] Augustine, Tractate 80.3 (on John 15:3) (Rettig, *Tractates on the Gospel of John 55–111*, 117–18).

[27] St. Irenaeus, *Against Heresies* 5.2.3 (ANF 1:528).

[28] For the development of the doctrine on the composition of matter and form in the sacraments, see P. Pourrat, *Theology of the Sacraments: A Study in Positive Theology* (St. Louis, MO: B. Herder, 1910), 51–92.

of Florence in the bull *Exsultate Deo*, which also mentions the proper minister as a third component:

> All these sacraments are realized by the presence of three components, namely, by things as the matter, by words as the form, and by the person of the minister conferring the sacrament with the intention of doing what the Church does. If any of these are lacking the sacrament is not realized.[29]

Fittingness of Bread and Wine

The essential matter for the Eucharist is what was used by Christ at the Last Supper. He would have celebrated the Last Supper with wheat bread and with wine from the grape, mixed with a little water. The *Code of Canon Law* (*Codex Iuris Canonici* [CIC]), canon 924, §1, specifies: "The most holy Eucharistic sacrifice must be offered with bread and with wine in which a little water must be mixed." Sections 2 and 3 of the canon state that the bread must be "only wheat and recently made so that there is no danger of spoiling." The wine must be "natural from the fruit of the vine and not spoiled."

Why did Christ pick wheat bread and grape wine to be the essential matter of this sacrament? Various reasons converge in this choice. First, bread and wine naturally represent all nourishment, and the Eucharist is the sacrament of spiritual nourishment. As water is the most common means of washing and thus is an apt symbol for the purification caused by Baptism, so bread and wine are among the most common forms of food and drink in the cultures of the world.[30] Secondly, bread and wine have a fitting appearance to represent Christ's Body and Blood. Their separate consecration sacramentally represents the separation of Christ's Body and Blood in His Passion.[31] This

---

[29] Council of Florence, *Exsultate Deo* (DS, 1312). In addition to the matter, form, and proper minister with the intention of realizing the sacrament, there must also be a proper subject who, if of the age of reason, intends to receive the sacrament.

[30] See *ST* III, q. 74, a. 1: "And the reasonableness of this is seen first, in the use of this sacrament, which is eating: for, as water is used in the sacrament of Baptism for the purpose of spiritual cleansing, since bodily cleansing is commonly done with water; so bread and wine, wherewith men are commonly fed, are employed in this sacrament for the use of spiritual eating."

[31] See *ST* III, q. 74, a. 1.

secondary symbolism of bread and wine is similar to the secondary symbolism of immersion into the baptismal water, which symbolizes participation in Christ's death and Resurrection. Third, bread and wine are made out of many grains of wheat and many grapes. This symbolizes the principal invisible effect of the Eucharist, which is the unity of the Church composed of many members that are bound together in charity in the communion of one Body.[32] This sense is indicated by St. Paul in 1 Corinthians 10:17: "Because there is one bread, we who are many are one body, for we all partake of the one bread."[33] St. Augustine explains, with reference to the words of John 6:55:

> He says, "For my flesh is food indeed, and my blood is drink indeed." For although by food and drink men strive for this, that they hunger not and thirst not, only this food and drink truly offer this; for it makes those by whom it is taken immortal and incorruptible, that is, the very society of saints, where there will be peace and full and perfect unity. For this reason, indeed, even as men of God knew this before us, our Lord, Jesus Christ, manifested his body and blood in those things which are reduced from many to some one thing. For the one is made into one thing from many grains, the other flows together into one thing from many grapes.[34]

In addition to representing the Passion, wine is also an apt symbol of one of the effects of Holy Communion, which is to inebriate the spirit by infusing it with supernatural charity and joy. St. Cyprian writes:

> Thus the Chalice of the Lord inebriates. . . . But because the inebriation of the Chalice and of the Blood of the Lord is

---

[32] See ibid. See also Lombard, *Sentences* IV, d. 8, ch. 7, no. 2: "It also has the likeness of a mystical thing, which is the unity of the faithful, because, just as one loaf of bread is made from many grains, and wine flows into one from many grapes, so the unity of the Church is composed out of the many persons of the faithful" (p. 45).

[33] *Didache* 9.4 also gives this ecclesial meaning: "Just as this broken bread was scattered upon the mountains and then was gathered together and became one, so may your church be gathered together from the ends of the earth into your kingdom" (Holmes, *The Apostolic Fathers: Greek Texts and English Translations*, 359).

[34] Augustine, *In Ioannis* 26.17 (Rettig, *Tractates on the Gospel of John, 11–27*, 274). For a good summary of the symbolism of the bread and wine, see Lombard, *Sentences* IV, d. 8, ch. 7, no. 2 (p. 45).

not such as the inebriation coming from worldly wine, when the Holy Spirit says in the Psalms: "Your chalice which inebriates," he adds, "how excellent it is!"[35] because, actually, the Chalice of the Lord so inebriates that it makes sober, that it raises minds to spiritual wisdom, that from this taste of the world each one comes to the knowledge of God and, as the mind is relaxed by that common wine and the soul is relaxed and all sadness is cast away, so, when the Blood of the Lord and the life-giving cup have been drunk, the memory of the old man is cast aside and there is induced forgetfulness of former worldly conversation and the sorrowful and sad heart which was formerly pressed down with distressing sins is now relaxed by the joy of the divine mercy.[36]

Wheat Bread

The bread for the Eucharist must be made of wheat for the sacrament to be valid. This is because wheat bread is the most common form of bread and because it was what was used by Christ at the Last Supper. St. Thomas explains:

> For the use of the sacraments such matter is adopted as is commonly made use of among men. Now among other breads wheaten bread is more commonly used by men; since other breads seem to be employed when this fails. And consequently Christ is believed to have instituted this sacrament under this species of bread. Moreover this bread strengthens man, and so it denotes more suitably the effect of this sacrament. Consequently, the proper matter for this sacrament is wheaten bread.[37]

Those who cannot tolerate wheat, such as people with celiac disease, should arrange to receive the chalice alone or arrange to receive a very low gluten host.

---

[35] See Ps 22 (23):5 in the *Vetus Latina* translation.

[36] St. Cyprian, Letter 63.11 (Donna, *Letters*, 210).

[37] *ST* III, q. 74, a. 3.

Bread Is Unleavened in the Latin Rite

In the Latin rite, the bread must be unleavened, according to CIC, canon 926. This practice reflects the fact that Christ instituted the Last Supper on the first night of Passover, and so He would have used unleavened bread. In the Eastern tradition, however, leavened bread is used.[38]

St. Thomas poses the question in the *Summa of Theology* as to whether the matter for the Eucharist is leavened or unleavened bread, and responds as follows:

> Two things may be considered touching the matter of this sacrament namely, what is necessary, and what is suitable. It is necessary that the bread be wheaten, without which the sacrament is not valid, as stated above. It is not, however, necessary for the sacrament that the bread be unleavened or leavened, since it can be celebrated in either.
>
> But it is suitable that every priest observe the rite of his Church in the celebration of the sacrament. Now in this matter there are various customs of the Churches: for, Gregory says: "The Roman Church offers unleavened bread, because our Lord took flesh without union of sexes: but the Greek Churches offer leavened bread, because the Word of the Father was clothed with flesh; as leaven is mixed with the flour." Hence, as a priest sins by celebrating with fermented bread in the Latin Church, so a Greek priest celebrating with unfermented bread in a church of the Greeks would also sin, as perverting the rite of his Church. Nevertheless the custom of celebrating with unleavened bread is more reasonable. First, on account of Christ's institution: for He instituted this sacrament "on the first day of the Azymes" (Matthew 26:17; Mark 14:12; Luke 22:7), on which day there ought to be nothing fermented in the houses of the Jews, as is stated in Exodus 12:15–19. Secondly, because bread is properly the sacrament of Christ's body, which was conceived without corruption, rather than of His Godhead, as will be seen later (76, 1, ad

---

[38] See Bruce Marshall, "What Is the Eucharist? A Dogmatic Outline," In Hans Boersma and Matthew Levering, eds., *The Oxford Handbook of Sacramental Theology* (New York: Oxford University Press, 2015), 504.

1). Thirdly, because this is more in keeping with the sincerity of the faithful, which is required in the use of this sacrament, according to 1 Corinthians 5:7: "Christ our Pasch is sacrificed: therefore let us feast . . . with the unleavened bread of sincerity and truth."

However, this custom of the Greeks is not unreasonable both on account of its signification, to which Gregory refers, and in detestation of the heresy of the Nazarenes,[39] who mixed up legal observances with the Gospel.[40]

Wine of the Grape

The wine for the Eucharist must be wine from the grape,[41] for this was what was used by Christ, as we can see in Matthew 26:29: "I shall not drink again of this fruit of the vine." Furthermore, wine from the grape is the most common form of wine.[42]

Mixture of Water with the Wine

The *Code of Canon Law* states that the Eucharist must be offered with "wine in which a little water must be mixed" (canon 924, §1). St. Thomas gives four reasons for the mixture of water with the wine. First, it reflects the actual usage of Jesus, according to the custom of

---

[39] The Nazarenes were Jewish Christians of the early Church who continued to practice the ceremonial laws of Moses. This would include the use of unleavened bread during Passover.

[40] *ST* III, q. 74, a. 4.

[41] See CIC, can. 924, §3: "The wine must be natural wine of the grape and not corrupt."

[42] *ST* III, q. 74, a. 5:

> This sacrament can only be performed with wine from the grape. First of all on account of Christ's institution, since He instituted this sacrament in wine from the grape, as is evident from His own words, in instituting this sacrament (Matt 26:29): "I will not drink from henceforth of this fruit of the vine." Secondly, because, as stated above (a. 3), that is adopted as the matter of the sacraments which is properly and universally considered as such. Now that is properly called wine, which is drawn from the grape, whereas other liquors are called wine from resemblance to the wine of the grape. Thirdly, because the wine from the grape is more in keeping with the effect of this sacrament, which is spiritual; because it is written (Ps 103:15): "That wine may cheer the heart of man."

the day.[43] Secondly, St. Thomas also sees the mixing of water with the wine as an allusion to the water and blood that came forth from Christ's pierced side, thus signifying His Passion. Third and most importantly, the water symbolizes our participation with Christ in His sacrifice and through the effects of Holy Communion. The mixing of water and wine thus symbolizes the ultimate effect of the Eucharist (*res tantum*), which is the unity of the Church with Christ. St. Cyprian writes: "We see that people are signified in the water, but in the wine the Blood of Christ is shown. But when water is mixed with wine in the Chalice, the people are united to Christ, and the multitude of the believers is bound and joined to Him in whom they believe."[44] Finally, St. Thomas sees the mixture of water into the wine as signifying the pledge of eternal life. As the water becomes wine when it is mixed, so our mortal nature will put on immortality through the work of Christ's redemption.[45]

The Council of Florence[46] and the *Catechism of the Council of Trent* give the same reasons. The latter explains:

---

[43] *ST* III, q. 74, a. 6: "It is believed with probability that our Lord instituted this sacrament in wine tempered with water according to the custom of that country."

[44] St. Cyprian, Letter 63.13 (Donna, *Letters*, 211). This text is quoted by St. Thomas in *ST* III, q. 74, a. 6, where he attributes it to Pope Julius (fourth synod of Braga, can. 1, which quotes St. Cyprian).

[45] *ST* III, q. 74, a. 6: "Fourthly, because this is appropriate to the fourth effect of this sacrament, which is the entering into everlasting life: hence Ambrose says (*De Sacram.* 5): 'The water flows into the chalice, and springs forth unto everlasting life.'"

[46] Council of Florence, *Exsultate Deo*, takes up the explanation of St. Thomas:

> Water is mixed in because . . . it is believed that our Lord himself instituted this sacrament with wine mixed with water. Furthermore, this is a fitting representation of our Lord's Passion. . . . For we read that both, that is, blood and water, flowed from the side of Christ. Finally, this is a fitting way to signify the effect of this sacrament, that is, the union of the Christian people with Christ. For, water represents the people, as the Apocalypse says: "Many waters . . . many peoples" [Rev 17:15]. According to the prescription of the canons, the Lord's chalice should be offered with wine mixed with water. For we see that the water represents the people and the wine manifests the blood of Christ. Thus, when wine and water are mixed in the chalice, the people are united with Christ, and the faithful people are closely joined to him in whom they believe. (DS, 1320)

To the sacramental wine the Church has always added water, because, as we know from various councils and particularly from St. Cyprian, our Lord himself did so. This mingling of wine and water also recalls the flow of both blood and water from his sacred side. And finally, because water is used in Revelation to signify the people (Rev 17:15), the mixture of water with wine signifies the union of the faithful with Christ their Head. This practice, derived from Apostolic tradition, has always been observed in the Catholic Church.[47]

The third meaning is indicated in the beautiful offertory prayer: "By the mystery of this water and wine may we come to share in the divinity of Christ who humbled himself to share in our humanity."[48]

In other words, the mixing of water and wine signifies first the union of the two natures in Christ: divinity symbolized by the wine and humanity symbolized by the water. But the Son of God assumed our humanity so that we would receive a share in His divinity. Thus the commingling of water and wine also signifies the divinization of man, who, through the mystery of the Eucharist, is given a share in the life of Christ and is inserted more deeply into the communion of the Church. The water added to the wine is not necessary for validity, but for licitness. Only a small quantity of water should be used.[49]

The Eucharist Must Be Consecrated under Both Species

Canon 927 of the *Code of Canon Law* states that "it is absolutely forbidden, even in extreme urgent necessity, to consecrate one matter without the other . . . or even both outside the eucharistic celebration." The dual consecration is necessary to realize the sacramental sign of Christ's sacrifice, for it sacramentally re-presents the separation of Christ's Blood from His Body. Without the consecration of both species, Christ's sacrifice would not be sacramentally realized.

---

[47] *CCT*, pt. 2, ch. 3, §16 (p. 218).

[48] *RM*, 529.

[49] See *CCT*, pt. 2, ch. 3, §17: "This addition of water to the wine is required for liceity; its deliberate omission is gravely sinful. However, such an omission would not invalidate the consecration. The priest must be careful, therefore, to add water to the wine; but at the same time he must add it in only small quantity" (p. 218).

The Essential Form of the Eucharist

As stated above, the notion of sacramental "form" refers to the words used in the celebration of the sacrament that specify the meaning of the sacramental sign more precisely than the material elements themselves can do, thereby signifying the substance of "what is effected in the sacrament."[50] The essential form does not include all of the words used in the sacramental liturgy, but only the substance of those words that directly express what the sacrament realizes as an efficacious sign.

Since the sacraments have been entrusted to her by the Lord, the Church has the power to shape the form and celebration of the sacraments while preserving their substance. The Council of Trent states this important principle:

> [The holy Council] declares that, in the administration of the sacraments—provided their substance is preserved—there has always been in the Church that power to determine or modify what she judged more expedient for the benefit of those receiving the sacraments or for the reverence due to the sacraments themselves—according to the diversity of circumstances, times, and places. This, moreover, is what the apostle seems to have indicated rather clearly when he said: "This is how one should regard us, as servants of Christ and stewards of the mysteries of God" [1 Cor 4:1].[51]

It follows from this principle that there can be different formulas used in different liturgical rites that express the same fundamental substance of the sacrament. A recent example of this shaping occurred when Paul VI established the words of the form in the Novus Ordo of the Roman rite as follows:

> However, for pastoral reasons, and in order to facilitate concelebration, we have ordered that the words of the Lord ought to be identical in each formulary of the Canon. Thus, in each Eucharistic Prayer, we wish that the words be pronounced thus: over the bread: ACCIPITE ET MANDUCATE EX HOC

---

[50] Ibid., §19 (p. 220).
[51] The Council of Trent, Doctrine of Communion under Both Kinds and the Communion of Little Children (session 21, July 16, 1562), ch. 2 (DS, 1728).

OMNES: HOC EST ENIM CORPUS MEUM, QUOD PRO VOBIS TRADETUR;[52] over the chalice: ACCIPITE ET BIBITE EX EO OMNES: HIC EST ENIM CALIX SANGUINIS MEI NOVI ET AETERNI TESTAMENTI, QUI PRO VOBIS ET PRO MULTIS EFFUNDETUR IN REMISSIONEM PECCATORUM. HOC FACITE IN MEAM COMMEMORATIONEM.[53] The words MYSTE-RIUM FIDEI, taken from the context of the words of Christ the Lord, and said by the priest, serve as an introduction to the acclamation of the faithful.[54]

The notion of essential form is tied to that of the validity of the sacraments. For a sacrament to be valid, there must be proper matter and the essential form, together with a proper minister who intends to do what the Church does.[55] If a minister alters the words such that the essential meaning is substantially changed, then the form is no longer valid. If the words are deliberately altered, but such that the meaning is not essentially changed, it will be valid but illicit.[56] What is significant is not the words taken materially, but their meaning, for sacraments are sacred signs that realize what they signify. St. Thomas explains: "The aforesaid words, which work the consecration, operate sacramentally. Consequently, the converting power latent under the forms of these sacraments follows the meaning, which is terminated in the uttering of the last word."[57]

---

[52] In English according to *RM*: "TAKE THIS, ALL OF YOU, AND EAT OF IT, FOR THIS IS MY BODY, WHICH WILL BE GIVEN UP FOR YOU."

[53] In English according to *RM*: "TAKE THIS, ALL OF YOU, AND DRINK FROM IT, FOR THIS IS THE CHALICE OF MY BLOOD, THE BLOOD OF THE NEW AND ETERNAL COVENANT, WHICH WILL BE POURED OUT FOR YOU AND FOR MANY FOR THE FORGIVE-NESS OF SINS. DO THIS IN MEMORY OF ME."

[54] Paul VI, Apostolic Constitution, *Missale Romanum* (1969), accessed June 28, 2017, http://w2.vatican.va/content/paul-vi/en/apost_constitutions/docu-ments/hf_p-vi_apc_19690403_missale-romanum.html.

[55] Council of Florence, *Exsultate Deo*: "All these sacraments are realized by the presence of three components, namely, by things as the matter, by words as the form, and by the person of the minister conferring the sacrament with the intention of doing what the Church does. If any of these are lacking the sacra-ment is not realized" (DS, 1312).

[56] See *Missale Romanum: Ex Decreto SS. Concilii Tridentini*, 1:lxvii.

[57] *ST* III, q. 78, a. 4, ad 3.

At first sight the essential form of the Eucharist may seem to be a simple and straightforward question, for the synoptic gospels and St. Paul give us, although with variants, the words used by Jesus in the institution of the Eucharist at the Last Supper, which indeed directly express "what is effected in the sacrament." The question, however, is more complicated than appears at first sight and has been the subject of considerable controversy between Catholic and Orthodox theologians.[58]

Patristic Witness on the Words of Consecration

The Fathers of the Church speak about this topic above all in the context of catechizing the newly baptized on the sacraments of Christian initiation. St. Ambrose, in his catechesis to the neophytes, as seen above, implies that the Eucharistic conversion is realized through the power of the words of Christ in the institution narrative, precisely because they are His words:

> Perhaps you say: "The bread I have here is ordinary bread." Yes, before the sacramental words are uttered this bread is nothing but bread. But at the consecration this bread becomes the body of Christ. Let us reason this out. How can something which is bread be the body of Christ? Well, by what words is the consecration effected, and whose words are they? The words of the Lord Jesus. All that is said before are the words of the priest: praise is offered to God, the prayer is offered up, petitions are made for the people, for kings, for all others. But when the moment comes for bringing the most holy sacrament into being, the priest does not use his own words any longer: he uses the words of Christ. Therefore, it is Christ's word that brings this sacrament into being.[59]

---

[58] For a good summary and analysis of this discussion, see Ibáñez, *L'Eucaristia, Dono e Mistero*, 503–10.

[59] Ambrose, *De Sacramentis*, 4.14 (Yarnold, *Awe-Inspiring Rites*, 132–33). See also *De Sacramentis* 4.21–22 (Yarnold, 135–36); St. Ambrose, *Explanatio Psalmi* 38.25: "If Christ now appears not to offer, nevertheless he himself is offered on earth because the body of Christ is offered. Indeed it witnesses itself that he offers in us, whose words consecrate the sacrifice that is offered" (Kilmartin, *The Eucharist in the West*, 19).

Gregory of Nyssa and St. John Chrysostom seem to maintain the same position. In his *Great Catechism*, St. Gregory of Nyssa writes:

> Rightly, then, do we believe that now also the bread which is consecrated by the Word of God is changed into the Body of God the Word. . . . It is at once changed into the body by means of the Word, as the Word itself said, "This is My Body."[60]

We have seen that St. John Chrysostom, in a sermon entitled "On the Betrayal of Judas," made a similar assertion:

> The priest is the representative when he pronounces those words, but the power and the grace are those of the Lord. "This is my Body," he says. This word changes the things that lie before us; and as that sentence "increase and multiply," once spoken, extends through all time and gives to our nature the power to reproduce itself; even so that saying "This is my Body," once uttered, does at every table in the Churches from that time to the present day, and even till Christ's coming, make the sacrifice complete.[61]

It is clear that Chrysostom regards the words of Christ spoken at the Last Supper as words of power no less than the divine words that underlie creation as the perennial foundation of nature's fruitfulness. As the words of creation continue to achieve their effect, so in an analogous way Christ's words once spoken—"This is my Body"—continue to resonate throughout the world in every Eucharistic liturgy in the sacramental proclamation, and they continue to work what Christ gave them to work at the Last Supper.

It has been argued that Chrysostom attributes the conversion of the elements not to the priest's words of the institution narrative in

---

[60] St. Gregory of Nyssa, *Great Catechism* [*Catechetical Oration*] 37.105–7, trans. William Moore and Henry Wilson (*NPNF2*, 5:505–6). See Michael Zheltov, "The Moment of Eucharistic Consecration in Byzantine Thought," in *Issues in Eucharistic Praying in East and West: Essays in Liturgical and Theological Analysis*, ed. Maxwell Johnson (Collegeville, MN: Liturgical Press, 2010), 282.

[61] St. John Chrysostom, *De Proditione Judae* [*On the Betrayal of Judas*], homily 1 and almost identical homily 2 (PG, 49:380, 389), in Quasten, *Patrology*, 3:481. See McKenna, *The Eucharistic Epiclesis*, 54.

the Mass, but solely to Christ's words said at the Last Supper, which would make the words of institution said by the priest unnecessary in the Mass.[62] But that would miss the nuance of his thought. It is necessary that a properly ordained minister make those words present for Christ's original utterance to work through them and touch our world today. As Christ's Baptism sanctified all waters and gave power of sanctification to the sacramental form used throughout the life of the Church, so Christ's words at the Last Supper gave those words a power that allows them to work in every time and place when said in His person.[63]

St. Thomas on the Form of the Eucharist

In his influential *Sentences*, Peter Lombard, citing the authority of St. Ambrose, taught that the form of the Sacrament of the Eucharist is comprised of Jesus's words of institution:

> As for the form, it is what he himself made known, saying: "This is my body"; and afterwards: "This is my blood." When these words are pronounced, the change of the bread and wine into the substance of the body and blood of Christ occurs; the rest is said to the praise of God.[64]

St. Thomas explains why it is fitting that the words of Christ at the institution are the essential form of the Eucharist:

> In this sacrament the consecration of the matter consists in the miraculous change of the substance, which can only be done by God; hence the minister in performing this sacrament has no other act save the pronouncing of the words. And because the form should suit the thing, therefore the form of

---

[62] See Robert Taft, "Mass Without the Consecration? The Historic Agreement on the Eucharist between the Catholic Church and the Assyrian Church of the East," *Worship* 77 (2003): 503–6; Nicholas V. Russo, "The Validity of the Anaphora of Addai and Mari: Critique of the Critiques," in Johnson, *Issues in Eucharistic Praying in East and West*, 30.

[63] See Zheltov, "The Moment of Eucharistic Consecration in Byzantine Thought," 283.

[64] Lombard, *Sentences* IV, d. 8, ch. 4 (p. 42). See also Paschasius, *De Corpore et Sanguine Domini* 15.12–23 (Paulus, CCCM, 16:92–93), cited here by Lombard.

this sacrament differs from the forms of the other sacraments in two respects. First, because the form of the other sacraments implies the use of the matter, as for instance, baptizing, or signing; but the form of this sacrament implies merely the consecration of the matter, which consists in transubstantiation, as when it is said, "This is My body," or, "This is the chalice of My blood." Secondly, because the forms of the other sacraments are pronounced in the person of the minister, whether by way of exercising an act, as when it is said, "I baptize thee," or "I confirm thee," etc.; or by way of command, as when it is said in the sacrament of order, "Take the power," etc.; or by way of entreaty, as when in the sacrament of Extreme Unction it is said, "By this anointing and our intercession," etc. But the form of this sacrament is pronounced as if Christ were speaking in person, so that it is given to be understood that the minister does nothing in perfecting this sacrament, except to pronounce the words of Christ.[65]

It is fitting that the words that constitute the essential form of the Eucharist be substantially Christ's own words, spoken in His person, rather than in the person of the Church or of the minister. This makes it clearer that a work is being done proper to divine omnipotence and according to Christ's institution. Furthermore, the words of the form should directly manifest the miraculous conversion of the bread and wine into His Body given for us and His Blood poured out for the forgiveness of sins, since that is what this sacrament does.[66] The words of institution fulfill both of these requirements.

With regard to the essential words in the consecration, St. Thomas poses the objection that none of the scriptural accounts give the exact words the Church uses. He answers that the words of consecration are a synthesis of the various words given in the four accounts and also states that it was not the intent of the Evangelists to transmit the exact form of the sacrament.[67] It seems that a better answer to this objection

---

[65] *ST* III, q. 78, a. 1.

[66] See *ST* III, q. 78, a. 2: "Now the form of a sacrament ought to denote what is done in the sacrament. Consequently the form for the consecration of the bread ought to signify the actual conversion of the bread into the body of Christ."

[67] *ST* III, q. 78, a. 3, ad 9: "The Evangelists did not intend to hand down the forms of the sacraments, which in the primitive Church had to be kept concealed, as Dionysius observes at the close of his book on the ecclesiastical hierarchy; their

is given by Louis Bouyer, who holds that the words of institution in the four accounts differ in details because the four accounts reflect the liturgical practice of the Church in different regions. These differences are accidental, and a liturgy celebrated according to any of them, as transmitted by apostolic Tradition, would be valid.[68] With regard to the sacraments in general, St. Thomas recognizes the principle that it is only the substance of the meaning that is essential in sacramental causality, and not a particular formula of words, for the sacraments cause as intelligible signs. In explaining that differences of language do not affect sacramental efficacy, he writes:

> As Augustine says,[69] the word operates in the sacraments "not because it is spoken," i.e., not by the outward sound of the voice, "but because it is believed" in accordance with the sense of the words which is held by faith. And this sense is indeed the same for all, though the same words as to their sound is not used by all. Consequently no matter in what language this sense is expressed, the sacrament is complete.[70]

This principle allows a significant degree of flexibility in sacramental form, which is regulated by the Church according to circumstances of local culture and other needs.

Magisterial Teaching on the Essential Form of the Eucharist

Beginning in the fourteenth and fifteenth centuries, the Eastern Orthodox theological tradition began to maintain that the essential form is comprised not only of Jesus's words in the institution narrative,

---

object was to write the story of Christ. Nevertheless nearly all these words can be culled from various passages of the Scriptures."

[68] See Bouyer, *Eucharist*, 157: "It does seem that [Joachim] Jeremias was right in explaining the divergencies of detail in the institution accounts that the New Testament has handed down to us by the fact that these were already different local liturgical formulations." See also Peter A. Kwasniewski, "Doing and Speaking in the Person of Christ: Eucharistic Form in the Anaphora of Addai and Mari," *Nova et Vetera* 4 (English), no. 2 (2006): 313–80, at 346.

[69] St Augustine, Tractate 80.3 (on John 15:3) (Rettig, *Tractates on the Gospel of John 55–111*, 118).

[70] *ST* III, q. 60, a. 7, ad 1.

but also (or exclusively) of the epiclesis that follows on Jesus's words in the Byzantine rite.[71] The issue of the essential form has not been solemnly and infallibly determined by the Magisterium, but there is a clear Magisterial teaching that the words of Jesus in the institution of the Eucharist constitute its essential form. The most important magisterial text in this regard is the Decree for the Armenians of the Council of Florence, which states:

> The form of this sacrament is the words of the Saviour with which he effected this sacrament; for the priest effects the sacrament by speaking in the person of Christ. It is by the power of these words that the substance of bread is changed into the body of Christ, and the substance of wine into his blood; in such a way, however, that the whole Christ is contained under the species of bread and the whole Christ under the species of wine.[72]

The Decree for the Jacobites of the same council is similar:

> But since in the aforesaid decree of the Armenians, the form of the words was not made explicit that the holy Roman Church, confirmed by the teaching and the authority of the Apostles Peter and Paul, has always been wont to use in the consecration of the Lord's Body and Blood, we decided it should be inserted into the present text: In the consecration of the body of the Lord, she uses this form of the words: "For this is my body." . . . As long as the substance of the bread remains, there should be no doubt whatsoever that it is immediately transubstantiated into the true body of Christ after the above-mentioned words of consecration of the body have been pronounced by the priest with the intention of confecting it.[73]

---

[71] For a discussion of the development and nuances of the Orthodox position, see Zheltov, "The Moment of Eucharistic Consecration in Byzantine Thought," 263–306. For a detailed discussion of this controversy, see Theophilus Spacil, *Doctrina Theologiae Orientis Separati De SS. Eucharistia*, 2 vols. (Rome: Pont. Institutum Orientalium Studiorum, 1929), 2:6–114; S. Salaville, "Épiclèse eucharistique," in *Dictionnaire de Théologie Catholique*, vol. 5 (1913), 247–265. See also Santogrossi, "Anaphoras without Institution Narrative," 27–59.

[72] Council of Florence, *Exsultate Deo* (DS, 1321).

[73] Council of Florence, Bull of Union with the Copts and the Ethiopians, *Cantate Domino* (1442) (DS, 1352).

The Council of Trent did not directly deal with this issue,[74] although it appears in the *Catechism of the Council of Trent*. With regard to the essential words for the species of bread, the *Catechism* states:

> From St. Matthew and St. Luke, as also from St. Paul, we know that the form of the sacrament consists of these words: "This is my body." . . . This form of consecration, as used by our Lord himself, has always been observed in the Catholic Church. We need not cite evidence from the Fathers in proof of this fact; it would be a practically endless enumeration of texts. Likewise, we will omit the decree of the Council of Florence, since it is readily available elsewhere. We need only refer to these further words of the Savior: "Do this in remembrance of me" (Lk 22:19; 1 Cor 11:24–25). What the Lord commanded to be done was not only what he did, but also what he said. For what he said was meant not only to signify but to effect what he did.
>
> That these words do in fact constitute the form is easily seen from reason alone. The form of a sacrament, as we have seen, is that which signifies what is effected in the sacrament. What is effected in the Eucharist is the changing of the bread into the true Body of the Lord. Since the words, "This is my Body," signify and effect that change, they therefore constitute the form of the Eucharist.[75]

With regard to the essential form for the chalice, the *Catechism of the Council of Trent* states:

> It must be held with certainty that the form for consecrating the chalice consists of these words: "This is the chalice of my

---

[74] The Council of Trent indirectly touches on this issue in the Decree Concerning the Most Holy Sacrament of the Eucharist (session 13, October 11, 1551), can. 4: "If anyone says that after the consecration the body and blood of our Lord Jesus Christ are not in the marvelous sacrament of the Eucharist but that they are there only in the use of the sacrament, while it is being received, and not before or after, . . . *anathema sit*" (DS, 1654). This canon is directed against those Protestants who hold that the real presence is restricted to the actual reception of Communion and does not intend to resolve the disputed question about when the consecration takes place, whether through the words of institution or the epiclesis. See also Pius VII, Brief *Adorabile Eucharistiae* (1822) (DS, 2718).

[75] *CCT*, pt. 2, ch. 3, §19 (p. 220).

blood of the new and eternal testament: the Mystery of Faith: which shall be shed for you and for many, to the remission of sins." . . . The truth of this form cannot be doubted, if we remember what has been already said regarding the consecration of the bread. As there, so also here, the words signifying and effecting a change of substance are exclusively the form. These words do just that: they declare that the substance of the wine is changed into the Blood of the Lord. Clearly, then, they—and they alone—constitute the form of this sacrament.[76]

The *Catechism of the Catholic Church*, §1353, sensitive to Orthodox concerns, states that the words of institution make Christ sacramentally present, as taught by the Council of Florence, but specifies that this happens through the power of the Holy Spirit, who is invoked in the epiclesis in Eucharistic Prayers:

> In the institution narrative, the power of the words and the action of Christ, and the power of the Holy Spirit, make sacramentally present under the species of bread and wine Christ's body and blood, his sacrifice offered on the cross once for all.

This same text of the *Catechism of the Catholic Church* also speaks of the importance of the epiclesis:

> In the epiclesis, the Church asks the Father to send his Holy Spirit (or the power of his blessing) on the bread and wine, so that by his power they may become the body and blood of Jesus Christ and so that those who take part in the Eucharist may be one body and one spirit (some liturgical traditions put the epiclesis after the anamnesis).

The Epiclesis and the Words of the Institution Narrative

As can be seen in the *Catechism of the Catholic Church*, §1353, the Holy Spirit is invoked in an epiclesis to realize two distinct but intimately interrelated effects: transubstantiation and the transformation of the faithful who receive Communion so as to build up the unity of the

---

[76] Ibid., §§21–22 (pp. 221–22).

Church. These two effects correspond to the *res et sacramentum*, which is the real presence, and the *res tantum*, which is the infusion of grace to build up the Mystical Body.

The epiclesis liturgically manifesting that transubstantiation, directly signified by the words of Christ in the institution narrative, is a miracle attributed to the power of the Holy Spirit and not to any natural cause. Furthermore, what the words of institution state in the indicative mood, the words of the epiclesis ask for to emphasize the supreme gratuitousness of the Eucharistic mystery. The institution narrative and the epiclesis are underlining two distinct aspects of a single reality. Because the liturgy is spoken in time, the institution narrative and the epiclesis cannot be simultaneous, and so the epiclesis must either precede or follow the institution narrative. However, they are expressing sequentially a single reality, for the causality of Christ's words and the power of the Holy Spirit operate simultaneously as instrumental and principal cause, respectively.[77]

The epiclesis manifests the principal efficient cause of transubstantiation, which is the power of the Holy Spirit. Although transubstantiation is the work of the divine omnipotence common to the Trinity, it is appropriated to the Holy Spirit as a supreme work of the divine love. For, since the Holy Spirit proceeds from the Father and Son as their mutual love, those works of God that especially manifest the divine love are appropriated to the Holy Spirit, as the archangel Gabriel attributed the realization of the Incarnation to the overshadowing of the Spirit.[78]

The words of Christ in the institution narrative, on the other hand, are an instrumental cause given power by the divine omnipotence that works through them, making what they say to be true. Although the liturgy pronounces the epiclesis either before or after the institution narrative, we should understand the action of Christ's words and the Spirit's power, invoked in the epiclesis, as simultaneous. The divine

---

[77] See Réginald Garrigou-Lagrange, *De Eucharistia et Paenitentia* (Turin: Marietti, 1948), 173–74; Kwasniewski, "Doing and Speaking in the Person of Christ," 317–22.

[78] See *ST* III, q. 32, a. 1: "The whole Trinity effected the conception of Christ's body: nevertheless, this is attributed to the Holy Ghost, for three reasons. First, because this is befitting to the cause of the Incarnation, considered on the part of God. For the Holy Ghost is the love of Father and Son, as stated in the First Part (q. 37, a. 1). Now, that the Son of God took to Himself flesh from the Virgin's womb was due to the exceeding love of God."

power appropriated to the Holy Spirit works through the words of Christ, realizing what they signify.

Liturgical texts are not meant to be read in a strictly chronological way. Liturgical texts, like the book of Revelation and other biblical texts, often speak of things that come later as if they were already actual, and of things already realized as if they were still coming into being. Robert Taft speaks of "the proleptic and reflexive nature of liturgical discourse,"[79] by which liturgical time is stretched, as it were, so that a reality can be anticipated and spoken of as actual while it is being prepared, as in the offertory,[80] and reflected upon afterward as if it were continually being actualized after it has already come to be. Jacques-Bénigne Bossuet makes a similar point, saying: "It is in order to make more vivid what is being accomplished that the Church speaks at every moment as if the entire action were being accomplished here and now, without wondering if the action has already been accomplished or is yet to be accomplished."[81] It is of the very nature of the liturgy that references to past, present, and future be intertwined, for in every sacrament, the past is recalled, a present event is enacted, and an eschatological hope is invoked.[82] One cannot read a liturgical text looking for chronological indications of when the Eucharistic conversion occurs, for that is not the intention of liturgical discourse. For example, the fact that the epiclesis occurs after the words of institution in many Eucharistic Prayers, as in the Byzantine rite,[83] should not

---

[79] Taft, "Mass Without the Consecration?" 495.

[80] The Offertory in the extraordinary form of the Roman rite speaks as if the sacrifice were already being offered: "Súscipe, sancta Trínitas, hanc oblatiónem, quam tibi offérimus ob memóriam passionis, resurrectiónis et ascensiónis Iesu Christi Dómini nostri" (*Missale Romanum: Ex Decreto SS. Concilii Tridentini*, 1:122).

[81] Jacques-Bénigne Bossuet, *Explications de quelques difficultés sur les prières de la messe à un nouveau catholique*, in *Oeuvres* 17 (Paris, 1864), 74–75, quoted in Santogrossi, "Anaphoras without Institution Narrative," 27–59, at 35.

[82] See *ST* III, q. 60, a. 3:

> A sacrament properly speaking is that which is ordained to signify our sanctification. In which three things may be considered; namely, the very cause of our sanctification, which is Christ's passion; the form of our sanctification, which is grace and the virtues; and the ultimate end of our sanctification, which is eternal life. And all these are signified by the sacraments. Consequently a sacrament is a sign that is both a reminder of the past, i.e. the passion of Christ; and an indication of that which is effected in us by Christ's passion, i.e. grace; and a prognostic, that is, a foretelling of future glory.

[83] The epiclesis comes after the institution narrative in the Byzantine liturgy of St.

be taken as an argument that the Eucharistic conversion has not yet occurred. The Roman Canon exhibits a similar phenomenon, anticipating the presence of Christ's Body and Blood before the words of institution and asking for the acceptance of the sacrifice after those words. Taft writes:

> Less smooth and unified in its redactional structure than the Antiochene anaphoral type, the Roman Canon does not first recite the Institution Narrative, then elucidate its meaning. Rather, it imbeds Jesus' words in a series of discrete prayers for the sanctification and acceptance of the oblation (which, theologically, are of course the same thing). Now some of these prayers even before the Words of Institution speak of the species in terms that can only refer to the Body and Blood of Christ, as if the gifts were already consecrated; and, conversely, after the Words of Institution speak in a way that could seem to imply the gifts are not yet consecrated.[84]

It has been inferred from this that, for the Fathers, the whole Eucharistic Prayer was considered consecratory.[85] This is true in the sense that the whole anaphora pertains to the consecration in the non-chronological manner described above. This explains why we can find Patristic texts that seem to attribute the Eucharistic change both to the words of institution and to the epiclesis without implying a contradiction.[86]

Basil (*PEER*, 119–20), the liturgy of St. John Chrysostom (*PEER*, 91–133), the Eucharistic Prayer given in the *Apostolic Tradition*, in the anaphora of St. James (*PEER*, 91–93), the liturgy of St. Mark (*PEER*, 65–66), the Third Maronite Anaphora of St. Peter, called *Sharar*, in (*PEER*, 48–50), the anaphora in book 8 of the Apostolic Constitutions (*PEER*, 110–11), etc. An epiclesis comes before the institution narrative in the Barcelona Papyrus (Zheltov, "The Anaphora and the Thanksgiving Prayer from the Barcelona Papyrus," 490).

[84] Taft, "Mass Without the Consecration?" 495. See also Russo, "The Validity of the Anaphora of Addai and Mari," 30.

[85] Taft, "Mass Without the Consecration?" 482–509, esp. 496–97; Jungmann, *The Mass of the Roman Rite*, 2:203–204n9. On this position, see Ibáñez, *L'Eucaristia, Dono e Mistero*, 507, with bibliography in 507n53.

[86] See John Damascene, *An Exact Exposition of the Orthodox Faith* 4.13 (Chase, 356–57), mentioned above in chapter 4, p. 175. See Yarnold, *Awe-Inspiring Rites of Initiation*, 49:

> There need, of course, be no inconsistency between the two views. The Holy Spirit effects the presence of Christ when we "do this in

Does this mean that there is no point in asking whether there is a part of the Eucharistic Prayer that can be considered to be the essential form of the sacrament? Is it simply a false problem that should be dismissed, or a problem foreign to the Patristic mentality, or to the very nature of the liturgy?[87] Not entirely, it seems to me. If it were only a question of chronological curiosity, then it might be less justified, although it would still be important for the Church to know when the Lord is present in His Body and Blood. In speaking about the essential form, however, we are not just posing a *chronological* question, but also asking if there is some part of the Eucharistic Prayer that directly expresses the sacramental action in a *uniquely authoritative and sacramental way*, such that it could be understood to be the *heart* of the Eucharistic Prayer that accomplishes what it says.[88] Although the Fathers do not pose the chronological question, which seems to be more of concern to modern Western culture, they do speak of the unique authority and power of Christ's own words, which, as words of power, effect what they signify through the Spirit's working through them.

The Anaphora of Addai and Mari

The biggest problem regarding the essential words of the form is the fact that the Assyrian Church of the East,[89] which was in communion

---

remembrance of (him)." A fully articulated liturgy should contain both a Supper-narrative and an Epiclesis. Disagreement comes only over the question, "At what moment does the change take place?"; but perhaps that is a question that should not be asked. Just as the Offertory and Eucharistic Prayer are two separate expressions of a single offering, so too the Supper-narrative and Epiclesis are two expressions of the same transformation of the bread and wine into Christ's body and blood.

[87] See Taft, "Mass Without the Consecration?" 495: "Liturgical language, the language of *theologia prima*, is typological, metaphorical, more redolent of Bible and prayer than of school and thesis, more patristic than scholastic, more impressionistic than systematic, more suggestive than probative. In a word, it is symbolic and evocative, not philosophical and ontological."

[88] See Cesare Giraudo, who speaks of the institution narrative as the beating heart of the Eucharistic Prayer, while seeking to avoid viewing it in isolation, in "La genesi anaforica del racconto istituzionale alla luce dell'anafora di Addai e Mari: tra storia delle forme e liturgia comparata," in *The Anaphoral Genesis of the Institution Narrative in Light of the Anaphora of Addai and Mari*, 426–29. Taft also speaks of the "centrality of the words of institution within the anaphoral context," ("Mass Without the Consecration?" 501).

[89] See Pontifical Council for Promoting Christian Unity, "Guidelines for Admission to the Eucharist between the Chaldean Church and the Assyr-

with Rome until the early fifth century when it fell into the Nestorian heresy, has continuously used an ancient Eucharistic Prayer that does not contain the words of institution: the Anaphora of Addai and Mari. This anaphora is thought to have originated in the third century[90] in Edessa of Mesopotamia and has recently been the subject of much discussion.[91] The Anaphora reflects a language of prayer closely tied to its Jewish origins.[92]

The Pontifical Council for Promoting Christian Unity published a document on this subject on July 20, 2001, entitled, "Guidelines for Admission to the Eucharist between the Chaldean Church and the Assyrian Church of the East."[93] This document grants the Catholic faithful of the Chaldean rite the permission in cases of pastoral necessity to attend Mass in the Assyrian Church of the East cele-

---

ian Church of the East," October 26, 2001, accessed June 27, 2017, http://www.vatican.va/roman_curia/pontifical_councils/chrstuni/documents/rc_pc_chrstuni_doc_20011025_chiesa-caldea-assira_en.html.

[90] Our earliest manuscript is from the tenth century. See William Macomber, "The Oldest Known Text of the Anaphora of the Apostles *Addai and Mari*," *Orientalia Christiana Periodica* 32 (1966): 335–71.

[91] See A. Gelston, *The Eucharistic Prayer of Addai and Mari* (Oxford: Clarendon Press, 1992); Taft, "Mass Without the Consecration?" 482–509; Uwe Michael Lang, "Eucharist without Institution Narrative? The 'Anaphora of Addai and Mari' Revisited," *Divinitas*, n.s., special edition (2004): 227–60 (also in *Die Anaphora von Addai und Mari: Studien zu Eucharistie und Einsetzungsworten*, ed. Uwe Michael Lang [Bonn: Verlag Nova & Vetera, 2007], 31–65); David Berger, "'Forma huius sacramenti sunt verba Salvatoris'—Die Form des Sakramentes der Eucharistie," *Divinitas*, n.s., special edition (2004): 171–99; Brunero Gherardini, "Le parole della Consacrazione eucaristica," *Divinitas*, n.s., special edition (2004): 141–69; Sarhad Jammo, "The Anaphora of the Apostles Addai and Mari: A Study of Structure and Historical Background," in *Studies on the Anaphora of Addai and Mari*, ed. Puthur, 1–34; Kwasniewski, "Doing and Speaking in the Person of Christ: Eucharistic Form in the Anaphora of Addai and Mari"; Russo, "The Validity of the Anaphora of Addai and Mari," 21–62; Santogrossi, "Anaphoras without Institution Narrative," 27–59; Giraudo, *The Anaphoral Genesis of the Institution Narrative*; Dominik Heringer, *Die Anaphora der Apostel Addai und Mari: Ausdrucksform einer eucharistischen Ekklesiologie* (Göttingen: V&R Unipress, 2013).

[92] See Stylianos Muksuris, "A Brief Overview of the Structure and Theology of the Liturgy of the Apostles Addai and Mari," *Greek Orthodox Theological Review* 43 (1998): 59–83.

[93] Pontifical Council for Promoting Chrisitan Unity, "Guidelines . . . between the Chaldean Church and the Assyrian Church of the East." On this document and its genesis, see Robert Taft, "The 2001 Vatican Addai and Mari Decision in Retrospect: Reflections of a Protagonist," in Giraudo, *The Anaphoral Genesis of the Institution Narrative*, 317–34.

brating the Anaphora of Addai and Mari, which lacks the institution narrative.[94] The pastoral issue hinges on the doctrinal question of whether this anaphora without the institution narrative constitutes a valid Mass.

A clarification of this document was issued by the Pontifical Council for Promoting Christian Unity on October 26, 2001, that gives a good statement of the theological problem:

> The Catholic Church considers the words of the Institution as a constitutive part of the Anaphora or Eucharistic Prayer. The Council of Florence stated "*The form of this sacrament are the words of the Saviour with which he effected this sacrament. A priest speaking in the person of Christ effects this sacrament. For, in virtue of those words, the substance of bread is changed into the body of Christ and the substance of wine into his blood*" (D.H. 1321). The same Council of Florence also characterised the

---

[94] Nevertheless, when Catholic faithful of the Chaldean rite are present, the Pontifical Council for Promoting Christian Unity's "Guidelines . . . between the Chaldean Church and the Assyrian Church of the East," §4, recommends that "the Assyrian minister is warmly invited to insert the words of the Institution in the Anaphora of Addai and Mari, as allowed by the Holy Synod of the Assyrian Church of the East." A fuller explanation of this recommendation is given in a subsequent document of the same Pontifical Council of Oct. 26, 2001, "Admission to the Eucharist in Situations of Pastoral Necessity," which explains the Guidelines:

> This possibility already exists in the Assyrian Church of the East. Indeed, the Holy Synod of the Assyrian Church of the East, assembled in 1978 in Baghdad, offered ministers in the Assyrian Church the option of reciting the words of the Institution in the Anaphora of Addai and Mari. Although this option does not affect the validity of the Anaphora of Addai and Mari, it might have a particular relevance from a liturgical, as well as an ecumenical viewpoint. From a liturgical viewpoint, this might be an appropriate means to bring the present use of the Anaphora of Addai and Mari into line with the general usage in every Eucharistic Prayer both in the Christian East and in the Christian West. From an ecumenical viewpoint, it might be an appropriate expression of fraternal respect for members of other Churches who receive Holy Communion in the Assyrian Church of the East and who are used, according to the theological and canonical tradition of their proper Church, to hear the recitation of the words of the Institution in every Eucharistic Prayer. (The October 26, 2001 document appears appended to the June 20 document at the same Vatican website location.)

words of the Institution as *"the form of words [forma verborum]
which the holy Roman Church [. . .] has always been wont to use
[semper uti consuevit] in the consecration of the Lord's body and
blood"* (D.H. 1352), without prejudice to the possibility of
some variation in their articulation by the Church. Although
not having any authority as to the substance of the sacraments,
the Church does have the power to determine their concrete
shaping, regarding both their sacramental sign (*materia*) and
their words of administration (*forma*) (cf. CCEO, can. 669).
Hence the doctrinal question about the validity of the Anaphora of Addai and Mari, when used in its short version without
a coherent Institution Narrative. Do the words of administration (*forma*) correspond to the conditions for validity, as
requested by the Catholic Church?

In other words, the question must be evaluated while keeping in
mind the teaching of the Council of Florence that the words of institution are the form of the sacrament and the principle that the Church
has a power over the concrete shaping of the matter and form of the
sacraments as long as their substance remains.[95]
The Congregation for the Doctrine of Faith studied the question
and, in January 2001, concluded that this anaphora can be considered
valid, based on three principal arguments.[96] These three arguments
are: (1) the antiquity of the anaphora and its intention to celebrate
the Eucharist in accordance with the intention of the Church, (2) the
fact that the Assyrian Church of the East is a particular church with
apostolic succession, and (3) the fact that "the words of Eucharistic
Institution are indeed present in the Anaphora of Addai and Mari,
not in a coherent narrative way and *ad litteram*, but rather in a dis-

---

[95] See the Council of Trent, Communion under Both Kinds and Communion of
Little Children (session 21), ch. 2 (DS, 1728).

[96] Pontifical Council for Promoting Chrisitan Unity, "Guidelines . . . between the
Chaldean Church and the Assyrian Church of the East," §3: "As the Catholic Church considers the words of the Eucharistic Institution a constitutive
and therefore indispensable part of the Anaphora or Eucharistic Prayer, a long
and careful study was undertaken of the Anaphora of Addai and Mari, from a
historical, liturgical and theological perspective, at the end of which the Congregation for the Doctrine of Faith on January 17th, 2001 concluded that this
Anaphora can be considered valid. H.H. Pope John Paul II has approved this
decision. This conclusion rests on three major arguments."

persed euchological way, that is, integrated in successive prayers of thanksgiving, praise and intercession. All these elements constitute a 'quasi-narrative' of the Eucharistic Institution."[97]

The document cites three principal passages from the anaphora that refer to the words of institution. The first makes explicit the Church's intention to offer the Body and Blood of Christ on the altar, for a remembrance:

> Do thou, O my Lord, in thy manifold and ineffable mercies, make a good and gracious remembrance for all the upright and just fathers who were pleasing before thee, *in the commemoration of the body and blood of thy Christ, which we offer to thee* upon the pure and holy altar, as thou hast taught us.[98]

In the second, the mystery that is being celebrated is said to be "the passion and death and resurrection of our Lord":

> We also, O my Lord, thy unworthy, frail and miserable servants who are gathered and stand before thee, and have received by tradition the example which is from thee, rejoicing and glorifying and exalting and commemorating and *celebrating this great and awesome mystery of the passion and death and resurrection of our Lord* Jesus Christ.[99]

---

[97] Ibid. This was basically the conclusion of Gelston, in *The Eucharistic Prayer of Addai and Mari*, 108–9: "There may be no formal Institution Narrative and no independent anamnesis as a separate section of the anaphora, but it cannot be denied that the substance of both such elements is clearly present in the anaphora in such a way as to suggest that it is of primary importance in determining the nature of what is being done." For an analysis and justification of the three principal arguments used in the "Guidelines," see Heringer, *Die Anaphora der Apostel Addai und Mari*.

[98] Gelston, *The Eucharistic Prayer of Addai and Mari*, 51–53 (my italics). Another translation is given by Mike Aquilina, *The Mass of the Early Christians*, 2nd ed. (Huntington, IN: Our Sunday Visitor, 2007), 190: "O Lord, through your many and ineffable mercies, make this memorial good and acceptable, with that of all the pious and righteous fathers who have been pleading before you in the commemoration of the body and blood of your Christ, which we offer to you upon your pure and holy altar, as you taught us."

[99] Gelston, *The Eucharistic Prayer of Addai and Mari*, 53–55 (my italics).

The third text is the epiclesis. Although it is does not directly mention the Body and Blood of Christ, this is implicit in the reference to "this offering," which has previously been identified as the "commemoration of the body and blood of thy Christ":

> And let thy Holy Spirit come, O my Lord, and rest upon this offering of thy servants, and bless it and sanctify it that it may be to us, O my Lord, for the pardon of sins, and for the forgiveness of shortcomings, and for the great hope of the resurrection from the dead, and for new life in the kingdom of heaven with all who have been pleasing before thee.[100]

The Pontifical Council's document then draws this conclusion:

> So the words of the Institution are not absent in the Anaphora of Addai and Mari, but explicitly mentioned in a dispersed way, from the beginning to the end, in the most important passages of the Anaphora. It is also clear that the passages cited above express the full conviction of commemorating the Lord's paschal mystery, in the strong sense of making it present; that is, the intention to carry out in practice precisely what Christ established by his words and actions in instituting the Eucharist.[101]

How Can a Eucharistic Prayer Be Valid without the Words of Institution?

We have seen the great fittingness of the fact that the substantial change of the elements be worked by the words of Christ, spoken in His person. Only in the words of institution does the priest speak in the person of Christ rather than in the person of the Church. Joseph Ratzinger writes:

> Thus a final point becomes evident: at the heart of the Canon is the narrative of the evening before Jesus' Passion. When this is spoken, then the priest is not recounting the story of

---

[100] Ibid., 55.
[101] Pontifical Council for Promoting Christian Unity, "Admission to the Eucharist in Situations of Pastoral Necessity."

something that is past, just recalling what happened then, but something is taking place in the present. "This *is* my Body" is what is said now, today. But these words are the words of Jesus Christ.[102]

Bouyer summarizes the results of ecumenical discussion on this point:

> Does it occur only by virtue of the *Verba Christi*, or through epiclesis? The only answer, according to tradition as a whole and aware of its origins, is that consecration takes place by virtue of the word of Christ when instituting the Eucharist, which the Church recalls formally in the heart of the invocation whereby it is entrusted to the strength of the mystery it commemorates. The joint commission of the Catholic Church and of the Orthodox Churches, with a view to a rapprochement, has been unanimous on this point.[103]

Does this mean that no Eucharist would be valid without Christ's words of the institution narrative? If a Eucharistic celebration did not contain the *substance of those words in some way*, then it could not be valid. The Pontifical Council for Promoting Christian Unity's 2001 document ties the validity of the Anaphora of Addai and Mari to the fact that the words of institution are in some sense *present and operative*, even though they are not spoken grammatically in the person of Christ. The principle still stands, then, that Christ's words are the form of the sacrament.[104] In the development of her liturgical Tradition, the Church has come to see that they are present most fittingly in a complete institution narrative, but according to this 2001 document,

---

[102] Ratzinger, *God Is Near Us*, 53–54. See also Jungmann, *The Mass of the Roman Rite*, 2:203: "The narrative of what once took place passes into the actuality of the present happening. There is a wonderful identification of Christ and the priest. In the person of the priest, Christ Himself stands at the altar, and picks up the bread, and lifts up 'this goodly chalice' (Psalm 22:5), *hunc praeclarum calicem*. Through this mode of speech clear expression is given to the fact that it is Christ Himself who is now active, and that it is by virtue of power deriving from Him that the transubstantiation which follows takes place."

[103] Louis Bouyer, *Dictionnaire Théologique* (Paris: Desclée, 1990), 68, trans. Guillaume Derville in *Eucharistic Concelebration: From Symbol to Reality* (Montreal: Wilson & Lafleur, 2011), 67.

[104] See Kwasniewski's excellent "Doing and Speaking in the Person of Christ."

they can also be said to be present in the Anaphora of Addai and Mari, although in a less fitting way, being implied rather than directly spoken in His person.

It might be asked who has the authority to determine whether Christ's words are present in a given Eucharistic Prayer, such as that of Addai and Mari. The Church must be able to recognize where her essential and constitutive elements are present, and thus she receives this power of discernment from the Lord, just as she receives the power to shape the matter and form of the sacraments—while preserving their substance—to accommodate changing conditions of time, place, and culture.[105]

Did the Anaphora of Addai and Mari Ever Have an Institution Narrative?

The argument has been made that the logic of the Anaphora presupposes that it once had an institution narrative, as can be seen by a comparison with related eastern liturgies, such as that of the Maronite anaphora of Peter III, called *Sharar*.[106] The central part of the Anaphora of Addai and Mari makes reference to the Body and Blood of

---

[105] See the Council of Trent, Communion under Both Kinds and Communion of Little Children (session 21), ch. 2 (DS, 1728). This power of the Church to shape the essential form of the sacraments while preserving their substance can be seen in a rather dramatic way in the reform of the liturgy decreed by Bl. Paul VI: Apostolic Constitution on the Sacrament of Confirmation, *Divinae Consortium Naturae*, AAS 63 (1971): 657–64; Paul VI, Apostolic Constitution *Sacram Unctionem Infirmorum* (1972); Apostolic Constitution Approving New Rites for the Ordination of Deacons, Priests, and Bishops (1968), in *Rites of Ordination of a Bishop, of Priests, and of Deacons*, 2nd typical ed. (Washington, DC: United States Conference of Catholic Bishops, 2003).

[106] See Lang, "Eucharist without Institution Narrative?"; Bouyer, *Eucharist*, 149–58; William Macomber, "The Maronite and Chaldean Versions of the Anaphora of the Apostles," *Orientalia Christiana Periodica* 37 (1971): 77–79; Macomber, "The Ancient Form of the Anaphora of the Apostles," in *East of Byzantium: Syria and Armenia in the Formative Period*, ed. N. G. Garsoïan, Y. G. Mathews, and R. W. Thomson (Washington, DC: Dumbarton Oaks, 1982), 73–88; Bernard Botte, "L'anaphore chaldeenne des Apotres," *Orientalia Christiana Periodica* 15 (1949): 259–76; Jungmann, *The Mass*, 133 ("Of the several attempts to explain this absence of the Institution narrative, the most tenable is the supposition that the narrative was dropped only at the time when the status of the epiclesis began to be exaggerated among the Nestorians, as A. Raes has proposed."); Alfons Raes, "Le récit de l'Institution eucharistique dans l'anaphore chaldéene et malabare des Apôtres," *Orientalia Christiana Periodica* 10 (1944): 216–26.

Christ, which is being offered on the altar according to the instruction of Christ ("as you taught us"):

> Do thou, O my Lord, in thy manifold and ineffable mercies, make a good and gracious remembrance . . . in the commemoration of the body and blood of thy Christ, which we offer to thee upon the pure and holy altar, *as thou hast taught us.*[107]

The institution narrative could logically be inserted at the end of this text. The words "as thou hast taught us" seem to be well suited to lead into the institution narrative. Furthermore, in order that the body and blood be offered, the institution narrative, with its command to "do this in memory of me," is presupposed. In fact, the Maronite anaphora of Peter III puts the institution narrative at this point:

> . . . commemoration of your body and your blood which we offer to you upon your living and holy altar, as you, our hope, have taught us in your holy and living gospel and have said: I am the bread of life which came down from heaven so that mortals may have life in me. We make, O Lord, the memorial of your passion *as you have taught us*: in that night when you were delivered up to the crucifiers, you took bread . . . [the institution narrative].[108]

There are also various arguments against the hypothesis that the Anaphora of Addai and Mari originally had an institution narrative.

---

[107] Gelston, *The Eucharistic Prayer of Addai and Mari*, 51–53.

[108] Translation from Jammo, "The Anaphora of the Apostles Addai and Mari," 4. See the position of the institution narrative in the reform of the Catholic Chaldean liturgy of the Anaphora of Addai and Mari, approved by the Holy See in 2006, which also puts the institution narrative after the words "as he taught us." The reformed Anaphora can be found in Sarhad Jammo, "The Chaldean Liturgy," Appendix 2: "The Reformed Anaphora of Addai and Mari," in *Emmanuel: The Book of Public Prayer, Selected from the Yearly Cycle of the Hudhra, with the Volume of Kahnayta, Which Is the Book of the Rites of All the Sacraments, as Celebrated in the Chaldean Church of the East* (San Diego, CA: Chaldean Catholic Diocese of St. Peter the Apostle, 2013), xci. Jammo, however, holds that the institution narrative was not original to Addai and Mari, even though he identifies this place in the Anaphora as most appropriate to it ("The Mesopotamian Anaphora of Addai & Mari: The Organic Dialectic between Its Apostolic Core and Euchological Growth," in Giraudo, *The Anaphoral Genesis of the Institution Narrative*, 416–18).

The most important is that none of our earliest manuscripts of this anaphora have an institution narrative, and it is hard to understand how it could have come to be omitted or removed if it was originally present. One can respond to this, with Bouyer and Bernard Botte, by pointing out its frequent omission in liturgical manuscripts:

> The liturgical manuscripts where these words do not appear are legion, even in cases where there is not the least doubt, if only according to the commentators of the period, about their compulsory presence in the celebration. This is actually the case in the West, with all the texts of the Gallican liturgy, with all the earliest texts of the Mozarabic liturgy, and in the East with many Syriac manuscripts, particularly among the Maronites. We should simply suppose that every celebrant knew the customary formula in a given rite by heart.[109]

Nevertheless, it still remains difficult to explain the constant tradition of the celebration of the anaphora without an institution narrative in the Assyrian Church of the East if the anaphora originally had one.[110]

Furthermore, the fact that the institution narrative fits well into the anaphora in the place mentioned above does not necessarily mean that it was originally there. It could mean that the inclusion of the institution narrative is in line with the interior logic of the Eucharistic Prayer "in its DNA," in the words of the eminent Jesuit liturgical

---

[109] Bouyer, *Eucharist*, 152.

[110] See Stephen B. Wilson, "The Anaphora of the Apostles Addai and Mari," in *Essays on Early Eastern Eucharistic Prayers*, ed. Paul F. Bradshaw (Collegeville, MN: Liturgical Press, 1997), 32: "The best argument against the missing narrative thesis is that the current text of AM does not contain one and it is unlikely that one would have dropped out with the increasing use and valuation of the narrative in later liturgical texts. A second argument in favor of the present form of AM is that its current structure has a certain structural and theological flow to it." Today, the more common view is that the Anaphora of Addai and Mari never had an institution narrative. See the studies in: Giraudo, *The Anaphoral Genesis of the Institution Narrative*; Russo, "The Validity of the Anaphora of Addai and Mari," 21–62; Jammo, "The Anaphora of the Apostles Addai and Mari," 1–34; Taft, "Mass Without the Consecration?" 482–509, at 489–90; Gabrielle Winkler, "A New Witness to the Missing Institution Narrative," in *Studia Liturgica Diversa: Studies in Church Music and Liturgy: Essays in Honor of Paul F. Bradshaw*, ed. Maxwell E. Johnson and L. Edward Phillips (Portland, OR: The Pastoral Press, 2004), 117; Bryan D. Spinks, *Worship: Prayers from the East* (Washington DC: Pastoral Press, 1994): 33–34.

theologian Cesare Giraudo.[111] But, Giraudo argues, it may have taken the Church more time to bring to completion this development of the liturgical Tradition than we are accustomed to imagine. The Anaphora of Addai and Mari would thus be a witness of the evolution of the Eucharistic Prayer before the inclusion of the institution narrative became the common tradition of the universal Church no later than the fourth century.[112]

Because of the difficulty of resolving the historical question of the original presence or absence of the institution narrative with certainty, the "Guidelines" of the Pontifical Council for Promoting Christian Unity wisely does not rely on a particular solution to this historical question, but on more general theological considerations contained in the three arguments mentioned above regarding the ancient roots of the Assyrian Church, its retention of apostolic succession, and the implicit presence of the institution narrative in the anaphora.

Hypothesis That the Institution Narrative Is a Later Development

It has been argued by some eminent liturgists that the inclusion of the institution narrative into Eucharistic Prayers became the general norm only in the third or fourth century.[113] The most important argument for this position is the fact that, as we have seen, the institution narrative is lacking in two of our earliest Eucharistic texts: the *Didache* and the Anaphora of Addai and Mari, as well as in the Gospel of John. An important support for this thesis is the fact that there are also other examples of Eucharistic Prayers that lack a complete institution nar-

---

[111] Giraudo, "La genesi anaforica del racconto istituzionale alla luce dell'anafora di Addai e Mari," 451.

[112] See Spinks, *Do This in Remembrance of Me*, 54: "The majority of scholars believe that the prayer never had an Institution Narrative and dates from a time before the narrative was regarded as a *sine qua non* of an anaphora."

[113] See Paul F. Bradshaw, "Did Jesus Institute the Eucharist at the Last Supper?" in Johnson, *Issues in Eucharistic Praying in East and West*, 1–19; Taft, "Mass Without the Consecration?" 490 ("Although theories on the origins and evolution of the pristine anaphora remain in flux, one point of growing agreement among representative scholars, Catholic and non, is that the Institution Narrative is a later embolism—i.e., interpolation—into the earliest eucharistic prayers"); and the important works of Cesare Giraudo, such as "La genesi anaforica del racconto istituzionale," 425–53, and *Eucaristia per la chiesa*, 329–60. Against this thesis, see E. J. Yarnold, "Anaphoras without Institution Narratives?" *Studia Patristica* 30 (1997): 395–410.

rative, and thus lack the words, "This is my body, . . . this is the chalice of my blood."[114]

This thesis that the inclusion of the institution narrative in Eucharistic Prayers is an early liturgical development that only gradually became universal is not impossible from a doctrinal perspective. If true, it would be a striking witness to the development of liturgical tradition in the Church, by which a form of worship comes to be felt as more fitting because it makes fully explicit what was previously present only in an implicit way. In this case, the institution narrative makes explicit what is implicitly presupposed in a text such as the Anaphora of Addai and Mari or other Syriac anaphoras with incomplete institution accounts that are no longer in use.[115]

On historical grounds, however, there are good reasons to think that the institution narrative was a key part of Eucharistic Prayers from the beginning.[116] The most important reason is the fact that the institution narrative is given to us in four parallel sources from the New Testament. As we have seen, St. Paul, a quarter of a century after Calvary, gives the words of Christ with a particular solemnity: "For I

---

[114] See Giraudo, "La genesi anaforica del racconto istituzionale," 440–450; *Eucaristia per la chiesa*, 345–59.

[115] See Giraudo, *Eucaristia per la chiesa*, 358–59:

> We have proposed: a) that the form of prayer should be considered anterior to the eucharistic institution account; b) that the genesis of the eucharistic institution account should be understood in the light of the liturgical dynamic of interpolation [by which a scriptural text is inserted into a prayer as an authoritative quotation, referred to by Giraudo as *embolism*]; c) that the early Church, having inherited this dynamic of interpolation from the Old Testament and from Judaism, needed a certain time to become aware of the effective possibility of putting it into practice with regard to the Scriptural text of the Eucharist, that is, the very words pronounced by the Lord Jesus *pridie quam pateretur*. (My translation.)

[116] With regard to the Roman canon, G. G. Willis shows that the Latin of the institution narrative seems to be more "primitive" than the other parts of the Eucharistic Prayer in that it completely lacks the rhythmic endings, called *cursus*, that mark the rest of the anaphora and, to a greater extent, the collects of the ancient Roman Sacramentaries (*Essays in Early Roman Liturgy* [London: SPCK, 1964], 113–17). This use of *cursus* became common in the liturgical prayers of the fourth and fifth centuries in Rome. This is a probable indication that the institution narrative had become fixed prior to the mid-fourth century and was considered too sacred to be stylistically modified. Willis writes: "*Quam oblationem* has two [rhythmic endings], but the Institution narrative . . . appears to have none at all. This seems to point to its being the earliest part of the Canon" (ibid., 116).

received from the Lord what I also delivered to you" (1 Cor 11:23).

Furthermore, it is reasonable to think that the four accounts of the institution of the Eucharist and their subtle variations—Paul and Luke on the one hand and Matthew and Mark on the other—may be colored by differences in the liturgical practices of the communities of the Evangelists and St. Paul.[117] This presupposes that the institution narrative was already present in the liturgical practice of the Apostolic age.

In the middle of the second century, St. Justin, in his *First Apology*, alludes to "the word of prayer that is from Christ" as effecting the conversion of the bread and wine into His Body and Blood and then goes on to cite the institution narrative.[118] This makes it very likely that the Eucharistic Prayer that Justin was describing in his *Apology* contained these words of Christ as their central core,[119] even though the prayer was not yet fixed in form.[120]

Furthermore, the fundamental similarity among the versions of the institution narrative in almost all Eucharistic Prayers,[121] otherwise often quite diverse, and its centrality[122] and solemnity, indicate that

---

[117] See Jeremias, *The Eucharistic Words of Jesus*, 109–25; Bouyer, *Eucharist*, 157; Benoit, *Jesus and the Gospel*, 1:96–97; Jungmann, *The Mass*, 5–6.

[118] Justin Martyr, *First Apology* 66 (Barnard, *St. Justin Martyr*, 70–71): "We have been taught that the food eucharistized through the *word of prayer that is from Him*, from which our blood and flesh are nourished by transformation, is the flesh and blood of that Jesus who became incarnate. For the Apostles in the memoirs composed by them, which are called Gospels, thus handed down what was commanded them: that Jesus took bread and having given thanks, said: 'Do this for my memorial, this is my body'; and likewise He took the chalice and having given thanks said: 'This is my blood.'" But see also Giraudo, *Eucaristia per la chiesa*, 345–46.

[119] See the discussions in Santogrossi, "Anaphoras without Institution Narrative," 31; Russo, "The Validity of the Anaphora of Addai and Mari," 31; Yarnold, "Anaphoras without Institution Narratives?" 407; Berger, "'Forma huius sacramenti sunt verba Salvatoris,'" 184–85.

[120] This is inferred from the fact that this text, *First Apology* 67, speaks of the presider praying "to the best of his ability" (Barnard, *St. Justin Martyr*, 71).

[121] See Robert Cabié, *The Eucharist*, trans. Matthew O'Connell (Collegeville, MN: Liturgical Press, 1986), 97: "It is at this point [institution narrative] that the various Eucharistic formularies resembled each other most closely, although we never find exactly the same wording twice."

[122] See Willis, *Essays in Early Roman Liturgy*, 128: "The recital of the institution is the core of all eucharistic prayers, and in every anaphora it is united to whatever precedes by the relative pronoun. This is a striking fact. . . . Thus the institution narrative is firmly embedded in a continuous action proceeding from the thanksgiving of the Preface."

this "beating heart"[123] of the Eucharistic Prayer constituted its core from the beginning.

Finally, given the scarcity of direct evidence of Eucharistic Prayers from the first two centuries and the acknowledged weakness of arguments based largely on silence, it is methodologically better to pre-suppose a development of the Eucharistic Prayer in continuity rather than in a radical discontinuity, which would be the case if the insti-tution narrative were generally introduced only in the third or fourth century.

MINISTER OF THE EUCHARIST

Only a priest can validly confect the Sacrament of the Eucharist.[124] It is validly but illicitly celebrated if the priest is impeded by canon law. The principal reason that the minister must be a validly ordained priest is that the Eucharist is essentially a sacrifice, as will be seen below. Sacrifice and priesthood are inseparably linked, for a priest is set apart from other men to make offerings to God on behalf of the whole community. This was already true in Israel. It is still more signif-icant in the New Covenant because the principal priest in every Mass is Christ Himself. The one who offers the sacrifice of the Eucharist must act *in persona Christi*.[125]

Luther on the Minister of the Eucharist

With far-reaching consequences, Martin Luther denied the sacramen-tality of Holy Orders, the distinction between the royal priesthood of the baptized and the ministerial priesthood, and the necessity of the ministerial priesthood for consecrating the Eucharist. These posi-tions were tied to his rejection of the sacrificial nature of the Mass, for priesthood and sacrifice mutually imply each other. Where there is a sacrifice, there must be a priesthood, and vice-versa. In *The Babylonian Captivity of the Church*, he wrote:

---

[123] Giraudo, "La genesi anaforica del racconto istituzionale," 429.

[124] See CIC, can. 900, §1: "The minister who is able to confect the sacrament of the Eucharist in the person of Christ is a validly ordained priest alone."

[125] See John Paul II, *EE*, §29.

> Let everyone, therefore, who knows himself to be a Christian,
> be assured of this, that we are all equally priests, that is to say,
> we have the same power in respect to the Word and the sac-
> raments. However, no one may make use of this power except
> by the consent of the community or by the call of a superior.
> . . . And therefore this "sacrament" of ordination, if it is any-
> thing at all, is nothing else than a certain rite whereby one is
> called to the ministry of the church. Furthermore, the priest-
> hood is properly nothing but the ministry of the Word. [126]

Luther thus held that the office of presiding over the Eucharist is
neither properly priestly nor given by a special sacrament imparting an
indelible priestly character, but a ministry given by the congregation
for a time.

The Church's response, however, is that Christ's will with regard to
the proper minister of the Eucharist, which stands at the very heart of
the Church, is properly known through the Church's constant Tradition. The Council of Trent responded with a definitive condemnation:

> If anyone says that there is in the New Testament no visible
> and external priesthood or that there is no power of conse-
> crating and offering the true Body and Blood of the Lord and
> of remitting and retaining sins, but only the office and bare
> ministry of preaching the gospel . . . let him be anathema.[127]

The principal reason that it is supremely fitting for Christ to have
instituted a special sacrament of Holy Orders giving a sacred power
to consecrate the Eucharist comes from the fact, rightly stressed by
Luther, that the High Priest in the New Covenant is properly Christ
Himself. In the Eucharist, an action is performed that can properly and principally be done only by Christ: making Himself present
through transubstantiation and offering Himself in sacrifice for our
redemption. For this reason, the essential form of the Eucharist is

---

[126] Martin Luther, *The Babylonian Captivity of the Church* (1520) (*LW*, 36:116). See
also *The Misuse of the Mass* (1522) (*LW*, 36:138): "Every true Christian really
ought to know that in the New Testament there is no outward, visible priest,
except those whom the devil has exalted and set up through human lies. We
have only one single priest, Christ."

[127] Council of Trent, Decree Concerning the Sacrament of Orders (session 23, July
15, 1563), can. 1 (DS, 1771).

made up of the words of Christ said in the *first person*.

No one can claim the right to speak Christ's words in the first person! Nor can any congregation give that right to someone.[128] Only Christ can give to another the power to act in His person. The sacrament of Holy Orders therefore highlights the primacy of the agency of Christ Himself in the Eucharist and the transcendence of the gift received. Needless to say, this point was not understood in the heat of the Reformation controversy. Joseph Ratzinger explains well:

> But these words are the words of Jesus Christ. No man can pronounce them for himself. No one can, for his own part, declare his body to be the Body of Christ, declare this bread to be his Body, speaking in the first person, the "I" of Jesus Christ. This saying in the first person—"my Body"—only he himself can say. If anyone were to dare to say, on his own behalf, that he saw himself as the self of Christ, this would surely be blasphemy. No one can endow himself with such authority; no one else can give it to him; no congregation or community can give it to him. It can only be the gift of the Church as a whole, the one whole Church, to whom the Lord has communicated himself. *For this reason the Mass needs the person who does not speak in his own name, who does not come on his own authority, but who represents the whole Church, the Church of all places and all ages, which has passed on to him what was communicated to her.*[129]

St. John Paul II also addresses this point in *Ecclesia de Eucharistia*:

> The ministry of priests who have received the sacrament of Holy Orders, in the economy of salvation chosen by Christ, makes clear that the Eucharist which they celebrate is *a gift which radically transcends the power of the assembly* and is in any event essential for validly linking the Eucharistic consecration to the sacrifice of the Cross and to the Last Supper.[130]

---

[128] See Congregation for the Doctrine of the Faith, Instruction on Certain Questions Concerning the Minister of the Eucharist, *Sacerdotium Ministeriale* (1983).

[129] Ratzinger, *God Is Near Us*, 54 (italics original).

[130] John Paul II, *EE*, §29 (italics original).

Study Questions

1. Explain the three levels in the Eucharist: outward sign (*sacramentum tantum*), inward reality and sign (*res et sacramentum*), and the reality of grace (*res tantum*).
2. In what sense can the sacraments be understood as instruments of Christ? Explain the notion of instrumental causality and how it applies to the sacraments.
3. How does the distinction between conjoined and extrinsic instruments apply to the Eucharist?
4. Explain the distinction between matter and form in the sacraments, and why both are necessary.
5. What are various reasons of fittingness for Jesus's choice to institute the Eucharist under the species of bread and wine?
6. Why is water mixed with the wine in the Eucharist?
7. What is the essential form of the Eucharist? Explain.
8. What is the role of the epiclesis in the Eucharistic Prayer?
9. Why does the Anaphora of Addai and Mari pose a theological problem for the theology of the Eucharist? What are the three reasons given by the Pontifical Council for Promoting Christian Unity in favor of the validity of the Anaphora of Addai and Mari?
10. Why is it fitting that the minister of the Eucharist be an ordained priest?

Suggestions for Further Reading

ST III, qq. 74, 78.

Kwasniewski, Peter A. "Doing and Speaking in the Person of Christ: Eucharistic Form in the Anaphora of Addai and Mari." *Nova et Vetera* (English) 4, no. 2 (2006): 313–80.

Lang, David P. *Why Matter Matters: Philosophical and Scriptural Reflections on the Sacraments.* Huntington, IN: Our Sunday Visitor, 2002.

Nutt, Roger. *General Principles of Sacramental Theology.* Washington, DC: Catholic University of America Press, 2017. Pp. 49–73, 99–137, 166–83.

Pontifical Council for Promoting Christian Unity. "Guidelines for Admission to the Eucharist between the Chaldean Church and the Assyrian Church of the East." July 20, 2001 (with a clarification from October 26, 2001, "Admission to the Eucharist in Situa-

tions of Pastoral Necessity"). Accessed June 29, 2017. http://www.
vatican.va/roman_curia/pontifical_councils/chrstuni/documents/
rc_pc_chrstuni_doc_20011025_chiesa-caldea-assira_en.html.
Zheltov, Michael. "The Moment of Eucharistic Consecration in Byzantine Thought." In *Issues in Eucharistic Praying in East and West:
Essays in Liturgical and Theological Analysis.* Edited by Maxwell
Johnson. Collegeville, MN: Liturgical Press, 2010. Pp. 263–306.

Part II

The Real Presence and Transubstantiation

✠

CHAPTER SIX

The Berengarian Controversy and Development of Eucharistic Theology

The Patristic period was full of controversy over many weighty doctrines, such as the Incarnation, the Trinity, original sin and the necessity of grace, and the use of images. Surprisingly, however, Eucharistic doctrines concerning Christ's real presence in the Eucharist and the substantial conversion of bread and wine into His Body and Blood were not key topics of controversy. Dispute began in the ninth century in France and returned in heightened form in the eleventh century in the dispute with Berengarius. This controversy and the effort to refute the doctrine of Berengarius enabled the Church to reach greater clarity on the doctrine of the real presence of Christ and the substantial conversion of the Eucharistic species.

St. Paschasius Radbertus

The ninth-century Eucharistic controversy began with a reaction to an important work on the Eucharist by St. Paschasius Radbertus, a monk of the monastery of Corbie in France who later became its abbot.[1] Surprisingly, Paschasius's treatise, *De Corpore et Sanguine Domini*, is the first complete treatise on the Eucharist that we have.[2] He further explained his Eucharistic doctrine in a letter to the monk Fredugardus

---

[1] For a summary of Paschasius's teaching, see O'Connor, *The Hidden Manna*, 85–90.

[2] Paschasius, *De Corpore et Sanguine Domini* (Paulus, CCCM, 16:viii). This work is dated to 831–833.

written toward the end of his life in order to defend his treatise from attack.

Paschasius's central thesis is that Christ is present in the Eucharist with the same Body that was born of the Virgin, crucified, and risen. It is that "body born of the Virgin Mary into which this [the Eucharist] is transferred, that which hung upon the cross, was buried in the tomb, rose from the dead, pierced the heavens and has now been made eternal high priest who daily intercedes for us."[3] We receive that very Body in the Eucharist to become members of His Mystical Body.

One of his arguments is that the Eucharist would be capable of giving us eternal life, according to Jesus's words in the sixth chapter of John, only if it is truly the flesh and blood of Him who is the eternal Life. In his letter to Fredugardus, he writes:

> If life did not exist in it [the Eucharist], then it could never be a source of life. Moreover, only that food which is the living and eternal God could give eternal life to those who receive it in a salutary way. . . . And therefore this sacrament that gives life has in itself that which it communicates to those who receive it worthily. And if life is in it, then it is the flesh and blood of that Living One in whom there truly is eternal life.[4]

Paschasius also points to a substantial conversion of the bread and wine when he says that "the body and blood of Christ are made from the *substance* of bread and wine through the power of the Spirit in His word."[5]

Although he neither does so in a systematic way nor uses a clear terminology, Paschasius also distinguishes and alludes to the three levels that later theologians will classify as *sacramentum tantum, res*

---

[3]   Ibid., 7 (Paulus, CCCM, 16:38; PL, 120:1285); see also 1.1 (Paulus, CCCM, 16:14–15): "And since he willed this to be, although He remains under the figure of bread and wine, it is to be believed that after the consecration there is nothing other than the flesh and blood of Christ. . . . And, to speak more marvelously, it is none other than that flesh that was born of Mary, suffered on the Cross, and rose from the tomb." See Mark G. Vaillancourt, "Sacramental Theology from Gottschalk to Lanfranc," in Boersma and Levering, eds., *The Oxford Handbook of Sacramental Theology*, 188.

[4]   Paschasius, *Epistola ad Fredugardum*, lns. 41–49 (Paulus, CCCM, 16:146).

[5]   Paschasius, *De Corpore et Sanguine Domini* 4.38–39: "Corpus Christi et sanguis virtute Spiritus in verbo ipsius ex panis vinique substantia efficitur" (Paulus, CCCM, 16:28).

et sacramentum, and *res tantum.* Although he is principally interested in the real presence (*res et sacramentum*) and its ecclesial effects (*res tantum*), he does not neglect the sacramental signs and their symbolism. In an interesting text, Paschasius explains that the Eucharist is both a figure and a truth or reality, but in different ways:

> Because this is a mystical sacrament, we do not deny that there is a figure. But if it is a figure, we must inquire into what way it can be truth. . . . But it appears to be a figure when it [the host] is broken, when in the visible species something else is understood than that which the vision and taste of the flesh perceives, while blood in the chalice is mixed together with water. On the other hand, this sacrament of faith is rightly said to be truth. It is truth therefore when the body and blood of Christ are made from the substance of bread and wine through the power of the Spirit in His word, and it is figure when the lamb is immolated daily as the priest does something externally at the altar in memory of his sacred Passion that was accomplished once.[6]

Here Paschasius distinguishes various ways in which the Eucharist is both sacred sign and reality. The appearances of the bread and wine are figures of the true reality of the Body and Blood, which they make present. The ritual oblation of Christ's Body and Blood on the altar by the priest is itself the image of another reality, which is Christ's bloody Passion, whose power and fruits are mysteriously made present. In other words, Paschasius has discerned not just one level of symbolism present—that of the appearances of bread and wine—but two. The separate oblation of the Body and Blood is the sacred sign of Christ's bloody immolation on Calvary, and it makes present the effects of Calvary, communicating to us the life of grace like a new tree of life.[7] Because the Body and Blood are not simply represented, but are made present, they are capable of representing and communicating further realities, such as Christ's Passion, the life of grace, and the building

---

6 Ibid., 4.25–42 (Paulus, CCCM, 16:28).

7 Paschasius does not speak in this passage directly of the *res tantum*, but he does so in many other places, such as *Epistula ad Fredugardum*, lns. 41–49 (Paulus, CCCM, 16:146; quoted above). See also *De Corpore et Sanguine Domini* 5.33–34 (CCCM, 16:32) and 7.35–45 (Paulus, CCCM, 16:39).

up of the Church. The Eucharist therefore is not a mere figure or shadow, as were the ceremonies of the Old Covenant,[8] but a supernatural reality that is an efficacious instrument of the grace it represents.

Paschasius's central thesis aroused an interesting discussion in the following decades. Those who focused on the symbolic meaning of the Eucharist accused him of saying that Christ is present in the Eucharist in the same way that a body is present in a place, such that He can be divided into parts, as with the teeth, a position that came to be known as "Capernaism."[9] Such a conception is what scandalized the disciples in Capernaum after the Bread of Life Discourse. Paschasius did not affirm that position, for although he states that Christ is corporally present in the Eucharist, he also says that Christ remains whole, entire, and unchanged throughout.[10] However, he did not sufficiently explain the unique and special mode of Christ's existence in the sacrament. Giving a better account of the sacramental mode of Christ's substantial presence in the Eucharist would be necessary to more clearly explain how Christ's Body in the Eucharist is indeed the Body born of the Virgin, crucified, and risen, which Paschasius rightly affirmed. In order to accomplish this theological task, however, a philosophical foundation would be necessary that would be developed only centuries later through the reappropriation of Aristotelian metaphysics in the High Middle Ages and perfected especially by St. Thomas Aquinas.

A fellow monk and former student of Paschasius named Ratramnus († ca. 870) wrote a work with the same title, *De Corpore et Sanguine Domini*, taking issue with Paschasius's Eucharistic realism.[11] He begins by posing two questions, prompted by questions from King Charles

---

[8] See Heb 10:1.

[9] Paschasius's thesis seems to have been criticized not only by Ratramnus (see below), but also by Gottschalk of Orbais (808–867) (*De Corpore et Sanguine Domini*, ed. Dom Cyril Lambot, in *Oeuvres théologiques et grammaticales de Godescalc D'Orbais* [Leuven, BE: Spicilegium Sacrum Lovaniense, 1945], 324–37), and Rabanus Mauro (ca. 780–856), *Poenitentiale* 33 (PL, 110:493). Paschasius's position was defended, on the contrary, by Hincmar of Reims (806–882), *De Cavendis Vitiis et Virtutibus Exercendis* 10 (PL, 125:928), and Haymo of Halberstadt († 853), *De Corpore* (PL, 118:815). See Vaillancourt, "Sacramental Theology from Gottschalk to Lanfranc," 189–191.

[10] Paschasius, *De Corpore et Sanguine Domini* 7.30–32 (Paulus, CCCM, 16:39). See Vaillancourt, "Sacramental Theology from Gottschalk to Lanfranc," 187.

[11] For the doctrine of Ratramnus, see John F. Fahey, *The Eucharistic Teaching of Ratramn of Corbie* (Mundelein, IL: Saint Mary of the Lake Seminary, 1951); Vaillancourt, "Sacramental Theology from Gottschalk to Lanfranc," 187–91.

the Bald. The first is whether the Eucharist contains the Body of Christ in figure or in truth. He says that some say that the Eucharist "is performed under no figure, or veil, but with the naked exhibition of the Truth itself; others testify that these things are contained under the figure of a mystery, and that it is one thing, which appears to the bodily senses, and another, upon which faith gazes."[12] It seems that Ratramnus (wrongly) understood Paschasius's position to be in favor of the first of these alternatives, whereas Ratramnus defends the second. In reality, this way of presenting the question makes it into a false dilemma, for Paschasius does not say that the Body and Blood is present under no figure; nor is the Catholic faith forced to choose between acknowledging a figure in the Eucharist and acknowledging the true reality of Christ's Body and Blood, for both are true at the same time, but in different ways. This false dilemma will return to cause confusion two centuries later when Berengarius, influenced by this text, poses the same dilemma.

Ratramnus then poses a second question that directly challenges Paschasius's central thesis: does the Eucharist contain the "very same Body which was born of Mary, suffered, died, and was buried, which rose again, ascended into heaven, and sits on the right hand of the Father"?[13] Contrary to Paschasius, Ratramnus answers negatively, for he concludes that no substantial change has taken place, since none can be empirically observed, and therefore the Eucharist contains Christ's Body only in a figure and in power, as in the other sacraments and in the Old Testament figures, such as the manna.[14] Thus Christ's presence is purely spiritual and is capable of spiritually nourishing us in the way that the other sacraments or Old Testament figures communicate salvation, but that is all.[15] In other words, Christ's presence in the Eucharist is not portrayed as essentially different from His presence by power in the other sacraments of the New or Old Covenant. A similar conception will reappear in some Protestant theologians.[16]

Similarly, Ratramnus understands the Eucharist as a pledge of

---

[12] Ratramnus, *De Corpore et Sanguine Domini* 2, in *The Book of Ratramn, the Priest and Monk of Corbey, Commonly Called Bertram, on the Body and Blood of the Lord*, trans. H. W. and W.C. C. (Oxford: John Henry Parker, 1838), 2.

[13] Ibid., 5 (p. 3).

[14] Ibid., 21–26 (pp. 12–15).

[15] Ibid., 47–48 (p. 26).

[16] See John Calvin, *Institutes of the Christian Religion*, bk. 4, ch. 14, nos. 1 and 23, trans. Henry Beveridge (Peabody, MA: Hendrickson Publishers, 2008), 843, 855.

Christ's promise of salvation, but one that remains distinct from that of which it is a pledge.[17] Ratramnus thus affirms that it is spiritual nourishment while denying that it truly contains, under the figure, the substance of Christ's Body and Blood, which theologians of the twelfth and thirteenth centuries will speak of as *res et sacramentum*.

In order to respond to Ratramnus, a sacramental theory needed to be developed with room for three levels and not just the two to which he refers, sacrament and reality. He affirms the sacramental sign and the grace communicated, but he seems to have no concept of an intermediate level of a reality that is invisibly present under the outward sign and is also a sign of the interior grace communicated. This idea, briefly alluded to by Paschasius, as we have seen, will be developed in the eleventh and twelfth centuries, following on Berengarius's appropriation of Ratramnus's thought.

Ratramnus's work seems to have had little influence until it reached Berengarius, who erroneously attributed the work to a more famous contemporary of Ratramnus, John Scotus Eriugena (ca. 815–877). Condemned with the positions of Berengarius, it disappeared again until shortly after the beginning of the Reformation when it aroused the interest of Protestant opponents of Eucharistic realism.

BERENGARIUS OF TOURS

The doctrine of transubstantiation was expressed more clearly when the Church had to combat the heresy of the denial of the Eucharistic conversion of the substance of the bread and wine into the substance of Christ. A denial of the real and substantial presence of Christ in the Eucharist became a serious problem in the West only in the eleventh century,[18] coinciding with a certain rationalist tendency of that time. Berengarius, who was a theologian and an expert in dia-

---

[17] Ratramnus, *De Corpore et Sanguine Domini* 89 (p. 47).

[18] The extent of the polemic can be seen from the introduction to a treatise attributed to Alberic of Monte Cassino: "The report recently brought to us, O most blessed Father, of the questioning that has arisen in regard to the body and blood of the Lord, has suddenly filled all this land to such an extent that not only clerics and monks, whose watchful attention should be devoted to such matters, but even the very laymen are chattering about it among themselves in the town squares" (Charles M. Radding, and Francis Newton, *Theology, Rhetoric, and Politics in the Eucharistic Controversy, 1078–1079: Alberic of Monte Cassino against Berengar of Tours* [New York: Columbia University Press, 2003], 127).

lectics, dared to deny the possibility of the Eucharistic conversion, which would later be called transubstantiation. Although claiming to hold the faith of the Church concerning the real presence, Berengarius firmly denied the conversion of the substance of bread and wine into the substance of Christ because he thought such a conversion was impossible.[19] He thought it was contradictory to affirm that the consecrated host becomes the body of Christ as it is in heaven. How could the body of Christ that is now in heaven, necessarily limited by space, be also on many altars and in numerous hosts?[20] Furthermore, he thought it was contradictory for the accidents of bread to remain while the substance of bread was changed into Christ. It seems that the reason for this denial was that his philosophy had no place for the distinction between substantial and accidental form, and thus between substance and accidents, for he seemed to identify the sensible accidental forms with the form, simply speaking.[21] Therefore, Berengarius thought he had no choice but to view the Eucharist, after the consecration, as a mere symbol or figure of Jesus Christ through which the faithful spiritually receive the Body and Blood of Christ "for faith and understanding," although the substance of bread and wine remain.[22] Berengarius tended to ridicule the simple Eucharistic faith of the common "mob," putting forth his view as the enlightened fruit of reason.[23] In rationalistic fashion, he exalted the

---

[19] See Lanfranc of Canterbury, *On the Body and Blood of the Lord*, ch. 4: "That teaching, however, by which we believe bread is converted into the true flesh of Christ, and wine into the true blood of Christ, you call nonsense" (trans. Mark G. Vaillancourt, FCMC, 10:39).

[20] See Berengarius, *De Sacra Coena adversus Lanfrancum* 37: "A portion of the flesh of Christ cannot be present on the altar . . . unless the body of Christ in heaven is cut up and a particle that has been cut off from it is sent down to the altar" (trans. Jaroslav Pelikan in *The Christian Tradition: A History of the Development of Doctrine* [Chicago: University of Chicago Press, 1978], 3:194).

[21] See Charles Sheedy, *The Eucharistic Controversy of the Eleventh Century Against the Background of Pre-Scholastic Theology* (Washington, DC: Catholic University of America Press, 1947), 66–69, 76–77; James Megivern, *Concomitance and Communion: A Study in Eucharistic Doctrine and Practice* (Fribourg, CH: University Press, 1963), 90.

[22] See the letter from Berengarius to Adelman, Bishop of Brescia quoted in O'Connor, *The Hidden Manna*, 100: "I am able to concede that, after the Consecration, the bread and wine themselves have become, for faith and understanding, the Body and Blood of Christ."

[23] See Berengarius, *De Sacra Coena adversus Lanfrancum Liber Posterior*, ed. A. F. and F. Th. Vischer (Berlin: Haude and Spener, 1834), 34–35, cited in Sheedy, *The Eucharistic Controversy of the Eleventh Century*, 50.

role of empirical reason over faith in investigating a mystery of faith.[24]

In answer to Berengarius, we can say that the Eucharistic conversion is unique and completely above the power of reason to verify. However, as will be seen in the following chapter, reason can respond that no contradiction is involved with regard to the place of the Body of Christ, for Christ is properly only in one place—heaven—in the way in which a body is circumscriptively measured by a place, by way of quantity and dimension.[25] He is in the Eucharist in a different way, by way of substance (as will be explained in the following chapter) "under" the accidents of the consecrated bread and wine, which are in their own proper places. Similarly, there is no contradiction in the miracle of the accidents of the bread and wine remaining without inhering in a substance, since the power of God can directly sustain them. For anything that a creature can do, God can also do. Thus as the substances of bread and wine sustain the accidents that inhere in them, God can also sustain them directly, without the aid of the substances of the bread and wine. Since these things are not contradictory, they are not impossible for God.

Because Berengarius asserted the impossibility of a substantial presence of Christ in the sacrament, he was understood by contemporaries to be denying the power of God to act above nature. Peter Lombard characterized the position of Berengarius and his followers in this way:

> These limit God's power according to the measure of natural things and contradict the truth more boldly and dangerously, asserting that the body of Christ or his blood is not there on the altar, nor is the substance of the bread and wine changed into the substance of the flesh and blood. They say that Christ said: "This is my body," in the same way in which the Apostle said: "The rock was Christ." For they say that the body of Christ is there only in the sacrament, that is, in the sign, and that it is only in the sign that he is eaten by us.[26]

---

[24] See Sheedy, *The Eucharistic Controversy of the Eleventh Century*, 50–60.

[25] "Circumscriptive" refers to the way in which the different parts of a body correspond with or are measured by different parts of its place. See thesis 12 in the Sacred Congregation of Studies' decree *Postquam Sanctissimus* (1914), giving 24 Thomistic theses: "It is also quantity that makes a body to be circumscriptively in one place and to be incapable, by any means, of such a presence in any other place."

[26] Lombard, *Sentences* IV, d. 10, ch. 1, no. 1 (p. 49).

It is not easy to understand the exact position of Berengarius. Although it is clear that he denied the substantial conversion that would later be called transubstantiation and denied that the Eucharist involves a miraculous action of God,[27] it is not clear in what way he understood Christ to be spiritually present in the sacrament. A contemporary theologian, Guitmund of Aversa, who wrote one of the finest responses to Berengarius, mentions that there were two opinions among the Berengarians. Both views asserted the continued presence of the bread and wine after the consecration. One view held that the bread and wine were merely symbols of Christ's body and blood. The other and more subtle view was that the bread and wine remain but Christ becomes present in them in an invisible way, which Guitmund refers to as "impanation":

> For all the Berengarians agree on this: the bread and wine are not changed essentially [*essentialiter*], but what I could wring from certain people was that they differ greatly on this point. Some say that absolutely nothing at all of the body and blood of the Lord is present in these sacraments, claiming that they are only shadows or figures. Others, however, ceding to the correct reasoning of the Church but not receding from foolishness—so that in some way they seem to be with us—say that the Lord's body and blood are truly contained there, but in a hidden way, and they are impanated—if I may say it in that way—so that they may be consumed. And they claim that this is the more subtle opinion of Berengarius himself.[28]

These two understandings of the doctrine of Berengarius will resurface in the Reformation, championed by Zwingli and Luther, respectively.

Berengarius's views caused scandal among the faithful, and he was repeatedly forced to recant. A synod in Rome in 1059 required

---

[27] See Sheedy, *The Eucharistic Controversy of the Eleventh Century*, 41.

[28] Guitmund of Aversa, *On the Truth of the Body and Blood of Christ in the Eucharist* 1.8 (trans. Mark Vaillancourt, FCMC, 10:97). Berengarius's major work, however, does not seem to support the impanation theory, but rather corresponds with the first interpretation, that Christ is present in the sacrament only figuratively. See Sheedy, *The Eucharistic Controversy of the Eleventh Century*, 76: "A presence of Christ's historical Body on the altar in some other way than through substantial change would be for him as contradictory as a presence through substantial change. The Body of Christ cannot possibly be in heaven and on earth at the same time."

Berengarius to swear to the following less than perfect formulation composed by Cardinal Humbert of Silva Candida:

> The bread and wine that are placed on the altar, after the consecration, are not only a sacrament, but also the true Body and Blood of our Lord Jesus Christ and that they are sensibly, not only in sacrament but in truth, touched and broken by the hands of priests and ground by the teeth of the faithful.[29]

This formulation focuses on the real presence: Christ is present not only as in a sacramental sign, but in His true Body and Blood. The declaration, however, does not mention the key point that Christ comes to be present through the *conversion of the substance* of bread and wine into the substance of Christ's Body and Blood. It also leaves open a potential "Capernaitic" misinterpretation by speaking of Christ's Body being really handled, broken, and chewed. It would have been more precise to say that the substance that is handled, broken, and chewed is nothing other than Christ's Body, present whole and indestructible under the appearances of the bread. It should not be thought that the Council was teaching that Christ's Body is actually changed by being handled, broken, and chewed. The sense in which this text must be understood is explained well by a text written after this synod by Guitmund of Aversa: "If the Host seems to be broken by the teeth or in some other way, we understand it to be unbroken, because we believe that the whole body is contained in each single part."[30]

Because Berengarius did not keep his oath to abjure his former view that denied the substantial conversion, he was obliged to swear another formula of faith twenty years later. In the Synod of Rome in 1079 under St. Gregory VII, Berengarius professed the following formula of faith that much more perfectly expresses the mind of the Church:

> I, Berengar, in my heart believe and with my lips confess that through the mystery of the sacred prayer and the words of our Redeemer the bread and wine that are placed on the altar are substantially changed [*substantialiter converti*] into the true

---

[29] Cardinal Humbert of Silva Candida, Synod of Rome, 1059 (DS, 690).

[30] Guitmund, *On the Truth of the Body and Blood of Christ in the Eucharist* 1.16 (Vaillancourt, FCMC, 10:105).

and proper and living flesh and blood of Jesus Christ, our Lord, and that after consecration it is the true body of Christ that was born of the Virgin and that, offered for the salvation of the world, was suspended on the Cross and that sits at the right hand of the Father, and the true blood of Christ, which was poured out from his side not only through the sign and power of the sacrament, but in its proper nature and in the truth of its substance.[31]

This profession of faith is a milestone because it is the first time a magisterial document puts forth the notion of *substantial conversion* as the key to understanding how Christ comes to be truly present in the Eucharist. Although the term "transubstantiation" is not used in this profession of faith, the notion of it is contained in the expression "substantially converted."

CONSEQUENCES OF THE BERENGARIAN CONTROVERSY FOR EUCHARISTIC THEOLOGY

The controversy with Berengarius ended up being extremely fruitful for the development of scholastic Eucharistic theology, and of scholastic theology in general. The errors of Berengarius, which came from a rationalist perspective and a poor philosophy, were met not by a fideist rejection of the use of reason in theology, but by a better use of reason under the tutelage of faith.

In the aftermath of the Berengarian controversy, three important

---

[31] Synod of Rome, February 11, 1079 (DS, 700). This profession of faith was prepared for by a similar profession given in a synod of 1075 in Poitiers:

> We believe in our hearts and profess with our lips that that bread and that wine which are set upon the altar for sacrifice, . . . after the consecration carried out there by the power of the Holy Spirit through the hand of the priest, is substantially transmuted into the true body and into the true blood of Christ—that is, into the very body that was born of the Virgin Mary, which suffered and was crucified for us, which rose from the dead, which sits at the right hand of God the Father, and into that same blood that flowed from his side as he hung on the cross, with no substance or nature of the bread and wine remaining beyond that likeness which we see there with our bodily eyes, that we might not abhor the sacrament by reason of the horror of the blood. (R. Somerville, "The Case against Berengar of Tours—A New Text," *Studi Gregoriani* 9 [1972]: 68–69).

Eucharistic treatises defending the traditional Eucharistic faith of the Church were written by Lanfranc of Canterbury (1005–1089),[32] Guitmund of Aversa († ca. 1090–1095),[33] and Alger of Liège (1055–1131).[34] The first two of these paved the way for the more perfect magisterial formulation of 1079, and all contributed to the subsequent doctrinal development culminating in Aquinas's writings on transubstantiation.

These and other anti-Berengarian authors of the eleventh and early twelfth centuries bring out at least six key points of Eucharistic theology. First, they underline the substantial change. Second, in order to uphold the conversion, they distinguish between the substance of the bread and wine that are converted and the accidents or appearances that remain. Third, they note the unique nature of the conversion, which is supremely miraculous. Fourth, they answer Berengarius' objections against a grossly realist understanding of the Eucharist, or Capernaism, by clarifying that Christ remains whole and entire under every part of the sacrament. Fifth, there is an implicit affirmation of the doctrine of concomitance, which will be explained below. Sixth, they contribute to a deeper understanding of the sign value of the Body and Blood in the Eucharist.

Substantial Conversion

All three of these theologians speak of the substantial conversion of the bread and wine into the Body and Blood of Christ as the central point of the controversy.[35] They also distinguish the substance that

---

[32] Lanfranc, *On the Body and Blood of the Lord* (Vaillancourt, FCMC, 10:29-87). Scholars date this work to roughly 1062, although the text of the Synod of Rome from 1079 was later inserted. See Vaillancourt's introduction (pp. 4–5); Vaillancourt, "Sacramental Theology from Gottschalk to Lanfranc," 196; Jean de Montclos, *Lanfranc et Bérenger: La controverse eucharistique du XIe siècle* (Leuven, BE: Spicilegium sacrum Lovaniense, 1971), 196–97, 249.

[33] Guitmund's *On the Truth of the Body and Blood of Christ in the Eucharist* has been dated to between 1073 and 1075 by Vaillancourt in his introduction (FCMC, 10:11). For a good summary of Guitmund's importance for Eucharistic theology, see O'Connor, *The Hidden Manna*, 106–10.

[34] Alger of Liège, *De Sacramentis Corporis et Sanguinis Dominici* (PL, 180:739–854). This work is dated to the second decade of the twelfth century.

[35] See Lanfranc, *On the Body and Blood of the Lord* 5 (Vaillancourt, FCMC, 10:41), in which he says Berengarius was forced to swear the oath of 1059 because Pope Nicholas concluded "that you taught that the bread and wine of the altar, after the consecration, remain in their former essences without a change of reality." Guitmund, in *On the Truth of the Body and Blood of Christ in the Eucharist* 1.8, sees this

changes from the appearances or accidents that remain. Lanfranc states this in a solemn way:

> We believe, therefore, that the earthly substances, which on the table of the Lord are divinely sanctified by the priestly ministry, are ineffably, incomprehensibly, miraculously converted by the workings of heavenly power into the essence of the Lord's body. The species and whatever other certain qualities of the earthly substances themselves, however, are preserved, so that those who see it may not be horrified at the sight of flesh and blood.[36]

Alger of Liège writes: "In an entirely new and unheard of way the substance of bread is so changed into the substance of the Body of Christ as to cease to be bread, except in appearance, while the body of Christ remains entirely unchanged."[37]

Guitmund further affirms that the substantial conversion is not a mere theological opinion, but the faith of the entire Church:

> For indeed, the belief that the bread and wine of the altar of the Lord are substantially changed [*substantialiter commutari*] into the body and blood of the Lord (not as Berengarius deliriously says, that they are only figures and shadows of the body and blood of the Lord, or that Christ is hidden or concealed within them) has been confirmed by the consent of the universal Church.[38]

Arguments for Substantial Conversion from Scripture and Tradition

Although the anti-Berengarians used philosophy to refute Berengarius's objections, the principal argument against him was not philosophical,

---

as the point that unified all the followers of Berengarius: "For all the Berengarians agree on this: the bread and wine are not changed essentially [*essentialiter*]" (Vaillancourt, FCMC, 10:97).

[36] Lanfranc, *On the Body and Blood of the Lord* 18 (Vaillancourt, FCMC, 10:66).

[37] Lanfranc, *On the Body and Blood of the Lord*, Sheedy (*The Eucharistic Controversy of the Eleventh Century*, 87).

[38] Guitmund, in *On the Truth of the Body and Blood of Christ in the Eucharist* 3.44 (Vaillancourt, FCMC, 10:207–8).

since we are dealing with a supreme mystery, but came from Scripture, the consensus of the Fathers, and the liturgy. Guitmund argued against impanation from the words of institution, and especially from the use of the demonstrative pronoun:

> The Lord Jesus himself destroys these Bread-minglers by the word of his mouth, when, taking the bread, giving thanks, and blessing it, he says: "This is my body." He does not say: "In this my body lies hidden." Neither did he say: "In this wine is my blood," but instead said: "this is my blood."[39]

Guitmund then makes an argument from the Roman Canon:

> Therefore, the Church of God separates them from herself, when, in the very canon of the Mass, from apostolic tradition she prays in this manner: "Which oblation, O God, we beseech you, that in every way, you deign to bless, accept, ratify, make holy and acceptable, so that for us it may become the body and blood of your most beloved Son, our Lord Jesus Christ." One does not pray that the body and blood might lie hidden within it, or that the body and blood might come into it, but that the oblation itself might become both the body and the blood.[40]

Distinction of Substance and Accidents

The anti-Berengarian authors bring out the distinction between substance and accidents, although without a uniform terminology, as a key to resolving the objections of Berengarius. Lanfranc's treatise is the earliest, and with regard to accidents, he speaks of the "qualities" and "appearances" of the bread and wine that remain: "Indeed, it is the same body as far as it concerns its essence, true nature, and its own excellence. It is not the same body in its appearance, however, if one is considering the species of bread and wine and the rest of the qualities mentioned above."[41]

In addition to the language of "appearances" (*species*) that remain,

---

[39] Ibid., 3.37 (Vaillancourt, FCMC, 10:200–01).
[40] Ibid.
[41] Lanfranc, *On the Body and Blood of the Lord* 18 (Vaillancourt, FCMC, 10:66).

both Guitmund and Alger speak more precisely of "accidents"[42] or "accidental qualities." Alger goes further than the others and specifies that God directly upholds the appearances/accidents in being: "The answer to this question is that as God is marvelous in all things, so is He in this; He causes the accidental qualities in His sacrament to exist of themselves, which in other things is impossible."[43]

This was the crux of the issue, for Berengarius's philosophy of nature had no room for this distinction. Ironically, although Berengarius put philosophical reason over faith as a point of method, he did this with a deeply flawed philosophy that had no place for the common sense distinction of substance and accidents.[44] His philosophy implicitly involves a kind of empiricism according to which the reality of a material thing is reduced to its observable qualities and quantity.

Miraculous and Unique Conversion

The anti-Berengarians all stress the ineffable and supremely mysterious nature of this conversion, which requires the omnipotence of

---

[42] See Guitmund, *On the Truth of the Body and Blood of Christ in the Eucharist* 3.28 (Vaillancourt, FCMC, 10:194).

[43] Alger of Liège, *De Sacramentis Corporis et Sanguinis Dominici* (PL, 180:809D–810A). This position is later defended in Lombard's *Sentences* IV, d. 12, ch. 1, no. 1:

> But if it be asked about the accidents which remain, namely species, taste, and weight, in what substance they inhere, it seems to me to be better to profess that they exist without a subject than that they are in a subject; because there is no substance there, apart from that of the Lord's body and blood, which is not joined to those accidents. For the body of Christ does not have their form, but the one in which he will appear at the judgment. And so those accidents, by which the body of Christ, which has its own form and nature, is hidden, remain subsistent through themselves, for the rite of the mystery, as an aid to taste and faith. (p. 60)

[44] See Sheedy, *The Eucharistic Controversy of the Eleventh Century*, 126–27:

> The "reason" upon which he built consisted in an immature philosophical system, the dialectics of the schools. Berengar simply did not know metaphysics, and yet his basic Eucharistic error was in the metaphysical order. His was a sensist metaphysics, the belief that the proper object of sensible experience is being in its totality, that the senses grasp not only the appearances of an object but also its essence, in a direct and immediate manner. Thus, the distinction between substance and accident was lost on him, and he was led to regard as absurd a doctrine which held for a change of substance while the accidents remained.

God. Other conversions involve the generation of a new subject, as in conception, or at least a modification of subject, as when food is digested and becomes part of our body, which is strengthened. In this conversion, on the contrary, all the change is on the part of the bread and wine, which are converted into an already existing subject, Christ, who remains unchanged. But although it is unique, it is not contradictory. Guitmund writes:

> To be sure, there is a difficulty which troubles some who believe that this change cannot occur, and it is this: in the physical world there is hardly any change in the whole of nature which is even remotely similar to it. For when one thing is substantially changed into another [*substantialiter transmutatur*], it is usually changed into that which did not exist before. . . . When, however, we say that the bread is changed, it is not changed into that which had not been flesh, but we confess that it is changed into the flesh which was already the flesh of Christ, without any increase in the flesh of the Lord himself. And although we do not deny that this change is difficult for us to understand in this age, it is, however, not difficult to believe.[45]

Guitmund goes on to analyze different kinds of change, and then he clarifies that this Eucharistic conversion is different from the kinds of change that we know of. He speaks of three kinds of coming into being: creation from nothing (and annihilation), accidental change, and substantial change from one substance into another that comes into being through the change (generation). The Eucharistic conversion is a fourth kind of change different from all of these. Although it is a substantial change, it is a change into an already existing substance (which is not changed thereby). Yet this is not pointless, because it makes Christ Himself to be present so that He can be immolated and received, but without suffering any change:

> The fourth change, however, is the one where that which exists passes into that which is no less existing, in the way that we believe by divine power bread and wine are changed [*commu-*

---

[45] Guitmund, *On the Truth of the Body and Blood of Christ in the Eucharist* 1.31 (Vaillancourt, FCMC, 10:117).

tari] by a certain unique power into Christ's own body [and blood]. And indeed this change is readily judged by believers to be far better, far more useful than the other three. Better indeed because that into which it is changed is divine flesh, which of all things is the best. More useful, moreover, because this change . . . Christ has established as a unique medicine for us.

Although this change involves a change of substance, it is like accidental change, but in reverse. There the accidents change but the substance remains. Here the substance changes, but the accidents remain.[46]

Transubstantiation

The anti-Berengarian theologians all speak of the substantial conversion in the Eucharist, but they lack a technical term to describe it. This lack is supplied in the second half of the twelfth century by the coining of the term *transubstantiatio*, which was used, among others, by Roland Bandinelli (ca. 1105–1181),[47] who became Pope Alexander III. Around 1180 Alan of Lille (ca. 1116–1202) defined the term as follows:

Transubstantiation is that type of change according to which both the matter and the substantial form are changed, while the accidents remain. Thus it is called transubstantiation because nothing of the substance remains, neither as regards matter nor substantial nature. This type of change occurs in the Consecration of the bread. For the bread is changed into the Body of Christ in such a way that nothing of the matter of bread remains; nor does the substance of bread remain. Rather, only certain accidental things remain, such as roundness, whiteness, taste.[48]

---

[46] See Vaillancourt, "Sacramental Theology from Gottschalk to Lanfranc," 197.

[47] See Ambrosius Gietl, ed., *Sententiae Magistri Rolandi*, in Alexander III, *Die Sentenzen Rolands, Nachmals Papstes* (Amsterdam, NL: Rodopi, 1969), 231. For the origins of the term, see Joseph Goering, "The Invention of Transubstantiation," *Traditio* 46 (1991): 147–70.

[48] Alan of Lille, *Contra Haereticos Libri Quatuor* 1.68 (PL, 210:360; translated in O'Connor, *The Hidden Manna*, 116–17).

The term first appears in a magisterial document in 1202, in a doctrinal letter by Pope Innocent III to Archbishop John of Lyon.[49] It was then used by the Fourth Lateran Council in 1215, called by Innocent III, in its definition against the Albigensians and Cathars:

> There is indeed one universal Church . . . in which the priest himself, Jesus Christ, is also the sacrifice. His Body and Blood are truly contained in the sacrament of the altar under the appearances of bread and wine, the bread being transubstantiated into the body by the divine power and the wine into the blood, to the effect that we receive from what is his what he has received from what is ours in order that the mystery of unity may be accomplished.[50]

The Second Council of Lyon (the fourteenth ecumenical council) in 1274 also used the term: "In this sacrament the bread is truly transubstantiated into the body of our Lord Jesus Christ, and the wine into his blood."[51]

Christ Remains Whole and Entire

In order to defend the faith of the Church against the Capernaistic error of gross or exaggerated realism that might be wrongly inferred from the language of the 1059 oath that Berengarius was required to swear, the anti-Berengarian theologians, especially Guitmund, explain that Christ is present whole and entire under each part of the appearances of the bread and wine, and that He is not changed by anything that happens to the Eucharist. This point is crucial for distinguishing the Catholic understanding from Capernaism. Guitmund writes:

---

[49] Innocent III, *Cum Marthae*: "You have asked who has added to the words of the formula used by Christ himself when he transubstantiated the bread and wine into His Body and Blood" (DS, 782). This letter was included in the Decretales of Gregory IX.

[50] Fourth Lateran Council, Definition against the Albigensians and Cathars (DS, 802). The Second Council of Lyon (fourteenth ecumenical council) also used the term in the Profession of Faith of Emperor Michael: "In this sacrament the bread is truly transubstantiated into the body of our Lord Jesus Christ, and the wine into his blood" (DS, 860).

[51] Profession of Faith of Emperor Michael Paleologus to Pope Gregory (DS, 860).

We are also able to say that he is as much in one little portion of the Host as he is in the whole Host. It is as when one reads about the manna, that neither he who gathered more had more, nor he who gathered less had less. Thus the whole Host is the body of Christ in such a way that each and every separate particle is the whole body of Christ. Three separate particles are not three bodies, but only one body. . . . In like manner, if the Host seems to be broken by the teeth or in some other way, we understand it to be unbroken, because we believe that the whole body is contained in each single part.[52]

In support of this view, Guitmund also cites a liturgical text, the preface used between Epiphany and Septuagesima Sunday:

Eternal God, [it is right and just] to offer you this victim of sacrifice, which is the salvific and ineffable sacrament of divine grace: which is offered by the many, and becomes the one body of Christ by the infusion of the Holy Spirit. Each receives Christ the Lord, and the whole Christ is in each portion; he is not diminished by each one of them, but instead offers the whole of himself in each one. Because of it, we who receive the communion of this holy bread and cup are made into the one body of Christ.[53]

Guitmund then gives two analogies to help explain how Christ can remain whole and entire even though there are many Masses and many hosts are divided and chewed. First, an interior thought remains whole and entire within us, even when it is put into words and communicated to many others.[54] Still more apt is the analogy of the soul,

---

[52] Guitmund, *On the Truth of the Body and Blood of Christ in the Eucharist* 1.16 (Vaillancourt, FCMC, 10:104–5).

[53] Gregory the Great, *Liber Sacramentorum*, "Dominica V post Theophaniam" (quoted in Guitmund, *On the Truth of the Body and Blood of Christ in the Eucharist* 1.17 [Vaillancourt, FCMC, 10:105]).

[54] Guitmund, *On the Truth of the Body and Blood of Christ in the Eucharist* 1.19: "For we know by daily experience that our intellect, that is, the word of our heart, when we clothe it, as it were, by the voice, while, hidden in our heart, it was known to us alone, now by means of the voice can be made known to others at one and the same time, while it still remains whole and entire within

which, remaining whole and entire, animates every part of the body, large or small:

> For certainly our soul itself, which is weighed down by a body that is corrupted, is not divided up piece by piece into individual members of the body, but is whole and integrally contained in each individual portion of the body, as St. Augustine most powerfully proves. Why would he who has bestowed such power upon our soul, so that it is simultaneously one and the same, and indivisible in each and every portion of its own body, not also be able to give that same dignity to his own flesh if he wished to? Is not his flesh just as powerful, so that it also could be whole and entire in the diverse portions of his body, which is the Church, since, just as the soul is the life of our body, so also is the flesh of the Savior (by all means many times better than our soul through the grace of God) in a similar way the life of the Church? Indeed, it is through the soul that the body lives temporally, but through the flesh of the Savior, the Church lives happily not just for a time, but forever.[55]

Concomitance

A consequence of the fact that Christ remains whole and unchanged in the Eucharist is the doctrine of "concomitance," which means "accompaniment." Since Christ is present whole and entire under every part of the sacramental species, where His Body is, there also is His Blood, and His entire personal reality.[56] William of Champeaux (ca. 1070–1121), teacher of Abelard and Hugh of St. Victor (1096–1141) and friend of St. Bernard, speaks about concomitance in his *Sentences*:

> It should be known that one who receives either species receives the whole Christ. For Christ is not received piecemeal or bit by bit, but whole, whether one receives both species

---

our heart. So also when the voice is heard equally by a thousand men so that, clothed as it is with the voice, our thought not only illuminates at the same time the hearts of all, but whole and entire touches the ears of all" (Vaillancourt, FCMC, 10:107).

[55] Ibid., 1.19 (Vaillancourt, FCMC, 10:108).

[56] For the development of the doctrine of concomitance, see Megivern, *Concomitance and Communion*.

or just one. Thus, because infants cannot eat bread, they are given communion from the chalice from which they receive the whole Christ.[57]

Alger, writing also at the beginning of the twelfth century, states likewise that "the whole Christ is received in the Flesh and the whole Christ in the Blood, and there are not two Christs divided, but one sole Christ under each species."[58]

Furthermore, because the whole Christ is received under either species, clearly one receives not only Christ's Body and Blood, but also His human soul and His divinity, which were separated at Christ's death but are now forever inseparable from His Body and Blood. William writes:

> Therefore, to hold that it is necessary [for the faithful] to receive under both species is clearly a heresy. . . . In both species the whole Christ is present who after the resurrection is totally . . . impassible, indivisible, such that the blood cannot exist without the flesh nor the flesh without the blood, nor either without the soul, nor the whole human nature without the Word of God which is personally united to it.[59]

But if the whole Christ is contained equally under either species, why then did Christ institute the sacrament under two species? William responds: "Both species are received distinctly, so that the memory of His Body that visibly hung from the Cross, and His Blood that flowed from His side with water, be maintained more firmly and made present."[60] Christ is made present under the two species to make sacramentally present His bloody sacrifice, consisting in the separation of His Blood from His Body.[61]

---

[57] William of Champeaux, *Sentences*, quoted in Odon Lottin, *Psychologie et morale aux XIIe et XIIIe siècles*, vol. 5 (Gembloux, BE: J. Duculot, 1959), 216–17 (my translation). It can be seen that, in the beginning of the twelfth century in France, Holy Communion was given to infants after their Baptism under the species of wine.

[58] Alger of Liège, *De Sacramentis Corporis et Sanguinis Dominici* 2.7 (PL, 180:825D-826A; in Sheedy, *The Eucharistic Controversy of the Eleventh Century*, 91).

[59] Lottin, *Psychologie et morale aux XIIe et XIIIe siècles*, 5:217 (my translation).

[60] Ibid., 5:216–17 (my translation).

[61] See Alger of Liège, *De Sacramentis Corporis et Sanguinis Dominici* 2.7: "Christ consecrated and gave His body and blood separately, not to divide His sub-

Res et Sacramentum: Three Levels in the Eucharist

One of the most significant fruits of the Eucharistic controversy with Berengarius was the distinction of three levels of sign and reality in the Eucharist, an insight that was then extended to other sacraments. Berengarius recognized only two levels: the sacramental sign and the reality of the grace of Christ received through faith in that sign. Indeed, together with his failure to distinguish substance and accidents, Berengarius's most crucial mistake was to make a strict dichotomy between sign or figure (*sacramentum*), on the one hand, and reality (*res*) or truth, on the other, presupposing that Christ could be present only in one or the other of these ways, but not both simultaneously.[62]

Where Berengarius posited a strict alternative between sign and reality, his theological opponents affirm that the Eucharist contains both sign and reality in a more complex way. Although they do not use the term, their thought paved the way for the development of the notion of *res et sacramentum,* which is crucial for sacramental theology. For Berengarius, however, the Eucharist is the sign alone (*sacramentum tantum*), which points to the glorious reality of Christ in heaven (*res sacramenti*), which it makes present only in the way that signs normally do, by way of a mental consideration.[63]

---

stance, so that they would receive two Christs, since in each they received the one Christ, but rather for the distinction of the figure, so that the bread that is crushed by the teeth could signify His flesh crushed in the Passion, and the wine poured in the mouths of the faithful could signify the blood that flowed from the side of Christ" (PL, 180:826A).

[62] See Colman O'Neill, *Sacramental Realism: A General Theory of the Sacraments* (Wilmington, DE: M. Glazier, 1983), 99: "Berengar was curiously modern in his cut-and-dried distinction between what is real and what is simply symbolic. If the bread and wine of the Eucharist, he argued, symbolize Christ and our union with him, then that is all there is to be said about it; Christ is present, but in symbol. . . . From this time on, the only way in which main-line theology could preserve the full mystery of the Eucharist was to make two classes of complementary statements about it, the first symbolic and the second realistic, with each in some way modifying the other." See also Megivern, *Concomitance and Communion,* 90, speaking of Berengarius: "His unquestioned presumption seems to have been that a sign by its very essence *must* be less than what it signifies. The possibility of a sign that actually contains the reality it signifies does not seem to have come under consideration."

[63] See Sheedy's excellent analysis of this:

In their scientific treatment of the Eucharist, medieval theologians inserted between the two elements *sacramentum tantum* and *res tantum,*

To combat Berengarius, the anti-Berengarian theologians of the eleventh and twelfth centuries point out first that the Eucharist is not just the sign or sacrament of an absent reality, but both a sacrament and a reality at the same time.[64] Hugh of St. Victor, for example, writes: "What then! Is the sacrament of the altar then not truth because it is a figure?"[65] Speaking of the substantial conversion, Alger writes: "The sacrament of the bread and wine is so changed as substantially to cease to be what it was before; its substance becomes the Body of Christ; its external appearance, however, remains, and *signifies* the Body of Christ *and contains it.*"[66] That is, the appearances of bread and wine that remain are a sacramental sign alone, but they contain the reality that they signify.

---

a third element, which is *sacramentum-et-res*, the true Body of Christ under the sacramental species. This middle element is totally lacking in Berengar's theology, and its presence in Lanfranc, Guitmund, and Alger is, we think, the key to the controversy concerning the Eucharist as sacrament. The stumbling block for Berengar was his inability to understand how the sacrament could be at one and the same time symbol and reality, and to save the symbol he abandoned the reality. . . . Thus the Eucharistic Body of Christ may be called the sacrament of the Body of Christ, not so as to relate the Eucharistic Body merely to the historical Body, but to the whole Christ, the Mystical body, since the final end and product of the sacrament is to bring about the incorporation of the faithful in Christ. The Body of Christ in the Eucharist is the sacrament of His Mystical body, which is the Church (*The Eucharistic Controversy of the Eleventh Century*, 118).

[64] Lanfranc states this clearly in *On the Body and Blood of the Lord* 8: "For you deny the flesh and blood, holding that whole reality exists solely as a sacrament. And we confess that it is a sacrament, and yet we faithfully and truthfully confess the reality of each as well" (Vaillancourt, FCMC, 10:46). He speaks about the symbolism of the Body of Christ in ch. 5: "The Church of Christ . . . believes that bread is converted into flesh, and wine is converted into blood. Yet the Church salubriously believes and truly recognizes that it is a sacrament of the Lord's Passion, a sacrament of divine propitiation, a sacrament of concord and unity, and finally, a sacrament of the flesh and blood assumed each in its own distinct and unique way from the Virgin" (Vaillancourt, FCMC, 10:40).

[65] Hugh of St. Victor, *On the Sacraments of the Christian Faith* 2.8.6 (Deferrai, 308). He continues: "Then neither is the death of Christ truth because it is a figure, and the resurrection of Christ is not truth because it is a figure. . . . The death of Christ was an example, that we die for sin, and His resurrection was an example, that we live for justice. On this account then was it not truth? . . . Why can the sacrament of the altar not be a likeness and truth? In one respect, indeed, a likeness; in another, truth."

[66] Alger of Liège, *De Sacramentis Corporis et Sanguinis Dominici* 1.8 (PL, 180:761A; in Sheedy, *The Eucharistic Controversy of the Eleventh Century*, 113).

Furthermore, there are two distinct levels of symbolism. The appearances of the bread and wine make present the reality of Christ, and that reality of the Body and Blood is itself a sign of the other effects of the Eucharist, such as our union with Him and our union with one another in the Mystical Body through that union with Him. Finally, the reality of Christ's Body and Blood is also a sign of the Passion of Christ and all that it has won for us; it is a sign of the New Covenant as Jesus says; and it is a sign of our future resurrection, since Christ is present in His glorified humanity.

To show that a reality can be the sign of other realities, Guitmund uses the example of Christ's human body in the mysteries of His earthly life. That human body was itself the sign of many things. St. Simeon referred to Jesus as a sign of contradiction. His being lost for three days and found in the Temple was a figure of His Passion and Resurrection. And all the acts of His earthly life were signs of how the members of the Church are to act. So likewise Christ's Body and Blood in the Eucharist is a sign of His Passion and Resurrection and of our union with His life in the Church.

Later medieval theologians refer to this invisible presence of Christ's Body and Blood as the *res et sacramentum*. It is a reality made present through the conversion of the bread and wine. At the same time, it is a sign of all the further benefits that Christ wills to give us in this sacrament. Hence, it is both a mysterious reality and a sign of other mysterious realities to be given to us through the reality of His Body and Blood.

In the first half of the twelfth century, Hugh of St. Victor, as seen above, gives a clear distinction of these three levels in the Eucharist:

> For although the sacrament is one, three distinct things are set forth there, namely, visible appearance, truth of body, and virtue of spiritual grace. . . . For what we see is the appearance of bread and wine, but what we believe under that appearance is the true body which hung on the cross and the true blood of Jesus which flowed from His side. We do not believe that through bread and wine the body and blood alone are signified but that under the appearance of bread and wine the true body and the true blood are consecrated, and that the visible appearance indeed is the sacrament of the true body and of the true blood, but that the body and blood are the sacrament of spiritual grace. Therefore, what is seen according

to appearance is the sacrament and the image of that which is believed according to the truth of the body, and what is believed according to the truth of the body is the sacrament of that which is perceived according to spiritual grace.[67]

Shortly thereafter, Peter Lombard gave this distinction still greater clarity, coining the classic terms that dominated discussion of the sacraments in the following centuries: *sacramentum tantum*, *res et sacramentum*, and *res tantum*. The theologians of the High Scholastic period, such as St. Thomas Aquinas, received this tripartite scheme as a precious inheritance from the Berengarian controversy through the theologians of the twelfth century.[68]

Fruits of the Controversy

In addition to this increase in the understanding of the dogma of the real presence and transubstantiation, the controversy over Berengarius also led to a beautiful growth in devotion to the Blessed Sacrament throughout the twelfth and thirteenth centuries, culminating in the Eucharistic teaching of St. Thomas Aquinas and the institution of the feast of Corpus Christi in 1264, for which St. Thomas wrote the liturgical office. On the negative side, however, Berengarius sowed the seeds of doubt that spread to others like John Wycliffe, a heretic of the late fourteenth century who was very influential on Martin Luther.

Study Questions

1. Contrast the positions of Paschasius Radbertus and his former student, Ratramnus, on the real presence.
2. What was the position of Berengarius on Christ's presence in the Eucharist? What were the principal roots of his error?

---

[67] Hugh of St. Victor, *On the Sacraments of the Christian Faith* 2.8.7 (Deferrari, 308–9).

[68] See Boyd Taylor Coolman, "The Christo-Pneumatic-Ecclesial Character of Twelfth-Century Sacramental Theology," in Boersma and Levering, eds., *The Oxford Handbook of Sacramental Theology*, 203: "One of the most significant contributions of the twelfth-century is the creation, consolidation, and then successful deployment of a tripartite framework for conceiving of the nature and the effects of the sacraments."

3. What were the key contributions made by Lanfranc of Canterbury, Guitmund of Aversa, and Alger of Liège to the theology of the Eucharist?

4. What are the key aspects in the profession of faith composed by Pope Gregory VII in 1079 that Berengarius had to profess?

5. Explain the three levels of the sacraments. How did the Berengarian controversy help to clarify this important doctrine?

Suggestions for Further Reading

Coolman, Boyd Taylor. "The Christo-Pneumatic-Ecclesial Character of Twelfth-Century Sacramental Theology." In Boersma and Levering, eds. *The Oxford Handbook of Sacramental Theology.* New York: Oxford University Press, 2015. Pp. 201–07.

King, R. F. "The Origin and Evolution of a Sacramental Formula: *Sacramentum Tantum, Res et Sacramentum, Res Tantum.*" *The Thomist* 31, no. 1 (1967): 21–82.

Lanfranc of Canterbury, *On the Body and Blood of the Lord*; and Guitmund of Aversa, *On the Truth of the Body and Blood of Christ in the Eucharist.* In FCMC 10. Translated by Mark G. Vaillancourt. Washington, DC: Catholic University of America Press, 2009.

Sheedy, Charles. *The Eucharistic Controversy of the Eleventh Century Against the Background of Pre-Scholastic Theology.* Washington, DC: Catholic University of America Press, 1947.

Vaillancourt, Mark G. "Sacramental Theology from Gottschalk to Lanfranc." In Boersma and Levering, eds., *The Oxford Handbook of Sacramental Theology.* Pp. 187–200.

✠

CHAPTER SEVEN

The Doctrine of
Transubstantiation according
to St. Thomas

The fruits of the Berengarian controversy, which began to appear in the decades after the condemnations of Berengarius, reached their full maturity in the Eucharistic treatise of St. Thomas Aquinas, which will be the focus of this chapter. His doctrine of transubstantiation, built on the distinction between the notions of substance and accident, is a beautiful example of the fertile interaction between Catholic theology and metaphysics.

THE DISTINCTION BETWEEN SUBSTANCE
AND ACCIDENTS

How does Christ come to be present in the Eucharist in this real and substantial way affirmed by the Church, given that we continue to perceive the appearances of bread and wine? This is a mystery of faith, a supernatural event beyond all natural forces, and thus it cannot be verified by scientific means or demonstrated by philosophy. We believe it solely because of what Christ said at the Last Supper and what He said earlier at the synagogue in Capernaum (John 6) and because the Church's infallible Magisterium has defined the sense of those words and the way they must be interpreted. However, some basic elements of the perennial philosophy must be brought in, not to prove the mystery, which is impossible, but to get the best understanding of what Christ has proclaimed and what the Church teaches about Christ's presence in the Eucharist. This philosophical analysis is also useful to show that a doctrine of the Church is not contradictory. For a mystery of faith, although it is above reason, can never be contrary to reason or in contradiction with itself.

First of all, we must distinguish between substance and accidents (appearances). The accidents of a thing are the changeable conditions which do not directly belong to the essence of the thing, but rather answer the question of *how* a thing is. We know a thing first by its accidents because our senses can perceive only the sensible accidents of things and not the substance per se. Accidents include the sensible aspects of color, taste, smell, sound, heat, texture, size, position, movement, and so on. They also extend to spiritual realities, such as knowledge, virtue, and grace. An accident is something whose nature is to exist *in a subject*: its nature is to have being not in itself, but in another. The being of an accident naturally depends on the being of the substance in which it exists.

"Substance" refers to the reality that underlies all the outward appearances or changeable "accidents" of a thing and gives it its identity. The term "substance" comes from the Latin to "stand under" because the substance is the reality that "stands under" the accidents. St. Thomas explains that substance has two properties, of which "the first is that it needs no external support but is supported by itself: wherefore it is said to subsist, as existing not in another but in itself. The second is that it is the foundation to accidents by sustaining them, and for this reason it is said to substand."[1]

Substance answers the question of *what* a thing is. It is the substance that has being in itself; the accidents have being through the substance. The substance is the whole and abiding subject in which the accidents inhere. St. Thomas defines substance as "something whose nature is . . . to have being *not in another*."[2] It is that which has being in itself, and it is the subject or foundation for the accidents of the thing.

The words uttered by Christ at the Last Supper, "This is my body. . . . This is the chalice of my blood," through the divine omnipotence, convert the *substance* of bread and wine into the *substance* of Christ's

---

[1] Thomas Aquinas, *De Potentia*, q. 9, a. 1, in *On the Power of God*, trans. English Dominican Fathers (Westminster, MD: Newman Press, 1952), 3:99. See John F. Wippel, *The Metaphysical Thought of Thomas Aquinas: From Finite Being to Uncreated Being* (Washington, DC: Catholic University of America Press, 2000), 205–06.

[2] *SCG* I, ch. 25, no. 10 (my italics).

Body and Blood. <u>The outward appearances or accidents of bread and wine, however, are miraculously suspended, remaining exactly what they were, but no longer inhering in a substance</u>. The pronoun "this" before the consecration refers to the substance of the bread. After the words of consecration have been uttered, "this" reality in the priest's hands has now become the Body of Christ.

THE EUCHARISTIC CONVERSION: TRANSUBSTANTIATION

How does Christ come to be really and substantially present in the Eucharist? The answer of the Church is that this occurs through a unique and marvelous *conversion* of the substance of the bread and wine on the altar into the substance of the Body and Blood of Christ. As seen above, the substantial conversion of the bread and wine on the altar into the Flesh and Blood of Jesus Christ was the central part of the oath that Berengarius was required to profess at the Synod of Rome in 1079 under St. Gregory VII,[3] and this conversion was referred to as transubstantiation by the Fourth Lateran Council in 1215.

Presence through Conversion or Local Movement?

St. Thomas theologically defends and illuminates the doctrine of transubstantiation by explaining that the only way that Christ's substantial presence after the consecration can come about without contradiction is through the *conversion* of the entire substance of the bread and wine into the entire substance of Christ's body and blood. This conversion is fittingly called *transubstantiation*, for it is the instantaneous conversion of one entire substance into another. In other words, St. Thomas argues that transubstantiation necessarily follows from the dogma of the real and substantial presence of Christ's Body and Blood in the Eucharist.

Are there any other options? Could Christ come to be present by *moving into* the bread and wine instead of through their conversion into Him? This is another logical alternative held by Martin Luther and some theologians of the eleventh and twelfth centuries,

---

[3] Synod of Rome, February 11, 1079 (DS, 700).

including some followers of Berengarius,[4] who sought to maintain the real presence while denying that any change happened with respect to the bread and wine. They held that the substance of the bread and the substance of the wine remain after the consecration and that Christ comes to be present *in addition to* them. Instead of the bread and wine being converted into Christ, this theory would imply a coming of Christ into the bread and wine. This position is often referred to as "consubstantiation," or "impanation." Consubstantiation implies simply that both substances, bread and Christ, are present together. Impanation implies, in addition, the idea that Christ has somehow assumed the bread and wine on the analogy of the hypostatic union.[5]

St. Thomas argues that consubstantiation is not compatible with the faith of the Church for two principal reasons. One argument, already given by many of Aquinas's predecessors, is based on the words used by Jesus in instituting the sacrament. Consubstantiation seems incompatible with the words of Christ that are the form of the sacrament: "This is my body."[6] If the substance of bread remained, Christ

---

[4] Peter Lombard refers to some theologians who held this position in his *Sentences* IV, d. 11, ch. 2, no. 6: "But others held that the substance of bread and wine remains there, and the body and blood of Christ is also there; and for this reason this substance is said to become that one, because where this one is, that one is also (which is a wonder). And they say that the very substance of bread or wine is the sacrament. But that no other substance is there except the body and blood of Christ is manifestly shown by the authorities above and below" (p. 56).

[5] See Boyd Taylor Coolman, "The Christo-Pneumatic-Ecclesial Character of Twelfth-Century Sacramental Theology," in Boersma and Levering, eds., *The Oxford Handbook of Sacramental Theology*, 205: "Generally speaking, 'consubstantiation' refers to any view that affirms the continuing, substantial reality of bread and wine, along with ('con') the substantial presence of Christ's body and blood. Impanation not only affirms the ongoing substantial presence of bread and wine along with body and blood, but also specifies a relationship between them, on analogy with the Incarnation (lit. 'being enfleshed')."

[6] *ST* III, q. 75, a. 2: "Secondly, because this position is contrary to the form of this sacrament, in which it is said: 'This is My body,' which would not be true if the substance of the bread were to remain there; for the substance of bread never is the body of Christ. Rather should one say in that case: 'Here is My body.' Thirdly, because it would be opposed to the veneration of this sacrament, if any substance were there, which could not be adored with adoration of latria." See also *SCG* IV, ch. 63, no. 5: "Furthermore, if the substance of the bread is simultaneous in this sacrament with the true body of Christ, Christ should rather have said: 'My body is here' than: 'This is My body.' For by 'here' one points to the substance of the bread, if it remains in the sacrament with the body of Christ."

would have had to say: "Here is my body"; "Here, where the bread is, there is also my body"; or "My body is in the bread." But instead He said: "*This* is my body."[7] The meaning has to be: "The substance present under these accidents—which was bread—is now my body." We generally use demonstrative pronouns to stand in a generic way for things or substances, as when we say that *this* is a cat or a dog.[8] Christ's words therefore imply a conversion of substance from one "this" into another "this."[9] If the substance of bread and wine continued to exist after the words of consecration, then those words of Christ would not be true, as St. Thomas points out, "for the substance of bread never is the body of Christ."[10] For those words to be true, the substance indicated by the pronoun "this" has to be simply Christ's body and nothing else.

St. Thomas also gives another more original and powerful argument against any position holding the continued existence of the substance of bread and wine after the consecration. This is a theological argument presupposing faith in the substantial presence of Christ in the Eucharist, but it makes use of a metaphysical analysis of how a substance can come to be present where it was not present before. The core of St. Thomas's reasoning, which is consistent throughout his career,[11] is that a substance can begin to be present in a new place

---

[7] As seen above (ch. 6, p. 246), this argument from St. Thomas based on the words of institution was made two centuries earlier by Guitmund of Aversa against Berengarius, in *On the Truth of the Body and Blood of Christ of Christ in the Eucharist* 3.37 (Vaillancourt, FCMC, 10:200–1).

[8] See *ST* III, q. 78, a. 5, ad 1, where St. Thomas says that the phrase, "this is my body," assigns "no noun on the part of the subject, but only a pronoun, which signifies substance in common, without quality, that is, without a determinate form."

[9] See *ST* III, q. 78, a. 5, ad 2: "The pronoun *this* does not indicate the accidents, but the substance underlying the accidents, which at first was bread, and is afterwards the body of Christ, which body, although not informed by those accidents, is yet contained under them."

[10] *ST* III, q. 75, a. 2.

[11] Aquinas first makes this argument in his commentary on the *Sentences* of Peter Lombard, *In IV Sent.*, d. 11, q. 1, a. 1, qla. 1:

It is impossible for something to exist now where it previously did not, without either itself changing or something else changing into it. . . . If therefore the body of Christ is truly under the sacrament now where previously it was not, it is necessary for some movement or mutation to have occurred. But according to this position [that the bread and wine remain after the consecration] no change occurs on the part of

in only two ways: by moving to the new place or by something already in that place converting into it.[12] In other words, something can begin to be present in a place either through local motion or through generation/conversion. For a substance to begin to be present somewhere, either it must undergo a change of place or something else must change into it. For example, fire can begin to be present in a room by being carried there from somewhere else, or it can begin to be present by being ignited there and transforming other things into itself, such as wood. Likewise, ash can begin to be present in a place by being

---

the bread. Therefore it would be necessary for the body of Christ to have changed at least through local movement, in order for it to be said that the body of Christ is now here. . . . But this altogether cannot be, because the body of Christ is consecrated simultaneously in different places, and thus it would be necessary that one and the same body be moved at the same time to different places. This is impossible, for it would mean that contrary movements would belong to the same body (or at least distinct movements of the same kind). That this is heretical is clear from the fact that it contradicts the truth of Scripture, for it would not be true to say: "This is my body," but rather: "Here is my body."

See also *SCG* IV, ch. 63; *ST* III, q. 75, a. 2.

[12] *ST* III, q. 75, a. 2:

I answer that, some have held that the substance of the bread and wine remains in this sacrament after the consecration. But this opinion cannot stand: first of all, because by such an opinion the truth of this sacrament is destroyed, to which it belongs that Christ's true body exists in this sacrament; which indeed was not there before the consecration. Now a thing cannot be in any place, where it was not previously, except by change of place, or by the conversion of another thing into itself; just as fire begins anew to be in some house, either because it is carried thither, or because it is generated there. Now it is evident that Christ's body does not begin to be present in this sacrament by local motion. First of all, because it would follow that it would cease to be in heaven: for what is moved locally does not come anew to some place unless it quit the former one. Secondly, because every body moved locally passes through all intermediary spaces, which cannot be said here. Thirdly, because it is not possible for one movement of the same body moved locally to be terminated in different places at the one time, whereas the body of Christ under this sacrament begins at the one time to be in several places. And consequently it remains that Christ's body cannot begin to be anew in this sacrament except by change of the substance of bread into itself. But what is changed into another thing, no longer remains after such change. Hence the conclusion is that, saving the truth of this sacrament, the substance of the bread cannot remain after the consecration.

carried there or by wood being converted into it by a fire. Similarly, a baby can begin to be present in a woman's womb either by being moved there, if it was artificially conceived in a test tube, or by being naturally conceived there through the union of the egg and sperm to form a new human being.

Applying these two alternatives to the Eucharist, the two options are that either (a) Christ's Body and Blood are *moved* into the bread and wine, which remain unchanged, or (b) that the bread and wine are *converted* into Christ's body and blood. Either the change is on the part of Christ (He is moved into the bread and wine), or it is on the part of the bread and wine (they are converted into Christ, who remains unchanged).[13] If neither the bread and wine nor Christ are changed, however, then Christ could not begin to be present where He was not present earlier. The key question, therefore, is whether, on the one hand, it is Christ who changes through local movement in some kind of consubstantiation or, on the other, the change is on the part of the bread and wine through conversion into Christ's Body and Blood. If we deny change on the part of Christ, such as movement, then we must affirm change or conversion on the part of the bread and wine. We cannot deny both without denying the real presence of Christ in the Eucharist.

It is clear that Christ does not begin to be present in the Eucharist through local motion, and this is for several reasons.[14] First, if that

---

[13] A third logical possibility, very rarely put forward, is that both the substances of bread and wine *and* Christ's body and blood are changed by the consecration. This seems to be the position of Germain Grisez, "An Alternative Theology of Jesus' Substantial Presence in the Eucharist," *Irish Theological Quarterly* 65 (2000): 111–31. Grisez excludes consubstantiation, for he holds that the substance of bread is transformed into Christ. However, his position is that the accidents of the bread and wine inhere in Christ after the consecration (123), which would mean that Christ's body is augmented with new dimensive quantity (that of each consecrated host) and new qualities (those of the bread and wine).

[14] The nucleus of St. Thomas's understanding that the real presence comes about through conversion rather than some kind of movement can be found in John Damascene, *An Exact Exposition of the Orthodox Faith* 4.13:

This [the eucharistic conversion] is not because that body which was taken up to heaven comes down from heaven, but because the very bread and wine are changed into the body and blood of God. However, should you inquire as to the manner in which this is done, let it suffice for you to hear that it is done through the Holy Ghost, just as it was through the Holy Ghost that the Lord made flesh subsist for Himself

were true, His Body would cease to be present in heaven, which is false. Second, His Body would have to pass through all the intervening places to get there, which would require some time. However, after the consecration of the Eucharist, we do not have to wait for Christ's Body to arrive from heaven.[15] Third, His Body could become present only in one place at a time, and thus He could not be present simultaneously in all the consecrated hosts throughout the world. The reason for this is that it seems contradictory for one and the same body to be in several entirely distinct places at the same time while still remaining one undivided body.

By eliminating the possibility of local movement, we have to hold instead that He becomes present through the other possibility, which is conversion of the bread and wine into Him.[16] Christ becomes present on the altar because the bread and wine become His Body and

---

and in Himself from the blessed Mother of God. . . . It is not amiss to say this, that just as bread by being eaten and wine and water by being drunk are naturally changed into the body of the person eating and drinking and yet do not become another body than that which the person had before, so in the same way are the bread of the offertory and the wine and water supernaturally changed into the body and blood of Christ by the invocation and coming down of the Holy Ghost. (FC 37 [Chase, 358])

[15] See *SCG* IV, ch. 63, nos. 3–4:

The first consideration we meet, then, is that of the way in which the true body of Christ begins to be under this sacrament. It is impossible, of course, that this take place by a local motion of the body of Christ. One reason is that it would follow that He ceases to be in heaven whenever this sacrament is performed. Another reason is that this sacrament could not be performed at the same time except in one place, since a local motion is not ended except at one term. Another reason, also, is that local motion cannot be instantaneous, but requires time. Consecration, however, is perfected in the ultimate instant of the pronouncement of the words. Therefore, one concludes by saying that the true body of Christ begins to be in this sacrament by the fact that the substance of the bread is converted into the substance of the body of Christ, and the substance of the wine into the substance of His blood.

[16] *SCG* IV, ch. 63, no. 5: "But thus appears the falsity of the opinion: not only of those who say that the substance of the bread exists simultaneously with the substance of Christ in this sacrament, but also of those who hold that the substance of bread is reduced to nothing or is resolved into prime matter. For on each of these positions it follows that the body of Christ does not begin to be in the sacrament except by local motion. And this is impossible, as we have shown."

Blood. An odd thing about this conversion, however, is that bread and wine are converted into a substance that *already exists*: Christ's Body and Blood, which are not generated or changed by this conversion. All the change is on the part of the substance of the bread and wine that become Christ's Body and Blood. Meanwhile, the accidents of the bread and wine remain what they were before.

The fact that transubstantiation involves the conversion of the bread and wine rather than the local movement of Christ into them is what makes possible the simultaneous celebration of many Masses throughout the world and the resulting real presence in many different tabernacles at the same time. There can be many simultaneous conversions of many different bodies of bread and wine into Christ's one Body in heaven. However, there cannot be many simultaneous local movements of the one Body of Christ into many different localities all at the same time.

Transubstantiation Is Not Annihilation

It is important to distinguish this substantial conversion from an annihilation of the bread and wine. The elements of bread and wine are not turned into nothingness, as some theologians have maintained,[17] but rather into Christ's Body and Blood. Christ's words—"this is my body"—do not signify the annihilation of anything, but rather that one substance, the bread, becomes another, Christ's Body, and similarly that the wine becomes His Blood. He did not say: "Let the bread cease to exist and let my Body take its place."

Furthermore, if the substances of bread and wine were simply annihilated, Christ would not be made present under their appearances, for then they would not be converted into Christ and He would have to become present through some kind of motion, which we have seen to be impossible. Aquinas writes:

> No way can be assigned whereby Christ's true body can begin to be in this sacrament, except by the change of the substance of bread into it, which change is excluded the moment we admit either annihilation of the substance of the bread, or dissolution into the original matter. Likewise no cause can be assigned for such dissolution or annihilation, since the effect

---

[17] See Lombard, *Sentences* IV, d. 11, ch. 2, no. 5 (p. 56).

of the sacrament is signified by the form: 'This is My body.' Hence it is clear that the aforesaid opinion is false.[18]

The Substantial Conversion Is Instantaneous

Because transubstantiation is a substantial change, it follows that it occurs in an instant. Changes can be gradual and continuous only when a given accidental form, such as heat or size, can receive a greater or lesser intensity or quantity. This is not the case with a substantial form, such as bread or the form of Christ's Body, which is either present or not.

Transubstantiation, however, is more radically instantaneous than other natural substantial changes because natural substantial change always presupposes a succession of changes in the disposition of the previous subject whose accidental forms are so modified that the substance can no longer retain its original substantial form. Transubstantiation, on the other hand, is not realized by successive changes in the disposition of the matter, but simply by the divine omnipotence changing one substance immediately into another. Aquinas writes:

> For these three reasons this conversion is instantaneous. First, because the substance of Christ's body which is the term of this conversion, does not receive more or less. Secondly, because in this conversion there is no subject to be disposed successively. Thirdly, because it is effected by God's infinite power.[19]

The Appearances of Bread and Wine Remain

Transubstantiation involves a twofold miracle: a miraculous *conversion* of substance and a *preservation* of the accidents. There is the complete and instantaneous conversion of the substance of bread and wine into Christ. Secondly, however, God continues to maintain the existence of all the appearances or accidents of the bread and wine, even though the substance of bread and wine that formerly sustained them in being has been converted into Christ's Body and Blood. This applies not only to sensible appearances but also to the natural action of the bread and wine in nourishing or even intoxicating. All the accidents of the

---

[18] *ST* III, q. 75, a. 3. See also *In* IV *Sent.*, d. 11, q. 1, a. 2.
[19] *ST* III, q. 75, a. 7.

bread and wine are preserved after transubstantiation, including quantity, quality, relation, place, time, action, and passion, which is their power to act on other bodies, such as our digestive system,[20] and to be acted upon by others, such as our teeth and digestive system. This means that there is no empirical difference at all between a consecrated and an unconsecrated host. All the empirical qualities (but not the substance) of the bread and wine remain after transubstantiation. No chemical or physical analysis could reveal any difference.

Why does God do this second miracle of preservation? First of all, the appearances of the bread and wine enable us to receive Christ as spiritual nourishment in a manner fitting for human nature and without the appearance of cannibalism! Aquinas explains:

> Spiritual effects were fittingly given under the likeness of things visible (as was said); therefore, spiritual nourishment of this kind is given to us under the appearances of the things which men rather commonly use for bodily nourishment. Bread and wine are of this sort. Accordingly, this sacrament is given under the appearances of bread and wine.[21]

Second, Christ wished His presence on our altars and in our tabernacles to be an article of faith and not of vision. He did not wish us to see His glorious Body made present by the words of consecration and, so, lose the merit of faith, which is firm belief in what is unseen. Thus He chose to have the appearances of bread and wine remain in the sacrament as *sacred veils*, suspended over His mysterious presence in the consecrated host. St. Thomas summarizes these reasons for the preservation of the appearances:

---

[20] See *ST* III, q. 77, a. 3: "Because, according to what was said above (a. 1), it is an effect of the divine power that the sacramental species continue in the being which they had when the substance of the bread and wine was present, it follows that they continue in their action. Consequently they retain every action which they had while the substance of the bread and wine remained, now that the substance of the bread and wine has passed into the body and blood of Christ. Hence there is no doubt but that they can change external bodies."

[21] *SCG* IV, ch. 61, no. 2. See Roch Kereszty, "Real Presence, Manifold Presence: Christ and the Church's Eucharist," *Antiphon* 6, no. 3 (2001): 29: "The accidents of bread and wine remain to signify that Christ is our spiritual nourishment. . . . The consecrated bread and wine do appear to the senses as bread and wine precisely to reveal to the eyes of faith that Christ's sacrificed and risen humanity became true food and drink for eternal life."

It is evident to sense that all the accidents of the bread and wine remain after the consecration. And this is reasonably done by Divine providence. First of all, because it is not customary, but horrible, for men to eat human flesh, and to drink blood. And therefore Christ's flesh and blood are set before us to be partaken of under the species of those things which are the more commonly used by men, namely, bread and wine. Secondly, lest this sacrament might be derided by unbelievers, if we were to eat our Lord under His own species. Thirdly, that while we receive our Lord's body and blood invisibly, this may redound to the merit of faith.[22]

Lanfranc of Canterbury, writing in the eleventh century in controversy with Berengarius, had similarly explained the continued appearances of the bread and wine: "The species and whatever other certain qualities of the earthly substances themselves, however, are preserved, so that those who see it may not be horrified at the sight of flesh and blood, and believers may have a greater reward for their faith at the sight."[23]

With regard to the preservation of the accidents, St. Thomas notes an important possible objection. Since accidents depend for their being on the substance in which they exist, it would seem that they could not subsist without their proper subject. But he answers: "An effect depends more on the first cause than on the second. And therefore by God's power, which is the first cause of all things, it is possible for that which follows to remain, while that which is first is taken away."[24] In other words, the power of God can do directly what any creature does and can supply for the lack of any created cause if the plan of the divine wisdom would be served thereby.[25] In this case, God's plan is served by His directly sustaining the existence of the accidents of bread and wine even though the substances of the bread and of the wine are no longer there to be the natural foundation of those accidents.

Two further objections can be made against the preservation of the appearances. First, it could seem that, in this way, God would be deceiving us, for by preserving the accidents of the bread and wine,

---

[22] *ST* III, q. 75, a. 5.

[23] Lanfranc of Canterbury, *On the Body and Blood of the Lord*, ch. 18 (Vaillancourt, FCMC, 10:66).

[24] *ST* III, q. 75, a. 5, ad 1.

[25] See Scheeben, *The Mysteries of Christianity*, 474–77.

He would be leading us to believe that their substance is there when it is not. St. Thomas responds by pointing out that our senses do not deceive us in seeing the appearances of bread and wine, for those appearances continue to exist after the consecration as they did before. Nor does our intellect deceive us, provided we have faith in the real presence:

> There is no deception in this sacrament; for the accidents which are discerned by the senses are truly present. But the intellect, whose proper object is substance as is said in *De Anima* 3, is preserved by faith from deception. . . . Faith is not contrary to the senses, but concerns things to which sense does not reach.[26]

Furthermore, it might be thought that it is simply contradictory for the accidents to remain without their proper substance,[27] for it belongs to the nature of an accident that it inhere in a substance and receive its being from that of the substance. That is true. But the fact that it is natural for accidents to inhere in their proper substance does not mean that it is impossible or contradictory for the accidents to be made to exist in an unnatural and miraculous state, deprived of their natural support in the substance of bread and wine, for God can work in creatures above their nature.[28]

---

[26] *ST* III, q. 75, a. 5, ad 2.

[27] St. Thomas poses this objection in *ST* III, q. 77, a. 1, obj. 2:

> Further, not even by miracle can the definition of a thing be severed from it, or the definition of another thing be applied to it; for instance, that, while man remains a man, he can be an irrational animal. For it would follow that contradictories can exist at the one time. . . . But it belongs to the definition of an accident for it to be in a subject, while the definition of substance is that it must subsist of itself, and not in another. Therefore it cannot come to pass, even by miracle, that the accidents exist without a subject in this sacrament.

[28] See *ST* III, q. 77, a. 1, ad 2:

> Since being is not a genus, then being cannot be of itself the essence of either substance or accident. Consequently, the definition of substance is not—*a being of itself without a subject*, nor is the definition of accident—*a being in a subject*; but it belongs to the quiddity or essence of substance *to have existence not in a subject*; while it belongs to the quiddity or essence of accident *to have existence in a subject*. But in this sacrament it is not in virtue of their essence that accidents are not in a subject, but through the Divine power sustaining them; and

If we seek an analogy, the unnatural state of the accidents of the bread and wine after the consecration is somewhat like the unnatural state of the human soul after death and before the resurrection. It is natural for a human soul to animate its proper human body. At death, however, the soul separates from the body that can no longer sustain it and continues to exist in an unnatural state, lacking an essential part. God somehow compensates for the lack of the sense faculties in the separated soul. The point of the analogy is to show that it is not contradictory for the accidents to be without their proper substance, as Berengarius thought. It is unnatural and miraculous, but not contradictory. Even God cannot do something contradictory, but He can bring about a state of affairs that transcends the natural order, and He does so for the sake of a supernatural good. St. Thomas explains:

> There is nothing to hinder the common law of nature from ordaining a thing, the contrary of which is nevertheless ordained by a special privilege of grace, as is evident in the raising of the dead, and in the restoring of sight to the blind; even thus in human affairs, to some individuals some things are granted by special privilege which are outside the common law. And so, even though it be according to the common law of nature for an accident to be in a subject, still for a special reason, according to the order of grace, the accidents exist in this sacrament without a subject, on account of the reasons given above.[29]

It might be objected, finally, that the accidents of the bread and wine after the consecration inhere in Christ's glorious Body. This solution would take away the necessity for positing the additional miracle of God sustaining the accidents of bread and wine without a subject in which they inhere.[30] Such a position is impossible, however, for it

---

consequently they do not cease to be accidents, because neither is the definition of accident withdrawn from them, nor does the definition of substance apply to them.

On God's action in directly sustaining the accidents of bread and wine see Levering, *Sacrifice and Community*, 156–60.

[29] *ST* III, q. 77, a. 1, ad 1.

[30] A position of this type has been advanced by Grisez, "An Alternative Theology of Jesus' Substantial Presence in the Eucharist," esp. 123. Grisez thinks that, on Thomas's account, the accidents would be the "accidents of nothing" or "so

would mean that Christ would be greatly (and grotesquely) altered by every act of transubstantiation, through which He would acquire new accidents proper to bread and wine and foreign to human nature. St. Thomas responds that "it is manifest that these accidents are not subjected in the substance of Christ's body and blood, because the substance of the human body cannot in any way be affected by such accidents; nor is it possible for Christ's glorious and impassible body to be altered so as to receive these qualities."[31] Christ is present under the accidents of the bread and wine but without being changed by them, as if He were their proper subject.[32]

Transubstantiation Is above Reason but Not against Reason

The Eucharist certainly cannot be explained by reason, but nevertheless, reason is equally impotent to show that Catholic doctrine on the Eucharist is contradictory or impossible. Certainly the Eucharist is naturally impossible, and in fact, it is the greatest miracle known to man. It is something entirely supernatural. But it is not contradictory.

The Council of Trent addresses this question in its definition of the real presence:

---

much of nothing" (114). This does not do justice to St. Thomas's account. It is central to his position that the accidents of the bread and wine after the consecration continue to have the same being that they formerly had prior to consecration. This means that they continue to have the being proper to the accidents of bread and wine. They are not accidents of nothing, but still of bread and wine, even though their proper subject no longer exists after transubstantiation. Furthermore, the appearances of bread and wine are the sacramental sign. They signify Christ present as spiritual nourishment, and thus they make Him present in that way. They can do this only if they retain their own being and ontological integrity as appearances of bread and wine (not of nothing, nor of Christ). Hence Aquinas's position that the appearances are miraculously sustained by God in the being they had formerly is crucial to the very nature of a sacrament.

[31] *ST* III, q. 77, a. 1.

[32] See Nicolas, *What Is the Eucharist?* 52–53: "We cannot say that the body of Christ is affected by the accidents of the bread. It does not acquire the extension of this host, it is not white, does not have its taste, etc. All these accidents remain foreign to it. Between it and them there is no relationship other than that of presence, of immanence. Thus I may break the host, but Christ is not broken in any way. He is simply present whole and entire in each of the two particles."

There is no contradiction in the fact that our Savior always sits at the right hand of the Father in heaven according to his natural way of existing and that, nevertheless, in his substance he is sacramentally present to us in many other places. We can hardly find words to express this way of existing; but our reason, enlightened through faith, can nevertheless recognize it as possible for God, and we must always believe it unhesitatingly.[33]

The Catholic doctrine of the real presence is not contradictory; it simply rests on the omnipotence of God and the divinity of Jesus Christ. Just as God can create the world out of nothing, so He can change one thing into another by His word. He who said at the beginning, "Let there be light," now says, "This is my body." And just as out of nothingness light was made, so now Jesus Christ is made present on the altar under the appearances of bread and wine.

An eleventh-century defender of the Eucharistic faith of the Church against the heresy of Berengarius made this point forcefully:

For if the very nature of all things has come to exist by the will of God, since it would be nothing at all [had God not made it], and if that nature has been formed into such a variety of different species of created things, how is it, then, that the nature of bread and wine now existing is able to resist the will of God so that one reality cannot be transferred into another? . . . If therefore, the stomach of a man or any animal whatsoever can change bread and wine, or whatever other food that is enclosed within it, into living flesh and living blood daily, is not God just as great, such that he can, by the power of the majesty of his presence and by the strength of his word, if he wishes, transform bread and wine into his flesh and blood?[34]

There is nothing contradictory about the substantial conversion of one substance into another instantaneously. It would be contradictory only to say simultaneously both that the bread is converted into the

---

[33] Council of Trent, On the Sacrament of the Eucharist (session 13), ch. 1 (DS, 1636).

[34] Guitmund, *On the Truth of the Body and Blood of Christ in the Eucharist* 1.9 (Vaillancourt, FCMC, 10:98–99).

Body and that it is not converted. Since God has dominion over being, He can take any being and make it into any other being of any kind. And God has no need of any gradual process of conversion to do this, as all creatures would. Nor does He need to make use of a substrate of this change, such as prime matter, as created agents would. Since He is the Lord of being, He can convert any being into any other being directly and immediately without there being any proper substrate of the change:

> Form cannot be changed into form, nor matter into matter by the power of any finite agent. Such a change, however, can be made by the power of an infinite agent, which has control over all being, because the nature of being is common to both forms and to both matters; and whatever there is of being in the one, the author of being can change into whatever there is of being in the other, withdrawing that whereby it was distinguished from the other.[35]

The technical term "transubstantiation" shows us that this conversion of the bread and wine into Christ is no ordinary conversion. It is a unique conversion that has no direct parallel in the natural world. This, of course, does not make it impossible, for God is not bound to obey the normal laws of nature: He framed that order through His omnipotence, and hence, He can also operate outside the natural order He has created.

Likewise, the omnipotence of God, which created the substance and appearances or accidents of things, such as the substance and accidents of bread and wine, is powerful also to miraculously disjoin what He put together in composing the natural order of things. For God has complete dominion over His creation. The only limit on God's omnipotence is contradiction, for even God cannot make a square circle or make something that is both bread and not bread at the same time and in the same way. After the consecration, the Eucharist is not both bread and not bread. It is Christ, and it is not bread. Only the accidents of bread remain, without the underlying substance of bread, for the substance has been converted into Christ. God, the creator of substance and accidents, can do this. Given that He could do this, how do we know that He did in fact do this? Because He Himself said so at the Last Supper: "This is my body."

---

[35] *ST* III, q. 75, a. 4, ad 3.

This truth is marvelously expressed in St. Thomas Aquinas's hymn, *Adoro te devote*:

> Sight, touch, and taste in Thee are each deceived;
> the ear alone most safely is believed:
> I believe all the Son of God has spoken
> than Truth's own word there is no truer token.[36]

And we believe it even though we see evidence to the contrary, for we know that the accidents of the bread and wine remain. Is this perhaps a contradiction? No, for accidents are one thing and substance is another. The accidents remain, whereas the substance is converted into Christ. There is no contradiction as long as we hold a real distinction between substance and accidents. And this distinction is a truth of common sense, for the accidents of things are subject to constant change, whereas the substance or essence remains the same until it ceases to be what it is and is transformed into something else.

Comparison between Transubstantiation, Natural Change, and Creation

In order to clarify the nature of transubstantiation, it is useful to compare it to natural substantial changes, such as conception or death, on the one hand, and to creation, on the other. Transubstantiation is distinct both from creation and from natural substantial changes.

Transubstantiation is similar to creation in that both are works proper to the divine omnipotence. The act of creation involves an operation not found in nature that brings something into being from nothing. Transubstantiation involves a conversion not found in nature in which the whole substance of one thing—both its substantial form and its matter—is changed directly into another preexisting substance. Both acts can be done only by God.

They differ, however, in that creation is not properly a change, for there is no preexisting subject that is changed into another being, whereas transubstantiation is a kind of change of one preexisting substance into another. And, since creation involves no preexisting subject, it does not actualize any preexisting potency of things. Transubstantiation, on the other hand, although it does not actualize a *natural*

---

[36] Thomas Aquinas, *Adoro Te Devote*, in Cantalamessa, *This Is My Body*, 13.

potency of bread and wine, it does actualize in them an *obediential* potency to become whatever God wills them to be. An obediential potency is not a natural potency in things, but rather simply the power of created being to be converted into whatever God wills it to become in obedience to His word.[37]

Transubstantiation is similar to natural substantial change, or transformation, in that both involve the conversion of one thing into another. Both changes also have a substrate that remains constant during the change. In natural change, matter is a necessary substrate that makes substantial change possible because only matter can receive a new form. In transubstantiation, on the other hand, the miraculously suspended accidents of the bread provide the "substrate," although without the matter (for that too, as part of the substance, is converted into Christ).

It should be noted that the term "substrate" is used improperly in the case of transubstantiation because the appearances do not "stand under" anything. Rather it is the substance, formerly of bread and wine, and after the consecration, that of Christ's Body and Blood, that "stand under" the appearances, which remain constant.[38] Nevertheless, it is the continued existence of the accidents that establishes the continuity between what was formerly the substance of bread and wine and is afterward the substance of Christ.

Transubstantiation is a more radical change than natural transformation, for it is not just the change of a substantial form in a given quantity of matter that remains constant, but rather, the instantaneous change of both substantial principles—substantial form and matter—into those of Christ's Body and Blood. It appears to the senses, however, to be no change at all, for the appearances retain the same being that they had before the change.

St. Thomas explains the similarities and differences between transubstantiation, natural transformation, and creation:

> This conversion of bread into the body of Christ has something in common with creation, and with natural transmutation, and in some respect differs from both. For the order of the terms

---

[37] For the notion of obediential potency, see *ST* III, q. 1, a. 3, ad 3; q. 11, a. 1; Lawrence Feingold, *The Natural Desire to See God according to St. Thomas Aquinas and His Interpreters* (Naples, FL: Sapientia Press, 2010), 101–65.

[38] To speak more properly, we could coin the term "suprastrate" to refer to the accidents that remain constant in this change "above" the hidden substance.

is common to these three; that is, that after one thing there is another (for, in creation there is being after non-being; in this sacrament, Christ's body after the substance of bread; in natural transmutation white after black, or fire after air); and that the aforesaid terms are not coexistent.

Now the conversion, of which we are speaking, has this in common with creation, that in neither of them is there any common subject belonging to either of the extremes; the contrary of which appears in every natural transmutation.

Again, this conversion has something in common with natural transmutation in two respects, although not in the same fashion. First of all because in both, one of the extremes passes into the other, as bread into Christ's body, and air into fire; whereas non-being is not converted into being. But this comes to pass differently on the one side and on the other; for in this sacrament the whole substance of the bread passes into the whole body of Christ; whereas in natural transmutation the matter of the one receives the form of the other, the previous form being laid aside. Secondly, they have this in common, that on both sides something remains the same; whereas this does not happen in creation: yet differently; for the same matter or subject remains in natural transmutation; whereas in this sacrament the same accidents remain.[39]

SACRAMENTAL MODE OF CHRIST'S PRESENCE

In order to more perfectly answer the objections of Berengarius, the theologians of the High Middle Ages had to give a more coherent account of the unique mode of presence of Christ in the Eucharist and how it was not in contradiction with the abiding local presence of Christ's Body in heaven. In other words, the task of theology was to show how one could coherently affirm that Christ is present in the Eucharist with the same Body that was born of Mary, nailed to the Cross, and risen from the dead, and yet avoid the gross realism that scandalized the disciples at Capernaum who thought that Christ was asking them to eat *pieces* of His flesh.[40] Aquinas accomplished this

---

[39] *ST* III, q. 75, a. 8.

[40] See, for example, Berengarius, *Epistola contra Almannum*, in Vaillancourt, "Sac-

theological task in an exemplary way by giving an account of Christ's presence in the sacrament according to the mode of *substance* rather than the mode of *dimensive quantity*. The latter is a property of bodies by which they are extended in three dimensions with parts outside of other parts capable of division and quantification that enables them to be localized in a particular place and measured and delimited by the surrounding bodies.

The Whole Christ Is Present under Each Part of the Sacred Species

Constant liturgical practice has maintained the mysterious property of the Eucharist by which the whole substance of Christ is present "under" any part of the appearances of bread and wine. If we break the consecrated host in half, Christ remains whole and entire in each half. And the same thing is true each time the consecrated host is subdivided. Christ is present whole and entire in every little particle of the host that remains on the paten and in every drop of the consecrated wine. This truth has great practical consequences for priests charged with responsibility for the Eucharist, and in general, for all those who distribute and receive Communion.

This truth of faith is admirably expressed in St. Thomas's hymn *Lauda Sion*: "The Sacrament has just been broken, fear not, but remember: there is as much contained in one fragment as in the whole. No rending of the reality but only of the sign takes place; neither the state nor the stature of what is signified is lessened."[41]

This unique property of the Eucharist can be understood by analogy to the way that the substances of the bread and wine were present under the visible appearances of the bread and wine. Before the consecration, the full nature and substance of bread was present under every part of the extension of the host, and similarly, the full nature and substance of the wine was present under any part of its dimensions. The *quantity* of the dimensions of the bread and wine would

---

ramental Theology from Gottschalk to Lanfranc," 195: "However, the position of the common crowd and Paschasius is no position at all, but insanity: that on the altar is a piece of flesh of the Lord, now broken in hands, now his extremities crushed by the teeth of men."

[41] Thomas Aquinas, *Lauda Sion*, trans. Victor Szczurek, in Charles Journet, *The Mass: the Presence of the Sacrifice of the Cross* (South Bend, IN: St. Augustine's Press, 2008), 167.

be changed by breaking the wafer or pouring out a drop, but not the *nature* or *substance* of the bread and wine, which would remain whole in each part, no matter how large or small, and would be unaffected by any division. Analogously, after the consecration, the full nature and substance of Christ's Body, whole and entire, is present under every part of that same extension of the appearances of bread and wine and is unaffected by any division of the dimensions of the sacred species.[42]

Perhaps the closest analogy to Christ's presence in the Eucharist whole and entire under any part of the appearances of the bread and wine is that of the human soul, which is fully present "in" every part of our body, making it alive and responsive to our wills. It is not a divisible part of the soul that is present in various parts of our body, but our whole soul, which forms an indivisible unity and cannot be divided into separate parts like the extension of our body. In like manner, Christ is present whole and entire, in an indivisible unity, "in" or "beneath" any part of the extension of the sacramental species (appearances) of bread and wine.[43]

However, although this analogy of the soul present in every part of the body is very helpful, it is nevertheless deficient, for the real presence of Christ in the Eucharist is altogether unique.[44] What is present is not just a purely spiritual reality like the human soul, but a physical body, including its accidents[45] (and of course also the soul and divinity of Christ).

---

[42] See Aquinas's commentary on 1 Cor 11, lec. 5, Marietti no. 664: "But as far as the nature of the substance is concerned, it is entire under each part of the dimensions. Hence, just before the consecration the whole truth of the substance and nature of bread was under each part of its dimensions, so after the consecration the whole body of Christ is under each part of the divided bread" (Larcher, *Commentary on the Letters of Saint Paul to the Corinthians*, 247–48).

[43] As seen above in chapter 6, pp. 251–52, this analogy was made by Guitmund in *On the Truth of the Body and Blood of Christ in the Eucharist* 1.19 (Vaillancourt, FCMC 10:108).

[44] See Thomas Aquinas, *In IV Sent.*, d. 10, q. 1, a. 3, qla. 3, ad 3, where he discusses this analogy and its limitations. See also Scheeben, *The Mysteries of Christianity*, 473.

[45] See Nicolas, *What Is the Eucharist?* 52: "In each consecrated host, it [the body of Christ] is present as is a substance to its accidents. Its presence is that of a body but the manner of this presence is not that in which a body is present. It is rather the manner in which a spirit is present." See also p. 54: "When we say that the substance of Christ's body is present, we are not to imagine it as deprived of its own proper accidents. Christ is there, whole and entire, as he is in heaven."

Christ Is Not Present in the Mode of Quantity

Christ's presence in the Eucharist is mysterious because He is present in a way distinct from the way a natural body is present in a place, with parts outside of parts and measured by the dimensive quantity of the surrounding bodies.[46] St. Thomas explains:

> Christ's body is not in this sacrament in the same way as a body is in a place, which by its dimensions is commensurate with the place; but in a special manner which is proper to this sacrament. Hence we say that Christ's body is upon many altars, not as in different places, but "sacramentally": and thereby we do not understand that Christ is there only as in a sign, although a sacrament is a kind of sign; but that Christ's body is here after a fashion proper to this sacrament.[47]

St. Thomas gives a fuller explanation of this mysterious property of the Eucharist in *ST* III, q. 76, a. 1, ad 3:

> As has been already stated (75, 5), after the consecration of the bread into the body of Christ, or of the wine into His blood, the accidents of both remain. From which it is evident that the dimensions of the bread or wine are not changed into the dimensions of the body of Christ, but substance into substance. And so the substance of Christ's body or blood is under this sacrament by the power of the sacrament, but not the dimensions of Christ's body or blood. Hence it is clear that the body of Christ is in this sacrament "by way of substance," and not by way of quantity. But the proper totality of substance is contained indifferently in a small or large quantity; as the whole nature of air in a great or small amount of air, and the whole nature of a man in a big or small individ-

---

[46] See Michael F. Brummond, "The Thomistic Notion of the Non-Local Presence of Christ in the Eucharist: Its Meaning and Place in Catholic Tradition," *Antiphon* 17, no. 3 (2013): 247–75.

[47] *ST* III, q. 75, a. 1, ad 1. This response is answering the following objection: "No body can be in several places at the one time. For this does not even belong to an angel; since for the same reason it could be everywhere. But Christ's is a true body, and it is in heaven. Consequently, it seems that it is not in very truth in the sacrament of the altar, but only as in a sign."

ual. Wherefore, after the consecration, the whole substance of Christ's body and blood is contained in this sacrament, just as the whole substance of the bread and wine was contained there before the consecration.

What does St. Thomas mean when he says that Christ is present in the Eucharist "by way of substance, and not by way of quantity"? This mysterious mode of presence is a consequence of transubstantiation. Before the consecration, the substance or essence of bread was present whole and entire under every part of the dimensions of the bread. At the completion of the words of consecration, the substance of bread is converted into the substance of Christ. This means that Christ comes to be present in the Eucharist in the same way that the substance or essence of bread was previously present under every part of the dimensions of the bread. Therefore, Christ is present in the Eucharist not in the way in which a body is present in a particular place by way of quantity and dimension, in which each part of the body is present in a different place, but in the way a soul or a nature is present in a body, which is whole and entire under every part of the sensible appearances.[48]

Concomitance

The words of consecration directly make Christ's Body present under the species of bread and His Blood present under the species of wine. However, since Christ's Body after the Resurrection is now inseparably united to His Blood and to His soul, these also are made present in the Eucharist by a natural accompaniment, or "concomitance." This means that the Body is necessarily accompanied by the Blood and the soul and that the precious Blood is necessarily accompanied by the Body and the soul.

Furthermore, Christ's divinity is inseparably united to every part of His sacred humanity by the hypostatic union. This union of the divinity with Christ's Body and Blood was not interrupted even in His death. The dead Body in the tomb was still the dead Body of the

---

[48] On Christ's presence in the Eucharist by way of substance rather than place, see Roger Nutt, "Faith, Metaphysics, and the Contemplation of Christ's Corporeal Presence in the Eucharist: Translation of St. Thomas Aquinas' Seventh Quodlibetal Dispute, Q. 4, A. 1 with an Introductory Essay," *Antiphon* 15, no. 2 (2011): 156–62; Levering, *Sacrifice and Community*, 149–55.

Second Person of the Trinity, and His separated soul was likewise still united to His divine Person. At the moment of his death on the Cross, Christ's Body and Blood were physically separated from each other and from His soul, although they all remained united to His divinity. In the moment of His glorious Resurrection, however, Christ's Body was again united to His Blood, and both were again animated by His human soul, and all three—Body, Blood, and soul—remain inseparably united to His divinity.

Therefore, the words of consecration, "This is my body," are not limited to producing this one effect by divine fiat—to make Christ's Body present—but they also indirectly make His Blood, soul, and divinity present,[49] because these are now inseparable from Christ's glorified human Body. The same thing occurs in the separate consecration of the wine. Although the power of the words is directly ordered to making Christ's Blood present, they also indirectly make His whole Body, soul, and divinity present in every drop of the consecrated species of wine.

St. Thomas holds that if Holy Mass had been celebrated on Holy Saturday before the Resurrection, while Christ's physical Body was still in the tomb, the words of consecration would have made Christ's inanimate Body present, separated from His soul and from His Blood but still united to His divinity. Likewise, the words of the consecration of the species of wine would have made only His Blood present, separated from His Body and from his soul but still united to the divinity.[50]

---

[49] See *ST* III, q. 76, a. 1, ad 1:

> Because the change of the bread and wine is not terminated at the Godhead or the soul of Christ, it follows as a consequence that the Godhead or the soul of Christ is in this sacrament not by the power of the sacrament, but from real concomitance. For since the Godhead never set aside the assumed body, wherever the body of Christ is, there, of necessity, must the Godhead be; and therefore it is necessary for the Godhead to be in this sacrament concomitantly with His body. Hence we read in the profession of faith at Ephesus (P. I., ch. 26): "We are made partakers of the body and blood of Christ, not as taking common flesh, nor as of a holy man united to the Word in dignity, but the truly life-giving flesh of the Word Himself."

[50] See *ST* III, q. 76, a. 1, ad 1: "His soul was truly separated from His body, as stated above (III, q. 50, a. 5). And therefore had this sacrament been celebrated during those three days when He was dead, the soul of Christ would not have been there, neither by the power of the sacrament, nor from real concomitance. But since 'Christ rising from the dead dies now no more' (Romans 6:9), His soul is always really united with His body. And therefore in this sacrament the

After the Resurrection, however, until the end of time, Christ's physical Body and Blood have been reunited to one another and to His soul, and all three are inseparably united to His divinity. Therefore, the words of consecration in every Mass make Christ's *entire reality as it currently exists*—His divine Person united to His living and breathing glorious Body—present under every part of the consecrated species.

This distinction between (a) what is present through the power of the words of the sacrament and (b) what is present by concomitance, is explained by St. Thomas as follows:

> It is absolutely necessary to confess according to the Catholic faith that the entire Christ is in this sacrament. But it should be borne in mind that something of Christ is in this sacrament in two ways: in one way through the power of the sacrament, and in another way through natural concomitance. Through the power of the sacrament, under the sacramental species there is that reality into which the pre-existing substance of bread and wine is directly converted. This is signified by the words of the form, which are efficacious in this as in the other sacraments, when it is said: "This is my body," or "This is my blood." But from natural concomitance, there is also in this sacrament whatever is united in reality with that in which the above-mentioned conversion terminates. For if any two things are united in reality, then wherever the one is really present, there the other must also be."[51]

The doctrine of concomitance has been infallibly taught in the Council of Trent, session 13, canon 3: "If anyone denies that in the venerable sacrament of the Eucharist *the whole Christ* is contained under each species and under each and every portion of either species when it is divided up: let him be anathema." For this reason, anyone who receives Communion under one or the other species has received Christ, whole and entire, with everything that forms part of His person. Thus it can be seen that the traditional custom in the Latin Church of distributing Communion only under the species of bread,

---

body indeed of Christ is present by the power of the sacrament, but His soul from real concomitance."

[51] *ST* III, q. 76, a. 1 (my translation from the Leonine edition).

motivated probably by the practical concern to avoid the spilling of the sacred Blood, does not deprive the faithful of any of the reality of Christ.[52]

Someone may wonder why Christ instituted the Eucharist under the two species of bread and wine if it is not necessary to receive Communion under both kinds. St. Thomas explains that the dual and separate consecration of the bread and wine is necessary for the fullness of the sacramental sign. For this double consecration sacramentally signifies Christ's violent death, consisting in the pouring out of His Blood for us on the Cross. The separate consecration is necessary for the sacramental representation of Christ's sacrifice, which is mystically made present in this way. The sacraments produce the invisible reality that they outwardly signify. Furthermore, the appearances of both bread and wine provide a more expressive sign of spiritual nourishment by including both food and drink.[53]

The Accidents of Christ's Body Are Made Present by Concomitance

It is important to distinguish what is made present in the Eucharist directly through the words of the form and what is present indirectly by concomitance. Only the substance of Christ's Body and Blood are made present *directly* through the power of the sacrament that works through the words of the form.[54] Everything else that belongs to Christ

---

[52] See the Council of Trent, On Communion under Both Kinds and the Communion of Little Children (session 21), ch. 3, and cans. 1–3 (DS, 1729, 1731–33).

[53] See *ST* III, q. 76, a. 2, ad 1: "Although the whole Christ is under each species, yet it is so not without purpose. For in the first place this serves to represent Christ's Passion, in which the blood was separated from the body; hence in the form for the consecration of the blood mention is made of its shedding. Secondly, it is in keeping with the use of this sacrament, that Christ's body be shown apart to the faithful as food, and the blood as drink." St. Thomas also mentions here that the separate consecration of Christ's Body and Blood is a sign of the fact that the Eucharist is instituted to redeem man both in his body and in his soul, which are represented respectively by Christ's Body and Blood, for blood is a natural sign of the principle of life: "Thirdly, it is in keeping with its effect, in which sense it was stated above (q. 74, a. 1) that 'the body is offered for the salvation of the body, and the blood for the salvation of the soul.'"

[54] See *ST* III, q. 76, a. 1, ad 3:

After the consecration of the bread into the body of Christ, or of the wine into His blood, the accidents of both remain. From which it is

is made present *indirectly* through concomitance. Since Christ's Body and Blood become present in the mode of substance rather than in the mode of quantity, it follows that everything that becomes present by concomitance is also made present *in the mode of substance*. This means that all of the *intrinsic accidents* of Christ's Body and Blood—His qualities, quantities, and relations—are also present by mode of substance, such that Christ is whole and entirely present under every part of the sacred species.

Oddly enough, even Christ's three-dimensional quantity is present in the mode of substance rather than in the mode of quantity. The proper mode of dimensive quantity is to be present with parts outside of other parts, such that the quantity is always divisible. Christ's quantity is present in the Eucharist, however, in the mode of substance, which means that His height, width, and breadth are present whole, entire, and indivisible under every part of the appearances of the consecrated bread and wine.[55] This explains how we can receive the whole of Christ's Body under the dimension of a tiny fragment of the consecrated host. St. Thomas writes:

> Since, then, the substance of Christ's body is present on the altar by the power of this sacrament, while its dimensive quantity is there concomitantly and as it were accidentally, therefore the dimensive quantity of Christ's body is in this sacrament, not according to its proper manner (namely, that the whole is in the whole, and the individual parts in individ-

---

evident that the dimensions of the bread or wine are not changed into the dimensions of the body of Christ, but substance into substance. And so the substance of Christ's body or blood is under this sacrament by the power of the sacrament, but not the dimensions of Christ's body or blood. Hence it is clear that the body of Christ is in this sacrament *by way of substance*, and not by way of quantity. But the proper totality of substance is contained indifferently in a small or large quantity; as the whole nature of air in a great or small amount of air, and the whole nature of a man in a big or small individual. Wherefore, after the consecration, the whole substance of Christ's body and blood is contained in this sacrament, just as the whole substance of the bread and wine was contained there before the consecration.

[55] See *ST* III, q. 76, a. 4: "Since the substance of Christ's body is not really deprived of its dimensive quantity and its other accidents, hence it comes that by reason of real concomitance the whole dimensive quantity of Christ's body and all its other accidents are in this sacrament."

ual parts), but after the manner of substance, whose nature is for the whole to be in the whole, and the whole in every part.[56]

It might be objected that it is impossible for both the dimensive quantity of Christ and that of the bread and wine to be present in the same place. How could Christ's dimensions be present without spreading out His Body and taking up the space in a way contrary to that of the bread and wine? [57] The answer is simple, even though it is impossible for us to imagine. There would be a problem only if they were both present in the same place *in the same way*. But the dimensions of the sacred species of bread and wine are present in the ordinary way of quantity, whereas Christ's dimensions are present in the way of substance, which means that they are present whole and entire under every part of the quantity of the species of bread and wine.[58] The fact that Christ is present in the mode of substance enables each of us to receive the whole Jesus Christ, and not just a part of Him.[59]

---

[56] *ST* III, q. 76, a. 4, ad 1.

[57] Grisez makes this objection in "An Alternative Theology of Jesus' Substantial Presence," 115:

> But what does it mean, for example, to say that a body really is of a certain size, but in the way characteristic of a substance, so that the body's size does not spread out its parts and make it too big to fit in a space smaller than it? After all, spreading out a body's parts is just what size does for it. And in general, what does it mean to say that accidents exist in the way a substance does, and so without determining the substance whose accidents they are? That is what accidents seem to do *per se*.

I would respond that the accidents of Christ's body do spread out the parts of His Body in heaven. However, they do not spread out His body in His sacramental presence, such that He can be present whole and entire under every part in the way that the substance of bread and wine was before the consecration.

[58] See *ST* III, q. 76, a. 4, ad 2: "Two dimensive quantities cannot naturally be in the same subject at the same time, so that each be there according to the proper manner of dimensive quantity. But in this sacrament the dimensive quantity of the bread is there after its proper manner, that is, according to commensuration: not so the dimensive quantity of Christ's body, for that is there after the manner of substance."

[59] Grisez, on the contrary, rejects the thesis that Christ's accidents are present in the mode of substance. In consequence, Christ would not be present whole and entire under every part of the sacred species, but would be present in the mode of quantity, with parts outside of parts. Furthermore, he holds that the accidents of bread and wine become the accidents of Christ after the consecration. According to Grisez, Christ would in fact be increased by additional matter in every transubstantiation and by new accidents that previously belonged to the

Christ is not localized by His own dimensional quantity in the Eucharist, but rather by the dimensions that belonged to the bread and wine before transubstantiation and remain afterward, sustained in being directly by God. In other words, Christ is present in the Eucharist under borrowed appearances and under *borrowed* dimensions[60] that localize Him and enable us to encounter and receive Him here on earth wherever there is a consecrated host.

The Cessation of Christ's Presence When the Sacred Species Are Corrupted

Christ remains present under the appearances of bread and wine as long as they are not corrupted such that they become the appearances of something else, as happens in our stomachs through digestion. For the accidents of bread and wine after the consecration retain the same

---

bread and wine. See "An Alternative Theology of Jesus' Substantial Presence in the Eucharist," esp. 123: "New *parts* of Jesus' body and blood are the immediate term of the transubstantiation of bread and wine. . . . The accidents of bread and wine that remain after the consecration become Jesus' accidents; they are accidents of the new parts of his body and blood into which the bread and wine have been changed." Furthermore, according to Grisez, when we receive communion, we receive an "integral part" of Christ, which would also change Him through the action of our teeth and digestion. For an excellent critique of Grisez's thesis and a defense of that of St. Thomas, see Stephen Brock, "St. Thomas and the Eucharistic Conversion," *The Thomist* 65, no. 4 (2001): 529–65.

[60] See *ST* III, q. 76, a. 4:

But every body occupying a place is in the place according to the manner of dimensive quantity, namely, inasmuch as it is commensurate with the place according to its dimensive quantity. Hence it remains that Christ's body is not in this sacrament as in a place, but after the manner of substance, that is to say, in that way in which substance is contained by dimensions; because the substance of Christ's body succeeds the substance of bread in this sacrament: hence as the substance of bread was not locally under its dimensions, but after the manner of substance, so neither is the substance of Christ's body. Nevertheless the substance of Christ's body is not the subject of those dimensions, as was the substance of the bread: and therefore the substance of the bread was there locally by reason of its dimensions, because it was compared with that place through the medium of its own dimensions; but the substance of Christ's body is compared with that place through the medium of foreign dimensions, so that, on the contrary, the proper dimensions of Christ's body are compared with that place through the medium of substance; which is contrary to the notion of a located body.

being that they had before the consecration. This means that the accidents can undergo corruption, just as they do in ordinary bread and
wine. When this happens, Jesus's Body and Blood will cease to be
present, for the sacramental sign will no longer be present, which is
the instrumental cause of the presence of Christ's Body and Blood.

The reality of Jesus's Body and Blood, of course, suffers no alter-
ation at all when the sacred species are corrupted. Their corruption
means simply that Christ's sacramental presence ends, just as the substance of ordinary bread and wine ceases to be present when their
accidents undergo a sufficient degree of corruption such that the substantial form can no longer be retained. St. Thomas explains:

> If there be such change on the part of the accidents as would
> not have sufficed for the corruption of the bread and wine,
> then the body and blood of Christ do not cease to be under
> this sacrament on account of such change, whether the change
> be on the part of the quality, as for instance, when the color or
> the savor of the bread or wine is slightly modified; or on the
> part of the quantity, as when the bread or the wine is divided
> into such parts as to keep in them the nature of bread or of
> wine. But if the change be so great that the substance of the
> bread or wine would have been corrupted, then Christ's body
> and blood do not remain under this sacrament; and this either
> on the part of the qualities, as when the color, savor, and other
> qualities of the bread and wine are so altered as to be incom-
> patible with the nature of bread or of wine; or else on the part
> of the quantity, as, for instance, if the bread be reduced to fine
> particles, or the wine divided into such tiny drops that the
> species of bread or wine no longer remain.[61]

In this regard, the Eucharist is similar to other consecrated objects,
for their consecration remains as long as the consecrated object is not
substantially changed.[62] The Eucharist transcends all other consecrated objects, for here alone, the consecration of the elements, as long
as the species remain uncorrupted, brings about the substantial presence of what is signified.

---

[61] *ST* III, q. 77, a. 4.

[62] See *ST* III, q. 76, a. 6, ad 2: "Thus are all other consecrations irremovable so
long as the consecrated things endure; on which account they are not repeated."

Transubstantiation Does Not Imply
Any Change in Christ

One of the keys to understanding the mystery of transubstantiation is that it does not involve any change in Christ: all the change is on the part of the substance of bread and wine, which are converted into Christ.[63] Christ Himself receives no change by transubstantiation. He is not bilocated, moved, multiplied, or divided. He is not increased by any additional matter in transubstantiation,[64] nor is anything changed in Him when the consecrated host is fractured or digested. He comes to be substantially present in the Eucharist not through a change *in* Him, but through a conversion of the bread and wine *into* Him.

Since this is a unique occurrence, we would look in vain for something similar in nature. An imperfect analogy can be made, however, with the Incarnation. The Incarnation did not make any change in the divine nature of the Word, which is immutable. All the change was on the part of the humanity that was assumed by the divine Person. The humanity thus gained an infinite dignity and a relation of union with the Person of the Word. Likewise, in the Eucharist, all the change is on the part of the substances of bread and wine that are converted into Christ.

Christ Himself, present in the Eucharist, is changed neither by the action of transubstantiation nor by anything that happens to the sacramental species, such as division or consumption. But, under every part of the dimensions of the sacramental species, Christ is made present, whole and unchanged.[65] Indeed, as mentioned above, the Eucharist

---

[63] See Bonaventure, *Commentaria in Librum Quartum Sententiarum*, d. 10, q. 1, ad 1: "God can convert many things into the body of Christ. For this reason the body of Christ is in many places, not by any change that happens in Christ, but rather [by the change] in the bread which is converted into Him" (*Opera Omnia* [Ad Claras Aquas: Typographia Collegii S. Bonaventurae, 1889], 4:217). See also Journet, "Transubstantiation," 737–39.

[64] See Lombard, *Sentences* IV, d. 11, ch. 2, nos. 1, 4: "Yet nothing is added to the body or blood, nor is the body or blood of Christ increased.... What the bread has been made is the body of Christ.... The body is not formed from it, as if from matter; but the substance is formed into the body and becomes it" (p. 55).

[65] See Scheeben, *The Mysteries of Christianity*, 473: "Is there any sense in which we may say that the sacramental existence of Christ's body is more glorious than the mode of existence natural to it? The sacramental existence is evidently the nobler inasmuch as the body of Christ in the Eucharist exists after the manner of higher substances, namely, the spiritual and the divine; the spiritual,

not only brings Him to us under the species of bread and wine but also, and more importantly, brings us to Him as He is in heaven! The Eucharist brings us to Him as He continues His heavenly life in all its fullness and freedom.

STUDY QUESTIONS

1. Why is the commonsense distinction between substance and accidents important for understanding the Eucharistic conversion?
2. What are two ways by which something can begin to be present somewhere?
3. Why does St. Thomas reject the option that Christ begins to be present in the Eucharist by some kind of movement?
4. Why is it necessary that Christ come to be present in the Eucharist by the conversion of the bread and wine into His Body and Blood?
5. Do the words of institution support the notion of consubstantiation?
6. What is meant by the term "transubstantiation?" Why is this a fitting term to describe the Eucharistic conversion?
7. Can transubstantiation be realized by any created power, or only by the omnipotence of God? Explain.
8. Why is it fitting that the appearances of bread and wine remain after the consecration?
9. St. Thomas says that Christ is present in the Eucharist not "by mode of place" but "by mode of substance." Explain.
10. Is Christ's whole substance present under either species? Explain.
11. What is meant by presence by "concomitance?"
12. Are Christ's accidents present in the Eucharist? Explain.
13. Does transubstantiation make any change in Christ?
14. Is Christ present in the Eucharist in the state of glory?
15. How is Christ's divinity present in the Eucharist?

---

because it is present whole and undivided in the entire host and in every part of it; the divine, because it is present in countless places, wherever the bread is consecrated."

SUGGESTIONS FOR FURTHER READING

Anscombe, G. E. M. "On Transubstantiation." In *Ethics, Religion and Politics: Collected Philosophical Papers of G. E. M. Anscombe*. Vol. 3. Oxford, UK: Blackwell, 1981. Pp. 107–12.

ST III, qq. 75–77.

SCG IV, chs. 61–68.

Journet, Charles. *The Mass: The Presence of the Sacrifice of the Cross*. Translated by Victor Szczurek. South Bend, IN: St. Augustine's Press, 2008. Pp. 150–69.

Levering, Matthew. *Sacrifice and Community: Jewish Offering and Christian Eucharist*. Malden, MA: Blackwell Publishing, 2005. Pp. 115–167.

Nicolas, Marie-Joseph. *What Is the Eucharist?* New York: Hawthorn Books, 1960. Pp. 46–56.

✣

CHAPTER EIGHT

Transubstantiation in Dispute: The Reformation and Its Legacy

PROTESTANT VIEWS ON THE PRESENCE OF CHRIST IN THE EUCHARIST

The Eucharistic controversies of the eleventh century, which had seemed to be satisfactorily put to rest by two centuries of prodigious theological work, culminating in the Eucharistic teaching of Aquinas, returned in full force at the beginning of the Reformation. There is no one Protestant position on the Eucharist, for the different Protestant leaders immediately split into various factions that considered each other heretical. The one thing uniting the Protestants with respect to Christ's presence in the Eucharist was their rejection of transubstantiation. They were united only in the belief that the substance of the bread and the wine continue to exist on the altar after the consecration. Martin Luther, however, vigorously maintained belief in Christ's real presence in the Eucharist *together with* the substances of the bread and wine, while more radical Protestants saw the Eucharist as a mere commemorative symbol.

Martin Luther's Position on the Real Presence

Luther's position on the Eucharist consists in attempting to maintain belief in the real presence while denying the Catholic dogma of transubstantiation, on the one hand, but also forcefully rejecting the more radical Protestant heresy of reducing Christ's presence in the Eucharist entirely to the level of a mere symbol, on the other.

It is not clear why, beginning in 1520, Luther rejected transubstantiation. Perhaps it was because of his study of nominalist theologians such as Pierre d'Ailly, a student of William of Ockham,[1] or because of the influence of John Wycliffe, who had denied transubstantiation in favor of consubstantiation,[2] or because of his passionate dismissal of scholastic theology in general, with its use of Aristotelian and Thomistic philosophical categories.[3] His rejection of transubstantiation is also connected with his opposition to the practice of Eucharistic adoration.[4] He also seemed to have various misunderstandings of transubstantiation, thinking that it implied an additional miracle of the annihilation of the substances of bread and wine or the creation of a new substance in which the accidents of bread and wine could inhere, notions to which he rightly objected but that are totally foreign to the Thomistic account.[5] Luther also rejected the doctrine of concom-

---

[1] Luther, *The Babylonian Captivity of the Church*:

Some time ago, when I was drinking in scholastic theology, the learned Cardinal of Cambrai [Pierre d'Ailly] gave me food for thought in his comments on the fourth book of the Sentences. He argues with great acumen that to hold that real bread and real wine, and not merely their accidents, are present on the altar, would be much more probable and require fewer superfluous miracles—if only the church had not decreed otherwise. When I learned later what church it was that had decreed this, namely the Thomistic—that is, the Aristotelian church—I at last found rest for my conscience in the above view, namely, that it is real bread and real wine, in which Christ's real flesh and real blood are present in no other way and to no less a degree than the others assert them to be under their accidents. I reached this conclusion because I saw that the opinions of the Thomists, whether approved by pope or by council, remain only opinions. (*LW*, 36:28–29)

[2] The Council of Constance in 1415 condemned three propositions of Wycliffe with regard to the presence of Christ in the Eucharist: 1) "The material substance of the bread and likewise the material substance of the wine remain in the sacrament of the altar"; 2) "The accidents of the bread do not remain without a subject in the same sacrament"; 3) "Christ is not in the same sacrament identically and really in his own bodily presence" (DS, 1151–53).

[3] Luther, *The Babylonian Captivity of the Church* (*LW*, 36:29).

[4] See Joseph Ratzinger, "The Problem of Transubstantiation," in *TL*, 227.

[5] See Mickey Mattox, "Sacraments in the Lutheran Reformation," in Boersma and Levering, eds., *The Oxford Handbook of Sacramental Theology*, 276; Luther, *The Babylonian Captivity of the Church*:

And why could not Christ include his body in the substance of the bread just as well as in the accidents? . . . Why is it not even more possible that the body of Christ be contained in every part of the substance

itance because it is based on understanding Christ's presence in the sacrament to be according to the mode of substance.[6]

Luther, however, did not hold the rejection of transubstantiation to be as decisive as the affirmation of the real presence.[7] He always vigorously maintained the real presence because of the force of the words of Christ in the institution of the Eucharist[8] and because he was too deeply and admirably attached to the humanity of Christ to surrender His presence in the sacrament,[9] although he admitted that he had been tempted to do so.[10] He wrote to the Christians of Strasburg in 1524:

> I confess that if Dr. Karlstadt, or anyone else, could have convinced me five years ago that only bread and wine were in the sacrament he would have done me a great service. At that time I suffered such severe conflicts and inner strife and torment that I would gladly have been delivered from them. I realized that on this point I could best resist the papacy. . . . But I am a captive and cannot free myself. The text is too powerfully present, and will not allow itself to be torn from its meaning by mere verbiage.[11]

---

of the bread? . . . Out of this has arisen that Babel of a philosophy of a constant quantity distinct from the substance, until it has come to such a pass that they themselves no longer know what are accidents and what is substance. For who has ever proved beyond the shadow of a doubt that heat, color, cold, light, weight, or shape are mere accidents? Finally, they have been driven to pretend that a new substance is created by God for those accidents on the altar, all on account of Aristotle, who says: "It is the nature of an accident to be in something," and endless other monstrosities. They would be rid of all these if they simply permitted real bread to be present. (*LW*, 36:32)

6   See Antonio Piolanti, "L'Eucaristia," in *Il Protestantesimo ieri e oggi*, ed. Antonio Piolanti (Rome: Libreria Editrice Religiosa F. Ferrari, 1958), 1097.

7   See Luther, *Confession Concerning Christ's Supper* (1528): "Now, I have taught in the past [*Babylonian Captivity* (*LW*, 36:28ff)] and still teach that this controversy is unnecessary, and that it is of no great consequence whether the bread remains or not. I maintain, however, with Wycliffe that the bread remains" (*LW*, 37:296).

8   See Althaus, *The Theology of Martin Luther*, 376–77, 382–91.

9   See ibid., 393–95.

10   See ibid., 376–77.

11   Luther, *Letter to the Christians at Strassburg in Opposition to the Fanatic Spirit* (*LW*, 40:68).

In the following years, Luther insisted on the real presence much more in the face of its denial by Huldrych Zwingli, Andreas Karlstadt, and others. In 1527 he wrote: "We believe precisely that his body is present, as his words say and indicate: 'This is my body.' . . . Over words we do not wish to argue, just so the meaning is retained that it is not mere bread that we eat in Christ's Supper, but the body of Christ."[12] Taking up the thought of the early Fathers, he too saw the humanity of Christ in the Eucharist as the medicine of immortality:

> It is a glory and praise of his inexpressible grace and mercy that he concerns himself so profoundly with us poor sinners and shows us such gracious love and goodness, not content to be everywhere in and around, above and beside us, but even giving us his own body as nourishment, in order that with such a pledge he may assure and promise us that our body too shall live forever, because it partakes here on earth of an everlasting and living food.[13]

Pushed by this controversy, Luther sought to justify the real presence while denying transubstantiation. This implies the position of "consubstantiation," which Luther put forward somewhat tentatively in 1520. As we have seen, this means that the bread and wine remain but that, somehow, Jesus comes into them through faith and coexists with them. Thus the consecrated host would be both bread and Christ at the same time. Luther compares the presence of Christ's Body in the Eucharist to the presence of Christ's divine nature in His humanity:

> In like manner, it is not necessary in the sacrament that the bread and wine be transubstantiated and that Christ be contained under their accidents in order that the real body and real blood may be present. But both remain there at the same time, and it is truly said: 'This bread is my body; this is my blood,' and vice versa. Thus I will understand it for the time being.[14]

---

[12] Luther, *That These Words of Christ, "This Is My Body," etc., Still Stand Firm Against the Fanatics* (*LW*, 37:65).

[13] Luther, *This Is My Body* (*LW*, 37:71).

[14] Luther, *The Babylonian Captivity of the Church* (*LW*, 36:35).

He further developed this view in a work of 1528, *Confession Concerning Christ's Supper*:

> For even though body and bread are two distinct substances, each one existing by itself, and though neither is mistaken for the other where they are separated from each other, nevertheless where they are united and become a new, entire substance, they lose their difference so far as this new, unique substance is concerned. As they become one, they are called and designated one object. It is not necessary, meanwhile, that one of the two disappear or be annihilated, but both the bread and the body remain, and by virtue of the sacramental unity it is correct to say, "This is my body," designating the bread with the word "this." For now it is no longer ordinary bread in the oven, but a "flesh-bread" or "body-bread," i.e., a bread which has become one sacramental substance, one with the body of Christ. Likewise with the wine in the cup. . . . For it is no longer ordinary wine in the cellar but "blood-wine," i.e., a wine which has been united with the blood of Christ in one sacramental substance.[15]

Luther was pushed to give a clearer defense of how denial of transubstantiation is compatible with Christ's real presence in the Eucharist by his growing conflict with and polemic against Zwingli and his followers in the years 1525–1528. Zwingli, who denied the real presence, proclaimed the impossibility of Christ's Body being in more than one place at the same time and saw Luther's position as contradictory. To counter this criticism, Luther sought to support his doctrine of consubstantiation with a doctrine sometimes referred to as "ubiquitism," which holds the omnipresence of the Body of Christ.[16] He reasoned that the humanity of Christ is united to the divinity and is seated at the right hand of the Father, and since the divinity and the right hand of the Father is omnipresent, giving being to all things, so also the humanity of Christ must be present in all things.

---

[15] Luther, *Confession Concerning Christ's Supper* (*LW*, 37:303).

[16] See Althaus, *The Theology of Martin Luther*, 398–99; Mattox, "Sacraments in the Lutheran Reformation," 279–80; Volker Leppin, "Martin Luther," in *A Companion to the Eucharist in the Reformation*, ed. Lee Palmer Wandel (Leiden/Boston: Brill, 2014), 52.

In consequence, therefore, He is also present in the Eucharist in the consecrated bread and the wine. In 1526, in a treatise written against Zwingli and his followers, he wrote:

> Moreover, we believe that Christ, according to his human nature, is put over all creatures [Eph 1:22] and fills all things, as Paul says in Eph 4:10. Not only according to his divine nature, but also according to his human nature, he is a lord of all things, has all things in his hand, and is present everywhere.[17]

In another treatise of 1527, he wrote:

> Christ's body is at the right hand of God; that is granted. The right hand of God, however, is everywhere, as you must grant from our previous demonstration. Therefore it surely is present also in the bread and wine at table. Now where the right hand of God is, there Christ's body and blood must be, for the right hand of God is not divisible into many parts but a single, simple entity. . . . Wherever and whatever God's right hand is in reality and in name, there is Christ, the Son of man.[18]

The third and final work of this polemic was his *Confession Concerning Christ's Supper* (1528), in which he wrote:

> Christ is God and man, and his humanity has become one person with God, and is thus wholly and completely drawn into God above all creatures, so that he remains perfectly united with him. How is it possible then, for God to be

---

[17] Luther, *The Sacrament of the Body and Blood of Christ—Against the Fanatics* (*LW*, 36:342–43).

[18] Luther, *That These Words of Christ, "This Is My Body," Etc., Still Stand Firm Against the Fanatics* (*LW*, 37:63–64). The text continues: "Even if Christ had never spoken or set forth these words at the Supper, 'This is my body,' still the words, 'Christ sits at the right hand of God,' would require that his body and blood may be there as well as at all other places, and that although there need be no transubstantiation or transformation of the bread into his body, it can well be present nonetheless, just as the right hand of God is not necessarily transformed into all things even though it is surely present and in them" (*LW*, 37:64). For Luther's defense of ubiquitism, see also *LW*, 37:227–235.

somewhere where Christ as man is not? How can it happen, without dividing the person, that God may be here without the humanity and there with the humanity? . . . If God and man are one person and the two natures are so united that they belong together more intimately than body and soul, then Christ must also be man wherever he is God.[19]

The obvious problem with this solution is that, if it were to prove anything, it would prove too much, for it would hold that the Body of Christ is present also in the unconsecrated host, and indeed in all of our food and in everything else, and that we should venerate all of reality as Catholics venerate the Blessed Sacrament. This doctrine, if applied consistently, would eliminate the distinction between the sacred and the profane, between the sacraments and nature.[20] Luther would counter this objection by saying that we give this worship to Christ's presence only in the Eucharist and not elsewhere because only there have we been instructed to do so by the word of Christ.

More fundamentally, the fact that the *divinity* of Christ is present in all places through His power, giving them being, in no way implies that the human body of Christ is equally present in all places, for the two natures of Christ remain distinct, each with its own properties.[21] The divinity is present everywhere spiritually by His power and knowledge, whereas Christ's human Body is present at a particular place through His dimensive quantity, which is proper to a body. Luther's error consists in confusing and fusing the two natures, which was the earlier heresy of monophysitism.

A consequence of Luther's defense of the real presence is his insistence, against Zwingli and others, that Christ is also received, although not unto salvation, by those who receive the sacrament unworthily: "Therefore the true, real body of Christ must of necessity be physically present in the bread which we break, and the unwor-

---

[19] Luther, *Confession Concerning Christ's Supper* (*LW*, 37:228–29). Luther's ubiquitism was taken up in later Lutheran confessional formulations; see *The Book of Concord: The Confessions of the Evangelical Lutheran Church*, ed. Theodore G. Tappert (Philadelphia, PA: Mühlenberg Press, 1959), 483, 586–87, 607.

[20] See Althaus, *The Theology of Martin Luther*, 399.

[21] See Leo the Great, Letter to Flavian of June 13, 449, *Lectis Dilectionis Tuae* ("Tome of Leo"): "For each nature does what is proper to each in communion with the other: the Word does what pertains to the Word, and the flesh to what pertains to the flesh" (DS, 294).

thy may partake of it physically, because they cannot partake of it spiritually."[22]

Huldrych Zwingli

Shortly after Luther rejected transubstantiation in favor of consubstantiation in 1520, a more radical Protestant position appeared that reduces Christ's "presence" in the Eucharist to a mere symbol to arouse and exercise faith. This view was first maintained by Ulrich (or Huldrych) Zwingli,[23] a Catholic priest (ordained 1506) turned Swiss Reformer, as well as by Luther's older colleague, Andreas Karlstadt, ordained a priest in 1510, and their followers. Luther blasted this group as heretics to whom he gave the name "Sacramentarians" or "fanatics."

This more radical group of Protestants who directly denied the real presence had a formidable task in explaining the meaning of the four words, "This is my body." Zwingli held that the "is" uttered by Christ should be interpreted to mean "signifies." Thus the words of Christ at the Last Supper should be understood as: "Take, eat, this bread *signifies* my body." The principal reason that he gives is that, otherwise, the Eucharist would imply a cannibalistic eating of Christ, just as the scandalized disciples of Capernaum thought.[24] That is, Zwingli implies that the only two options are a merely symbolic interpretation or a crude realism (Capernaism) that is untenable. Another argument used by Zwingli is that Christ's Body left the earth at His Ascension and, thus it is impossible for it to be locally present on the

---

[22] Luther, *Confession Concerning Christ's Supper* (*LW*, 37:354). See Althaus, *The Theology of Martin Luther*, 400.

[23] For Zwingli's Eucharistic teaching, see Carrie Euler, "Huldrych Zwingli and Heinrich Bullinger," in Wandel, *A Companion to the Eucharist in the Reformation*, 57–74.

[24] Zwingli, *On the Lord's Supper*, art. 1: "For if the 'is' is to be taken literally, then we must eat the body of Christ with its flesh, bones, veins, nerves, marrow and other members which I will forbear to mention. . . . If Christ spoke literally and not figuratively, then of necessity it follows that his body is eaten literally and perceptibly, as Berengarius was forced to confess: but all believers know very well that they do not eat the body of Christ in that way. . . . For God never deceives us. If he did speak literally, we should perceive the body" (Bromiley, *Zwingli and Bullinger*, 199). He wrote earlier in the same work: "If he is present literally and essentially in the flesh, then in the flesh he is torn apart by the teeth and perceptibly masticated. We cannot evade the issue by saying: 'With God all things are possible'" (p. 190).

altar at the same time that it is present in heaven.[25] Zwingli does not seem to be aware of the Thomistic teaching on Christ's presence in the Eucharist according to the mode of substance.

On the basis of John 6:43, Zwingli holds that eating Christ's Body and drinking His Blood means simply believing in Him.[26] The Eucharist is the "sign itself that by which those who rely upon the death and blood of Christ mutually prove to their brethren that they have this faith. The meaning of Christ's words becomes perfectly plain to this effect: 'This feast signifies or is the symbol by which you will recall that my body ... was given for you.'"[27] From John 6:51, Zwingli concludes:

> From these words we learn clearly that the flesh of Christ is the food and hope of the human heart, simply in that he was slain for us. For what is produced of flesh is flesh (John 3:6). The flesh of Christ, therefore, being eaten, cannot produce anything but flesh. Yet the flesh of Christ in dying for us makes that person spiritual ... who rests upon his death. I conclude, therefore, that this bread of which Christ speaks is simply this: that Christ was delivered up to death for our life.[28]

Zwingli also compares the Eucharist with a wedding ring that a husband gives to his spouse to remind her of him during his absence. In a work written to win the favor of the king of France, he writes:

---

[25] Zwingli, *On the Lord's Supper*: "He sits at the right hand of the Father, he has left the world, he is no longer present with us. And if these words are true, it is impossible to maintain that his flesh and blood are present in the sacrament" (Bromiley, *Zwingli and Bullinger*, 214–15). Zwingli rightly opposes the Lutheran doctrine of ubiquitism. His argument is valid against Luther, but it does not address the Thomistic doctrine that Christ is present circumscriptively only in heaven.

[26] Zwingli, *On the Lord's Supper*: "It follows then that to feed on Christ's body is to believe in him who was given up to death on our behalf. . . . The primitive Fathers, and we ourselves . . . have shown quite clearly that in the teaching brought before us in John 6:43 when Christ referred to eating his flesh and drinking his blood he simply meant believing in him as the one who has given his flesh and blood for our redemption and the cleansing of our sins" (Bromiley, *Zwingli and Bullinger*, 198–99).

[27] Zwingli, Letter to Matthew Alber Concerning the Lord's Supper (Nov. 1524), trans. Henry Preble, in *Huldrych Zwingli: Writings*, vol. 2 (Allison Park, PA: Pickwick Publications, 1984), 139.

[28] Ibid., 133.

The ring with which your majesty was betrothed to the queen your consort is not valued by her merely according to the value of the gold: it is gold, but it is also beyond price, because it is the symbol of her royal husband. For that reason she regards it as the king of all her rings, and if ever she is naming and valuing her jewels she will say: This is my king, that is, the ring with which my royal husband was betrothed to me. It is the sign of an indissoluble union and fidelity. In the same way the bread and wine are the symbols of that friendship by which God is reconciled to the human race in and through his Son. We do not value them according to their intrinsic worth, but according to the greatness of that which they represent.... Indeed, it is in fact the body of Christ, but only in name and signification, or, as we now say, sacramentally.[29]

For Zwingli, the Eucharist is but a symbol of the communion that we have with Christ in faith through the power of His death for us. Thus Christ's words of institution should be taken to mean that the bread that Christ gave to His disciples *signifies* His Body that was given for us on Calvary.

This interpretation was clearly violating the evident sense of the words, "This is my body." Furthermore, we may answer that God is somewhat more powerful than the husband in Zwingli's analogy, who could give only a ring to his wife. The miracle of the Eucharist, in which Christ leaves His very self as an inheritance to His Church, is perfectly in accordance with God's omnipotence and infinite love for man. Zwingli has reduced Christ to the level of a mere mortal man who works no miracle in the Eucharist, and his position continues the rationalist line begun by Berengarius four hundred and fifty years earlier.

A more meritorious part of Zwingli's Eucharistic teaching was his battle against Luther's doctrine of the omnipresence of Christ's Body, which he saw to be a Christological heresy. He rightly says: "It belongs only to the divine nature of Christ to be ubiquitous. Otherwise Christ could not have ascended up bodily into heaven."[30] Zwingli's argument against "ubiquitism," however, is not an argument against the real

---

[29] Zwingli, *An Exposition of the Faith* (1531), in Bromiley, *Zwingli and Bullinger*, 262–63.

[30] Zwingli, *On the Lord's Supper* (Bromiley, *Zwingli and Bullinger*, 219).

presence, for there is another way in which Christ can be truly present under the species of bread and wine—transubstantiation—which, of course, Zwingli opposed no less vehemently than he did Luther's ubiquitism.

John Calvin

John Calvin[31] has a position on the Eucharist that is more radical than Luther's but differs from Zwingli's by emphasizing a dynamic encounter with Christ through the sacrament. He hoped this would make it more acceptable to the Lutherans so as to take away the division among the Protestants. He wrote to Philip Melanchthon:

> It is of the utmost importance that no suspicion of the divisions that are among us come to the attention of future centuries. For it is the most ridiculous thing imaginable that after dividing ourselves from the rest of the world, we were so little in agreement among ourselves right from the beginning of our Reform.[32]

On the one hand, Calvin denies consubstantiation, any local presence of Christ in the Eucharist, or any omnipresence of the Body of Christ such as Luther had affirmed. Like Berengarius and Zwingli, Calvin thought the Catholic dogma of the real presence was in contradiction with the glorious state of Christ's Body physically present in heaven,[33] and he held that Christ is present in the Eucharist only

---

[31] For Calvin's theology of the Eucharist, see Kilian McDonnell, *John Calvin, the Church, and the Eucharist* (Princeton, NJ: Princeton University Press, 1967); Brian Gerrish, *Grace and Gratitude: The Eucharistic Theology of John Calvin* (Minneapolis, MN: Fortress Press, 1993); Nicholas Wolterstorff, "John Calvin," in Wandel, *A Companion to the Eucharist in the Reformation*, 97–113.

[32] John Calvin, Letter to Philip Melanchthon, cited in E. Mangenot, *Dictionnaire de théologie catholique: contenant l'exposé des doctrines de la théologie catholique, leurs preuves et leur histoire/commencé sous la direction de A. Vacant; continué sous celle de E. Mangenot; avec concours d'un grand nombre de collaborateurs*, "Eucharistie," (Paris: Letouzey et Ané, 1903–1950), 5:1342.

[33] See John Calvin, *Institutes*, bk. IV, ch. 17, no. 23: "As we cannot at all doubt that it is bounded according to the invariable rule in the human body, and is contained in heaven, where it was once received, and will remain till it return to judgment, so we deem it altogether unlawful to bring it back under these corruptible elements, or to imagine it everywhere present" (Beveridge, 902).

as a symbol, but one that nevertheless has *a power to strengthen our faith*. Calvin emphasizes the presence of a spiritual power of Christ in the Eucharist that Zwingli did not so clearly acknowledge. Calvin maintains a certain mysterious "dynamic" and "spiritual" presence of Christ in the Eucharist *through faith* and the action of the Holy Spirit, which implies not that Christ becomes present in the bread, coming physically down to us, but that the faithful who receive the bread are brought spiritually in faith to an encounter with Christ in heaven.[34] Calvin writes:

> They are greatly mistaken in imagining that there is no presence of the flesh of Christ in the Supper, unless it be placed in the bread. They thus leave nothing for the secret operation of the Spirit, which unites Christ himself to us. Christ does not seem to them to be present unless he descends to us, as if we did not equally gain his presence when he raises us to himself.[35]

Calvin is aware of the Scholastic distinction of three levels in the Eucharist that were introduced by Peter Lombard to refute the position of Berengarius. Calvin denies, however, that Christ's Body and Blood can be considered *res et sacramentum* precisely because, like Berengarius, he denies that it is properly contained in the sacrament. After quoting Lombard's distinction between the Body and Blood that is the *res et sacramentum* and the spiritual nourishment that is the *res tantum*, Calvin writes:

> To his distinction between the flesh of Christ and the power of nourishing which it possesses, I assent; but his maintaining it to be a sacrament, and a sacrament contained under the bread, is an error not to be tolerated. Hence has arisen that false interpretation of sacramental eating, because it was imagined

---

[34] See Michael Allen, "Sacraments in the Reformed and Anglican Reformation," in Boersma and Levering, eds., *The Oxford Handbook of Sacramental Theology*, 292: "Calvin argued that the fellowship occurred by the Spirit's drawing the believer up to the local presence of Christ in the heavenly places, rather than by the incarnate Son being present to multiple earthly spatialities. He continued to oppose the doctrine of ubiquity even in affirming a real presence through the instrument of the sacrament." See also Piolanti, "L'Eucaristia," 1102.

[35] Calvin, *Institutes*, bk. IV, ch. 17, no. 31 (Beveridge, 918).

that even the wicked and profane, however much alienated from Christ, eat his body. But the very flesh of Christ in the mystery of the Supper is no less a spiritual matter than eternal salvation.[36]

It can be seen from this text that Calvin, like Zwingli, differs from Luther in also holding that those who receive the host unworthily do not actually receive His real presence. Since Calvin denies that Christ is properly "in the bread" or in the outward elements of the sacrament and holds that it is faith that brings the believer to Christ in receiving the sacrament, it makes sense that Calvin holds that those who receive without faith or without the action of the Spirit do not actually receive Christ.[37] Only the worthy actually encounter the heavenly Christ through the instrumentality of the sacrament.

Because he denies a local presence of Christ in the Eucharist, and because the words of institution speak of a taking rather than of an adoration, Calvin also, like the other Protestant leaders, forbids the adoration of Christ in the sacrament:

Had all their thoughts been kept in due subjection to the word of God, they certainly would have listened to what he himself has said, "Take, eat, and drink," and obeyed the command by which he enjoins us to receive the sacrament, not worship it. Those who receive without adoration, as commanded by God, are secure that they deviate not from the command.[38]

The *Westminster Confession* from 1646 gives an authoritative formulation of the Calvinist position:

[No. 5:] . . . The outward elements in this sacrament, duly set apart to the uses ordained by Christ, have such relation to him crucified, as that truly, yet sacramentally only, they are sometimes called by the name of the things they represent, to wit, the body and blood of Christ; albeit, in substance and nature,

---

[36] Calvin, *Institutes*, bk. IV, ch. 17, no. 33 (Beveridge, 920).

[37] See ibid.

[38] See ibid., no. 35 (Beveridge, 923). Benedict XVI has a powerful response to a position like that of Calvin's, in *Sacramentum Caritatis*, §66, examined below in chapter 16, p. 597.

they still remain truly, and only, bread and wine, as they were before.

No. 6: That doctrine which maintains a change of the substance of bread and wine, into the substance of Christ's body and blood (commonly called transubstantiation) by consecration of a priest, . . . is repugnant, not to Scripture alone, but even to common-sense and reason; overthroweth the nature of the sacrament; and hath been, and is the cause of manifold superstitions. . . .

No. 7: Worthy receivers . . . do then also inwardly by faith, really and indeed, yet not carnally and corporally, but spiritually, receive and feed upon Christ crucified, and all benefits of his death; the body and blood of Christ being then not corporally or carnally in, with, or under the bread and wine; yet as really, but spiritually, present to the faith of believers in that ordinance.[39]

Calvin is saying that, by receiving the Eucharist in faith, one receives the spirit of Christ and a certain power of Christ to vivify our faith. This is indeed true, but, from the Catholic perspective, it is much too little. The problem with Calvin's position lies in what he denies: Christ's substantial and corporeal presence in the Eucharist. All of the sacraments have the spiritual power to give us the grace of Christ and strengthen our faith. However, the Eucharist not only contains the power of Christ to give grace, but also contains Christ Himself, whole and entire, the author of grace and the author of our faith.

Anglican View

Although the Anglican Church allows great doctrinal liberty to her members, common Anglican doctrine on the Eucharist is taken from both Luther and Calvin and was formulated in the *Thirty-Nine Articles of the Church of England* (1563).[40] Anglicans (and Episcopalians) generally teach that Christ is "really present" in the Eucharist, but

---

[39] *Westminster Confession* (1646), art. 29, nos. 5–7, in *Creeds of the Churches: A Reader in Christian Doctrine from the Bible to the Present*, ed. John H. Leith, rev. ed. (Richmond, VA: John Knox Press, 1973), 226.

[40] See James F. Turrell, "Anglican Theologies of the Eucharist," in Wandel, *A Companion to the Eucharist in the Reformation*, 139–58.

they reject transubstantiation,[41] and like Calvin, they generally restrict His presence to the moment in which the Eucharist is consumed in faith, and only for the person who consumes it in faith. This view is contained in articles 28 and 29 of the Thirty-Nine Articles. Article 28 states:

> [Only] to such as rightly, worthily, and with faith, receive the same, the Bread which we break is a partaking of the Body of Christ; and likewise the Cup of Blessing is a partaking of the Blood of Christ. . . . And the mean whereby the Body of Christ is received and eaten in the Supper, is Faith.[42]

Article 29 specifies that only believers actually receive the Body of Christ:

> The wicked, and such as be void of a lively faith, although they do visibly press with their teeth (as Saint Augustine saith) the Sacrament of the Body and Blood of Christ; yet in no wise are they partakers of Christ: but rather, to their condemnation, do eat and drink the sign or Sacrament of so great a thing.[43]

The real presence conceived in this way is a presence that has lost its objective and ontological dimension and tends toward the Calvinist view that the Eucharist is only a dynamic and faith-sustaining symbol of Christ.

This doctrine has great practical consequences regarding the cult of the Eucharist. One immediate consequence of this subjective interpretation of the real presence was the general Anglican rejection of Eucharistic adoration and prayer before the Blessed Sacrament.

---

[41] See *Thirty-Nine Articles of the Church of England* (1563), art. 28: "Transubstantiation (or the change of the substance of Bread and Wine) in the Supper of the Lord, cannot be proved by Holy Writ; but is repugnant to the plain words of Scripture, overthroweth the nature of a Sacrament, and hath given occasion to many superstitions" (*Creeds of the Churches*, 276).

[42] Ibid.

[43] Ibid., art. 29.

The Council of Trent on Christ's Presence in the Eucharist

The Council of Trent responded to various Protestant errors concerning Christ's presence in the Eucharist in its thirteenth session. Trent's Decree on the Eucharist begins by affirming that "after the consecration of the bread and wine, our Lord Jesus Christ, true God and man, is truly, really, and substantially contained under the appearances of those perceptible realities."[44] The substantial presence of Christ in the Eucharist is thus a dogma of faith.

Trent also affirms that Christ's substantial presence in the Eucharist does not contradict the fact that Christ "always sits at the right hand of the Father in heaven according to his natural way of existing."[45] This implies that Christ's sacramental mode of presence is distinct from the natural way that a body is present in a place. The text goes on to emphasize that this sacramental mode of presence escapes our imagination and capacity of expression: "We can hardly find words to express this way of existing; but our reason, enlightened through faith, can nevertheless recognize it as possible for God."[46]

After defining the substantial presence of Christ in the Eucharist, Trent defines transubstantiation to be the way in which Christ becomes substantially present. It is defined as the change of the whole substance of bread and wine into that of Christ's Body and Blood. Trent also teaches, like St. Thomas, that the doctrine of transubstantiation follows from the words of Jesus at the Last Supper:

> Because Christ our Redeemer said that it was truly his body that he was offering under the species of bread, it has always been the conviction of the Church of God, and this holy council now again declares, that, by the consecration of the bread and wine, there takes place a change of the whole substance of bread into the substance of the body of Christ our

---

[44] Council of Trent, On the Sacrament of the Eucharist (session 13), ch. 1 (DS, 1636). See the corresponding can. 1: "If anyone denies that the body and blood, together with the soul and divinity, of our Lord Jesus Christ and, therefore, the whole Christ is truly, really, and substantially contained in the sacrament of the most holy Eucharist, but says that Christ is present in the Sacrament only as in a sign or figure, or by his power: let him be anathema" (DS, 1651).

[45] Ibid., ch. 1 (DS, 1636).

[46] Ibid.

Lord and of the whole substance of wine into the substance of his blood. This change the holy Catholic Church has fittingly and properly named transubstantiation.[47]

Consubstantiation is definitively condemned in canon 2: "If anyone says that in the most holy sacrament of the Eucharist the substance of bread and wine remains together with the body and blood of our Lord Jesus Christ, . . . let him be anathema."[48] The same canon also condemns those who deny transubstantiation and asserts the fittingness of the term itself to express the content of the Eucharistic conversion:

> If anyone . . . denies that wonderful and unique change of the whole substance of the bread into his body and of the whole substance of the wine into his blood while only the species [appearances] of bread and wine remain, a change which the Catholic Church very fittingly calls transubstantiation, let him be anathema.[49]

The Council of Trent chose to use the word "species" instead of the more technical term "accident." *Species* should be understood here to mean perceptible forms or empirical accidents. Aristotle's hylomorphic theory and the distinction of substance and accidents provide the general conceptual framework in which the conciliar Fathers were working.[50]

Trent also solemnly teaches the doctrine of concomitance, and it distinguishes what is made present directly through the power of the words of consecration from what is made present by concomitance:

---

[47] Ibid., ch. 4 (DS, 1642).

[48] Ibid., can. 2 (DS, 1652).

[49] Ibid.

[50] See Ibáñez, *L'Eucaristia, Dono e Mistero*, 296–301. See also Edward Schillebeeckx, *The Eucharist*, trans. N. D. Smith (New York: Sheed and Ward, 1968), 57–58: "There is a great deal of evidence to show that there was not one of the fathers of the Council who did not think of the dogma in Aristotelian terms.... This does not imply any sanctioning by the Church of an Aristotelian philosophy; nonetheless, the whole Aristotelian doctrine of substance and accidents was the framework of thought within which the fathers of the Council reflected about faith." See also E. Gutwenger, "Substanz und Akzidenz in der Eucharistielehre," *Zeitschrift für katholische Theologie* 83 (1961): 257–306.

This has always been the belief of the Church of God that immediately after the consecration the true body and blood of our Lord, together with his soul and divinity, exist under the species of bread and wine. The body exists under the species of bread and the blood under the species of wine by virtue of the words. But the body, too, exists under the species of wine, the blood under the species of bread, and the soul under both species in virtue of the natural connection and concomitance by which the parts of Christ the Lord, who has already risen from the dead to die no more, are united together. Moreover, the divinity is present because of its admirable hypostatic union with the body and the soul.[51]

This doctrine of concomitance is the foundation of the Council's teaching on the legitimacy of the Church's practice of distributing Communion under just one species:

Although our Redeemer at the Last Supper ... instituted and distributed this sacrament to the apostles under two species: nevertheless, it must be confessed that even under only one of the two species the whole and entire Christ and the true sacrament is received; and, therefore, with respect to the fruit of the sacrament, those who receive under only one species are not deprived of any grace necessary for salvation.[52]

Trent also condemns the idea common to Reformed and Anglican traditions that would limit Christ's presence in the sacrament to the moment that it is received in faith:

If any one says that after the consecration the body and blood of our Lord Jesus Christ are not in the marvelous sacrament of the Eucharist but that they are there only in the use of the sacrament, while it is being received, and not either before or after, and that in the consecrated hosts or particles that are

---

[51] Council of Trent, On the Sacrament of the Eucharist (session 13), ch. 3 (DS, 1640); see also can. 3 (DS, 1653).

[52] Council of Trent, On Communion under Both Kinds and the Communion of Little Children (session 21), ch. 3 (DS, 1729).

preserved or are left over after communion the true body of the Lord does not remain, let him be anathema.[53]

The Council of Trent also vigorously reaffirmed the great merit of Eucharistic adoration:

> There remains, therefore, no room for doubting that all the faithful of Christ, in accordance with the perpetual custom of the Catholic Church, must venerate this most holy Sacrament with the worship of *latria* that is due to the true God. Nor is it to be less adored because it was instituted by Christ the Lord to be received. For in it we believe that the same God is present whom the eternal Father brought into the world, saying: "Let all God's angels worship him" [Heb 1:6; from Ps 97:7], whom the Magi fell down to worship, and whom, finally, the apostles adored in Galilee, as Scripture testifies [cf. Matt 28:17].[54]

The corresponding canon condemns those who deny that the Eucharist should be the object of adoration and special liturgical honor:

> If anyone says that . . . the Sacrament therefore is not to be honored with special festive celebrations or solemnly carried in processions according to the praiseworthy universal rite and custom of the holy Church; or that it is not to be publicly exposed for the people's adoration and that those who adore it are idolaters, let him be anathema.[55]

Tragically, almost all Protestants, despite their differences, tend to agree in rejecting Eucharistic adoration.[56]

---

[53] Council of Trent, On the Sacrament of the Eucharist (session 13), can. 4 (DS, 1654).

[54] Ibid., ch. 5 (DS, 1643).

[55] Ibid., can. 6 (DS, 1656).

[56] For the Reformed and Presbyterian tradition, see the *Westminster Confession*, art. 29, no. 4: "Worshiping the elements, the lifting them up, or carrying them about for adoration . . . are all contrary to the nature of this sacrament, and to the institution of Christ" (*Creeds of the Churches*, 226).

Summary of the Principal Truths on the Real Presence Defined by the Council of Trent

1) Christ is present in the Eucharist, whole and entire, with a substantial presence.[57]

2) At the words of consecration, the substances of the bread and the wine are converted into the substance of Christ's Body and Blood, a unique conversion fittingly called "transubstantiation."[58] Only this doctrine offers a coherent explanation of the real and substantial presence of our Lord in the Most Blessed Sacrament.

3) The substances of the bread and wine do not remain after the consecration.[59]

4) Christ's substantial presence under the consecrated species remains[60] as long as the appearances of bread and wine have not been corrupted and transformed into something else (as occurs in digestion after some minutes).

5) Christ is contained whole and entire under each species through concomitance. The faithful who receive only under one species still receive the whole Christ. Furthermore, Christ is present whole and entire in every part of either species.[61] Thus a broken particle of the host or a drop of wine from the chalice contains the whole Christ.

6) Christ present in the Eucharist is entitled to the adoration and the worship of *latria* proper to God alone. Because the Eucharist deserves the worship of *latria*, it is very fitting for the Church to institute and promote forms of Eucharistic adoration.[62]

---

[57] Council of Trent, On the Sacrament of the Eucharist (session 13), ch. 3 and can. 1 (DS, 1641, 1651).

[58] Ibid., ch. 4 and can. 2 (DS, 1642, 1652).

[59] Ibid., can. 2 (DS, 1652).

[60] Ibid., can. 4 (DS, 1654).

[61] Ibid., ch. 3 and can. 3 (DS, 1641, 1653).

[62] Ibid., ch. 5 and can. 6 (DS, 1643–44, 1656).

Jansenism

The Jansenists were a heretical strain of Catholics active in the seventeenth and eighteenth centuries who, influenced by Michael Baius,[63] sought to incorporate certain Calvinist ideas, particularly regarding grace and free will, into the Catholic faith. With regard to the Eucharist, they introduced two errors. They were fiercely opposed to frequent Communion by the faithful, thus denying proper access to the fountain of grace that is the Eucharist.[64] In addition, without directly denying the doctrine of transubstantiation, they simply proposed to let the term fall into oblivion, teaching the fact of the real presence without mentioning that word or the substantial conversion. This pastoral strategy was condemned by Pius VI in the bull *Auctorem Fidei* (1794) as "pernicious and injurious to the exposition of the truth of the Catholic faith with regard to the dogma of transubstantiation and such as to promote heresy."

Paul VI, in *Mysterium Fidei* (1965), §24, likewise maintains the importance of the term "transubstantiation":

> And so the rule of language which the Church has established through the long labor of centuries, with the help of the Holy Spirit, and which she has confirmed with the authority of the Councils, and which has more than once been the watchword and banner of orthodox faith, is to be religiously preserved, and no one may presume to change it at his own pleasure or under the pretext of new knowledge.

---

[63] See the condemnation of 80 errors of Michael Baius by Pius V in 1567 (DS, 1901–80).

[64] See Antoine Arnauld, *De la fréquente communion*, 7th ed. (Paris: Pierre le Petit, 1683).

Twentieth-Century Challenge to Transubstantiation: "Transsignification"

In the mid-twentieth century, certain Catholic theologians[65] attempted to reinterpret transubstantiation on the basis of an idealist philosophy, replacing the venerable term of "transubstantiation" with "transsignification" or "transfinalization."[66] Although these terms have a different philosophical foundation than the positions of Berengarius, Zwingli, or Calvin, they move in the same direction.

The theologians who proposed this new theory were influenced by certain tenets of the philosophy of existentialism, according to which the *objective* "being" of things is not considered a meaningful category, and the "substance" of things is identified with the *significance* they hold for us socially and historically.[67] This goes together with a rejection not only of an Aristotelian philosophy of nature, but also of the meaningfulness of the commonsense categories of "substance" and "accidents."[68] According to this idealist and subjectivist philosophical

---

[65] See Schillebeeckx, *The Eucharist*; Charles Davis, "Understanding the Real Presence," in *The Word in History: The St. Xavier Symposium*, ed. T. Patrick Burke (New York: Sheed and Ward, 1966), 154–78; Piet Schoonenberg, "Christus' tegenwoordigheid voor ons," *Verbum* 31 (1964): 393–415; J. de Baciocchi, "Présence eucharistique et transsubstantiation," *Irénikon* 32 (1959): 139–61. See also the review of the German edition of Schillebeeckx's book by Joseph Ratzinger in *TL*, 243–48.

[66] See Piet Schoonenberg, "Presence and Eucharistic Presence," *Cross Currents* 17 (Winter 1967): 39–54, at 54: "Through this consecration, Christ is not dragged out of heaven, in a spatial way, nor is there a physical or chemical change in the bread and wine. What happens is a change of signs; the transubstantiation is a transfinalization or a transignification, but this takes place in the depths which only Christ, in his most real self-giving, reaches." The section on the Eucharist in the Dutch Catechism, *De Nieuwe Katechismus: geloofsverkondiging voor volswassenen* (*The New Catechism: Proclamation of the Faith for Adults*) (Hilversum, NL: Brand, 1966), 391–408, shows the influence of this theological position. For an excellent overview of this general position, its development, proponents, philosophical presuppositions, and theological weaknesses, see Ibáñez, *L'Eucaristia, Dono e Mistero*, 390–409.

[67] See, for example, Schillebeeckx, *The Eucharist*, 130–32. For a study of the philosophical foundations of this controversy, see Notger Slenczka, *Realpräsenz und Ontologie: Untersuchung der ontologischen Grundlagen der Transsignifikationslehre* (Göttingen: Vandenhoeck & Ruprecht, 1993).

[68] See Schillebeeckx, *The Eucharist*, 94: "It had already become clear in the period between the two world wars that transubstantiation was in need of

position, the real presence, together with all objective realities, loses its objective meaning, and transubstantiation becomes equated with transsignification. For example, Edward Schillebeeckx writes:

> The Eucharist . . . takes the form of a commemorative meal in which the usual secular significance of the bread and wine is withdrawn and these become bearers of Christ's gift of himself. . . . In this commemorative meal, bread and wine become the subject of a new *establishment of meaning*, not by men, but by the living Lord *in* the Church, through which they become the *sign* of the real presence of Christ giving himself to us.[69]

This explanation is not false in what it affirms—a change in the meaning of the sacramental signs—but rather in what it leaves out—an objective but mysterious change on the level of the *substance* of bread and wine independent of the faith of those present. Catholic proponents of transsignification affirm the reality of Christ's presence in the Eucharist, but what is lacking is the clear affirmation of a *substantial* presence as distinct from a symbolic one.[70]

Bl. Paul VI, in *Mysterium Fidei*, speaks at some length about the various ways, apart from transubstantiation, in which Christ is really

---

reinterpretation. The facts of modern physics had shaken the neo-scholastic speculations about the concept of substance to their foundations. This heralded the change from an approach to the Eucharist by way of natural philosophy to the anthropological approach. . . . The quantum theory in physics made many neo-scholastics realize that the concept substance could not be applied to material reality—or at the most that the whole of the cosmos could be seen as only one great substance." See the response to this kind of argumentation by Roger Nutt in "Faith, Metaphysics, and the Contemplation of Christ's Corporeal Presence in the Eucharist," 159: "To assert, as Schillebeeckx does, that the developments of modern science, and quantum theory in physics in particular, necessitated that theologians move away from the concept of substance, indicates that, consciously or unconsciously, quantity and substance have been erroneously equated: indeed, the proper object of the empirical sciences is, precisely, quantitative entities located in space, as quantitative."

[69] Schillebeeckx, *The Eucharist*, 137. See the insightful critique of transsignification theories by Kereszty, "Real presence, Manifold Presence," 23–36.

[70] See Schillebeeckx, *The Eucharist*, 155: "In referring to a 'metaphysical dimension,' as, for example, in my conclusion that, according to the Tridentine dogma, this dimension forms an essential part of our faith in Christ's real 'presence' in the Eucharist, all I mean is that Christ's eucharistic presence is a *reality*. I am not affirming that this reality is to be found behind the phenomenal appearance, but that it appears *in* the phenomenon to the believer."

present in His Church. He is present in the prayer of the faithful, in their works of mercy, in those who live in charity, in the preaching, in the Word of God, in all the sacramental actions of the Church. Only in the Eucharist, however, is Christ substantially present in His humanity:

> These various ways in which Christ is present fill the mind with astonishment and offer the Church a mystery for her contemplation. But there is another way in which Christ is present in His Church, a way that surpasses all the others. . . . This presence is called "real" not to exclude the idea that the others are "real" too, but rather to indicate presence par excellence, because it is substantial and through it Christ becomes present whole and entire, God and man. And so it would be wrong for anyone to try to explain this manner of presence by dreaming up a so-called "pneumatic" nature of the glorious body of Christ that would be present everywhere; or for anyone to limit it to symbolism, as if this most sacred Sacrament were to consist in nothing more than an efficacious sign "of the spiritual presence of Christ and of His intimate union with the faithful, the members of His Mystical Body."[71]

As in the case of Berengarius, an explanation of the Eucharist in terms of transsignification or transfinalization tends to reduce the richness of the Eucharist from the three levels—sacramental sign, the mystery of Christ's Body and Blood made present and offered in sacrifice, and the grace of sanctification and ecclesial unity—to two: sacramental sign and the ultimate effect of the Eucharist that is the unity of the Church. The substantial presence of Christ's Body and

---

[71] Paul VI, Encyclical Letter on the Holy Eucharist, *Mysterium Fidei* (1965), §§38–39. See also *CCC*, §1374, which explains the doctrine of the real presence of Christ in the Eucharist by stressing that this presence is not only real but also *substantial*: "In the most blessed sacrament of the Eucharist 'the body and blood, together with the soul and divinity, of our Lord Jesus Christ and, therefore, *the whole Christ is truly, really, and substantially contained.*' This presence is called 'real'—by which is not intended to exclude the other types of presence as if they could not be 'real' too, but because it is presence in the fullest sense: that is to say, it is a *substantial* presence by which Christ, God and man, makes himself wholly and entirely present." For a discussion of these various forms of presence, see Colman O'Neill, *New Approaches to the Eucharist* (New York: Alba House, 1967), 70–79.

Blood (the *res et sacramentum*), and in consequence the substantial presence of Christ's sacrifice on Calvary, are downplayed and reinterpreted only on the level of signs, if not directly excluded.[72]

Paul VI, in *Mysterium Fidei*, called attention to these errors that were beginning to circulate among theologians. He writes:

> For We can see that some of those who are dealing with this Most Holy Mystery in speech and writing are disseminating opinions on Masses celebrated in private or on the dogma of transubstantiation that are disturbing the minds of the faithful and causing them no small measure of confusion about matters of faith, just as if it were all right for someone to take doctrine that has already been defined by the Church and consign it to oblivion or else interpret it in such a way as to weaken the genuine meaning of the words or the recognized force of the concepts involved.
>
> To give an example of what We are talking about, it is not permissible . . . to concentrate on the notion of sacramental sign as if the symbolism—which no one will deny is certainly present in the Most Blessed Eucharist—fully expressed and exhausted the manner of Christ's presence in this Sacrament; or to discuss the mystery of transubstantiation without mentioning what the Council of Trent had to say about the marvelous conversion of the whole substance of the bread into the Body and the whole substance of the wine into the Blood of Christ, as if they involve nothing more than "transignification," or "transfinalization" as they call it; or, finally, to propose and act upon the opinion that Christ Our Lord is no longer present in the consecrated Hosts that remain after the celebration of the sacrifice of the Mass has been completed.
>
> Everyone can see that the spread of these and similar opinions does great harm to belief in and devotion to the Eucharist.[73]

---

[72] See the sympathetic but penetrating critique of this theological thesis by O'Neill, *New Approaches to the Eucharist*, 113–26, esp. 119: "But where does the Eucharistic sacrifice appear in this approach? It is here, I feel, that the weakest point in the new theory is to be discovered, even when it is viewed exclusively from within its own terms of reference. . . . This is the startling omission in the new theory."

[73] Paul VI, *Mysterium Fidei*, §§10–12.

Paul VI goes on to explain that the Eucharistic consecration certainly brings about a change of meaning and finality, for the consecrated bread and wine no longer point to physical nourishment, but spiritual. This change of meaning (transsignification) comes about, however, because of an ontological change by which the old realities—the substances of bread and wine—have been converted into the substance of the Body and Blood of Christ. The ontological change is the foundation for the change in meaning and finality:

> As a result of transubstantiation, the species of bread and wine undoubtedly take on a new signification and a new finality, for they are no longer ordinary bread and wine but instead a sign of something sacred and a sign of spiritual food; but they take on this new signification, this new finality, precisely because they contain a new "reality" which we can rightly call *ontological*. For what now lies beneath the aforementioned species is not what was there before, but something completely different; and not just in the estimation of Church belief but in reality, since once the substance or nature of the bread and wine has been changed into the body and blood of Christ, nothing remains of the bread and the wine except for the species—beneath which Christ is present whole and entire in His physical "reality," corporeally present, although not in the manner in which bodies are in a place.[74]

In other words, Christ's Body and Blood are present in themselves in the sacrament, and because they are present, they are signs of their proper effects of sanctification and ecclesial unity. That is precisely the idea of *res et sacramentum*, which is simultaneously both a new and mysterious *reality* and a *sign*. The Body and Blood are both ontological *realities* and *signs* of the grace that they confer. A sacramental theory that puts all the emphasis on the aspect of signification tends to leave out the ontological dimension of *res et sacramentum*, which is foundational.

Paul VI reaffirmed Trent's teaching on transubstantiation again in 1968 in the Credo of the People of God. Every theological explanation of the mystery must affirm that the bread and wine objectively cease

---

[74] Ibid., §46 (DS, 4413; italics original).

to exist after the consecration, having been changed into the reality of His Body and Blood:

> Christ cannot be thus present in this sacrament except by the change into His body of the reality itself of the bread and the change into His blood of the reality itself of the wine, leaving unchanged only the properties of the bread and wine which our senses perceive. This mysterious change is very appropriately called by the Church transubstantiation. Every theological explanation which seeks some understanding of this mystery must, in order to be in accord with Catholic faith, maintain that in the reality itself, independently of our mind, the bread and wine have ceased to exist after the Consecration, so that it is the adorable body and blood of the Lord Jesus that from then on are really before us under the sacramental species of bread and wine, as the Lord willed it, in order to give Himself to us as food and to associate us with the unity of His Mystical Body.[75]

STUDY QUESTIONS

1. What is the position of Martin Luther on Christ's presence in the Eucharist?
2. What is "ubiquitism?"
3. What is the position of Huldrych Zwingli on Christ's presence in the Eucharist?
4. What is the position of John Calvin on Christ's presence in the Eucharist?
5. What is the Anglican position on Christ's presence in the Eucharist?
6. What did the Council of Trent solemnly teach concerning transubstantiation?
7. What are the other principal teachings of Trent on the presence of Christ in the Eucharist?

---

[75] Paul VI, Apostolic Letter on the Credo of the People of God, *Solemni Hac Liturgia* (1968), §25.

8. Christ is present in His Church in many ways. What is unique about the presence of Christ in the Eucharist? What is meant by "substantial presence"?

9. What does Bl. Paul VI say about transsignification in *Mysterium Fidei*?

Suggestions for Further Reading

Allen, Michael. "Sacraments in the Reformed and Anglican Reformation." In Boersma and Levering, eds., *The Oxford Handbook of Sacramental Theology*. New York: Oxford University Press, 2015. Pp. 283–97.

Althaus, Paul. *The Theology of Martin Luther*. Translated by Robert C. Schultz. Philadelphia, PA: Fortress Press, 1966. Pp. 375–403.

Mattox, Mickey L. "Sacraments in the Lutheran Reformation." In Boersma and Levering, eds., *The Oxford Handbook of Sacramental Theology*. Pp. 269–82.

O'Neill, Colman. *New Approaches to the Eucharist*. New York: Alba House, 1967. Pp. 65–126.

Bl. Paul VI. Encyclical on the Eucharist, *Mysterium Fidei*. September 3, 1965.

Ratzinger, Joseph. "The Problem of Transubstantiation." In *Theology of the Liturgy: The Sacramental Foundation of Christian Existence. Joseph Ratzinger Collected Works*. Vol. 11. San Francisco: Ignatius Press, 2014. Pp. 218–42.

Schillebeeckx, Edward. *The Eucharist*. Translated by N. D. Smith. New York: Sheed and Ward, 1968.

PART III

�֍

SACRIFICE

✠

CHAPTER NINE

The Sacrifice of the Mass

SACRIFICE IS A FUNDAMENTAL
ACT OF RELIGION

We have seen above that the Eucharist was instituted for three fundamental ends. It is the sacrament of Christ's presence among us, the sacrament of Christ's expiatory sacrifice on Calvary that He has given to His Church, and the sacrament of spiritual nourishment. In this chapter we shall focus on the Eucharist as the Christian sacrifice. First, however, we need to reflect on the nature and purpose of sacrifice as a central act of religious worship present in almost all religions.

The classical philosophers consider religion to be a moral virtue by which we give to God what is due to Him[1] and thus "bind ourselves back" to Him, as the etymology of the word suggests.[2] Religion is, in

---

[1] *ST* II-II, q. 81, a. 4:

> Since virtue is directed to the good, wherever there is a special aspect of good, there must be a special virtue. Now the good to which religion is directed, is to give due honor to God. Again, honor is due to someone under the aspect of excellence: and to God a singular excellence is competent, since He infinitely surpasses all things and exceeds them in every way. Wherefore to Him is special honor due: even as in human affairs we see that different honor is due to different personal excellences, one kind of honor to a father, another to the king, and so on. Hence it is evident that religion is a special virtue.

[2] See Lactantius, *The Divine Institutes* 4.28: "We are fastened and bound to God by this bond of piety, whence religion itself takes its name" (trans. Mary Francis McDonald [Washington, DC: Catholic University of America Press, 1964], 318); Augustine, *De Vera Religione* 55.111: ". . . bind [*religare*] our souls to him alone without superstition. Hence, it is believed, religion derives its name"

fact, the most exalted aspect of the moral virtue of justice, by which we give to each one his due.[3] And what is due to God, our Creator, Lord, and Redeemer? The principal things that are due from us to God are spiritual acts: supreme praise, honor, gratitude, obedience to His commands, faith, hope, charity, and readiness to do all that serves to manifest His glory and His love. And when we have sinned, contrition and the desire to make reparation are due to God. These spiritual acts are a kind of interior sacrifice or gift of self to God, and they are the heart of the virtue of religion, which is the habitual attitude of seeking to give fitting glory to God.

Man, however, is not a pure spirit, and so it is fitting for him to express the spiritual worship of the heart by means of external and sensible signs of the interior worship.[4] The most important of these exterior acts of the virtue of religion is sacrifice.[5] For this reason, sac-

---

(trans. J. H. S. Burleigh [South Bend, IN: Regnery Gateway, 1979], 105); *ST* II-II, q. 81, a. 1:

> Religion may be derived from *religare* (*to bind together*), wherefore Augustine says [*De Vera Religione* 55.113]: "May religion bind us to the one Almighty God." However, whether religion take its name from frequent reading, or from a repeated choice of what has been lost through negligence, or from being a bond, it denotes properly a relation to God. For it is He to Whom we ought to be bound as to our unfailing principle; to Whom also our choice should be resolutely directed as to our last end; and Whom we lose when we neglect Him by sin, and should recover by believing and protesting our faith.

[3] *ST* II-II, q. 81, a. 6: "Whatever is directed to an end takes its goodness from being ordered to that end; so that the nearer it is to the end the better it is. Now moral virtues . . . are about matters that are ordered to God as their end. And religion approaches nearer to God than the other moral virtues, in so far as its actions are directly and immediately ordered to the honor of God. Hence religion excels among the moral virtues."

[4] See *ST* I-II, q. 101, a. 2: "Divine worship is twofold: internal, and external. For since man is composed of soul and body, each of these should be applied to the worship of God; the soul by an interior worship; the body by an outward worship: hence it is written (Ps 83: 3): 'My heart and my flesh have rejoiced in the living God.' And as the body is ordained to God through the soul, so the outward worship is ordained to the internal worship."

[5] See Odo Casel, *The Mystery of Christian Worship*, ed. Burkhard Neunheuser (New York: Crossroad, 1999), 19:

> There is no religion without sacrifice. Religion is the ordering between God and his creature; God bends down to man, and man climbs up toward God; by his taking it and passing it into his possession God makes the sacrifice holy and consecrates it. If the offerer is stained with

rifice is something readily understood by most cultures of human history. To modern Western culture, on the contrary, ritual sacrifice seems totally foreign, a throwback to primitive times left far behind, in which crude and bloodthirsty conceptions of religion governed human societies.

The fundamental purpose of all sacrifice offered to God is to sensibly return something to God to express the spiritual ordering of our souls to Him so as to enter into fellowship with Him. St. Augustine gave a classic analysis of sacrifice in book 10 of *The City of God*. Speaking of pagan and Jewish animal sacrifices, he said: "We are to understand that the significance of those acts was precisely the same as that of those now performed amongst us—the intention of which is that we may cleave to God and seek the good of our neighbor for the same end. Thus the visible sacrifice is the sacrament, the sacred sign, of the invisible sacrifice."[6]

In sacrifice, we externally offer to God something that symbolically represents and accompanies the interior ordering of our heart to God in seeking to give Him His due and to repair for our offenses against Him. Having a bodily and a social dimension, we need to manifest the interior sacrifice with our bodies and through the offering of exterior things in a visible and social way. The external sacrifice is the sacred sign or sacrament[7] of the interior sacrifice of the heart by which one gives oneself wholly to God.[8] The inner sacrifice of the

---

sin, and thereby retarded in his sacrifice, the act must become first of all one of reparation. In this case it is carried out first in the form of a purification to make the sacrifice properly acceptable. "Without bloodshed there is no forgiveness" and no sacrifice of sinful man. The sacrifice made pure by reparation can find its way up to God.

[6] Augustine, *City of God* 10.5 (Bettenson, 377). For the context of St. Augustine's definition, see Uwe Michael Lang, "Augustine's Conception of Sacrifice in *City of God*, Book X, and the Eucharistic Sacrifice," *Antiphon* 19, no. 1 (2015): 29–51.

[7] Sacrifice has the nature of a sacrament, taken in the broad sense, in which there is an exterior sign that represents an interior sacred reality. See *ST* III, q. 22, a. 2; de la Taille, *The Mystery of Faith*, 1:9.

[8] See *ST* II-II, q. 85, a. 2: "The sacrifice that is offered outwardly represents the inward spiritual sacrifice, whereby the soul offers itself to God according to the words of the Psalmist (Ps 50:19), 'A sacrifice to God is an afflicted spirit,' since, as stated above (q. 81, a. 7; q. 85, a. 2), the outward acts of religion are directed to the inward acts." See Forrest, *The Clean Oblation*, 9, who gives a good summary of the Thomistic understanding of sacrifice: "Sacrifice may be described as an offering made to God by a priest, in the name of the people,

contrite heart is more important, but our human nature also requires a sensible manifestation of what occurs in the heart, and thus we need to offer God visible sacrifices, just as we offer visible tokens of our love, gratitude, and sorrow to our loved ones.[9] St. Cyril of Alexandria writes: "For in our sacrifices, we to a certain extent immolate and offer our soul, as in an image, to God, when we die to the world and to the wisdom of the flesh, when we mortify our vices and are, so to speak, crucified with Christ; and thus living a pure and holy life, we spend our days in submission to His holy will."[10] The invisible interior sacrifice is given visible, social, and objective expression in the exterior sacrifice, as our sensible and social nature demands.

Under this general purpose of an external sign to establish fellowship with God, we can distinguish four distinct purposes for which offerings are made: to express adoration by manifesting God's dominion over creation; to return some part of His gifts in thanksgiving for all that we have received; to make propitiation for sin by offering something by way of satisfaction; and to offer something to obtain a particular blessing from God and implore His aid. These purposes can be summarized as adoration, thanksgiving, propitiation, and supplication (which are the same ends of prayer in general).[11] These purposes of sacrifice are accomplished by returning to God a symbolic part of His gifts to us.

St. Thomas explains the purpose of sacrifice as the exterior and sensible manifestation of the ordering of oneself and the world to God alone, as the last end of all creation:

> In offering up sacrifices man proclaims that God is the first principle of the creation of all things, and their last end, to which all things must be directed. And since, for the human

---

of a gift which represents in some way human life. The outward offering of this visible gift signifies the inward offering or consecration of human life to God—the giving to God of 'our whole heart.'" See Nicolas, *What Is the Eucharist?* 58–62.

[9] See *ST* II-II, q. 85, a. 1: "Hence it is a dictate of natural reason that man should use certain sensibles, by offering them to God in sign of the subjection and honour due to Him, like those who make certain offerings to their lord in recognition of his authority. Now this is what we mean by a sacrifice."

[10] Cyril of Alexandria, *De Adoratione in Spiritu et Veritate* 11 (PG, 68:769; English trans. in de la Taille, *The Mystery of Faith*, 1:8–9).

[11] See Pius XII, *Mediator Dei*, §§3, 71–74.

mind to be rightly directed to God, it must recognize no first author of things other than God, nor place its end in any other; for this reason it was forbidden in the Law to offer sacrifice to any other but God.[12]

Sacrifice and Oblation

The word "sacrifice," which corresponds to the Latin *sacrificium*, comes from *sacrum facere*, to make something sacred or consecrated to God.[13] An object is made sacred when something is done to it that removes it from ordinary human ownership and dedicates it to God. The same is true for making a person sacred. Sacrifice thus includes two aspects: (1) it is *offered* to God as an oblation, which means subtraction from man's ordinary use and being given over to divine worship; and (2) it is somehow *changed* to sensibly manifest God's exclusive dominion, as when an animal is immolated. Sacrifice, therefore, is an oblation offered to God, in which the transfer of dominion to God is sensibly manifested by some change. St. Thomas explains:

> A sacrifice, properly speaking, requires that something be done to the thing which is offered to God, for instance animals were slain and burnt, the bread is broken, eaten, blessed. The very word signifies this, since *sacrifice* is so called because a man does something sacred [*facit sacrum*]. On the other hand an oblation is properly the offering of something to God even if nothing be done thereto, thus we speak of offering money or bread at the altar, and yet nothing is done to them. Hence every sacrifice is an oblation, but not conversely. First-fruits are oblations, because they were offered to God, according to Deuteronomy 26, but they are not a sacrifice, because nothing sacred was done to them. Tithes, however, are neither a sacrifice nor an oblation, properly speaking, because they are not offered immediately to God, but to the ministers of divine worship.[14]

---

[12] *ST* I-II, q. 102, a. 3.

[13] See Isidore of Seville, *Etymologies* 6.19.38: "Sacrifice, *sacrificium*, is as if *sacrum factum*, the sacred thing having been done" (*The Etymologies of Isidore of Seville*, trans. Stephen A. Barney [Cambridge: Cambridge University Press, 2006]).

[14] *ST* II-II, q. 85, a. 3, ad 3.

Placing the victim or oblation on the altar, which expresses divine dominion and acceptance of the gift, represents the transfer of dominion of the sacrificial offering to God. If the victim is an animal, the transfer to God's dominion is expressed by the pouring out of blood, which represents the life, and/or by burning in fire. The word "sacrifice" can be applied to the action of the sacred offering or to the victim that is offered. St. Isidore writes: "The sacrifice is the victim and anything burned or placed on the altar. Everything given to God is either dedicated or consecrated."[15]

Interestingly, neither ancient Judaism nor pagan religions offered to God in sacrifice things that do not sustain life, such as gold or jewels. Sacrifices were made from organic things that sustain human life, such as bread, wine, and the flesh of animals. Of all the things offered in sacrifice, the lifeblood of the animal was the most important[16] and considered sacred because it most directly represents the life of the animal, and thus our life. For this reason, God did not allow the people to consume the blood of the animal that was offered, but commanded that it all be poured out in sacrifice.[17]

What is offered in sacrifice represents the life of the one offering. This offering of nourishment and blood thus represents several things at once. It represents our dependence on God as the source of life and our need to offer what is highest in order to give thanks and supplication, to make satisfaction for sin, and to represent the complete gift of self that we are called to make back to God. Finally, the sacrifice of that which sustains life, together with the lifeblood, most perfectly represents the sacrifice of Christ, whose blood was poured out for our redemption in order to win us a share in His divine life.

---

[15] See Isidore of Seville, *Etymologies* 6.19.30.

[16] See Heb 9:22: "Indeed, under the law almost everything is purified with blood, and without the shedding of blood there is no forgiveness of sins."

[17] See Lev 17:11–12: "For the life of the flesh is in the blood; and I have given it for you upon the altar to make atonement for your souls; for it is the blood that makes atonement, by reason of the life. Therefore I have said to the sons of Israel, No person among you shall eat blood, neither shall any stranger who sojourns among you eat blood." See Yerkes, *Sacrifice in Greek and Roman Religions and Early Judaism*, 44: "Blood, to all ancient men, was symbolic, never of death, always of life. Blood and life were synonymous."

The Offering of Sacrifice to God Belongs to Natural Law

In contemporary society, most people have no awareness that the offering of sacrifice to God is a central act of the virtue of religion and thus a good and morally obligatory thing. Even Catholics who attend Mass are generally unaware that they are participating in an infinite offering to God or that that is the principal reason why there is a Sunday Mass obligation. The more society becomes secularized, the more the notion of sacrifice and its obligation becomes foreign and difficult to grasp. Clearly there is a great need for catechesis about the meaning, glory, and obligation of offering sacrifice to God.

Wherever we find human culture, however, we find the existence of religion with sacrifice and priesthood.[18] All religions offer some type of sacrifice to God. Even where a religion has become terribly perverted and distorted, as in religions that offered human sacrifice, treating an innocent human being as a scapegoat,[19] we still find the true belief that it is necessary to offer sacrifice to God on account of sin[20] at the hands of priests who have been consecrated or set aside for this purpose. Nevertheless, the universality of this religious practice shows at least that reason naturally understands the duty of offering sacrifice. For this reason, theologians like St. Thomas Aquinas considered the offering of some kind of sacrifice to God to be a precept of the natural law that a reasonable person can discover in conscience.[21]

Reason, Aquinas argues, especially through the experience of our weakness and indigence, is naturally able to grasp the existence of a higher being (God) by whom we are governed and to whom we turn for aid, wisdom, and mercy. Reason also naturally grasps the general principle that those who are governed must honor, obey, and be subject

---

[18] See Lawrence Feingold, *The Mystery of Israel and the Church*, vol. 2, *Things New and Old* (St. Louis, MO: Miriam Press, 2010), 92–96, from which this section was drawn.

[19] See the analysis of sacrifice by René Girard, a mature and concise expression of which is presented in *The One by Whom Scandal Comes*, trans. Malcolm B. DeBevoise (East Lansing, MI: Michigan State University Press, 2014), 33–48. For a very concise summary, see Robert Daly, *Sacrifice Unveiled: The True Meaning of Christian Sacrifice* (London: Continuum/T. and T. Clark, 2009), 205.

[20] See Heb 5:1.

[21] See *ST* II–II, q. 85, a. 1, sc: "At all times and among all nations there has always been the offering of sacrifices. Now that which is observed by all is seemingly natural. Therefore the offering of sacrifices pertains to the natural law."

to those who govern. Furthermore, man grasps that it is fitting that his subjection be represented in external and sensible signs, for this is proper to human nature.[22] Social life always involves giving visual and external representation to social relations; why should this be less true with regard to our relationship with God, King of creation? Just as we accord special signs to kings and nations, expressing our allegiance to their sovereignty in various ways, as in the crowning of a king, the giving of the keys of a city to the conquering monarch, or pledging allegiance to the flag, so too it is fitting that we represent our dependence on God, interior loyalty and subservience to Him, and our desire for reconciliation and union with Him through exterior symbols such as the offering of sacrifice. This is the purpose of the cult and the sacrifices offered to God. For example, the Israelites were ordered to offer to God the first fruits of their harvests and flocks as a sign of recognition of God's absolute dominion and bounty. Sacrifice, therefore, can be offered only to God, for He alone has absolute dominion over creation and is the first source of all good. For this reason, the martyrs chose to die rather than offer sacrifice to the emperors or false gods.

When sin has been committed, sacrifice to God is due for an additional reason. To manifest repentance from sin, it is fitting to offer God a special sensible sacrifice of penitence and satisfaction.[23]

---

[22] *ST* II–II, q. 85, a. 1:

> Natural reason tells man that he is subject to a higher being, on account of the defects which he perceives in himself, and in which he needs help and direction from someone above him: and whatever this superior being may be, it is known to all under the name of God. Now just as in natural things the lower are naturally subject to the higher, so too it is a dictate of natural reason in accordance with man's natural inclination that he should tender submission and honor, according to his mode, to that which is above man. Now the mode befitting to man is that he should employ sensible signs in order to signify anything, because he derives his knowledge from sensibles. Hence it is a dictate of natural reason that man should use certain sensibles, by offering them to God in sign of the subjection and honor due to Him, like those who make certain offerings to their lord in recognition of his authority. Now this is what we mean by a sacrifice, and consequently the offering of sacrifice is of the natural law.

[23] See Joseph Ratzinger, *The Spirit of the Liturgy*, trans. John Saward (San Francisco: Ignatius Press, 2000), 33: "If 'sacrifice' in its essence is simply returning to love and therefore divinization, worship now has a new aspect: the healing of wounded freedom, atonement, purification, deliverance from estrangement. The essence of worship, of sacrifice—the process of assimilation, of growth in love, and thus the way into freedom—remains unchanged. But now it assumes

Penitence is an act of the will of sorrow for sin, and sensible satisfaction would be a physical offering made to the offended party that represents this interior sorrow and compensates for the offense caused by the sin. The ancient religions of the world, including ancient Israel, typically represented this interior sorrow by the offering of the blood of sacrificial animals.[24] This sensibly represents the debt that has been incurred, the pardon that is implored, and the satisfaction that is offered.

The blood of sacrificial animals, of course, cannot of itself make atonement or reestablish justice between God and man, as stated in Hebrews 10:1–4:

> For since the law has but a shadow of the good things to come instead of the true form of these realities, it can never, by the same sacrifices which are continually offered year after year, make perfect those who draw near.... For it is impossible that the blood of bulls and goats should take away sins.

Such sacrifices, by their very inadequacy, in some way profess man's implicit desire for a better sacrifice that could truly reestablish the order disrupted by sin.

The Priesthood, Mediation, and Sacrifice

Sacrifice implies the person of a priest who offers the sacrifice. Sacrifice and priesthood are inseparably linked. The central idea of the priesthood is that the priest serves as a mediator between God and man. This mediation works in both an ascending and descending direction.[25] The priest's ascending mediation involves his offering to God of gifts

---

the aspect of healing, the loving transformation of broken freedom, of painful expiation."

[24] See Heb 9:22: "Unless blood is shed, there can be no remission of sins." See also Fulton Sheen, *The Priest Is Not His Own* (San Francisco: Ignatius Press, 2004), 12.

[25] See *ST* III, q. 22, a. 1: "The office proper to a priest is to be a mediator between God and the people. This occurs inasmuch as he bestows divine things on the people, wherefore *sacerdos* (priest) means a giver of sacred things (*sacra dans*), ... and again, insofar as he offers up the people's prayers to God, and, in a manner, makes satisfaction to God for their sins." For texts that apply this distinction of ascending and descending mediation to the sacraments, see *ST* III, q. 60, a. 5; q. 63, a. 1.

on behalf of the people and sacrifices for their sins, as well as offering the adoration, thanksgiving, and petitions of the entire people. The central act of this ascending mediation is the priestly offering of sacrifice. The Letter to the Hebrews (5:1) defines the mediation of the priest in this way: "For every high priest chosen from among men is appointed to act on behalf of men in relation to God, to offer gifts and sacrifices for sins." The priesthood is thus essentially linked with sacrifice.

This ascending mediation seeks to propitiate God and thereby to receive gifts from Him that can be distributed to the people. Thus there is also a descending mediation, by which gifts of grace and knowledge are transmitted from God to man through the mediation of the priest. The Eucharist most perfectly realizes these two forms of mediation.[26] The priest, acting in the person of Christ, offers up the infinite sacrifice of Calvary to God the Father. At the same time, Holy Communion is the greatest sacramental means by which grace is brought down to the faithful. The descending mediation—the distribution of spiritual gifts—presupposes the ascending mediation by which the perfect sacrifice is offered to God.

Since sacrifice and priesthood belong not only to the Old and New Covenants but also to the natural religions of the world, we can thus distinguish three fundamental forms of priesthood by which specially designated persons offer sacrifice and serve as mediators in the things of God: (a) under natural law in the natural religions of the world; (b) in the Old Testament; and (c) the priesthood of Christ as exercised by Christ Himself and continued in the Catholic Church.

THE SACRIFICE OF CALVARY

In virtue of the hypostatic union, by which Christ is at once true man and true God, the Messiah was able to offer a sacrifice that was not only an external and sensible *figure* of the homage and propitiation due to God (like all the sacrificial offerings of animals offered under the Law) but rather true homage and propitiation of infinite value in both its *internal* and its *external* dimensions. Christ's suffering and death on Calvary constitutes the one true sacrifice symbolized by all

---

[26] See Hubert Van Zeller, *The Mass in Other Words: A Presentation for Beginners* (Springfield, IL: Templegate, 1965), 26–27.

the bloody animal sacrifices. It alone offers proper satisfaction for sin by giving to God something more pleasing than all sin is displeasing. St. Thomas writes:

> Now it is the proper effect of sacrifice to appease God; just as man likewise overlooks an offence committed against him on account of some pleasing act of homage shown him. . . . And in like fashion Christ's voluntary suffering was such a good act that, because of its being found in human nature, God was appeased for every offence of the human race with regard to those who are made one with the crucified Christ.[27]

It should be noticed that St. Thomas teaches that Christ's sacrifice offers satisfaction not by virtue of a punishment, destruction, or deprivation received in our place, but rather because of its supreme goodness in charity, by reason of which it serves to compensate for all sin's violation thereof. The infinite value of the sacrifice of Calvary comes from the charity by which it is offered, from the divine dignity of the victim offered, from the totality of the holocaust of the victim,[28] from the dignity of the priest offering it, from the unity of the priest and victim, and finally, from the unity of the mediator with God, to whom it is offered, and with mankind, *for* whom it is offered. The sacrifice of Calvary is maximum or infinite in each of these respects.

The Son of God has infinite dignity both as victim being offered and as priest offering. He offers Himself with unlimited charity, both for the glory of His Father and for the love of all men, for whom He offers Himself. Every man can say with St. Paul that the Son of God "loved me and gave himself for me" (Gal 2:20). The holo-

---

[27] See *ST* III, q. 49, a. 4, esp. ad 2–3.

[28] See *ST* III, q. 48, a. 2:

> He properly atones for an offence who offers something which the offended one loves equally, or even more than he detested the offence. But by suffering out of love and obedience, Christ gave more to God than was required to compensate for the offence of the whole human race. First of all, because of the exceeding charity from which He suffered; secondly, on account of the dignity of His life which He laid down in atonement, for it was the life of One Who was God and man; thirdly, on account of the extent of the Passion, and the greatness of the grief endured.

caust is maximum and superabundant[29] because He offers Himself
to the worst and most humiliating kind of death with total freedom,
holding nothing back. As John says in John 13:1, which introduces
the Last Supper and the Passion: "having loved his own who were in
the world, he loved them to the end." Furthermore, the unity is total
both between priest and victim, and between the priest, who is God
the Son, and God the Father to whom it is offered. The unity is also
maximum between the priest and those for whom He offers Himself.
In His Incarnation He has become the new Adam—the new head
of mankind, for whom He offers Himself. In the sacrifice of Calvary,
Christ offered Himself in union with all human suffering, redeeming it and giving to it a redemptive sacrificial value when offered in
communion with His. As we read in Hebrews 4:15, "For we have not
a high priest who is unable to sympathize with our weaknesses, but
one who in every respect has been tempted as we are, yet without sin."

St. Augustine highlights the unity of the sacrifice:

> Now there are four things to be considered in every sacrifice:
> whom it is offered to, whom it is offered by, what it is that is
> offered, and whom it is offered for. And this one true medi-
> ator, in reconciling us to God by his sacrifice of peace, would
> remain one with him to whom he offered it, and make one
> in himself those for whom he offered it, and be himself who
> offered it one and the same as what he offered.[30]

The sacrifice of Calvary therefore has an infinite value of reparation, for it gives infinitely more glory to God than all human sin put
together gives offense. This sacrifice of Calvary was the true sacrifice
prefigured in all the other sacrifices in the history of the world, the
one sacrifice that is efficacious in itself. Therefore, it is reasonable to
think that after Calvary no more exterior sacrifices would be necessary, for the sacrifice of Calvary fulfilled all the purposes of sacrifice,
including propitiation for sin. And this is true. No more animal sacrifices are necessary, for they simply prefigured the sacrifice of Calvary.

---

[29] The superabundance can be seen from the fact that one drop of blood of God
Incarnate would have been sufficient to redeem us, as the Church sings in the
hymn *Adoro Te Devote*: "Cuius una stilla salvum facere / Totum mundum quit
ab omni scelere."

[30] Augustine, *The Trinity* 4.3.19, trans. Edmund Hill (Hyde Park, NY: New City
Press, 1991), 166–67.

For this reason, the sacrifices of the Mosaic Law lost their principal reason for being, which was to prefigure the sacrifice of Calvary and the Mass. This was symbolically manifested by the rending of the veil of the Temple on Good Friday as our Lord expired on the Cross. It is not unreasonable to think that it was also symbolized in the destruction of the Temple some forty years later and the consequent cessation of the Jewish sacrificial rites.

THE SACRIFICE OF THE CHURCH

It is fitting, however, that the New Covenant not be without a sacrifice. But how can this be if the sacrifice of Calvary puts an end to sacrifice? The divine answer is that the New Covenant should have a sacrifice that is the same as Calvary, one by which the Church offers herself in offering her Lord.

Christ did not want His Church to be merely the *beneficiary* of His sacrifice, but also a *co-offerer*. He wanted her to be able to enter into the glorification of His Father accomplished by His sacrifice, for, as we have seen, the offering of sacrifice to God is both a duty and an inner need of man, a law written on our hearts. It was not enough for Christ to sacrifice Himself for His Bride. He wanted his Bride to be able to offer to the Father, together with Him, the perfect sacrifice. And since His Bride was to remain on earth until His Second Coming, He wanted her to be able to offer the perfect sacrifice in every place until His return.[31]

So, on the night before He died, Jesus wished to leave a perfect sacrifice to His Church. But what sacrifice could He give to His Church to offer to God, since He Himself in person was about to offer

---

[31] See Scheeben, *The Mysteries of Christianity*, 494:

> As head of the human race, . . . He also represents all the members of this vast body before God. And as He offers Himself in His own person to God as an infinitely perfect and agreeable sacrifice, so He associates His entire mystical body with Himself and in Himself in this consecration, and His mystical body in turn is to offer the God-man, and itself in Him, to God as one great sacrifice. Thus the sacrifice offered by the individual men in whom the God-man is harbored likewise becomes infinitely precious and agreeable in God's sight. As Christ the head continues His divine life in His members, so He is also to continue His divine sacrifice in them.

everything to the Father on the Cross? He could not give His Church a figure or prophecy of His own sacrifice, as God did to ancient Israel, for the figures were fulfilled on Calvary. Nor could He give the Church, His Bride, merely a symbol or remembrance of His great sacrifice, for that would be too little.

The solution was worthy of both the divine wisdom and the divine omnipotence. Christ willed to leave to his Church the same sacrifice that He offered His Father on Good Friday. By instituting the miracle of transubstantiation, Christ made Himself present in the Eucharist as the divine Victim, the *same* Victim who was offered in a bloody manner on Calvary. Furthermore, by instituting the priesthood at the same moment, He arranged to be continually present as High Priest offering His own Body and Blood in the sacrifice of the Mass through the ministerial priests ordained to act *in persona Christi* throughout the ages until His second coming. Nothing less than the Sacred Heart of Jesus Himself, burning with love for man, is present, mystically immolated together with His entire humanity and offered in this holy and immaculate sacrifice.

He is offered, however, not in the cruel and bloody manner of Calvary, in which His Blood was physically separated from His Body, but in an unbloody and sacramental fashion worthy of the Heart of God, in which His Blood is *sacramentally* separated from His Body, for, having risen from the dead, His Body and Blood can be physically separated no more. A second difference is that, on Calvary, Christ alone offered Himself. In the Mass, He allows Himself to be offered by His whole Mystical Body through His ordained ministers.

St. John Paul II explains: "This sacrifice is so decisive for the salvation of the human race that Jesus Christ offered it and returned to the Father only *after he had left us a means of sharing in it* as if we had been present there. Each member of the faithful can thus take part in it and inexhaustibly gain its fruits."[32] In this way, the whole Church can participate in the ascending movement of glorification by which Christ offers Himself and the whole of creation and history, now redeemed, to His Father:

> Because even when it is celebrated on the humble altar of a country church, the Eucharist is always in some way celebrated *on the altar of the world*. It unites heaven and earth. It

---

[32] John Paul II, *EE*, §11 (italics original).

embraces and permeates all creation. The Son of God became man in order to restore all creation, in one supreme act of praise, to the One who made it from nothing. He, the Eternal High Priest who by the blood of his Cross entered the eternal sanctuary, thus gives back to the Creator and Father all creation redeemed. He does so through the priestly ministry of the Church, to the glory of the Most Holy Trinity. Truly this is the *mysterium fidei* which is accomplished in the Eucharist: the world which came forth from the hands of God the Creator now returns to him redeemed by Christ.[33]

Trinitarian Dimension of the Sacrifice of Calvary and the Mass

The Sacrifice of Calvary is the supreme sacrifice ultimately because of its Trinitarian nature.[34] Mankind is reconciled with the Father through the self-donation of the Son[35] and in the Spirit, who is given to us through the Sacrifice of the Son. Christ's sacrifice manifests the structure of the Trinitarian life. The Father sends the Son, who gives Himself back totally to the Father, imparting the Spirit of reconciliation, who is the bond of love between the Father and Son. Christ's sacrifice is thus supremely relational and interpersonal and is designed to include mankind by incorporation into His ecclesial Body. Thus we are enabled to enter into the great sacrifice in the Person of the Son.

The Trinitarian dimension of the sacrifice of Calvary is mirrored in the sacrifice of the Church. The Son is offered to the Father through the Holy Spirit who descends on the bread and wine to make them His Body and Blood, and who also descends on the faithful so that they can offer themselves to the Father with the Son and in His likeness.[36]

---

[33] Ibid., §8 (italics original).

[34] For this Trinitarian theme, see Daly, *Sacrifice Unveiled*, 6–14; Daly, "Sacrifice Unveiled or Sacrifice Revisited: Trinitarian and Liturgical Perspectives," *Theological Studies* 64, no. 1 (2003): 24–42; Kilmartin, *The Eucharist in the West*, 381–83.

[35] For sacrifice as self-donation, see Daly, *Sacrifice Unveiled*, 11.

[36] See Oliver Treanor, "Apostolicity and the Eucharist," *Communio* 39, no. 4 (2012): 569–86, at 583:

Thus the Eucharist is a two-directional dynamism: a centrifugal force that jettisons and distributes all the self-giving that is personhood in

This Trinitarian dimension is manifested in the prayers of the Eucharistic liturgy, which are directed predominantly to the Father, through Christ made incarnate by the power of the Holy Spirit, and in the unity and sanctification given by the Holy Spirit.[37] A good example of this can be seen in Eucharistic Prayer IV:

> And you so loved the world, *Father* most holy, that in the fullness of time you sent your Only Begotten *Son* to be our Savior. Made incarnate by the *Holy Spirit* and born of the Virgin Mary He shared our human nature. . . . And that we might live no longer for ourselves but for him who died and rose again for us, he sent the *Holy Spirit* from you, *Father*, as the first fruits for those who believe, so that, bringing to perfection his work in the world, he might sanctify creation to the full. Therefore, O Lord, we pray: may this same *Holy Spirit* graciously sanctify these offerings, that they may become the Body and Blood of our Lord Jesus Christ.[38]

The Trinitarian structure of the Eucharist comes into focus most clearly in the epiclesis prayer, which has a twofold purpose. The priest implores the Father to send the Holy Spirit, first to transform the bread and wine to make them into the Body and Blood of the Son, and secondly to transform the lives of the faithful by sanctifying them

---

God, and a centripetal force that draws all human personhood into the communion of the Trinity. A spiraling-out and a spiraling-in, a reaching-towards and a bringing-back-again of all that was lost or unloved or dead. The language of the Eucharist is the language of the trinitarian relations *ad intra*: the breathing out and the breathing in of the Father and the Son in the Holy Spirit, the processional distinction, the inseparable union. It is the language too of the divine missions: the sending forth of the Son and the Spirit and their return home to the Father, their witness complete, the redemption accomplished. It is, finally, the language of apostolicity: the appointment and commissioning of disciples, sent to gather the new Israel into the one body of Christ, Temple of the Holy Spirit.

[37] See, for example, Eucharistic Prayer II, Preface (*RM*, 645), which is also the Common Preface VI (*RM*, 620): "It is truly right and just, our duty and our salvation, always and everywhere to give you thanks, Father most holy, through your beloved Son, Jesus Christ, your Word through whom you made all things, whom you sent as our Savior and Redeemer, incarnate by the Holy Spirit and born of the Virgin."

[38] Eucharistic Prayer IV (*RM*, 657–58; my italics).

more perfectly into the unity of the Body of Christ, so making of them an offering to the Father in the Son. Eucharistic Prayer III makes this explicit: "May he [the Holy Spirit] make of us an eternal offering to you, so that we may obtain an inheritance with your elect."[39]

In the Latin rite, these two purposes of the epiclesis are separated, such that the first occurs before the institution narrative while the second follows it, after the anamnesis. In most other Eucharistic Prayers, such as in the Byzantine rite, these two petitions for the action of the Holy Spirit are put together to emphasize the parallelism of the Spirit's action on the gifts on the altar and in the hearts of the faithful.[40]

THEOLOGICAL REFLECTION ON THE SACRIFICE OF THE MASS

The Fathers and Medieval Theologians on the Sacrifice of the Mass

As we have seen, the Fathers of the Church and the early liturgical texts see the Eucharist as the realization of the prophecy of Malachi 1:11, the pure oblation offered among the Gentiles.[41] The sacrificial nature of the Eucharist is a common patrimony of the Patristic age[42] and is affirmed numerous times in all Eucharistic Prayers, especially in the anamnesis, in which, remembering His Paschal mystery, the "bread of eternal life and the chalice of everlasting salvation"[43] are offered to the Father. The Fathers and the early Eucharistic Prayers affirm the oneness of the Mass with the sacrifice of Calvary, of which it is the sacramental or mystical image,[44] and they affirm that it is a bloodless

---

[39] Eucharistic Prayer III (*RM*, 653).

[40] See Cesare Giraudo, *Eucaristia per la chiesa*, 436–42.

[41] See *Didache* 14; Justin Martyr, *Dialogue with Trypho* 41.

[42] *Didache* 14, in a brief paragraph, refers to the Mass as a sacrifice four times. See Robert Louis Wilken, *The First Thousand Years: A Global History of Christianity* (New Haven, CT: Yale University Press, 2012), 34–35.

[43] Roman Canon, in *RM*, 641.

[44] See Cyprian, Letter 63.9: "The Blood of Christ is not offered if wine is lacking in the Chalice and that the Sacrifice of the Lord is not celebrated with lawful sanctification unless the Oblation and our Sacrifice correspond to the Passion" (Donna, *Letters*, 208).

sacrifice[45] and a "spiritual worship," according to Romans 12:1,[46] but they do not directly pose the questions as to *how* it is one with Calvary, how exactly it realizes the definition of sacrifice, and how Christ is immolated in the Mass.

An exceptional text is the well-known commentary of St. John Chrysostom on Hebrews 9:24–26, in which he says:

> For we always offer the same Lamb, not one now and another tomorrow, but always the same one, so that the sacrifice is one. . . . As then while offered in many places, He is one body and not many bodies; so also [He is] one sacrifice. He is our High Priest, who offered the sacrifice that cleanses us. We now offer that victim which was then offered, which cannot be exhausted.[47]

The sacrifice of Calvary and the Mass are one because the same Victim is offered and the same High Priest offers.

Since the sacrificial aspect of the Mass had not been challenged in any major way until well after their time, the scholastic theologians of the Middle Ages also do not dedicate much space to explaining and defending this dogma.[48] In general, they teach that the Mass, making present the real Body and Blood of Christ, is a true sacrifice identified with that of Calvary, of which it is a commemoration or sacramental image in which the same Victim is offered, although now glorious and incapable of death again.

Guitmund of Aversa writes:

---

[45] The Eucharistic Prayer attributed to Sarapion, Egyptian bishop from the mid-fourth century, speaks of the eucharist as a "bloodless offering": "Fill also this sacrifice with your power and your partaking: for to you we offered this living sacrifice, this bloodless offering" (*PEER*, 77).

[46] See the Liturgy of St. John Chrysostom: "We offer you also this reasonable and bloodless service" (*PEER*, 133).

[47] John Chrysostom, *In Epistolam ad Hebraeos Homiliae* 17 (*NPNF*1, 14:447, 449; I have slightly modified the translation), quoted in John Paul II, *EE*, §12.

[48] See Kilmartin, *The Eucharist in the West*, xxiv: "The question of eucharistic realism was officially settled for the Latin Church in the period of early scholasticism and subsequently confirmed by the Council of Trent. In contrast, the theology of eucharistic sacrifice remained in an embryonic state up through the thirteenth century."

For as often as the celebration of the body and blood of the Lord occurs, truly we do not kill Christ again, but instead we commemorate his death in and through that celebration. . . . The celebration of the body and blood of the Lord is a sign of the Passion of Christ. . . . For, when we say in the celebration of the body of the Lord, "Christ is immolated," no one should take this carnally according to the letter. For Christ has died once, "now he does not die, death no longer has power over him" (Rom 6:9). . . . For the celebration is not the Lord's Passion itself, but rather a commemoration of the Lord's Passion, now symbolically carried out.[49]

Alger of Liège, in his great treatise on the Eucharist, writes:

It must be plain to us that if our daily oblation were other than that once offered in Christ, it would not be true, but would be superfluous. For since that oblation once offered in Christ is really true, because truly it is eternal life, and since of itself alone it is sufficient to confer that life on us, if there were another offering, what other life could it promise or confer? For another offering would need to confer another salvation. . . . Hence as another salvation is an impossibility, that oblation of Christ once made and our daily oblation must be the same: so that this same offering is not superfluous to itself, but is ever sufficient and ever necessary. . . . Our sacrifice is the image of His: the very same, always the very same. . . . There in the reality of the Passion in which he was killed for us, here in the figure and imitation of that Passion, in which Christ does not suffer again really, but the memorial of His actual true Passion is daily repeated for us. . . . Although the offering of Christ in the past was real, and our daily offering on the altar is figurative, nevertheless here, as well as there, we have absolutely the same grace of our salvation.[50]

---

[49] Guitmund of Aversa, *On the Truth of the Body and Blood of Christ in the Eucharist* 2.25 (Vaillancourt, FCMC 10:146–47).

[50] Alger of Liège, *De Sacramentis Corporis et Sanguinis Dominici* 1.16 (PL, 180:786–787), trans. de la Taille, *The Mystery of Faith*, vol. 2, *The Sacrifice of the Church* (New York: Sheed & Ward, 1950), 209–10.

Alger thus holds, first, that the Mass is not a different sacrifice from Calvary, which would be superfluous, but the "very same." Secondly, the Mass is the same sacrifice because it is the (sacramental) *image* of the sacrifice of Calvary. Thus Christ does not suffer again in the Mass, but His Passion is sacramentally represented. Thirdly, even though Christ is not slain again, the grace of eternal life won on Calvary is made present through the Mass, for "we have absolutely the same grace of our salvation."

In the fourth book of his extremely influential *Sentences*, Peter Lombard poses the question of "whether Christ is immolated every day" in every Mass, or whether "he was immolated only once." He answers by affirming both sides of the dilemma while distinguishing two modes of offering the same thing:

> To this, it may briefly be said that what is offered and consecrated by the priest is called sacrifice and oblation, because it is a remembrance and representation of the true sacrifice and the holy immolation made on the altar of the cross. And indeed Christ died only once, namely on the cross, and there he was immolated in himself; but he is daily immolated in the sacrament, because in the sacrament is made a remembrance of what was done once. . . . It is gathered that what is done at the altar is and is called a sacrifice; and that Christ was offered once, and is offered every day; but in one way then, in another now.[51]

In other words, the Mass is a sacrifice because it is a sacramental representation of the sacrifice of Calvary. Thus it is said to be the same sacrifice, even though the mode of offering differs, for in the Mass it is offered in a sacramental way. He also goes on to show that it is not a *mere* representation, but one capable of granting the same fruits as that of Calvary: the grace of the forgiveness of sins. For since we sin daily, it is fitting, as the Fathers observed, that Christ's sacrifice be offered daily.[52] Lombard's view of the Eucharistic sacrifice became

---

[51] Peter Lombard, *Sentences* IV, dist. 12, ch. 5, nos. 1, 4 (pp. 64–65).

[52] Lombard quotes Ambrose, *De Sacramentis* 4.6.28; John Chrysostom, *In Epistolam ad Hebraeos Homiliae* 17.3; and Paschasius, *De Corpore et Sanguine Domini* 9.

the standard account of later medieval theologians, up to the time of the Reformation.[53]

St. Thomas on the Sacrifice of the Mass

The Mass Is the "Representative Image" of the Passion

Like his contemporaries, St. Thomas does not dedicate much space to explaining and defending the sacrificial nature of the Mass and its relation to Calvary because, in his time, it was not yet a disputed question. He states that the Mass is a sacrifice in itself because in it a victim (*hostia*) is offered up to God in an ascending movement of glorification and propitiation.[54] But how is it the same sacrifice as Calvary? St. Thomas's answer has two parts: it is the same sacrifice because (a) it is Calvary's sacramental and living representation (b) that is efficacious in making present Calvary's fruits of grace. Let us begin by looking at the first half of this answer: sacramental representation of Calvary.

In discussing the names of the Eucharist, St. Thomas says that it is called the sacrifice of the Mass because it represents that of Calvary: "This sacrament has a threefold significance: one with regard to the past, inasmuch as it is commemorative of Our Lord's Passion, which was a true sacrifice, as stated above (q. 48, a. 3), and in this respect it is called a *Sacrifice*."[55] In the reply to the third objection in this article, he also specifies that it not only represents the Passion but also contains its Victim: "This sacrament is called a *Sacrifice* inasmuch as it represents the Passion of Christ; but it is termed a *Host* [*hostia*] inasmuch as it contains Christ, Who is a host ... of sweetness [Eph 5:2]."[56] The Mass, therefore, is not a *mere* representation or commemoration of Calvary, but uniquely efficacious in that it contains the same Victim[57]

---

[53] See Francis Clark, *Eucharistic Sacrifice and the Reformation* (Westminster, MD: Newman Press, 1960), 78–80.

[54] *ST* III, q. 79, a. 5: "This sacrament is both a sacrifice and a sacrament; it has the nature of a sacrifice inasmuch as it is offered up; and it has the nature of a sacrament inasmuch as it is received. And therefore it has the effect of a sacrament in the recipient, and the effect of a sacrifice in the offerer, or in them for whom it is offered."

[55] *ST* III, q. 73, a. 4.

[56] *ST* III, q. 73, a. 4, ad 3.

[57] See also *ST* III, q. 22, a. 3, ad 2: "The Sacrifice which is offered every day in the Church is not distinct from that which Christ Himself offered, but is a

and, as Thomas makes clear in other articles, makes Calvary's effects of grace and union present.

St. Thomas also touches on the sacramental representation of the Passion in asking why Christ instituted the sacrament under two species. In his commentary on 1 Corinthians 11, he says: "This sacrament is presented under two species . . . on account of its signification. For it is the memorial of the Lord's passion, through which the blood of Christ was separated from his body; that is why in this sacrament the blood is offered separately from the body."[58] In the *Summa theologiae*, he makes the same point: "Although the whole Christ is under each species, yet it is so not without purpose. For in the first place this serves to *represent Christ's Passion, in which the blood was separated from the body*; hence in the form for the consecration of the blood mention is made of its shedding."[59]

He deals with the sacrificial aspect more directly in *ST* III, question 83, article 1, in which he asks whether Christ is sacrificed in this sacrament. He argues that the Mass is said to be a sacrifice first (following Lombard) because it is the "representative image" of the Sacrifice of Calvary[60] and second because it efficaciously imparts the fruits of the Passion that it represents.[61] In other words, it is a sacra-

---

commemoration thereof. Wherefore Augustine says (*De Civ. Dei* 10): 'Christ Himself both is the priest who offers it and the victim: the sacred token of which He wished to be the daily Sacrifice of the Church.'"

[58] Commentary on 1 Corinthians 11, lec. 5, Marietti no. 653, in Larcher, trans., *Commentary on the Letters of Saint Paul to the Corinthians*, 244. See also lec. 6, Marietti no. 681 (p. 254).

[59] See also *ST* III q. 78, a. 3, ad 2: "As was said above (ad 1; q. 76, a. 2 ad 1), the *blood consecrated apart expressly represents Christ's Passion*, and therefore mention is made of the fruits of the Passion in the consecration of the blood rather than in that of the body." See also *In* IV *Sent.*, d. 11, q. 2, a. 1, q. 1.

[60] For an interpretation of this article and the meaning of "representative image" here, see Thierry-Dominique Humbrecht, "L'eucharistie, 'représentation' du sacrifice du Christ, selon saint Thomas," *Revue Thomiste* 98 (1998): 355–86; Štěpán Martin Filip, "*Imago Repræsentativa Passionis Christi*: St. Thomas Aquinas on the Essence of the Sacrifice of the Mass," trans. Roger Nutt, *Nova et Vetera* (English) 7 (2009): 405–38.

[61] These two reasons for the identification of the sacrifice of the Mass and Calvary are summarized in the following article (*ST* III, q. 83, a. 2): "In the celebration of this mystery, we must take into consideration the representation of Our Lord's Passion, and the participation of its fruits." See also the reply to the first objection in this article (*ST* III, q. 83, a. 2, ad 1), in which he explains why the Eucharist is celebrated daily: "Christ's Passion is recalled in this sacrament, inasmuch as its effect flows out to the faithful; but at Passion-tide Christ's

mental sacrifice because it is a sacred sign of Christ's sacrifice that realizes and makes present the sacred mystery that it signifies.

> The celebration of this sacrament is said to be the immolation of Christ for two reasons. First, because, as St. Augustine says to Simplician: "Images are customarily called by the names of the things of which they are images, as when we see a painting or mural we say, 'that is Cicero, that is Sallust.'"[62] The celebration of this sacrament, as was said above [q. 79, a. 1], is a certain representative image of the Passion of Christ, which is His true immolation, and therefore the celebration of this sacrament is said to be the immolation of Christ. For this reason St. Ambrose, commenting on Hebrews 10, says: "In Christ the sacrificial victim was offered once, having the power to effect eternal salvation. What therefore do we do? Do we not offer each day in memory of his death?"
>
> Secondly it is called a sacrifice with regard to the effect of His Passion, because by this sacrament we are made participants of the fruit of the Lord's Passion. Hence in one of the Sunday *Secrets* (Ninth Sunday after Pentecost) we say: "Whenever the memorial of this sacrifice is celebrated, the work of our redemption is accomplished." With regard therefore to the first reason, it can be said that Christ is immolated even in the figures of the Old Testament. . . . But according to the second reason it is proper to this sacrament alone that Christ is immolated in its celebration.[63]

As a representation of the sacrifice of Calvary, the Mass is similar to the rites of the Old Covenant that prefigured Calvary. Those rites were true sacrifices in that a victim was offered to God to represent the interior oblation of the heart, and they also prefigured the great sacrifice of Calvary. As representations of Calvary, the sacrificial rites

---

Passion is recalled inasmuch as it was wrought in Him Who is our Head. This took place but once; whereas the faithful receive daily the fruits of His Passion: consequently, the former is commemorated but once in the year, whereas the latter takes place every day, both that we may partake of its fruit and in order that we may have a perpetual memorial."

[62] Augustine, *Miscellany of Questions in Response to Simplician* 2.3.2, in *Responses to Miscellaneous Questions* (Hyde Park, NY: New City Press, 2008), 226.

[63] *ST* III, q. 83, a. 1 (my translation).

of the Old Covenant can be said to be one with it in a certain respect. It is striking how lofty a view St. Thomas has of the sacrifices and sacraments of the Old Covenant.[64]

The Mass, however, is an infinitely more perfect representation of the sacrifice of Calvary than were the Old Testament rites. Although St. Thomas does not directly state this in this article (*ST* III, q. 83, a. 1), it is clearly the case, since the Mass contains the same Victim[65] and is offered by the same High Priest who offered the sacrifice of Calvary.[66] The Mass represents the sacrifice of Calvary by making present the Victim of Calvary in His true Body and Blood that were separated at His death. Their physical separation is represented in the Mass by the separate consecration of the Body and the Blood. The typological sacrifices of the Old Covenant represented Calvary through the bloody physical death of other victims brought about by the separation of their blood from their body. The Mass has the same Victim as Calvary, but His death is present only in sacramental representation and in its effects, and not in its bloody historical reality.

The bloody immolation of Calvary thus stands between two series of sacrificial rites that point to it and derive their dignity from it. It was prefigured beforehand by all the sacrifices of the Old Covenant and, less perfectly, by the sacrifices of the natural religions of the world. After Good Friday it is made sacramentally present through the Eucharist's unbloody sacramental image of the bloody immolation of Calvary.[67] These two series do not stand on the same plane, however, because they are separated by the central event of salvation history, the historical coming of the Word Incarnate and the realization of His Paschal mystery. The sacrifices of the Old Covenant served to make

---

[64] See also *ST* III, q. 60, a. 2, ad 2: "The sacrifice of the Paschal Lamb signified Christ's Sacrifice whereby we are made holy: and suchlike are properly styled sacraments of the Old Law."

[65] See *ST* III, q. 73, a. 4, ad 3.

[66] See *ST* III, q. 83, a. 1, ad 3: "The priest also bears Christ's image, in Whose person and by Whose power he pronounces the words of consecration, as is evident from what was said above (q. 82, aa. 1, 3). And so, in a measure, the priest and victim are one and the same." See also *ST* III, q. 78, aa. 1, 4; q. 64, a. 1.

[67] See David Fagerberg, *Consecrating the World: On Mundane Liturgical Theology* (Kettering, OH: Angelico Press, 2016), 33–34: "The liturgy celebrates the Paschal mystery, and that mystery stands at the center of a timeline that stretches between the protological alpha and the eschatological omega. Everything leads up to it, and everything flows out of it. By its anamnetic and epicletic link to the Paschal mystery, liturgy brings heavenly activity to earth."

contact with the future event of Calvary through foreshadowing it in faith and hope. The sacrifice of the Mass enables the faithful of the New Covenant to make spiritual contact with the mystery as already actualized and operative in the present.

We can compare the Mass to the prefigurative rites of the Old Testament as, respectively, we can compare "image/icon" to "shadow," according to Hebrews 10:1: "For since the law has but a *shadow* of the good things to come instead of the *true image*[68] [*imago*; εἰκών] of these realities, it can never, by the same sacrifices which are continually offered year after year, make perfect those who draw near." The "image/icon" refers to the cult of the New Covenant, whereas that of the Old Covenant is spoken of as "shadow," for it foreshadows Christ without yet making Him present.

When St. Thomas uses the term *imago repraesentativa* in *ST* III, question 83, article 1, we should understand it according to the terminology of Hebrews 10:1. The sacrifice of the Mass is not a mere "shadow" of the sacrifice of Calvary, as were the sacrifices of paschal lambs, but rather its sacramental *image* or icon. St. Thomas explains the difference between shadow and image in *ST* I-II, question 101, article 2:

> For under the Old Law, neither was the Divine Truth manifest in Itself, nor was the way leading to that manifestation as yet opened out, as the Apostle declares (Heb 9:8). Hence the external worship of the Old Law needed to be figurative not only of the future truth to be manifested in our heavenly country, but also of Christ, Who is the way leading to that heavenly manifestation. But under the New Law this way is already revealed: and therefore it needs no longer to be foreshadowed as something future, but to be brought to our minds as something past or present: and the truth of the glory to come, which is not yet revealed, alone needs to be foreshadowed. This is what the Apostle says (Heb. 10:1): "The Law has a shadow of the good things to come, not the very image of the things." For a shadow is less than an image; so that the image belongs to the New Law, but the shadow to the Old.

---

[68] The RSV translates εἰκών as "true form."

For St. Thomas, the notion of "image" implies not a mere generic likeness, but a *specific* likeness. In explaining in what sense man is created "in the image of God," he writes:

> Not every likeness, not even what is copied from something else, is sufficient to make an image; for if the likeness be only generic, or existing by virtue of some common accident, this does not suffice for one thing to be the image of another. . . . But the nature of an image requires likeness in species; thus the image of the king exists in his son: or, at least, in some specific accident.[69]

Thus, when St. Thomas refers to the Mass as the "representative image" of Calvary, this should be taken in a strong sense, signifying a specific and not a merely generic likeness. Whereas the Old Testament sacrifices could be shadows (generic likenesses) of the sacrifice of Calvary, it is the privilege of the sacrifice of the New Covenant to be the proper "representative image" of the sacrifice of Calvary. Its specific likeness comes from the fact that it contains the same crucified Victim (now glorified) and is offered by the same High Priest for the same ends.

The Sacrifice of the Mass Applies the Effects of the Passion

St. Thomas teaches that, in addition to being its sacramental image, the Mass is one with the sacrifice of Calvary because it applies and makes present its proper effects such that the faithful "are made participants of the fruit of the Lord's Passion."[70] This point is not fully developed in the treatise on the Eucharist in the *Summa theologiae*, but it had been explained earlier in the treatise on Christ's priesthood and Passion.

Although the bloody sacrifice of Calvary cannot be repeated, the fruits of it can be applied throughout the time of the Church because its infinite value has an eternal dimension. Even though the sacrifice of Calvary took place in time, its value is not limited and contained in

---

[69] *ST* I, q. 93, a. 2. See Roger Nutt, *General Principles of Sacramental Theology*, 61–62.

[70] *ST* III, q. 83, a. 1.

the past but transcends all times, just as Christ's priesthood is eternal, transcending the limits of His earthly life.[71] The sacrifice of the Mass is the preeminent ordinary means of actualizing and applying the fruits of the sacrifice of Calvary, making that bloody sacrifice that was offered nearly 2,000 years ago perpetually active and fruitful in the world today and in every time and place in which the Mass is celebrated.

The reason that the sacrifice of Calvary has a certain eternal power and cannot be limited to that one moment of history is that it is the supreme earthly act of a divine Person. St. Thomas sees Christ's humanity and all of His human acts as instruments of His divinity in working our salvation.[72] God ordinarily makes use of created agents as instruments of His providence. Christ's humanity and human acts, however, have a higher dignity and power than any other instruments of our salvation because of the hypostatic union. Hence, they can be called *conjoined* rather than *external* instruments.[73] As our brain, hands, and lips are instruments that are more powerful than external instruments because they are substantially joined to us, so Christ's

---

[71] See *ST* III, q. 22, a. 5, ad 2 and 3:

> Although Christ's passion and death are not to be repeated, yet the virtue of that Victim endures forever; for, as it is written (Heb. 10:14), "by one oblation He hath perfected forever them that are sanctified." . . . As to the unity of this sacrifice, it was foreshadowed in the Law in that, once a year, the high-priest of the Law entered into the Holies, with a solemn oblation of blood, as set down in Lev 16:11. But the figure fell short of the reality in this, that the victims (in the figure) had not an everlasting virtue, for which reason these sacrifices were renewed every year.

[72] See *ST* III, q. 19, a. 1: "In Christ the human nature has its proper form and power whereby it acts; and so has the Divine. Hence the human nature has its proper operation distinct from the Divine, and conversely. Nevertheless, the Divine Nature makes use of the operation of the human nature, as of the operation of its instrument; and in the same way the human nature shares in the operation of the Divine Nature, as an instrument shares in the operation of the principal agent."

[73] See *ST* III, q. 62, a. 5: "A sacrament works to cause grace in the manner of an instrument, of which there are two kinds. One kind is separate, as in the case of a stick; the other is united, as a hand. Now the separate instrument is moved by means of the united instrument, as a stick by the hand. The principal efficient cause of grace is God Himself, in comparison with whom Christ's humanity is a united instrument, whereas the sacrament is a separate instrument. It is necessary, therefore, that the saving power in the sacraments be derived from Christ's divinity through His humanity" (my translation).

human acts are divine instruments of salvation that are immeasurably more powerful than any others because they are acts of a divine Person. Because of this union with divinity these acts transcend the limited time in which they were accomplished and have an eternal power proportionate to the divine Person whose works they are. Christ's human acts can thus be seen as instrumental efficient causes of the divine act of our salvation that are capable of "touching" us today even though they were completed in the past. They are, as St. Thomas says, conjoined instruments of the Godhead.

If this is true of all of Christ's human actions, it is especially true of His Passion, which is also the meritorious[74] and exemplar cause of our salvation. Thus the Passion, even though it belongs to past time in historical reality, has an infinite instrumental power to work human salvation.[75] St. Thomas says it operates "by way of efficiency, inasmuch as Christ's flesh, wherein He endured the Passion, is the instrument of the Godhead, so that His sufferings and actions operate with Divine power for expelling sin."[76] The power of the Passion is applied concretely to human beings throughout the course of history in a spiritual rather than a physical way, through the virtue of faith and the reception of the sacraments,[77] and particularly through the sacrifice of the Mass. When treating the effects of the Eucharist, St. Thomas says that, because the Eucharist is the sacramental representation of the Passion, "this sacrament works in man the effect which Christ's Passion wrought in the world."[78] He then quotes St. John Chrysostom's commentary on John 19:34: "The Mysteries have their source

---

[74] See *ST* III, q. 48, a. 1.

[75] See *ST* III, q. 48, a. 6: "There is a twofold efficient agency—namely, the principal and the instrumental. Now the principal efficient cause of man's salvation is God. But since Christ's humanity is the *instrument of the Godhead*, as stated above (q. 43, a. 2), therefore all Christ's actions and sufferings operate instrumentally in virtue of His Godhead for the salvation of men. Consequently, then, Christ's Passion accomplishes man's salvation efficiently." For a development of St. Thomas's doctrine in this regard, see Damian Fandal, *The Essence of the Eucharistic Sacrifice* (River Forest, IL: Aquinas Library, 1960); Mannes M. Matthijs, *De Aeternitate Sacerdotii Christi et de Unitate Sacrificii Crucis et Altaris* (Rome: Pontificia Studiorum Universitas a Sancto Thoma Aquinate in Urbe, 1963).

[76] *ST* III, q. 49, a. 1.

[77] See *ST* III, q. 48, a. 6, ad 2: "Christ's Passion, although corporeal, has yet a spiritual effect from the Godhead united: and therefore it secures its efficacy by spiritual contact—namely, by faith and the sacraments of faith." See Nicolas, *What Is the Eucharist?* 69–70.

[78] *ST* III, q. 79, a. 1.

from there, so that when you approach the awesome chalice you may come as if you were about to drink from His very side."[79]

Cardinal Cajetan on the Sacrifice of the Mass

The great Thomist theologian Cardinal Cajetan (Thomas de Vio, 1469–1534) was among the first Catholic theologians to respond to the rejection of the sacrificial nature of the Mass by Martin Luther and Huldrych Zwingli at the outbreak of the Reformation. He deals with this question in two brief tractates, both of which stress the unity of the sacrifice of the Mass and that of Calvary.

In the earlier treatise, Cajetan makes an analogy between the real presence in the Mass of Christ's Body and Blood, on the one hand, and His sacrifice of Calvary, on the other. Transubstantiation makes the same Body and Blood present on the altar that were present on the Cross and are now present in heaven. The mode of presence differs, however. On the altar, they are present in the mode of substance, but not in the mode of quantity, as seen above in chapter 7, whereas they were present on the Cross and are now present in heaven in the mode of quantity proper to bodies. We can say something analogous about the sacrifice. The sacrifice is the same on Calvary and on the altar, but the mode of presence differs. Cajetan explains this difference of mode by saying: "Then it was offered corporeally and now it is offered spiritually. Then it was offered in the reality of death, now it is offered in the mystery of death."[80]

Cajetan then makes a distinction between the real presence of Christ as He is offered in the Eucharist and the sacramental presence of His death: "Christ is both signified and contained in this sacrifice; His death however is signified but not contained. Therefore it does not occur that Christ dies every time this sacrifice is offered, although He is contained and offered in it."[81] We can say that Christ's sacrifice is signified and made present in the Mass (in a spiritual mode), whereas His death is signified but not contained, although its fruits are made present and applied to the world in a spiritual manner.

In his second and longer treatise, Cajetan further stresses the

---

[79] John Chrysostom, *Homily* 85 (Goggin, *Commentary on Saint John*, 435).

[80] Cajetan, *Tractatus De Erroribus Contingentibus in Eucharistiae Sacramento* 9, in Thomas de Vio Cajetanus, *Opuscula Omnia* (repr., Hildesheim/Zürich/New York: Georg Olms Verlag, 1995), 145.

[81] Ibid.

unity of the Victim in the sacrifice of Calvary and in the Mass, with a difference of the mode of offering, in that one is bloody and the other unbloody:

> The unity of the Victim is the foundation of truth that allows one to understand the different passages of Sacred Scripture regarding the sacrifice and priesthood of the New Testament. This one Victim was sacrificed simply and absolutely [*simpliciter et absolute*] only once on the Cross by Christ Himself. In a certain respect, however, He is sacrificed by Christ through ministers each day in His Church. Thus in the New Testament there is a bloody Victim and an unbloody Victim. The bloody Victim is Jesus Christ offered once only on the altar of the Cross for the sins of the entire world; the unbloody Victim instituted by Christ is His Body and Blood under the species of bread and wine. . . . The bloody and unbloody Victim, nevertheless, are not two victims, but one only, for the reality of the Victim is one and the same. The Body of Christ on our altar is none other than the Body of Christ offered on the Cross; and the Blood of Christ on our altar is none other than the Blood of Christ poured out on the Cross. But the manner of immolating this one Victim differs. . . . This unbloody mode, however, was instituted not for itself as a disparate mode of sacrifice, but solely as referring to the bloody Victim of the Cross. For all who can understand and see that a thing which does not exist except for another is but one thing with that other, it follows that one cannot affirm the existence in the New Testament of two sacrifices, two victims, two oblations, two immolations. . . . There is rather only one Victim, offered once only on the Cross, which endures by way of immolation through the daily repetition of the rite instituted by Christ in the Eucharist.[82]

Notice that Cajetan does not say that Christ's sacrifice is repeated. Only the sacrificial *rite* is repeated that Christ instituted at the Last Supper, by which His sacrifice once and for all continues to be made

---

[82] Cajetan, *Tractatus De Missae Sacrificio et Ritu adversus Lutheranos, ad Clement VII*, ch. 6, in *Opuscula Omnia*, 287 (my translation modifying that given in Journet, *The Mass*, 83–84).

present in a new and unbloody way. Although the Victim of the sacrifice of Calvary and of the altar is one and the same, Cajetan carefully distinguishes the differences in the mode of offering. First, the sacrifice of Calvary was offered under its proper species (bloody), whereas that of the Mass is offered under sacramental species, and thus is said to be "unbloody." Secondly, the sacrifice of Calvary was a sacrifice in itself, whereas the Mass is a sacrifice not from itself but through its intrinsic relation to the sacrifice of the Cross, which it was instituted to sacramentally represent and memorialize. Thus Calvary could be said to be an *absolute* sacrifice, whereas the Mass is essentially *relative* to it. Third, although the Victim of Calvary is equally contained in both, only the sacrifice of Calvary brought about Christ's death, whereas in the Mass it is sacramentally signified but not physically brought about. Fourth, the sacrifice of Calvary, by its very nature, is incapable of repetition, whereas Christ instituted the sacrifice of the altar to be repeated daily in every place to bring about the participation of the Church in the offering.

The Council of Trent on the Sacrifice of the Mass

After Martin Luther's vehement rejection of the sacrificial nature of the Mass in 1520, which will be discussed in the following chapter, it became necessary for Catholic theologians to defend more explicitly the general consensus on the sacrifice of the Mass and its unity with Calvary. The Council of Trent gave a dogmatic response without entering into the theological differences among reputable Catholic theologians:

> He then, our Lord and God, was once and for all to offer himself by his death on the altar of the Cross to accomplish for them an everlasting redemption. But, because his priesthood was not to end with his death, at the Last Supper "on the night when he was betrayed" [1 Cor 11:23], in order to leave to his beloved Spouse the Church a visible sacrifice (as the nature of man demands)—by which the bloody sacrifice that he was once for all to accomplish on the Cross would be re-presented, its memory perpetuated until the end of the world, and its salutary power applied for the forgiveness of the sins that we daily commit—declaring himself constituted

a priest forever according to the order of Melchizedek, he offered his body and blood under the species of bread and wine to God the Father, and, under the same signs, gave them to partake of to the disciples (whom he then established as priests of the New Covenant) and ordered them and their successors in the priesthood to offer, saying: "Do this in remembrance of me," etc., as the Catholic Church has always understood and taught.[83]

In this solemn text, the Council of Trent states that the sacrifice of the Mass "re-presents" the sacrifice of Calvary. This should be understood in the sense of "making present again." The sacrifice of the Mass makes the sacrifice of Calvary present on our altars, perpetuating it throughout the ages.[84] The Mass is not a theatrical "representation" of another sacrifice, as if it were a *mere* commemoration.[85] Nor is it a sacrifice different from Calvary. There is only one sacrifice that is offered day by day: the very sacrifice of Calvary, made present, "re-presented." How is this done? How can the sacrifice of the Mass in all the churches of the world be the same as that of Calvary? The Council of Trent explains: "It is one and the same victim; the same person now offers it by the ministry of His priests, who then offered Himself on the cross, the manner of offering alone being different."[86]

The sacrifice of the Mass is identical with Calvary because it contains the same Victim, who is mystically immolated, and because it is offered by the same High Priest, Jesus Christ, through the sacramental ministry of His ordained priests who act in His person. It cannot be a new bloody sacrifice, because Jesus Christ in His glorious body cannot die again. His bloody immolation cannot be repeated, and so

---

[83] Council of Trent, On the Sacrifice of the Mass (session 22), ch. 1 (DS, 1740).

[84] See Second Vatican Council, Constitution on the Sacred Liturgy, *Sacrosanctum Concilium*, §47: "Our Saviour instituted the Eucharistic Sacrifice of his body and blood, in order to perpetuate the sacrifice of the Cross throughout time, until he should return." See also John Paul II, *EE*, §11: "The Eucharist is indelibly marked by the event of the Lord's passion and death, of which it is not only a reminder but the sacramental re-presentation. It is the sacrifice of the Cross perpetuated down the ages."

[85] See Council of Trent, On the Sacrifice of the Mass (session 22), can. 3: "If anyone says that the sacrifice of the Mass is . . . a simple commemoration of the sacrifice accomplished on the Cross, but not a propitiatory sacrifice . . . let him be anathema" (DS, 1753).

[86] Ibid., ch. 2 (DS, 1743).

the Mass re-presents that bloody immolation of Calvary through an unbloody sacramental separation of His Blood from His Body. Only in this unbloody mode of offering does the sacrifice of the Mass differ from Calvary. Otherwise they are the same through the identity of the Victim and Priest.

Post-Tridentine Catholic Theories on What Constitutes the Sacrifice of the Mass

After the Council of Trent there was a vigorous discussion among Catholic theologians on what essentially constitutes the Mass as a true sacrifice.[87] The basis of the discussion, generally accepted by all, was the idea that in a sacrifice, something is not only offered to God, but in some way is also modified or destroyed.

The answer to this question can be framed in different ways. One path is to hold that the immolation in the Mass is a sacramental representation of the bloody sacrifice of Calvary. In this way of understanding it, the Mass is a true sacrifice because it is the real and present offering of the abiding Victim immolated physically in the sacrifice of Calvary, but immolated only in sacramental signs in the Mass. A second path is to seek to identify a new real, although unbloody, immolation in every celebration of the sacrifice of the Mass. As we have seen, St. Thomas, in harmony with the Fathers and medieval doctors, took the first path, which was followed also by Cardinal Cajetan and the Council of Trent. Many post-Tridentine theologians of the sixteenth to the nineteenth centuries took the second path.

St. Robert Bellarmine framed the problem by putting forth the thesis that "a true and real sacrifice requires the true and real death, or destruction, of the thing offered."[88] This thesis comes from the notion

---

[87] For a summary of the various theories proposed by Catholic theologians, see Edward F. Dowd, *A Conspectus of Modern Catholic Thought on the Essence of the Eucharistic Sacrifice* (Washington, DC: Catholic University of America, 1937); Clark, *Eucharistic Sacrifice and the Reformation*, 250–60; Journet, *The Mass*, 252–67; Emmanuel Doronzo, *Tractatus Dogmaticus de Eucharistia*, 2:967–1033; Ibáñez, *L'Eucaristia, Dono e Mistero*, 330–67.

[88] Robert Bellarmine, *Controversiarum de Sacramento Eucharistiae* 5.2:

A true sacrifice requires that what is offered to God in sacrifice be clearly destroyed, that is, so changed that it ceases to be what it was before. This is how it most differs from a simple oblation.... It seems that there are two reasons for this. One is to signify the death of Christ.

of ritual sacrifice as it was understood in the religious cultures of the world. If this principle is accepted, as it was by most Catholic theologians of the time, the problem then is how to explain how there is a true destruction of the Victim offered in the Mass.

Eminent Catholic theologians in the post-Tridentine period offered different hypotheses on what constituted the modification or destruction of the offering in the sacrifice of the Mass.[89] Bellarmine argued that this destruction occurred in the Communion by the priest, by which Christ's Eucharistic presence would be terminated.[90] This theory found few followers.[91] A crucial problem with this position is that it would make Christ's immolation in the Mass essentially different from that on Calvary: every Mass (and every Communion) would add a new real immolation, although unbloody. The unity of the sacrifice of the Mass and Calvary would thereby be impaired. Second, this position confuses the essence of the sacrifice and the reception of its fruit in the priest's Communion, which, although they form an integral whole, remain distinct and complementary aspects of the Eucharist.[92] Third, the dual consecration would contribute nothing to the immolation conceived in this way. Although it should therefore be rejected that Communion constitutes the essence of the Eucharistic sacrifice, it is true that Communion serves as a symbol of Christ's sacrificial gift of self. He has given Himself to be our spiritual nour-

---

The second is that sacrifice is the supreme confession of our subjection to God and the supreme external cult that can be given. A supreme confession requires not only that the use of a thing be offered to God, but also even its substance. (*Opera Omnia*, ed. Justinus Fèvre, vol. 4 [Paris: Vivès, 1873], 305–06)

[89] See Trent Pomplun, "Post-Tridentine Sacramental Theology," in Boersma and Levering, eds., *The Oxford Handbook of Sacramental Theology*, 348–61, esp. 352–54.

[90] Robert Bellarmine, *Controversiarum de Sacramento Eucharistiae* 5.27: "That this is the essential part is demonstrated by the fact that in the whole celebration of the Mass . . . there is no other real destruction of the victim other than this. That a real destruction is necessary has been demonstrated above" (*Opera Omnia*, 4:366).

[91] The Salmanticenses (here "John of the Annunciation") follow Bellarmine's position in *De Eucharistiae Sacramento*, disp. 13, dub. 2, no. 30, in *Cursus Theologicus*, vol. 18 (Paris: Apud Victorem Palmé, 1882), 782.

[92] See Journet, *The Mass*, 254n19: "Everybody today admits that the essence of the sacrifice of the Mass is situated in the moment of the consecration, and that the reason for Communion is to allow us to enter more deeply into the sacrificial drama."

ishment. There are many elements in the liturgical rite, such as the fractioning of the host, that symbolize the sacrifice of Calvary without constituting properly the essence of the sacrifice.

John Cardinal de Lugo (1583–1660),[93] followed most prominently in the nineteenth century by Johann Baptist Cardinal Franzelin, S.J. (1816–1886), held that the immolation in the Mass consists in Christ being present in the Eucharist in an ignoble and humbled state, appearing as mere nourishment.

This reflection can be helpful for understanding Christ's self-emptying in the Eucharist and for appreciating the love of Christ that leads Him to wish to be present to us in this way. But as an explanation of how Christ is essentially immolated in the sacrament, this thesis should be rejected. First, like that of Bellarmine, it would make every Mass a new immolation, essentially different from that of Calvary. The essential nature of the dual consecration would also be lost. Furthermore, Christ is not really changed at all by the consecration, even though He can be said to take on the appearances of bread and wine.

The great nineteenth-century theologian Matthias Joseph Scheeben, although a former pupil of Franzelin, argues against his teacher, showing that Christ is actually present in the Eucharist in a more noble state, closer to the divine omnipresence, in that He is whole and entire and impassible under every part of the sacred species, and is simultaneously in all the places of the world where there is a consecrated host.[94]

Leonardus Lessius, S.J. (1554–1623) held that the double consecration was the immolation, for it would result in the separation of Christ's body and blood on the altar, but for the fact of Christ's impassibility after the Resurrection.

Another theory, that of the great Jesuit theologian Francisco Suárez (1548–1617), saw the consecration as the modification of the oblation, which consisted not in a destruction of the thing offered, but rather its change for the better, by which the bread and wine were transformed into the Body and Blood of Christ.[95] The problem with this proposal is that the change and destruction is not on the part of Christ but on that of the bread and wine. The sacrifice that is offered

---

[93] John Cardinal de Lugo, *De Eucharistia*, disp. 19, sect. 5.

[94] Scheeben, *The Mysteries of Christianity*, 473.

[95] This theory was followed, at least in part, in the nineteenth century by Scheeben, in *The Mysteries of Christianity*.

to the Father in the Mass, however, is not that of bread and wine, but of Christ's Body and Blood, as witnessed by the faith of the Church and the liturgical texts of Eucharistic Prayers.[96]

These theories positing a real immolation in every Mass were very popular from the seventeenth through the nineteenth centuries, but they have been generally abandoned in the last century.[97] The most serious general problem with these theories is that they impair the unity of the sacrifice of the Mass and of Calvary. For if Christ is immolated in the Mass in a new way, as by being consumed in Communion or being brought into a state of humiliation under the appearances of bread and wine, then this immolation in the Mass would not be same as that on Calvary, but would differ essentially. Although these theories were worked out in part to answer Protestant objections, it seems that they simply sharpen the Protestant accusation that Catholics are seeking to add some new immolation to that of Calvary, as if it were insufficient.

An additional general problem with these theories lies in their common presupposition that death or destruction is regarded as the essence of sacrifice. This appears to be an innovation compared with the classical doctrine proposed by the Fathers and medieval doctors. It is true that St. Thomas held that a sacrifice, as the etymology implies, is distinguished from a simple oblation from the fact that something is done to the offering to symbolize its consecration and transfer to God in token of the interior offering of the heart. This may involve physical death or destruction as an expressive means of transfer, but the emphasis should be on the positive gift that is given to God. For sacrifice is an external sign not of substitutionary punishment, annihilation, or destruction, but of the gift of self that is given to God. The blood of sacrificial animals symbolizes the life that is given to God and not death or destruction, which God says that He does not desire.[98]

---

[96] Suarez's position is criticized by the Salmanticenses on this account in *De Eucharistiae Sacramento*, disp. 13, dub. 2, nos. 32, 783–784: "Non sufficit immutatio panis, sed aliqua etiam mutatio admitti debet in ipso Christo, si est res oblata per verum sacrificium, ut catholice fateri debemus."

[97] See Nicolas, *What Is the Eucharist?* 65–66.

[98] See Wis 1:13–14: "God did not make death, and he does not delight in the death of the living. For he created all things that they might exist, and the creatures of the world are wholesome." See Michael McGuckian, *The Holy Sacrifice of the Mass: A Search for an Acceptable Notion of Sacrifice* (Chicago, IL: Hillenbrand Books, 2005), 99.

Gabriel Vázquez, S.J. (1549–1604), a contemporary of Suárez, argued against the preceding positions that support a new and real immolation in the Mass and took the more traditional path mentioned above, arguing that the Mass is a sacrifice through its relation to the sacrifice of Calvary. He distinguished two kinds of sacrifices: absolute and relative. The former is a sacrifice in and from itself; the latter is a sacrifice that commemorates another, from which it draws its sacrificial nature. The Mass is a relative commemorative sacrifice sacramentally imitating the absolute sacrifice of Calvary.[99] The difficulty with this theory is that not every representation of a sacrifice is held to be a sacrifice. Neither a painting of Calvary nor a Passion play is a sacrifice. Why is the representation of Calvary in the Mass a sacrifice?[100] He responds to this objection by noting that the Mass is not a *mere* representation because Christ, the Victim of Calvary, is truly contained and offered in the sacrifice of the Mass.[101] Vazquez's thesis is clearly much more in harmony with that of the Fathers and medieval doctors than the explanations of the other theologians mentioned above, who posit a new real immolation in every Mass, distinct from that of Calvary. His theory could be improved, however, by highlighting the eternal efficacy of the sacrifice of Calvary that is being made present and applied to the world through the Mass.

This debate over the nature of the immolation of Christ in the Mass continued vigorously through the first half of the twenti-

---

[99] See Gabriel Vázquez, *Commentarium in 3 Partem S. Thomae*, disp. 220, ch. 3, no. 25 (Lugduni, 1631), 3:394, quoted in Doronzo, *De Eucharistia*, vol. 2, *De Sacrificio*, 972:

> It should be noted that there are two kinds of sacrifice. One is absolute, namely that which is not the commemoration of another sacrifice. The other kind can be called relative or commemorative, the sole example of which we have in the sacrifice of the altar, which can be said to be commemorative. And even though in this there is no alteration of that which is offered in this way, we still find the true manifestation of the divine omnipotence, as in an absolute sacrifice. Thus the true notion of sacrifice applies to this no less than to an absolute and bloody sacrifice.

[100] See the objection leveled against Vásquez by the Salmanticenses, *De Eucharistiae Sacramento*, disp. 13, dub. 2, no. 32: "Although it is indeed the commemoration and representation of the sacrifice of the Cross, nevertheless it is necessary to confess that it is in itself truly and properly a sacrifice, and not merely the representation of a sacrifice. Nor do the heretics deny the latter" (*Cursus Theologicus*, 18:783).

[101] Vásquez, *Commentarium in 3 Partem*, disp. 222, ch. 8, no. 66, 3:416, quoted in Doronzo, *De Eucharistia*, 2:972–73.

eth century. An interesting contribution to the debate was made by Maurice de la Taille (1872–1933) in his work, *Mysterium Fidei*, written in 1921. His contribution lies in distinguishing more clearly the notions of oblation (offering) and immolation. He sees the Last Supper as the moment of ritual oblation of the bloody immolation on Calvary. In every Mass, the Church joins in the ritual oblation of the Victim immolated on Calvary. In this view, the Mass and Calvary, like the Last Supper and Calvary, form a whole composed of oblation and immolation.[102] In every Mass, according to de la Taille, there is a new sacramental oblation of the Victim already immolated on Calvary, but not a new immolation. The difficulty in this intriguing hypothesis is that it seems to make an excessive distinction between ritual oblation and immolation. It seems that it would be better to see the sacrifice of the Mass as the sacramental re-presentation of *both* Christ's interior oblation *and* his exterior immolation on Calvary.[103]

The Thomistic revival begun by Leo XIII[104] that marked the first half of the twentieth century worked to foster a renewal of the authentic position of St. Thomas Aquinas on this question of the essence of the sacrifice of the Mass. Various prominent theologians stressed the fact that the Mass is a sacramental re-presentation or commemoration of the sacrifice of Calvary, truly making Calvary and its eternal efficacy sacramentally present, and not a new immolation. Important contributions were made by Louis Cardinal Billot,[105] Odo Casel,[106] Anscar

---

[102] For a recent appreciation of the contribution of the Eucharistic theology of de la Taille, see Michon M. Matthiesen, "De la Taille's *Mysterium Fidei*: Eucharistic Sacrifice and Nouvelle Théologie," *New Blackfriars* 94 (2013): 518–39, esp. 531–36; Matthiesen, *Sacrifice as Gift: Eucharist, Grace, and Contemplative Prayer in Maurice de la Taille* (Washington, DC: Catholic University of America Press, 2013).

[103] See Pius XII, *Mediator Dei*, §68: "The august sacrifice of the altar, then, is no mere empty commemoration of the passion and death of Jesus Christ, but a true and proper act of sacrifice, whereby the High Priest *by an unbloody immolation offers Himself* a most acceptable victim to the Eternal Father, as He did upon the cross" (my italics).

[104] See Leo XIII, Encyclical Letter, *Aeterni Patris* (1879). On the topic of the Sacrifice of the Mass, see Leo XIII, *Mirae Caritatis*.

[105] Ludovicus Billot, *De Ecclesiae Sacramentis: Commentarius in Tertiam Partem S. Thomae*, 7th ed. (Rome: Apud Aedes Universitatis Gregorianae, 1931), 1:604–40.

[106] Casel, *The Mystery of Christian Worship*. For an interpretation and assessment of the significance of Casel's contribution, see Kilmartin, *The Eucharist in the West*, 268–91; Ibáñez, *L'Eucaristia, Dono e Mistero*, 344–52.

Vonier,[107] and Charles Cardinal Journet,[108] all of which served to highlight the Mass as the sacramental and mysterious presence of Calvary throughout the life of the Church. This theological work prepared for a magisterial presentation by Pius XII of this Thomistic doctrine on the sacrifice of the Mass.

Mediator Dei on the Sacrifice of the Mass

In his 1947 encyclical on the liturgy, *Mediator Dei*, Pius XII gives an authoritative statement on the twofold question of how the Mass is a true sacrifice and also, in essence, the same sacrifice as that of Calvary. The encyclical affirms the position held by Lombard and St. Thomas that the Mass is a relative sacrifice that is one with Calvary through being a sacramental representation of it that applies its fruits to the world. It offers no support for the theories positing a real immolation distinct from Calvary in every Mass.[109]

Following the Council of Trent, *Mediator Dei,* §68 says that the Mass is "no mere empty commemoration of the passion and death of Jesus Christ, but a true and proper act of sacrifice." It is a true sacrifice because a true priest, Jesus Christ, "by an unbloody immolation offers Himself a most acceptable victim to the Eternal Father, as He did upon the cross." It is also the same sacrifice as Calvary for the reason given by Trent, which is that the same Priest offers the same Victim:

> The priest is the same, Jesus Christ, whose sacred Person His minister represents. Now the minister, by reason of the sacerdotal consecration which he has received, is made like to the High Priest and possesses the power of performing actions in virtue of Christ's very person. Wherefore in his priestly activity he in a certain manner "lends his tongue, and gives his hand" to Christ.[110]

---

[107] Anscar Vonier, *A Key to the Doctrine of the Eucharist* (Bethesda, MD: Zaccheus, 2003).

[108] Journet, *The Mass.* On Journet's teaching on the Sacrifice of the Mass, see Roger Nutt, "The Application of Christ's One Oblation: Charles Journet on the Mass, the Real Presence, and the Sacrifice of the Cross," *Nova et Vetera* (English) 8, no. 3 (2010): 665–81.

[109] For an interpretation of the teaching of *Mediator Dei* on the essence of the sacrifice of the Mass, see Ibáñez, *L'Eucaristia, Dono e Mistero*, 368–71.

[110] John Chrysostom, *In Joann. Hom.* 86.4.

Likewise the victim is the same, namely, our divine Redeemer in His human nature with His true body and blood.[111]

Although the sacrifice of the Mass is essentially the same as that of Calvary in that both have the same Victim and Priest, *Mediator Dei* develops the teaching of Trent that there is a difference in the mode of offering. On Calvary, the immolation was bloody, whereas in the Mass, that bloody immolation is sacramentally represented through the separate consecration of the bread and the wine into the Body and Blood of Christ:

> The manner, however, in which Christ is offered is different. On the cross He completely offered Himself and all His sufferings to God, and the immolation of the victim was brought about by the bloody death, which He underwent of His free will. But on the altar, by reason of the glorified state of His human nature, "death shall have no more dominion over Him," and so the shedding of His blood is impossible; still, according to the plan of divine wisdom, the sacrifice of our Redeemer is shown forth in an admirable manner by external signs which are the symbols of His death.
>
> For by the "transubstantiation" of bread into the body of Christ and of wine into His blood, His body and blood are both really present: now the eucharistic species under which He is present symbolize the actual separation of His body and blood. Thus the commemorative representation of His death, which actually took place on Calvary, is repeated in every sacrifice of the altar, seeing that Jesus Christ is symbolically shown by separate symbols to be in a state of victimhood.[112]

In other words, the separate conversion of the bread and wine into Christ's Body and Blood sacramentally or mystically *re-present* the real separation of the Blood from the Body of Christ in His death on Calvary.

The words of consecration, uttered in the person of Christ, are the means of effecting the Eucharistic sacrifice. As seen above, St. Gregory of Nazianzen likens these words of the consecration to a mystical knife

---

[111] Pius XII, *Mediator Dei*, §§69–70.
[112] Ibid., §70.

that immolates the Lamb of God. He writes to a fellow bishop: "Cease not both to pray and to plead for me when you draw down the Word by your word, when with a bloodless cutting you sever the body and blood of the Lord, using your voice for the sacrificial knife."[113]

In summary, the sacrifice of the Mass is identical with that of Calvary in three ways: the Victim is Jesus Christ, through the miracle of transubstantiation; the priest who offers is Jesus Christ, through the ministerial priest; and the ends for which the Mass is offered are the same—to give supreme glory to God, to give thanks, to satisfy for all sin, and to make supplication for all our needs.

One obvious difference, however, between the sacrifice of the Mass and that of Calvary is the mode of offering. On Calvary, Christ made use of the hands of his executioners to effect His bloody sacrifice. In the Mass, no executioners or torturers are at work, but Christ Himself is present and offering Himself as He did then, but now through the priests of His Mystical Body.[114] The same sacrifice is offered in an "unbloody" manner, in a sacramental way, through the words of consecration that effect a mystical separation of body and blood, for death no longer has any physical hold over Christ.

A second fundamental difference is that Christ alone (with His Mother, St. John, and the other disciples at the foot of the Cross) offered the sacrifice of Calvary, whereas the Church, through her priests, offers the sacrifice of the Mass with Christ and offers herself with Him.

After *Mediator Dei*, the post-Tridentine question on the essence of the sacrifice of the Mass was basically resolved and ceased to be a burning subject of theological debate. St. John Paul II masterfully summarizes the teaching of Trent and *Mediator Dei* in *Ecclesia de Eucharistia*, §12:

> The Mass makes present the sacrifice of the Cross; it does not add to that sacrifice nor does it multiply it. What is repeated is its memorial celebration, its "commemorative representation," which makes Christ's one, definitive redemptive sacrifice

---

[113] Gregory Nazianzen, Letter 171 to Amphilochius (*NPNF2*, 7:469).

[114] See Masure, *The Sacrifice of the Mystical Body*, 35: "She [the Church] would thus take possession of the sacrifice of the Cross in all its essentials: not as deriving from the executioners and the Jews, but as emanating from the will of the Son and of the Father."

always present in time. The sacrificial nature of the Eucharistic mystery cannot therefore be understood as something separate, independent of the Cross or only indirectly referring to the sacrifice of Calvary.

This teaching clearly excludes the post-Tridentine theories, mentioned above, that consider the immolation of the Mass as distinct in nature from the immolation of the Cross such that the Mass could add something to Calvary. The Mass, rather, makes sacramentally present in our time the "one definitive redemptive sacrifice."

Three Levels of the Eucharistic Sacrifice

We have seen above that one of the fruits of the Berengarian controversy was the realization that the Eucharist could not be described simply in terms of sacramental sign and hidden reality. The anti-Berengarian theologians maintained that there are two distinct kinds of hidden reality in the Eucharist: Christ's Body and Blood and the grace that builds up the unity of the Mystical Body. The hidden reality of Christ's Body and Blood is also an efficacious sign of that grace and unity. Scholastic theologians of the twelfth century thus worked out a threefold scheme to speak about the sacraments. There is a visible sacramental sign (*sacramentum tantum*), an intermediate level that is both a hidden reality and an invisible sign (*res et sacramentum*), and that which is a supernatural reality and not a sign (*res tantum*). From the time of Peter Lombard on, Scholastic theologians applied this threefold scheme to the Eucharist considered as a sacrament.

The Eucharist, however, is also a sacrifice. Are there also three levels in its sacrificial aspect? Although this was not developed by the medieval theologians, the answer must be affirmative.[115] Just as the Church's sacraments are richer and more complex than other sacred signs, so too the Church's sacrifice is richer and more complex than other ritual sacrifices.

We have seen that the sacramental sign (*sacramentum tantum*) is composed of the matter of bread and wine and the essential form

---

[115] Some twentieth-century theologians use this terminology with regard to the Eucharist in its sacrificial dimension. Masure, *The Sacrifice of the Mystical Body*, 23, speaks about the presence of the sacrifice of the Cross as *res et sacramentum*, and de la Taille, in *The Mystery of Faith*, 2:217–18, gives a fuller explanation.

given by Christ's words at the Last Supper. These words clearly indicate that the bread and wine sacramentally signify Christ's Body and Blood precisely as given over and poured out for the forgiveness of sins. The second level, *res et sacramentum*, properly speaking, should be understood not simply as the real presence of Christ's Body and Blood, but as His Body and Blood *immolated* on Calvary and *offered* in the Mass, as is clear in the words of consecration and in the symbolism of the separate consecration of the elements. Although Christ is not physically immolated in the Mass as He was on the Cross—for He dies no more—He remains for all eternity as the glorious immolated Victim of Calvary.[116] His Resurrection and Ascension do not undo His glorious Passion. This is manifested in the fact that Christ rose from the dead retaining the glorious wounds of His Passion. It is also manifested in the words of consecration, which speak of His Body as "given up" for us and His Blood as "poured out . . . for the forgiveness of sins." The Body made present on the altar is the one given up for us, and the Blood made present is that which was poured out for us. On the level of *res et sacramentum*, there is not a new immolation, but rather the personal reality of Christ, who was made—and eternally remains—the Victim of Calvary given "for the life of the world."[117]

The third level, the interior *reality alone* (*res tantum*), is what is signified by the *res et sacramentum*. In every sacrifice the reality signified by the exterior sacrifice is the interior oblation of the heart that is offered to God to glorify Him. Thus we can speak of the *reality alone* of the sacrifice of the Mass as the interior oblation of the heart of Christ on Calvary, to which the faithful join the interior oblation of their hearts. The *res tantum* would also include the glorification of God the Father by the Son and the effect of propitiation that results from the Sacrifice.[118] This will be examined in chapters 11 and 12 below.

---

[116] See David W. Fagerberg, "Divine Liturgy, Divine Love," *Letter & Spirit* 3 (2007): 95–112, at 102: "The victim who is made present on the altar is an immolated victim, so when the Church gives him over to the Father it is a real sacrifice. But the victim made present on the altar is already an immolated victim, so we do not add to his victimhood. That is how it can be affirmed, as Catholic teaching always has, that our 'new' sacrifice of the Mass does not add something new (in the sense of 'additional') to the cross."

[117] See John 6:51.

[118] See the fine analysis by de la Taille, *The Mystery of Faith*, 2:217:

For in every true sacrifice . . . two things are to be considered; one is the *reality and sign* (*res et signum*), the other the *reality only* (*res tantum*).

The three levels of the Eucharist, considered both as (1) sacrament of spiritual nourishment and (2) as sacramental sacrifice, are represented in the following diagram:

	1. Sacrament of spiritual nourishment	2. Sacramental sacrifice
Sensible sacramental sign (*sacramentum tantum*)	Bread and wine	Separate consecration
(Invisible) reality and sign (*res et sacramentum*)	Body and Blood	Offering of Christ's Body and Blood
Interior reality alone (*res tantum*)	Grace and charity; unity of the Church in charity	Interior self-donation of the heart—of Christ and the faithful who participate in the sacrifice

Christ's Sacrifice Transcends Time

The law that governs the sacraments of the Church is that they are efficacious signs that truly make present the supernatural reality that they represent. Since the sacramental signs represent not only Christ's presence in His Body and Blood but also the separation of His Body and Blood that occurred in His Passion, it follows that the reality of Christ's immolation is truly made present and offered to the Father in every Mass. But how can this be? What does it mean to say that an historical event two thousand years past can be made present?

We have seen that transubstantiation makes Christ present in the same Body that was nailed to the Cross and the same Blood that poured from His wounds and His pierced side. It makes Christ present as the Victim who was crucified for our redemption, and that same

---

The *reality only* is our internal immolation. The *reality and sign* is our giving over to God, by an action apparent to the senses, of a victim either already immolated, or of a victim actually now submitted to immolation, or to be immolated in the future. This external giving is a *sign* in as much as our internal dedication is denoted by it; it is a true *reality* in as much as in itself it is a real genuine handing over and dedication of some external gift.

abiding Victim is offered to the Father in every Mass, even though the event of death is not repeated, nor could it be.[119]

Although the event of Christ's Passion belongs to past time, it also transcends time in a way that no other historical event ever could because it is the culminating action of the life of the eternal incarnate Son. As the Word made flesh, His actions have an infinite and eternal value, both in meriting all salvation and in being the ultimate exemplar or archetype of the life of redeemed mankind.[120] And if this is true of all the mysteries of Christ's life, it is especially true of the Paschal mystery to which all the other actions of His life were oriented. St. Thomas writes:

> Christ's Passion had a virtue which was neither temporal nor transitory, but everlasting, according to Heb. 10:14: "For by one oblation He hath perfected for ever them that are sanctified." And so it is evident that Christ's Passion had no greater efficacy then than it has now.[121]

In the sixteenth century, Melchior Cano (1509–1560) eloquently expressed this power of Christ's Paschal mystery to transcend all time, connecting it with the sacrifice of the Mass:

> If Christ offering Himself on the Cross did not subtract Himself from our presence, but perpetually hung on the Cross before the eyes of all the faithful in every place and time, . . . we would not need an exemplar or image of that victim. For although that offering made by Christ in the past and the visible slaying is over, it is still so acceptable to God, so everlasting in its power, that it is just as effective in the sight of the

---

[119] See O'Connor, *The Hidden Manna*, 309: "The killing and offering of the Victim has passed; the Victim who was killed and offered remains, now alive but Victim still. The past is irretrievable, but it always lives on in those it has affected. Any Jewish man or woman who lived through the concentration camps is marked forever with victimhood, even though the actual persecution is over. So, too, with the Victim of *the* Holocaust, the God-Man." See also Nicolas, *What Is the Eucharist?* 67–68.

[120] See John Paul II, *EE*, §5: "In the paschal event and the Eucharist which makes it present throughout the centuries, there is a truly enormous 'capacity' which embraces all of history as the recipient of the grace of the redemption."

[121] *ST* III, q. 52, a. 8.

Father today as it was on the day when the Blood gushed from the pierced side. Hence we offer now, and truly offer Christ, the same victim of the cross. . . . In very truth this sacramental image and exemplar in no way prevents our offering here and now that same blood of the Cross, just as if it were now shed in our presence.[122]

Joseph Ratzinger makes a similar point:

This true sacrifice that turns us all into sacrifice, in other words, unites us with God and causes us to become godlike, is indeed fixed and founded on an historical event but does not lie behind us as a thing in the past but, rather, becomes contemporary with and accessible to us in the community of the believing, praying Church, in its sacrament: this is what "sacrifice of the Mass" means.

Luther's error lay, I am convinced, in a false concept of historicity, in a misunderstanding of what is unrepeatable. Christ's sacrifice is not behind us as a thing of the past. It touches all times and is present to us. Eucharist is not merely the distribution of something but is, rather, the presence of Christ's Paschal Mystery, which transcends and unites all times. When the Roman Canon cites Abel, Abraham and Melchisedech and describes them as concelebrants of the Eucharist, it does so in the conviction that in them, too, those great men offering sacrifice, Christ was passing through time, or perhaps, more precisely, that in their search they were going forth to meet Christ.[123]

The *CCC*, §1085 further illuminates the same idea:

His Paschal mystery is a real event that occurred in our history, but it is unique: all other historical events happen once, and then they pass away, swallowed up in the past. The Paschal

---

[122] Melchior Cano, *De Locis Theologicis* 12.11, in *Opera*, ed. Hyacintho Serry (Patavii, 1762), 378 (my translation on the basis of that given in de la Taille, *The Mystery of the Faith*, 2:117).

[123] Joseph Ratzinger, "The Theology of the Liturgy," in *TL*, 555–56. See also Jungmann, *The Mass*, 102–08.

mystery of Christ, by contrast, cannot remain only in the past, because by his death he destroyed death, and all that Christ is—all that he did and suffered for all men—participates in the divine eternity, and so transcends all times while being made present in them all. The event of the Cross and Resurrection *abides* and draws everything toward life.

Christ's Paschal mystery transcends time in a unique way because it is the act of a divine and eternal Person who is present to all times. Although it occurred in the midst of time, it impacts every time and place in human history by destroying the power of death, meriting the grace of sharing in the divine life, offering perfect worship to the Father, and engrafting into history the power of the Resurrection. The Paschal mystery is the meritorious and exemplar cause of all human salvation and of every grace given to mankind after the Fall. Because the Paschal mystery impacts all time, it cannot remain imprisoned in the past but is eternally powerful to touch and elevate our present.

But if all time is touched by the effects of Christ's Passion and Resurrection, how does the Mass make the Paschal mystery present in a unique way, different from that hidden way by which it is mysteriously present in all times and places? In the Mass, the immolation of Christ is made present in both its ascending and its descending movements of mediation *in a sacramental way*—that is, by a sacred sign that realizes what it represents. Even though the Paschal mystery is present to our world outside of the Mass through the hidden action of grace, the Mass makes it present in a sacramental mode whereby it is sensibly manifested and solemnly offered by the Church, and thereby endowed with unique efficacious power to glorify God and draw down graces won by Christ on Calvary to our world today.[124] This efficacious power

---

[124] Jacques Maritain tried to take this idea a step further in an essay in *Untrammeled Approaches*, vol. 20, *Collected Works* (Notre Dame, IN: University Notre Dame Press, 1997), 350–80. He reasoned that since Christ's sacrifice on Calvary is present in the divine eternity, God could miraculously make that historical time present again in every Mass. In other words, he proposed that the past time of the sacrifice of Calvary is somehow made *ontologically present* in the Mass through the divine omnipotence. Our time is miraculously made to touch that past time which is always present in the divine eternity. It seems to me that this proposal obscures the sacramental mode in which Calvary is made present. For St. Thomas, a past event is made present by having the *substance* and *eternal*

is proper to the queen of the sacraments of the New Covenant. Since every Mass makes present the eternal power of Calvary, the Mass remains *ever new* throughout the centuries. The collect for the liturgy for Thursday of the Lord's Supper says that Jesus "has entrusted to the Church a sacrifice that is new for all eternity."[125]

The Mass Makes Present the Whole of the Paschal Mystery: Death, Resurrection, and Ascension

Since Christ is made present in the Eucharist as He is when Mass is celebrated, and since Christ has been glorified in His Resurrection, the Eucharist also makes the Resurrection present.[126] Jesus is made present as the glorified Victim eternally acceptable to God. The Resurrection pertains to the sacrifice insofar as it has manifested that God has accepted the offering and gives us a pledge of our future glory. The sacrifice is essentially the victim offered, immolated, and accepted by God such that it can become for us the bread of life. Christ's Resurrection therefore pertains to the Eucharistic sacrifice as the sign of its acceptance, as the current state of the Victim who is made present and given to us as our spiritual nourishment, full of glorious life, and as the pledge of our future participation in His Resurrection.[127]

St. John Paul II, in *Ecclesia de Eucharistia*, §14, explains this presence of Christ's Resurrection in the sacrifice:

---

power of the event made present through a sacramental *image*, but not by having the past *time* itself made present, which is what Maritain seems to be proposing. For a critique of this idea, see Nicolas, *What Is the Eucharist?* 66: "Time is not like space. What is past no longer exists in the form dominated by time which is implied by the historical facts of suffering and death. Co-existence between yesterday and today is not possible."

[125] Thursday of the Lord's Supper, Evening Mass, collect (*RM*, 299).

[126] For the importance of the Resurrection of Christ in the Eucharist, see Gustave Martelet, *The Risen Christ and the Eucharistic World*. On the development of this doctrine in twentieth-century magisterial teaching, see Langevin, *From Passion to Paschal Mystery*.

[127] See Scheeben, *The Mysteries of Christianity*, 520: "On the cross the flesh of Christ had to be offered in its earthly nature, as otherwise it could not suffer. At the resurrection it had to be glorified, in order to complete the holocaust. But in the Eucharist it must display its efficacy as the holocaust already consummated by death and resurrection, together with the power that has wrought full regeneration in the midst of redeemed mankind."

Christ's passover includes not only his passion and death, but also his resurrection. This is recalled by the assembly's acclamation following the consecration: "*We proclaim your resurrection.*" The Eucharistic sacrifice makes present not only the mystery of the Saviour's passion and death, but also the mystery of the resurrection which crowned his sacrifice. It is as the living and risen One that Christ can become in the Eucharist the "bread of life" (John 6:35, 48), the "living bread" (John 6:51).

Even at the Last Supper, just as His Passion was sacramentally anticipated, so too the victory of the Resurrection was already mysteriously made present in the Father's acceptance of the sacrifice of the Son. Benedict XVI explains this in *Sacramentum Caritatis* §10:

> In the prayer of praise, the *Berakah*, he does not simply thank the Father for the great events of past history, but also for his own "exaltation." In instituting the sacrament of the Eucharist, Jesus anticipates and makes present the sacrifice of the Cross and the victory of the resurrection.

Christ's Ascension is also involved in the Eucharist in at least two respects.[128] First, the Body we receive in Communion is that Body that has ascended and sits in glory at the right hand of the Father in heaven, sending us His Spirit and communicating to us the fruits of the redemption.[129] Communion thus is a perfect pledge of our future resurrection and glorification. Second, the Victim that is offered to the Father in every Mass is one who has already passed through the veil of this creation and has ascended into heaven and sits at the right

---

[128] See de la Taille, *The Mystery of Faith*, 1:196–201.

[129] See O'Neill, *New Approaches to the Eucharist*, 34–35:

> By explicitly locating the Mass-sacrifice in the mystery of the risen Christ we leave no doubt that this sacrifice is dependent on the unique sacrifice of Christ and is derived from the gift of the Spirit sent into the world by the Christ ascended to his Father. . . . It is within the sphere of this communication of Christ's paschal mystery that there is a sacramental representation of the unique sacrifice. And such a sacramental dimension is given this unique sacrifice in order that the faithful, who have not yet risen, not yet received the full fruits of redemption, may participate in the sacrifice.

hand of the Father, from which place He continually intercedes for us, according to Hebrews 7:25: "Consequently he is able for all time to save those who draw near to God through him, since he always lives to make intercession for them."[130]

It is fitting, therefore, that, in the anamnesis of Eucharistic Prayers, we remember not only the Passion but also the glorious mysteries. In the Roman Canon (Eucharistic Prayer I), for example, in the anamnesis right after the consecration, the priest prays: "As we celebrate the memorial of the blessed Passion, the Resurrection from the dead, and the glorious Ascension into heaven of Christ, your Son, our Lord."[131]

STUDY QUESTIONS

1. St. Thomas Aquinas holds that the offering of sacrifice is a precept of natural law. Why is the offering of sacrifice necessary?
2. Explain the ascending and descending aspects of priestly mediation.
3. Give three reasons why Christ's sacrifice on Calvary perfectly atones (makes satisfaction) for all the sins of the world.
4. Give five reasons why Christ's sacrifice on Calvary is the most perfect sacrifice that is possible.
5. Why does Christ's sacrifice on Calvary alone accomplish what all the sacrifices of the Mosaic Law could merely prefigure?
6. In what sense does the sacrifice of Calvary and the Mass have a Trinitarian dimension?
7. Why did Christ wish to give to His Church a sacrifice that would be offered until the end of time? Was the sacrifice of Calvary not sufficient?
8. In what way are the sacrifice of the Mass and the sacrifice of Calvary one?
9. What do the Council of Trent and *Mediator Dei* say about this?
10. In what way does the sacrifice of the Mass differ from Calvary?

---

[130] See also Heb 9:11–12: "But when Christ appeared as a high priest of the good things that have come, then through the greater and more perfect tent (not made with hands, that is, not of this creation) he entered once for all into the Holy Place, taking not the blood of goats and calves but his own blood, thus securing an eternal redemption." See also Heb 10:12. St. Thomas refers to Christ's intercession from heaven in *ST* III, q. 57, a. 6.

[131] Eucharistic Prayer I (*RM*, 641).

11. When is the sacrifice of the Mass sacramentally realized? What is the significance of the separate consecration of the species of bread and wine? Why must the Mass never be celebrated with just one of the elements (bread or wine alone)?

12. How is Christ's Paschal mystery able to transcend time so as to become present in every Mass?

13. In what sense does the Mass make present the whole of the Paschal mystery: Passion and death, Resurrection, and Ascension?

Suggestions for Further Reading

Council of Trent. Session 22, September 7, 1562 (DS, 1738–44 and 1751–54).

———. Session 23, July 15, 1563 (DS, 1764).

De la Taille, Maurice, S.J. *The Mystery of Faith*. Vol. 1, *The Sacrifice of Our Lord*. New York: Sheed & Ward, 1940.

Journet, Charles. *The Mass: The Presence of the Sacrifice of the Cross*. Translated by Victor Szczurek. South Bend, IN: St. Augustine's Press, 2008. Pp. 1–91.

Masure, Eugène. *The Christian Sacrifice*. Translated by Illtyd Trethowan. London: Burns & Oates, 1944.

Nicolas, Marie-Joseph. *What Is the Eucharist?* New York: Hawthorn Books, 1960. Pp. 57–75.

Pius XII. Encyclical on the Sacred Liturgy, *Mediator Dei*. November 20, 1947. See esp. §§67–79.

Vonier, Anscar. *A Key to the Doctrine of the Eucharist*. Bethesda, MD: Zaccheus, 2003.

✣

CHAPTER TEN

Objections to the Sacrificial Nature of the Mass

M artin Luther was not the first theologian to deny the sacrificial nature of the Mass. It had been previously denied by the English theologian John Wycliffe (1320–1384). It was with Luther, however, that the attack on the sacrifice of the Mass received much greater theological importance, due to its connection with the issue of justification and the nature of the Gospel.

Luther's attack on the sacrificial aspect of the Mass began in 1520 with his work *The Babylonian Captivity of the Church*, in which the Mass, understood as a "good work and a sacrifice," is presented as the third captivity of the Church and an invention of the devil,[1] although he admitted that it was seen as a sacrifice for centuries by the Tradition of the Church.[2] The sacrifice of the Mass was intimately connected in Luther's mind with the central notion of justification and served as the clearest practical illustration of the

---

[1] See Luther, *The Babylonian Captivity of the Church* (*LW*, 36:35–57). His position is further developed in *The Misuse of the Mass* (*LW*, 36:133–230, especially 162–98).

[2] See Luther, *The Babylonian Captivity of the Church*: "There is no opinion more generally held or more firmly believed in the church today than this, that the mass is a good work and a sacrifice. . . . I am attacking a difficult matter, an abuse perhaps impossible to uproot, since through century-long custom and the common consent of men it has become so firmly entrenched that it would be necessary to abolish most of the books now in vogue, and to alter almost the entire external form of the churches and introduce, or rather reintroduce, a totally different kind of ceremonies" (*LW*, 36:35–36). See also John Calvin, *Institutes*, bk. IV, ch. 18, no. 1: "He [Satan] blinded almost the whole world in the belief that the Mass was a sacrifice and oblation for obtaining the remission of sins" (Beveridge, 934).

Catholic understanding of salvation that he opposed, for he saw it as the quintessential attempt to procure salvation through a work rather than through faith alone.[3] This connection explains the passion that surrounded this issue in the sixteenth century. What Catholics saw as the summit of the Church's life and the supreme glorification of God, Luther and the entire Reformation viewed as an abomination deeply contrary to God's will.[4] Although Protestants differed with regard to the real presence, they all were united from the beginning in rejecting that the Mass is a sacrifice that makes present the sacrifice of Calvary. This became a central focus of the Reformation.[5]

OBJECTIONS OF LUTHER AND CALVIN TO THE SACRIFICE OF THE MASS

Argument from the Definition of a Sacrament and the Rejection of "Works"

Given the immense importance of the issue, it is worthwhile to reflect on Luther's reasons, which he outlines most clearly in his work *The Misuse of the Mass* (1522). His most central reason has to do with the dialectical opposition between law and faith (or law and gospel). This dialectic contrasts a relation to God through giving against one accomplished through receiving. The law is seen by Luther as the attempt

---

[3] See Francis Clark, *Eucharistic Sacrifice and the Reformation* (Westminster, MD: Newman Press, 1960), 103–10.

[4] See Joseph Ratzinger, "Is the Eucharist a Sacrifice?" trans. Michael J. Miller, in *TL*, 207:

> Although the question about the sacrificial character of the Eucharist is not in the foreground of the Catholic-Protestant theological dialogue today, it is nevertheless one of the decisive differences that gave the schism during the century of the Reformation its distinctive character, its spiritual and theological depth.... For Luther, the Mass, that is, the Eucharist understood as a sacrifice, is idolatry, an abomination, because it is a regression from the newness of Christianity back into pagan sacrificial practices; for a Catholic, it is the Christian way of glorifying God together through Christ in the Church. In fact, for Luther, the dispute about the Mass is only one illustration of the basic problem of justification; although he sees in it a perversion of the true nature of Christian faith and thinks that the center of Christianity is thereby destroyed and turned upside down.

[5] See Clark, *Eucharistic Sacrifice and the Reformation*, 99–101.

to justify oneself through works that one gives to God, whereas the gospel is *receiving* the gift of God's favor through the Cross of Christ. Joseph Ratzinger has given a good analysis of Luther's position and the theological concern underlying it:

> In the final analysis, for him there are only two opposing ways of relating to God: the way of the law and the way of faith. . . . The direction of faith is diametrically opposite to that of the law: it is receiving divine favor, not offering gifts. Consequently, Christian worship by its very nature can be receiving only, not giving; it is acceptance of God's saving deed in Christ Jesus, which suffices once for all. This means then, conversely, that Christian worship is by its very nature distorted, indeed, is turned into its very opposite, when offering is reintroduced instead of thanksgiving. . . . From this vantage-point, it is understandable that Luther saw in the idea of the Sacrifice of the Mass a denial of grace, a revolt of human autonomy, the backsliding from faith into the law that Paul fought so keenly.[6]

This dialectic between law and faith is operative in Luther's understanding of a sacrament. Since he sees the Gospel as essentially the reception of God's promise without the attempt to justify oneself by giving something back to God, he understands sacraments solely as signs attesting to God's promise of the forgiveness of sins.[7] A sacrament, for Luther, is essentially a visual or sensible promise of the core message of the Gospel, which is the forgiveness of our sins through faith in Christ's work of redemption on Calvary.[8] It follows that Luther acknowledges only what we can call the descending aspect of the sacraments, by which a promised blessing from God to man is attested, and he resolutely denies any ascending movement by which sacrifice is offered to God. He writes:

---

[6] Ratzinger, "Is the Eucharist a Sacrifice?" in *TL*, 207–08.

[7] See Luther, *The Babylonian Captivity of the Church*, where Luther defines sacraments as "those promises [of God] which have signs attached to them" (*LW*, 36:124).

[8] See Luther, *The Misuse of the Mass*: "Here [in the words of Institution] you see clearly that no work of satisfaction or sacrifice of reconciliation is of any use; only faith in the given body and the shed blood reconciles. Not that faith does the reconciling in and of itself, but it lays hold on and obtains the reconciliation which Christ has performed for us" (*LW*, 36:177).

> Sacrifice and promise are further apart than sunrise and sunset. A sacrifice is a work in which we present and give to God something of our own. The promise, however, is God's word, which gives to man the grace and mercy of God. So it is not merely false, but also incomprehensible to human reason to make out of God's promise a human sacrifice, and out of the word of divine majesty a work of a lowly creature.[9]

Or again:

> How can we then, out of this pledge and seal of God given to us as a gift, make a sacrifice and work of our own? Who among men would be so foolish as to sacrifice the seal on a letter, in which something is promised to him, to the one who makes the promise?[10]

The same point is made by comparison with Baptism:

> Who has ever been so mad as to regard baptism as a good work, or what candidate for baptism has believed that he was performing a work which he might offer to God on behalf of himself and communicate to others? If, then, there is no good work that can be communicated to others in this one sacrament and testament, neither will there be any in the mass, since it too is nothing else than a testament and sacrament.[11]

A first response has to do with Luther's understanding of sacrifice as a "good work," which he takes as a merely human action by which man offers something of his own to God in order to gain His favor. If the Mass were nothing more than a human work offered to God, then Luther would be right. But do Catholics regard the Mass as a "good work" in that sense? Christ instituted the Mass so that the Church can participate in offering an act of worship that infinitely transcends mere human activity and time itself. The Mass is the total self-offering of the Son of God to His Father in the Holy Spirit, and the Church's faithful are given the gift of being able to associate themselves with it.

---

[9] Ibid. (*LW*, 36:169).
[10] Ibid. (*LW*, 36:174).
[11] Luther, *The Babylonian Captivity of the Church* (*LW*, 36:48).

The Mass, therefore, is essentially a *theandric* action of Christ, joined by His Mystical Body, in which nothing less than Christ Himself is offered to the Father.[12]

A second response is that Luther's understanding of justification as purely passive underlies his rejection of the sacrificial dimension of the Mass. This understanding of justification precludes cooperation by the faithful in Christ's work of redemption and glorification of the Father. Catholic theology, on the contrary, holds that Christ has granted to His Mystical Body the privilege of participating in His work of glorification and redemption.[13] This participation, of course, is utterly subordinate to His grace and redeeming work and can be seen as its crown. Just as a good teacher is valued by his power to

---

[12] See Pius XII, *Mediator Dei*, §68: "The august sacrifice of the altar, then, is no mere empty commemoration of the passion and death of Jesus Christ, but a true and proper act of sacrifice, whereby the High Priest by an unbloody immolation offers Himself a most acceptable victim to the Eternal Father, as He did upon the cross." See also Second Vatican Council, *Sacrosanctum Concilium*, §7 ("Rightly, then, the liturgy is considered as an exercise of the priestly office of Jesus Christ"); Pius XII, *Mediator Dei*, §20 ("The sacred liturgy is, consequently, the public worship which our Redeemer as Head of the Church renders to the Father, as well as the worship which the community of the faithful renders to its Founder, and through Him to the heavenly Father. It is, in short, the worship rendered by the Mystical Body of Christ in the entirety of its Head and members"). See also Jungmann, *The Mass*, 112–13: "What is correctly connoted by this offering, however, is not an independent, autonomous action of the Church, an action proceeding purely from human power. It is an action proceeding from divine power and divine grace: 'from the many gifts you have given us' (*de tuis donis ac datis*). It is performed totally with the power communicated to the Church by Jesus Christ . . . as sharer in his priesthood. . . . So it is then that in the sacrifice of the Mass, Christ and the Church are at work together."

[13] See O'Neill, *New Approaches to the Eucharist*, 35:

> There is a close connection between this teaching [on the sacrifice of the Mass] and the Catholic doctrine of justification; and it is here that the sense of the principle of cooperation becomes clear. Because the Church believes that the faithful are *interiorly* transformed by grace (and in this *personal* way have the justice of Christ imputed to them), she consequently teaches that they can, always under and with Christ, cooperate freely and responsibly in their own salvation. This is a work of grace (that is, given by God); it is brought about, therefore, by the cross of Christ. Yet it is accomplished in such a way that it enables the Christian personally and actively to share in the unique and fundamental act of Christian atonement and worship which took place on Calvary.

make teachers, so the perfect Redeemer is one who can transform others, through His grace, into participants in the work of redemption and glorification. This is the heart of the mystery of the Church. The redeemed Body is vitally joined to its Head, from which all sanctification and glorification flow. Through this mysterious union with her Head and Bridegroom in the Mystical Body, the Bride can join sacramentally in the perfect offering worked by her Head.

Third, Luther's notion of justification shapes his understanding of the sacraments as essentially a *promise* with a sign attached to it.[14] A better definition of sacrament is that it is a sacred sign of man's effective sanctification through Christ[15] that realizes what it symbolizes. Man's sanctification, however, is twofold: it begins with the reception of God's grace and the forgiveness of sins, but it culminates in the task of giving back glory to Him through the exercise of virtue, which is made possible through cooperation with that grace.[16] We could refer to these two aspects as passive and active sanctification. It does not seem to be reasonable to think that the sacraments should be efficacious only in transmitting grace from God to man and contain no aid for man to give glory to God through Christ.[17] In other words, there is no reason why a sacrament should be only descending in its movement and not also ascending. St. Thomas Aquinas, contrary to Luther, sees a double finality in the sacraments of the New Covenant: "The sacraments of the New Law are ordained for a twofold purpose, namely, as a remedy for sin, and for the Divine worship."[18]

---

[14] See Luther, *The Babylonian Captivity of the Church* (*LW*, 36:124).

[15] See *ST* III, q. 60, a. 2, where he defines a sacrament as a "sign of a holy thing so far as it makes men holy."

[16] See *ST* I-II, q. 111, a. 2, on the distinction between operative and cooperative grace.

[17] See *ST* III, q. 63, a. 6 ("The sacraments of the New Law are ordained for a twofold purpose, namely, as a remedy for sin, and for the Divine worship"); q. 60, a. 5 ("In the use of the sacraments two things may be considered, namely, the worship of God, and the sanctification of man: the former of which pertains to man as referred to God, and the latter pertains to God in reference to man"); q. 62, a. 5; q. 65, a. 1.

[18] *ST* III, q. 63, a. 6. St. Thomas then explains that the aspect of divine worship, although in some way common to all the sacraments, is preeminently contained in the Eucharist: "Now a sacrament may belong to the Divine worship in three ways: first in regard to the thing done; secondly, in regard to the agent; thirdly, in regard to the recipient. In regard to the thing done, the Eucharist belongs to the Divine worship, for the Divine worship consists principally therein, so far as it is the sacrifice of the Church."

Christ, as the perfect mediator between God and man, works in both an ascending and a descending direction. As mediator, His task is not only to win grace for us but also to enable us to fulfill our end, which is to perfectly glorify God and offer Him pleasing worship. It is fitting that Christ's mediation in both directions be carried out sacramentally and liturgically, through sacred efficacious signs.

Furthermore, Catholics believe that the Eucharist is unique among the sacraments in being both a sacrifice and a sacrament, and thus it alone was instituted not only to be received as a means of sanctification but also to be something infinite—Christ's sacrifice—that we can offer to God to glorify Him.[19]

Argument from the Eucharist as Christ's Testament

Luther supports this general notion of sacrament as the sign or pledge of a promise by considering the word διαθήκη in the institution narratives, which Luther translates as "testament":

> Let this stand, therefore, as our first and infallible proposition—the mass or Sacrament of the Altar is Christ's testament [Luke 22:20; 1 Cor 11:25]. . . . You see, therefore, that what we call the mass is a promise of the forgiveness of sins made to us by God, and such a promise as has been confirmed by the death of the Son of God. For the only difference between a promise and a testament is that the testament involves the death of the one who makes it.[20]

Presupposing this idea that the Eucharist is essentially Christ's testament, Luther offers a parable to illustrate that it is not something that can be offered back to God, for that would be like offering back to God His own promised inheritance:

> If a prince were to allot his property to you and give you a written testament of his last will as a pledge, and he did

---

[19] See *ST* III, q. 79, a. 5: "This sacrament is both a sacrifice and a sacrament; it has the nature of a sacrifice inasmuch as it is offered up; and it has the nature of a sacrament inasmuch as it is received. And therefore it has the effect of a sacrament in the recipient, and the effect of a sacrifice in the offerer, or in them for whom it is offered."

[20] Luther, *The Babylonian Captivity of the Church* (*LW*, 36:37–38).

this out of kindness and goodness because of your poverty, demanding nothing from you except that you love and accept the testament with gratitude and joy and keep it intact; and if you were to go and offer the testament back to him, so as to increase his property and not your own, and you wished to be honored as a benefactor, while he would be disgraced by accepting something from you, a poor beggar: would you not be considered mad and foolish and lacking in understanding? ... This is the situation with the papist clergy when compared to the divine majesty because they consider the mass a sacrifice and presume to enrich God with his own promise. O abomination of all abominations![21]

In response, it is better to translate the word διαθήκη in all four institution narratives as "covenant" rather than "testament."[22] Jesus is instituting a new and definitive covenant between God and man. Covenants in the Old Testament were always sealed with the blood of animals offered to God and consumed by the faithful as a sign of the covenant fellowship with God.[23] Therefore, when Christ's Blood is said to be the "blood of the covenant," recalling Exodus 24:8, or "the New Covenant in His blood," this is clearly a reference to the sacrificial nature of the Eucharist as the sacrifice that seals the New Covenant between God and man, establishing communion. The "blood of the covenant" is sacrificial blood.[24]

Second, Christ's gift of Himself to us in the Eucharist is the greatest gift God could give, for it is the gift of Himself. Thus it is worthy

---

[21] Luther, *The Misuse of the Mass* (*LW*, 36:170).

[22] See Jungmann, *The Mass*, 9: "Here the Greek word *diatheke* must be (and now generally is) understood not to mean testamentary decree, as Luther wrongly supposed even in the words of the institution of the Eucharist."

[23] See Thomas Aquinas, commentary on 1 Corinthians 11, lec. 6, no. 678: "It should be noted that in antiquity the custom was that they would pour out the blood of some victim to confirm a pact. ... Therefore, just as the Old Testament or pact was confirmed by the figural blood of bulls, so the New Testament or pact was confirmed in Christ's blood, which was poured out in the passion. And in the cup the sacrament is so contained" (Larcher, *Commentary on the Letters of Saint Paul to the Corinthians*, 253).

[24] See Ratzinger, "Is the Eucharist a Sacrifice?" in *TL*, 212: "The idea of sacrifice unquestionably enters into the Last Supper event through the concept of 'blood of the covenant': the liturgy of the life and death of Jesus Christ is interpreted as a covenantal sacrifice, which adopts the Mosaic first step at a higher level."

not only for human recipients but also for God. Christ is worthy not only to be received by us but also to be offered to God.

Third, we can turn the parable back against Luther's use of it. If a king or benefactor gives to someone the gift of a great estate, the beneficiary would be morally obligated in gratitude to return some fruit of the estate to the giver of the gift. We see this in Jesus's parable of the tenant farmers. In such a case, however, only part of the fruit could be returned to the benefactor. Jesus has found a better solution for us. He gives us something better than a fruitful estate. He gives us Himself in such a way that He can be offered back to His Father, whole and entire and also received by each of the faithful, whole and entire. It is only in material things that a division among multiple recipients causes a lessening of the portions. Spiritual goods can be distributed to many without loss to the giver and without any lessening of the shares among the recipients, and the whole can be returned to the giver without loss to the recipients.

Objection That the Eucharist Is a Banquet Rather Than a Sacrifice

Luther seeks to support his denial of the sacrificial aspect of the Mass through Christ's words of institution, in which Jesus uses words referring to reception and eating, rather than to offering:

> When he says "take" he makes you thereby possessors of the gifts which he has given and broken. Therefore the word "take" does not admit of anything being sacrificed. It indicates rather that the gift which you take comes to you from God.[25]

Similarly, Luther assumes that the order to eat and drink is incompatible with the offering of sacrifice:

> "Eat and drink." That is all that we are to do with the sacrament. Therefore he breaks it, gives it, and tells us to take it, so that we eat and drink it and in so doing remember him and besides proclaim his death. Likewise Paul knew of no other work in this sacrament than eating and drinking [1 Cor 11:26]. ... But what we eat and drink we do not sacrifice; we keep it

---

[25] Luther, *The Misuse of the Mass* (*LW*, 36:172–73).

for ourselves and consume it.... To sacrifice to God and to be consumed by us are not compatible ideas. The Levites, indeed, took the offerings of the people of Israel, but they did not eat any of that which was to be sacrificed to God.[26]

Luther thus thinks that the idea that the Mass is a sacrifice is in contradiction with its aspect of communion and banquet:

We eat it completely, and offer it completely to God; that is as much as to say that when we offer it, we do not consume it, and when we consume it, we do not offer it. Hence, since we do both, we do neither. Who ever heard of such foolishness? It is all self-contradictory.[27]

John Calvin makes a similar argument:

While the Supper itself is a gift of God, which was to be received with thanksgiving, the sacrifice of the Mass pretends to give a price to God to be received as satisfaction. As widely as giving differs from receiving, does sacrifice differ from the sacrament of the Supper.[28]

The Catholic position, held by all of Christian antiquity, as seen in the Fathers of the Church and manifested in liturgies of all rites, is that the Mass is both a sacrifice offered to God and a supreme gift received from Him in a sacred banquet. The Victim is first mystically immolated and offered to God, and then given to the faithful to consume. These two aspects are not contradictory, but rather complementary, and they happen at two different moments. The Mass is essentially a *sacrificial banquet*, both sacrifice and banquet.[29] Similarly, the Mass is essentially constituted by *both* an ascending *and* a descending movement. That which is offered to God in an ascending movement is also received by the faithful in a descending movement of the giving of grace.

---

[26] Ibid. (LW, 36:173).

[27] Ibid. (LW, 36:174).

[28] Calvin, *Institutes*, bk. IV, ch. 18, no. 7 (Beveridge, 938).

[29] See John Paul II, *EE*, §48: "The 'banquet' always remains a sacrificial banquet marked by the blood shed on Golgotha."

Furthermore, Luther knew that many sacrifices mandated by the Law of Moses were both offered to God and consumed, at least in part, by Levites or the faithful. The most evident example is the paschal lamb that was immolated and offered to God in the Temple on the 14th of Nisan and then consumed entirely by the faithful on that evening. The paschal lamb, as the closest Old Testament type of the Eucharist, is a good illustration that the Eucharist was intended by Jesus to be both a sacrifice and a communion banquet. Similarly, peace offerings were also consumed by the faithful after being offered to God.[30]

Additionally, the notions of sacrifice and sacrificial banquet are intrinsically linked in the religious history of mankind.[31] The purpose of sacrifice is to bring about a reconciliation or fellowship between God and man, which is exemplified or represented by the sharing of a meal with God Himself. This is done by the fact that the sacrificial offering is first given to God, and then returned by God to the faithful to be consumed by them.

Finally, we have seen above that the words of institution are full of sacrificial overtones. As John Paul II states in *Ecclesia de Eucharistia*, §12: "Jesus did not simply state that what he was giving them to eat and drink was his body and his blood; he also expressed its *sacrificial meaning* and made sacramentally present his sacrifice which would soon be offered on the Cross for the salvation of all."[32] Christ affirms not only that we are to consume His Body and Blood, but also that His Body is "given for us" and that the Blood is "poured out for many."

---

[30] The bread of the Presence, for example, as mandated in Lev 24:5–9, was first offered to the Lord and then consumed by the priests. It was this bread of the Presence already offered to the Lord that was eaten by King David and his men in 1 Sam 21:4–6, to which Jesus refers in Matt 12:3–6.

[31] See, for example, Louis Bouyer, *Rite and Man: Natural Sacredness and Christian Liturgy*, trans. Joseph Costelloe (Notre Dame, IN: University of Notre Dame Press, 1963), 82–83: "Catholic theologians in modern times have taken great pains, but quite uselessly, to prove to Protestants that the Eucharist can *also* be a sacrifice, *even though* it is obviously a meal. . . . This shows on the part of both Protestants and Catholics a strange misunderstanding of ancient Christian tradition and the common customs of mankind. The very opposite is true. In antiquity the Eucharist was seen as the sacrifice of the Christians *because* it was the sacred meal of the Christian community." See also Yerkes, *Sacrifice in Greek and Roman Religions and Early Judaism*, 4–5; Levering, *Sacrifice and Community*, 65; Berman, *The Temple* 128–33.

[32] Italics original.

Jesus's words make it clear that there is a double giving of His Body and Blood. That which Jesus tells us to take and eat is "given *for us*." That which we are given to drink is "poured out for many for the forgiveness of sins" (Matt 26:28). But the pouring out of blood for the forgiveness of sins is the description of a sacrificial offering given to God on behalf of the faithful. In other words, the Body and Blood are given or poured out *for us* first in sacrifice, and then given *to us* to consume in communion.

Luther's objection that the Mass is essentially a banquet rather than a sacrifice seems to strike a chord also with many Catholics today because they rightly wish to highlight the communal dimension of the Mass. A banquet, at least at first sight, seems to be much more communal than a sacrifice. Furthermore, we have many natural experiences of communal banquets but none of sacrifices.

In reality, the offering of sacrifice, like feasting, is essentially a communal action, for it is offered by the community gathered together for worshipping and honoring God. This is emphasized by St. Augustine's definition of sacrifice as "every act that is designed to unite us to God in a holy fellowship."[33] The sacrifice of the Mass, however, is immeasurably more communal than the sacrifices of the religions of the world because it involves entering into the Trinitarian communion. In the sacrifice of the Mass, we are enabled to join with God the Son in offering Himself and ourselves to God the Father in the unity of the Holy Spirit. Furthermore, in the offering of the Mass, we put ourselves in union with the whole Mystical Body, even though they are not all present, as the Eucharistic Prayers manifest.[34] The communal nature of the sacrifice culminates in the Eucharistic banquet in which we receive the self-gift of a divine Person. The reception of that gift, however, enables us to enter more deeply into the interior dimension of sacrifice, which is to give ourselves back to the Father with the Son in the Spirit. Sacrifice and banquet together constitute a vital circle of giving and receiving the divine Love.

---

[33] Augustine, *City of God* 10.6 (Bettenson, 379). See Schönborn, *The Source of Life*, 77–78.

[34] See, for example, Eucharistic Prayer III: "You never cease to gather a people to yourself, so that from the rising of the sun to its setting a pure sacrifice may be offered to your name" (*RM*, 650).

Argument That the Mass as Sacrifice Implies an Angry God in Need of Appeasement

Another argument given by Luther against the sacrificial nature of the Mass is that the offering of sacrifice implies that God is angry and in need of appeasement, which is contrary to the Gospel and to the goodness of God evident in the gift of Communion:

> Furthermore, he who sacrifices wishes to reconcile God. But he who wishes to reconcile God considers him to be angry and unmerciful. And whoever does this does not expect grace or mercy from him, but fears his judgment and sentence. . . . Nothing can be more directly opposed to the profitable use of the sacrament than the teaching of the papists and these harmful consciences who believe that God is angry and needs to be appeased by this sacrifice. But if God were not so gracious and merciful, he would never have poured out so rich a treasure and given us such a precious gift.[35]

The best response to this objection is that God's graciousness and mercy is shown most in giving us not merely something to receive but also something to give back, for it is "more blessed to give than to receive" (Acts 20:35). Of ourselves, we have nothing to give to God that is capable of giving Him His due, nothing proportionate both to His goodness to us and to our offense against Him in sin. So God gives us something that we can give back that is proportionate to His own goodness—His Son. In other words, He gives us His only Son not only to receive but also, first, to give back in an ascending movement of praise, thanksgiving, satisfaction, and supplication. After participating in the offering of the Son to the Father and offering ourselves with Him, we are blessed to receive Him back in Communion as our glorious Bridegroom. In general, the best way to aid someone is to restore their dignity by making them able to offer something. Christ does this perfectly by enabling us to offer the sacrifice of the Mass with Him.

Secondly, the fact that the Mass is a propitiatory sacrifice does not mean that God is an angry or unmerciful God. A propitiatory sacrifice is one that is pleasing to God, and thereby serves to make satisfaction for sin and restore justice. In the Mass, we are able to give

---

[35] Luther, *The Misuse of the Mass* (*LW*, 36:175).

to God something more pleasing than sin is displeasing: Jesus Christ who offers Himself and associates us in His offering. This is a sign not of God's anger, but of His unspeakable graciousness and mercy in restoring our dignity. Reconciliation is not a burden, but rather a grace.

Objection That the Sacrifice of the Mass Implies That Christ Would Be Killed Again in Every Mass

John Calvin adds another important objection. If the Mass is a sacrifice, it seems that Jesus must be killed in every Mass:

> It is necessary that the victim which is offered be slain and immolated. If Christ is sacrificed at each Mass, he must be cruelly slain every moment in a thousand places. This is not my argument, but the apostle's: "Nor yet that he should offer himself often"; "for then must he often have suffered since the foundation of the world" (Heb 9:25, 26).[36]

The Council of Trent responded to this objection by distinguishing between a bloody and an unbloody mode of sacrifice.[37] Christ was offered on Calvary by a bloody sacrifice in which His Blood was physically separated from His Body so as to bring about His violent death. In the Mass Christ is the same Victim who is offered, but here His Blood is separated from the Body not physically, because Christ

---

[36] Calvin, *Institutes*, bk. IV, ch. 18, no. 5 (Beveridge, 937). The same objection was made by Thomas Cranmer (1489–1556), in "An Answer to a Crafty and Sophistical Cavillation Devised by Stephen Gardiner," in *Writings and Disputations of Thomas Cranmer Relative to the Sacrament of the Lord's Supper*, vol. 1 of *Works*, ed. John Cox (Cambridge: University Press, 1844), 348: "The papists, to excuse themselves, do say that they make no new sacrifice, nor none other sacrifice than Christ made, . . . but they say that they make the selfsame sacrifice for sin that Christ himself made. And here they run headlong into the foulest and most heinous error that ever was imagined, . . . then followeth it of necessity that they every day slay Christ and shed His blood." Zwingli made a similar charge against the sacrificial nature of the Mass, for he equated sacrifice with killing. See Keith D. Lewis, "'Unica Oblatio Christi': Eucharistic Sacrifice and the First Zürich Disputation," *Renaissance and Reformation*, n.s., 17, no. 3 (1993): 19–42.

[37] Council of Trent, Doctrine Concerning the Sacrifice of the Mass (session 22), ch. 2: "In this divine sacrifice that is celebrated in the Mass, the same Christ who offered himself once in a bloody manner on the altar of the Cross is contained and is offered in an unbloody manner" (DS, 1743).

can die no more, but under sacramental signs. Sacramental separation takes the place of physical separation of Body and Blood.[38]

Calvin's objection presupposes that every sacrifice has to involve a physical death. Sacrifice, however, is a symbolic act that visibly represents the interior oblation of the heart through the outward sign of a created good given to God and transferred to His dominion. The interior oblation of the heart of Christ is the same both on Calvary and in the Mass, for Christ's interior dispositions do not change, since "Jesus Christ is the same yesterday, today and forever" (Heb 13:8). The exterior representation of the interior oblation differs, however, in the Mass and on Calvary. On Calvary the Victim was transferred to the dominion of God by a physical death that could occur only once. In the Mass, that same interior oblation of the Victim is outwardly represented by the sacramental separation of Christ's Body and Blood in the separate consecration of the two species. This sacramental immolation can occur as many times as there are priests to offer the Mass in every time and place.

Roger Nutt has argued that Calvin's objection stems from a misunderstanding of the nature of a sacrament as a sacred sign that efficaciously makes present what it represents.[39] The Mass is a *sacramental* sacrifice, the "representative image"[40] of the sacrifice of Calvary. A sacramental image does not stand in competition with the sacred reality or event of which it is the image, nor does it seek to duplicate or multiply the event.[41] Rather, it serves precisely to bring about a living contact with the event of Calvary that is capable of mysteriously bridging every gap of time and place, enabling members of the Church in every century and country to participate in history's central event, which, as the sacrifice of the Incarnate Word and Lord of history, transcends all times and places.

As transubstantiation does not multiply bodies of Christ, but rather makes the one Body present to us under the appearances of bread and wine, so the sacrifice of the Mass does not multiply Christ's death or slay Him again and again, but likewise makes that one sacrifice present on every altar through the separate consecration of bread

---

[38] See Pius XII, *Mediator Dei*, §70.
[39] See Roger Nutt, *General Principles of Sacramental Theology*, 84–87.
[40] *ST* III, q. 83, a. 1.
[41] See Journet, *The Mass*, 32: "The sacrifice-institution, in our eyes, does not multiply the sacrifice-event; it multiplies the real presences of the sacrifice-event."

and wine into His one Body that was given for us, and His Blood that was poured out for the forgiveness of sins. The sacrifice of the Mass absolutely depends on the mystery of transubstantiation. Since Calvin denied transubstantiation, it is inevitable that the sacrificial nature of the Mass would likewise be denied. Without the real presence of the Body and Blood of the Victim of Calvary, we cannot have the sacramental *image* of the sacrifice of Calvary, but only a mere commemoration or shadow.

Objection That the Sacrifice of the Mass Would Detract from Calvary

What does the repetition of the offering of the Mass add if Calvary was completely sufficient and indeed infinitely superabundant? Does not the repetition detract from the dignity of the sacrifice of Calvary?

There are several answers to this crucial objection. First, Christ wants our participation in His glorification of the Father. He did not become man simply to take our place, but to raise us up and to make us one with Him. And if we are to become one with Him, we have to join Him in the offering of His supreme sacrifice and in the perfect worship of God that this entails.

In play here are two different ways of conceiving Christ's relationship with mankind that can be categorized as "substitution" and "participation." Did the Word become flesh to take our place in receiving punishment for sin and thus winning forgiveness? Or did He become man to give us a share in His divinity, charity, justice, and His perfect glorification of the Father? If we understand Christ's sacrifice as substitutionary punishment, then the Mass as a sacrifice will no longer make sense. Christ has already substituted for us on Calvary, and now we are free from the burden of sacrifice and merit. If, on the other hand, God desires our participation, then Christ's work was not finished on Calvary, but rather continues throughout the time of the Church as we continue to be drawn into a deeper participation in Christ's glorification of the Father in the sacrifice of the Mass.

A second answer has to do with our human condition, which is not content with merely abstract knowledge. Our human nature, which is both bodily and spiritual, requires frequent sensible manifestations of the invisible truths that we believe. Truths not frequently manifested outwardly fail to make an impression on men's lives. This is why our Savior instituted the seven sacraments as sensible outward signs and instituted the Mass as a solemn liturgical re-presentation and prolongation of the one sacrifice of Calvary, which would be offered "from the rising of the sun to its setting," according to the prophecy of Malachi 1:11.

The Eucharist makes the very sacrifice of our redemption—the center of all human history and the culmination of the yearning and history of Israel—present in our own lives. Mere historical knowledge of events in the distant past remains shadowy for us. We were not present at the sacrifice of Calvary. The Eucharist takes this weakness and need of human nature into account, suspending, as it were, the natural limitations of space and time. St. John Paul II writes: "In this gift Jesus Christ entrusted to his Church the perennial making present of the Paschal mystery. With it he brought about a mysterious 'oneness in time' between that *Triduum* and the passage of the centuries."[42]

A third way to answer this objection is to reflect on the relationship between a sacrament and the mystery that it makes present. Like the other sacraments, the Sacrament of the Eucharist is not in competition with the reality it represents—the Paschal mystery—but rather it glorifies that reality precisely by sacramentally extending its presence to touch us in our own time and place.[43] In other words, the sacramental presence of Christ and His sacrifice is entirely subordinated to the historical reality of Christ's Paschal mystery, and gives us mysterious access to it so that we can share in the offering and in its fruits.[44]

Thus we see that the real presence of Christ in the Eucharist does not diminish the importance of the visible presence of Christ through

---

[42] John Paul II, *EE*, §5.

[43] See *ST* III, q. 61, a. 1, ad 3: "Christ's Passion is a sufficient cause of man's salvation. But it does not follow that the sacraments are not also necessary for that purpose: because they obtain their effect through the power of Christ's Passion; and Christ's Passion is, so to say, applied to man through the sacraments according to the Apostle (Rom. 6:3): 'All we who are baptized in Christ Jesus, are baptized in His death.'"

[44] See Masure, *The Sacrifice of the Mystical Body*, 12: "The Mass presupposes the Cross to which it is related, but the reverse of this is not true. Far from derogating from the value of the Cross the Eucharist pays homage to it since without the reality of Calvary it could not achieve its purpose which is to contain the mystery and realize its fruits. It is identified with the mystery and consequently cannot detract from it any more than a man could ever be in opposition to the principle which gives him his own life and existence." See also Nutt, *General Principles of Sacramental Theology*, 94.

the Incarnation during His earthly life. On the contrary, because that incarnate presence was the most important event in the world, Christ wanted to extend it and make it available to all men. The same consideration applies to His Passion. Because His Passion was the most important act in the history of the world, Christ wanted to make all men capable of entering into a mysterious contact with it in the Eucharist and of offering it with Him.

A fourth answer is that God willed that the merits won for us once and for all on Calvary be applied to our souls chiefly through the holy sacrifice of the Mass, for, as the liturgy proclaims, "whenever the memorial of this sacrifice is celebrated the work of our redemption is accomplished."[45] Pius XII quotes this liturgical text in *Mediator Dei*, §79: "The august sacrifice of the altar is, as it were, the supreme instrument whereby the merits won by the divine Redeemer upon the cross are distributed to the faithful: 'as often as this commemorative sacrifice is offered, there is wrought the work of our Redemption.'" In each Mass, however, only some of that merit is concretely applied to us or distributed to us. This will be explained more fully below in chapter 12 on the fruits of the Mass.

The repetition of the Mass does not increase the merit of Christ's act of propitiation, for the merit of the sacrifice of Calvary was infinite, and thus it was capable of "purchasing" the redemption of all men who ever lived and would come into the world. However, this merit must be applied to our souls individually and progressively as we progressively sanctify ourselves.[46]

---

[45] Prayer over the Offerings, Holy Thursday Mass of the Lord's Supper (*RM*, 462). This liturgical text is quoted by St. Thomas in his article on the sacrifice of the Mass in *ST* III, q. 83, a. 1, as well as by the Second Vatican Council in *Sacrosanctum Concilium*, §2, which states that, through the liturgy, "the work of our redemption is accomplished"; *Lumen Gentium*, §3 ("As often as the sacrifice of the cross in which Christ our Passover was sacrificed, is celebrated on the altar, the work of our redemption is carried on"); *Presbyterorum Ordinis*, §13 ("In the mystery of the Eucharistic Sacrifice, in which priests fulfill their greatest task, the work of our redemption is being constantly carried on"); and by *The General Instruction of the Roman Missal*, §2 (*RM*, 19). It is also quoted by John Paul II in *EE*, §§11 and 21.

[46] Pius XII explains this in *Mediator Dei*, §77:

> This purchase, however, does not immediately have its full effect; since Christ, after redeeming the world at the lavish cost of His own blood, still must come into complete possession of the souls of men. Wherefore that the redemption and salvation of each person and of future

The constant sacramental re-presentation in the Church of the one sacrifice of Calvary, far from diminishing the value of the Cross, serves to impress upon the faithful the centrality of Christ's sacrifice, which is the center of history and the cause of all our hope.[47] The sacrifice of Calvary is so absolutely central and all-important that Christ wished it also to be the center of all our worship, the means of sanctifying the Lord's Day, and the fountain from which all graces flow, a fountain from which we can drink every day of our lives, so that we may live constantly from it and penetrate deeper into its mystery day by day, week by week.[48] May we all be able to say with John Paul II: "Holy Mass is the absolute center of my life and of every day of my life."[49]

Reactions against the Sacrificial Nature of the Mass in Theology of the Last Century

Is the Mass a Banquet Rather Than a Sacrifice?

In the last century, various Catholic theologians have advanced critiques against a sacrificial understanding of the Mass, privileging the notion of banquet over sacrifice. The eminent Catholic liturgist Josef A. Jungmann, S.J. (1889–1975) states this objection as it was often posed in the middle of the twentieth century:

---

generations unto the end of time may be effectively accomplished, and be acceptable to God, it is necessary that men should individually come into vital contact with the sacrifice of the cross, so that the merits, which flow from it, should be imparted to them. In a certain sense it can be said that on Calvary Christ built a font of purification and salvation which He filled with the blood He shed; but if men do not bathe in it and there wash away the stains of their iniquities, they can never be purified and saved.

[47] See *CCC*, §1085; Joseph Ratzinger, "The Theology of the Liturgy," in *TL*, 555–56.

[48] Pius XII, *Mediator Dei*, §79.

[49] John Paul II, Address in honor of the 30th anniversary of *Presbyterorum Ordinis*, §4 (*L'Osservatore Romano* English edition, November 15, 1995, p. 7). Benedict XVI quoted this and made it his own in his address to the clergy of Rome on May 13, 2005 in the Basilica of St. John Lateran.

In many places the idea has emerged that the meal, the social meal must be considered as the one and only basic form of the Mass; it is not the sacrifice, but the meal which determines the basic form of the Holy Mass. There is a table; bread and wine are put on it, one eats and one drinks. What are we to say to this?[50]

Is the Mass primarily a banquet or a sacrifice? Have the dominant currents of Catholic theology since the Reformation betrayed the original institution of Christ by unduly privileging the sacrificial aspect of the Mass?[51] Jungmann goes on to answer the objection that he posed above:

But if we look at the whole of the Mass-liturgy, where the Word, the word of thanksgiving, of praise, of consecration is decisive, which through the Word becomes an *Oblatio rationabilis*, then one cannot overlook the fact that the Mass is essentially and, I would say, predominantly an offering, planned as a sacrifice, which overflows in the form of a meal. The meal is previously consecrated and carried to God. This movement to God, the *Eucharistia*, determines the entire character of the celebration.[52]

The sensible sacramental sign includes the matter of both bread and wine, which points to the dimension of spiritual nourishment or banquet, and also the words of the form, which clearly express a sacrificial meaning, as explained above. The words of the form, however, carry the principal weight because they clarify and determine the meaning of the sacramental sign. As Jungmann says: "In the sacramental sacrifice, the sacramental sign is of two kinds: what one sees and

---

[50] Jungmann, *The Eucharistic Prayer*, 36.

[51] See Ratzinger, "The Theology of the Liturgy," in *TL*, 543: "Stefan Orth, in the vast panorama of a bibliography of recent works devoted to the theme of sacrifice, believed he could make the following statement as a summary of his research: 'In fact, many Catholics themselves today ratify the verdict and the conclusions of Martin Luther, who says that to speak of a sacrifice is 'the greatest and most appalling horror' and a 'damnable idolatry;' this is why we want to refrain from all that smacks of sacrifice" (the citation is from Orth, "Renaissance des Archaischen? Das neuerliche theologische Interesse am Opfer," *Herder Korrespondenz* 55 [2001]: 195–200, at 198).

[52] Jungmann, *The Eucharistic Prayer*, 36–37.

what one hears. And what one hears is the factor that determines the meaning of what one sees. . . . The entire Eucharistic Prayer expresses a God-ward movement, an offering."[53]

It is helpful to look at the Passover as the principal Old Testament type of the Mass. There is no doubt that the Passover was a sacred meal. Its sacred character, however, came from the fact that it was a sacrificial banquet in which the paschal lamb was first immolated and offered to God, and then received by the faithful as a sign of the reconciliation with God achieved by the sacrifice. The people's consumption of the victim signified participation in the sacrifice and in the sacredness of the victim dedicated to God as a sign of Israel's own dedication to the covenant and to its Lord. Sacrifice is not an afterthought or accidental aspect of the Jewish Passover in its original form when the sacrifice could still be offered in the Temple. Nor can the sacrifice be identified with the meal, for the meal is the culmination of the sacrifice, which it presupposes and brings to completion.

Has Christ Done Away with Cultic Sacrifice?

Some Catholic theologians of the past fifty years have maintained that the Eucharist can indeed be called a sacrifice, but only by radically reversing and "demythologizing" the meaning of the word. According to David N. Power (1932–2014),[54] the Eucharist does not stand

---

[53] Jungmann, *The Mass*, 139. See also John Paul II, *Dominicae Cenae*, §9 ("The Eucharist is above all else a sacrifice. . . . All who participate with faith in the Eucharist become aware that it is a 'sacrifice,' that is to say, a 'consecrated Offering.' For the bread and wine presented at the altar and accompanied by the devotion and the spiritual sacrifices of the participants are finally consecrated, so as to become truly, really and substantially Christ's own body that is given up and His blood that is shed"); and Apostolic Letter, *Mane Nobiscum Domine* (2004), §15 ("There is no doubt that the most evident dimension of the Eucharist is that it is a *meal*. . . . Yet it must not be forgotten that the Eucharistic meal also has a profoundly and primarily *sacrificial* meaning"; italics original).

[54] See David N. Power, *The Eucharistic Mystery: Revitalizing the Tradition* (New York: Crossroad, 1993), 320–21:

> When Justin Martyr said that Christians did indeed have a sacrifice but that it was no other than the thanks rendered for redemption in the death of Christ, his words recast religious reality in a new mould. They said something startling about the way to God that eliminated cultic sacrifice from the picture and placed the grateful memory of the cross in its stead and replaced the rites of sacrifice with the table of Christ's body and blood. . . . Later theology pointed to the death of Christ as

in continuity with the cultic sacrifices of man's religious history, for these involved a "mythical" view of man's relation to an angry God who needs to be appeased. Such a view of sacrifice was abolished by Christ's Paschal mystery,[55] which radically transformed the notion of sacrifice such that it no longer signifies the offering of a victim to God, but now is taken in the metaphorical sense of honoring God through a manifestation of praise, thanksgiving, and self-giving. To continue to understand the Mass as a propitiatory sacrifice is to remain in the realm of the cultic sacrifices.

It should be noted that this position would put the Christian sacrifice in opposition to the sacrifices of the world, rather than in typological continuity with them. It would involve a hermeneutic of rupture with the religious history of mankind, including that of Israel, rather than a relation of typological fulfillment.[56] Such a

---

the highest sacrifice in which all other sacrifices are fulfilled and for that reason rendered obsolete. That was not the meaning of the word as it was applied to the Eucharist and to the death of Christ in early writers, nor the meaning of taking the language of offering into the thanksgiving prayer itself. All ritual offerings ceased because of the way in which the Word Incarnate had wrestled with humankind's alienation from God in death and sin. Christ's pasch and its Eucharist were not one, albeit the highest form, in a series. They were outside the series, a totally different kind of reality. One could call them sacrifices because they realized superabundantly the end and purpose of sacrifice. To do this is to take sacrifice apart and to point to a different reality as the way to God. . . . The religious awe and power associated with cultic sacrifice was transferred to the memorial Eucharist, to the death remembered, to lives lived in obedience to this gospel, and to the witness of the martyrs.

For an insightful critique of the position of Power, see Matthew Levering, "John Paul II and Aquinas on the Eucharist," in *John Paul II & St. Thomas Aquinas*, ed. Michael Dauphinais and Matthew Levering (Naples, FL: Sapientia Press of Ave Maria University, 2006), 209–31, and "A Note on Joseph Ratzinger and Contemporary Theology of the Priesthood," *Nova et Vetera* (English) 5, no. 2 (2007): 271–84.

[55] This position is also maintained by Kilmartin, *The Eucharist in the West*, 184: "The problem with all theologies of the Mass of the post-Reformation period originates in the search for the grounds of sacrifice in the rite itself, and not in the representation of the sacrifice of the cross. Catholic theology did not take seriously enough the fact that 'sacrifice' in the history-of-religions sense was abolished with the Christ-event. In the Christ-event, sacrificial activity on the part of the creature is reduced to the obedience of Jesus before the Father, even unto death."

[56] For a penetrating critique of this type of position—a hermeneutic of rupture with regard to sacrifice—in contemporary theology, see Levering, *Sacrifice and Community*, esp. 1–28.

view is clearly not in harmony with the principle that "grace does not destroy nature"[57] or natural virtue but rather elevates and perfects it. The Catholic theological tradition, on the contrary, has understood the Mass as the supernatural elevation and perfection of man's natural religious duty to offer sacrifice to God as an exterior sign of his interior self-donation to Him. In becoming man, Christ has put Himself in solidarity with mankind's religious sense, enabling sacrifice finally to perfectly fulfill its fourfold goal of glorification, thanksgiving, supplication, and satisfaction for sin.

If one holds that the Eucharist is not a sacrifice in the cultic sense of an act in which a victim is offered to God, in what sense is the Mass still a sacrifice? In this view, it seems that the "sacrifice" coincides entirely with the aspect of banquet. According to Edward Kilmartin (1923–1994), the sacrifice of the Mass is precisely the meal as the sign of Christ's total self-offering to us, which provides the model of our Christian life:

> In the action of the Eucharist, the sacrifice of Christ is proclaimed by word and represented and applied to the community in the giving over of the eucharistic gifts as food. The outward form of the representation of the sacrificial offering of Jesus is not a sacrificial rite in the commonly understood sense, but the distribution of his body and blood as food of life. The basic structure is the sacrifice of self-offering in the signs of food.
>
> The Eucharist renders present the reality of the mystery of the cross in the form of a sacramental memorial meal of the Church. As sacrifice of the Church, it is disclosed as a sharing in the one sacrifice of Jesus. The goal of the Eucharist is the self-offering of the whole Church, head and body. . . . The visible sign of the sacrifice is the meal. There is the offering and sharing of the body and blood of Christ as food.[58]

It is undeniable that the self-offering of Jesus is the heart of the Eucharist. Nevertheless, it is important to distinguish the two aspects of this self-offering that we have referred to as ascending and descending. In this text of Kilmartin, the two aspects are conflated or blurred

---

[57] *ST* I, q. 1, a. 8, ad 2.
[58] Kilmartin, *The Eucharist in the West*, 199.

together, giving the impression that the sacrifice is Christ's offering of Himself *to us* under the appearances of food, rather than His self-offering to His Father.[59] Jesus first offers Himself *for* us in an ascending motion *to the Father*, as He is sacrificed "for the life of the world" (John 6:51), and then He offers Himself *to* us to be our life.[60] There is sacrifice and communion, and the latter presupposes the former. The Church is invited to join in both aspects: offering Jesus to the Father in sacrifice and herself with Him, and receiving the sacrificial Victim in Communion. For this reason, we cannot identify the sacrifice with the sacred banquet, but rather we should see them as complementary movements of ascending and descending mediation.

Contrary to the views of Power and Kilmartin, in which the Mass is a sacrifice in a metaphorical and non-cultic sense, St. John Paul II, in harmony with the whole Tradition, teaches that the Mass is a sacrifice "in the strict sense" of the word, as a religious offering made to God.[61] It is a true sacrifice not principally because Christ is offered to us as our spiritual nourishment, but because it contains Christ's self-offering to the Father, in which His Mystical Body is called to share. John Paul writes:

> By virtue of its close relationship to the sacrifice of Golgotha, the Eucharist is *a sacrifice in the strict sense*, and not only in a general way, as if it were simply a matter of Christ's offering himself to the faithful as their spiritual food. The gift of his love and obedience to the point of giving his life (cf. John 10:17–18) is in the first place a gift to his Father. Certainly it is a gift given for our sake, and indeed that of all humanity (cf. Matt 26:28; Mk 14:24; Lk 22:20; John 10:15), yet it is *first and foremost a gift to the Father*: "a sacrifice that the Father accepted, giving, in return for this total self-giving by his Son, who 'became obedient unto death' (Phil 2:8), his own

---

[59] See O'Neill, *New Approaches to the Eucharist*, 66.

[60] This double giving is well stated in CIC, can. 899, §1: "In it [the celebration of the Eucharist] Christ the Lord, by the ministry of a priest, offers Himself, substantially present under the forms of bread and wine, to God the Father and gives Himself as spiritual food to the faithful who are associated with His offering."

[61] John Paul II, *EE*, §13. See Levering, "John Paul II and Aquinas on the Eucharist," 226: "The pope thus rules out the strictly metaphorical sense of sacrifice that would focus, as Power does, on the memorial meal."

paternal gift, that is to say the grant of new immortal life in the resurrection."

In giving his sacrifice to the Church, Christ has also made his own the spiritual sacrifice of the Church, which is called to offer herself in union with the sacrifice of Christ.[62]

Is the Sacrificial Aspect of the Mass a Later Development?

Many Catholic theologians hold that there is a sacrificial dimension of the Mass but that it is a later development that deeply modified the original form of the Mass as practiced in the first Christian communities. Paul Bradshaw gives a hypothetical reconstruction of how this development came about. The starting point is not just the Last Supper, but rather all the meals that the disciples shared with Jesus. It is reasonable to think that the early Christian community would have continued to hold communal meals as they had with Jesus:

> I believe that the regular sharing of meals was fundamental to the common life of the first Christian communities, as it apparently had been to Jesus' own mission. At these meals they would have experienced an eschatological anticipation of God's kingdom, one of the primary marks of which was that the hungry are fed and many come from East and West to feast (Matt 8:11; Luke 13:29), and they would have responded by calling upon Jesus to return, crying *Marana tha* (1 Cor 16:22; Didache 10.6; Rev 22:20). They would have recalled stories of Jesus eating—not just with his disciples but scandalously with tax collectors and sinners. They would have recollected that he had miraculously fed large multitudes with small quantities of food. And they would have remembered that he had once, perhaps in relation to one of these feeding miracles, associated his own flesh with bread. At least some communities of impoverished Christians, whose staple food would have been bread and little else and whose meals generally did not include wine, came to associate what they called the breaking of bread with feeding on the flesh of Jesus.[63]

---

[62] John Paul II, *EE*, §13 (italics original).

[63] Bradshaw, "Did Jesus Institute the Eucharist at the Last Supper?" 17–18.

How then did the Christian communal meal become associated with Christ's sacrifice and with the Last Supper? Bradshaw thinks that St. Paul was the key architect of this transformation:

> Someone, however, possibly St. Paul himself, did begin to associate the sayings of Jesus with the supper that took place on the night before he died, and interpreted them as referring to the sacrifice of his body and blood and to the new covenant that would be made through his death. This interpretation had some influence within the churches founded by Paul and possibly beyond. It certainly reached the author of Mark's Gospel, who inserted a version of the sayings into his already existing supper narrative, perhaps because he was compiling his account of Jesus in Rome, where the Christians were particularly subject to sporadic persecution and so the association of their own spiritual meals with the sacrificed body and blood of their Savior would have been especially encouraging to believers facing possible martyrdom themselves, however novel to them was this juxtaposition of the two traditions. But this combination does not otherwise seem to have been widely known in early Christianity. It was only much later, as the New Testament books gained currency and authority, that it began to shape both the catechesis and the liturgy of the churches, and to shift the focus of Eucharistic thought from feeding to sacrifice.[64]

Bradshaw's reconstruction of the emergence of the Mass as sacrifice is untenable first of all because it leaves aside the crucial data that we have in our four parallel accounts of the institution of the Eucharist, regarding them as secondary, and instead offers a reconstruction that is almost entirely hypothetical and unsupported by the data of the New Testament.[65] St. Paul introduces his account of the

---

[64] Ibid., 18–19.
[65] See Ratzinger, "The Theology of the Liturgy," in *TL*, 545:

> The problem has been aggravated by the fact that the most recent movement of "enlightened" thought goes much farther than Luther: whereas Luther still took literally the accounts of the institution and made them, as the *norma normans*, the basis of his efforts at reform, the hypotheses of historical criticism have long since caused a broad erosion of the texts. The accounts of the Last Supper are seen as the

institution of the Eucharist, written about a quarter of a century after the Last Supper, with words that solemnly emphasize that he is transmitting something certain—Apostolic Tradition that he himself has received: "For I received from the Lord what I also delivered to you" (1 Cor 11:23).[66] We have seen above that the language of the institution narratives is steeped in sacrificial concepts and terminology. From the beginning, the Mass appears to us as the sacrifice of the New Testament and the realization of the prophecy of Malachi 1:11.

---

product of the liturgical construction of the community; behind the texts an historical Jesus is sought who could not have been thinking of the gift of His Body and Blood or understood His Cross as a sacrifice of expiation; we should, rather, imagine a farewell meal that included an eschatological perspective.

See also Ratzinger, *The Feast of Faith*, 43–44 (*TL*, 306–07):

At one point, however, we must disagree with Schürmann. His thesis, that the apostolic Eucharist is a continuation of Jesus' daily table fellowship with his disciples, was limited to the question of the structural origin of the celebration, but it is used by many people who wish to deny that anything was "instituted" at the Last Supper and who assume that the Eucharist originated more or less exclusively in Jesus' meals with sinners. This view identifies the Eucharist of Jesus with a strictly Lutheran doctrine of justification, namely, the pardoning of the sinner; ultimately, among those who see Jesus' eating with sinners as the only solid fact about the historical Jesus which has come down to us, the whole of Christology and theology is reduced to this one factor. It results in a view of the Eucharist which has nothing in common with primitive Christianity. Whereas Paul says that those who approach the Eucharist in sin "eat and drink judgment" upon themselves (1 Cor 11:29) and pronounces an anathema to protect the Eucharist from abuse (1 Cor 16:22), proponents of this view see it as the essence of the Eucharist that it is available to all without distinction and without conditions. . . . The fact that this thesis contradicts the entire eucharistic inheritance of the New Testament indicates the wrong-headedness of its basic assumption: the Christian Eucharist was not understood in the context of Jesus' eating with sinners.

[66] See Jeremias, *The Eucharistic Words of Jesus*, 186: "Of all forms of the account of the Lord's Supper that of Mark shows by far the strongest Semitic speech coloring; the Lukan form has already been more assimilated to Greek style; in Paul—although his account is the oldest from a literary perspective—the graecizing has advanced the farthest. This result is of far-reaching significance for the question of the age of the tradition of the eucharistic words of Jesus." On the date of Paul's account in 1 Cor 11 and its sources, see ibid., 188. Although Paul's account of the institution narrative is the earliest of the four New Testament texts, the oral tradition on which the synoptic accounts are based is still more primitive.

But if, for the sake of argument, we accept Bradshaw's reconstruction of the emergence of the Mass understood as a sacrifice, should this change the way we should understand the Mass? Bradshaw thinks so:

> Does any of this matter? Is it important whether the ultimate roots of Jesus' sayings may lie in the life-giving feeding of those who were hungry rather than in primary association with his imminent death? Did not that sacrificial death also come to be viewed by Christians as life-giving, and therefore to an equal degree as spiritually nourishing? Was anything really lost? I think so. While I believe it was, and is, perfectly legitimate for Christians to interpret Jesus' sayings in relation to his death, whenever and wherever they may have first been uttered, yet I believe a valuable balanced insight was lost by an excessive focus on the power of his sacrificed body and blood and a consequent diminishing of the value of his living and nourishing flesh and blood. In particular, it led in the course of time to a decline in the reception of communion, as that came to be seen as less important for believers than the offering of the Eucharistic sacrifice—to a disproportionate emphasis, if you like, on altar rather than on table.[67]

Bradshaw's conclusion presupposes that communion and sacrifice are related in such a way that a greater emphasis on the one would inevitably lead to a lesser emphasis on the other. We must choose: altar or table. Excessive emphasis on the sacrificial dimension is held responsible for diminishing the appreciation of Communion in the Middle Ages and up to our time.

I would respond that the notions of sacrifice and communion are not inversely related such that an emphasis on one necessarily detracts from the other, even though that may sometimes happen in practice. When that happens, it is a symptom of a misunderstanding of the relationship between sacrifice and communion, for they are complementary aspects of one integral whole in which the aspects of presence, sacrifice, and spiritual nourishment are intimately tied up with one another and presuppose each other.

Because Jesus is truly present and offered, the Eucharist is a sacrifice that culminates in a sacrificial banquet in which one has

---

[67] Bradshaw, "Did Jesus Institute the Eucharist at the Last Supper?" 19.

communion with the Victim, with God, with whom reconciliation has been made by the sacrifice, and with all those who share in the sacrifice in the communion of the Church. Christ's Flesh is life-giving not only because it is the Flesh of the Second Person of the Trinity but also because it has been sacrificed "for the life of the world" (John 6:51). The sacrifice does not detract from the life-giving nature of Christ's Flesh, but adds a new title to its vital power and enables us to receive life in Him as its fruit.

The immensity of the sacrificial dimension of the Mass is measured by the magnitude of the fruit of communion that it wins, which is the reception of the Flesh of Jesus given for the life of the world that binds us with Him and one another in the Spirit. The reception of Communion then enables the recipient to offer himself in a deeper and more Christlike way to the Father. Communion thus perfects the movement of sacrifice, just as the sacrifice prepares for a more perfect union.

Or to put it another way, the greatness of the Eucharist lies in the fact that it perfectly unites the ascending and descending movements that make up religion and Christ's perfect mediation between man and God. God is glorified by the Church through the ascending movement of the sacrificial offering of the Word made flesh, and man is sanctified in the Church through the blessing of Holy Communion with that life-giving and Spirit-imparting Body. The ascending movement is ordered to the descending, and vice versa, creating a "vital circle." The sacrifice prepares for Communion, and each Communion nourishes the Church in the likeness of Christ so that she can give herself more fully in the sacrifice of her Head.

Study Questions

1. Why does Luther acknowledge only a descending or receptive dimension to the sacraments?

2. How is Luther's understanding of the sacraments connected with his rejection of the sacrificial dimension of the Mass?

3. How can one respond to Luther's objection that the Lord's Supper is essentially a banquet in which we are to "take," "eat," and "drink," and thus not an offering or sacrifice?

4. How can one respond to the objection that the sacrifice of the Mass implies the false image of an angry God?

5. Is Christ killed again in every Mass?
6. How can one respond to the objection that the sacrifice of the Mass and its multiplication detracts from the centrality of the sacrifice of Calvary?
7. How can one respond to the objection that Christ's Passion has put an end to cultic sacrifice?

Suggestions for Further Reading

Calvin, John. *Institutes of the Christian Religion*. Translated by Henry Beveridge. Peabody, MA: Hendrickson, 2008. Bk. IV, ch. 18 (pp. 933–45).

Journet, Charles. *The Mass: The Presence of the Sacrifice of the Cross*. Translated by Victor Szczurek. South Bend, IN: St. Augustine's Press, 2008. Pp. 1–91.

Jungmann, Josef A. *The Mass: An Historical, Theological, and Pastoral Survey*. Edited by Mary E. Evans. Translated by Julian Fernandes. Collegeville, MN: The Liturgical Press, 1976. Pp. 82–84, 97–121, 138–52.

Levering, Matthew. "John Paul II and Aquinas on the Eucharist." In *John Paul II & St. Thomas Aquinas*. Edited by Michael Dauphinais and Matthew Levering. Naples, FL: Sapientia Press of Ave Maria University, 2006. Pp. 209–31.

———. *Sacrifice and Community: Jewish Offering and Christian Eucharist*. Malden, MA: Blackwell Publishing, 2005. Pp. 1–28.

Luther, Martin. *The Babylonian Captivity of the Church*. In *LW*. 36:35–57.

———. *The Misuse of the Mass*. In *LW*. 36:133–230, especially 162–98.

Ratzinger, Joseph. "Is the Eucharist a Sacrifice?" In *TL*. Pp. 207–17.

✠

CHAPTER ELEVEN

The Participation of the Faithful in Offering the Sacrifice of the Mass

THE COMMON PRIESTHOOD OF THE FAITHFUL

Communal Nature of Sacrifice

One reason that it is difficult for modern man to understand the Eucharistic sacrifice is that sacrifice by its very nature is a social and public action in which an interior oblation is represented exteriorly and socially, and presented to God by a community through the mediation of a priest. Modern society, on the contrary, tends to conceive of religious acts as exclusively personal and individual.

There are two reasons for the communal nature of sacrifice. First of all, man is a social creature. Therefore it is fitting that God be adored, be thanked, be petitioned, and have satisfaction made not only by isolated individuals but by whole communities or societies. Each one of us needs to do these things as a member of society in its different levels. Secondly, sacrifice offered to God is not only an essentially social act but also one that, by its very nature, binds society more closely together by expressing the common orientation of society to its proper end, which is union with God and the manifestation of His glory and goodness through sharing in them. Sacrifice, therefore, serves to "re-bind"[1] society with God and the members of society with one another. Sacrifice has a binding power in both the vertical and

---

[1] The etymological meaning of "religion" is to "bind back again": re-ligare.

the horizontal dimensions. It can bind members of a society together because it first binds society with its ultimate unifying principle, which is God. It follows that rightly ordered sacrifice is a foundational principle for constituting a society as "city of God" in the Augustinian sense, meaning a society ordered to the glory of God rather than of man.[2]

The social aspect of sacrifice is manifested by being offered on behalf of the community by one who represents the community in its relations with God. This is the task of the priest who acts as a mediator between God and man, according to Hebrews 5:1: "For every high priest chosen from among men is appointed to act on behalf of men in relation to God, to offer gifts and sacrifices for sins." Without a visible priesthood by which some act on behalf of the whole community is made, sacrifice would lose its essential social dimension. If every individual offered his own sacrifice, serving as his own priest, there would be no offering by the community as a whole and sacrifice would not help society to be bound together by offering something in common to its Lord.

The fact that the priest is offering the sacrifice on behalf of the people does not mean that the people for whom sacrifice is offered are not involved in the sacrifice. As stated above, every person has a moral duty to give to God His due through offering sacrifice. The role of the priest is not to *substitute* for the people in the offering, but to *represent* them by offering on their behalf, in such a way that the people offer sacrifice together *through* the hands of the priest. In every ritual sacrifice, therefore, we can distinguish a ministerial priest who offers on behalf of the community and the people as a whole who offer through him.

Furthermore, as mentioned above, every ritual sacrifice, by its nature, is an external sign of the interior oblation of the hearts of the faithful. This interior oblation is not just that of the priest, but that of the people who offer through the priest and on behalf of whom sacrifice is offered. The logic of sacrifice requires that each person make his own interior act of self-offering and intend that it be represented by the external bodily sacrifice that is offered on the people's behalf by the priest, who is their mediator before God. Thus the people consent to the offering of the victim as the sign of their own interior act that they are making together with the community.

In other words, in the offering of sacrifice, not everything is del-

---

[2]   See Augustine, *City of God* 10.6; 10.25; 12.9; 14.28; 15.21.

egated to the priest. <u>The external offering alone is delegated so that</u> <u>there can be one external offering for the many.</u> The interior offering <u>of the heart, however, cannot be delegated to the priest, for all of the</u> <u>faithful must order and offer themselves to God personally through</u> <u>the gift of their wills, conforming themselves to His will.</u> This is the reality represented by the external offering.

The distinction between the priest who sacrifices and the people who sacrifice through the priest is common to religious societies in general. We can speak of a ministerial priesthood and a "common priesthood" of the whole people, using the word analogically. The ministerial priest is a priest in the proper sense of the word, one who offers an external sacrifice on behalf of the community to represent their interior sacrificial offering, which implies that they too share in performing a priestly role, but one that is carried out interiorly. Although common to religious societies in general, we see this distinction made explicit in Israel and the Church.

The Common Priesthood of the Faithful in Israel

The Mosaic Law stipulates that there be a ministerial priesthood taken from the sons of Aaron. The whole of Israel, however, is spoken of as a priestly people. In Exodus 19:5–6, at the foot of Mount Sinai, God tells the people of Israel: "if you will obey my voice and keep my covenant, you shall be my own possession among all peoples; for all the earth is mine, and you shall be to me a kingdom of priests and a holy nation." Even though only the descendants of Aaron were subsequently made ministerial priests, the entire people of Israel exercised a "common priesthood" by which they were to offer the interior sacrifice of obedience to God in faith, hope, and charity, manifested externally in the offering of the ritual victims through the ministry of the Levitical priesthood. Through their common priesthood, the whole people participated in glorifying God through the offering of a sacrifice pleasing to Him. The people's participation in the offering of sacrifice is also manifested in their consuming a part of what was offered. This was most visible in the sacrifice of the paschal lamb and in peace offerings.

The fact that the sacrifices of Israel were offered by the faithful to represent the interior offering of the heart can also be seen in the fact that God is not always pleased with the sacrifices of Israel. Sometimes this is because Israel does not offer an exterior worship in accordance with what God has requested, as in the case of the golden calf or the sacrifices of the Northern Kingdom denounced by the prophets.[3] At other times, however, the sacrifices are unwelcome not because of anything irregular in the exterior offering but because the hearts of the people are not turned to the Lord. The exterior sacrifices are meant to represent the offering of the heart, and when this is not the case, such offerings are said to be an abomination to the Lord. Isaiah 1:11–15 states this in graphic terms:

> What to me is the multitude of your sacrifices?
>   says the LORD;
> I have had enough of burnt offerings of rams
>   and the fat of fed beasts;
> I do not delight in the blood of bulls,
>   or of lambs, or of he-goats.
>   . . . I cannot endure iniquity and solemn assembly.
> Your new moons and your appointed feasts
>   my soul hates;
> they have become a burden to me,
>   I am weary of bearing them.
> When you spread forth your hands,
>   I will hide my eyes from you;
> even though you make many prayers,
>   I will not listen;
> your hands are full of blood.

Here God is not saying that the sacrifices of the Israelites were deficient because of a defect in the exterior offering. The problem was the lack of purity of heart in the faithful. Since the nature of sacrifice demands the sacrifice of the heart as the primary thing, not all sacrifices are pleasing to God.

The Common Priesthood of the Faithful in the New Covenant

The Church inherited from Israel the awareness that the new People of God is a priestly people called to offer spiritual sacrifices, the distinction between the ministerial and the common priesthood, and the

---

[3]   See, for example, 1 Kings 13.

understanding that the exterior sacrifice offered by the ministerial priest is to be an image of the interior oblation of the heart of the faithful.

Speaking of the dignity of the baptized faithful, 1 Peter 2:9 quotes Exodus 19:6: "But you are a chosen race, a *royal priesthood*,[4] a holy nation, God's own people, that you may declare the wonderful deeds of him who called you out of darkness into his marvelous light." The whole Church is spoken of as having a common or royal priesthood, a priesthood belonging to the whole kingdom because Christ gave His sacrifice to the whole Church to be her offering. All the faithful share in Christ's priesthood in the sense that they are called to offer up the interior holocaust of hearts made pure and of their Christian lives, spiritually joined to the sacrifice of Christ made present on our altars in the holy Mass, and so call down blessings upon men.[5]

Exodus 19:6 is also alluded to in Revelation 1:5–6: "To him who loves us and has freed us from our sins by his blood and made us a kingdom, priests to his God and Father"; and Revelation 5:9–10 points to it as well: "Worthy are you to take the scroll and to open its seals, for you were slain and by your blood you ransomed men for God from every tribe and tongue and people and nation, and have made them a kingdom and priests to our God, and they shall reign on earth." The royal priesthood of the faithful is depicted here as the great fruit of the sacrifice of the Lamb who was slain. Christ the High Priest, by offering Himself in sacrifice, has engendered a priestly kingdom to offer the same Lamb through His ministerial priests.

Spiritual Sacrifices of the Common Priesthood

Since the faithful have been given this great dignity of the common priesthood, they are called to offer spiritual sacrifices through Christ. Every act of charity is said to be an acceptable sacrifice. The letters of St. Paul and the Letter to the Hebrews exhort the faithful to offer such sacrifices. Hebrews 13:15–16 speaks of the faithful offering a

---

4   Exod 19:6 is quoted according to the Septuagint, which translates "kingdom of priests" (מַמְלֶכֶת כֹּהֲנִים) with "royal priesthood" (βασίλειον ἱεράτευμα).

5   See *ST* III, q. 82, a. 1, ad 2: "A devout layman . . . has a spiritual priesthood for offering spiritual sacrifices, of which it is said (Ps 50:19): 'A sacrifice to God is an afflicted spirit'; and (Rom 12:1): 'Present your bodies a living sacrifice.' Hence, too, it is written (1 Pt 2:5): 'A holy priesthood, to offer up spiritual sacrifices.'"

"sacrifice of praise" through their lives: "Through him then let us continually offer up a sacrifice of praise to God, that is, the fruit of lips that acknowledge his name. Do not neglect to do good and to share what you have, for such sacrifices are pleasing to God."

An example of a spiritual sacrifice is given in Philippians 4:18, which uses sacrificial language to speak of the gifts given by the community of the Philippians to St. Paul in captivity: "I am filled, having received from Epaphroditus the gifts you sent, a fragrant offering, a sacrifice acceptable and pleasing to God."

St. Paul also speaks of the royal priesthood of the faithful and the offering of the sacrifice of their own Christian lives in Romans 12:1: "I appeal to you therefore, brethren, by the mercies of God, to present your bodies as a living sacrifice, holy and acceptable to God, which is your spiritual worship."[6] By speaking of our bodies as a living sacrifice, the entire bodily dimension of the Christian life is included in what can and should be offered to God. The term *logikḗ latreía*, translated here rather inadequately as "spiritual worship," is very rich. It could also be translated as "worship in the Logos," which means worship in Christ and His Spirit. The whole of the Christian life and the entire scope of the double commandment of love pertain to this worship in the Logos that is our living sacrifice.

This is a theme particularly dear to the Fathers. St. Peter Chrysologus, for example, speaking on Romans 12:1, writes:

> Listen now to what the Apostle urges us to do. "I appeal to you," he says, "to present your bodies as a living sacrifice." By this exhortation of his, Paul has raised all men to priestly status. . . . Each of us is called to be both a sacrifice to God and his priest. Do not forfeit what divine authority confers on you. Put on the garment of holiness, gird yourself with the belt of chastity. Let Christ be your helmet, let the cross on your forehead be your unfailing protection. Your breastplate

---

[6]   For the relationship of Rom 12:1 to the Eucharist, see Jeremy Driscoll, O.S.B., "Worship in the Spirit of Logos: Romans 12:1–2 and the Source and Summit of Christian Life," *Letter & Spirit* 5 (2009): 77–101; Robert Daly, S.J., *Sacrifice Unveiled: The True Meaning of Christian Sacrifice* (London: Continuum and T. and T. Clark, 2009), 57–58. For an interpretation of Romans 12:1–2 as a reversal of Romans 1:18–32, see Michael Thompson, *Clothed with Christ: The Example and Teaching of Jesus in Romans 12.1–15.13* (Sheffield, UK: JSOT Press, 1991), 80–85.

should be the knowledge of God that he himself has given you. Keep burning continually the sweet smelling incense of prayer. Take up the sword of the Spirit. Let your heart be an altar. Then, with full confidence in God, present your body for sacrifice. God desires not death, but faith; God thirsts not for blood, but for self-surrender; God is appeased not by slaughter, but by the offering of your free will.[7]

St. Augustine characteristically gives an ecclesial reading to Romans 12:1, interpreting the word "body" also as the ecclesial body of the Church. In *The City of God* 10.6 he writes:

It follows that the whole of that redeemed city, that is, the congregation or communion of saints, is offered as a universal sacrifice to God through the High Priest who, 'taking the form of a servant,' offered Himself in His passion for us that we might be the body of so glorious a Head. . . . When, therefore, the Apostle had exhorted us to present our bodies as a sacrifice, living, holy, pleasing to God—our spiritual service . . . he went on to remind us that it is we ourselves who constitute the whole sacrifice. . . . Such is the sacrifice of Christians: "We, the many, are one body in Christ."[8]

St. Augustine then identifies this ecclesial spiritual worship, in which the whole Body of the Church offers herself, with the sacrifice of the Mass: "This is the Sacrifice, as the faithful understand, which the Church continues to celebrate in the sacrament of the altar, in which it is clear to the Church that she herself is offered in the very offering she makes to God."[9] Christ cannot be offered apart from the Body of which He is the Head. The offering of the Christian life of the faithful, therefore, is intrinsic to the Mass, for the Head and the Body cannot be separated.

Benedict XVI has a rich commentary on Romans 12:1 in his

---

[7] Peter Chrysologus, Sermon 108 (PL, 52:499–500), in the *Liturgy of the Hours*, Tuesday of the Fourth Week of Easter, Office of Readings, 2nd Reading.

[8] Augustine, *City of God* 10.6, in *The City of God, Books VIII–XVI*, trans. G. G. Walsh and G. Monahan, FC 14 (Washington, DC: Catholic University of America Press, 1952), 126–27. See the commentary on this text by Lang, "Augustine's Conception of Sacrifice in *City of God*," 29–51, esp. 42–45.

[9] Augustine, *City of God* 10.6 (Walsh and Monahan, 127).

apostolic exhortation *Sacramentum Caritatis*, in which he develops St. Augustine's ecclesial interpretation and applies it to the participation of the faithful in the Mass:

> Here the eucharistic celebration appears in all its power as the source and summit of the Church's life, since it expresses at once both the origin and the fulfilment of the new and definitive worship of God, the *logiké latreía*. Saint Paul's exhortation to the Romans in this regard is a concise description of how the Eucharist makes our whole life a spiritual worship pleasing to God: "I appeal to you therefore, my brothers, by the mercies of God, to present your bodies as a living sacrifice, holy and acceptable to God, which is your spiritual worship" (Rom 12:1). In these words the new worship appears as a total self-offering made in communion with the whole Church. The Apostle's insistence on the offering of our bodies emphasizes the concrete human reality of a worship which is anything but disincarnate. The Bishop of Hippo goes on to say that "this is the sacrifice of Christians: that we, though many, are one body in Christ. The Church celebrates this mystery in the sacrament of the altar, as the faithful know, and there she shows them clearly that in what is offered, she herself is offered."[10] Catholic doctrine, in fact, affirms that the Eucharist, as the sacrifice of Christ, is also the sacrifice of the Church, and thus of all the faithful. This insistence on sacrifice—a "making sacred"—expresses all the existential depth implied in the transformation of our human reality as taken up by Christ (cf. Phil 3:12).[11]

The unity of the Church and her entire life is offered in every Mass, for Christ cannot be separated from His members and their concrete life. The Church prays, furthermore, that the unity of the members with their Head and with one another will be deepened through the sacrifice and increased as the fruit of the sacrifice. Finally, Holy Communion helps to solidify that unity by nurturing the faithful in charity. Pope Benedict goes on to stress the totality of the Christian life that is offered by the faithful in every Mass:

---

[10] Ibid.

[11] Benedict XVI, *Sacramentum Caritatis*, §70.

Christianity's new worship includes and transfigures every aspect of life: "Whether you eat or drink, or whatever you do, do all to the glory of God" (1 Cor 10:31). Christians, in all their actions, are called to offer true worship to God. Here the intrinsically eucharistic nature of Christian life begins to take shape. The Eucharist, since it embraces the concrete, everyday existence of the believer, makes possible, day by day, the progressive transfiguration of all those called by grace to reflect the image of the Son of God (cf. Rom 8:29ff.). There is nothing authentically human—our thoughts and affections, our words and deeds—that does not find in the sacrament of the Eucharist the form it needs to be lived to the full. Here we can see the full human import of the radical newness brought by Christ in the Eucharist: the worship of God in our lives cannot be relegated to something private and individual, but tends by its nature to permeate every aspect of our existence. Worship pleasing to God thus becomes a new way of living our whole life, each particular moment of which is lifted up, since it is lived as part of a relationship with Christ and as an offering to God. The glory of God is the living man (cf. 1 Cor 10:31). And the life of man is the vision of God.[12]

The old form of the Roman Pontifical's liturgy for the consecration of an altar set forth this inner sacrifice of the faithful with which Holy Mother Church desires us to approach her altars: "At this . . . altar let innocence be in honor, let pride be sacrificed, anger slain, impurity and every evil desire laid low, let the sacrifice of chastity be offered in place of doves, and instead of the young pigeons the sacrifice of innocence."[13] These are the spiritual sacrifices of the faithful that Holy Church wishes to be joined to the immaculate sacrifice of her Redeemer.

---

[12] Ibid. The last two sentences are quoting Irenaeus, *Against Heresies* 4.20.7.

[13] *The Roman Pontifical* [rites performed by a bishop], Consecration of an altar, Preface, cited in *Mediator Dei*, §100.

*The Common and the Ministerial Priesthood
According to* Lumen Gentium

While emphasizing the common or royal priesthood of the faithful, the Church's Magisterium clearly distinguishes it from the ministerial priesthood deriving from the sacrament of Holy Orders, which alone gives the power to consecrate the Eucharist in the person of Christ. The Second Vatican Council, in *Lumen Gentium*, §10, teaches:

> Though they differ essentially and not only in degree, the common priesthood of the faithful and the ministerial or hierarchical priesthood are none the less ordered one to another; each in its own proper way shares in the one priesthood of Christ. The ministerial priest, by the sacred power he enjoys, teaches and rules the priestly people; acting in the person of Christ, he makes present the eucharistic sacrifice, and offers it to God in the name of all the people. But the faithful, in virtue of their royal priesthood, join in the offering of the Eucharist. They likewise exercise that priesthood in receiving the sacraments, in prayer and thanksgiving, in the witness of a holy life, and by self-denial and active charity.

The common priesthood of the faithful and the ministerial priesthood are both ordered toward the Eucharist, which is "the fount and apex of the whole Christian life,"[14] but in two complementary ways. The ministerial priesthood makes the Eucharistic sacrifice and Victim present through Christ's words of consecration. Through priestly character, the ministerial priest acts in the person of Christ, enabling Christ Himself to act as the eternal High Priest in every Mass, offering Himself through the ministry of His ordained priests. Christ, who is man and God, has the singular capacity to perform acts at once divine and human, which are called *theandric* acts. Through the sacrament of Holy Orders, the priest too participates in this singular privilege of the Word made flesh. The priest, acting in the person of Christ in saying the words of consecration, performs the divine act of bringing Christ into the world through the miracle of transubstantiation, and of offering Him as the acceptable Victim on behalf of the Church in sacrifice for the sins of the world.

---

[14] Second Vatican Council, *Lumen Gentium*, §11.

Through the sacrifice of the priest, all the faithful, through their common priesthood, can put themselves in solidarity with the offering of their Head so that they too "offer the Divine Victim to God, and offer themselves along with It."[15] The common priesthood of the faithful presupposes the ministerial priesthood, is nourished by it, and cooperates with it. Without the ministerial priesthood, the Church would never be able to offer the sacrifice of the Mass, and thus the faithful would not be able to participate in that offering by making the internal offering of their own lives in conjunction with the divine Victim on the altar. The ordained priest offers the sacrifice of Christ in the name of the people and for the people, and he associates their interior offering of themselves with Christ's offering of Himself, offering both together up to God. In this way the sacrifices of the faithful receive an incalculable increase in value and dignity.

The Common Priesthood in the Prayers of the Eucharistic Liturgy

It is striking how frequently the Eucharistic liturgy emphasizes that the offering is made by the whole Church and not just by the priest acting in the person of Christ.[16] The common priesthood of the faithful is first expressed in the Offertory prayers of the Roman rite when the priest says: "Pray, brethren that my sacrifice and yours may be acceptable to God, the almighty Father." He says "my sacrifice and yours" for two reasons. First, it shows that the faithful also offer the

---

[15] Ibid.

[16] See Pius XII, *Mediator Dei*, §87:

> Moreover, the rites and prayers of the eucharistic sacrifice signify and show no less clearly that the oblation of the Victim is made by the priests in company with the people. For not only does the sacred minister, after the oblation of the bread and wine when he turns to the people, say the significant prayer: "Pray brethren, that my sacrifice and yours may be acceptable to God the Father Almighty;" but also the prayers by which the divine Victim is offered to God are generally expressed in the plural number: and in these it is indicated more than once that the people also participate in this august sacrifice inasmuch as they offer the same. The following words, for example, are used: "For whom we offer, or who offer up to Thee . . . We therefore beseech thee, O Lord, to be appeased and to receive this offering of our bounded duty, as also of thy whole household. . . . We thy servants, as also thy whole people . . . do offer unto thy most excellent majesty, of thine own gifts bestowed upon us, a pure victim, a holy victim, a spotless victim."

sacrifice. But he does not simply say "our sacrifice," in order to distinguish the way in which the sacrifice is offered by the ministerial priest in the person of Christ and on behalf of the whole Church from the way it is offered by the faithful gathered around him, each of whom offers his own personal interior oblation together with that of Christ.

In the invitatory dialogue that marks the beginning of Eucharistic Prayers, all of the faithful are called to lift up their hearts (*sursum corda*) to the Lord, to whom the sacrifice is being offered. This stresses the interior participation of all the faithful in the sacrificial action as it begins to unfold.

In the Roman Canon, the twofold offering of priest and people is expressed in the prayer: "Remember, Lord, your servants and all gathered here, whose faith and devotion are known to you. For them, *we offer you* this sacrifice of praise *or they offer it for themselves and all who are dear to them.*"[17] Again, the text distinguishes and affirms both the offering by the priest and the offering of the faithful as members of Christ's Body.[18] The unity in distinction of the common and ministerial priesthoods is also manifested in the prayers of offering that surround the consecration. Before the institution narrative, the priest prays: "Lord, we pray: graciously accept this oblation of our service, *that of your whole family.*"[19] Right after the consecration (in the anamnesis) the priest prays: "We, your servants *and your holy people, offer* to your glorious majesty from the gifts that you have given us, this pure victim."[20] It is not insignificant that the prayers expressing offering are in the plural rather than the singular.[21]

That the sacrifice of the Mass is offered by the faithful is also indicated in the Roman Canon when the priest prays that the sacrifice be found acceptable:

---

[17] *RM*, 636. The "or" here, translating the Latin "vel," should be understood in the inclusive sense, meaning "and."

[18] See Jungmann, *The Eucharistic Prayer*, 14: "What is so striking is that the Mass appears in the liturgy at once and before all else as our sacrifice, and so it appears throughout: we bring gifts, we beg for acceptance, we prepare my sacrifice and your sacrifice."

[19] *RM*, 638.

[20] *RM*, 641.

[21] Jungmann, *The Eucharistic Prayer*, 30: "All the prayers which constitute the proper official Mass liturgy are in the plural without exception." See also p. 31: "We may observe, however, that to say these prayers in the name of all, and thus in the plural, was not considered sufficient. One also made sure of the express assent and joint action of the congregation."

> Be pleased to look upon these offerings with a serene and kindly countenance, and to accept them, as once you were pleased to accept the gifts of your servant Abel the just, the sacrifice of Abraham, our father in faith, and the offering of your high priest Melchizedek, a holy sacrifice, a spotless victim.[22]

At first sight, this prayer seems strange. Why should we pray that the sacrifice be acceptable like those of Abel, Abraham, and Melchizedek, when we are speaking about the sacrifice of Christ made present on the altar? How can Christ's sacrifice be compared with those of sinners and mere men? And why should we pray for the acceptance of a sacrifice that has infinite value in itself? Did not the Father manifest the acceptance of Christ's sacrifice in His glorious Resurrection and Ascension? If the Mass were only the sacrifice of Christ Himself, then such a prayer would be unfitting and inexplicable. But since the Mass is the sacrifice offered by the Church and all the faithful, the petition is deeply meaningful. In order that a sacrifice be found acceptable to God, both the interior and the exterior offering must be pleasing to Him. The interior sacrifice of the heart must be sincere, and the exterior sacrifice must be proportioned to it as a worthy sign of the interior offering. We have seen that the Old Testament sacrifices were sometimes said to be unacceptable, indeed abominable, to God because of the lack of interior self-donation of the faithful. In the same way, the Church prays that the offering of the New Covenant may be acceptable despite the sins of the faithful. It is always acceptable in the divine Victim, but it may not be completely acceptable in the interior dimension of the self-donation of the faithful. Jungmann writes:

> From this point the form of the offering prayers after the consecration becomes intelligible, and especially the phrasing of the second prayer of offering, the *Supra quae*. We have often been astonished and even objected to the fact that we human beings beg God to accept the sacrifice of His Son, and in so doing compare this incomparable Sacrifice with the sacrifices which Abel and Abraham and Melchisedech offered. That would of course be meaningless and lacking in reverence if it concerned only the sacrifice which Christ offers. But

---

[22] *RM*, 641.

Christ's sacrifice is not concerned. His sacrifice has already been accepted, and accepted definitively. But it is the sacrifice which we offer with Him here and now that is concerned, and we offer this sacrifice in a worthy manner only when we possess that inner conviction of mind of which this sacrifice is the sign, and when we possess at least as perfect an obedience, and an attitude of mind as full of surrender, as the patriarchs.[23]

Joseph Ratzinger also makes this connection between this prayer for the acceptance of the Eucharistic sacrifice and the participation of the faithful in the sacrifice, citing the key text of Romans 12:1:

Its aim, as St. Paul says in the text already referred to, is that "our bodies" (that is, our bodily existence on earth) become "a living sacrifice", united to the Sacrifice of Christ (cf. Rom 12:1). That is the only explanation of the urgency of the petitions for acceptance that characterize every Christian liturgy. . . . This Sacrifice is only complete when the world has become the place of love, as St. Augustine saw in his *City of God*. Only then, as we said at the beginning, is worship perfected and what happened on Golgotha completed. That is why, in the petitions for acceptance, we pray that representation become a reality and take hold of us. That is why, in the prayers of the Roman Canon, we unite ourselves with the great men who offered sacrifice at the dawn of history: Abel, Melchizedek, and Abraham.[24]

After mentioning the sacrifice of the patriarchs, the Roman Canon continues this theme of acceptance by imploring that the sacrifice may "be borne by the hands of your holy Angel to your altar on high in the sight of your divine majesty, so that all of us, who through this participation at the altar receive the most holy Body and Blood of your Son, may be filled with every grace and heavenly blessing."[25] This text beautifully manifests the double movement of ascent and descent. We

---

[23] Jungmann, *The Eucharistic Prayer*, 17. See also Ludovicus Billot, *De Ecclesiae Sacramentis: Commentarius in Tertiam Partem S. Thomae*, 7th ed. (Rome: Apud Aedes Universitatis Gregorianae, 1931), 1:602.

[24] Joseph Ratzinger, *The Spirit of the Liturgy*, 58–59.

[25] *RM*, 641.

pray that the sacrifice ascend in a movement of self-donation from the physical altar to the heavenly altar, so that we may receive from heaven a participation in the Victim, source of all blessing.[26]

Petitions that the holy sacrifice be acceptable to God are found in other Eucharistic Prayers. In the Maronite Third Anaphora of St. Peter, called *Sharar*, right after the institution narrative the priest prays:

> Grant us to gain life through your life-giving death that we may stand before you in purity and serve you in holiness and offer that sacrifice to your Godhead, that it may be pleasing to the will of your majesty. . . . May our prayers ascend in your sight, and your mercy descend on our petitions, and let that sacrifice be acceptable before you.[27]

Here the acceptability of the sacrifice is clearly tied to the holiness of those who offer.

The participation of the faithful in offering the sacrifice is also eloquently manifested in the anamnesis and epiclesis of Eucharistic Prayer III of the Roman rite:

> Therefore, O Lord, as we celebrate the memorial of the saving Passion of your Son, his wondrous Resurrection and Ascension into heaven, and as we look forward to his second coming, we offer you in thanksgiving this holy and living sacrifice. Look, we pray, upon the oblation of your Church and, recognizing the sacrificial Victim by whose death you willed to reconcile us to yourself, grant that we, who are nourished by the Body and Blood of your Son and filled with his Holy Spirit, may become one body, one spirit in Christ. May he make of us an eternal offering to you.[28]

This text begins, in the anamnesis, with the sacrifice of His Passion, the sacramental memorial of which is offered to the Father as a "holy

---

[26] See Cabié, *The Eucharist*, 102: "The petition [that the faithful receive the fruits of the Eucharist] is here mediated through the image of the two altars and the twofold movement associated with them: the offering of human beings ascends to God and then comes back in blessing upon those who approach the table of sacrifice."

[27] Third Maronite Anaphora of St. Peter, called *Sharar* (*PEER*, 48).

[28] *RM*, 653.

and living sacrifice." This sacrifice is then said to be the "oblation of the Church," for Christ has given it to her to offer to the Father. In the epiclesis the Church asks through the merits of this oblation that reconciled mankind to God and through the grace of Communion that we may be filled with the Holy Spirit so as to become one body that is made into "an eternal offering" like unto His. Cardinal Schönborn comments that this Eucharistic Prayer "speaks first of the sacrifice of Christ, then of the sacrifice offered by the Church, and third of the sacrifice that we ourselves must become."[29]

The Sacrifices of the Faithful Are Offered on the Altar of the Body of Christ

The altar represents the divine acceptance of a victim offered in sacrifice. The altar thus signifies the sanctification of the victim that is offered. On what altar are the sacrifices of the faithful offered? That is the same as asking what sanctifies them and manifests their acceptance. The answer is simple: the sacrifices of the Mystical Body are sanctified by the sacrifice of the Head and are offered together with it. Thus we can think of the sacrifices of the faithful as being offered on the altar that is the Body of Christ Himself. For, in the Mass, Christ is ultimately Priest, Victim, and Altar.[30] The faithful therefore can think of putting their personal sacrifices on the paten that holds the Body of Christ and of "offering them up" to the Father on the "Altar" of Christ's own Body.

Benedict XVI spoke about the practice of "offering up" the daily sacrifices of life in his encyclical on Christian hope, *Spe Salvi* (2007), §40:

> There used to be a form of devotion—perhaps less practised today but quite widespread not long ago—that included the idea of "offering up" the minor daily hardships that continually strike at us like irritating "jabs", thereby giving them a meaning. . . . What does it mean to offer something up? Those who did so were convinced that they could insert these little annoyances into Christ's great "com-passion" so that

---

[29] Schönborn, *The Source of Life*, 71.
[30] See the extensive discussion of the theme of Christ as the altar of His sacrifice by de la Taille, *The Mystery of Faith*, 1:215–34.

they somehow became part of the treasury of compassion so greatly needed by the human race. In this way, even the small inconveniences of daily life could acquire meaning and contribute to the economy of good and of human love. Maybe we should consider whether it might be judicious to revive this practice ourselves.

The best way of inserting the sacrifices of the Christian life into Christ's great "com-passion" is to offer them during the Eucharistic sacrifice as our interior oblation that is represented by Christ's sacrifice, placing them on the altar of His own Body to be offered to the Father.

A natural opportunity for the faithful to spiritually unite the sacrifice of their lives with the Mass is during the Offertory, in which the material gifts of the faithful are presented. The Offertory thus symbolically represents the contribution of the faithful and of creation to the sacrifice.[31] The Offertory prayers in the Novus Ordo, drawing on the Jewish blessings before meals, mention that we offer the fruit of the earth and of the vine, representing creation, and of the work of human hands. In the consecration, this work of human hands will be transformed into Christ. This exterior gift is an image of our interior offering. St. John Paul II explains this profound meaning of the offertory rite in *Dominicae Cenae*, §9:

---

[31] See Marie-Joseph Nicolas, *What Is the Eucharist?* 71:

> The victim of the sacrifice of the Mass takes up into himself all our personal offerings. It is one of the essential principles of the Treatise on the Redemption (and we might call it the principle of Co-redemption) that men, far from being dispensed by the sacrifice of Christ from offering themselves in sacrifice, are rather made capable by it of doing so. The imperfect victims which we are, are given value by their union with the perfect victim. By offering himself through the instrumentality of men, Christ offers men themselves with him. This is admirably expressed by the offertory rite.

See also Jungmann, *The Mass*, 121: "The well-structured Offertory, with at least an intimation of the sacrifice about to take place, is a valuable occasion for all participants to realize what the Mass as the Church's sacrifice should be: an expression of the God-ward orientation of our whole life with all its joys and sorrows, its hopes and longings; an acknowledgement that all this is mingled and united with the sacrifice that Christ, our High Priest, has offered and continues to offer with us."

Although all those who participate in the Eucharist do not confect the sacrifice as he [the ministerial priest] does, they offer with him, by virtue of the common priesthood, their own spiritual sacrifices represented by the bread and wine from the moment of their presentation at the altar. For this liturgical action, which takes a solemn form in almost all liturgies, has a "spiritual value and meaning." The bread and wine become in a sense a symbol of all that the eucharistic assembly brings, on its own part, as an offering to God and offers spiritually.[32]

Human works are elevated in Christ to the supernatural level as works of supernatural charity, and thus they become an acceptable sacrifice to God.[33]

The most profound and unsurpassable model for the participation of the faithful in offering the sacrifice is given by Mary's participation in offering her Son's sacrifice at the foot of the Cross,[34] joined by John, Mary Magdalene, and Mary of Clopas (see John 19:25–26). Pius XII teaches that Mary, "always more intimately united with her Son, offered Him on Golgotha to the Eternal Father for all the children of Adam, sin-stained by his unhappy fall, and her mother's rights and her

---

[32] John Paul II, *Dominicae Cenae*, §9.

[33] See Jungmann, *The Eucharistic Prayer*, 26:

> The sacrifice of Christ is not of course enacted here; but in every sense the offertory does prepare the way for it. He Himself has so arranged it that we should take the things of this earth in order to offer His sacrifice. We, the Church, should go before Him with our earthly gifts from which He deigns to prepare His gifts. . . . The sacrifice which we offer, however sacred and heavenly it is, does not sway above our heads in the clouds, but the material world is made use of, material creation is reverenced in it, and it is made holy and brought back to God. Secondly, our human life in particular is taken up in these gifts; the work of our hands, the food from which we live and therefore our life itself. Our earthly life on this earth, with all its wants and necessities, is caught up in these earthly gifts; but in gifts the value of which has been raised up to the value of heavenly gifts with which nothing can be compared.

[34] See John Paul II, *EE*, §56: "Mary, throughout her life at Christ's side and not only on Calvary, made her own *the sacrificial dimension of the Eucharist*. . . . In her daily preparation for Calvary, Mary experienced a kind of 'anticipated Eucharist'—one might say a 'spiritual communion'—of desire and of oblation, which would culminate in her union with her Son in his passion, and then find expression after Easter by her partaking in the Eucharist which the Apostles celebrated as the memorial of that passion" (italics original).

mother's love were included in the holocaust."[35] The Second Vatican Council, in *Lumen Gentium*, §58, likewise speaks of Mary's union with the sacrifice of her Son:

> The Blessed Virgin . . . faithfully persevered in her union with her Son unto the cross, where she stood, in keeping with the divine plan, grieving exceedingly with her only begotten Son, uniting herself with a maternal heart with His sacrifice, and lovingly consenting to the immolation of this Victim which she herself had brought forth.

As Mary interiorly offered the bloody sacrifice of Calvary to the Father as the price of our redemption, to which she joined her own inner sorrow of compassion, similarly the faithful are given the opportunity to join in the offering of Christ to the Father, adding to it their own crosses and compassion.[36]

MAGISTERIAL TEXTS ON THE COMMON PRIESTHOOD AND ACTIVE PARTICIPATION IN THE MASS

Pius XII's *Mediator Dei* on the Participation of the Faithful in the Mass

Not a few magisterial texts of the twentieth century emphasize that all the baptized faithful, by being inserted into Christ through Baptismal character, are called to join in Christ's priestly offering of Himself to the Father in the sacrifice of the Mass. Pius XII explains the participation of all the faithful in offering the sacrifice of the Mass in several texts from *Mediator Dei*. He cites the prayers of the Roman Canon of the Mass to show how the lay faithful participate spiritually in offering the sacrifice by uniting their intention with that of the priest, giving their interior consent to the offering made through his hands:

---

[35] Pius XII, Encyclical Letter, *Mystici Corporis* (1943), §110.

[36] See John Paul II, *EE*, §58: "In the Eucharist the Church is completely united to Christ and his sacrifice, and makes her own the spirit of Mary."

"Not only," says Innocent III of immortal memory, "do the priests offer the sacrifice, but also all the faithful: for what the priest does personally by virtue of his ministry, the faithful do collectively by virtue of their intention." We are happy to recall one of St. Robert Bellarmine's many statements on this subject. "The sacrifice," he says "is principally offered in the person of Christ. Thus the oblation that follows the consecration is a sort of attestation that the whole Church consents in the oblation made by Christ, and offers it along with Him."[37]

In *Mediator Dei*, §§98–99, Pius XII emphasizes a second aspect of the participation of the faithful in the sacrifice. They are to unite the interior oblation of their entire Christian lives in union with Christ's self-oblation:

In order that the oblation by which the faithful offer the divine Victim in this sacrifice to the heavenly Father may have its full effect, it is necessary that the people add something else, namely, the offering of themselves as a victim. . . . For the Prince of the Apostles wishes us, as living stones built upon Christ, the cornerstone, to be able as "a holy priesthood, to offer up spiritual sacrifices, acceptable to God by Jesus Christ" (1 Pet 2:5). St. Paul the Apostle addresses the following words of exhortation to Christians . . . "I beseech you therefore, . . . that you present your bodies, a living sacrifice, holy, pleasing unto God, your reasonable service" (Rom 12:1). . . . With the High Priest and through Him they offer themselves as a spiritual sacrifice, . . . and each one should consecrate himself to the furthering of the divine glory, desiring to become as like as possible to Christ in His most grievous sufferings.

In order for the faithful to engage in these two aspects of their participation in the offering of the sacrifice (uniting their hearts with Christ's self-offering through the action of the priest and uniting to His sacrifice the offering of their own lives) the faithful must seek, insofar as they can, to have the same dispositions that Christ had when He offered Himself:

---

[37] Pius XII, *Mediator Dei*, §86.

It is, therefore, desirable, Venerable Brethren, that all the faithful should be aware that to participate in the eucharistic sacrifice is their chief duty and supreme dignity, and that not in an inert and negligent fashion, giving way to distractions and day-dreaming, but with such earnestness and concentration that *they may be united as closely as possible with the High Priest*, according to the Apostle, "Let this mind be in you which was also in Christ Jesus."[38] And together with Him and through Him let them make their oblation, and in union with Him let them offer up themselves.

It is quite true that Christ is a priest; but He is a priest not for Himself but for us, when in the name of the whole human race He offers our prayers and religious homage to the eternal Father; He is also a victim and for us since He substitutes Himself for sinful man. Now the exhortation of the Apostle, "Let this mind be in you which was also in Christ Jesus," requires that *all Christians should possess, as far as is humanly possible, the same dispositions as those which the divine Redeemer had when He offered Himself in sacrifice*: that is to say, they should in a humble attitude of mind, pay adoration, honor, praise and thanksgiving to the supreme majesty of God. Moreover, it means that they must assume to some extent the character of a victim, that they deny themselves as the Gospel commands, that freely and of their own accord they do penance and that each detests and satisfies for his sins. It means, in a word, that we must all undergo with Christ a mystical death on the cross so that we can apply to ourselves the words of St. Paul, "With Christ I am nailed to the cross."[39]

Active Participation in the Mass according to Vatican II

This participation of the faithful in the offering of Christ as Priest and Victim is the principal meaning of the Second Vatican Council's call to the faithful to participate more actively and deeply in the liturgy. *Sacrosanctum Concilium*, §14 brings the notion of "active participation" to the forefront and connects it directly to the royal priesthood of the faithful:

---

[38] Phil 2:5.
[39] Pius XII, *Mediator Dei*, §§80–81 (my italics).

Mother Church earnestly desires that all the faithful should be led to that fully conscious, and active participation in liturgical celebrations which is demanded by the very nature of the liturgy. Such participation by the Christian people as "a chosen race, a royal priesthood, a holy nation, a redeemed people" (1 Pet. 2:9; cf. 2:4–5), is their right and duty by reason of their baptism.

In the restoration and promotion of the sacred liturgy, this full and active participation by all the people is the aim to be considered before all else; for it is the primary and indispensable source from which the faithful are to derive the true Christian spirit; and therefore pastors of souls must zealously strive to achieve it, by means of the necessary instruction, in all their pastoral work.

What is the principal way in which this is realized? *Sacrosanctum Concilium*, §48 clarifies the nature of active participation in the Mass:

The Church, therefore, earnestly desires that Christ's faithful, when present at this mystery of faith, should not be there as strangers or silent spectators; on the contrary, through a good understanding of the rites and prayers they should take part in the sacred action conscious of what they are doing, with devotion and full collaboration. They should be instructed by God's word and be nourished at the table of the Lord's body; they should give thanks to God; *by offering the Immaculate Victim, not only through the hands of the priest, but also with him, they should learn also to offer themselves.*[40]

Lumen Gentium, §11 states: "Taking part in the Eucharistic Sacrifice, which is the source and summit of the whole Christian life, they offer the divine Victim to God, and offer themselves along with it." *Presbyterorum Ordinis*, §5 teaches likewise:

The Most Blessed Eucharist contains the entire spiritual boon of the Church, that is, Christ himself, our Pasch and Living Bread, by the action of the Holy Spirit through his very flesh vital and vitalizing, giving life to men who are thus invited and

---

[40] My italics.

encouraged to offer themselves, their labors and all created things, together with him. In this light, the Eucharist shows itself as the source and the apex of the whole work of preaching the Gospel. . . . Thus the Eucharistic Action, over which the priest presides, is the very heart of the congregation. So priests must instruct their people to offer to God the Father the Divine Victim in the Sacrifice of the Mass, and to join to it the offering of their own lives.

Lumen Gentium, §34 discusses the nature of this offering. The faithful participate in the priestly office of Christ through the offering of all their sacrifices, concerns, labors, and joys to God the Father together with the Body of Christ in the Eucharist. In this way, their secular activities are invested with a supernatural redemptive merit. The Church's holiness depends on the living force of this doctrine in the lives of all the faithful:

> For besides intimately linking them to His life and His mission, He also gives them a sharing in His priestly function of offering spiritual worship for the glory of God and the salvation of men. . . . For all their works, prayers and apostolic endeavors, their ordinary married and family life, their daily occupations, their physical and mental relaxation, if carried out in the Spirit, and even the hardships of life, if patiently borne—all these become "spiritual sacrifices acceptable to God through Jesus Christ" (1 Pet 2:5). *Together with the offering of the Lord's body, they are most fittingly offered in the celebration of the Eucharist.* Thus, as those everywhere who adore in holy activity, the laity consecrate the world itself to God.[41]

The Church here teaches that our participation in the Eucharist is deeply linked to the mystery of suffering in union with Christ. We

---

[41] My italics. This text is quoted in *CCC*, §901 and in John Paul II, *Christifideles Laici* (1988), §14, which also states: "The lay faithful are sharers in the *priestly mission*, for which Jesus offered himself on the cross and continues to be offered in the celebration of the Eucharist for the glory of God and the salvation of humanity. Incorporated in Jesus Christ, the baptized are united to him and to his sacrifice in the offering they make of themselves and their daily activities (cf. Rom 12:1, 2)."

are to offer ourselves to God as "victims" of propitiation together with Christ immolated on the altar.

One of the most profound truths of the Catholic faith is the secret of the sanctification of suffering in union with Christ's Passion. There is no suffering so great that it cannot be joined to those of Christ and thereby made such that we can bear it together with Him. This uniting of our sufferings can be done in simple prayer, but the most efficacious way is through our presence at the Holy sacrifice of the Mass, for Christ Himself is there mystically immolated for love of us on the altar. Furthermore, we unite ourselves with the divine Victim not only in the pain of our lives but also in every act of fidelity to the Christian life, even the most joyous. There is no reality in the Christian life (except sin) that cannot be united to the Eucharist. This uniting of our sufferings and affections with those of Christ concerns both dimensions of the Eucharist as sacrifice and as sacrament of communion. We are to unite ourselves with Christ both in the offering of His sacrifice to God the Father and in receiving the fruit of that sacrifice.

It is striking how many times the documents of Vatican II emphasize the mission of the faithful to interiorly participate in offering the Eucharistic sacrifice. But has this been implemented?[42] Have the faithful been instructed that they are called to offer the divine Victim to the Father together with the offering of their own Christian lives? Indeed, this is the principal reason for the duty to attend Mass on Sundays and holy days of obligation. But even if they cannot attend Mass or receive Holy Communion, the faithful can still frequently offer the sacrifice of the altar in a spiritual way on the altars of their hearts, uniting themselves to the sacrifice of all the Masses celebrated throughout the Catholic world, as in the petitions of the Divine Mercy chaplet.

We have seen that our participation in the priestly office of Christ has two movements: ascending and descending. Together with our High Priest, we offer our love and sufferings up to God. This is the ascending movement. And together with Him, we implore God's blessings down upon us, which includes the blessing of being able to suffer something worthily through love of Christ, to bear with love the crosses that come our way, the blessing of uniting our souls with Him in charity, and the blessing of being an instrument of grace

---

[42] A key work emphasizing the interior dimension of active participation in the liturgy is Ratzinger, *The Spirit of the Liturgy*, 171–77.

for others. In other words, the graces that descend as a result of our ascending movements of prayer and works are ordered ultimately to a renewed ascending movement of glorification of God. We plead for blessings so that we may be made more worthy of offering our hearts up to God. Charity can come to rest finally only in God, not in ourselves. We need God's gifts so as to be better able to give ourselves back to Him.

Our participation in Christ's priestly office also has an essential social dimension. We ought not only to offer up our own sacrifices but also to make those of all our brothers our own through the bond of charity. Through our union in Christ with all mankind, we can offer up vicariously the sufferings of those who do not know the purpose of suffering, offering the hearts of all men to God, and especially those of our family members, friends, associates, and so on. Likewise, we must plead for grace for all, especially those closest to us. And there is no better means than the sacrifice of the Mass, in which our holy desires are immolated together with the Sacred Heart of the Redeemer.

It can be seen that the greater the inner participation of the faithful in Christ's sacrifice through faith, hope, charity, and all the supernatural virtues, the greater will be their contribution in the co-offering of Christ's sacrifice in the Mass, and thus the greater will be their glorification of God and the personal fruit derived from the Mass, enriching the Church. As Pius XII teaches in *Mediator Dei*, §102:

> All the elements of the liturgy, then, would have us reproduce in our hearts the likeness of the divine Redeemer through the mystery of the cross, according to the words of the Apostle of the Gentiles, "With Christ I am nailed to the cross. I live, now not I, but Christ liveth in me" (Gal 2:19–20). Thus we become a victim, as it were, along with Christ to increase the glory of the eternal Father.

Christ offered a sacrifice of infinite value in His immolation on Calvary. He wills, however, that His Mystical Body, the Church, share in His riches, and thus He calls the Church to participate ever more deeply in His own sacrifice by incorporating their lives into His offering. This inner participation, which is by no means limited to the time Mass is celebrated, is the fruit of communion that Christ wants to see from us. He wants His Church to be intimately associated in His saving act.

It seems that Martin Luther did not understood this point, even though he spoke of the common priesthood of the faithful as if it were the only type of Christian priesthood. He would not admit that Christ willed the Church to have a share in offering His sacrifice, and for this reason, the personal and interior sacrifices of Christians lost their co-redemptive value in the Protestant scheme. It seems that the Protestant tradition has not been coherent in insisting on a common priesthood and yet denying that the faithful are called to offer up prayers and sacrifice through the mediation of that priesthood.

However, this participation of the Church in Christ's sacrifice does not lower Christ's dignity. Far from it, for it shows that Christ's redemption ennobles the Church so as to make her a true spouse, capable of mystically sharing in the merits and sacrifices of her Bridegroom and Redeemer. Christ has redeemed the Church in His blood so as to make her pure and immaculate, giving her the power to offer spiritual sacrifice to the Lord, through Him, with Him, and in Him.

Active Participation in the Mass and the New Evangelization

If the Catholic laity were to live the teaching of the Second Vatican Council on the participation of the faithful in the sacrifice of the Mass, the situation of the Church, the world, and the New Evangelization would radically change for the better. We need to bring our society, with all its aspects of hope and tragedy, to the altar to offer it up to the Father with Christ who offers Himself and is offered by the priest and the whole Church. Although He is a sacrifice of infinite value, Christ does not want to be offered alone! He gave His sacrifice to the Church so that we could add our lives, our dreams, our efforts (even when they end in apparent failure and the Cross), our loves and sorrows, our humiliations and trials, our forgiveness and acts of mercy, to be placed on the altar with Him and be offered to the Father with Him.

The totality of life that ought to be offered in the Eucharist by every member of the faithful is powerfully expressed by the great Orthodox theologian Alexander Schmemann:

> All rational, spiritual and other qualities of man, distinguishing him from other creatures, have their focus and ultimate fulfillment in this capacity to bless God, to know, so to speak, the meaning of the thirst and hunger that constitutes his

life. "*Homo sapiens*," "*homo faber*". . . yes, but, first of all, "*homo adorans*." The first, the basic definition of man is that he is *the priest*. He stands in the center of the world and unifies it in his act of blessing God, of both receiving the world from God and offering it to God—and by filling the world with this Eucharist, he transforms his life, the one that he receives from the world, into life in God, into communion with Him. The world was created as the "matter," the material of one all-embracing Eucharist, and man was created as the priest of this cosmic sacrament.[43]

The ancient Greek philosophers understood man as a microcosm, a little universe, because he unites in himself the spiritual and the physical creation. In his role as priest, a human being offers himself, as a microcosm, and the whole world of which he is an image and a connecting link or bridge between the material and the spiritual, in Christ, the Word through whom all was framed.

To implement Vatican II and carry out the New Evangelization, we need to wake up what we could call the sleeping giant, which is the great crowd of lay Catholics.[44] Everyone is called to participate,

---

[43] Alexander Schmemann, *For the Life of the World* (Crestwood, NY: St. Vladimir's Seminary Press, 1973), 15.

[44] See Alexander Schmemann, *The Eucharist*, trans. Paul Kachur (Crestwood, NY: St. Vladimir's Seminary Press, 1987), 113–14:

> With each passing century, an understanding of the Church has intensified in which she is experienced above all as the clergy's "serving" of the laity, the satisfaction by the clergy of the "spiritual needs" of the faithful. It is precisely in this perception of the Church that we must seek the cause of those two chronic illnesses of church consciousness that run like a red thread through the entire history of Christianity: "clericalism" and "laicism," which usually takes the form of "anticlericalism." . . . This "clericalization" of the Church, the reduction of "ministry" to the clergy alone and the consequent atrophy in the consciousness of the laity, led to the gradual demise of the sacrificial perception of the Church herself and of the sacrament of the Church—the Eucharist. The conviction that the priest serves on behalf of the laity and, so to speak, in their place led to the conviction that he serves for them, for the satisfaction of their "religious needs," subordinate to their religious "demand." . . . The overwhelming majority of the laity (supported in this, alas, all too often by the clergy and the hierarchy) sense the Church as existing for themselves but do not sense themselves as the Church transformed and eternally being transformed into a sacrifice and offering to God, into participants in the sacrificial ministry of Christ.

not in outwardly great and extraordinary things, but above all in the Eucharistic life, by which we bring all our dreams, hopes, and daily efforts, things big and little, to the altar to offer them to the Father with Christ, and so to call down the Father's blessing on them and on the whole world. If each one of us were to do this more deeply, it would change the world, although in ways that may remain hidden until the Last Judgment.

Ars Celebrandi *and Active Participation*

The active participation of the faithful is fostered above all by the reverent and faithful celebration on the part of the priestly minister.[45] Benedict XVI called attention to this in his post-synodal apostolic exhortation *Sacramentum Caritatis* (2007), §38:

> In the course of the Synod, there was frequent insistence on the need to avoid any antithesis between the *ars celebrandi*, the art of proper celebration, and the full, active and fruitful participation of all the faithful. The primary way to foster the participation of the People of God in the sacred rite is the proper celebration of the rite itself. The *ars celebrandi* is the best way to ensure their *actuosa participatio*. The *ars celebrandi* is the fruit of faithful adherence to the liturgical norms in all their richness; indeed, for two thousand years this way of celebrating has sustained the faith life of all believers, called to take part in the celebration as the People of God, a royal priesthood, a holy nation.

When the priest celebrates Mass with an awareness of what he is offering, the faithful will be drawn into the interior dimension of the sacrifice.[46] In addition, when the priest is attentive to the liturgical

---

[45] See Peter Elliott, "*Ars Celebrandi* in the Sacred Liturgy," in *The Sacred Liturgy: Source and Summit of the Life and Mission of the Church—The Proceedings of the International Conference on the Sacred Liturgy, Sacra Liturgia 2013*, ed. Alcuin Reid (San Francisco: Ignatius Press, 2014), 69–85.

[46] See Malcolm Cardinal Ranjith, "Towards an *Ars Celebrandi* in the Liturgy," *Antiphon* 13, no. 1 (2009): 7–17, esp. 10: "At its roots, the *ars celebrandi* is . . . not so much a matter of a series of actions put together in a harmonious unity as much as a deeply interior communion with Christ—the art of conforming to Christ the High Priest and His sacrificial and salvific action. . . . There can be no true *ars celebrandi* unless every priest is, first and foremost, touched and

norms, attention is taken away from his person and drawn to the liturgical action itself. The importance of faithfully observing the liturgical norms is emphasized in *Sacramentum Caritatis*, §40:

> Emphasizing the importance of the *ars celebrandi* also leads to an appreciation of the value of the liturgical norms. The *ars celebrandi* should foster a sense of the sacred and the use of outward signs which help to cultivate this sense, such as, for example, the harmony of the rite, the liturgical vestments, the furnishings and the sacred space. The eucharistic celebration is enhanced when priests and liturgical leaders are committed to making known the current liturgical texts and norms, making available the great riches found in the *General Instruction of the Roman Missal* and the *Order of Readings for Mass*. Perhaps we take it for granted that our ecclesial communities already know and appreciate these resources, but this is not always the case. These texts contain riches which have preserved and expressed the faith and experience of the People of God over its two-thousand-year history. Equally important for a correct *ars celebrandi* is an attentiveness to the various kinds of language that the liturgy employs: words and music, gestures and silence, movement, the liturgical colours of the vestments. By its very nature the liturgy operates on different levels of communication which enable it to engage the whole human person. The simplicity of its gestures and the sobriety of its orderly sequence of signs communicate and inspire more than any contrived and inappropriate additions. Attentiveness and fidelity to the specific structure of the rite express both a recognition of the nature of Eucharist as a gift and, on the part of the minister, a docile openness to receiving this ineffable gift.

---

profoundly motivated by his faith in the Lord and in the grandeur of the tasks the Lord entrusts to him." See also Owen Vyner, "Friendship with the Fairest of the Children of Men: Relating the *Ars celebrandi* to *Actuosa participatio*," *Antiphon* 14, no. 3 (2010): 261–72.

Sunday Mass: Obligation and Glory

Most Catholics are aware, although this cannot be taken for granted, that there is an obligation to participate in Mass on Sundays and holy days of obligation. Yet, for very many, this is felt as an external and legalistic imposition. A huge pastoral task in the New Evangelization is revitalizing the meaning of the Sunday Mass obligation and communicating its real content.

Joseph Ratzinger illustrated our current pastoral challenge by drawing a contrast with attitudes from the early Church. He speaks of a group of Christian martyrs in AD 304 who were arrested for attending Sunday Mass. In the Acts of their martyrdom, they justified their violation by saying: "Without the Day of the Lord we cannot exist."[47] He comments:

> Such a witness from the dawn of Church history could easily give rise to nostalgic reflections if one contrasts it with the lack enthusiasm for Sunday service typical of the middle-European Christian. . . . Instead of "without Sunday we cannot exist," Sunday obligation appears only as an imposed Church law, an *external* necessity. Then, like all duties coming from the outside, it is cropped more and more until only the requirement remains to have to attend a half-hour ritual that is becoming ever more remote. Asking when and why one can be excused from it ultimately becomes more important than asking why one should regularly celebrate it.[48]

The Sunday Mass obligation, as the early Christian martyrs were aware, comes from the incredible dignity that the faithful have in co-offering the sacrifice. It is notable that the Sunday obligation is not for Holy Communion but for participation in the sacrifice. This shows the primacy of the sacrificial dimension of the Mass and the fact that the Mass is first an offering to God before it is a banquet.[49]

Why Sunday? The Resurrection of our Lord took place on Sunday,

---

[47] Joseph Ratzinger, "The Resurrection as the Foundation of Christian Liturgy—On the Meaning of Sunday for Christian Prayer and Christian Life," in *TL*, 187–206, at 188.

[48] Ibid., 188–89.

[49] See John Paul II, *Dominicae Cenae*, §9: "The Eucharist is above all else a sacrifice."

the first day of the week. This is fitting because it shows that this central event of history constitutes a "new creation" and a new beginning, as it were. On the first day, God began creation with the command "Let there be light." In the Resurrection of Christ, a spiritual light was ignited that will never be extinguished. The glorious light of Christ's redemption entered our world on that Sunday of Easter. The entrance of that light into the world is celebrated liturgically every year in the Easter Vigil Mass, the most solemn Mass of the year, which begins with the lighting of the Easter candle and the proclamation of the light of the Messiah: *lumen Christi*. This is the meaning of the Christian celebration of Sunday, the first day of the week,[50] the day of the new creation.

In his apostolic letter *Dies Domini*, John Paul II explains this typology of Sunday that celebrates the original creation of light and the new creation of the light of faith through Christ's Resurrection from the dead and looks forward to His Second Coming in glory:

> It is *Easter* which returns week by week, celebrating Christ's victory over sin and death, the fulfilment in him of the first creation and the dawn of "the new creation" (see 2 Cor 5:17). It is the day which recalls in grateful adoration the world's first day and looks forward in active hope to "the last day," when Christ will come in glory (see Acts 1:11; 1 Thes 4:13–17) and all things will be made new (see Rev 21:5). . . . Therefore, in commemorating the day of Christ's Resurrection not just once a year but every Sunday, the Church seeks to indicate to every generation the true fulcrum of history, to which the mystery of the world's origin and its final destiny leads.[51]

Dies Domini, §24 further develops this idea:

> Christian thought spontaneously linked the Resurrection, which took place on "the first day of the week," with the first

---

[50] See John Paul II, Apostolic Letter on Keeping the Lord's Day Holy, *Dies Domini* (1998), §26.

[51] Ibid., §§1–2. For a good commentary on this Apostolic Letter, see James Massa, "Building Communion on the Lord's Day: An Appraisal of John Paul II's *Dies Domini,*" *Antiphon* 8, no. 3 (2003): 13–20. For the significance of Sunday as the "eighth day," see Ratzinger, *The Feast of Faith*, 45 (*TL*, 308), and *The Spirit of the Liturgy*, 92–98 (*TL*, 56–60).

day of that cosmic week (see Gen 1:1–2:4), which shapes the creation story in the Book of Genesis: the day of the creation of light (see 1:3–5). This link invited an understanding of the Resurrection as the beginning of a new creation, the first fruits of which is the glorious Christ, "the firstborn of all creation" (Col 1:15) and "the firstborn from the dead" (Col 1:18).

The Sunday Mass obligation is first and foremost a duty to order creation, in Christ, back to God, in a movement of praise and thanksgiving. One day—the Lord's Day—is set aside to give meaning to all days and times, thereby sanctifying time. The Church has always understood the sanctifying of the Lord's Day as essentially bound up with the celebration of Holy Mass. Already in the Acts of the Apostles,[52] and more clearly in the Apology of St. Justin Martyr,[53] we see the celebration of the Mass preeminently on the "first day of the week," which is Sunday, the day on which the Lord rose.

The Mass sanctifies time by fulfilling the purpose of creation itself. Through creation, things move out from God into existence, but their purpose is to return again to Him through glorifying Him. This creates the circle of *exitus* and *reditus*. The sacrifice of the Mass is the greatest return of glory to God possible in this stage of history before Christ's Second Coming. The faithful are enabled to offer the infinite and divine Victim to the Father and offer themselves as well.

The very act of making this offering, in a profound sense, is a liberation from the constraints of time and history because, in the sacrifice of the Mass, time and history have fulfilled their goal, which is to make a perfect return to the Creator. It is the nature of time that each moment has to pass away into a succeeding one, and thus it would seem that time, by its very nature, is imperfect and unfulfilled because it is fleeting. The world of work shares in this imperfection of time. Human work is always incomplete and pressing. The Mass fulfills the true notion of leisure,[54] in which one is free from constraints and deadlines because one is doing that which is the goal of time itself, the glorification of God, by offering Christ and the Christian life—which cannot be separated from Him—back to the Lord. The Mass

---

[52] Acts 20:7–8; 1 Cor 16:1–2.

[53] Justin Martyr, *First Apology* 67 (Barnard, *St. Justin Martyr*, 71).

[54] See Josef Pieper, *Leisure, the Basis of Culture*, trans. Gerald Malsbary (South Bend, IN: St. Augustine's Press, 1998).

redeems time in another sense as well: not only does it realize the end of creation, but it outweighs the disorder that human free will has put into creation through sin.

PARTICIPATION OF THE FAITHFUL AND CHURCH ARCHITECTURE

The *Domus Ecclesiae*

The fact that the sacrifice of the Mass is offered by the whole Church and not just by the priest can be seen in the radical difference of design between Christian churches and pagan temples. A Christian church had to accommodate the faithful gathered together with the priest in the offering of the sacrifice. Pagan temples did not typically have an interior place for the faithful. The sanctuary was small with room only for the priests and their attendants and the statue of the divinity. Even the Temple in Jerusalem had only courtyards and vestibules for the faithful; there was no space for them in the interior room with the priests.[55]

Jewish synagogues, on the contrary, were built for the gathering together of the faithful in prayer. For this reason the church buildings

---

[55] See Jungmann, *The Eucharistic Prayer*, 29:

> In ancient pagan religious worship it was not essential, although there were exceptions, for the people to take part in the act of worship. For this there existed a priesthood which looked after everything. Even the place of worship was laid out in accordance with this idea. It was not a room in which people could gather, but an ancient temple housing in its interior quite a small sanctuary, a gloomy cell, where the picture of the gods was placed. The rest of the building was concerned simply with external decoration. . . . Even in Jerusalem the temple was only slightly different, but at least there were vestibules, spare places in front of the sanctuary which were meant for the people. In Christianity the place appointed for worship was originally, and still is, essentially a place for the assembled people, for the *Ecclesia* . . . a priestly people . . . which through Christ has access to God.

See also Ratzinger, *The Spirit of the Liturgy*, 62 (*TL*, 37): "In the Old Covenant, the high priest performed the rite of atonement in the Holy of Holies. None but he was allowed to enter, and even he could do so only once a year. Similarly, the temples of all the other religions are usually not meeting places for worshippers but cultic spaces reserved to the deity."

in the early Church were modeled not on pagan temples, nor even on the Temple in Jerusalem, but on the Jewish synagogue and on Roman basilicas, which were public buildings with space for the people.[56] The Christian church soon came to be called the *domus ecclesiae*, which could be translated as "the house of the assembled church."[57]

Symbolic Significance of "Orientation" in the Liturgy

A proper understanding of "orientation" in the liturgy can help the faithful enter more deeply into their mission of offering the sacrifice of the Mass through their common priesthood. We have seen that the faithful offer the sacrifice together with the priest, although in a distinct way. This means that, during the Eucharistic Prayer, the direction of worship is entirely *ascending to the Lord*, on the part of both the priest and the faithful, in one united action of sacrificial worship.

The liturgy has the mission to manifest in exterior signs the worship that is taking place. Since the central worship of the Mass is the offering of the holy sacrifice of the Son of God to His Father in the power of the Holy Spirit, it is crucial that the liturgy help the faithful to come to active participation in that central event. External signs should help the faithful become aware and take possession of their priestly mission, which they exercise together with the ministerial priest, although in different ways, for only he acts in the person of Christ. External signs should indicate a common orientation to God of both priest and people, together with a distinction of roles.

The liturgy of the Word, which is directed to the edification of the

---

[56] See Bouyer, *Rite and Man*, 167:

> Even before its adaptation by the Christians for their churches, the Jews used for their synagogues the basilical type of building, which had been spread by the Romans throughout the empire. This public building, employed for all kinds of assemblies, had nothing religious about it. Both the synagogue and the church, however, took over this type of building since it was essential to both religions that worship should not be restricted to the clergy, even though this were done in the name of the people, but rather that it should be an act of the people themselves. . . . At the same time the sanctuary, without ceasing to be the house of God, became the house of the assembled people, or, as the Christians described it, the *domus ecclesiae*.

[57] See Ratzinger, *The Spirit of the Liturgy*, 62 (*TL*, 37).

faithful, is fittingly marked off from the offering of sacrifice, which is directed to the glorification of God. The descending movements of the liturgy of the Word and the distribution of Communion should be visibly distinguished from the ascending movement of the sacrifice. A traditional way in which this is done is through a distinction of orientation in which the priest or lector turns toward the people (*versus populum*) in the liturgy of the Word, and then all, priest and people, turn to the Lord (*versus Dominum*) when the sacrifice is being offered to Him.[58] This common turning toward the Lord has two dimensions. It involves turning upward to heaven and turning forward to the Second Coming; it is an orientation that is both ascending and eschatological.

Especially in the first millennium of the history of the Church, this orientation to the Lord was expressed by a general orientation of both priests and people to the geographical east during prayer. This orientation of prayer modified the Jewish custom of praying in the direction of the Temple in Jerusalem.[59] Louis Bouyer comments that this turn to the east "indicates that they had definitely substituted for the earthly Jerusalem the heavenly Jerusalem that is our mother, of which the Apostle speaks, and they were waiting to see it descend

---

[58] See Joseph Ratzinger, in his foreword to Uwe Michael Lang, *Turning Towards the Lord: Orientation in Liturgical Prayer* (San Francisco: Ignatius Press, 2004), 11: "Josef Andreas Jungmann . . . emphasized that what was at issue was not the priest turning away from the people, but, on the contrary, his facing the same direction as the people. The Liturgy of the Word has the character of proclamation and dialogue, to which address and response can rightly belong. But in the Liturgy of the Eucharist the priest leads the people in prayer and is turned, together with the people, towards the Lord." See also Ratzinger, *The Feast of Faith*, 139–45 (*TL*, 388–92).

[59] See Bouyer, *Rite and Man*, 168, in which he gives a description of the orientation of prayer in a Jewish synagogue of the early Christian era:

The rabbi who presided over the assembly with the assistance of the "ancients," the *presbyteroi*, was seated near the center of the nave on a platform known in Greek as a *bema*. His seat, which was called the "chair of Moses," was placed at the center of the *bema*. . . . When praying, all, including the people, faced the empty apse. In all the ancient synagogues, the building was so constructed that the apse marked the direction of Jerusalem. Thus in the prayer of the liturgy, the people and the rulers were found turned toward the sole *naos* [sanctuary containing the presence of the deity] in which the presence was believed to dwell with Israel . . .

that is, the Temple in Jerusalem.

from heaven with Christ in His Parousia, which had become symbolized for them by the East."[60]

St. John Damascene gives a good explanation of this eastward orientation of prayer:

> Since God is spiritual light and Christ in sacred Scripture
> is called "Sun of Justice" and "Orient,"[61] the East should be
> dedicated to His worship. . . . Scripture says: "And the Lord
> had planted a paradise in Eden to the east; wherein he placed
> man whom he had formed," and whom He cast out, when he
> had transgressed, and made him to live . . . in the west. Thus it
> is that, when we worship God, we long for our ancient father-
> land and gaze toward it. The tabernacle of Moses had the veil
> and the propitiatory to the east. . . . And when he [Jesus] was
> taken up, He ascended to the east and thus the Apostles wor-
> shiped Him and thus He shall come in the same way as they
> had seen Him going into heaven,[62] as the Lord Himself said:
> "As lightning comes from the east and shines as far as the west:
> so will be the coming of the Son of man" (Matt 24:27). And so,
> while we are awaiting Him, we worship toward the east. This
> is, moreover, the unwritten tradition of the Apostles, for they
> have handed many things down to us unwritten.[63]

St. Augustine emphasizes that this turn to the east helps teach the
faithful to turn interiorly to God:

---

[60] Ibid., 170.

[61] See Mal 4:2; Zech 3:8; Luke 1:78.

[62] Acts 1:11.

[63] John Damascene, *De Fide Orthodoxa* 4.12 (Chase, 353–54). St. Thomas summarized Damascene's teaching in *ST* II-II, q. 84, a. 3, ad 3:

> There is a certain fittingness in adoring towards the east. First, because
> the Divine majesty is indicated in the movement of the heavens which
> is from the east. Secondly, because Paradise was situated in the east
> according to the Septuagint version of Gen 2, and so we signify our
> desire to return to Paradise. Thirdly, on account of Christ Who is
> the light of the world, and is called "the Orient" (Zech 6:12), "Who
> mounteth above the heaven of heavens to the east" (Ps 67:34), and is
> expected to come from the east, according to Matt 24:27, "A lightning
> cometh out of the east, and appeareth even into the west; so shall also
> the coming of the Son of Man be."

For the purpose of signifying this truth, when we stand at prayer we face the East, where the rise of the heavens begins. This is not to signify that God is dwelling there, as though He had forsaken the other parts of the world—for God is present everywhere, not in habitations of place but in power of majesty. It is done so that the mind may be admonished to turn toward God while its body is turned toward a heavenly body.[64]

This eastward orientation of Christian prayer applied also to the Eucharistic Prayer, which is the preeminent prayer of the Church.[65]

In the Latin rite of the second millennium (as occasionally in the first), an orientation to geographical east is often no longer maintained so that churches can be laid out in the way most suitable to the local setting. Instead, the Latin rite generally maintained an orientation, during the Eucharistic Prayer, to the apse behind the altar, which, whatever its geographical direction, symbolizes the east. It can be called "liturgical east." This practice symbolized the fact that the whole Church, Head and members, hierarchy and faithful, are turned toward God the Father, through Christ and in Christ and in expectation of the glorious return of Christ, the sun of justice who is symbolized by the dawn. By having the priest and people share a common orientation toward the Cross, toward God, the liturgy manifests the participation of the faithful in the priesthood of Christ, which is exercised by the ministerial priest *in persona Christi*.

The Church in worship is like a ship (which is the etymological origin of the word "nave") directed toward liturgical east, toward the parousia. The ship is led by the ministerial priests, who offer the sacrifice of the Church in the person of Christ, but its numerous crew is composed of the faithful, who offer that same sacrifice together with the priest. Or we may liken the Church in worship to an army in

---

[64] Augustine, *De Sermone Domini in Monte* 2.5.18, on Matt 6:9, in *Commentary on the Lord's Sermon on the Mount with Seventeen Related Sermons*, trans. D. J. Kavanagh, FC 11 (Washington, DC: Catholic University of America Press, 1951), 125–26.

[65] See Klaus Gamber, *The Reform of the Roman Liturgy: Its Problems and Background*, trans. Klaus D. Grimm (Fort Collins, CO: Roman Catholic Books, n.d.), 80–84; Bouyer, *Rite and Man*, 175. But see the critique of some of Gamber's claims by Robin M. Jensen, "Recovering Ancient Ecclesiology: The Place of the Altar and the Orientation of Prayer in the Early Latin Church," *Worship* 89, no. 2 (2015): 99–124.

battle array, led by her general and captains, all facing a common goal, symbolized by the apse at the end of the sanctuary, which, in the early Church, generally coincided with the geographical east.

The ministerial priesthood and the royal priesthood of the faithful, although essentially distinct, share the same orientation toward God, toward the parousia. Since the royal priesthood depends on the ministerial priesthood, it is fitting that the faithful stand behind the priest in the nave and join their spiritual sacrifices to that of Christ offered through the priest.

In his classic work, *The Spirit of the Liturgy*, Joseph Ratzinger speaks of the symbolic significance of the orientation of the priest in the liturgy.[66] Where the priest faces the people, there can be a danger that the faithful may concentrate too much on the person of the priest who is celebrating and forget that the entire Eucharistic liturgy is oriented vertically toward God the Father and eschatologically oriented to the parousia. This danger can be remedied in various ways. One way is for Mass to be celebrated at times *versus absidem* ("to the apse"), accompanied by a catechesis explaining the orientation of the Mass to the Lord, the eschatological dimension of the liturgical orientation, and the common priesthood of the faithful. An alternative and complementary proposal to restore awareness of the Eucharist's theocentric orientation is, when celebrating toward the people, for priest and faithful to focus on the altar cross as the fulcrum of the sacrificial offering. Ratzinger writes:

> Ought we really to be rearranging everything all over again? Nothing is more harmful to the liturgy than a constant activism, even if it seems to be for the sake of genuine renewal. I see a solution in a suggestion. . . . Facing east . . . was linked with the "sign of the Son of Man," with the Cross, which announces the Lord's Second Coming. That is why very early on the east was linked with the sign of the Cross. Where a direct common turning toward the east is not possible, the

---

[66] Ratzinger, *The Spirit of the Liturgy*, 74–84 (*TL*, 44–51). See also Lang, *Turning Towards the Lord*; Gamber, *The Reform of the Roman Liturgy*, 77–89; Robert Cardinal Sarah, "Towards an Authentic Implementation of *Sacrosanctum Concilium*," presented at Sacra Liturgia UK 2016, July 5, 2016, accessed July 5, 2017, http://www.sacraliturgia.org/2016/07/robert-cardinal-sarah-towards-authentic.html. On the historical aspect, see Stefan Heid, "The Early Christian Altar—Lessons for Today," in Reid, *The Sacred Liturgy*.

cross can serve as the interior "east" of faith. It should stand in the middle of the altar and be the common point of focus for both priest and praying community. In this way we obey the ancient call to prayer: "*Conversi ad Dominum*," Turn toward the Lord! In this way we look together at the One whose death tore the veil of the Temple—the One who stands before the Father for us and encloses us in his arms in order to make us the new and living Temple. Moving the altar cross to the side to give an uninterrupted view of the priest is something I regard as one of the truly absurd phenomena of recent decades. Is the cross disruptive during Mass? . . . The Lord is the point of reference. He is the rising sun of history.[67]

Many people think that the orientation *versus populum* was required by the Second Vatican Council. This is incorrect; *Sacrosanctum Concilium* makes no reference to this question.[68] The *General Instruction on the Roman Missal* (GIRM) touches on the subject of orientation very briefly in §299, discussing the position of the altar in newly constructed churches. The official Latin text reads: "Altare exstruatur a pariete seiunctum, ut facile circumiri et in eo celebratio versus populum peragi possit, quod expedit ubicumque possibile sit."[69] The standard English translation reads: "The altar should be built separate from the wall, in such a way that it is possible to walk around it easily and that Mass can be celebrated at it facing the people, which is desirable wherever possible."[70] It seems that this translation is inaccurate. The Latin relative pronoun "quod," which is neuter, should be taken to refer back, not to *celebratio*, which is feminine, but to the main clause—"Altare exstruatur a pariete seiunctum,"—and to the verb, *possit*. In other words, that which is said to be expedient or "desirable whenever possible" is that

---

[67] Ratzinger, *The Spirit of the Liturgy*, 83–84 (in *TL*, 51).

[68] See Ratzinger, foreword to Lang, *Turning Towards the Lord*, 9 (*TL*, 393). The celebration of Mass *versus populum* was first advocated, it seems, by Martin Luther in 1526 in *The German Mass and the Order of Worship* (Gamber, *Reform of the Roman Liturgy*, 77–78).

[69] *Missale Romanum: Ex Decreto Sacrosancti Œcumenici Concilii Vaticani II Instauratum Auctoritate Pauli PP. VI Promulgatum Ioannis Pauli PP. II Cura Recognitum*, Editio Typica Tertia (Vatican City: Libreria Editrice Vaticana, 2008), 68. The phrase, "quod expedit ubicumque possibile sit," was added in the revised edition in 2000.

[70] *RM*, 68.

that "the altar be built separate from the wall" so that it is *possible* (*possit*) to walk around it (as in incensing) and possible for Mass to be celebrated *versus populum*. In addition, if the GIRM really intended to mandate a celebration *versus populum* wherever possible, this section on the position of the altar would seem to be an inconspicuous place for such an important rubric. A better translation, therefore, would be: "The altar should be built separated from the wall, which is advantageous wherever possible, so that one can walk around the altar easily and there can be celebration facing the people."[71]

Various other rubrics in the GIRM, furthermore, seem to presuppose that the priest is not necessarily facing *versus populum*. For example, the celebrant is instructed to turn to the people at certain times, which would be superfluous if the priest were always facing the people.[72]

The interpretation of §299 of the GIRM was the subject of a *dubium* and an official response from the Congregation for Divine Worship on September 25, 2000.[73] It was asked whether "§299 of the

---

[71] My translation. See also John Hunwicke, "Guest Editorial," *Sacred Music* 127, no. 4 (Winter 2001): 3: "Would you like a Latin lesson? Consider the phrase: *quod expedit ubicumque possibile sit. Quod* is neuter. So it cannot possibly have as its antecedent *celebratio (versus populum)*, which is feminine. *Quod* clearly refers to the preceding sentence as a whole, where the crucial term is *possit*. In GIRM this verb is commonly used for things which are genuinely optional—as in the preceding two and following two paragraphs (297–298 and 300–301). Paragraph 299 says: 'The High Altar [not, be it observed, every altar] should be constructed away from the wall, so that the option is open [*possit*] of walking easily around it and using it for Mass facing the people. This [i.e., having the altar free-standing so that the options are open] is desirable wherever possible.'" See also Christopher M. Cullen, S.J., and Joseph W. Koterski, S.J., "The New IGMR and Mass *versus Populum*," *Homiletic and Pastoral Review* (June 2001), 51–54; Lang, *Turning Towards the Lord*, 25–26.

[72] The instruction to be "standing facing the people" is given in GIRM §146 (at the *Orate, fratres*); §154 (at the greeting of peace); and §157 (at the *Ecce agnus Dei*). This is in contrast to §158, which stipulates that the priest consumes the host "standing facing the altar." This implies that to be *facing the people* and to be *facing the altar* are not always the same, as they would be when one is celebrating *versus populum*. See Lang, *Turning Towards the Lord*, 23–24.

[73] See the summary of this document by Joseph Ratzinger, in his foreword to Lang, *Turning Towards the Lord*, 9–10 (*TL*, 393). Speaking of §299 of the GIRM and the clause "which is desirable wherever possible" he writes:

> This was taken in many quarters as hardening the 1969 text to mean that there was now a general obligation to set up altars facing the people "wherever possible." This interpretation, however, was rejected

Instituto Generalis Missalis Romani constitutes a norm according to which, during the Eucharistic liturgy, the position of the priest *versus absidem* [facing toward the apse] is to be excluded." The answer was "negative," and an explanation was then given. First, the document explains how §299 should be understood:

> It is in the first place to be borne in mind that the word *expedit* does not constitute an obligation, but a suggestion that refers to the construction of the altar *a pariete sejunctum* ["detached from the wall"] and to the celebration *versus populum* ["toward the people"]. The clause *ubi possibile sit* ["where it is possible"] refers to different elements, as, for example, the topography of the place, the availability of space, the artistic value of the existing altar, the sensibility of the people participating in the celebrations in a particular church, etc. It reaffirms that the position toward the assembly seems more convenient inasmuch as it makes communication easier (cf. the editorial in *Notitiae* 29 [1993] 245—49), without excluding, however, the other possibility.[74]

In addition, the response speaks about the theological meaning of orientation and possible misunderstandings. Regardless of whether it is celebrated toward the people or toward the apse, the Eucharistic sacrifice is always directed *to the Lord* and never directed *to the people*:

> However, whatever may be the position of the celebrating priest, it is clear that the Eucharistic Sacrifice is offered to the one and triune God, and that the principal, eternal, and high priest is Jesus Christ, who acts through the ministry of the priest who visibly presides as His instrument. The litur-

---

by the Congregation for Divine Worship on 25 September 2000, when it declared that the word *"expedit"* ("is desirable") did not imply an obligation but only made a suggestion. The physical orientation, the Congregation says, must be distinguished from the spiritual. Even if a priest celebrates *versus populum*, he should always be oriented *versus Deum per Iesum Christum.* . . . For this reason the Congregation warns against one-sided and rigid positions in this debate.

[74] Congregation for Divine Worship and the Discipline of the Sacraments, "On the Orientation of the Priest at Mass" (Prot. Prot. No. 2036/00/L), Sept. 25, 2000 (English translation in *Adoremus Bulletin* [online edition] 6, no. 9 [Dec 2000–Jan 2001]).

gical assembly participates in the celebration in virtue of the common priesthood of the faithful which requires the ministry of the ordained priest to be exercised in the Eucharistic Synaxis. The physical position, especially with respect to the communication among the various members of the assembly, must be distinguished from the interior spiritual orientation of all. It would be a grave error to imagine that the principal orientation of the sacrificial action is [toward] the community. If the priest celebrates *versus populum*, which is legitimate and often advisable, his spiritual attitude ought always to be *versus Deum per Jesus Christum* ["toward God through Jesus Christ"], as representative of the entire Church. The Church as well, which takes concrete form in the assembly which participates, is entirely turned *versus Deum* [toward God] as its first spiritual movement.[75]

The document wisely concludes by stating that a "rigid position" absolutizing one solution should be avoided.[76] Familiarity with the wealth of the liturgical heritage of the Church better enables the faithful to learn the deeper meaning of the Mass, not only through conceptual instruction but also through the proper liturgical means of sensible signs that externally and worthily represent the interior and invisible reality that is taking place.

I would add that it should not be taken for granted that the faithful understand this spiritual orientation of the Eucharistic sacrifice *to the Lord*. In reality, very many of the faithful have never heard it explained that the Mass is a sacrifice directed to God. Many have been instructed to think of the Mass as a fraternal meal and have a vague idea that sacrifices belong to a barbarous age of mankind that has been left far behind. Precisely for this reason it is highly expedient that the visual impression of the Eucharistic Prayer sensibly manifest the ascending and eschatological direction of the prayer to God. A fundamental principle of the liturgy is that visible and spiritual ori-

---

[75] Ibid.

[76] Ibid.: "There is no need to give excessive importance to elements that have changed throughout the centuries. What always remains is the event celebrated in the liturgy: this is manifested through rites, signs, symbols and words that express various aspects of the mystery without, however, exhausting it, because it transcends them. Taking a rigid position and absolutizing it could become a rejection of some aspect of the truth which merits respect and acceptance."

entation should coincide as much as possible. The more society is secularized, the more valuable it is that the radically theocentric orientation of the liturgy be outwardly manifested. Ratzinger states: "If the liturgy appears first of all as the workshop for our activity, then what is essential is being forgotten: God. For the liturgy is not about us, but about God. Forgetting about God is the most imminent danger of our age."[77] Robert Cardinal Sarah echoed this point in an address from 2016 entitled "Towards an Authentic Implementation of *Sacrosanctum Concilium*":

> I wish to underline a very important fact here: God, not man is at the center of Catholic liturgy. We come to worship Him. The liturgy is not about you and I; it is not where we celebrate our own identity or achievements or exalt or promote our own culture and local religious customs. The liturgy is first and foremost about God and what He has done for us. . . . The Council Fathers did not arrive in Rome in October 1962 with the intention of producing an anthropocentric liturgy.[78]

Do the faithful adequately understand the theocentrism of the Mass? If not, the celebration of the liturgy should be made to more effectively manifest its intrinsic spiritual orientation toward God, especially in the liturgy's apex, which is the Eucharistic sacrifice. Cardinal Sarah writes:

> I believe that it is very important that we return as soon as possible to a common orientation, of priests and the faithful turned together in the same direction—Eastwards or at least towards the apse—to the Lord who comes, in those parts of the liturgical rites when we are addressing God. This practice is permitted by current liturgical legislation. It is perfectly legitimate in the modern rite. Indeed, I think it is a very important step in ensuring that in our celebrations the Lord is truly at the centre.[79]

---

[77] Joseph Ratzinger, preface to Alcuin Reid, *The Organic Development of the Liturgy*, in *TL*, 593.

[78] Sarah, "Towards an Authentic Implementation of *Sacrosanctum Concilium*," 5.

[79] Ibid., 21. The text continues with a plea to priests and bishops:

> And so, dear Fathers, I humbly and fraternally ask you to implement this practice wherever possible, with prudence and with the necessary

Study Questions

1. Why does sacrifice have a communal dimension?
2. What texts of Scripture manifest the common priesthood of the faithful in Israel and the Church?
3. What is the distinction between the common priesthood of the faithful and the ordained priesthood? How are they related to each other?
4. How do the faithful participate in the offering of the sacrifice?
    a. Why does the priest pray "that *my sacrifice and yours* may be acceptable to God, the almighty Father"? What other texts of the Roman Canon (or other Eucharistic Prayers) make reference to the participation of the faithful in offering the sacrifice?
    b. Explain the teaching of Pius XII in *Mediator Dei* on the participation of the faithful in the Eucharistic sacrifice.
    c. Explain *Lumen Gentium*, §11: "Taking part in the Eucharistic Sacrifice, which is the source and summit of the whole Christian life, they offer the divine Victim to God, and *offer themselves along with it.*"
5. What is the meaning of Vatican II's call for "active participation" of the faithful in the Mass?
6. Explain the reasons for the Sunday Mass obligation.

---

catechesis, certainly, but also with a pastor's confidence that this is something good for the Church, something good for our people. . . . Dear Fathers, we should listen again to the lament of God proclaimed by the prophet Jeremiah: "they have turned their backs to me and not their faces" (2:27). Let *us* turn again towards the Lord! Since the day of his Baptism, the Christian knows only one direction: the Orient. "You entered to confront your enemy, for you intended to renounce him to his face. You turned toward the East (*ad Orientem*), for one who renounces the devil turns towards Christ and fixes his gaze directly on Him" (From the beginning of the Treatise *On the Mysteries* by Saint Ambrose, Bishop of Milan).

I very humbly and fraternally would like to appeal also to my brother bishops: please lead your priests and people towards the Lord in this way, particularly at large celebrations in your dioceses and in your cathedral. Please form your seminarians in the reality that we are not called to the priesthood to be at the centre of liturgical worship ourselves, but to lead Christ's faithful to him as fellow worshippers united in the one same act of adoration. Please facilitate this simple but profound reform in your dioceses, your cathedrals, your parishes and your seminaries.

7. What is meant by the term "orientation" in the liturgy? What is the symbolic significance of facing east (geographical or liturgical) in the Eucharistic Prayer?

Suggestions for Further Reading

Benedict XVI. Apostolic Exhortation *Sacramentum Caritatis*. February 22, 2007. See §§38–42.

John Paul II. Apostolic Letter *Dies Domini*. May 31, 1998.

Lang, Uwe Michael. *Turning Towards the Lord: Orientation in Liturgical Prayer*. San Francisco: Ignatius Press, 2004.

Pius XII. Encyclical on the Sacred Liturgy *Mediator Dei*. November 20, 1947. See §§80–115.

Ratzinger, Joseph. *Theology of the Liturgy: The Sacramental Foundation of Christian Existence*. San Francisco: Ignatius Press, 2014. Pp. 31–52; 106–10; 187–206; 371–95; 582–88.

Sarah, Robert Cardinal, "Towards an Authentic Implementation of *Sacrosanctum Concilium*," presented at Sacra Liturgia UK 2016 Conference, London, England, July 2016. Accessed July 5, 2017. https://drive.google.com/file/d/0B8CZzED2HiWJNzdaOE9ycVI4ekU/view.

✠

CHAPTER TWELVE

Fruits of the Sacrifice
of the Mass

THE MERITS OF THE SACRIFICE OF CALVARY
ARE APPLIED BY THE MASS

We have seen that the sacrifice of the Mass actualizes the sacrifice of Calvary, re-presenting it in the life of the Church in every time and place, from the rising to the setting of the sun (Mal 1:11). It makes Calvary present by allowing the Church to participate in Christ's act of offering to the Father, and also by enabling Calvary's effects of grace to be poured out abundantly on the Church and the world in a descending movement. Like Calvary, the sacrifice of the Mass is essentially an ascending movement of glorification. But the ascending movement, in addition to glorifying God, aims to achieve reconciliation between God and man, which will result in God showering the world with graces, which are the fruits of the sacrifice. Every Mass applies to the world some of the effects won universally by the sacrifice of Calvary. We could compare the sacrifice of Calvary to a fountain and the sacrifice of the Mass, celebrated in many times and places, to streams flowing out from that one fountain to water many places and provide drink for many.

The Council of Trent addressed the relationship between the fruits of the sacrifice of Calvary and the Mass:

> The fruits of this oblation (the bloody one, that is) are received in abundance through this unbloody (oblation). By no means, then, does the latter detract from the former. Therefore it is rightly offered according to apostolic tradition, not only for the sins, punishments, satisfaction, and other necessities of

the faithful who are alive, but also for those who have died in Christ but are not wholly purified.[1]

Because the sacrifice of the Mass applies the fruits of the sacrifice of the Cross to mankind in a given time and place, the Mass depends on the sacrifice of Calvary as an instrumental and particular cause depends on a principal and universal cause.[2] As Michelangelo's chisel does not detract from the sculptor's power, but rather applies it in a particular way, so the Mass, as a sacramental instrument, does not detract from the source of its power—the Passion of Christ—but makes it present, applying it to the world here and now.[3]

All of the sacraments apply the merits won through the sacrifice of Calvary. The Mass does so in a special way, in that it alone is not only a sacrament that transmits the grace that it represents but also a sacrifice that is pleasing to God so as to call down graces upon the *whole world*, even on those who are not able to receive the sacraments. Thus these fruits of the sacrifice are not exhausted in the reception of Holy Communion, but extend far more widely.[4] It is in this way, for example, that the Mass can benefit the faithful departed in purgatory.

In his encyclical on the liturgy, *Mediator Dei*, Pius XII explains the relationship between the sacrifice of Calvary, the sacraments in general, and the Mass. Speaking of the redemption accomplished in Christ's Passion, he writes:

> This purchase, however, does not immediately have its full effect; since Christ, after redeeming the world at the lavish cost of His own blood, still must come into complete posses-

---

[1] Council of Trent, On the Sacrifice of the Mass (session 22), ch. 2 (DS, 1744).

[2] See Colman O'Neill, *New Approaches to the Eucharist*, 34–35.

[3] See Nicolas, *What Is the Eucharist?* 58: "Just as the Eucharist is not another body of Jesus but the bringing to us of his bodily presence, so too the Mass is not another sacrifice, another immolation of his body, but this sacrifice and this immolation made present and actual in our hands. And it follows that the Mass is the efficacy of the sacrifice applied to the actual and present needs of the world."

[4] See Council of Trent, On the Sacrifice of the Mass (session 22), can. 3: "If anyone says that the Sacrifice of the Mass . . . benefits only those who communicate; and that it should not be offered for the living and the dead, for sins, punishments, satisfaction, and other necessities: let him be anathema" (DS, 1753).

sion of the souls of men. Wherefore, that the redemption and salvation of each person and of future generations unto the end of time may be effectively accomplished, and be acceptable to God, it is necessary that men should individually come into vital contact with the sacrifice of the cross, so that the merits, which flow from it, should be imparted to them. In a certain sense it can be said that on Calvary Christ built a font of purification and salvation which He filled with the blood He shed; but if men do not bathe in it and there wash away the stains of their iniquities, they can never be purified and saved.[5]

The task of the Church is to bring all men into contact with the streams of grace that flow from Calvary. This is done principally through the sacraments of the Church:

> The cooperation of the faithful is required so that sinners may be individually purified in the blood of the Lamb. For though, speaking generally, Christ reconciled by His painful death the whole human race with the Father, He wished that all should approach and be drawn to His cross, especially by means of the sacraments and the eucharistic sacrifice, to obtain the salutary fruits produced by Him upon it.[6]

If all the sacraments distribute the graces won on Calvary, this is done in a supreme way in the Mass:

> The august sacrifice of the altar is, as it were, the supreme instrument whereby the merits won by the divine Redeemer upon the cross are distributed to the faithful: "as often as this commemorative sacrifice is offered, there is wrought the work of our Redemption."[7] This, however, so far from lessening the

---

[5] Pius XII, *Mediator Dei*, §77.

[6] Ibid., §78. In this paragraph, Pius XII quotes his earlier encyclical *Mystici Corporis*, §44: "When dying on the cross, [Jesus] bestowed upon His Church, as a completely gratuitous gift, the immense treasure of the redemption. But when it is a question of distributing this treasure, He not only commits the work of sanctification to His Immaculate Spouse, but also wishes that, to a certain extent, sanctity should derive from her activity."

[7] *Roman Missal* (prior to the liturgical reform after the Second Vatican Council),

dignity of the actual sacrifice on Calvary, rather proclaims and renders more manifest its greatness and its necessity, as the Council of Trent declares. Its daily immolation reminds us that there is no salvation except in the cross of our Lord Jesus Christ and that God Himself wishes that there should be a continuation of this sacrifice "from the rising of the sun till the going down thereof," so that there may be no cessation of the hymn of praise and thanksgiving which man owes to God, seeing that he required His help continually and has need of the blood of the Redeemer to remit sin which challenges God's justice.[8]

Four Ends of the Sacrifice of the Mass

Catholic tradition speaks of four ends of the Mass, four ends that are common to the entire liturgy, to prayer, and, in fact, to all religion. These four ends are adoration by which God is glorified, thanksgiving, petition, and expiation of sin. The Mass realizes each of these four ends in a supreme way.

Sacrifice of Praise

Ex opere operato,[9] the Mass gives infinitely greater glory to God than any other meritorious act that we can perform, for it is the very sacrifice of Calvary sacramentally made present on our altars, in which the Word Incarnate offers Himself for the salvation of men, moved by maximum charity.[10] By devoutly celebrating Mass, participating in

---

Secret of the Ninth Sunday after Pentecost. Currently, Prayer over the Offerings, Holy Thursday Mass of the Lord's Supper and Second Sunday of Ordinary Time (*RM*, 303, 462).

[8] Pius XII, *Mediator Dei*, §79.

[9] See O'Neill, *New Approaches to the Eucharist*, 42: "Whereas, in its application to the other sacraments, this phrase refers to the gift of grace given through the sacrament to the ('disposed') recipient, when applied to the Mass it denotes the manifold pleading for grace which is characteristic of a sacrifice. It directs attention specifically to the active presence of Christ the priest in the Mass, which brings with it an infinite ennoblement of the Church's worship."

[10] See Pius XII, *Mediator Dei*, §71: "The first of these [ends of the Eucharistic sacrifice] is to give glory to the Heavenly Father. From His birth to His death Jesus Christ burned with zeal for the divine glory; and the offering of His blood

Mass, or having Mass offered, we give immeasurably more glory to God than by any other means, for the sacrifice of the Mass makes present Christ's glorification of God on Calvary. This end of the Mass is most clearly expressed in the doxology that concludes Eucharistic Prayers, as in the Roman Canon: "Through him, and with him, and in him, O God, almighty Father, in the unity of the Holy Spirit, all glory and honor is yours, for ever and ever."[11] The Sanctus, likewise, is an eloquent expression of adoration leading into the heart of the Eucharistic Prayer, in which we join in with the Church triumphant in her eternal chorus of praise.

Sacrifice of Thanksgiving

The Mass is also the most perfect means of giving thanks to God for all of His benefits. From this end of the Mass comes its name, Eucharist, which is the Greek word for "thanksgiving." As Pius XII wrote in *Mediator Dei*, §72:

> Only the divine Redeemer, as the eternal Father's most beloved Son whose immense love He knew, could offer Him a worthy return of gratitude. This was His intention and desire at the Last Supper when He "gave thanks." He did not cease to do so when hanging upon the cross, nor does He fail to do so in the august sacrifice of the altar, which is an act of thanksgiving or a "eucharistic" act; since this "is truly meet and just, right and availing unto salvation."

Psalm 116:12–13 prefigures the power of thanksgiving of the Eucharistic chalice: "What shall I render to the Lord for all His bounty to me? I will lift up the cup of salvation and call on the name of the Lord." This end of the Mass, present throughout, is exemplified in the Preface of Eucharistic Prayers, in which God is praised for His work of creation, redemption, and the particular mystery being celebrated in the liturgy of the day.

---

upon the cross rose to heaven in an odor of sweetness. To perpetuate this praise, the members of the Mystical Body are united with their divine Head in the eucharistic sacrifice, and with Him, together with the Angels and Archangels, they sing immortal praise to God and give all honor and glory to the Father Almighty."

[11] *RM*, 643.

Sacrifice of Impetration

The Mass is also the supreme *impetratory* sacrifice. This means that the sacrifice of the Mass is the best way to present our petitions before God, for in the Mass the Blood of Christ is poured out for us, the Blood that "speaks more graciously than the blood of Abel" (see Heb 12:24). However, this impetratory effect also depends on the strength of the faith, hope, and charity with which we offer up the Mass. This impetratory aspect of the Mass is manifested in a solemn way in the universal prayer on Good Friday and in more condensed form in the intercessions within the Eucharistic Prayer.[12] St. Cyril of Jerusalem explains this aspect in one of his mystagogical homilies:

> Then, when the spiritual sacrifice—this worship without blood—has been completed, we beg God over the sacrifice of propitiation for general peace among the churches, for the right order of the world, for the kings, for soldier and allies, for the sick and the afflicted, and in short we all make entreaty and offer this sacrifice for all who need help.[13]

The Mass Is a Propitiatory Sacrifice Benefitting the Living and the Dead

The Mass is the most perfect expiatory or propitiatory sacrifice that can be offered or even conceived, for it is the expiation of Jesus Christ, true God and true man, for all the sins of the world.[14] All our personal sacrifices have immeasurably greater value before God when we offer them through the sacrifice of Calvary and of the altar.

The Mass is efficacious in expiating the two consequences of sin, which are the guilt of sin and the temporal punishment due to sin.

---

[12] See the prayer for the universal Church in the Roman Canon: "Be pleased to grant her peace, to guard, unite and govern her throughout the whole world, together with your servant N. our Pope and N. our Bishop, and all those who, holding to the truth, hand on the catholic and apostolic faith" (*RM*, 635).

[13] Cyril of Jerusalem, *Mystagogic Catecheses* 5.8 (Yarnold, *Awe-Inspiring Rites*, 93).

[14] Pius XII, *Mediator Dei*, §73: "Likewise He daily offers Himself upon our altars for our redemption, that we may be rescued from eternal damnation and admitted into the company of the elect. This He does, not for us only who are in this mortal life, but also 'for all who rest in Christ, who have gone before us with the sign of faith and repose in the sleep of peace.'"

This distinction comes from the fact that every sin involves an offense to God (guilt of sin) and some disorder that is introduced into the world and human relationships.[15] The offense to God is taken away by sincere repentance and sacramental absolution. The disorder that has been brought into the world, however, requires that some satisfaction be made to reestablish order. This can be done in this life through acts of charity and penance or after this life in purgatory, and this satisfaction is referred to as "temporal punishment for sin."[16]

While it is true that guilt for sin is forgiven directly only through contrition and the sacraments of Baptism and Penance, the power of those sacraments to forgive sin is gained only through the merits of the sacrifice of Calvary, which is renewed on the altar. The propitiatory effect of the sacrifice of the Mass is principally to call down God's mercy on sinners so that He may send them His grace of contrition and conversion and lead them to make use of the grace of the sacraments of Penance and Communion. Even the most hardened sinner may be converted through the graces merited by the sacrifice of Calvary and applied to the world through the Eucharistic sacrifice. If we are aware that we are in a state of mortal sin, we must not receive Communion before receiving valid absolution in Confession,[17] but it

---

[15] On the twofold consequences of sin, see *CCC*, §1472:

> To understand this doctrine and practice of the Church, it is necessary to understand that sin has a double consequence. Grave sin deprives us of communion with God and therefore makes us incapable of eternal life, the privation of which is called the "eternal punishment" of sin. On the other hand every sin, even venial, entails an unhealthy attachment to creatures, which must be purified either here on earth, or after death in the state called Purgatory. This purification frees one from what is called the "temporal punishment" of sin. These two punishments must not be conceived of as a kind of vengeance inflicted by God from without, but as following from the very nature of sin. A conversion which proceeds from a fervent charity can attain the complete purification of the sinner in such a way that no punishment would remain.

See also *ST* III, q. 86, a. 4.

[16] See *CCC*, §1473: "The forgiveness of sin and restoration of communion with God entail the remission of the eternal punishment of sin, but temporal punishment of sin remains. While patiently bearing sufferings and trials of all kinds and, when the day comes, serenely facing death, the Christian must strive to accept this temporal punishment of sin as a grace. He should strive by works of mercy and charity, as well as by prayer and the various practices of penance, to put off completely the 'old man' and to put on the 'new man.'"

[17] See CIC, can. 916, discussed below in chapter 14, pp. 540–42.

is still most profitable for us to participate in Mass to implore God's forgiveness of our sins and the grace of repentance.

This effect of the Mass of winning graces of conversion and repentance leading to the forgiveness of sins is witnessed above all in the words of the institution narrative over the chalice: "the blood of the new and eternal covenant, which will be poured out for you and for many for the forgiveness of sins."[18] It is also seen in many Eucharistic Prayers in the epiclesis for the sanctification of the faithful. For example, the ancient Maronite anaphora called *Sharar* states: "For the sins, faults, and defects of us all, we offer this pure and holy offering."[19] The Divine Mercy Chaplet offers the following prayer: "Eternal Father, I offer you the Body and Blood, Soul and Divinity of Your dearly beloved Son, Our Lord Jesus Christ, in atonement for our sins and those of the whole world. For the sake of His sorrowful Passion, have mercy on us and on the whole world."

The sacrifice of the Mass also remits some of the temporal punishment due to sin, which otherwise would have to be expiated in purgatory. This propitiatory effect can be applied both to the living (the members of the Church who are in a state of grace) and to those suffering in purgatory. Indeed, offering the holy Mass for the relief of the holy souls in purgatory is the most efficacious means of aiding them, for the Mass obtains this effect *ex opere operato*, through the direct action of Christ the High Priest. Nevertheless, many Masses may have to be offered, depending on the dispositions of those for whom it is offered and the greatness of the debt against God's justice.

The existence of this potent propitiatory effect of the Mass on behalf of the living and the dead, vehemently denied by Luther and all Protestants, was defined in the Council of Trent:

> In the divine sacrifice that is offered in the Mass, the same Christ who offered himself once in a bloody manner on the altar of the cross is present and is offered in an unbloody manner. Therefore, the holy Council teaches that this sacrifice is truly propitiatory, so that if we draw near to God with an upright

---

[18] *RM*, 647.

[19] Third Maronite Anaphora St. Peter, called *Sharar* (*PEER*, 46). See Cesare Giraudo, who highlights the frequent presence of prayers for the forgiveness of sins in the epiclesis of sanctification, in "L'eucaristia: premio per i sani o medicina per i malati? Nuovi orizzonti di teologia a partire dalle anafore d'Oriente e d'Occidente," *La Civiltà cattolica* 166 (September 26, 2015): 480–93.

heart and true faith, with fear and reverence, with sorrow and repentance, through it "we may obtain mercy and find grace to help in time of need" [Heb 4:16]. For the Lord, appeased by this oblation, grants grace and the gift of repentance, and he pardons wrongdoings and sins, even grave ones. For it is one and the same victim: He who now makes the offering through the ministry of priests and he who then offered Himself on the cross; only the manner of offering is different.[20]

The denial of the propitiatory effect of the Mass was definitively condemned by Trent in canon 3 of session 22, on the Eucharistic Sacrifice:

If anyone says that the Sacrifice of the Mass is merely an offering of praise and thanksgiving, or that it is a simple memorial of the sacrifice offered on the cross, and not propitiatory, or that it benefits only those who communicate; and that it should not be offered for the living and the dead, for sins, punishments, satisfaction, and other necessities: let him be anathema.[21]

The Council of Trent, in its Decree on Purgatory, also affirmed that the souls in purgatory are aided by the offering of the sacrifice of the Mass: "There is a purgatory and . . . the souls detained there are helped by the acts of intercession of the faithful, and especially by the acceptable Sacrifice of the Altar."[22]

The reason that the offering of the sacrifice of the Mass is propitiatory is simply that it is the offering of Christ Himself, sacramentally immolated. The sacramental offering makes the sacrifice of Calvary present to our own time and place, as transubstantiation makes Christ's own substance present under the sacramental species. And if the Mass makes the sacrifice of Calvary sacramentally present, how could it not be propitiatory, or pleasing to God, and thus uniquely capable of drawing down the graces won by that sacrifice?

St. Cyril of Jerusalem offers an early witness of the propitiatory

---

[20] Council of Trent, On the Sacrifice of the Mass (session 22), ch. 2 (DS, 1743).

[21] Ibid., can. 3 (DS, 1753).

[22] Council of Trent, Decree Concerning Purgatory (session 25, December 4, 1563) (DS, 1820).

nature of the Mass, as he explains to the neophytes why the Mass is offered for the living and the dead.[23] After mentioning the petitions for the deceased in the Eucharistic Prayer, he says:

> After that, we pray on behalf of the holy fathers and bishops and in general all amongst us already gone to their rest, for we believe that these souls will obtain the greatest help if we make our prayers for them while the holy and most awesome sacrifice is being offered.
>
> I should like to use an illustration to persuade you of the truth of this, for I know that many of you are saying: "how is a soul which has quitted this world, whether in sin or not, helped by being mentioned in the prayers?" Well, surely if a king had exiled some opponents, and their friends wove a garland and presented it to him on behalf of those who had been penalized, would not he relax their punishment? It is the same when we make our entreaties to God on behalf of the dead, even if they are sinners. But we do not weave a garland; we offer Christ who has been slain for our sins, and so we appease the merciful God both on their behalf and on ours.[24]

St. Monica alluded to the propitiatory power of the Mass when speaking to her sons shortly before her death: "Bury this body anywhere. Let its care give you no concern. One thing only do I ask of you, that you remember me at the altar of the Lord, wherever you may be."[25] St. Augustine comments: "She knew that on it the Holy Victim is offered; by means of which 'the decree against us, which was hostile to us,' is cancelled. . . . To this sacrament of our redemption Thy handmaid bound her soul with the bond of faith."[26] After her death, St. Augustine mentions that "the sacrifice of our redemption was offered for her."[27]

St. Augustine speaks of the sacrifice of the Mass offered for the

---

[23] For Patristic thought and practice on offering the sacrifice of the Mass for the faithful departed, see Christian D. Washburn, "The Value of Offering Sacrifice for the Dead in the Thought of the Fathers of the Church," *Antiphon* 16, no. 3 (2012): 154–78.

[24] Cyril of Jerusalem, *Mystagogic Catecheses* 5.9–10 (Yarnold, *Awe-Inspiring Rites*, 93–94).

[25] Augustine, *Confessions* 9.11.27, trans. V. J. Bourke, FC 21 (Washington, DC: Catholic University of America Press, 1953), 254.

[26] Ibid., 9.13.36 (Bourke, 261).

[27] Ibid., 9.12.32 (Bourke, 257).

faithful departed in his *Faith, Hope and Charity* (also known as the *Enchiridion*):

> And it cannot be denied that the souls of the dead obtain relief through the piety of their living friends, when they have the Sacrifice of the Mediator offered for them, or when alms are given in the Church on their behalf. But these things benefit those only who during their lives merited that these services should one day help them. For there is a manner of life neither so good as not to need such helps after death, nor so bad that they cannot be of benefit. . . . When, therefore, sacrifices either of the altar or of alms of any kind are offered for all the baptized dead, they are thank offerings for the very good; for those who were not very bad they are propitiatory offerings; and, though for the very bad they have no significance as helps for the dead, they do bring a measure of consolation to the living. And those who actually receive such profit, receive it in the form either of a complete remission of sin, or of at least an amelioration of their sentence.[28]

Two centuries later, St. Isidore of Seville referred to the practice of offering the sacrifice of the Mass for the faithful departed as an apostolic tradition:

> We believe that it is a tradition from the apostles themselves that the sacrifice is offered for the repose of the faithful departed or to pray for them, because this is maintained throughout the whole world. The Catholic Church holds this everywhere. For if it did not believe that the faithful departed are forgiven their sins, it would not give alms for their souls or offer sacrifice to God.[29]

---

[28] Augustine, *Faith, Hope and Charity*, trans. L. A. Arand, ed. Johannes Quasten and Joseph C. Plumpe, ACW 3 (New York: Newman Press, 1947), 103–104. See also St. Augustine, Sermon 172.2: "It is not to be doubted, though, that the dead can be helped by the prayers of holy Church, and the eucharistic sacrifice" (*Sermons [148–183] on the New Testament*, trans. Edmund Hill, WSA, pt. III [Homilies], vol. 5 [New Rochelle, NY: New City Press, 1992], 252).

[29] Isidore of Seville, *De Ecclesiasticis Officiis* 1.18.11, trans. T. L. Knoebel, ACW 61 (New York: Newman Press, 2008), 44.

Eucharistic Prayers commonly state that the sacrifice is being offered for the living and the dead. The ancient Maronite anaphora called *Sharar* begins: "We offer to you, God our Father, Lord of all, an offering and a commemoration and a memorial in the sight of God, living from the beginning and holy from eternity, for the living and the dead, for the near and the far."[30] The Roman Canon prays: "Grant them, O Lord, we pray, and all who sleep in Christ, a place of refreshment, light and peace."[31]

PARTICULAR FRUITS OF THE SACRIFICE OF THE MASS

The sacrifice of the Mass is above all an act of homage to God by Christ and the Church. Its primary thrust is to glorify and thank God and offer an infinite expiatory satisfaction for sin. Thus it is primarily an ascending movement from man to God.[32] In offering the expression of adoration, thanksgiving, contrition, and supplication, it also calls down—through its aspects of propitiation and petition—a shower of blessings from God to men.

Since Christ is the High Priest who offers Himself in every Mass through the hands of His ordained ministers, it follows that the Mass has an efficacy in achieving its four ends—adoration, thanksgiving, supplication, and propitiation—that does not depend on the sanctity of the ordained priest or even on his being in a state of grace. A Mass celebrated by a priest in grave sin is still the sacrifice of Calvary made present on our altars. This intrinsic efficacy of the Mass, as of all the other sacraments, is expressed in Catholic theology by saying that the sacraments are efficacious *ex opere operato*, which means by the fact of being rightly performed.[33] This efficacy, furthermore, is distinct from the fruitfulness of Holy Communion. Every valid Mass is efficacious

---

[30] Third Maronite Anaphora of St. Peter, called *Sharar* (*PEER*, 46).

[31] *RM*, 642.

[32] See Nicolas, *What Is the Eucharist?* 73: "It is customary to insist on the fact that each Mass is a new application of the virtue of the sacrifice of the Cross. But we must not forget that the 'virtue' of the sacrifice of the Cross is above all its direct power over the Heart of God, its value as perfect worship. . . . Every Mass contains in itself, in all its fullness, the adoration of Christ, his thanksgiving, his desire to make reparation, but as passing through the Church, through us, and so making our religion and our offering his own."

[33] See *CCC*, §§1127–28:

in the way that a sacrifice is efficacious, as an ascending movement of praise and self-offering that is pleasing to God. It is intrinsically efficacious first in offering supreme praise and thanksgiving to God, and also by having a propitiatory effect for the forgiveness of sins and for calling forth the bestowal of God's blessings on the world.

These blessings or fruits of the Mass benefit three classes of recipients. First of all, there is a *general fruit* that benefits the whole Church, for it is offered by the Head of the Mystical Body, Jesus Christ, on behalf of the whole mystical Body, which includes both the living and the dead. Thus it benefits the suffering souls in purgatory, shortening their time of purgation. It even has effects on those who are outside the Church, who are all potential members, propitiating God on their behalf so that they may be given the grace of conversion. This is true of every valid Mass.[34]

This general effect is manifested in all Eucharistic Prayers. In Eucharistic Prayer IV of the Roman rite, the priest prays: "as we await his coming in glory, we offer you his Body and Blood, the sacrifice acceptable to you which brings salvation to the *whole world*."[35] This general intention always includes the Pope and the bishops, on whom the welfare of the whole Church depends. In the Byzantine liturgy of

---

Celebrated worthily in faith, the sacraments confer the grace that they signify. They are *efficacious* because in them Christ himself is at work. . . . The Father always hears the prayer of his Son's Church which, in the epiclesis of each sacrament, expresses her faith in the power of the Spirit. . . .

[§1128] This is the meaning of the Church's affirmation that the sacraments act *ex opere operato* (literally: 'by the very fact of the action's being performed'), i.e., by virtue of the saving work of Christ, accomplished once for all. It follows that 'the sacrament is not wrought by the righteousness of either the celebrant or the recipient, but by the power of God' [*ST* III, q. 68, a. 8]. From the moment that a sacrament is celebrated in accordance with the intention of the Church, the power of Christ and his Spirit acts in and through it, independently of the personal holiness of the minister. Nevertheless, the fruits of the sacraments also depend on the disposition of the one who receives them.

See also Ludovicus Billot, *De Ecclesiae Sacramentis: Commentarius in Tertiam Partem S. Thomae*, 7th ed. (Rome: Apud Aedes Universitatis Gregorianae, 1931), 1:597–98.

[34] See *RM*, General Instruction, §2 (p. 19): "The Priest also prays that the Body and Blood of Christ may be a sacrifice which is acceptable to the Father and which brings salvation to the whole world."

[35] *RM*, 660.

St. Basil, there is a beautiful petition for the whole Church: "We pray you, Lord, remember your holy, catholic, and apostolic Church from one end of the world to the other, and grant it the peace which you purchased by the precious blood of your Christ, and establish this holy house until the consummation of the age, and grant it peace."[36]

Secondly, the Mass has a *special fruit* that corresponds to the special intentions for which it is offered by the priest.[37] This normally corresponds to the intention for which the priest has received a Mass stipend, which is a sign of the interior desire of the faithful who offer it. Again, it can be offered both for the living, to implore graces, and for the dead, for the remission of the temporal punishment of the holy souls in purgatory. Having the Mass celebrated for this intention is a great work of charity for our loved ones who have passed away.

Finally, there is a *personal fruit* for the priest who celebrates with devotion and for all who are present with devotion. The greater the devotion of priest and faithful, the greater will be their personal fruit.[38] A holy priest is a great aid to the faithful in this respect, for he helps them to increase the fervor and reverence with which they participate in the Mass. It should be observed that this personal fruit is independent from receiving Communion. Even those who, for whatever reason, cannot receive Communion can gain this fruit from devout participation in the Mass. Of course, the devout reception of Communion adds to the personal fruit of those who participate in the offering.

Eucharistic Prayer IV gives a good summary of the particular, special, and general fruit of the Mass, by listing those for whom the Mass is offered:

---

[36] Byzantine Liturgy of St. Basil (*PEER*, 120).

[37] See O'Neill, *New Approaches to the Eucharist*, 43: "A second implication of Christ's ecclesial offering concerns directly the *ex-opere-operato* efficacy of the Mass. The Church can *apply* the Mass, as Christ's sacrifice, to certain people. This is shown primarily from the fact that the Church does so."

[38] The importance of the devotion of the faithful in receiving the fruits of the Mass can be seen, for example, in the Collect for the 34th Week of Ordinary Time: "Stir up the will of your faithful, we pray, O Lord, that, striving more eagerly to bring your divine work to fruitful completion, they may receive in greater measure the healing remedies your kindness bestows" (*RM*, 194). See also the Prayer over the Offerings for the First Sunday of Lent: "Give us the right dispositions, O Lord, we pray, to make these offerings" (*RM*, 216).

Therefore, Lord, remember now all for whom we offer this sacrifice: especially your servant N. our Pope, N. our Bishop, and the whole Order of Bishops, all the clergy, those who take part in this offering, those gathered here before you, your entire people, and all who seek you with a sincere heart. Remember also those who have died in the peace of your Christ and all the dead, whose faith you alone have known.[39]

Eucharistic Prayer I likewise summarizes those for whom the Mass is offered, while putting a special emphasis on the devotion of the faithful who are present and their intentions:

Bless these gifts, these offerings, these holy and unblemished sacrifices, which we offer you firstly for your holy catholic Church. Be pleased to grant her peace, to guard, unite and govern her throughout the whole world, together with your servant N. our Pope and N. our Bishop, and all those who, holding to the truth, hand on the catholic and apostolic faith. Remember, Lord, your servants N. and N. and all gathered here, whose faith and devotion are known to you. For them, we offer you this sacrifice of praise or they offer it for themselves and all who are dear to them: for the redemption of their souls, in hope of health and well-being, and paying their homage to you, the eternal God, living and true.[40]

Why Does the Church Celebrate Many Masses If Every Mass Has Infinite Value?

Since the Mass is the sacrifice of Calvary made present on our altars, every Mass in itself has an infinite value of adoration, thanksgiving, supplication, and propitiation on account of the spotless Victim who offers Himself. Why, then, does the Church multiply the celebrations of Holy Mass? If every Mass has an infinite value, what is gained from multiplying the number of Masses that are celebrated?

In order to answer this, we have to consider the reason Christ instituted the Mass. He instituted it not to duplicate or add to the value of Calvary, but to allow His Church to participate in the offer-

---

[39] *RM*, 661.
[40] *RM*, 635–36.

ing of His one sacrifice and in the application of its effects.[41] The
Eucharist allows the Church and all her members to frequently join in
offering the infinite sacrifice of her Head, in which the Church herself
and the lives and hearts of the faithful are also offered. This ascending
movement of the self-offering of Christ, head and members, glorifies
God immeasurably. We who are finite and temporal need to participate frequently in offering God the infinite Gift of His Son.

Secondly, from the point of the descending fruits of the Mass, it
is also desirable to multiply Masses so that more graces will be show-
ered on the world. Even though every Mass has an infinite value in its
ascending movement of glorification, it does not follow that every Mass
calls down an infinite number of graces. That would not be possible,
for all the graces that God gives to the world are finite in number and
intensity.[42] No matter how much grace God actually gives, He could
always still give more. Therefore, a finite amount of graces from the
infinite merits of Calvary are offered to the faithful through every Mass.

Granted that the graces won by a given Mass are finite, what
determines their greater or lesser quantity and intensity? God is obviously free to give as He wills, but it is fitting that the value of grace
and mercy won by every Mass be dependent not only on Christ but
also on the devotion of those who participate in the offering and those
for whom it is offered.

We have seen above that in every sacrifice we can distinguish the
interior oblation of the faithful who are offering the sacrifice through
a ministerial priest from the victim who is offered on their behalf to
sensibly represent the interior offering of the heart. In every Mass
the Victim who is offered and the High Priest who offers (through
a ministerial priest) is a divine Person whose acts are both humanly
and divinely perfect and have infinite value in glorifying, thanking,
pleading, and propitiating the Father. The interior oblation of the
faithful, however, is always imperfect and finite. Thus we can say that
every Mass is infinite because it is the sacramental re-presentation of
Christ's sacrifice, but finite with regard to the Church's participation
in His sacrifice. For this reason, as seen in the preceding chapter, the
Roman Canon prays to the Father: "Be pleased to look upon these

---

[41] See John Paul II, *EE*, §12: "The Mass makes present the sacrifice of the Cross;
   it does not add to that sacrifice nor does it multiply it. What is repeated is its
   memorial celebration, its 'commemorative representation' (*memorialis demonstratio*),
   which makes Christ's one, definitive redemptive sacrifice always present in time."

[42] See *ST* III, q. 7, a. 11.

offerings with a serene and kindly countenance." On the part of Christ, the oblation is infinitely acceptable. But since the Mass exists so that we may participate in Christ's offering, and since our offering is imperfect, we pray for the acceptance of our offering.

With regard to the effect of satisfaction of each Mass that is offered for the souls of the faithful departed for the remission of the temporal punishment due to their sins, St. Thomas holds that we have to consider not so much the infinite perfection of the Victim who is offered, but the interior devotion of the faithful for whom it is offered and who offer it, which is always finite. He writes:

> But in so far as it is a sacrifice, it has a satisfactory power. Yet in satisfaction, the affection of the offerer is weighed rather than the quantity of the offering. Hence Our Lord says (Mark 12:43: cf. Luke 21:4) of the widow who offered two mites that she cast in more than all. Therefore, although this offering suffices of its own quantity to satisfy for all punishment, yet it becomes satisfactory for them for whom it is offered, or even for the offerers, according to the measure of their devotion.[43]

It may happen, therefore, that many Masses need to be offered for a given soul in purgatory, according to the greater or lesser degree of interior devotion they had at the time of death. In response to an objection, St. Thomas clarifies that "if part of the punishment and not the whole be taken away by this sacrament, it is due to a defect not on the part of Christ's power, but on the part of man's devotion."[44]

---

[43] *ST* III, q. 79, a. 5. Bl. Duns Scotus assigns a different reason for the finite effects of the Mass and the consequent necessity for the multiplication of Masses. He held that the Mass has only a finite value on account of the Church as the proximate offerer. See Scotus, *Quodlibet* XX, no. 22: "The Mass is not equal in worth to the passion of Christ. . . . When the Eucharist is offered it is not the will of Christ, as if he were the proximate offerer, that determines the measure of its acceptability; but rather it is the collective will of the Church, the merit of which is of finite degree" (Francis Clark, *Eucharistic Sacrifice and the Reformation* [Westminster, MD: Newman Press, 1960], 325). The problem with Scotus's position is that Christ, as the High Priest, is the principal offerer of every Mass, and the ministerial priest who acts in His Person is acting as His living instrument. The value of an effect should be calculated not from the dignity of an instrument but from the dignity of the principal agent, who in this case is Christ. See Ibáñez, *L'Eucaristia, Dono e Mistero*, 243–45; Edward Kilmartin, *The Eucharist in the West*, 160–61, 166–68.

[44] *ST* III, q. 79, a. 5, ad 3.

Although the power of the Mass is potentially infinite on account of the Victim, we inevitably take hold of it in a finite manner according to the measure of our interior disposition. Charles Journet writes:

> The Church enters into the mystery of the Mass as into the sun, which overshadows her on all sides. . . . The application of the Mass is measured first of all by the fervor of those who, through Christ, with Christ and in Christ, pray for the salvation of the world. It is further conditioned, however, to a certain degree by the disposition of those very ones for whom we pray: by their present dispositions if they are living; by their previous devotion if they are dead.[45]

That the application of the fruits of the Mass depends on the measure of faith and devotion of those for whom it is offered is implied in the prayer of the Roman Canon: "Remember, Lord, your servants and all gathered here, whose faith and devotion are known to you. For them, we offer you this sacrifice of praise, or they offer it for themselves and all who are dear to them: for the redemption of their souls, in hope of health and well-being, and paying their homage to you, the eternal God, living and true."[46]

Since each Mass applies a finite amount of blessings and graces on the world, the multiplication of the acts of offering the sacrifice of the Mass brings down more blessings on the world. St. Thomas writes: "But the oblation of the sacrifice is multiplied in several masses, and therefore the effect of the sacrifice and of the sacrament is multiplied."[47] Properly speaking, we do not say that the sacrifice is multiplied, for that is essentially the same in every Mass, as Christ's Body is one in every consecrated host. What is multiplied are the sacramental acts of offering the one sacrifice through the ministry of the Church, each of which draws down on the world graces merited by the one sacrifice of Calvary.[48]

---

[45] Journet, *The Mass*, 117–32, esp. 126 and 128.

[46] *RM*, 636.

[47] *ST* III, q. 79, a. 7, ad 3.

[48] See again John Paul II, *EE*, §12, quoted above in note 41 of this chapter. He continues here: "The sacrificial nature of the Eucharistic mystery cannot therefore be understood as something separate, independent of the Cross or only indirectly referring to the sacrifice of Calvary."

The Logic of Superabundance

The Lord's intentions with regard to the offering of the Mass seem to follow the same logic of superabundance that can be observed throughout the work of Christ. Even though something lesser would have been sufficient, He would leave nothing undone. As St. Thomas says in the hymn *Adoro te devote*, Christ could have redeemed us with one drop of His Blood. Why then all the Blood that was shed in the Passion? Why the greatest suffering that the world has known?[49] In the same way, Christ could have given His Church a lesser sacrifice that did not contain His own self-offering. But He has chosen to give us a superabundant offering, more pleasing to God than all sins are displeasing because it is the offering of His Son. And, having given us the Mass, He could have willed that it be offered only once or rarely. But in the same logic of superabundance, He gives us the Mass to be offered daily in every place by every priest.

With regard to the multiplication of Masses, the right question is not whether a smaller number would be sufficient, but rather how the Church should best conform to the Lord's logic of superabundance.

Martin Luther's Rejection of the
Fruits of the Mass

Since Luther rejected the sacrificial nature of the Mass, it makes sense that he thought it could have fruits only for those who hear the Mass with faith, and that it could not be offered for others. This follows from seeing the sacraments solely as promises from God to the faithful and as excluding any ascending aspect of giving glory to God and offering Him a propitiatory sacrifice. Luther argues by strictly equating the Mass with Baptism. Just as Baptism affects only the one who receives it, and as it cannot be offered for the dead or the conversion of others, so likewise the Mass:

> Hence it is a manifest and wicked error to offer or apply the mass for sins, for satisfactions, for the dead, or for any needs whatsoever of one's own or of others. You will readily see the obvious truth of this if you firmly hold that the mass is a divine promise, which can benefit no one, be applied to no

---

[49] See *ST* III, q. 46, a. 6.

one, intercede for no one, and be communicated to no one, except only to him who believes with a faith of his own. Who can receive or apply, in behalf of another, the promise of God, which demands the personal faith of each one individually?[50]

The *Augsburg Confession* of 1530, a fundamental Lutheran confessional document, condemns the Catholic conception of the sacrifice of the Mass and the Catholic practice of having Masses offered for souls in purgatory. It implies that Catholic theology taught that the sacrifice of Calvary atoned only for original sin whereas the Mass atones for personal sins:

> It was taught that our Lord Christ had by his death made satisfaction only for original sin, and had instituted the Mass as a sacrifice for other sins. This transformed the Mass into a sacrifice for the living and the dead, a sacrifice by means of which sin was taken away and God was reconciled. . . . Out of this grew the countless multiplication of Masses, by the performance of which men expected to get everything they needed from God. Meanwhile faith in Christ and true service of God were forgotten.[51]

This objection presupposes an erroneous understanding of the relationship between the sacrifice of Calvary and the Mass that was never the common doctrine of Catholic theologians. Calvary and the Mass are not partial causes of our salvation in competition with one another, as if they forgive different kinds of sins, for Calvary alone is the universal cause of salvation. The multiplication of Masses is a good thing not because they add something to the merit of Calvary, but because each Mass, in addition to glorifying God, applies to our world graces won by the infinite merits of Calvary.

The Value of "Private" Masses

A consequence of the fact that the priest offers the Mass in the person of Christ Himself is that every Mass involves the entire mystical Body,

---

[50] Martin Luther, *The Babylonian Captivity of the Church* (*LW*, 36:48).

[51] *Augsburg Confession*, ch. 24, in *Creeds of the Churches: A Reader in Christian Doctrine from the Bible to the Present*, ed. John H. Leith, rev. ed. (Richmond, VA: John Knox Press, 1973), 84–85.

Head and members. For Christ, the Head of the Mystical Body, offers the immaculate sacrifice of His Body and Blood for the redemption of His Bride, the whole Church, which includes the living members (the "Church Militant"), and the faithful departed in purgatory (the "Church Suffering"), and He wills to associate the whole Church in His sacrifice to glorify His Father. The Mass is also offered for all men, all of whom are potential members of the Church. Thus every Mass, even if the priest is celebrating alone, "is not robbed of its social effects."[52] So-called "private" Masses, in which there is no presence of the faithful, are still public acts of the Church and retain the infinite value of the sacrifice of Christ renewed on the altar. This is very important. The Mass is still the sacrifice of Christ given to His Church, no matter how many or few of the faithful are present to benefit by it.[53] Joseph Ratzinger highlights the "catholic" dimension of every Mass:

> Universality is an essential feature of Christian worship. It is the worship of an open heaven. It is never just an event in the life of a community that finds itself in a particular place. No, to celebrate the Eucharist means to enter into the openness of a glorification of God that embraces both heaven and earth, an openness effected by the Cross and Resurrection. Christian liturgy is never just an event organized by a particular group or set of people or even by a particular local Church.[54]

Luther, in consequence of his denial of the sacrificial nature of the Mass, logically rejected the celebration of "private Masses,"[55] and he

---

[52] Pius XII, *Mediator Dei*, §97. See also the Council of Trent, On the Sacrifice of the Mass (session 22), ch. 6: "Those Masses in which the priest alone communicates sacramentally . . . should also be considered as truly common . . . because they are celebrated by a public minister of the Church not only for himself, but for all the faithful who belong to the Body of Christ" (DS, 1747).

[53] See the profound discussion of this question by O'Neill, *New Approaches to the Eucharist*, 39–62.

[54] Joseph Ratzinger, *The Spirit of the Liturgy*, 49 (in *TL*, 30).

[55] Luther, *The Babylonian Captivity of the Church*: "When a priest celebrates public mass, he should determine to do nothing else than to commune himself and others by means of the mass. . . . The private mass does not differ in the least from the ordinary communion which any layman receives at the hand of the priest, and has no greater effect" (*LW*, 36:54). His position is further developed in *De Abroganda Missa Privata Martini Lutheri Sententia* (1521), in *D. Martin Luthers Werke: Kritische Gesammmtausgabe*, 127 vols. (Weimar, DE: H.

was followed in this by John Calvin.[56] Starting in the middle of the twentieth century, some Catholic theologians have reformulated this position in more nuanced form.[57] In response to this trend, Paul VI reaffirmed the value of so-called "private Masses" in his encyclical on the Eucharist, *Mysterium Fidei* (1965), saying: "It is not permissible to extol the so-called 'community' Mass in such a way as to detract from Masses that are celebrated privately."[58] Benedict XVI, in his post-synodal apostolic exhortation *Sacramentum Caritatis*, §80, again defended the value of the celebration of Mass even when none of the faithful are present:

> To this end I join the Synod Fathers in recommending "the daily celebration of Mass, even when the faithful are not present." This recommendation is consistent with the objectively infinite value of every celebration of the Eucharist, and is motivated by the Mass's unique spiritual fruitfulness. If celebrated in a faith-filled and attentive way, Mass is formative in the deepest sense of the word, since it fosters the priest's configuration to Christ and strengthens him in his vocation.

EUCHARISTIC CONCELEBRATION

Sacramental Eucharistic concelebration can be defined as a Eucharistic celebration in which two or more priests participate in a common priestly oblation, such that each is acting in the person of Christ

---

Böhlau, 1883–2009), 8:411–476; *Receiving Both Kinds in the Sacrament* (1522) (*LW*, 36:257); and especially in *The Private Mass and the Consecration of Priests* (1533) (*LW*, 38:147–14). In the last work, Luther recounts, perhaps as a literary device, that he came to this position after a nocturnal visitation of Satan in which Satan debated with him and successfully convinced him to abolish private Masses, for Luther, in terror, could not counter his arguments (*LW*, 38:149–58). See Jacques-Bénigne Bossuet, *History of the Variations of the Protestant Churches* (Fraser. MI: American Council on Economics and Society, 1997), 115–16.

[56] See John Calvin, *Institutes*, bk. IV, ch. 18, no. 8: "Wherever there is no breaking of bread for the communion of the faithful, there is no Supper of the Lord, but a false and preposterous imitation of the Supper. But false imitation is adulteration. Moreover, the adulteration of this high ordinance is not without impiety. In private masses, therefore, there is an impious abuse" (Beveridge, 939).

[57] See Karl Rahner and Angelus Häussling, *The Celebration of the Eucharist*, trans. W. J. O'Hara (New York: Herder and Herder, 1968), 99–106.

[58] Paul VI, *Mysterium Fidei*, §11 (DS, 4411).

in realizing and offering the Eucharistic sacrifice.[59] This entails each priest pronouncing the words of consecration. Distinct from concelebration in the proper or sacramental sense is the practice of "ceremonial concelebration," in which one or more priests join the main presider in the liturgical rite but without themselves pronouncing the words of consecration. In this case, only the main celebrant (the bishop) is acting in the person of Christ and offering the Eucharistic sacrifice.

Concelebration, whether sacramental or ceremonial, has a place in liturgical rites of both East and West and goes back to the early Church. We see it attested to in the letters of St. Ignatius of Antioch.[60] The primary purpose of concelebration, whether ceremonial or sacramental, is to manifest the hierarchical unity of the priesthood under the bishop, which culminates in offering the sacrifice of the Mass.[61] Concelebration is especially appropriate on solemn occasions in which the bishop is joined by members of the presbyterate, although it is not limited to such events.

It seems that sacramental, as opposed to ceremonial, concelebration was a practice that developed in the Roman rite.[62] In the history

---

[59] This definition is based on that given by Bouyer, *Dictionnaire Théologique*, 84. See also Derville, *Eucharistic Concelebration*, 5.

[60] See Ignatius of Antioch, *Letter to the Philadelphians* 4: "Take care, therefore, to participate in one Eucharist. . . . There is one altar, just as there is one bishop, together with the council of presbyters and the deacons" (*The Apostolic Fathers*, trans. M. Holmes, 3rd ed. [Grand Rapids, MI: Baker Academic, 2007], 239. See also his *Letter to the Smyrnaeans* 8.

[61] See Second Vatican Council, *Presbyterorum Ordinis*, §7: "All priests, in union with bishops, so share in one and the same priesthood and ministry of Christ that the very unity of their consecration and mission requires their hierarchical communion with the order of bishops. At times in an excellent manner they manifest this communion in liturgical concelebration as joined with the bishop when they celebrate the Eucharistic Sacrifice."

[62] Outside the Roman rite, concelebration was traditionally ceremonial. See Jungmann, *The Mass of the Roman Rite*, 1:196n6: "In the Orient (ceremonial) concelebration was customary and common from time immemorial, but it is only in the Uniate groups that the joint pronouncing of the words of consecration was added, apparently not till the start of the 18th century and then under the influence of Rome, which recognized no other type than the sacramental concelebration." See also Alcuin Reid, foreword to Joseph de Sainte-Marie, *The Holy Eucharist: The World's Salvation; Studies on the Holy Sacrifice of the Mass, Its Celebration and Its Concelebration* (Leominster, UK: Gracewing, 2015), xxix: "Sacramental concelebration is a late Western imposition on the venerable Eastern custom of ceremonial concelebration." See also Paul Tirot, "La con-

of the Latin rite, sacramental concelebration was used in the rite of priestly ordination to manifest the unity of the presbyterate under the bishop,[63] as well as on Holy Thursday, for the same reason. Furthermore, from at least the eighth until the twelfth century, the cardinal presbyters of Rome sacramentally concelebrated with the Pope on solemn liturgical occasions.[64]

Concelebration and the Fruits of the Mass

How does the current practice of concelebration affect the fruits of the Mass? It may seem that concelebration, as opposed to individual priests celebrating the Mass separately, could have a negative effect in this regard by reducing the number of Masses that are celebrated.[65] Furthermore, it could be asked why each concelebrating priest may receive a stipend for Mass intentions.

At first sight, it would seem that the fruits of the Mass are multiplied by multiplying Masses. Since concelebrating priests participate in bringing about only one consecration (or one act of transubstantiation),[66] it would seem that a concelebrated Mass is simply one Mass. Thus some have argued that the fruits of a concelebrated Mass—its value in glorifying God, making satisfaction for sin, and calling down graces on the earth—are the same as those of any other Mass offered by one priest alone. This would imply that the common practice of concelebration would be reducing the number of Masses, and thus

---

célébration et la tradition de l'Église," *Ephemerides Liturgicae* 101 (1987): 33–59.

[63] See *ST* III, q. 82, a. 2: "When a priest is ordained he is placed on a level with those who received consecrating power from Our Lord at the Supper. And therefore, according to the custom of some Churches, as the apostles supped when Christ supped, so the newly ordained co-celebrate with the ordaining bishop."

[64] See Jungmann, *The Mass of the Roman Rite*, 1:196n6: "On five great feasts of the year each of the Cardinal priests who surround the altar of the pope carries three hosts on a corporal and together with the pope, speaks over these the entire Canon including the words of consecration." This practice is mentioned by Innocent III in *De Sacro Altaris Mysterio* 4.25 (PL, 217:874): "It was customary for the Cardinal priests to stand beside the Roman Pontiff and to celebrate together with him."

[65] See Joseph de Sainte-Marie, *The Holy Eucharist*.

[66] See Thomas Aquinas, *In* IV *Sent.*, d. 13, q. 1, a. 2, qla. 2, ad 1: "Since intention is required for the completion of the sacraments, and since all [the concelebrants] have the intention to make one consecration, there is no more than one consecration there."

reducing the fruits of the Mass. If this were the case, it would seem that the current pastoral practice of frequent concelebration in the Latin rite would be a matter of great concern.[67]

To resolve this question, it is important to distinguish between the multiplication of Masses and the multiplication of *acts of priestly offering*. The fruits of the Mass *ex opere operato* are multiplied, it seems, precisely by multiplying the acts of priestly offering.[68]

At issue here are two ways of considering the action of priests sacramentally concelebrating a Mass. One way would be to suppose that each priest is acting as a partial cause of the consecration whose contribution is supplemented by each of the other concelebrating priests. Another way would be to consider each priest as a total rather than a partial cause of the consecration and the sacrifice. The first way of understanding concelebration would be like four men pulling one and the same object or four musicians playing one string quartet.[69] In such cases, there would be only one merit for the group, split up between them. It is harder to find an analogy for the second way of considering concelebration. We could imagine four scientists formulating the same theory at the same time independently of each other. In such a case, each would be a total cause of the one theory and, thus, each would have a full merit, even though only one theory was formulated.

Which model is more fitting for this case? I hold that the second way of considering the matter is correct. There is no reason to think that

---

[67] This is the position of Joseph de Sainte-Marie, *The Holy Eucharist*, and Rudolf Michael Schmitz, "La concelebrazione eucaristica," in *Il Mistero Eucaristico*, ed. Antonio Piolanti (Vatican City: Libreria Editrice Vaticana, 1983), 501–20.

[68] See de la Taille, *The Mystery of Faith*, 1:141: "There are just as many sacrifices as there are priestly offerings."

[69] This view of concelebrants as partial causes is maintained by Peter Kwasniewski, "Celebration vs. Concelebration: Theological Considerations":

When two priests concelebrate one Mass, a *single* act of sacrifice is made present through both of them together, acting in tandem as one instrument—as when several men pull on a rope together, there is *one* pulling of the rope, and one effect, e.g., that a heavy stone be pulled. In contrast, when two priests celebrate two Masses, Christ makes present anew, through *each* of them, His sacrifice to the Father; for us men and for our salvation, He has twice renewed His oblation at their consecrated hands. This multiplies the graces poured forth into the world from the Lord's most holy soul, the fountain of all gifts. (*New Liturgical Movement*, September 1, 2014, accessed July 6, 2017, http://www.newliturgicalmovement.org/2014/09/celebration-vs-concelebration.html#.V64UgZMrJTY) sacramental concelebration makes each concelebrant a partial cause, as if he were doing some fraction of the consecration and sacrifice. On the contrary, there is every reason to think that each concelebrating priest is acting as a total cause whose power extends to the entire effect of consecration and sacrifice. Several priests are simultaneously realizing the same consecration in such a way that each one is a total cause of the one consecration, equally making the one Victim present in His sacramental immolation. This is because each priest is acting *in persona Christi*, which enables each one to be the sufficient and total cause of the entire effect.[70] Each one says the words of the sacramental form through which God's omnipotence operates. The concelebrants do not divide up the words of consecration. Each priest simultaneously pronounces all the words of the essential form, and each has a fullness of power from sacramental character to say them so that they realize what they signify through the overshadowing power of the Holy Spirit. With regard to the act performed *in persona Christi*, each priest does neither more nor less than they would do if celebrating individually, and neither more nor less than any other concelebrant. Christ works through them equally such that they all offer the same sacrifice.

An analogy for this can be found in a mysterious aspect of Christ's presence in the Eucharist, which is a presence whole and entire under every host and every part of the host. As Christ is able to be present whole and entire in a great multiplicity of hosts, so too His action of sacrificial oblation can be present whole and entire in many priestly agents, whether they are celebrating together in a concelebration or apart in individual celebrations. Thus it seems that in a concelebration there are many priestly acts of sacrificing, even though there is but one act of transubstantiation of each species and one Victim placed on the altar.

This poses another question. What determines the multiplication of the fruits of the Mass? Is it the number of priestly acts of sacrificing or the number of distinct times that the Victim is made present on the altar? In other words, does the multiplication of the fruits of the Mass follow the number of priestly acts of offering sacrifice, which are multiple in a concelebration, or simply the number of times that transubstantiation is enacted and the one Victim is made present in His Body and Blood, which is only once in a concelebrated Mass?

---

[70] See Joseph Kleiner, "Théologie de la concélébration," *Esprit et vie* 90 (1980): 551; Tirot, "La concélébration et la tradition de l'Église," 57–59.

I think that it is much more reasonable to connect the multiplication of the fruits of the Mass with the number of priestly offerings.[71] In every Mass it is the same Jesus who is offered as Victim. He is never multiplied. Similarly, in every Mass Christ's sacrifice is essentially one, identical with Calvary. What is capable of being increased is the number of sacramental *priestly acts* by which the *same* infinite Victim is sacrificed *in persona Christi*, actualizing and making present His one sacrifice throughout the life of the Church. These *priestly acts of sacrificing* are multiplied both when multiple priests concelebrate and when they celebrate individually. There are no fewer priestly acts of offering sacrifice when one hundred priests sacramentally concelebrate than when one hundred priests offer Mass individually. There is a lessening of the priestly acts of offering, however, when one hundred priests assist at the Mass of another or concelebrate ceremonially (without pronouncing the words of consecration), as opposed to celebrating individually or sacramentally concelebrating.

This position follows from the teaching of Pius XII in two important discourses of 1954 and 1956 that touch on the subject of sacramental and ceremonial concelebration. The key principle used by Pius XII in both discourses is this: "With regard to the offering of the Eucharistic Sacrifice, the actions of Christ, the High Priest, are as many as are the priests celebrating." In the address of 1954, Pius XII was responding to a theological opinion put forth in an article of 1949 in which Karl Rahner proposed that the fruits of the Mass would be essentially the same whether (a) a number of priests gathered together celebrated individual Masses, (b) only one celebrated and the others assisted at that Mass, or (c) they concelebrated.[72] Pius XII said that this thesis was erroneous:

---

[71] See Tirot, "La concélébration et la tradition de l'Église," 58, who argues that the Thomist understanding that each concelebrant acts as a total rather than a partial cause (a position common among Thomists of the sixteenth and seventeenth centuries, such as the Salmanticenses) implies that a concelebrated Mass has the same fruit as would be gained by the same number of individual Masses as there are concelebrants. See Salmanticenses, *De Eucharistiae Sacramento*, disp. 2, dub. 4, no. 68, and disp. 12, dub. 2, no. 7, in *Cursus Theologicus*, vol. 18 (Paris: Apud Victorem Palmé, 1882), 148–49, 740.

[72] Karl Rahner, "Multiplication of Masses," *Orate Fratres* 24 (1950): 553–62, esp. 558: "From the understanding we have gained concerning the manner in which the Mass achieves its effects, it follows also that in regard to the measure of the so-called 'fruits of the Sacrifice,' it is of itself of no consequence in which one of the possible ways one takes part in the mass—whether by priestly celebration, by lay

An assertion which is being made today, not only by laymen but also at times by certain theologians and priests and spread about by them, ought to be rejected as an erroneous opinion: namely, that the offering of one Mass, at which a hundred priests assist with religious devotion, is the same as a hundred Masses celebrated by a hundred priests. That is not true. With regard to the offering of the Eucharistic Sacrifice, the actions of Christ, the High Priest, are as many as are the priests celebrating, not as many as are the priests reverently hearing the Mass of a Bishop or a priest; for those present at the Mass in no sense sustain, or act in, the person of Christ sacrificing, but are to be compared to the faithful layfolk who are present at the Mass.[73]

Pius XII emphasizes that there is an essential difference, a difference in the nature of the act performed, between a priest celebrating Mass and the same priest merely assisting at a Mass celebrated by another. In the former case, the priest is acting in the person of Christ offering sacrifice, but not in the latter. Christ's priestly oblation is sacramentally multiplied only when the priest says the words of consecration *in persona Christi*. Thus, when a hundred priests hear the Mass of another without celebrating themselves, Christ's sacrificial offering is not sacramentally multiplied as it would be if they were all to celebrate Mass themselves.

Although Pius XII did not directly address the question of concelebration in the discourse of 1954, the principle that he laid down has clear implications for the theology of concelebration. For while there is an essential difference in the nature of the act between a priest celebrating Mass and the same priest only assisting at Mass celebrated by another, the same difference is not seen when comparing a priest sacramentally concelebrating and a priest celebrating Mass individually. In the latter comparison, both priests are acting equally *in persona Christi*, sacramentally making present Christ's sacrificial oblation, for

---

assistance, by concelebration, or by furnishing the material of sacrifice (stipend)." This is an English translation of part of Rahner's original article published in *Zeitschrift für katholische Theologie* 71 (1949): 257–17. This article was then taken up and revised in Rahner and Häussling, *The Celebration of the Eucharist*.

[73] Pius XII, Address to Cardinals, Archbishops, and Bishops Gathered in Rome for Ceremonies in Honor of Our Lady, November 2, 1954 (English translation in *The Pope Speaks* 1 [1954]: 378; Latin original in *AAS* 46 [1954]: 666–77, here 669).

"the actions of Christ, the High Priest, are as many as are the priests celebrating, not as many as are the priests reverently hearing the Mass of a Bishop or a priest."

The implications of Pius XII's teaching with regard to concelebration were made more explicit in an address of 1956 to the International Congress on Pastoral Liturgy, in which he repeated the passage quoted above from his 1954 discourse and specified again that the error condemned in the earlier address stems from a failure to distinguish between (1) the objective nature of the act performed (celebrating Mass *in persona Christi*, as opposed to merely assisting at Mass celebrated by another) and (2) the subjective fruits received from the Mass, which will vary according to the dispositions of each, and which can be known only by God.[74] He writes:

> We therefore repeat it: the decisive question (for concelebration as for the Mass of a single priest) is not to know the fruit the soul draws from it, but the nature of the act which is performed: does or does not the priest, as minister of Christ, perform "*actio Christi se ipsum sacrificantis et offerentis*?"[75]

When the priest says the words of consecration in the Person of Christ, Christ offers Himself through the instrumentality of His priestly minister. Pius XII makes it clear that this occurs also when a priest sacramentally concelebrates, as long as he personally says the words of consecration *in persona Christi*:

> According to this, the central element of the Eucharistic Sacrifice is that in which Christ intervenes as "*se ipsum offerens*"—to adopt the words of the Council of Trent.[76] That happens at the consecration when, in the very act of transubstantiation worked by the Lord, the priest-celebrant is "*personam Christi*

---

[74] Pius XII, Address to the International Congress of Pastoral Liturgy at Assisi, September 22, 1956 (English translation from *The Pope Speaks* 3, no. 3 [Winter 1956–57]: 278; French original in *AAS* 48 (1956): 716).

[75] Ibid. (English, p. 280; original French, p. 718). The text continues: "Likewise, in celebration and concelebration, one must see whether, along with the necessary interior intention, the celebrant completes the external action, and, above all, pronounces the words which constitute the '*actio Christi se ipsum sacrificantis et offerentis.*'"

[76] Council of Trent, On the Sacrifice of the Mass (session 22), (DS, 1740).

gerens." Even if the consecration takes place without pomp and in all simplicity, it is the central point of the whole liturgy of the sacrifice, the central point of the "*actio Christi cuius personam gerit sacerdos celebrans,*" or "*sacerdotes concelebrantes*" in the case of a true concelebration. . . . In reality the action of the consecrating priest is the very action of Christ Who acts through His minister. In the case of a concelebration in the proper sense of the word, Christ, instead of acting through one minister, acts through several.[77]

It is clear therefore that the principle given in the earlier discourse also applies to concelebrating priests: "The actions of Christ, the High Priest, are as many as are the priests celebrating." In a concelebration, since Christ is acting through many ministers instead of one, His act of sacrificing is sacramentally multiplied through the multiple ministers.[78]

Pius XII then goes on to emphasize the necessity that concelebrating priests individually (and simultaneously) pronounce the words of consecration.

This fact raises the important point: "What intention and what exterior action are required to have a true concelebration and simultaneous consecration?" On this subject let Us recall what We said in our Apostolic Constitution "*Episcopalis Consecrationis*" of November 30, 1944. We there laid down that in an episcopal consecration the two Bishops who accompany the consecrator must have the intention of consecrating the Bishop-elect, and that, consequently, they must perform the exterior actions and pronounce the words by which the power and the grace to transmit are signified and transmitted. It is, then, not sufficient for them to unite their wills with that of

---

[77] Pius XII, Address to the International Congress of Pastoral Liturgy at Assisi (English, p. 279). See *ST* III, q. 82, a. 2, ad 2: "If each individual priest were acting in his own power, then other celebrants would be superfluous, since one would be sufficient. But whereas the priest does not consecrate except as in Christ's stead; and since many are *one in Christ* (Gal 3:28); consequently it does not matter whether this sacrament be consecrated by one or by many, except that the rite of the Church must be observed."

[78] The bloody act of sacrifice realized on Calvary cannot be multiplied. What is capable of sacramental multiplication are the sacramental acts of oblation realized by the sacred ministers in pronouncing the words of consecration in the person of Christ.

the chief consecrator, and to declare that they make his words and actions their own. They must themselves perform the actions and pronounce the essential words.

The same thing likewise happens in concelebration in the true sense. It is not sufficient to have and to indicate the will to make one's own the words and actions of the celebrant. The concelebrants must themselves say over the bread and the wine, "This is my Body," "This is my Blood." Otherwise, their concelebration is purely ceremonial.[79]

The question of concelebration was also addressed in a response of the Holy Office of 1957. The question was posed as to whether priests could be considered to concelebrate if they did not pronounce the words of consecration. The response was negative, and the reason given was that, "from the institution of Christ, only he validly celebrates who pronounces the words of consecration."[80]

As long as each concelebrating priest is pronouncing the essential words of the consecration with the intention to act in the person of Christ, they are each truly offering the sacrifice of the Mass. Thus there will be as many acts of offering as there are concelebrating priests. This is the theological basis for the canonical permission for each concelebrant to receive a Mass stipend, according to §1 of canon 945 in the *Code of Canon Law*.

Vatican II and Post-Conciliar Magisterial Texts on Concelebration

The Second Vatican Council, in *Sacrosanctum Concilium*, §57, called for increasing the occasions in which Eucharistic concelebration is permitted in order to better manifest the unity of the priesthood and hierarchical communion with the bishop.[81] It also stipulated that

---

[79] Pius XII, Address to the International Congress of Pastoral Liturgy at Assisi (English, pp. 279–80).

[80] Response of the Holy Office of March 8, 1957, in *AAS* 49 (1957): 370 (DS, 3928).

[81] Second Vatican Council, *Sacrosanctum Concilium*, §57 extends permission for concelebration to the following cases:

1.
   a) on the Thursday of the Lord's Supper, not only at the Mass of the Chrism, but also at the evening Mass.

"each priest shall always retain his right to celebrate Mass individually, though not at the same time in the same church as a concelebrated Mass, nor on Thursday of the Lord's Supper."[82]

Eucharistic concelebration is also mentioned in *Presbyterorum Ordinis*, §7, which speaks about the intimate hierarchical communion between the bishop and his presbytery:

> All priests, in union with bishops, so share in one and the same priesthood and ministry of Christ that the very unity of their consecration and mission requires their hierarchical communion with the order of bishops. At times in an excellent manner they manifest this communion in liturgical concelebration as joined with the bishop when they celebrate the Eucharistic Sacrifice.[83]

The *Code of Canon Law* regulates concelebration in canon 902:

> Unless the welfare of the Christian faithful requires or suggests otherwise, priests can concelebrate the Eucharist. They are completely free to celebrate the Eucharist individually, however, but not while a concelebration is taking place in the same church or oratory.

Study Questions

1. What are the four principal ends of the sacrifice of the Mass?
2. What does it mean that the Mass is a propitiatory sacrifice?

---

    b) at Masses during councils, bishops' conferences, and synods;
    c) at the Mass for the blessing of an abbot.
  2. Also, with permission of the ordinary, to whom it belongs to decide whether concelebration is opportune:
    a) at conventual Mass, and at the principal Mass in churches when the needs of the faithful do not require that all priests available should celebrate individually;
    b) at Masses celebrated at any kind of priests' meetings, whether the priests be secular clergy or religious.

[82] Ibid.

[83] See also Sacred Congregation of Rites, Instruction on Eucharistic Worship, *Eucharisticum Mysterium* (1967), §47, which commends the practice of concelebration "unless it conflicts with the needs of the faithful."

3. Why is the Mass offered for the living and the dead? How does the offering of the Mass aid the faithful departed?

4. Who is benefited by the celebration of the Holy Mass? (Distinguish three beneficiaries.)

5. Does every Mass have infinite value? If so, why is it good that many Masses are celebrated? Explain.

6. What is the principal purpose of concelebration?

7. What is the difference between sacramental and ceremonial concelebration?

8. Is it reasonable to think that the practice of frequent concelebration, insofar as it diminishes the number of individual Masses celebrated, reduces the fruits of the Mass?

9. How many sacramental priestly acts of offering are made in a concelebrated Mass?

Suggestions for Further Reading

De la Taille, Maurice, S.J. *The Mystery of Faith.* Vol. 2, *The Sacrifice of the Church.* New York: Sheed & Ward, 1950.

Derville, Guillaume. *Eucharistic Concelebration: From Symbol to Reality.* Montreal: Wilson & Lafleur, 2011.

Journet, Charles. *The Mass: The Presence of the Sacrifice of the Cross.* Translated by Victor Szczurek. South Bend, IN: St. Augustine's Press, 2008. Pp. 93–132.

Pius XII. Encyclical on the Sacred Liturgy *Mediator Dei.* November 20, 1947. See §§71–79.

Part IV

Communion

✠

Effects of Holy Communion

COMMUNION AND SACRIFICE

It is not by accident that the Eucharist is both the Church's sacrifice and the sacrament of communion. There is a most intimate relationship between the offering and communion in the sacrifice, a link that is found in Judaism and ancient religions in general. Many of the sacrifices commanded by the Mosaic Law involve receiving in communion, by the priests or the offerers, a part of what was offered to God.[1] The clearest example of this is the Passover lamb, which was sacrificed on behalf of each household and consumed by them.

In 1 Corinthians 10:18, St. Paul expresses the meaning of the people's partaking of the victim: "Consider the people of Israel; are not those who eat the sacrifices partners in the altar?" The ritual consumption of the victim manifests one's solidarity with what has been offered to God and one's interior configuration with it. St. Thomas makes this point in answer to the question of whether the priest is bound to partake of the sacrifice:

> The Eucharist is not only a sacrament, but also a sacrifice. Now whoever offers sacrifice must be a sharer in the sacrifice, because the outward sacrifice he offers is a sign of the inner sacrifice whereby he offers himself to God, as Augustine says (*City of God* 10). Hence by partaking of the sacrifice he shows that the inner one is likewise his.[2]

---

[1] See Berman, *The Temple*, 128–33.
[2] *ST* III, q. 82, a. 4.

Maurice de la Taille explains this connection: "For the man who ate of the sacrifice, by communion with the victim sacrificed to God, became himself, so to speak, a victim sacrificed to God."[3] For this reason, Charles Cardinal Journet writes: "'The Lord's Banquet,' yes, but one calculated to immerse us actively in 'the Lord's Sacrifice.'"[4]

Joseph Ratzinger likewise stresses the intimate connection between sacrifice and the sacrificial meal:

> Throughout the entire history of religions, sacrifice and meal are inseparably united. The sacrifice facilitates *communio* with the divinity, and men receive back the divinity's gift in and from the sacrifice. This is transformed and deepened in many ways in the mystery of Jesus Christ: here the sacrifice itself comes from the incarnate love of God, so that it is God who *gives himself*, taking man up into his action and enabling him to be both gift and recipient.[5]

Hans Urs von Balthasar eloquently expresses the same idea: "The Eucharist presupposes the cross of Christ, but the Eucharist has as its goal our total, crucifying gift."[6]

Communion in the sacrifices of Judaism and natural religions expresses three fundamental ideas. First, it symbolizes a union with the sacrificial victim that is offered. Second, it represents communion with God, to whom the sacrifice is offered and with whom peace has been established through the sacrifice offered and accepted. Thus there is a table fellowship established and nourished with God Himself! This table fellowship expresses the essence of the covenant between God and man that is being celebrated. Third, it represents communion among all who share in the sacrificial meal, binding them together in the household of God.[7]

In this connection of sacrifice and communion, it is important to

---

[3] De la Taille, *The Mystery of Faith*, 1:19.
[4] Journet, "Transubstantiation," 736.
[5] Ratzinger, *The Feast of Faith*, 93–94.
[6] Hans Urs von Balthasar, "Eucharist: Gift of Love," *Communio* 43, no. 1 (2016): 139–53, at 145. The text continues: "How many of those who go forward for Communion realize that? However, to follow this and say that it would be better to not draw near would be false. For where could we accept the love that the Lord demands of us unless he first gives us his own love?"
[7] De la Taille, *The Mystery of Faith*, 1:19–20.

understand that there is an order: the sacrifice precedes the communion, and the communion is the culmination and fruit of the sacrifice.[8] The communion in the sacrifice presupposes that God has first been propitiated by the sacrifice, which enables the faithful to enter into deeper intimacy with Him.

If sacrifice and communion are deeply interrelated in the worship of Israel, that is still more true of the worship of the Church. As we have seen, the sacrifice of the altar re-presents the sacrifice of Calvary, which truly wins reconciliation between God and man such that man can enter into intimacy with God by coming to share in His life. There is no more perfect way to share in the divine life than by receiving the sacrificial Victim offered for the life of the world, the Victim who has in Himself the divine life that is communicated to us in Holy Communion. In this way, the ascending and descending directions of divine worship come together in the proper order. First glory is given to God in an ascending movement, and then blessings from God come to men in a descending movement, which in turn makes possible a more perfect ascending movement of self-donation.

In contemporary Western society, the perception of this link between sacrifice and communion is extremely dim. The faithful are generally unaware that Mass is a sacrifice and that Jesus is first offered in sacrifice to the Father before being received in Communion. Even theologians often contrast these aspects of the Mass—sacrifice and banquet—as if they were separate aspects that stand in competition with one another for the proper emphasis. A key pastoral task, therefore, is to restore the sense of the intimate connection and continuity between the two complementary aspects. The Mass is not just any banquet, but a *sacrificial banquet*[9] in which we receive the Lamb who first is offered in sacrifice as an efficacious sign of our own interior sacrifice.

St. John Paul II, in *Ecclesia de Eucharistia*, §16, stresses the unity of sacrifice and banquet:

> The saving efficacy of the sacrifice is fully realized when the Lord's body and blood are received in communion. The Eucharistic Sacrifice is intrinsically directed to the inward union of the faithful with Christ through communion; we

---

[8] See ibid., 1:20–22.

[9] See John Paul II, *EE*, §48: "The 'banquet' always remains a sacrificial banquet marked by the blood shed on Golgotha."

receive the very One who offered himself for us, we receive his body which he gave up for us on the Cross and his blood which he "poured out for many for the forgiveness of sins" (Matt 26:28).

To worthily receive the Lamb who is sacrificed we must seek to reproduce in ourselves the interior self-offering of the Lamb, for we receive communion *to become what we receive.* This is the key principle governing worthy reception of Holy Communion.[10]

EFFECTS OF HOLY COMMUNION

Since the Eucharist is the source and summit of the Church's life, it follows that Holy Communion is maximally beneficial to the faithful who receive it with the right dispositions, which means being in a state of grace, repentant of one's sins, and having faith in Christ's presence in the Eucharist. Since we receive Christ Himself in His entirety as our spiritual nourishment in Communion, there is nothing greater that can be imagined or conceived this side of heaven.

Witness of Eucharistic Prayers on the Graces of Communion

A good picture of the effects of Holy Communion is given by the Eucharistic Prayers (ordinarily in the second part of the epiclesis) in which the Church implores the Holy Spirit to sanctify the faithful who partake of the sacrament. The Roman Canon is characteristically sober in its petition for the effects of Communion, asking that "all of us, who through this participation at the altar receive the most holy Body and Blood of your Son, may be filled with every grace and heavenly blessing."[11] Eastern Eucharistic Prayers give a fuller picture of the effects of Holy Communion. The ancient Anaphora of Addai and Mari prays that the Holy Spirit descend upon the offering "that it may be to us, Lord, for remission of debts, forgiveness of sins, and the

---

[10] See, for example, Augustine, Sermon 229A, 1: "What you receive is what you yourselves are, thanks to the grace by which you have been redeemed" (Hill, *Sermons [184–229Z] on the Liturgical Seasons,* 270).

[11] *RM,* 641.

great hope of resurrection from the dead, and new life in the kingdom of heaven, with all who have been pleasing in your sight."[12] The Alexandrian Anaphora of St. Mark is still more detailed, praying that the Holy Spirit descend upon the offerings "that they may become to all of us who partake of them for faith, for sobriety, for healing, for renewal of soul, body, and spirit, for fellowship in eternal life and immortality, for the glorifying of your all-holy name, for forgiveness of sins."[13] The epiclesis in book 8 of the *Apostolic Constitutions*, probably from the fourth century, prays "that those who partake of it may be strengthened to piety, obtain forgiveness of sins, be delivered from the devil and his deceit, be filled with the Holy Spirit, become worthy of your Christ, and obtain eternal life, after reconciliation with you, almighty Master."[14]

From these texts, we see that Holy Communion sanctifies the communicants with every grace and blessing, such as piety and temperance, the forgiveness of sins, reconciliation with God, strength against the devil and his temptations, the gift of the Holy Spirit, resurrection, and the eternal life of the kingdom of God in communion with the whole Mystical Body.

Sacramental Grace

All of the sacraments communicate sanctifying grace *ex opere operato* to all those who validly receive them without posing an obstacle (such as lack of repentance or faith). It is proper to Baptism to open the door to grace, removing the obstacle of original sin and imparting the supernatural life for the first time. Penance restores it if it was lost through mortal sin, and the other sacraments communicate an increase of sanctifying grace. Of these, the Eucharist preeminently gives grace because it was instituted precisely to be the ordinary means of progressive nourishment in the life of grace and charity, and therefore should be received frequently.

In addition to the common effect of imparting sanctifying grace, each sacrament also gives particular effects of grace that are proper to the purpose for which that sacrament was instituted. The particular effects given by each sacrament are generally referred to as "sacra-

---

[12] Anaphora of Addai and Mari (*PEER*, 43).

[13] Alexandrian Anaphora of St. Mark (*PEER*, 66).

[14] *Apostolic Constitutions* 8 (*PEER*, 111).

mental grace."[15] St. Thomas speaks about sacramental grace in various articles in which he asks whether the sacraments give an effect of grace distinct from sanctifying grace, the infused virtues, and the gifts of the Holy Spirit. He consistently answers that sacramental graces flow from sanctifying grace, the infused virtues, and the gifts, but differ from them by being a special effect of a particular sacrament that was instituted for a specific end. The exact nature of these special aids proper to each sacrament, however, is not entirely clear.

In his early work *De Veritate* (*On Truth*), St. Thomas sees the distinction between the different sacramental graces as lying in the different ways that grace provides a remedy to sin and its consequences.[16] The general defects caused by sin are a certain habitual complacency with sin in the will and a lack of fervor, ignorance in the practical intellect, weakness and lack of constancy in the irascible appetite, and disordered inclinations in the concupiscible appetite.[17] Thus sacramental graces would strengthen the soul against these various consequences of sin, according to the particular purpose of each sacrament. The Eucharist accomplishes this effect, as will be seen below, by attracting the soul to a greater fervor of charity.

In his mature treatment of sacramental grace in the *Summa theologiae* III, question 62, article 2, St. Thomas simply states that

---

[15] See *CCC*, §1129: "'Sacramental grace' is the grace of the Holy Spirit, given by Christ and proper to each sacrament. The Spirit heals and transforms those who receive him by conforming them to the Son of God."

[16] Thomas Aquinas, *De Veritate*, q. 27, a. 5, ad 12:

> Just as different virtues and different gifts of the Holy Spirit are directed to different actions, so too the different effects of the sacraments are like different medicines for sin and different shares in the efficacy of our Lord's passion, which depend upon sanctifying grace, as do the virtues and gifts. . . . But the defects of sin, against which the sacraments are instituted, are hidden. Hence the effects of the sacraments do not have a proper name but go by the name of grace, for they are called sacramental graces, and the sacraments are distinguished on the basis of these graces as their proper effects. Those effects, moreover, belong to sanctifying grace, which also is joined to those effects. Thus along with their proper effects they have a common effect, sanctifying grace, which is given by means of the sacraments to one who does not have it and increased by them in one who does. (Schmidt, *Truth*, 3:343–44)

See also St. Thomas's treatment of this topic in his commentary on the *Sentences* of Peter Lombard: *In II Sent.*, d. 26, a. 1, ad 5; *In IV Sent.*, d. 1, q. 1, a. 4, qla. 5; *In IV Sent.*, d. 7, a. 2, a. 2, qla. 3.

[17] See *ST* I-II, q. 85, a. 3.

sacramental graces give divine assistance in living that aspect of the Christian life to which that sacrament is ordered. Since all the sacraments are ordered in some way to remedying the effects of sin, this response would coincide with his earlier text. However, one could argue that the purpose of the sacraments is not only remedying sin but also imparting a share in the divine life and aiding the recipient to live that supernatural life in the world according to his state of life. Thus the divine assistance is not limited to remedying defects deriving from sin but also includes positive aids by which the Holy Spirit moves us to do good. In this article, St. Thomas writes:

> Grace, considered in itself, perfects the essence of the soul, in so far as it is a certain participated likeness of the Divine Nature. And just as the soul's powers flow from its essence, so from grace there flow certain perfections into the powers of the soul, which are called virtues and gifts, whereby the powers are perfected in reference to their actions. Now the *sacraments are ordained unto certain special effects which are necessary in the Christian life*: thus Baptism is ordained unto a certain spiritual regeneration, by which man dies to vice and becomes a member of Christ: which effect is something special in addition to the actions of the soul's powers: and the same holds true of the other sacraments. Consequently just as the virtues and gifts confer, in addition to grace commonly so called, a certain special perfection ordained to the powers' proper actions, so does *sacramental grace confer, over and above grace commonly so called, and in addition to the virtues and gifts, a certain Divine assistance in obtaining the end of the sacrament.* It is thus that sacramental grace confers something in addition to the grace of the virtues and gifts.[18]

St. Thomas does not specify the precise nature of the "divine assistance" given by sacramental grace, other than that it is something added to habitual or sanctifying grace and the virtues and gifts and that it is ordered to the particular end of each sacrament.[19] What might this

---

[18] *ST* III, q. 62, a. 2 (my italics).

[19] For a good summary of various theories of what constitutes sacramental grace, see Antonio Miralles, *I sacramenti cristiani: trattato generale*, 2nd ed. (Rome: Apollinare studi, 2008), 254–62. See also Charles Schleck, "St. Thomas on the Nature of Sacramental Grace," *The Thomist* 18, no. 1 (1955): 1–30 (concluded

be? In addition to sanctifying grace and the habitual supernatural gifts that flow from it—the theological virtues, infused moral virtues, and gifts of the Holy Spirit—we also need *actual grace*,[20] which is a divine impulse that moves our spiritual faculties, *illuminating* our intellect to grasp supernatural truths and *attracting* our will to desire and choose supernatural goods. Every action and affection ordered to our supernatural end has its origin in the impulses given to us by actual grace. It is reasonable to think, therefore, that sacramental grace includes the giving of actual grace ordered to the end of each sacrament.[21] Each sacrament must somehow bring about a series of actual graces ordered to the specific purpose of that sacrament, as long as no obstacle, such as unrepented mortal sin, blocks the divine action. Some theologians explain this by saying that each sacrament gives a kind of covenantal "right" to the graces ordered to its purpose.[22]

All of the sacraments are ordered to configuration with Christ, but they differ by giving a participation in different aspects of Christ's mission. Whenever God gives a particular mission, He grants the grace to accomplish the mission. Sacramental grace can be understood, therefore, as the grace to accomplish the different missions that result from different aspects of configuration with Christ. Baptism and Confirmation give a series of graces that make it possible to participate in the three offices of Christ as prophet, priest, and king. Baptism does this in an initial manner, conferring graces to strengthen faith and

---

in no. 2: 242–78); Robert Reginald Masterson, "Sacramental Graces: Modes of Sanctifying Grace," *The Thomist* 18 (1955): 311–72.

[20] For the distinction between sanctifying grace and actual graces, see *CCC*, §2000: "Sanctifying grace is an habitual gift, a stable and supernatural disposition that perfects the soul itself to enable it to live with God, to act by his love. *Habitual grace*, the permanent disposition to live and act in keeping with God's call, is distinguished from *actual graces*, which refer to God's interventions, whether at the beginning of conversion or in the course of the work of sanctification."

[21] The thesis that sacramental graces consist in a series of actual graces was maintained by Cardinal Cajetan in his commentary on *ST* III, q. 62, a. 2, no. 2, in *Opera Omnia Sancti Thomae Aquinatis*, Leonine ed., vol. 12 (Rome: Typographia poliglotta S. C. de Propaganda Fide, 1906), 23.

[22] See Joseph A. de Aldama, "On the Sacraments in General," in *Sacrae Theologiae Summa*, vol. 4A, *On the Sacraments in General: On Baptism, Confirmation, Eucharist, Penance and Anointing*, 3rd ed., trans. Kenneth Baker (Ramsey, NJ: Keep the Faith, 2015), 43–45, esp. 43: "These *helps* will be given at the opportune time, that is, when they are demanded by the end of the sacrament. However, the *right* to them is permanent, according as it is rooted in habitual grace, so it is also lost with it."

receive the other sacraments. Confirmation gives graces that enable the recipients to be mature witnesses of Christ in a hostile world, *actively* participating in His threefold mission of building up the Church. Similarly, matrimony[23] and Holy Orders give graces ordered to a holy exercise of the exalted missions they confer. The sacrament of Penance gives actual graces to avoid the sins confessed, to strengthen contrition, to make reparation for sin, and to overcome its effects and wounds. Anointing of the Sick gives actual graces to sanctify the experience of weakness and suffering and to prepare the soul for death through a strengthening of hope and a more complete overcoming of the remnants of sin. The Eucharist, finally, gives actual graces ordered to its proper ends, which are the enkindling of greater charity for God and neighbor, and the glorification of God through offering the sacrifice of the Christian life in union with Christ's Paschal mystery.

Sacramental Grace and Docility to God's Inspirations

It seems likely, however, that the sacramental graces proper to each sacrament are not limited only to a series of actual graces that are given as we need them. Since actual graces require our cooperation so that they can result in free and meritorious action,[24] it would be fitting

---

[23] For the sacramental grace of the Sacrament of Matrimony, see Pius XI, Encyclical Letter on Christian Marriage, *Casti Connubii* (1930), §40:

> By the very fact, therefore, that the faithful with sincere mind give such consent, they open up for themselves a treasure of sacramental grace from which they draw supernatural power for the fulfilling of their rights and duties faithfully, holily, perseveringly even unto death. Hence this sacrament not only increases sanctifying grace, the permanent principle of the supernatural life, in those who, as the expression is, place no obstacle (*obex*) in its way, but also adds particular gifts, dispositions, seeds of grace, by elevating and perfecting the natural powers. By these gifts the parties are assisted not only in understanding, but in knowing intimately, in adhering to firmly, in willing effectively, and in successfully putting into practice, those things which pertain to the marriage state, its aims and duties, giving them in fine right to the actual assistance of grace, whensoever they need it for fulfilling the duties of their state.

[24] See *ST* I-II, q. 111, a. 2. See also Lawrence Feingold, "God's Movement of the Soul through Operative and Cooperative Grace," in *Thomism and Predestination: Principles and Disputations*, ed. Steven A. Long, Roger W. Nutt, and Thomas Joseph White (Washington, DC: Catholic University of America Press, 2017), 166–91.

for the sacraments to give not only the actual graces that are ordered to the purpose of each sacrament but also a habitual docility to be receptive and cooperate with them. Since everything is received according to the mode of the receiver, no less important than the actual graces received are the interior dispositions that incline the recipient to be docile to those graces and act on them through active cooperation. St. Thomas understands the gifts of the Holy Spirit as the vehicles for this docility to the inspirations of actual grace. In explaining the necessity of the gifts of the Holy Spirit, St. Thomas writes:

> Now it is evident that whatever is moved must be proportionate to its mover: and the perfection of the mobile as such, consists in a disposition whereby it is disposed to be well moved by its mover. Hence the more exalted the mover, the more perfect must be the disposition whereby the mobile is made proportionate to its mover: thus we see that a disciple needs a more perfect disposition in order to receive a higher teaching from his master. Now it is manifest that human virtues perfect man according as it is natural for him to be moved by his reason in his interior and exterior actions. Consequently man needs yet higher perfections, whereby to be disposed to be moved by God. These perfections are called gifts, not only because they are infused by God, but also because by them man is disposed to become amenable to the Divine inspiration.[25]

This docility or receptivity to particular movements of actual grace depends on sanctifying grace and charity.[26] We are docile to what we love. The more we love our teachers, the more we are capable of being instructed by them. If this is true of human teachers, it is still more true of the inward Teacher, the Paraclete.[27] It is reasonable to think

---

[25] *ST* I-II, q. 68, a. 1.

[26] See *ST* I-II, q. 68, a. 5: "Now the Holy Spirit dwells in us by charity, according to Rom 5:5: 'The charity of God is poured forth in our hearts by the Holy Ghost, Who is given to us,' even as our reason is perfected by prudence. Wherefore, just as the moral virtues are united together in prudence, so the gifts of the Holy Ghost are connected together in charity: so that whoever has charity, has all the gifts of the Holy Ghost, none of which can one possess without charity."

[27] See John 14:26: "But the Counselor, the Holy Spirit, whom the Father will send in my name, he will teach you all things, and bring to your remembrance all that I have said to you."

that sacramental grace strengthens this docility that comes from grace and charity by focusing it according to the mission of each sacrament. This is in harmony with St. Thomas's assertion that sacramental grace flows from sanctifying grace and presupposes it.[28]

Thus it seems reasonable to hold that the sacraments give gifts of docility to the Holy Spirit in a way proper to the particular purpose of each sacrament to help the recipient be habitually docile to the actual graces sent by God to aid them in carrying out the ecclesial mission given by a particular sacrament. This thesis helps explain how the proper effects of the sacraments come forth from the action of the Holy Spirit in the soul.[29] Many texts in the liturgy, such as the epiclesis for the sanctification of the faithful, refer to this action of the Holy Spirit. In the case of the Eucharist, this docility will be to all the inspirations of God that lead us to the manifold exercise of charity.

Connection between Sacramental Grace and the "Inward Reality and Sign"

There is an intimate connection between the "inward reality and sign" (*res et sacramentum*) in each sacrament and the sacramental graces proper to that sacrament. The key principle governing the sacraments is that they efficaciously produce the grace they signify. Since the *res et sacramentum* is itself an invisible and durable sign, it efficaciously produces (as an instrumental cause) what it signifies as long as no obstacle blocks it from achieving its effect. Better dispositions in the recipient, however, will enable it to achieve greater efficaciousness.

In the three sacraments that give an indelible character—Baptism, Confirmation, and Holy Orders—that character abides in the soul as an efficacious sign of the grace to accomplish the mission conferred by the sacrament. As long as one remains in a state of grace, it is reasonable to hold that the character draws down the actual graces ordered to the carrying out of the mission of the sacrament. In Holy Matrimony, the indissoluble sacramental marital bond is the *res et sacramentum*, and it likewise abides to draw down the graces necessary for fulfilling the mission of marriage.

In the case of the Eucharist, unlike the other sacraments, the inward reality and sign (*res et sacramentum*) abides for only a short

---

[28] See *De Veritate*, q. 27, a. 5, ad 12.
[29] See Miralles, *I sacramenti cristiani*, 226–49.

time in the recipient before the sacramental species are corrupted by
the process of digestion. Despite the brevity of the presence of this
inward reality and sign in the recipient, the Eucharist has a unique,
unsurpassable dignity because this inward reality is not a quality of the
recipient, as in the other sacraments, but the very Body and Blood of
Christ and His Paschal mystery. For this reason, the Eucharist sanctifies those who worthily receive it by configuring them with the heart
of Christ and His sacrificial love, and with the life of grace, charity,
reconciliation, and communion that He won for us by His Paschal
mystery, ultimately communicating to us the Life that is to flower into
eternal life.

The sacramental grace proper to the Eucharist, as the sacrament
of charity, therefore, is to nourish the soul with the ardor of sacrificial
love for God and neighbor, configuring one with the love of Christ.
Above all, the Eucharist helps us deepen our union with God through
this marriage feast with the Son. And because it causes us to grow in
the love of God, the Eucharist binds the Church together in charity,
and also aids the soul to grow in deeper contrition and interior conversion. It thus further nourishes and develops the proper effect of the
sacrament of Penance.

St. Thomas on the Effects of Communion

In *ST* III, question 79, article 1, St. Thomas explains the effects of
Communion according to four aspects of the Eucharist: it contains
the real presence of Christ, it is the sacrifice of the Cross, it is the
sacrament of spiritual nourishment, and it is the sacrament of ecclesial
unity. All four of these ways of understanding the Eucharist converge
in manifesting the effects of grace, reconciliation, and divinization
that Holy Communion produces in a rightly disposed recipient.

The Eucharist Sanctifies by Substantially Containing Christ

First, since Christ Himself is substantially present in this sacrament,
and since He came to bring grace into the world by becoming man, we
receive in this sacrament both Christ Himself and that grace that He
came to give us, according to the measure in which we are disposed
to receive it. We can infer the effects of Communion, therefore, from
reflecting on the various purposes of the Incarnation. We have seen in

the first chapter of the present book that Christ became man to free us from sin, death, and the dominion of Satan; to fill us with a share in His divine life; and to bring us into a filial and spousal union with the Triune God. The Fathers frequently teach that the Son of God took on a mortal human nature so that we might be brought to share in His divine nature and be made into sons and daughters of God.[30] Holy Communion is the chief sacramental means to bring about this divine interchange. We receive His Body and Blood so as to be nourished by His divine life. St. Thomas writes:

> The effect of this sacrament ought to be considered, first of all and principally, from what is contained in this sacrament, which is Christ; Who, just as by coming into the world, He visibly bestowed the life of grace upon the world, according to John 1:17: "Grace and truth came by Jesus Christ," so also, by coming sacramentally into man, causes the life of grace, according to John 6:58: "He that eateth Me, the same also shall live by Me." Hence Cyril says on Luke 22:19: "God's life-giving Word by uniting Himself with His own flesh, made it to be productive of life. For it was becoming that He should be united somehow with bodies through His sacred flesh and precious blood, which we receive in a life-giving blessing in the bread and wine."

We have seen above in chapter 5 that the sacraments are instruments of God in imparting grace and that, whereas the other sacraments are "separated instruments" like a chisel in the hand of a sculptor, the Eucharist contains the humanity of Christ, which is a *conjoined* instrument of the divinity. Because of this, the Eucharist is the most perfect instrument to bring about in us a progressive configuration with the perfect humanity of Christ and a sharing in His divinity.

---

[30] See Irenaeus, *Against Heresies* 3.19.1: "For it was for this end that the Word of God was made man, and He who was the Son of God became the Son of man, that man, having been taken into the Word, and receiving the adoption, might become the son of God" (*ANF*, 1:448). See also Thomas Aquinas, *Opusculum 57, In Festo Corporis Christi*, lec. 1: "The only-begotten Son of God, wishing to make us participants in his divinity, assumed our nature so that, having been made man, He might make men gods" (*Liturgy of the Hours*, feast of Corpus Christi, Office of Readings, 2nd Reading).

The Eucharist Makes Present Christ's Passion

Secondly, the Eucharist sanctifies by applying the effects of Christ's Passion, the cause of all justification and grace, to those who receive Him. By receiving His immolated Flesh and Blood, we have the effects of Christ's Passion applied to us, for we receive Christ in solidarity with His sacrifice that has just been offered. Communion is a union not only with the Person of Christ but also with His sacrifice. Therefore, Holy Communion progressively brings about in the well-disposed recipient all the effects that Christ's Passion has won for us: forgiveness, reconciliation, and sanctification. St. Thomas explains:

> This sacrament works in man the effect which Christ's Passion wrought in the world. Hence, Chrysostom says on the words, "Immediately there came out blood and water" (John 19:34): "Since the sacred mysteries derive their origin from thence, when you draw nigh to the awe-inspiring chalice, so approach as if you were going to drink from Christ's own side." Hence our Lord Himself says (Matt 26:28): "This is My blood . . . which shall be shed for many unto the remission of sins."[31]

The other sacraments sanctify us by applying the grace merited in Christ's Passion. The Eucharist has preeminence in giving grace because it is not a separated instrument of the Passion, but sacramentally makes present the sacrifice of Calvary that merited our salvation and all sanctification and contains the glorious Victim of Calvary. Again, the other sacraments are separated instruments of the crucified and risen Lamb, but in the Eucharist, we receive that Lamb Himself. The Eucharist, therefore, is the perfect instrument for configuring us with the Passion and all its fruits.

The Eucharist Sanctifies by Way of Spiritual Nourishment

Third, this sacrament is received as spiritual food and drink and thus offers spiritual sustenance in the very life of grace and charity. St. Thomas writes:

---

[31] *ST* III, q. 79, a. 1.

Thirdly, the effect of this sacrament is considered from the way in which this sacrament is given; for it is given by way of food and drink. And therefore this sacrament does for the spiritual life all that material food does for the bodily life, namely, by sustaining, giving increase, restoring, and giving delight. Accordingly, Ambrose says (*De Sacramentis* 5): "This is the bread of everlasting life, which supports the substance of our soul." And Chrysostom says (Hom. 46 on John): "When we desire it, He lets us feel Him, and eat Him, and embrace Him." And hence our Lord says (John 6:56): "My flesh is meat indeed, and My blood is drink indeed."[32]

The other sacraments dispense graces through separated sacramental instruments. The Eucharist is the most perfect form of spiritual nourishment conceivable because the nourishment in grace comes from receiving the very Author of all grace. Christ could have devised a way to nourish us with grace through receiving something other than Himself. In the Eucharist, however, he gives us a share in His divine Life in the most perfect way by giving us nothing other than Himself, who is "the way, the truth, and the life" (John 14:6). And, because the Eucharist contains the "desire of the everlasting hills" (Gen 49:26), it refreshes and consoles the soul in a preeminent manner.

The Eucharist Is the Sacrament of Ecclesial Charity

Fourth, in Holy Communion we receive the grace of ecclesial unity and the bond of charity. This can be seen from the very nature of the sacramental species of bread and wine, which are produced through a union of many parts: the bread is one substance from many grains, and the wine is one substance from many grapes. This sacramental sign of unity makes real what is signified:

Fourthly, the effect of this sacrament is considered from the species under which it is given. Hence Augustine says (Tract. 26 on John): "Our Lord betokened His body and blood in things which out of many units are made into some one whole: for out of many grains is one thing made," that is, bread; "and many grapes flow into one thing," that is, wine. And therefore

---

[32] Ibid.

he observes elsewhere (Tract. 26 on John): "O sacrament of piety, O sign of unity, O bond of charity!"[33]

The other sacraments also nurture ecclesial communion, each in its own way,[34] but the Eucharist is preeminent here as well because it nourishes that unity by the fact that the many members all receive the same Christ and are brought to share in the same divine life of the Son of God. Every member of the Church receives the same divine Bridegroom and is progressively configured to His peace.

Increase of Sanctifying Grace

The principal effect of Holy Communion is to nourish the participation in the divine life that we initially receive in Baptism. Because sanctifying grace is a habitual sharing in the divine life or nature (2 Pet 1:4), that sharing or participation admits of countless degrees. No matter how much grace one already has received, God can always increase it still more. Even though Mary was said by the angel to be full of grace at the time of the Annunciation, she could still increase in grace every day of her earthly life.

We cannot give grace to ourselves, for it is a share of God's life. He has established three principal ways that we can grow in it: sacraments, merit, and prayer. We can pray for an increase of grace, and we can merit its increase through doing works animated by charity. The principal way, however, is through the sacraments. And of all the sacraments, Holy Communion was instituted directly to nourish the life of grace.[35] As food nourishes the natural life of the body, so the Body

---

[33] Ibid.

[34] See Second Vatican Council, *Lumen Gentium*, §11.

[35] See *ST* III, q. 79, a. 1, ad 1:

> This sacrament has of itself the power of bestowing grace; nor does anyone possess grace before receiving this sacrament except from some desire thereof; from his own desire, as in the case of the adult; or from the Church's desire in the case of children, as stated above (q. 73, a. 3). Hence it is due to the efficacy of its power, that even from desire thereof a man procures grace whereby he is enabled to lead the spiritual life. It remains, then, that when the sacrament itself is really received, grace is increased, and the spiritual life perfected: yet in different fashion from the sacrament of Confirmation, in which grace is increased and perfected for resisting the outward assaults of Christ's enemies. But by

and Blood of Christ nourish the life of Christ in our souls and bodies. Both the sacramental sign of bread and wine and the *res et sacramentum* of the Body and Blood signify, in different ways, the nourishing of Christ's life in us, which is sanctifying grace. St. Leo the Great speaks eloquently of the sanctification worked by Holy Communion:

> This partaking in the body and blood of Christ means nothing else than that we should pass over into what we have taken in. Since we have died with him and are buried with him and are risen with him, let us bear him through all things both in spirit and in flesh, as the Apostle says: "You have died, and your life is hidden with Christ in God" (Col 3:3).[36]

Each person receives a different degree of sanctifying grace through Holy Communion, for each one receives according to one's dispositions of desire and thirst for union with Christ in the sacrament. We can apply Jesus's saying: "For to him who has will more be given" (Mark 4:25).

Increase of Charity

The Eucharist, as the sacrament of charity, is especially ordered to nourish charity in both its vertical and horizontal dimensions of love for God and neighbor.[37] Charity is especially tied to sanctifying grace, such that the two are always born together and grow together, and they are lost together if we fall into mortal sin. They are strictly tied together, for God is love, and any increase in our participation in the divine nature will bring about an increase in our ability to love as God loves.

Once again, the sacramental sign indicates this effect of charity by the fact that Christ gives Himself to us whole and entire to be received directly into our bodies in a nuptial way. In the Eucharist, Christ feeds us with His own Body and Blood, which is the most expressive sign of the love that the Eucharist produces in the faithful who are rightly dis-

---

this sacrament grace receives increase, and the spiritual life is perfected, so that man may stand perfect in himself by union with God.

[36] Leo the Great, Sermon 63 (Freeland and Conway, 277).

[37] On the nourishing of charity as the principal effect of the Eucharist according to Aquinas, see Spezzano, *The Glory of God's Grace*, 320–23.

posed.[38] As with sanctifying grace, we cannot increase faith, hope, and charity in ourselves by our own acts, but their increase can be gained through prayer, merit, and the sacraments, especially the Eucharist.

Leo XIII, in his encyclical on the Eucharist, *Mirae Caritatis* (1902), writes:

> That genuine charity, therefore, which knows how to do and to suffer all things for the salvation and the benefit of all, leaps forth with all the heat and energy of a flame from that most holy Eucharist in which Christ Himself is present and lives, in which He indulges to the utmost His love towards us, and under the impulse of that divine love ceaselessly renews His Sacrifice. And thus it is not difficult to see whence the arduous labours of apostolic men, and whence those innumerable designs of every kind for the welfare of the human race which have been set on foot among Catholics, derive their origin, their strength, their permanence, their success.[39]

St. Thomas also holds that, in addition to giving an increase in the virtue of charity, the sacramental grace of Holy Communion stimulates the will to make more fervent *acts* of affective and effective love. As seen above, the sacramental grace of the Eucharist gives actual graces ordered to the exercise of charity and an increased docility to cooperate with those graces. St. Thomas expresses this with an eloquence clearly based on personal experience:

> This sacrament confers grace spiritually together with the virtue of charity. Hence Damascene (*De Fide Orthod.* 4) compares this sacrament to the burning coal which Isaias saw (6:6): "For a live ember is not simply wood, but wood united to fire; so also the bread of communion is not simple bread,

---

[38] See John Chrysostom, Homily 46, on John 6:41–53: "And to show the love He has for us He has made it possible for those who desire, not merely to look upon Him, but even to touch Him and to consume Him and to fix their teeth in His Flesh and to be commingled with Him; in short, to fulfill all their love. Let us, then, come back from that table like lions breathing out fire, thus becoming terrifying to the Devil, and remaining mindful of our Head and of the love which He has shown for us" (FC 33, Goggin, *Commentary on Saint John*, 468–69).

[39] Leo XIII, *Mirae Caritatis*, §13.

but bread united with the Godhead." But as Gregory observes in a Homily for Pentecost, "God's love is never idle; for, wherever it is, it does great works." And consequently through this sacrament, as far as its power is concerned, not only is the habit of grace and of virtue bestowed, but it is furthermore aroused to act, according to 2 Cor. 5:14: "The charity of Christ presseth us."[40]

Since we receive Christ in His act of giving Himself *to the end*, Communion nourishes us with that same ecstatic love by configuring us with what we have received. Holy Communion progressively enables us to say with St. Paul in Galatians 2:20: "It is no longer I who live, but Christ who lives in me; and the life I now live in the flesh I live by faith in the Son of God, who loved me and gave himself for me."[41] St. Thomas describes this effect of ecstatic love that carries us out of ourselves into Christ:

> It belongs to charity to transform the lover into the beloved, because charity is such that it brings about ecstasy, as Dionysius says. And since the increase of virtues caused by this sacrament comes about through the changing of the one eating into the spiritual food eaten, therefore to this sacrament is specially attributed the increase of charity rather than an increase of other virtues.[42]

Increase of Faith, Hope, the Infused Moral Virtues, and Gifts of the Holy Spirit

Charity never grows alone. Together with sanctifying grace and charity, the faithful receive an increase of the theological virtues of faith and hope. Every increase in sanctifying grace will bring an increase in our conformity with God's revealed truth, which is faith, and an increase in our hope to fully share in God's life in heaven.

Together with the theological virtues, the infused moral virtues

---

[40] *ST* III, q. 79, a. 1, ad 2.

[41] For this theme of Eucharistic ecstasy, see the excellent article by Peter Kwasniewski, "Aquinas on Eucharistic Ecstasy: From Self-Alienation to Gift of Self," *Nova et Vetera* (English) 6, no. 1 (2008): 157–204.

[42] Thomas Aquinas, *In IV Sent.*, d. 12, q. 2, a. 1, qla. 1, ad 3 (trans. Kwasniewski, "Aquinas on Eucharistic Ecstasy," 190).

(supernatural prudence, justice, fortitude, and temperance) also grow in our souls, for charity is their queen and animating principle.[43] The same is true of the seven gifts of the Holy Spirit mentioned in Isaiah 11:2–3: wisdom, understanding, counsel, knowledge, fortitude, piety, and fear of the Lord. St. Thomas explains that the root of all of these gifts is charity, for charity as friendship with God gives a connatural ability to be docile to the Beloved of the soul and His gentle impulses in our interior.[44] Therefore, to the degree that the Eucharist nourishes charity, it also strengthens our habitual docility to the Holy Spirit, which is the essence of the seven gifts of the Spirit.

Communion and the Forgiveness of Sins

Eucharistic Prayers, in the epiclesis for the sanctification of the faithful, frequently mention the forgiveness of sins as a primary effect of Communion.[45] This is interpreted by Innocent III to mean that devout reception of the Eucharist "blots out venial sins and wards off mortal sins."[46] Both effects are made possible by the infusion of charity. This does not mean, of course, that all mortal sins are effectively warded off, nor that all venial sins are actually forgiven, for the infusion of charity is according to the measure of the disposition of the communicant and both effects require our free and active cooperation.

The forgiveness of venial sins through reception of Holy Communion comes through an infusion of charity that attracts the soul to further conformity with the will of God, leading it to repent (at least implicitly) for certain habits of venial sin that it sees to be contrary to God's will and to make a purpose of amendment in that regard.[47]

---

[43] See *ST* I-II, q. 65, a. 2.

[44] See *ST* I-II, q. 68, a. 5: "Just as the moral virtues are united together in prudence, so the gifts of the Holy Spirit are connected together in charity, so that whoever has charity has all the gifts of the Holy Spirit, none of which can be possessed without charity."

[45] See Cesare Giraudo, "L'eucaristia: premio per i sani o medicina per i malati?" esp. 488–91.

[46] Innocent III, *De Sacro Altaris Mysterio*, bk. 4, ch. 44 (PL, 217:885), quoted by Thomas Aquinas in *ST* III, q. 79, a. 4, sc.

[47] St. Thomas explains this effect of Communion in *ST* III, q. 79, a. 4:

> Two things may be considered in this sacrament: the sacrament itself, and the reality of the sacrament. It appears from both that this sacrament has the power of forgiving venial sins. For this sacrament is

Venial sins will be forgiven to the degree that there is a movement of true contrition for them that includes a resolve to avoid those sins in the future.

Experience shows that contrition for one venial sin does not have to include contrition for other venial sins, for we can resolve to combat some venial sins without making the resolve to eliminate others.[48] That is, we can remain attached to some venial sins while sincerely repenting of others. Mortal sins, on the other hand, are always forgiven together, because, unlike venial sins, they all involve a turning away from God as our final end.[49] The infusion of charity requires that all of them be repudiated, for all are directly and gravely contrary to love for God above all. Venial sins, on the contrary, do not imply that the soul makes something else other than God into its final end, and thus they are not opposed to the very existence of charity, as mortal sin is, but rather to its fervor and perfection. Thus an infusion of charity increases the fervor of the will and freely attracts it to combat, at least in part, what is opposed to the perfection of charity. St. Thomas says: "Venial sins, although not opposed to the habit of charity, are nevertheless opposed to the fervor of its act, which act is kindled by this

---

received under the form of nourishing food. Now nourishment from food is requisite for the body to make good the daily waste caused by the action of natural heat. But something is also lost daily of our spirituality from the heat of concupiscence through venial sins, which lessen the fervor of charity, as was shown [II-II, q. 24, a. 10]. And therefore it belongs to this sacrament to forgive venial sins. Hence Ambrose says (De Sacramentis 5) that this daily bread is taken "as a remedy against daily infirmity." The reality of this sacrament is charity, not only as to its habit, but also as to its act, which is kindled in this sacrament; and by this means venial sins are forgiven. Consequently, it is manifest that venial sins are forgiven by the power of this sacrament.

[48] See *ST* III, q. 87, a. 1, ad 1.

[49] See *ST* I-II q. 71, a. 4; q. 72, a. 5 ("He who, by sinning, turns away from his last end, if we consider the nature of his sin, falls irreparably, and therefore is said to sin mortally and to deserve eternal punishment: whereas when a man sins without turning away from God, by the very nature of his sin, his disorder can be repaired, because the principle of the order is not destroyed; wherefore he is said to sin venially, because he does not sin so as to deserve to be punished eternally"); q. 88, a. 1 ("The defect of order to the last end cannot be repaired through something else as a higher principle, as neither can an error about principles. Wherefore such sins are called mortal, as being irreparable. On the other hand, sins which imply a disorder in things referred to the end, the order to the end itself being preserved, are reparable. These sins are called venial").

sacrament; by reason of which act venial sins are blotted out."[50]

Future sins are also warded off by an increase of charity, which is the best defense against all temptations and all the attacks of the enemy and of our disordered inclinations. St. Thomas explains:

> Sin is the spiritual death of the soul. Hence man is preserved from future sin in the same way as the body is preserved from future death of the body: and this happens in two ways. First of all, in so far as man's nature is strengthened inwardly against inner decay, and so by means of food and medicine he is preserved from death. Secondly, by being guarded against outward assaults; and thus he is protected by means of arms by which he defends his body.
>
> Now this sacrament preserves man from sin in both of these ways. For, first of all, by uniting man with Christ through grace, it strengthens his spiritual life, as spiritual food and spiritual medicine, according to Psalm 103:5: "(That) bread strengthens man's heart." Augustine likewise says (Tract. 26 in Joan.): "Approach without fear; it is bread, not poison." Secondly, inasmuch as it is a sign of Christ's Passion, whereby the devils are conquered, it repels all the assaults of demons. Hence Chrysostom says (Hom. 46 in Joan.): "Like lions breathing forth fire, thus do we depart from that table, being made terrible to the devil."[51]

It is in this sense that St. Thomas interprets the words of John 6:50: "This is the bread which comes down from heaven, that a man may eat of it and not die." The Eucharist gives us the spiritual power to ward off any mortal sin, which causes the death of the soul.

Although worthy reception of the Eucharist gives us the means to ward off future sin, it does not automatically achieve that effect because our free will during this earthly life is not yet fully confirmed in good, as is the case of the blessed who see God. The Eucharist gives us the grace to avoid all grave sin or even deliberate venial sin, but our will can still resist that grace if we so choose.[52]

---

[50] *ST* III, q. 79, a. 4, ad 1.

[51] Ibid., a. 6.

[52] See ibid., ad 1: "The effect of this sacrament is received according to man's condition: such is the case with every active cause in that its effect is received in matter according to the condition of the matter. But such is the condition

By nourishing us with charity, Holy Communion also gives strength to resist the temptations of the enemy. This effect is indicated in the fourth-century Eucharistic Prayer in the *Apostolic Constitutions*, in which the priest prays that those who partake of the sacrifice "be delivered from the devil and his deceit."[53]

Holy Communion and Spiritual Consolation

Reception of Holy Communion, by giving an infusion of charity, also generally refreshes the soul with spiritual consolation. As food not only nourishes the body but also restores energy and gives delight, so Communion not only nourishes the spiritual life with charity but also consoles and delights the soul and gives new fervor to its movement of self-giving. Reception of the perfect Victim enables us to embrace Him and His Cross and grow in love for Him, and it strengthens the soul in its resolve to offer itself back to God. In his text for the office of Corpus Christi, St. Thomas writes:

> No one can fully express the sweetness of this sacrament, in which spiritual delight is tasted at its very source, and in which we renew the memory of that surpassing love for us which Christ revealed in his passion.[54]

In *ST* III, question 79, article 1, ad 2, St. Thomas describes the spiritual effects of the Eucharist in a similar way: "Hence it is that the soul is spiritually nourished through the power of this sacrament, insofar as it is spiritually gladdened, and as it were inebriated with the sweetness of the divine Goodness, according to Song 5:1: 'Eat, O friends, and drink, and be inebriated, my dearly beloved.'" In the dark night of the soul, however, for purposes of purification, God can suspend this consolation so that the soul does not experience it.[55]

---

of man on earth that his free-will can be bent to good or evil. Hence, although this sacrament of itself has the power of preserving from sin, yet it does not take away from man the possibility of sinning."

[53] *Apostolic Constitutions* 8 (*PEER*, 111).

[54] Thomas Aquinas, *Opusculum 57, In Festo Corporis Christi*, lec. 4 (*Liturgy of the Hours*, feast of Corpus Christi, Office of Readings, 2nd Reading).

[55] See, for example, Thérèse of Lisieux, *Story of a Soul: The Autobiography of St. Thérèse of Lisieux*, trans. John Clarke, 3rd ed. (Washington, DC: ICS, 1996), 172.

The presence of venial sin to which one is still attached does not completely block the principal spiritual effects of the Eucharist, which are an increase of the habits of sanctifying grace and charity, but such an attachment obviously makes us less receptive to graces that God is giving us, and thus it may also block this infusion of spiritual joy and interior consolation, insofar as the mind is distracted from devotion by the venial sin.[56]

J. R. R. Tolkien, in a letter to his son Michael, wrote an unforgettable passage on the consolation given by Holy Communion:

> Out of the darkness of my life, so much frustrated, I put before you the one great thing to love on earth: the Blessed Sacrament. . . . There you will find romance, glory, honour, fidelity, and the true way of all your loves on earth, and more than that: Death. By the divine paradox, that which ends life, and demands the surrender of all, and yet by the taste—or foretaste—of which alone can what you seek in your earthly relationships (love, faithfulness, joy) be maintained, or take on that complexion of reality, of eternal endurance, which every man's heart desires.[57]

Indwelling of the Trinity and Holy Communion

An increase of grace and charity bring about a still greater benefit, which is the deepening and nourishing of the Indwelling of God in the soul. At first it might seem that the Indwelling is not something that can increase. St. Thomas, however, shows how this deepening

---

[56] See *ST* III, q. 79, a. 8:

> Venial sins can be taken in two ways: first of all as past, secondly as in the act of being committed. Venial sins taken in the first way do not in any way hinder the effect of this sacrament. For it can come to pass that after many venial sins a man may approach devoutly to this sacrament and fully secure its effect. Considered in the second way, venial sins do not utterly hinder the effect of this sacrament, but merely in part. For, it has been stated above (q. 79, a. 1), that the effect of this sacrament is not only the obtaining of habitual grace or charity, but also a certain actual refreshment of spiritual sweetness; which is indeed hindered if anyone approach to this sacrament with mind distracted through venial sins; but the increase of habitual grace or of charity is not taken away.

[57] J. R. R. Tolkien, *The Letters of J. R. R. Tolkien*, ed. Humphrey Carpenter (New York: Houghton Mifflin Harcourt, 2000), 53–54.

is possible. The Indwelling can be understood as a new presence of God in the soul as its Beloved. It is common Scholastic teaching that God is in all things in three ways: upholding them in being, exercising dominion over them in His omnipotence, and knowing them perfectly.[58] None of these can be increased. In addition to these three ways, however, God is present to us in a still better way if we are in a state of grace and have the virtue of charity. In that case He is present to us in a *relational* way as our Beloved who is present *in the temple of our hearts*. If we are in a state of grace, we habitually love God, and so He is present in our hearts as the object of our habitual love. In the three kinds of presence mentioned above, God is present in all things as a *cause* is present in its effect, but in the Indwelling He is present as the *object* of the heart's habitual movement, which ought to grow in intensity throughout our lives.

St. Thomas explains this as follows:

> God is said to be in a thing in two ways; in one way after the manner of an efficient cause; and thus He is in all things created by Him; in another way He is in things as the object of operation is in the operator; and this is proper to the operations of the soul, according as the thing known is in the one who knows; and the thing desired in the one desiring. In this second way God is especially in the rational creature, which knows and loves Him actually or habitually. And because the rational creature possesses this prerogative by grace, as will be shown later, He is said to be thus in the saints by grace.[59]

The beloved is present in the will as the term or goal of the will's movement of benevolent love. Unlike other beloved persons, however, God can make His presence known in the heart of the one who loves Him by giving gentle inspirations to lead us to love Him more. The more the soul grows in love for God, the more docile it becomes to these inspirations of the Indwelling Guest. This relational presence of God as the Beloved in the temple of a loving heart admits of unlimited degrees, according to the degrees of charity. By nourishing us with charity, therefore, the Eucharist nourishes the Indwelling of the Trinity in the soul.

---

[58] See *ST* I, q. 8, a. 2.
[59] *ST* I, q. 8, a. 3. See also *ST* I, q. 43, a. 3.

It is fitting that it was just after the Last Supper and the first Communion of the Apostles that Jesus explained the Indwelling of the divine Persons in John 14–16. First He promises the gift of the Spirit in John 14:15–17:

> If you love me, you will keep my commandments. And I will pray the Father, and he will give you another Counselor, to be with you for ever, even the Spirit of truth, whom the world cannot receive, because it neither sees him nor knows him; you know him, for he dwells with you, and will be in you.

Then Jesus promises that He too will abide with them, and that the Father is in Him as He is in the Father. Thus the Father will indwell also: "In that day you will know that I am in my Father, and you in me, and I in you. . . . If a man loves me, he will keep my word, and my Father will love him, and we will come to him and make our home with him" (John 14:20, 23). It is significant that Jesus prefaces this promise of the Indwelling of the three divine Persons with the condition that we love Him and keep His commandments, for the Indwelling presupposes the life of charity and is meant to grow continually in intimacy.

By nourishing us with sanctifying grace and charity, worthy reception of the Eucharist builds up, day by day, the life of the Trinity in the faithful. Thus its proper effect is to enable those who receive Communion worthily to say with St. Paul in Galatians 2:20: "I have been crucified with Christ; it is no longer I who live, but Christ who lives in me; and the life I now live in the flesh I live by faith in the Son of God, who loved me and gave himself for me." Or as Jesus says in John 6:56–57: "He who eats my flesh and drinks my blood abides in me, and I in him. As the living Father sent me, and I live because of the Father, so he who eats me will live because of me." In other words, the proper effect of the Eucharist is the intensifying of the Indwelling of Christ in the soul and of the soul in Christ, and where Christ indwells, there also are the Father and the Holy Spirit.

John Paul II alludes to this effect of the Eucharist in *Ecclesia de Eucharistia*, §22:

> Incorporation into Christ, which is brought about by Baptism, is constantly renewed and consolidated by sharing in the Eucharistic Sacrifice, especially by that full sharing which

takes place in sacramental communion. We can say not only that *each of us receives Christ*, but also that *Christ receives each of us*. He enters into friendship with us: "You are my friends" (John 15:14). Indeed, it is because of him that we have life: "He who eats me will live because of me" (John 6:57). Eucharistic communion brings about in a sublime way the mutual "abiding" of Christ and each of his followers: "Abide in me, and I in you" (John 15:4).

As Christ comes to indwell more profoundly in us through Holy Communion, we can say that Communion progressively perfects the invisible missions of the Son and the Holy Spirit. A divine Person is said to be "sent" into the world when a divine Person who proceeds from another—the Son from the Father and the Holy Spirit from the Father and the Son—begins to be present in the world in a way in which He was not previously present.[60] The Second Person of the Trinity was visibly sent into the world in His Incarnation, and the Spirit was visibly sent on Pentecost. Both the Son and the Spirit are invisibly sent into the world through sanctifying grace[61] and the Indwelling. Holy Communion, therefore, by nourishing the Indwelling of the divine Persons, perfects the invisible missions of the Son and the Holy Spirit.[62] Although the Father also indwells, He is not said to be sent by another because He does not eternally

---

[60] See *ST* I, q. 43, a. 1.

[61] See *ST* I, q. 43, a. 3: "The divine person is fittingly sent in the sense that He exists newly in anyone; and He is given as possessed by anyone; and neither of these is otherwise than by sanctifying grace."

[62] This idea is developed by Matthias Scheeben in *The Mysteries of Christianity*, 528:

> The oneness of substance and life existing between the Father and the Son is transmitted to us and reproduced in us most perfectly by the Eucharist. In particular, the Eucharist is the agency that effects the real and perfect mission of the divine persons to the outer world. Above all it crowns the Son's mission to us on this earth. For in the Eucharist the Son unites Himself to us in the most perfect way, to give us in general the power to become sons of God, and also to make us one Son of God by incorporating us in Himself. In the Eucharist we likewise perceive the real and intimate mission of the Holy Spirit. For, since the Holy Spirit, the Spirit of the Son, is really united to the Son's body, in which He reposes and dwells, He also comes to us in the same body, to unite Himself to us therein to communicate Himself to us, and to give Himself to us as our own.

proceed from another divine Person, but rather is the eternal font of the divine life.

Although, on the level of the *res et sacramentum*, we are receiving the humanity of the Second Person of the Trinity, in the *res tantum*, we receive an increase in the Indwelling of all three divine Persons. As the *res et sacramentum* is the sign and cause of the *res tantum*, so reception of Christ's Body and Blood is the instrumental cause of the increase of the life of the Blessed Trinity in us.

Since the Son is in the Father and vice versa, as the Son becomes present in the soul, so does the Father. And as our hearts are configured by charity with the heart of Christ, the Father is made intimately and progressively present in our hearts as the object of our filial love. And, since the humanity of Christ was maximally permeated by the sanctification of the Holy Spirit, the reception of Christ's humanity efficaciously communicates the Holy Spirit with which He was full and whom He came to send. Matthias Scheeben develops this point with vigor:

> He [the Spirit] lives on in the Son's flesh and blood with His fire and His vitalizing energy, as proceeding from the Son, and fills the sacred humanity with His own being to sanctify and glorify it. Particularly in the Eucharist He glorifies and spiritualizes the Son's human nature like a flaming coal, so that it takes on the qualities of sheer fire and pure spirit. Straightway He makes use of the Eucharist as an instrument to manifest His sanctifying and transforming power to all who come into contact with it, and as a channel to communicate Himself to all who receive it and feast upon it.[63]

Many Eucharistic Prayers, especially in the second part of the epiclesis, pray that the faithful be filled with the Holy Spirit as a result of Holy Communion. In the epiclesis of the Eucharistic Prayer given in the *Apostolic Constitutions*, the priest prays, "Send down your Holy Spirit upon this sacrifice . . . that those who partake of it may . . . be filled with the Holy Spirit."[64]

St. John Paul II, in *Ecclesia de Eucharistia*, §17, speaks of the Spirit

---

[63] Scheeben, *The Mysteries of Christianity*, 529.

[64] *Apostolic Constitutions* 8 (*PEER*, 111). This anaphora is generally dated to the second half of the fourth century.

being imparted through Holy Communion, citing St. Ephrem and the Byzantine liturgy of St. John Chrysostom:

> Through our communion in his body and blood, Christ also grants us his Spirit. Saint Ephrem writes: "He called the bread his living body and he filled it with himself and his Spirit. . . . He who eats it with faith, eats Fire and Spirit. . . . Take and eat this, all of you, and eat with it the Holy Spirit. For it is truly my body and whoever eats it will have eternal life."[65] The Church implores this divine Gift, the source of every other gift, in the Eucharistic epiclesis. In the Divine Liturgy of Saint John Chrysostom, for example, we find the prayer: "We beseech, implore and beg you: send your Holy Spirit upon us all and upon these gifts . . . that those who partake of them may be purified in soul, receive the forgiveness of their sins, and share in the Holy Spirit."[66] . . . Thus by the gift of his body and blood Christ increases within us the gift of his Spirit, already poured out in Baptism and bestowed as a "seal" in the sacrament of Confirmation.

Normally, we associate the giving of the Holy Spirit with Confirmation, where the Spirit comes to transform the confirmed faithful into active members of the Church. In Communion, the Spirit is given by way of spiritual nourishment, feeding us with an increase of the Indwelling and its effects of ecclesial unity.

Receiving the three divine Persons should not be imagined as something static, but rather supremely dynamic, active, and relational. Through the Indwelling, the relations of the divine Persons are reproduced and intensified in us. We receive the Son of God in His humanity so as to be configured more deeply as sons and daughters of the Father through the power of the Holy Spirit, who proceeds as the love of the Father and Son and infuses in us the spirit of loving sonship by which we can say, "Abba, father."[67]

The Holy Spirit proceeds in the divine life by way of the operation of love, as the mutual love breathing forth from the Father and the

---

[65] Ephrem, *Sermo IV in Hebdomadam Sanctam*; Corpus Scriptorum Christianorum Orientalium 413 (CSCO, Scriptores Syri 182), 55.

[66] Divine Liturgy of Saint John Chrysostom, anaphora.

[67] See Rom 8:15.

Son. Holy Communion configures us to this procession of love of the Spirit by strengthening in us the impetus of love for God and neighbor. This strengthening of our supernatural love enables us to return more powerfully to our source,[68] the Trinitarian life, and to order all things more coherently to that end. In this way Communion enables us to enter more deeply into the sacrifice of Christ, offering the world and ourselves to God in a more perfect way.

Sacrament of Ecclesial Unity

The Eucharist is the sacrament of communion in two ways, for it strengthens our union both with Christ and with the Church. Communion with the Church is created by the members' common union with Christ in charity. In *ST* III, question 73, article 4, St. Thomas writes:

> With regard to the present it has another meaning, namely, that of ecclesiastical unity, in which men are aggregated through this Sacrament; and in this respect it is called "Communion" or Synaxis. For Damascene says (*De Fide Orth.* 4) that "it is called Communion because we communicate with Christ through it, both because we partake of His flesh and Godhead, and because we communicate with and are united to one another through it.

The vertical union with Christ given through Holy Communion is the privileged means of building the horizontal communion of all those who have been received into union with Christ. Union with Christ creates the communion of Christians.

As the sacrament of spiritual nourishment, the Eucharist builds up the communion of the Church by nourishing us with the divine life, from which flows fraternal charity, through which enemies are

---

[68] St. John Chrysostom describes this effect of Communion of igniting the impetus of love through the communication of the Spirit as a spiritual fire: "Indeed, here lies the body of the Lord, not wrapped in swaddling-clothes as formerly, but attired completely with the Holy Spirit.... Don't you know that this table is full of spiritual fire, and just as springs gush forth the force of water, so too does the table contain a certain mysterious flame?" (*Homily Concerning Blessed Philogonius*, in Wendy Mayer and Pauline Allen, *John Chrysostom* [London and New York: Routledge, 2000], 192, 194).

reconciled, differences overcome, and gifts shared. As the sharing in a communal banquet establishes a bond between the participants in that banquet, so the Eucharist works to supernaturally bind together those who share in the heavenly banquet of Christ's Body and Blood. This happens, however, not only through sharing in the same meal but also through being transformed into what we receive. By nourishing charity with one's neighbor, the Eucharist gives graces that lead to mutual reconciliation and enhanced communion, and the overcoming of divisions caused by sin. In a particular way, the Eucharist nourishes the capacity of the soul to forgive injuries and love one's enemies.

All the members of the Body receive the same life of the Head and Bridegroom of the Church so as to be given, progressively, one mind and heart in Christ. Only members of the ecclesial Body of Christ can receive His Eucharistic Body and so come to live ever more from the life of the Head of the Body of which they are members. Paschasius Radbertus eloquently expresses this ecclesial dimension of Holy Communion:

> They consume Him worthily who are in His Body, for only the Body of Christ in pilgrimage is to be fed on His own flesh and so learn to hunger after nothing but Christ, thirst for nothing but Christ, think of nothing but Christ, nor live on anything else, nor be anything but the Body of Christ.[69]

St. Cyril of Alexandria beautifully develops this ecclesial effect of Communion in his commentary on John 17:21, in which Jesus prays that His disciples be one in Him as He is one with the Father. St. Cyril poses the question of how this prayer can be realized. He answers that the Eucharist is the mystical means by which this unification of the faithful in Christ is accomplished, for all the faithful receive the one Body of Christ:

> In order that we too may be mixed together and come into unity with God and one another, even though the difference between each of us makes us exist individually in terms of our bodies and souls, the Only Begotten manufactured a means for that to happen, devised by his wisdom and the will of the

---

[69] Paschasius, *De Corpore et Sanguine Domini* 1.7.19–24 (Paulus, CCCM, 16:38).

Father. By one body, that is, his own, he blesses those who believe in him through mystical participation and makes them to be of the same body as himself and one another. Who could divide or separate from their natural union with one another those who are bound together through his one holy body into unity with Christ? If "we all partake of the one bread" (1 Cor 10:17), then we are all made one body, since Christ cannot be divided. . . . We are all united in the one Christ through his holy body since we receive the one indivisible body in our own bodies. . . . If we are all members of the same body with one another in Christ—and not only with one another but also with him who is in us through his flesh—is it not obvious that we all are one both with one another and with Christ?[70]

Secondly, St. Cyril develops the ecclesial effect from the fact that all are also given to drink of the one Spirit in Holy Communion: "Just as the power of his holy flesh makes those in whom it dwells one body, in the same way I think that the one Spirit of God, who dwells indivisibly in all, gathers everyone into a spiritual unity."[71]

This unifying effect of the Spirit is manifested in Eucharistic Prayer III, in which the priest prays: "Grant that we who are nourished by his body and blood may be filled with his Holy Spirit, and become one body, one spirit in Christ." Since the Holy Spirit is the soul of the Church, unifying the members with a common impetus of love, the increased communication of the Spirit works to make us more fully "one body, one spirit in Christ."[72]

Since ecclesial unity is the work of the Spirit, normally this prayer for the unity of the Church as the fruit of Communion occurs in the second part of the epiclesis.[73] In the Byzantine liturgy of St. Basil,

---

[70] Cyril of Alexandria, *Commentary on John*, 2:304–05.

[71] Ibid., 305.

[72] *RM*, 653. See also the corresponding prayer in Eucharistic Prayer II, which reads: "Humbly we pray that, partaking of the Body and Blood of Christ, we may be gathered into one by the Holy Spirit. Remember, Lord, your Church, spread throughout the world, and bring her to the fullness of charity, together with N. our Pope and N. our Bishop and all the clergy" (*RM*, 648).

[73] In the Roman Canon, however, the petition for the unity of the Church occurs in the first part of the prayer: "Bless these gifts, these offerings, these holy and unblemished sacrifices, which we offer you firstly for your holy catholic Church. Be pleased to grant her peace, to guard, unite and govern her throughout the whole world, together with your servant N. our Pope and N. our Bishop,

after the epiclesis over the Body and Blood, the priest prays: "Unite with one another all of us who partake of the one bread and the cup into fellowship with the one Holy Spirit."[74]

Holy Communion also nourishes the recipient with the fruits of the Spirit, which St. Paul speaks of as "love, joy, peace, patience, kindness, goodness, faithfulness, gentleness, self-control" (Gal 5:22–23). By their very nature, the fruits of the Spirit work to bring about ecclesial unity and peace.[75]

The increase in charity imparted by Holy Communion works to build up the bonds of communion not only with the Church militant on earth but also with the Church in purgatory and the Church triumphant, with whom we share the same divine life and the same end of heavenly beatitude. Many liturgical prayers, such as the Sanctus, proclaim how the Eucharist unites the Church militant and triumphant in a common worship. St. John Paul II emphasizes this:

> This is an aspect of the Eucharist which merits greater attention: in celebrating the sacrifice of the Lamb, we are united to the heavenly "liturgy" and become part of that great multitude which cries out: "Salvation belongs to our God who sits upon the throne, and to the Lamb!" (Rev 7:10). The Eucharist is truly a glimpse of heaven appearing on earth. It is a glorious ray of the heavenly Jerusalem which pierces the clouds of our history and lights up our journey.[76]

It would seem that Holy Communion also increases our communion with those who, even though outside the visible Church, are living in a state of grace and possess habitual charity. By increasing charity, Holy Communion nourishes the members of the Church in the ability

---

and all those who, holding to the truth, hand on the catholic and apostolic faith" (*RM*, 635).

[74] Byzantine Liturgy of St. Basil (*PEER*, 120). This ecclesial effect of Holy Communion is developed at greater length in the epiclesis of the Anaphora of James: "That they may become to all who partake of them . . . for strengthening Your holy, [catholic and apostolic] Church, which You founded on the rock of faith, that the gates of hell should not prevail against it, rescuing it from every heresy, and from the stumbling-blocks of those who work lawlessness, [and from the enemies who rose and rise up,] until the consummation of age" (*PEER*, 93).

[75] See John Meinert, "*Alimentum Pacis*: The Eucharist and Peace in St. Thomas Aquinas," *Nova et Vetera* (English) 14, no. 4 (2016): 871–90.

[76] John Paul II, *EE*, §19.

to attract those who are outside the visible Church and to evangelize by the example of a living charity.

It was not by accident that Christ gave the "new commandment" to love one another as He has loved us (John 13:34) just after giving the disciples their first Holy Communion, which strengthens our capacity to love as Christ does. Similarly, later that same evening, Christ solemnly prayed for the unity of His disciples in His high priestly prayer in John 17:21–23:

> That they may all be one; even as you, Father, are in me, and I in you, that they also may be in us, so that the world may believe that you have sent me. The glory which you have given me I have given to them, that they may be one even as we are one, I in them and you in me, that they may become perfectly one.

What is the glory that Jesus says He has given to His disciples? It seems reasonable to connect this with the fact Jesus had just given the fruits of His Paschal mystery to the disciples in associating them in His sacrifice and giving them His Body and Blood in Holy Communion. And He did so to transform them into unity with Himself and with one another, thereby building up His Church.

Corpus Mysticum *and* Corpus Verum

The terms *corpus mysticum* and *corpus verum* have been used in theology to refer to the Body of Christ in its two senses of the Church and the Eucharist. Henri de Lubac studied the evolution of these terms[77] and found that there has been a reversal of meaning over the centuries. This should not be surprising, given the intimate relationship between Eucharistic and ecclesial communion. Originally, the word *mysticum* signified "sacramental." Thus the *corpus mysticum* referred to the sacramental Body of Christ in the Eucharist, and the *corpus verum* referred to the Church as the Body of Christ. Reception of the sacramental Body is the means by which the faithful are built into the Body of Christ. In the second millennium, the term *mysticum* tended to refer

---

[77] Henri de Lubac, *Corpus Mysticum: The Eucharist and the Church in the Middle Ages*, trans. Gemma Simmonds (Notre Dame, IN: University of Notre Dame Press, 2007).

instead to the ecclesial body, being understood no longer in the sense of "sacramental," but of the "mystery" of grace. As Ratzinger explains:

> In the vocabulary of the Fathers, *mysticum* did not mean "mystical" in the modern sense, but rather "pertaining to the mystery, the sphere of the sacrament." Thus the phrase *corpus mysticum* was used to express the sacramental Body, the corporeal presence of Christ in the Sacrament. According to the Fathers, that Body is given to us, so that we may become the *corpus verum*, the real Body of Christ. Changes in the use of language and the forms of thought resulted in the reversal of these meanings. The Sacrament was now addressed as the *corpus verum* . . . while the Church was called the *corpus mysticum*, the "Mystical Body," "mystical" here meaning no longer "sacramental" but "mysterious." . . . As we saw above, the Blessed Sacrament contains a dynamism, which has the goal of transforming mankind and the world into the New Heaven and New Earth, into the unity of the risen Body. This truth was not seen so vividly as before. . . . The Eucharistic Body of the Lord is meant to bring us together, so that we become his "true Body." But the gift of the Eucharist can do this only because in it the Lord gives us *his true Body*. Only the true Body in the Sacrament can build up the true Body of the new City of God.[78]

There is no contradiction between the two senses of the Body of Christ because the sacramental Body, made present and offered in the sacrifice of the Mass and received in Holy Communion, creates the ecclesial Body of Christ.[79] St. Hilary says: "Christ is the Church, bearing it wholly within Himself by the sacrament of His body."[80] Ratzinger writes:

---

[78] Joseph Ratzinger, *The Spirit of the Liturgy*, 86–88.

[79] The twofold epiclesis in the Anaphora of St. Basil and other eastern Eucharistic Prayers eloquently expresses this relationship. First, one prays that the Holy Spirit come upon the gifts, making them into the Body and Blood of Christ. This first request, however, is ordered to the second: so that we may be made into one ecclesial Body. See Cesare Giraudo, *Eucaristia per la chiesa*, 436–38.

[80] Hilary, *Tractatus super Psalmos* 125.6 (*CSEL*, 22:609), in Scheeben, *The Mysteries of Christianity*, 486.

Eucharist is never merely an *event à deux*, a dialogue between Christ and me. The goal of Eucharistic communion is a total recasting of a person's life, breaking up a man's whole "I" and creating a new "We." Communion with Christ is of necessity a communication with all those who are his: it means that I myself become part of this new "bread" which he creates by transubstantiating all earthly reality.[81]

The State of Glory as an Effect of Communion

In the Bread of Life Discourse, Jesus says that eternal life is the ultimate and principal effect of the Eucharist: "He who eats my flesh and drinks my blood has eternal life, and I will raise him up at the last day" (John 6:54). For this reason, St. Ignatius of Antioch spoke of the Eucharist as the "medicine of immortality."[82] This eschatological dimension of the Eucharist is clearly expressed in the epiclesis of the ancient Anaphora of Addai and Mari:

> May there come, O Lord, your Holy Spirit and rest upon this oblation of your servants, and bless and hallow it, that it may be to us, O Lord, for the pardon of offences and forgiveness of sins and for the great hope of resurrection from the dead and for the new life in the kingdom of heaven with all those who have been pleasing in your presence.[83]

This eschatological dimension of the Eucharist is a consequence of the fact that Communion nourishes us with sanctifying grace, which is the seed of future glory. Since sanctifying grace is a participation in the divine life, St. Thomas says that "grace is nothing else than a beginning of glory in us."[84] Everyone who dies in a state of grace will rise in glory. So the Eucharist, by directly communicating sanctifying grace, which

---

[81] Joseph Ratzinger, *Behold the Pierced One: An Approach to a Spiritual Christology*, trans. Graham Harrison (San Francisco: Ignatius Press, 1986), 89.

[82] Ignatius of Antioch, Letter to the Ephesians 20, in *The Apostolic Fathers: Greek Texts and English Translations*, trans. Michael Holmes, 3rd ed. (Grand Rapids, MI: Baker Academic, 2007), 199.

[83] Anaphora of Addai and Mari, in Elavanal, "The Pneumatology of the Anaphora of Addai and Mari Especially in Its Epiclesis," 153–54 (see 162–66 for a commentary on the eschatological dimension of this epiclesis).

[84] *ST* III, q. 24, a. 3, ad 2.

is the life of Christ, indirectly communicates the future life of glory.

As we have seen, St. Thomas argues that we can determine the effects of the Eucharist from what it sacramentally contains, which is Christ Himself and His Passion. It will therefore bring us the communication of His life, which was merited for us by His Passion.[85] The ultimate reality that Christ won for us is eternal life: the beatific vision, the glorious resurrection of our bodies, and the communion of the saints. Thus the Eucharist will have that effect in us as long as its efficacy is not blocked by unrepented mortal sin.

There is a great fittingness, furthermore, in the fact that sanctifying grace is given to us through reception of the Body of the Risen Christ.[86] Since the Eucharist contains Christ's glorious and resurrected

---

[85] See *ST* III, q. 79, a. 2:

In this sacrament we may consider both that from which it derives its effect, namely, Christ contained in it, as also His Passion represented by it; and that through which it works its effect, namely, the use of the sacrament, and its species. Now as to both of these it belongs to this sacrament to cause the attaining of eternal life. Because it was by His Passion that Christ opened to us the approach to eternal life, according to Heb 9:15: "He is the Mediator of the New Testament; that by means of His death . . . they that are called may receive the promise of eternal inheritance." Accordingly in the form of this sacrament it is said: "This is the chalice of My blood, of the New and Eternal Testament." In like manner the refreshment of spiritual food and the unity denoted by the species of the bread and wine are to be had in the present life, although imperfectly; but perfectly in the state of glory.

[86] See Ratzinger, *TL*, 289:

Resurrection means quite simply that the body ceases to be a limit and that its capacity for communion remains. Jesus could rise from the dead, and did rise from the dead, because he had become, as the Son and as the One who loved on the Cross, the One who shares himself wholly with others. To have risen from the dead means to be communicable; it signifies being the one who is open, who gives himself. And on that basis we can understand that Jesus, in the speech about the Eucharist that John has handed down to us, puts the Resurrection and the Eucharist together and that the Fathers say that the Eucharist is the medicine of immortality. Receiving Communion means entering into communion with Jesus Christ; it signifies moving into the open through him who alone could overcome the limits and thus, with him and on the basis of his existence, becoming capable of resurrection oneself.

See also John Paul II, *EE*, §14: "The Eucharistic Sacrifice makes present not only the mystery of the Saviour's passion and death, but also the mystery of the resurrection which crowned his sacrifice. It is as the living and risen One that Christ can become in the Eucharist the 'bread of life.'"

Body, which we receive into our bodies like a seed that is received into the earth, it makes sense that this seed of glory will produce an effect of glory in its proper time, which is the general resurrection.[87] St. Gregory of Nyssa expresses this vividly:

> For just as if you would mix something deadly with something healthy, what is combined is rendered harmless, so also Christ's immortal body, when it is within him who eats, changes the whole mortal body into its own nature. . . . It is clear that otherwise it is impossible that our body be immortal, unless it is made to participate in incorruption through a communion with what is immortal.[88]

St. Athanasius makes the same point: "Since His body has become immune from corruption, without any doubt it has been made the cause of our own incorruptibility."[89] Leo XIII also writes: "And in the frail and perishable body that divine Host, which is the immortal Body of Christ, implants a principle of resurrection, a seed of immortality, which one day must germinate."[90] John Paul II writes: "This pledge of the future resurrection comes from the fact that the flesh of the Son of Man, given as food, is his body in its glorious state after the resurrection. With the Eucharist we digest, as it were, the 'secret' of the resurrection."[91]

From the sacramental sign of spiritual nourishment we deduce the same conclusion. The Eucharist is spiritual nourishment for the journey of this life that has heaven as its goal. The sacramental sign of bread and wine also symbolizes the satisfaction of every upright hunger and thirst, which will take place in eternal life.[92]

---

[87] As seen above, St. Irenaeus makes this argument in *Against Heresies* 5.2.3: "How can they affirm that the flesh is incapable of receiving the gift of God, which is life eternal, which [flesh] is nourished from the body and blood of the Lord, and is a member of Him?" (*ANF*, 1:528).

[88] Gregory of Nyssa, *Oratio Catechetica* 37, in Michon Matthiesen, *Sacrifice as Gift: Eucharist, Grace, and Contemplative Prayer in Maurice de la Taille* (Washington, DC: Catholic University of America Press, 2013), 150.

[89] Athanasius, *Epistula Heortastica* 11.14 (PG, 26:1411), in de la Taille, *The Mystery of Faith*, 2:177.

[90] Leo XIII, *Mirae Caritatis*, §9.

[91] John Paul II, *EE*, §18.

[92] See St. Augustine's commentary on John 6:56, *In Ioannis Evangelium* 26.17: "For although by food and drink men strive for this, that they hunger not and

Finally, the sacramental sign symbolizes the communion of saints, for the bread and wine is made into one whole from many grains of wheat and grapes. The Eucharist will thus produce this fraternal communion in us. Here on earth that communion is imperfect, but the Eucharist will bring us to a perfect communion as long as we pose no violent obstacle to its efficacy through grave sin.

Since the Eucharist is the pledge and harbinger of future glory, frequent worthy reception of the Eucharist is the best means of growing in Christian hope. Leo XIII writes:

> By this same Sacrament our hope of everlasting blessedness, based on our trust in the divine assistance, is wonderfully strengthened. For the edge of that longing for happiness which is so deeply rooted in the hearts of all men from their birth is whetted even more and more by the experience of the deceitfulness of earthly goods, by the unjust violence of wicked men, and by all those other afflictions to which mind and body are subject. Now the venerable Sacrament of the Eucharist is both the source and the pledge of blessedness and of glory, and this, not for the soul alone, but for the body also. For it enriches the soul with an abundance of heavenly blessings, and fills it with a sweet joy which far surpasses man's hope and expectations; it sustains him in adversity, strengthens him in the spiritual combat, preserves him for life everlasting, and as a special provision for the journey accompanies him thither.[93]

It might be objected that Baptism also, according to the teaching of St. Thomas, has the effect of giving us eternal life and making us an heir of heaven. If this comes first through Baptism, how is eternal life the proper effect of the Eucharist? The best answer is that Baptism is the gateway into the Church, intrinsically orders the faithful to the Eucharist to be nourished with Christ's life, and infuses an implicit desire for Communion. St. Thomas explains: "By Baptism a man is ordained to the Eucharist, and therefore from the fact of children being baptized, they are destined by the Church to the Eucharist;

---

thirst not, only this food and drink truly offer this; for it makes those by whom it is taken immortal and incorruptible, that is, the very society of saints, where there will be peace and full and perfect unity" (Rettig, *Tractates on the Gospel of John 11–27*, 274).

[93] Leo XIII, *Mirae Caritatis*, §9.

and just as they believe through the Church's faith, so they desire the Eucharist through the Church's intention, and, as a result, receive its reality."[94]

In summary, Holy Communion gives us Jesus Christ and, together with Him, all supernatural gifts, which include an increase of sanctifying grace, charity, fervor, the gifts of the Holy Spirit, and the Indwelling of the Trinity. We also obtain the forgiveness of venial sin insofar as we repent of it through the aid of the grace obtained, the warding off of future sins, an actual spiritual refreshment or consolation that comes from an infusion of charity, a deepening of the bond of ecclesial unity, and the pledge of eternal life.

Spiritual Communion

The Fathers and Doctors of the Church teach that the effects of the grace of the Eucharist can be obtained not only from sacramental reception of Holy Communion but also from a fervent desire to receive the sacrament. This is not unique to the Eucharist, but applies also to Baptism, Confirmation,[95] and Penance.

St. Thomas treats spiritual communion in *ST* III, question 73, article 3. He asks whether reception of the Eucharist is necessary for salvation and answers that actual reception of the sacrament is not necessary for salvation. However, one must in some way receive the reality of the sacrament (*res sacramenti*), which is participation in the unity of the Mystical Body. This can be received by desire for the sacrament even by those who cannot receive Jesus sacramentally. Interestingly, as seen above, St. Thomas explains that even infants receive this effect of the sacrament by an implicit desire that comes from their baptismal incorporation into Christ:

> Two things have to be considered in this sacrament, namely, the sacrament itself, and what is contained in it. Now it was stated above [q. 73, a. 1, obj. 2] that the reality [*res*] of the sacrament is the unity of the mystical body, without which there can be no salvation; for there is no entering into salvation outside the Church, just as in the time of the deluge there was

---

[94] *ST* III, q. 73, a. 3.
[95] See *ST* III, q. 72, a. 6, ad 1.

none outside the Ark, which denotes the Church, according to 1 Peter 3:20–21. And it has been said above [q. 68, a. 2], that before receiving a sacrament, the reality of the sacrament can be had through the very desire of receiving the sacrament. Accordingly, before actual reception of this sacrament, a man can obtain salvation through the desire of receiving it, just as he can before Baptism through the desire of Baptism, as stated above [q. 68, a. 2]. Yet there is a difference in two respects. First of all, because Baptism is the beginning of the spiritual life, and the door of the sacraments; whereas the Eucharist is, as it were, the consummation of the spiritual life, and the end of all the sacraments, as was observed above [q. 63, a. 6]: for by the sanctification of all the sacraments preparation is made for receiving or consecrating the Eucharist. Consequently, the reception of Baptism is necessary for starting the spiritual life, while the receiving of the Eucharist is required for its consummation; by partaking not indeed actually, but in desire, as an end is possessed in desire and intention.

He also mentions spiritual communion in *ST* III, question 79, article 1, ad 3. Here he specifies that spiritual communion can be explicit, as in those who desire to receive the sacrament of which they are aware, but also implicit, as in those who know about the sacrament only in an obscure way through figures and types. In this way, the Eucharist was received spiritually by the Israelites, aided by the types in the Old Covenant that prefigured the Eucharist:

As stated above [q. 73, a. 3], the effect of the sacrament can be secured by every man if he receive it in desire, though not in reality. Consequently, just as some are baptized with the Baptism of desire, through their desire of baptism, before being baptized in the Baptism of water; so likewise some eat this sacrament spiritually ere they receive it sacramentally. Now this happens in two ways. First of all, from desire of receiving the sacrament itself, and thus are said to be baptized, and to eat spiritually, and not sacramentally, they who desire to receive these sacraments since they have been instituted. Secondly, by a figure: thus the Apostle says (1 Cor 10:2), that the fathers of old were "baptized in the cloud and in the sea," and that "they did eat . . . spiritual food, and . . . drank

. . . spiritual drink." Nevertheless, sacramental eating is not useless, because the actual receiving of the sacrament produces more fully the effect of the sacrament than does the desire thereof, as stated above of Baptism [q. 69, a. 4, ad 2].

Whenever we cannot attend Mass or receive Holy Communion, we can still frequently offer the sacrifice of the altar in a spiritual way on the altars of our hearts, uniting ourselves to all the sacrifices of the Mass celebrated throughout the world. In a similar way, we can make frequent spiritual communions throughout the day. Pope Pius XII praises the practice of spiritual communion in *Mediator Dei*, §117:

> She wishes in the first place that Christians—especially when they cannot easily receive holy communion—should do so at least by desire, so that with renewed faith, reverence, humility and complete trust in the goodness of the divine Redeemer, they may be united to Him in the spirit of the most ardent charity.

John Paul II speaks of the great value of spiritual communion in *Ecclesia de Eucharistia*, §34:

> The Eucharist thus appears as the culmination of all the sacraments in perfecting our communion with God the Father by identification with his only-begotten Son through the working of the Holy Spirit. With discerning faith a distinguished writer of the Byzantine tradition voiced this truth: in the Eucharist "unlike any other sacrament, the mystery [of communion] is so perfect that it brings us to the heights of every good thing: here is the ultimate goal of every human desire, because here we attain God and God joins himself to us in the most perfect union."[96] Precisely for this reason it is good to *cultivate in our hearts a constant desire for the sacrament of the Eucharist*. This was the origin of the practice of "spiritual communion," which has happily been established in the Church for centuries and recommended by saints who were masters of the spiritual life.

---

[96] Nicolas Cabasilas, *Life in Christ*, IV, 10: (*Sources Chretienne*, 355:270).

However, if the faithful can receive sacramental communion, obviously that is far preferable. Thus the Council of Trent exhorted the faithful "when they attend Mass to communicate not only by a spiritual communion but also by a sacramental one, so that they may obtain more abundant fruit from this most holy sacrifice."[97]

St. Teresa of Ávila earnestly recommends the practice of spiritual communion in *The Way of Perfection*:

> When you do not receive Communion, daughters, but hear Mass, you can make a spiritual communion. Spiritual communion is highly beneficial; through it you can recollect yourselves in the same way after Mass, for the love of this Lord is thereby deeply impressed on the soul. If we prepare ourselves to receive Him, He never fails to give in many ways which we do not understand. It is like approaching a fire; even though the fire may be a large one, it will not be able to warm you well if you turn away and hide your hands. . . . But it is something else if we desire to approach Him. If the soul is disposed (I mean, if it wants to get warm), and if it remains there for a while, it will stay warm for many hours.[98]

St. Alphonsus Liguori also strongly recommends the practice of spiritual communion. One of his most popular devotional books is *Visits to the Blessed Sacrament and the Blessed Virgin Mary*. He encourages the faithful to make a visit to Jesus in the Blessed Sacrament every day and gives a brief meditation for each day of the month. He recommends that the visit to the Blessed Sacrament be accompanied by a spiritual communion and offers the following prayer:

> My Jesus, I believe that You are present in the Most Blessed Sacrament. I love You above all things, and I desire to receive You into my soul. Since I cannot now receive You sacramentally, come at least spiritually into my heart. I embrace You as

---

[97] Council of Trent, On the Sacrifice of the Mass (session 22), ch. 6, quoted in Pius XII, *Mediator Dei*, §118.

[98] Teresa of Ávila, *The Way of Perfection* 35.1, in *The Collected Works of St. Teresa of Ávila*, vol. 2, trans. Otilio Rodriguez, O.C.D. and Kieran Kavanaugh, O.C.D. (Washington, DC: ICS, 2000), 174–75.

if You were already come, and I unite myself wholly to You. Never permit me to be separated from You.[99]

No particular form of words is required for a spiritual communion. It consists essentially in the fervent desire of the heart to be united with Jesus in deep and intimate union.

In the practice of spiritual communion, it is very beneficial to begin with an act of perfect contrition. St. Alphonsus introduces this in the prayer that he gives before each visit:

> My Jesus, I love You with my whole heart. I am very sorry for having so many times offended Your infinite goodness. With the help of Your grace, I purpose never to offend You again. And now, unworthy though I am, I consecrate myself to You without reserve.[100]

Is Spiritual Communion Possible for a Person in a State of Mortal Sin?

Can those who are not in a state of grace, and who are thus unable to receive sacramental communion, make a spiritual communion? Properly speaking, no. A spiritual communion is a reception of the effects of Holy Communion through a sincere and efficacious desire for the sacrament. The principal spiritual effect of Holy Communion is an increase of sanctifying grace and charity. This increase presupposes that one is already in a state of grace. Just as physical nourishment presupposes physical life, so supernatural nourishment presupposes that supernatural life is already present (which is what is meant by the "state of grace").

It follows that spiritual communion presupposes justification. In the unbaptized, this can come about through "baptism of desire." In the baptized who have lost the state of grace through mortal sin, justification comes through the sacrament of Penance or an act of perfect contrition with the desire and intention to sacramentally confess one's grave sins, unless one is invincibly ignorant of the sacrament, in which case the act of perfect contrition alone is sufficient.

---

[99] Alphonsus Liguori, *Visits to the Blessed Sacrament and the Blessed Virgin Mary* (Rockford, IL: TAN Books, 2000), 2–3.

[100] Ibid., 1–2.

Thus if a Catholic is unable to receive sacramental Communion because of a mortal sin that is not yet confessed, he or she could make a spiritual communion after making an act of perfect contrition with the intention of going to sacramental confession. This act of perfect contrition must include the resolution to avoid grave sin and the proximate voluntary occasions of it.

What if a Catholic is unwilling to make such a resolution to avoid a habitual grave sin, such as sexual relations with a person to whom he or she is not validly married, pornography use, or contraception? Such people should go to Mass and pray for the grace of conversion so that they will be able to make such a resolve, be sacramentally forgiven, and eventually receive Communion. This is a true desire for Communion, and it will undoubtedly be greatly beneficial, but it is not yet a desire that is capable of anticipating the principal spiritual effects of Communion.

In other words, it is important to distinguish two kinds of desire for Communion: one of a person in grace who is disposed to receive the proper effects of sacramental Communion, and another of a person who is not yet disposed to receive those effects.[101] Only the former is properly a spiritual communion. The other is a desire for Communion that is not yet efficacious because it is lacking proper contrition, although it is an excellent prayer and a good disposition for receiving that contrition.

Something similar is the case with regard to desire for Baptism. Not every desire for Baptism or its effects is such that it is properly said to be a "baptism of desire." An efficacious desire for baptism that anticipates the principal effect of the sacrament of Baptism must be accompanied by an act of perfect contrition as well as some act of faith, hope, and charity, according to the possibilities of the person.[102]

---

[101] See Benoît-Dominique de La Soujeole, O.P., "Communion sacramentelle et communion spirituelle," *Nova et Vetera* 86 (2011): 147–53; Paul Jerome Keller, O.P., "Is Spiritual Communion for Everyone?" *Nova et Vetera* (English) 12, no. 3 (2014): 631–55; John Corbett et al., "Recent Proposals for the Pastoral Care of the Divorced and Remarried: A Theological Assessment," *Nova et Vetera* (English) 12, no. 3 (2014): 616–17.

[102] This is clarified in a letter from the Holy Office to Archbishop Cushing of Boston, August 8, 1949: "Nor must it be thought that any kind of desire of entering the Church suffices for one to be saved. It is necessary that the desire by which one is related to the Church be animated by perfect charity. The implicit desire can produce no effect unless a person has supernatural faith" (DS, 3872).

Study Questions

1. What is sacramental grace?
2. How does the sacramental grace of the Eucharist differ from that of the other sacraments?
3. Summarize the effects of Holy Communion.
4. How does Holy Communion contribute to the forgiveness of venial sins?
5. How does Holy Communion ward off future sins?
6. Explain how Holy Communion increases the Indwelling of the Holy Trinity.
7. Why is Communion the seed of eternal life?
8. How does Holy Communion build up the communion of the Church?
9. (a) What is received by a rightly disposed desire for the Eucharist (spiritual communion)? (b) Why is it better to receive the Eucharist sacramentally rather than spiritually, if possible?
10. Can one who is not in a state of grace make a spiritual communion? Explain with a distinction.

Suggestions for Further Reading

ST III, q. 79, aa. 1–8; q. 73, a. 3.

John Chrysostom. Homily 46 on John 6:41–53. In *Commentary on Saint John the Apostle and Evangelist: Homilies 1–47*. Translated by T. A. Goggin. FC 33. Washington, DC: Catholic University of America Press, 1957. Pp. 468–72.

John Paul II. *EE.* §§16–24, 34, 40.

Leo XIII. Encyclical on the Holy Eucharist *Mirae Caritatis*. May 18, 1902.

Nutt, Roger. *General Principles of Sacramental Theology*. Washington, DC: Catholic University of America Press, 2017. Pp. 138–50.

CHAPTER FOURTEEN

Holy Communion Presupposes Ecclesial Communion, Invisible and Visible

HOLY COMMUNION PRESUPPOSES ECCLESIAL COMMUNION

From our earliest Patristic testimonies we see that limits have been placed on Eucharistic Communion. The *Didache* gives this directive: "On the Lord's own day gather together and break bread and give thanks, having first confessed your sins so that your sacrifice may be pure. But let no one who has a quarrel with a companion join you until they have been reconciled, so that your sacrifice may not be defiled."[1] St. Justin, in the middle of the second century, gives three conditions for the reception of Holy Communion. One must be baptized, believe in the faith of the Church, and live a Christian life: "And this food is called among us eucharist, of which no one is allowed to partake except one who believes that the things which we teach are true, and has received the washing that is for the remission of sins and for rebirth, and who so lives as Christ handed down."[2] In the Byzantine liturgy, this limitation on Communion is expressed in the words of the priest before Communion: "Holy things for the holy."[3] As the sacrament of spiritual nourishment that builds up the supernatural life

---

[1] *Didache* 14, in Holmes, trans. *The Apostolic Fathers: Greek Texts and English Translations*, 365–67.

[2] Justin Martyr, *First Apology* 66 (Barnard, *St. Justin Martyr*, 70).

[3] See Meletius Michael Solovey, *The Byzantine Divine Liturgy: History and Commentary*, trans. Demetrius Emil Wysochansky (Washington, DC: Catholic University of America Press, 1970), 312–13.

of the Church, Holy Communion presupposes that one already has that supernatural life through the sacraments of Baptism and Penance.

Reception of the Eucharist presupposes ecclesial communion in two dimensions: invisible and visible. Visible ecclesial communion comes from the sacrament of Baptism and also involves being in communion with the successor of Peter and the bishops in communion with him. Invisible ecclesial communion comes from being in a state of grace. First we will look at the requirement of invisible communion.

WHY BEING IN A STATE OF GRACE IS A NECESSARY CONDITION FOR RECEIVING COMMUNION

We have seen that there is an intimate relationship between the sacrificial aspect of the Mass and Holy Communion. This relationship is crucial for understanding the meaning of Communion and the conditions for receiving it. Reception of Holy Communion is not simply a banquet; it is a sacrificial banquet that implies communion in the complete self-donation of Christ and a sharing in the interior dispositions of His heart.[4] If a person's interior disposition radically contradicts Christ's holocaust, then it would be profoundly false to partake of the sacrifice so as to strengthen a configuration that is not actually desired.[5]

St. Paul speaks in very strong terms about unworthy reception of the Eucharist in 1 Corinthians 11:26–30:

> For as often as you eat this bread and drink the chalice, you proclaim the Lord's death until he comes. Whoever, therefore, eats the bread or drinks the cup of the Lord in an unworthy manner will be guilty of profaning the body and blood of the Lord. Let a man examine himself, and so eat of the bread and

---

[4] See John Paul II, *EE*, §48: "The 'banquet' always remains a sacrificial banquet marked by the blood shed on Golgotha."

[5] See John Chrysostom, Homily on the Betrayal of Judas, no. 6: "Give up your enmity, that you may obtain healing from the table. You approach that Victim before whom we all must stand in awe, that holy Victim, and so show respect for what that offering teaches you. Christ lies slain there. And for what reason was he slain? Why? To reconcile heaven and earth, to make you a friend even of the angels" (PG, 49:381; in de la Taille, *The Mystery of Faith*, 2:101).

drink of the cup. For any one who eats and drinks without discerning the body eats and drinks judgment upon himself. That is why many of you are weak and ill, and some have died. But if we judged ourselves truly, we should not be judged. But when we are judged by the Lord, we are chastened so that we may not be condemned along with the world.

Unworthy communion is so serious because we are receiving Christ Himself, crucified for our sins, in a bodily union. This sacramental union presupposes that one is invisibly united to Him in charity as a bride to a bridegroom. To receive in mortal sin would be to "not discern," or to directly contradict, the kind of total union given by sacramental reception. It would also fail to "discern" that the Body received is that of the crucified Victim, and that reception of the Victim implies that one is interiorly configured with His sacrificial self-giving by living in accordance with His commandment of love.

In his commentary on 1 Corinthians 11, St. Thomas gives two reasons why one must be in a state of grace to receive Communion. The first is based on the fact that the Eucharist was instituted to be our spiritual nourishment, which can be received only by those who are already alive in the Spirit: "This sacrament is spiritual food, as baptism is spiritual birth. But one is born in order to live, but he is not nourished unless he is already alive. Therefore, this sacrament does not befit sinners who are not yet alive by grace; although baptism befits them."[6]

The second reason is that the Eucharist is the sacrament of the consummation of unity with Christ and the Church. This presupposes that one is already united with Christ and with the Church through charity. Otherwise, there would be a grave contradiction between one's life and the meaning and content of the sacrament. St. Thomas refers to this as "lying to the sacrament."[7] A lie is graver according to the dignity of the truth that is falsified,[8] which here involves one's final end:

Furthermore, "the Eucharist is the sacrament of love and ecclesial unity," as Augustine says in *On John*. Since, there-

---

[6]   Thomas Aquinas, Commentary on 1 Cor 11, lec. 7, Marietti no. 691, in Larcher, *Commentary on the Letters of Saint Paul to the Corinthians*, 258.

[7]   *ST* III, q. 80, a. 4.

[8]   See *CCC*, §2484.

fore, the sinner lacks charity and is deservedly separated from the unity of the church, if he approaches this sacrament, he commits a falsehood, since he is signifying that he has charity, but does not.[9]

St. Thomas further develops this argument in *ST* III, question 80, article 4:

> In this sacrament, as in the others, that which is a sacrament is a sign of the reality of the sacrament. Now there is a twofold reality of this sacrament, as stated above (q. 73, a. 6): one which is signified and contained, namely, Christ Himself; while the other is signified but not contained, namely, Christ's mystical body, which is the fellowship of the saints. Therefore, whoever receives this sacrament, expresses thereby that he is made one with Christ, and incorporated in His members; and this is done by living faith, which no one has who is in mortal sin. And therefore it is manifest that whoever receives this sacrament while in mortal sin, is guilty of lying to this sacrament, and consequently of sacrilege, because he profanes the sacrament: and therefore he sins mortally.

When St. Thomas says that Christ's mystical body is the reality of the sacrament (*res tantum*), he is referring primarily to the invisible communion worked by living faith, which means faith enlivened by charity.

John Paul II addresses the issue of unworthy communion in *Ecclesia de Eucharistia*, §§36–38:

> Invisible communion, though by its nature always growing, presupposes the life of grace, by which we become "partakers of the divine nature" (2 Pet 1:4), and the practice of the virtues of faith, hope and love. Only in this way do we have true communion with the Father, the Son and the Holy Spirit. Nor is faith sufficient; we must persevere in sanctifying grace and love, remaining within the Church "bodily" as well as "in our heart"; what is required, in the words of Saint Paul, is "faith working through love" (Gal 5:6).
> Keeping these invisible bonds intact is a specific moral

---

[9]   Thomas Aquinas, commentary on 1 Cor 11, lec. 7 (Larcher, 259).

duty incumbent upon Christians who wish to participate fully in the Eucharist by receiving the body and blood of Christ. The Apostle Paul appeals to this duty when he warns: "Let a man examine himself, and so eat of the bread and drink of the cup" (1 Cor 11:28). Saint John Chrysostom, with his stirring eloquence, exhorted the faithful: "I too raise my voice, I beseech, beg and implore that no one draw near to this sacred table with a sullied and corrupt conscience. Such an act, in fact, can never be called 'communion,' not even were we to touch the Lord's body a thousand times over, but 'condemnation,' 'torment' and 'increase of punishment.'"

Along these same lines, the *Catechism of the Catholic Church* rightly stipulates that "anyone conscious of a grave sin must receive the sacrament of Reconciliation before coming to communion." I therefore desire to reaffirm that in the Church there remains in force, now and in the future, the rule by which the Council of Trent gave concrete expression to the Apostle Paul's stern warning when it affirmed that, in order to receive the Eucharist in a worthy manner, "one must first confess one's sins, when one is aware of mortal sin."

The two sacraments of the Eucharist and Penance are very closely connected. Because the Eucharist makes present the redeeming sacrifice of the Cross, perpetuating it sacramentally, it naturally gives rise to a continuous need for conversion, for a personal response to the appeal made by Saint Paul to the Christians of Corinth: "We beseech you on behalf of Christ, be reconciled to God" (2 Cor 5:20). If a Christian's conscience is burdened by serious sin, then the path of penance through the sacrament of Reconciliation becomes necessary for full participation in the Eucharistic Sacrifice.

Judas as an Example of Unworthy Communion

The New Testament perhaps provides a witness of an unworthy Communion in the very first celebration of the sacrament at the Last Supper, in the person of Judas. St. Thomas discusses this in *ST* III, question 81, article 2.

Hilary, in commenting on Matthew 26:17, held that Christ did not give His body and blood to Judas. And this would have been quite proper, if the malice of Judas is considered. But since Christ was to serve us as a pattern of justice, it was not in keeping with His teaching authority to sever Judas, a hidden sinner, from Communion with the others without an accuser and evident proof. Lest the Church's prelates might have an example for doing the like, and lest Judas himself being exasperated might take occasion of sinning. Therefore, it remains to be said that Judas received our Lord's body and blood with the other disciples, as Dionysius says (*Ecclesiastical Hierarchy* 3), and Augustine (Tract. 62 on John).

In reply to the second objection in this article, he likewise states:

The wickedness of Judas was known to Christ as God; but it was unknown to Him, after the manner in which men know it. Consequently, Christ did not repel Judas from Communion; so as to furnish an example that such secret sinners are not to be repelled by other priests.

In general, with regard to the distribution of Communion to those who are in a state of mortal sin, St. Thomas writes:

A distinction must be made among sinners: some are secret; others are notorious, either from evidence of the fact, as public usurers, or public robbers, or from being denounced as evil men by some ecclesiastical or civil tribunal. Therefore Holy Communion ought not to be given to open sinners when they ask for it. . . . But if they be not open sinners, but occult, then Holy Communion should not be denied them if they ask for it. For since every Christian, from the fact that he is baptized, is admitted to the Lord's table, he may not be robbed of his right, except from some open cause. . . . Nevertheless a priest who has knowledge of the crime can privately warn the secret sinner, or warn all openly in public, from approaching the Lord's table, until they have repented of their sins and have been reconciled to the Church; because after repentance and reconciliation, Communion must not be refused even to public sinners, especially in the hour of death. Hence in the [3rd] Council of Carthage [can. 35] we read: "Reconciliation is not to be denied to stage-players or actors, or others of the sort, or to apostates, after their conversion to God."[10]

St. John Chrysostom speaks on preparation for Holy Communion in a homily given five days before the feast of Christmas. Thinking that many would come to communion not properly disposed, he urged them to make use of the remaining days to reconcile themselves with God:

> But as it is, many of the faithful have arrived at such a degree of silliness and neglect that, although they're full of countless evils, and because they take no thought whatsoever for themselves, they approach this table on feast days in a random and frivolous fashion. They don't know that the time of communion doesn't consist of a feast and a celebration, but of a clear conscience and a life free of reproach. Just as the ordinary person who has nothing on their conscience ought to approach communion every day, so it's unsafe for the person who's overpowered by sin and doesn't repent to approach even on a feast day. For approaching once a year isn't going to free us from reproach, if we approach unworthily; but it's precisely this that damns us all the more, namely that when we approach on that one occasion we're not even then approaching with a clear conscience. . . . Don't you know that this table is full of spiritual fire, and just as springs gush forth the force of water, so too does the table contain a certain mysterious flame? So don't approach it if you're carrying stubble, wood or dry grass, in case you cause a bigger blaze and you burn your soul as it takes communion. But bring precious stones, gold, silver, in order to make the material more pure, in order to go back home having derived a great deal of profit.[11]

---

[10] *ST* III, q. 80, a. 6.

[11] John Chrysostom, *Homily Concerning Blessed Philogonius*, in Wendy Mayer and Pauline Allen, *John Chrysostom* (London and New York: Routledge, 2000), 193–94. St. Catherine of Siena presents our Lord explaining unworthy communion in a powerful way:

> But anyone who would approach this gracious sacrament while guilty of deadly sin would receive no grace from it, even though such a person would really be receiving me as I am, wholly God, wholly human. But do you know the situation of the soul who receives the sacrament

RECIPIENTS OF HOLY COMMUNION AND UNWORTHY COMMUNION: CANONS 916 AND 915 OF THE *CODE OF CANON LAW*

Canon law has the task of codifying the limits on Communion. Some of these limits are not intrinsic to the sacrament. For example, in the current norms for the Latin rite, canon 919 requires that one must have fasted for one hour from any food and drink except water and medicine before receiving Communion. Section 3 of this canon states: "The elderly, the infirm, and those who care for them can receive the Most Holy Eucharist even if they have eaten something within the preceding hour." In addition, one cannot receive more than twice in one day, and the second Holy Communion must be in the context of a "eucharistic celebration in which the person participates" (can. 917), except in the case of Viaticum (can. 921, §2). Intrinsic limits on the recipient of Communion, which come from the very nature of the sacrament, are that the recipient be a baptized member of the faithful, in a state of grace (can. 916), and not "obstinately persevering in manifest grave sin" (can. 915).

Canon 916

Canon 916 of the *Code of Canon Law* gives the most important criterion for licit reception, which is freedom from mortal sin:

> A person who is conscious of grave sin is not to celebrate Mass or receive the body of the Lord without previous sacramental confession unless there is a grave reason and there is

---

unworthily? She is like a candle that has been doused with water and only hisses when it is brought near the fire. The flame no more than touches it but it goes out and nothing remains but smoke. Just so, this soul brings the candle she received in holy baptism and throws the water of sin over it, a water that drenches the wick of baptismal grace that is meant to bear the light. And unless she dries the wick out with the fire of true contrition by confessing her sin, she will physically receive the light when she approaches the table of the altar, but she will not receive it into her spirit. If the soul is not disposed as she should be for so great a mystery, this true light will not graciously remain in her but will depart, leaving her more confounded, more darksome, and more deeply in sin. (*The Dialogue of Catherine of Siena* trans. Suzanne Noffke, O.P., [Mahwah, NJ: Paulist Press, 1980], 208–09)

no opportunity to confess; in this case the person is to remember the obligation to make an act of perfect contrition which includes the resolution of confessing as soon as possible.

Grave reason to celebrate Mass (and thus to receive Communion as celebrant) would be the duty of pastors to their faithful. When sacramental confession is impossible before the celebration of Mass, the priest must make an act of perfect contrition with the intention of receiving the sacrament of Penance as soon as possible.

The faithful do not ordinarily have grave reason to receive Communion, for its principal effect can be gained by a spiritual communion made after an act of perfect contrition. Therefore, if a member of the faithful who does not have a pastoral duty to celebrate Mass is aware of grave sin, ordinarily he must receive sacramental absolution prior to Holy Communion. Although an act of perfect contrition with the intention of going to Confession as soon as possible would restore the state of grace and remove the danger of sacrilege, this would not be sufficient for receiving Holy Communion, according to canon 916, unless there existed a grave reason for receiving and grave difficulty in receiving the sacrament of Penance first. Such a Communion that follows an act of perfect contrition but is done without grave reason would be illicit, although not sacrilegious. Without an act of perfect contrition, however, such a Communion would be both illicit and sacrilegious.[12]

The content of canon 916 is based on the decree of the Council of Trent:

> It is not right that anyone should participate in any sacred functions except in a holy manner. Certainly, then, the more Christians are aware of the holiness and the divinity of this heavenly sacrament, the more careful they should be not to receive it without great reverence and sanctity, especially since we read in the apostle the fearful words, "Those who eat and drink unworthily without discerning the body of the Lord, eat and drink judgment upon themselves" (1 Cor 11:29). Therefore, whoever desires to communicate must be reminded of the

---

[12] See the commentary on can. 916 by Davide Mussone in *L'eucaristia nel codice di diritto canonico: Commento ai Can. 897–958* (Vatican City: Libreria Editrice Vaticana, 2002), 84–87.

precept: "Let them examine themselves" (1 Cor 11:28). Now ecclesiastical usage declares that this examination is necessary, that no one conscious of mortal sin, however contrite he may seem to himself, should approach the Holy Eucharist without a previous sacramental confession. This, the holy Synod has decreed, is always to be observed by all Christians, even by those priests on whom by their office it may be incumbent to celebrate, provided the recourses of a confessor be not lacking to them. But if in an urgent necessity a priest should celebrate without previous confession, let him confess as soon as possible.[13]

Canon 915

If a person presents himself for Holy Communion who is publicly and notoriously living in a state of sin or has been excommunicated or interdicted, then canon 915 is to be applied: "Those who have been excommunicated or interdicted after the imposition or declaration of the penalty and others obstinately persevering in manifest grave sin are not to be admitted to holy communion." Before refusing to administer Holy Communion, pastors are to meet with the persons concerned and explain the Church's teaching to them in a prudent and gentle way.[14]

The reason for canon 915 is to avoid both the sacrilege of the communicant and the great danger of scandal for the faithful, who would tend to conclude either that the Catholic Church does not hold that the public sin in question is indeed sinful or that it does not matter if one is in a state of grace for receiving Communion.[15]

---

[13] Council of Trent, On the Sacrament of the Eucharist (session 13), ch. 7 (DS, 1646). See CIC, can. 916.

[14] See Pontifical Council for Legislative Texts, *Declaration Concerning the Admission to Holy Communion of Faithful Who Are Divorced and Remarried* (2000), §3: "Naturally, pastoral prudence would strongly suggest the avoidance of instances of public denial of holy communion. Pastors must strive to explain to the concerned faithful the true ecclesial sense of the norm in such a way that they would be able to understand it or at least respect it" (*Origins* 30, no. 11 [Aug. 17, 2000]: 174–75, at 175).

[15] See the commentary on this canon by Raymond Cardinal Burke, "Canon 915: The Discipline Regarding the Denial of Holy Communion to Those Obstinately Persevering in Manifest Grave Sin," *Periodica de re canonica* 96 (2007): 3–58, accessed July 7, 2017, http://www.ewtn.com/library/CANONLAW/burkcompol.htm.

John Paul II comments on this canon in *Ecclesia de Eucharistia,* §37:

> The judgment of one's state of grace obviously belongs only to the person involved, since it is a question of examining one's conscience. However, in cases of outward conduct which is seriously, clearly and steadfastly contrary to the moral norm, the Church, in her pastoral concern for the good order of the community and out of respect for the sacrament, cannot fail to feel directly involved. The *Code of Canon Law* refers to the situation of a manifest lack of proper moral disposition when it states that those who "obstinately persist in manifest grave sin are not to be admitted to Eucharistic communion."[16]

With regard to Catholic politicians who are involved in formal cooperation in evil concerning abortion or euthanasia, Cardinal Ratzinger provided some prudent guidelines to the American Catholic bishops in 2004:

> Regarding the grave sin of abortion or euthanasia, when a person's formal cooperation becomes manifest (understood, in the case of a Catholic politician, as his consistently campaigning and voting for permissive abortion and euthanasia laws), his pastor should meet with him, instructing him about the Church's teaching, informing him that he is not to present himself for Holy Communion until he brings to an end the objective situation of sin and warning him that he will otherwise be denied the Eucharist.[17]

---

[16] See Burke, "Canon 915," 11: "With the words, 'cannot fail to feel directly involved,' the Roman Pontiff clarified the obligation, on the part of the Church, to take action, when a person who remains in grievous and public sin approaches to receive Holy Communion. The obligation in question is distinct from the obligation of the person to examine his conscience regarding grave sin before approaching, which is treated in can. 916."

[17] Joseph Cardinal Ratzinger, Fifth Principle in *Worthiness to Receive Holy Communion: General Principles,* Memorandum to Cardinal McCarrick, accessed July 7, 2017, http://www.ewtn.com/library/curia/cdfworthycom.htm.

POST-CONCILIAR MAGISTERIUM ON COMMUNION FOR THE DIVORCED AND CIVILLY REMARRIED

There is a rich magisterial teaching on the controversial question of reception of Holy Communion by those who are divorced and civilly remarried.[18]

John Paul II, *Familiaris Consortio*, §84

St. John Paul II dealt with this issue in some depth in §84 of his apostolic exhortation on the Role of the Christian Family in the Modern World, *Familiaris Consortio* (1981). We can summarize his position in two fundamental points. The first point is that a valid marriage is the "only right place" for the conjugal act, in order for it to be what it was meant to be in God's plan. Therefore, those who have been divorced and civilly remarried without an annulment can receive sacramental absolution and Communion only if they resolve to practice continence and seek to avoid giving scandal. Generally, this means the termination of cohabitation. Sometimes, however, there are new obligations springing from children (or other circumstances) in the second, invalid union that would make it imprudent to separate. In such cases one can continue cohabitation and resolve to practice continence through the aid of God's grace. Such couples can receive absolution and Communion, but they should avoid receiving Communion where they might give scandal. This can generally be avoided by receiving in another parish where their situation is not known.

On the other hand, sacramental absolution or Communion is not a possibility in cases in which the partners have not resolved to avoid relations within an invalid marriage and thus are living in an objec-

---

[18] See the sensitive presentation of this question by Christoph Cardinal Schön-born, *The Source of Life*, 147–52. See also George Cardinal Pell, "Foreword," in Stephan Kampowski and Juan José Pérez-Soba, *The Gospel of the Family: Going Beyond Cardinal Kasper's Proposal in the Debate on Marriage, Civil Re-Marriage and Communion in the Church* (San Francisco: Ignatius Press, 2014), 9: "One insurmountable barrier for those advocating a new doctrinal and pastoral discipline for the reception of Holy Communion is the almost complete unanimity of two thousand years of Catholic history on this point. It is true that the Orthodox have a long-standing but different tradition, forced on them originally by their Byzantine emperors, but this has never been the Catholic practice."

tively disordered state without a firm purpose of amendment. John Paul II writes:

> However, the Church reaffirms her practice, which is based upon Sacred Scripture, of not admitting to Eucharistic Communion divorced persons who have remarried. They are unable to be admitted thereto from the fact that their state and condition of life objectively contradict that union of love between Christ and the Church which is signified and effected by the Eucharist. Besides this, there is another special pastoral reason: If these people were admitted to the Eucharist, the faithful would be led into error and confusion regarding the Church's teaching about the indissolubility of marriage.
>
> Reconciliation in the sacrament of Penance which would open the way to the Eucharist, can only be granted to those who, repenting of having broken the sign of the Covenant and of fidelity to Christ, are sincerely ready to undertake a way of life that is no longer in contradiction to the indissolubility of marriage. This means, in practice, that when, for serious reasons, such as for example the children's upbringing, a man and a woman cannot satisfy the obligation to separate, they "take on themselves the duty to live in complete continence, that is, by abstinence from the acts proper to married couples."[19]

This teaching rests on several firm foundations. First, it rests on the doctrine of the indissolubility of marriage. A valid sacramental consummated marriage cannot be dissolved by any power on earth. Secondly, the only proper place for the sexual act is in the state of total mutual self-donation constituted by a valid and indissoluble marriage. Third, Holy Communion necessarily presupposes that one is in a state of grace, for it is the sacrament whose purpose is to nourish the bond of communion that already exists between Christ and the soul. Fourth, it rests on the nature of sacramental absolution, which cannot be given without a firm resolve to break with the sin. Fifth, it also rests on the need to avoid giving grave scandal.

---

[19] John Paul II, Apostolic Exhortation on the Role of the Christian Family in the Modern World, *Familiaris Consortio* (1981), §84. The last quoted text is taken from John Paul II, Homily at the Conclusion of the 6th General Assembly of the Synod of Bishops, §7 (October 25, 1980) (*AAS* 72 (1980): 1082).

The *Catechism of the Catholic Church*, §1650 reaffirms this teaching:

If the divorced are remarried civilly, they find themselves in a situation that objectively contravenes God's law. Consequently, they cannot receive Eucharistic communion as long as this situation persists. For the same reason, they cannot exercise certain ecclesial responsibilities. Reconciliation through the sacrament of Penance can be granted only to those who have repented for having violated the sign of the covenant and of fidelity to Christ, and who are committed to living in complete continence.

The teaching was reaffirmed in the 1994 letter to the bishops of the Catholic Church *Concerning the Reception of Holy Communion by the Divorced and Remarried Members of the Faithful* by the Congregation for the Doctrine of the Faith. Referring to *Familiaris Consortio*, §84, it states:

When for serious reasons, for example, for the children's upbringing, a man and a woman cannot satisfy the obligation to separate, they "take on themselves the duty to live in complete continence, that is, by abstinence from the acts proper to married couples." In such a case they may receive holy communion as long as they respect the obligation to avoid giving scandal.

. . . At the same time [*Familiaris Consortio*] confirms and indicates the reasons for the constant and universal practice, "founded on Sacred Scripture, of not admitting the divorced and remarried to Holy Communion." The structure of the Exhortation and the tenor of its words give clearly to understand that this practice, which is presented as binding, cannot be modified because of different situations.[20]

---

[20] Congregation for the Doctrine of the Faith, *Letter to the Bishops of the Catholic Church Concerning the Reception of Holy Communion by the Divorced and Remarried Members of the Faithful* (1994), §4. Cardinal Ratzinger, as prefect of the CDF, returned to this question in a document of 1998, which was an introduction to volume 17 of a series produced by the CDF on this issue entitled "Documenti e studi": *On the Pastoral Care of the Divorced and Remarried* (Vatican City: Libreria Editrice Vaticana, 1998), 20–29.

The Church returned to this question in 2000 in a document of the Pontifical Council for Legislative Texts, *Declaration Concerning the Admission to Holy Communion of Faithful Who Are Divorced and Remarried*, which reaffirms the teaching of *Familiaris Consortio*, §84. It states that the canonical practice given in canons 915 and 916 has its foundation in divine law:

> The prohibition found in the cited canon [915], by its nature, is derived from divine law and transcends the domain of positive ecclesiastical laws: the latter cannot introduce legislative changes which would oppose the doctrine of the Church. The scriptural text on which the ecclesial tradition has always relied is that of St. Paul: . . . (1 Cor 11:27–29).
>
> . . . In the concrete case of the admission to Holy Communion of faithful who are divorced and remarried, the scandal, understood as an action that prompts others toward wrongdoing, affects at the same time both the sacrament of the Eucharist and the indissolubility of marriage. That scandal exists even if such behavior, unfortunately, no longer arouses surprise: in fact it is precisely with respect to the deformation of the conscience that it becomes more necessary for Pastors to act, with as much patience as firmness, as a protection to the sanctity of the Sacraments.[21]

Pastoral Solicitude for the Divorced and Civilly Remarried

The second fundamental point in St. John Paul's treatment of this issue is that the Church must make serious pastoral efforts to accompany the faithful who are divorced and civilly remarried so that they do not feel abandoned or rejected by the Church:

> Since this is an evil that, like the others, is affecting more and more Catholics as well, the problem must be faced with resolution and without delay. The synod fathers studied it expressly. The Church, which was set up to lead to salvation all people and especially the baptized, cannot abandon to their

---

[21] Pontifical Council for Legislative Texts, *Declaration Concerning the Admission to Holy Communion of Faithful Who Are Divorced and Remarried*, §1 (p. 174).

own devices those who have been previously bound by sacramental marriage and who have attempted a second marriage. The Church will therefore make untiring efforts to put at their disposal her means of salvation.[22]

John Paul II explains that one must discern the differences among those who find themselves in this tragic situation. Some have been unjustly abandoned by their first spouse, whereas others have been the cause of the breakdown of the first marriage. Some enter a second union moved largely by concern for the welfare of their children. These differences require different kinds of attention.[23] However, in all cases both pastors and all the faithful are "earnestly called" to seek to reach out to them to "make sure that they do not consider themselves as separated from the Church, for as baptized persons they can and indeed must share in her life":

> They should be encouraged to listen to the word of God, to attend the Sacrifice of the Mass, to persevere in prayer, to contribute to works of charity and to community efforts in favor of justice, to bring up their children in the Christian faith, to cultivate the spirit and practice of penance and thus implore, day by day, God's grace. Let the Church pray for them, encourage them and show herself a merciful mother and thus sustain them in faith and hope.
>
> . . . At the same time she shows motherly concern for these children of hers, especially those who, through no fault of their own, have been abandoned by their legitimate partner.
>
> With firm confidence she believes that those who have rejected the Lord's command and are still living in this state will be able to obtain from God the grace of conversion

---

[22] John Paul II, *Familiaris Consortio*, §83.

[23] See ibid., §84: "Pastors must know that for the sake of truth they are obliged to exercise careful discernment of situations. There is, in fact, a difference between those who have sincerely tried to save their first marriage and have been unjustly abandoned and those who, through their own grave fault, have destroyed a canonically valid marriage. Finally, there are those who have entered into a second union for the sake of the children's upbringing and who are sometimes subjectively certain in conscience that their previous and irreparably destroyed marriage had never been valid."

and salvation, provided that they have persevered in prayer, penance and charity.[24]

The CDF also reiterated this point in the 1994 *Letter to the Bishops Concerning the Reception of Holy Communion by the Divorced and Remarried Members of the Faithful*. The document reminds the bishops of the desire expressed by St. John Paul II for pastoral action in support of the faithful in such irregular marital situations:

> . . . with solicitous charity to do everything that can be done to strengthen in the love of Christ and the Church those faithful in irregular marriage situations. Only thus will it be possible for them fully to receive the message of Christian marriage and endure in faith the distress of their situation. In pastoral action one must do everything possible to ensure that this is understood not to be a matter of discrimination but only of absolute fidelity to the will of Christ who has restored and entrusted to us anew the indissolubility of marriage as a gift of the Creator. It will be necessary for pastors and the community of the faithful to suffer and to love in solidarity with the persons concerned so that they may recognize in their burden the sweet yoke and the light burden of Jesus [cf. Matt 11:30]. Their burden is not sweet and light in the sense of being small or insignificant, but becomes light because the Lord—and with him the whole Church—shares it. It is the task of pastoral action, which has to be carried out with total dedication, to offer this help, founded in truth and in love together. [25]

---

[24] Ibid. This teaching is quoted in *CCC*, §1651:

> Toward Christians who live in this situation, and who often keep the faith and desire to bring up their children in a Christian manner, priests and the whole community must manifest an attentive solicitude, so that they do not consider themselves separated from the Church, in whose life they can and must participate as baptized persons: "They should be encouraged to listen to the Word of God, to attend the sacrifice of the Mass, to persevere in prayer, to contribute to works of charity and to community efforts for justice, to bring up their children in the Christian faith, to cultivate the spirit and practice of penance and thus implore, day by day, God's grace" (*Familiaris Consortio*, §84).

[25] CDF, *Letter to the Bishops of the Catholic Church Concerning the Reception of Holy Communion by the Divorced and Remarried Members of the Faithful*, §10. In §9, the document explains that reception of Communion contrary to the norms

Pope Benedict XVI, *Sacramentum Caritatis*, §29

This doctrine was revisited in Benedict XVI's post-synodal apostolic exhortation *Sacramentum Caritatis* (2007), which reconfirms the teaching of *Familiaris Consortio*:

> The synod of bishops confirmed the Church's practice, based on Sacred Scripture (cf. Mk 10:2–12), of not admitting the divorced and remarried to the sacraments, since their state and their condition of life objectively contradict the loving union of Christ and the Church signified and made present in the Eucharist.
>
> ...Where the nullity of the marriage bond is not declared and objective circumstances make it impossible to cease cohabitation, the Church encourages these members of the faithful to commit themselves to living their relationship in fidelity to the demands of God's law, as friends, as brother and sister; in this way they will be able to return to the table of the Eucharist, taking care to observe the Church's established and approved practice in this regard. This path, if it is to be possible and fruitful, must be supported by pastors and by adequate ecclesial initiatives.[26]

Benedict reiterates St. John Paul II's concern that the divorced and civilly remarried be the object of the Church's pastoral solicitude:

> Yet the divorced and remarried continue to belong to the Church, which accompanies them with special concern and encourages them to live as fully as possible the Christian life through regular participation at Mass, albeit without receiving communion, listening to the word of God, eucharistic adoration, prayer, participation in the life of the community, honest dialogue with a priest or spiritual director, dedication

---

of the Church cannot be beneficial: "Receiving Eucharistic Communion contrary to ecclesial communion is therefore in itself a contradiction. Sacramental communion with Christ includes and presupposes the observance, even if at times difficult, of the order of ecclesial communion, and it cannot be right and fruitful if a member of the faithful, wishing to approach Christ directly, does not respect this order."

[26] Benedict XVI, *Sacramentum Caritatis*, §29.

to the life of charity, works of penance, and commitment to the education of their children.[27]

He also spoke of the need to devote more pastoral attention to marriage preparation.[28] He addresses the issue of those who have doubts about the validity of their first marriage, but have not received an annulment, and exhorts each diocese to "have a sufficient number of persons with the necessary preparation, so that the ecclesiastical tribunals can operate in an expeditious manner. I repeat that it is a grave obligation to bring the Church's institutional activity in her tribunals ever closer to the faithful."[29] This concern is fully shared by Pope Francis and motivated his motu proprio *Mitis Iudex Dominus Iesus* (2015), which reforms the *Code of Canon Law* regarding the process for determining the nullity of a marriage.

Pope Francis, *Amoris Laetitia*

Pope Francis treats this delicate topic of Communion with regard to those who are divorced and remarried above all in the eighth chapter of his post-synodal apostolic exhortation, *Amoris Laetitia* (2016). He emphasizes the need for a pastoral approach that can assist those in irregular marital situations to respond to the action of grace in their lives so as to gradually come into conformity with God's plan for marriage and the family:

---

[27] Ibid.

[28] Ibid.:

> The Synod also recommended devoting maximum pastoral attention to training couples preparing for marriage and to ascertaining beforehand their convictions regarding the obligations required for the validity of the sacrament of Matrimony. Serious discernment in this matter will help to avoid situations where impulsive decisions or superficial reasons lead two young people to take on responsibilities that they are then incapable of honoring. The good that the Church and society as a whole expect from marriage and from the family founded upon marriage is so great as to call for full pastoral commitment to this particular area. Marriage and the family are institutions that must be promoted and defended from every possible misrepresentation of their true nature, since whatever is injurious to them is injurious to society itself.

[29] Ibid.

"In considering a pastoral approach toward people who have contracted a civil marriage, who are divorced and remarried, or simply living together, the Church has the responsibility of helping them understand the divine pedagogy of grace in their lives and offering them assistance so they can reach the fullness of God's plan for them," something which is always possible by the power of the Holy Spirit.[30]

Or again:

Discernment must help to find possible ways of responding to God and growing in the midst of limits. By thinking that everything is black and white, we sometimes close off the way of grace and of growth, and discourage paths of sanctification which give glory to God. Let us remember that "a small step, in the midst of great human limitations, can be more pleasing to God than a life which appears outwardly in order, but moves through the day without confronting great difficulties."[31]

A part of this pastoral approach is the attempt to integrate those in irregular marital situations, as much as would be possible without scandal, into the life of the Christian community.[32] This applies, of course, especially to their children.[33]

Much discussion has been given to *Amoris Laetitia*, §305, which, following *CCC*, §1753, speaks of cases in which culpability for objectively grave sins is diminished through ignorance or lack of full deliberation:

---

[30] Francis, Post-Synodal Exhortation on Love in the Family, *Amoris Laetitia* (2016), §297.

[31] Francis, *Amoris Laetitia*, §305. The quotation is from Pope Francis, Apostolic Exhortation on the Proclamation of the Gospel in Today's World, *Evangelii Gaudium* (2013), §44.

[32] See Francis, *Amoris Laetitia*, §299: "I am in agreement with the many Synod Fathers who observed that 'the baptized who are divorced and civilly remarried need to be more fully integrated into Christian communities in the variety of ways possible, while avoiding any occasion of scandal. The logic of integration is the key to their pastoral care, a care which would allow them not only to realize that they belong to the Church as the body of Christ, but also to know that they can have a joyful and fruitful experience in it.'"

[33] Ibid.: "This integration is also needed in the care and Christian upbringing of their children, who ought to be considered most important."

Because of forms of conditioning and mitigating factors, it is possible that in an objective situation of sin—which may not be subjectively culpable, or fully such—a person can be living in God's grace, can love and can also grow in the life of grace and charity, while receiving the Church's help to this end.

In other words, it can happen that a person is habitually committing an objectively grave sin but is lacking full knowledge of the gravity of the sin or full deliberation.[34] Thus, although there is grave matter, one of the other two conditions for mortal sin are lacking.[35] In such a case, is it possible to give absolution to a penitent who does not make a firm purpose of amendment to avoid such a sin in the future, granting it precisely because of the absence of either full knowledge or full consent? Footnote 351, the subject of much controversy, seems to imply that this can sometimes be the case:

In certain cases, this can include the help of the sacraments. Hence, "I want to remind priests that the confessional must not be a torture chamber, but rather an encounter with the Lord's mercy" (*Evangelii Gaudium*, 44). I would also point out that the Eucharist "is not a prize for the perfect, but a powerful medicine and nourishment for the weak" (47).

In interpreting footnote 351, it must be borne in mind that the phrase "help of the sacraments" applies principally to the sacrament of Penance and refers only to the case in which there is question of a sin that is objectively grave but not gravely culpable because of a lack

---

[34] See ibid., §301: "The Church possesses a solid body of reflection concerning mitigating factors and situations. Hence it can no longer simply be said that all those in any 'irregular' situation are living in a state of mortal sin and are deprived of sanctifying grace. More is involved here than mere ignorance of the rule. A subject may know full well the rule, yet have great difficulty in understanding 'its inherent values,' or be in a concrete situation which does not allow him or her to act differently and decide otherwise without further sin."

[35] See Rocco Buttiglione, "The Joy of Love and the Consternation of Theologians: Some Comments on the Apostolic Exhortation *Amoris Laetitia*," *L'Osservatore Romano*, July 19, 2016, accessed June 14, 2017, http://www.osservatoreromano. va/en/news/joy-love-and-consternation-theologians; Buttiglione, "*Amoris laetitia*: Risposte ai critici," *Lateranum* 83, no. 1 (2017): 191–240, at 193; Antonio Spadaro, "The Demands of Love: A Conversation with Cardinal Schönborn about 'The Joy of Love,'" *America* 215, no. 4 (2016): 23–27.

of full knowledge or deliberation. What might this look like? In the case of lack of full knowledge of the sinfulness of a certain behavior through inculpable ignorance, a confessor could ask the penitent the following question: If you came to understand that such a behavior is gravely contrary to God's will, would you firmly resolve to break it off? If a person answered negatively, then such a person would clearly not be disposed to receive absolution. If they resolved affirmatively and promised to use appropriate means to come to full knowledge of the moral law and to pray for that understanding from God, then this might be a case in which the teaching of footnote 351 could be applied and absolution could be given validly.

The obligation would remain for the penitent to embark on a path of the formation of conscience in that regard through prayer and catechesis. Without a firm commitment to come to understand God's will and act on it, though, sacramental absolution would not be valid, for inculpable ignorance presupposes that a person is not gravely negligent in seeking the truth.[36] It seems therefore that one could not long remain inculpably ignorant in such a case. Furthermore, the confessor must make it clear that those who receive sacramental absolution in cases like this have a grave obligation to avoid giving scandal by receiving Communion where their situation might be known.[37]

Supposing that absolution would be valid in such a case, is this the best option? Would it be better in some cases to give absolution only if the person makes a firm resolve to avoid such a sin that is

---

[36] See *CCC*, §1791: "This ignorance can often be imputed to personal responsibility. This is the case when a man 'takes little trouble to find out what is true and good, or when conscience is by degrees almost blinded through the habit of committing sin' (*Gaudium et spes* 16). In such cases, the person is culpable for the evil he commits."

[37] Spiritual communion should be explained and recommended in such cases. See Benedict XVI, *Sacramentum Caritatis*, §55: "Even in cases where it is not possible to receive sacramental communion, participation at Mass remains necessary, important, meaningful and fruitful. In such circumstances it is beneficial to cultivate a desire for full union with Christ through the practice of spiritual communion." On the importance of avoiding scandal, see the text (cited above) of the Pontifical Council for Legislative Texts, *Declaration Concerning the Admission to Holy Communion of Faithful Who Are Divorced and Remarried*, §1: "In the concrete case of the admission to holy communion of faithful who are divorced and remarried, the scandal, understood as an action that prompts others toward wrongdoing, affects at the same time both the sacrament of the eucharist and the indissolubility of marriage. That scandal exists even if such behavior, unfortunately, no longer arouses surprise."

objectively grave but for which they are not fully culpable at present? It seems that there is no one answer to such a question, for it depends on the disposition of the penitent and other circumstances.[38] On the one hand, the aid of the sacraments, if they can be received fruitfully, cannot be underestimated. On the other hand, the confessor has a grave duty to aid the penitent to correct an erroneous conscience, which always remains a tragedy,[39] to resolve to avoid objectively grave sin, and to progress in the arduous path of conversion. Needless to say, in such a case, the confessor should follow the guidelines given by the Magisterium and his bishop.[40]

INTERCOMMUNION (*COMMUNICATIO IN SACRIS*)

The Eucharist, as we have seen, is a sacrament that nourishes ecclesial communion as one of its primary effects. It also expresses that communion and presupposes it, in order to nourish it. For this reason, both concelebration of the Mass and reception of Holy Communion presuppose both visible and invisible ecclesial communion. Visible

---

[38] See Francis, *Amoris Laetitia*, §304: "It is true that general rules set forth a good which can never be disregarded or neglected, but in their formulation they cannot provide absolutely for all particular situations. At the same time, it must be said that, precisely for that reason, what is part of a practical discernment in particular circumstances cannot be elevated to the level of a rule. That would not only lead to an intolerable casuistry, but would endanger the very values which must be preserved with special care." See also Buttiglione, "*Amoris laetitia*: Risposte ai critici," 198–99.

[39] See *CCC*, §1793: "If . . . the ignorance is invincible, or the moral subject is not responsible for his erroneous judgment, the evil committed by the person cannot be imputed to him. It remains no less an evil, a privation, a disorder. One must therefore work to correct the errors of moral conscience." On the tragic aspect of invincible ignorance, see Joseph Ratzinger, "Conscience and Truth," presented at the 10th Workshop for the American Bishops, February 1991, in Dallas, TX, published as *Conscience and Truth* (Braintree, MA: Pope John XXIII Medical-Moral Research and Education Center, 1991).

[40] See *Amoris Laetitia*, §300: "Priests have the duty to 'accompany [the divorced and remarried] in helping them to understand their situation according to the teaching of the Church and the guidelines of the bishop.'" See also Buttiglione, "*Amoris laetitia*: Risposte ai critici," 198–99. For an example of guidelines set by a bishop for his diocese, see Archbishop Charles Chaput, "Pastoral Guidelines for Implementing *Amoris Laetitia* in the Archdiocese of Philadelphia," July 1, 2016, accessed July 7, 2017, http://archphila.org/wp-content/uploads/2016/06/AOP_AL-guidelines.pdf.

ecclesial communion involves visible unity in faith, sacraments, and governance, which implies professing the same faith, recognizing the same sacraments, and being subject to the Church's hierarchical order of governance, which means being in communion with the successor of Peter and the bishops in communion with him.[41]

John Paul II addresses the question of intercommunion in *Ecclesia de Eucharistia*, §35. He states that participation in the Eucharist does not create a new unity, but is rather an expression and strengthening of an already existing participation in both the visible and invisible communion of the Church.

> The celebration of the Eucharist, however, cannot be the starting-point for communion; it presupposes that communion already exists, a communion which it seeks to consolidate and bring to perfection. The sacrament is an expression of this bond of communion both in its *invisible* dimension, which, in Christ and through the working of the Holy Spirit, unites us to the Father and among ourselves, and in its *visible* dimension, which entails communion in the teaching of the Apostles, in the sacraments and in the Church's hierarchical order. The profound relationship between the invisible and the visible elements of ecclesial communion is constitutive of the Church as the sacrament of salvation. Only in this context can there be a legitimate celebration of the Eucharist and true participation in it. Consequently it is an intrinsic requirement of the Eucharist that it should be celebrated in communion, and specifically maintaining the various bonds of that communion intact.

It follows that concelebration with those not in full visible communion with the Church and intercommunion cannot be understood as a means of bringing about the unity of the Church with those who are not yet in full visible communion with her. Concelebration always presupposes full ecclesial communion.[42] Reception of Holy Communion, however, admits certain exceptions from the general norm for the

---

[41] See Oliver Treanor, "Apostolicity and the Eucharist," *Communio* 39, no. 4 (2012): 569–86.

[42] See CIC, can. 908: "Catholic priests are forbidden to concelebrate the Eucharist with priests or ministers of Churches or ecclesial communities which do not have full communion with the Catholic Church."

sake of the salvation of souls, but not for the promotion of ecumenical unity. The general legislation on sacramental intercommunion with non-Catholics is given in canon 844 of the *Code of Canon Law*:

1. Catholic ministers may licitly administer the sacraments to Catholic members of the Christian faithful only and, likewise, the latter may licitly receive the sacraments only from Catholic ministers with due regard for parts 2, 3, and 4 of this canon, and can. 861, part 2.

2. Whenever necessity requires or genuine spiritual advantage suggests, and provided that the danger of error or indifferentism is avoided, it is lawful for the faithful for whom it is physically or morally impossible to approach a Catholic minister, to receive the sacraments of penance, Eucharist, and anointing of the sick from non-Catholic ministers in whose churches these sacraments are valid.

3. Catholic ministers may licitly administer the sacraments of penance, Eucharist and anointing of the sick to members of the oriental churches which do not have full communion with the Catholic Church, if they ask on their own for the sacraments and are properly disposed. This holds also for members of other churches, which in the judgment of the Apostolic See are in the same condition as the oriental churches as far as these sacraments are concerned.

4. If the danger of death is present or other grave necessity, in the judgment of the diocesan bishop or the conference of bishops, Catholic ministers may licitly administer these sacraments to other Christians who do not have full communion with the Catholic Church, who cannot approach a minister of their own community and on their own ask for it, provided they manifest Catholic faith in these sacraments and are properly disposed.[43]

John Paul II comments on §4 in *Ecclesia de Eucharistia*:

These conditions, from which no dispensation can be given, must be carefully respected, even though they deal with specific individual cases, because the denial of one or more truths

---

[43] This corresponds to can. 671 in the *Code of Canons of the Eastern Churches*.

of the faith regarding these sacraments and, among these, the truth regarding the need of the ministerial priesthood for their validity, renders the person asking improperly disposed to legitimately receiving them. And the opposite is also true: Catholics may not receive communion in those communities which lack a valid sacrament of Orders.

The faithful observance of the body of norms established in this area is a manifestation and, at the same time, a guarantee of our love for Jesus Christ in the Blessed Sacrament, for our brothers and sisters of different Christian confessions— who have a right to our witness to the truth—and for the cause itself of the promotion of unity.[44]

STUDY QUESTIONS

1. Why does the offering of sacrifice fittingly go together with communion in the sacrifice?
2. Why is it gravely wrong to receive Communion in a state of mortal sin?
3. Explain the content of canons 915 and 916.
4. Explain the Church's teaching on Communion for divorced and civilly remarried Catholics.
5. How should the Church accompany those who find themselves in an irregular marital situation?
6. When can Communion (as well as Confession and Anointing of the Sick) be offered by a Catholic priest to non-Catholics, and when can it be received by Catholics from a non-Catholic minister?
7. Explain the following phrase of St. John Paul II from *Ecclesia de Eucharistia*, §35: "The celebration of the Eucharist, however, cannot be the starting-point for communion; it presupposes that communion already exists, a communion which it seeks to consolidate and bring to perfection."

---

[44] John Paul II, *EE*, §46.

Suggestions for Further Reading

Benedict XVI. Post-Synodal Apostolic Exhortation *Sacramentum Caritatis*. February 22, 2007. See §29.

Congregation for the Doctrine of the Faith, *Letter to the Bishops of the Catholic Church concerning the Reception of Holy Communion by the Divorced and Remarried Members of the Faithful*. September 14, 1994.

John Paul II. Encyclical *Ecclesia de Eucharistia*. April 17, 2003. See §§35–46.

———. Post-Synodal Apostolic Exhortation *Familiaris Consortio*. November 22, 1981. See §84.

Pope Francis. Post-Synodal Apostolic Exhortation *Amoris Laetitia*. April 8, 2016. Ch. 8.

Ratzinger, Joseph Cardinal. *Worthiness to Receive Holy Communion: General Principles*. Memorandum to Cardinal McCarrick (July, 2004). Accessed July 6, 2017. http://www.ewtn.com/library/curia/cdfworthycom.htm.

Schönborn, Christoph Cardinal. *The Source of Life*. Translated by Brian McNeil. New York: Crossroad, 2007. Pp. 138–61.

✠

CHAPTER FIFTEEN

Reception of Holy Communion

FREQUENCY OF COMMUNION

The Church teaches that it is good for the faithful to receive Holy Communion frequently—weekly and even daily. This practice is recorded in Scripture and in the Church Fathers, continued to be recommended in the medieval period, and was especially encouraged by the Council of Trent. St. Pope Pius X officially promoted this practice in his decree on frequent Communion, *Sacra Tridentina Synodus* (1905).[1]

The fittingness of daily reception of Communion is prefigured by the manna that was eaten every day by the Israelites in the desert. The daily Eucharistic celebration is also prefigured in the daily sacrifice in the Temple of two lambs, one in the morning and one in the evening, and of bread and wine.[2] The fittingness is also implied in the very nature of the Eucharist as spiritual nourishment. Why should we nourish our souls much less frequently than our bodies?

Early Church

There is much reason to think that Holy Communion was received frequently, and often indeed daily, in the early Church. Daily communion is hinted at in a brief sketch of the primitive Church in Acts 2:46: "And day by day, attending the temple together and breaking

---

[1] Sacred Congregation of the Council, Decree on Frequent and Daily Reception of Holy Communion, *Sacra Tridentina Synodus*, December 20, 1905 (*ASS* 38 [1905]: 400–406; English translation in R. Kevin Seasoltz, *The New Liturgy: A Documentation, 1903–1965* [New York: Herder and Herder, 1966], 11–15).

[2] See Num 18:1–8.

bread in their homes, they partook of food with glad and generous hearts, praising God and having favor with all the people. And the Lord added to their number day by day those who were being saved." In the middle of the third century, St. Cyprian says: "We who are in Christ, daily receive the Eucharist as the food of salvation."[3] St. Basil, in the mid-fourth century, writes, "It is commendable and most beneficial to communicate and partake of the Body and Blood of Christ every single day."[4] St. Ambrose, a contemporary of St. Basil, says to the neophytes:

> What is it the apostle says about every time you receive it? "As often as we receive it, we herald the death of the Lord." If we herald his death, we herald the remission of sins. If whenever his blood is shed, it is shed for the remission of sins, I ought always to receive him so that he may always forgive sins. Since I am always sinning, I always need the medicine.[5]

In a sermon attributed to St. Augustine and quoted by St. Thomas, there is a beautiful and balanced exhortation to daily Communion: "Receive daily that it may profit you daily. . . . So live as to deserve to receive it daily." [6]

St. John Chrysostom also exhorts the faithful to receive daily if they have a clear conscience: "Just as the ordinary person who has nothing on their conscience ought to approach communion every day, so it's unsafe for the person who's overpowered by sin and doesn't repent to approach even on a feast day."[7] We can see, however, from Chrysostom's homily, dated to circa AD 386, that many of the faithful at that time were in the habit of receiving Communion only once a year on a solemnity such as Christmas or Easter. In another homily he said: "In vain do we stand before the altar; there is no one to partake."[8]

---

[3] Cyprian, *De Dominica Oratione* 18 (PL, 4:531). See also Tertullian, *De Idololatria* 7 (PL, 1:669).

[4] Basil, *Epistula* 93 (PG, 32:484).

[5] Ambrose, *De Sacramentis* 4.28, in (Yarnold, *Awe-Inspiring Rites*, 140).

[6] Augustine, Sermon 84.3 (PL, 39:1908–9), quoted in *ST* III, q. 80, a. 10.

[7] John Chrysostom, Homily Concerning Blessed Philogonius, in Wendy Mayer and Pauline Allen, *John Chrysostom* (London and New York: Routledge, 2000), 194.

[8] John Chrysostom, Homilies on Ephesians 3.4 (*NPNF*1, 13:64). See Jungmann, *The Mass of the Roman Rite*, 2:361.

Medieval Period

In the early seventh century in Spain, St. Isidore of Seville speaks about the frequency of reception of Holy Communion. For those in a state of grace who receive with devotion and humility, daily reception is a good thing, in accordance with the petition of the Lord's Prayer regarding our daily bread:

> Some say that the Eucharist ought to be received daily unless some sin comes in the way; for, at the Lord's command, we request that this bread be given to us daily, saying: "Give us each day our daily bread" [Luke 11:3]. They say this well if they receive it with reverence and devotion and humility, and if they do not perform this action proudly, believing in the presumption of their own righteousness.[9]

St. Isidore clarifies that venial sins should not keep one from approaching Communion, for too much abstinence from the Eucharist keeps the soul from drawing near to the source of life.[10]

St. Thomas mentions that he agrees with Ambrose and Augustine that the Eucharist should be received daily because of the power it has in itself to strengthen our spiritual life and heal our spiritual wounds.

---

[9] Isidore of Seville, *De Ecclesiasticis Officiis* 1.18.7, trans. T. L. Knoebel, ACW 61 (New York: Newman Press, 2008), 43.

[10] Ibid., 1.18.8:

> On the other hand, if there are such sins that would move them back from the altar as if dead, penance is to be accomplished first and then this salvific medication is to be received. "For whoever eats in an unworthy manner eats and drinks judgment against themselves" [1 Cor 11:27, 29]. And this is to receive unworthily—if one receives at the very time that one ought to be doing penance. On the other hand, if the sins are not so great that it is judged one ought to be kept from communion, one should not separate oneself from the medicine of the Lord's body, lest, the abstaining person being prohibited for a long time, he would be separated from the body of Christ. It is clear that they live who draw near to his body. Thus, it is to be feared, lest, while one is separated for a long time from the body of Christ, one would remain separated from salvation, the Lord himself saying: "unless you eat the flesh of the Son of Man and drink his blood, you have no life in you" [John 6:54]. Thus, whoever has presently ceased from sinning ought not to stop from communicating.

However, he recognizes with Augustine that this cannot be recommended unless the recipient has the proper dispositions:

> There are two things to be considered regarding the use of this sacrament. The first is on the part of the sacrament itself, the virtue of which gives health to men; and consequently it is profitable to receive it daily so as to receive its fruits daily. Hence Ambrose says (*De Sacramentis* 4): "If, whenever Christ's blood is shed, it is shed for the forgiveness of sins, I who sin often, should receive it often: I need a frequent remedy." The second thing to be considered is on the part of the recipient, who is required to approach this sacrament with great reverence and devotion. Consequently, if anyone finds that he has these dispositions every day, he will do well to receive it daily. Hence, Augustine after saying, "Receive daily, that it may profit thee daily," adds: "So live, as to deserve to receive it daily." But because many persons are lacking in this devotion, on account of the many drawbacks both spiritual and corporal from which they suffer, it is not expedient for all to approach this sacrament every day; but they should do so as often as they find themselves properly disposed. Hence it is said in *De Ecclesiasticis Dogmatibus* 53: "I neither praise nor blame daily reception of the Eucharist."[11]

What this means is that, when one is properly disposed, frequent reception is praiseworthy, but one cannot blame those who are unable to receive frequently, as long as they fulfill the obligation of receiving Communion once a year, according to the obligation imposed by the Fourth Lateran Council in 1215.

---

[11] *ST* III, q. 80, a. 10. *De Ecclesiasticis Dogmatibus* (*On Church Doctrine*) is now attributed to Gennadius († ca. 496), although formerly it was attributed to St. Augustine. On the frequency of Communion, see also St. Thomas's commentary on 1 Cor 11, lec. 7, Marietti no. 699: "From the fact that those who receive this sacrament spiritually acquire life, some are drawn to receive this sacrament frequently. But from the fact that those who receive unworthily acquire judgment upon themselves, many are deterred and rarely receive. Both seem commendable. . . . But because of themselves love is preferred to fear, it seems more commendable to receive more frequently rather than more rarely" (Larcher, *Commentary on the Letters of Saint Paul to the Corinthians*, 261).

The Sixteenth Century and the Council of Trent

In a letter commending the establishment of a confraternity of the Blessed Sacrament, St. Ignatius of Loyola laments the state of Eucharistic devotion in his time:

> In the early Church members of both sexes received Communion daily as soon as they were old enough. But soon devotion began to cool and Communion became weekly. Then, after a considerable interval of time, as devotion became cooler still, Communion was received on only three of the principal feasts of the year, each one being left to his own choice and devotion to receive oftener.... And finally, because of our weakness and indifference, we have ended with once a year. You would think we are Christian only in name, to see us so calmly accepting the condition to which the greater part of the world has come.[12]

In a letter to a female religious, St. Ignatius recommended her to practice daily Communion:

> As to daily Communion, we should recall that in the early Church everybody received daily, and that up to this time there has been no written ordinance of Holy Mother Church, nor objection by either positive or Scholastic theologians against anyone receiving daily Communion, should his devotion move him thereto.... The witness on which we can rely is our own conscience. What I mean is this. After all, it is lawful for you in the Lord if, apart from evident mortal sins or what you can judge to be such, you think that your soul derives help and is inflamed with love for our Creator and Lord, and you receive with this intention, finding by experience that this spiritual food soothes, supports, settles, and preserves you for His greater service, praise and glory, you may without doubt receive daily; in fact, it would be better for you to do so.[13]

---

[12] Ignatius of Loyola, Letter to the townspeople of Azpeitia, 1540, in *Letters of St. Ignatius of Loyola*, trans. William J. Young (Chicago: Loyola University Press, 1959), 45.

[13] Ignatius, Letter to Theresa Rejadella, November 15, 1543, in *Letters*, 71–72.

The Council of Trent earnestly recommends frequent devout reception of Communion. First, the Council explains that there are three ways of receiving Communion: sacramentally only, spiritually only, and both sacramentally and spiritually. One receives sacramentally only if one receives it in a state of mortal sin and thus is unable to obtain any spiritual fruit from it. One receives spiritually only if one makes a spiritual communion. Communion is received both spiritually and sacramentally when it is received sacramentally by a person who is rightly disposed so as to receive its spiritual fruit. A spiritual communion, obviously, is better than a Communion that is only sacramental (but unfruitful). But a Communion that is both sacramental and spiritual is best.[14] Hence, the Council recommends that the faithful live in such a way that they can frequently receive the "Bread of Angels":

> Keeping in mind the great majesty and the most excellent love of our Lord Jesus Christ . . . who gave us his flesh to eat, may all Christians have so firm and strong a faith in the sacred mystery of his body and blood, may they worship it with such devotion and pious veneration, that they will be able to receive *frequently* their 'super-substantial bread.' May it truly be the life of their souls and continual health for their minds.[15]

The *Catechism of the Council of Trent* further explains the three kinds of reception of the Eucharist. Those who receive only sacramentally "receive no benefit from its participation; rather, as the Apostle says, they 'eat and drink judgment upon themselves' (1 Cor 11:29)." The second group includes all those who "share in this sacrament out of desire—even if the desire is itself only implicit. From this faith and love they derive certainly very many of its benefits." However, the

---

[14] See the Council of Trent, On the Sacrament of the Eucharist (session 13), ch. 8: "As regards the use, our Fathers have correctly and appropriately distinguished three ways of receiving this holy sacrament. They teach that some receive it only sacramentally because they are sinners. Others receive it only spiritually; they are the ones who, receiving in desire the heavenly bread put before them, with a living faith 'working through love,' experience its fruit and benefit from it. The third group receive it both sacramentally and spiritually; they are the ones who examine and prepare themselves beforehand to approach this divine table, clothed in the wedding garment" (DS, 1648).

[15] Ibid., (DS, 1649).

third way of receiving Communion sacramentally and spiritually is clearly far superior. Hence, the Catechism draws a strong conclusion in favor of frequent Communion:

> Those, therefore, who are able, after due preparation, actually to receive the sacrament of the Body and Blood of the Lord, but do not do so, because they prefer to receive holy Communion in a spiritual manner only, are clearly choosing a way which is only second best, and are thereby depriving themselves of inestimable gifts.[16]

After the Council of Trent, the Jesuits became the principal promoters of frequent Communion. In the mid-seventeenth century, a contrary position was vehemently maintained by the Jansenists. Its leading proponent was Antoine Arnauld, who wrote a work opposing frequent Communion, *De la fréquente communion*, published in 1643.[17] Due to the influence of Jansenism, the frequency of Communion declined further.

St. Pius X

St. Pius X promulgated the definitive teaching on frequent Communion in the decree *Sacra Tridentina Synodus*, On Frequent and Daily Reception of Holy Communion, on December 20, 1905. In this document, he encourages daily Communion, and describes the necessary dispositions for worthy reception.

A first argument in favor of frequent, and even daily, Communion is taken from the figure of the manna in the desert and from the Lord's Prayer, in which we ask for our "daily bread," which principally signifies the Eucharist:

> From this comparison of the Food of angels with bread and with manna, it was easily to be understood by His disciples that, as the body is daily nourished with bread, and as the Hebrews were daily fed with manna in the desert, so the Christian soul might daily partake of this heavenly bread and be refreshed

---

[16] *CCT*, p. 241.

[17] See Antoine Arnauld, *De la fréquente communion* (DS, 2316–23). Eight propositions from this book were condemned by the Holy Office in 1690.

thereby. Moreover, we are bidden in the Lord's Prayer to ask for "our daily bread" by which words, the holy Fathers of the Church all but unanimously teach, must be understood not so much that material bread which is the support of the body as the Eucharistic bread which ought to be our daily food.[18]

Secondly, the purpose of the sacrament is principally to be a strengthening of the soul in grace and charity and an antidote against the sins that attack us daily. It is not a reward for established virtue, but the most central means for us to grow in it. Since we always need that help, it should be received frequently, and even daily, as long as we have right dispositions:

> The desire, in fact, of Jesus Christ and of the Church that all the faithful of Christ approach the sacred banquet daily consists above all in this, that the faithful of Christ being joined with God through the sacrament may receive from it the strength to restrain passion, to wash away the little faults that occur daily, and to guard against more grievous sins to which human frailty is subject; not principally, however, to render honor and veneration to God or as a sort of compensation or reward for the virtues of those who receive.[19]

Therefore, St. Pius X determines that "frequent and daily communion ... must be open to all the faithful of whatever class or condition, so that none who is in the state of grace and approaches the holy table with a right and pious intention may be turned away from it."[20] A right intention to receive Communion is defined as follows: "that a person approach the holy table, not from routine, vanity, or human motives, but because he wishes to please God, to be more closely united with him in charity, and to overcome his infirmities and defects by means of this divine remedy."[21]

With regard to venial sin, Pius X insists that it does not disqualify one from receiving Communion, although "it is extremely desirable that those who practice frequent and daily Communion be free from

---

[18] *Sacra Tridentina Synodus* (Seasoltz, *New Liturgy*, 11).

[19] *Sacra Tridentina Synodus* (DS, 3375).

[20] Ibid. (DS, 3379).

[21] Ibid. (DS, 3380).

venial sins, or at least from fully deliberate ones, and from all attachment to them, yet it is enough that they be free from mortal sins and resolved never to sin again."[22]

Finally he emphasizes the need for a "solid preparation" before Communion, and afterward, "a proper thanksgiving, according to each one's strength, conditions, and duties."[23]

J. R .R. Tolkien, in a letter to his son Michael, wrote about the inestimable value of frequent reception of Holy Communion:

> The only cure for sagging or fainting faith is Communion. Though always Itself, perfect and complete and inviolate, the Blessed Sacrament does not operate completely and once for all in any of us. Like the act of Faith it must be continuous and grow by exercise. Frequency is of the highest effect. Seven times a week is more nourishing than seven times at intervals.[24]

In that same letter, Tolkien refers to St. Pius's decree on frequent Communion as "the greatest reform of our time. . . . I wonder what state the Church would now be but for it."[25]

COMMUNION FOR CHILDREN

Another disputed question resolved by St. Pius X concerns the proper age for the first reception of Holy Communion by children in the Latin rite. This is currently treated by the *Code of Canon Law* in canon 913.[26] When danger of death is present, it is sufficient that a child be

---

[22] Ibid. (DS, 3381).

[23] Ibid. (DS, 3382).

[24] J. R. R. Tolkien, Letter of November 1, 1963, in *The Letters of J.R.R. Tolkien*, ed. Humphrey Carpenter (New York: Houghton Mifflin Harcourt, 2000), 338–39.

[25] Ibid., 339. See Robert F. Taft, *Beyond East and West: Problems in Liturgical Understanding*, 2nd ed. (Rome: Edizioni Orientalia Christiana, Pontifical Oriental Institute, 1997), 105: "The greatest and most successful liturgical reform in Catholic history is surely the movement for the restoration of frequent communion, sanctioned by Pius X in 1906." See Joseph Dougherty, *From Altar-Throne to Table: The Campaign for Frequent Holy Communion in the Catholic Church* (Lanham, MD: Scarecrow Press, 2010).

[26] CIC, can. 913, §1: "The administration of the Most Holy Eucharist to children requires that they have sufficient knowledge and careful preparation so that they understand the mystery of Christ according to their capacity and are able

capable of understanding the difference between the Eucharist and ordinary food and receive it with reverence. In normal situations, there should be an additional preparation so that children can understand the mystery that they are receiving according to their age, and come to it with devotion.

The key magisterial text regarding the age for the reception of First Communion is the decree published by the Sacred Congregation of the Discipline of the Sacraments on August 8, 1910, *Quam Singulari*. The text begins with Christ's desire that the little children come to Him:

> The pages of the Gospel plainly testify to the special love which Christ showed while on earth to the little ones. It was his delight to be in their midst. He laid his hands upon them. He embraced and blessed them. He was indignant when they were repulsed by his disciples and reprimanded the latter in the following words: "Suffer the little children to come unto me, and forbid them not, for of such is the kingdom of God" (Mk 10:13–16). How highly he prized their innocence and simplicity of soul he shows when, calling a little one, he said to his disciples: "Amen I say to you, unless you be converted and become as little children, you shall not enter into the kingdom of heaven" (Mt 18:3–5).[27]

In the first millennium, the Church, east and west, administered Communion to nursing infants at their Baptism (under the species of wine) and frequently thereafter.[28] This practice, which continues

---

to receive the body of Christ with faith and devotion"; and §2: "The Most Holy Eucharist, however, can be administered to children in danger of death if they can distinguish the body of Christ from ordinary food and receive communion reverently."

[27] Sacred Congregation of the Discipline of the Sacraments, Decree on First Communion, *Quam Singulari* (1910) (*AAS* 2 [1910]: 577–83), in Seasoltz, *The New Liturgy*, 17.

[28] See *Quam Singulari*:

> The Catholic Church from the beginning took care to bring Christ to the little ones through eucharistic communion, which was given even to the sucklings. This as was prescribed in almost all the ancient rituals till the thirteenth century, was done at baptism, and the same custom prevailed for a long time in some places; it is still in vogue with the Greeks and Orientals. But to avoid all danger, lest the children should spit

in the Eastern rites, gradually shifted in the Latin rite by the thirteenth century to reception of First Communion at the age of reason,
a change solidified by the decree of the Fourth Lateran Council that
made Confession and Communion obligatory once a year only upon
reaching the age of reason.[29]

Despite this clear norm, the age of First Communion tended to be
further postponed by considering the age of reason for the Eucharist
to be later than that for the sacrament of Penance.[30] The result was
that children were needlessly deprived of the spiritual nourishment of
the Eucharist, its infusion of charity, and the protection against sin
afforded by it. The decree states:

> This custom, by which, under the plea of safeguarding the
> august sacrament, the faithful were kept away from the same,
> was the cause of many evils. It happened that the innocence
> of childhood, torn away from the embraces of Christ, was
> deprived of the sap of interior life; from which it also fol-
> lowed that youth destitute of this strong help, surrounded by
> so many snares, having lost its candor, fell into vice before
> ever tasting of the sacred mysteries. And even though a more
> thorough instruction and an accurate sacramental confession
> should precede the first holy communion, which does not
> happen everywhere, yet the loss of first innocence is always
> to be deplored and might have been avoided by receiving the
> holy Eucharist in more tender years.
>
> Not less is the custom, which exists in many places, to
> be condemned, according to which children are not allowed
> to receive the sacrament of penance before they are admitted

---

out the consecrated host, the custom obtained from the beginning of
giving the holy Eucharist under the species of wine alone. The infants
did not, however, receive holy communion only at baptism, but they
frequently afterward partook of the divine repast. For it was the custom
in many churches to give communion to the children immediately after
the communion of the adults. (Seasoltz, *The New Liturgy*, 17)

[29] Fourth Lateran Council (1215), ch. 21 (DS, 812).

[30] See *Quam Singulari*: "But in establishing the year when children come to the
use of reason many errors and deplorable abuses have crept in, in the course of
time. There were those who considered one age necessary for the sacrament of
penance, another for holy eucharist. . . . And thus . . . the age of ten years was
fixed for receiving first holy communion in some places, in others fourteen
years and even more were required" (Seasoltz, *The New Liturgy*, 18).

to communion, or else absolution is not given to them. . . . Such injury is caused by those who insist on an extraordinary preparation for first holy communion, more than is reasonable, not realizing that this kind of precaution proceeds from the errors of the Jansenists, who maintain that holy Eucharist is a reward, not a remedy for human frailty. The Council of Trent holds a different opinion when it teaches that it is "an antidote by which we are freed from daily faults and preserved from mortal sins,"[31] which doctrine has lately been inculcated by a decree[32] . . . in which daily approach to communion is opened to all, both old and young, two conditions only being required, the state of grace and a right intention. Neither does it appear reasonable that while formerly even sucklings received the remnant of the sacred particles, at present an extraordinary preparation should be required from the children who are in the happy state of innocence.[33]

The decree *Quam Singulari* successfully reversed the long trend of excessively postponing First Communion and, together with the decree *Sacra Tridentina Synodus* on frequent Communion, was of great benefit to the life of the Church.

The Congregation for Divine Worship and the Discipline of the Sacraments' 2004 Instruction *Redemptionis Sacramentum* gives the following guidelines on preparation for First Communion and its celebration:

The First Communion of children must always be preceded by sacramental confession and absolution. Moreover First Communion should always be administered by a Priest and never outside the celebration of Mass. Apart from exceptional cases, it is not particularly appropriate for First Communion to be administered on Holy Thursday of the Lord's Supper. Another day should be chosen instead, such as a Sunday between the Second and the Sixth Sunday of Easter, or the Solemnity of the Body and Blood of Christ, or the Sundays of Ordinary Time, since Sunday is rightly regarded as the day

---

[31] Council of Trent, On the Sacrament of the Eucharist (session 13), can. 2.

[32] *Sacra Tridentina Synodus*.

[33] *Quam Singulari* (Seasoltz, *The New Liturgy*, 18–19).

of the Eucharist. "Children who have not attained the age of reason, or those whom" the Parish Priest "has determined to be insufficiently prepared" should not come forward to receive the Holy Eucharist. Where it happens, however, that a child who is exceptionally mature for his age is judged to be ready for receiving the Sacrament, the child must not be denied First Communion provided he has received sufficient instruction.[34]

VIATICUM

Viaticum is one of the three last rites of the Church, together with Anointing of the Sick and Penance. It refers to the administration of Holy Communion to those in danger of death. The Latin word means "provisions for a journey." Here the journey is to eternal life. The Church earnestly desires that those who are in danger of death be nourished by Viaticum, according to the *Code of Canon Law*, canons 921 and 922:

> The Christian faithful who are in danger of death from any cause are to be nourished by holy communion in the form of Viaticum.

> Even if they have been nourished by holy communion on the same day, however, those in danger of death are strongly urged to receive communion again.

> While the danger of death lasts, it is recommended that holy communion be administered often, but on separate days.

> Holy Viaticum for the sick is not to be delayed too long; those who have the care of souls are to be zealous and vigilant that the sick are nourished by Viaticum while fully conscious.

Children in danger of death can and should receive Viaticum as long as they are capable of distinguishing the Eucharist from ordinary food and can receive it reverently, according to canon 913, §2.

---

[34] Congregation for Divine Worship and the Discipline of the Sacraments, Instruction on Certain Matters to Be Observed or to Be Avoided Regarding the Most Holy Eucharist, *Redemptionis Sacramentum* (2004), §87.

THE RECEPTION OF COMMUNION

Communion Under Both Species

St. Thomas Aquinas treats the question of Communion under both species in *ST* III, question 80, article 12, in which he asks whether it is lawful to receive the Body of Christ without the precious Blood. In support, he cites the "custom of many churches for the body of Christ to be given to the communicant without His blood."[35] He then answers that the common practice in the Latin rite of the faithful to receive only the Body of Christ, without the chalice, was due to practical considerations, so as to facilitate the distribution of Communion and lessen the chance of spilling the precious blood:

> Two points should be observed regarding the use of this sacrament, one on the part of the sacrament, the other on the part of the recipients; on the part of the sacrament it is proper for both the body and the blood to be received, since the perfection of the sacrament lies in both, and consequently, since it is the priest's duty both to consecrate and finish the sacrament, he ought on no account to receive Christ's body without the blood.
>
> But on the part of the recipient the greatest reverence and caution are called for, lest anything happen which is unworthy of so great a mystery. Now this could especially happen in receiving the blood, for, if incautiously handled, it might easily be spilt. And because the multitude of the Christian people increased, in which there are old, young, and children, some of whom have not enough discretion to observe due caution in using this sacrament, on that account it is a prudent custom in some churches for the blood not to be offered to the reception of the people, but to be received by the priest alone.

The Council of Trent defined that it is not necessary for the faithful to receive Communion under both species and that the full effects of grace are given by Communion under either species:

---

[35] *ST* III, q. 80, a. 12, sc.

> This holy Synod . . . declares and teaches that laymen, and clerics when not consecrating, are not obliged by any divine precept to receive the sacrament of the Eucharist under both species; and that neither can it by any means be doubted, without injury to faith, that Communion under either species is sufficient for them unto salvation.[36]

The reason for this is that "it must be confessed that Christ whole and entire and a true sacrament is received even under either species alone, and that on that account, as far as regards its fruit, those who receive only one species are not to be deprived of any grace which is necessary for salvation."[37]

The Council of Trent also declared that the Church has the power to determine in different ways, in accordance with what is suggested by the circumstances of the times, whatever does not pertain to the essence of the sacraments.[38] This principle is then applied to the question of Communion under both species.

The Second Vatican Council, in *Sacrosanctum Concilium*, §55, provides for the possibility of distributing Communion under both kinds to the laity of the Latin rite:

> The dogmatic principles which were laid down by the Council of Trent remaining intact, Communion under both kinds may be granted when the bishops think fit, not only to clerics and religious, but also to the laity, in cases to be determined by the Apostolic See.

The current *Code of Canon Law*, canon 925, states simply: "Holy Communion is to be given under the form of bread alone, or under both species according to the norm of the liturgical laws, or even under the form of wine alone in a case of necessity."

The *General Instruction on the Roman Missal* gives the general principles governing Communion under both kinds:

---

[36] Council of Trent, On Communion under Both Kinds and the Communion of Little Children (session 21), ch. 1 (DS, 1726–27).

[37] Ibid., ch. 3 (DS, 1729).

[38] Ibid., ch. 2 (DS, 1728).

Holy Communion has a fuller form as a sign when it takes place under both kinds. For in this form the sign of the Eucharistic banquet is more clearly evident and clearer expression is given to the divine will by which the new and eternal Covenant is ratified in the Blood of the Lord, as also the connection between the Eucharistic banquet and the eschatological banquet in the Kingdom of the Father.

Sacred pastors should take care to ensure that the faithful who participate in the rite or are present at it, are made aware by the most suitable means possible of the Catholic teaching on the form of Holy Communion as laid down by the Ecumenical Council of Trent. Above all, they should instruct the Christian faithful that the Catholic faith teaches that Christ, whole and entire, and the true Sacrament, is received even under only one species, and hence that as regards the resulting fruits, those who receive under only one species are not deprived of any grace that is necessary for salvation.

Furthermore, they should teach that the Church, in her administration of the Sacraments, has the power to lay down or alter whatever provisions, apart from the substance of the Sacraments, that she judges to be more readily conducive to reverence for the Sacraments and the good of the recipients, in view of changing conditions, times, and places. However, at the same time the faithful should be instructed to participate more readily in this sacred rite, by which the sign of the Eucharistic banquet is made more fully evident.[39]

The *Norms for the Distribution and Reception of Holy Communion Under Both Kinds in the Dioceses of the United States of America* (2001) cautions against an excessive use of extraordinary ministers, which might mean limiting the distribution of Communion under both species or using intinction (the dipping of the host in the chalice and then distributing on the tongue):

In practice, the need to avoid obscuring the role of the priest and the deacon as the ordinary ministers of Holy Communion by an excessive use of extraordinary ministers might in some circumstances constitute a reason either for limiting the

---

[39] *GIRM*, §§281–282. Further guidelines are given in *GIRM*, §§281–284.

distribution of Holy Communion under both species or for using intinction instead of distributing the Precious Blood from the chalice.[40]

The Congregation for Divine Worship and the Discipline of the Sacraments' 2004 *Redemptionis Sacramentum* observes similarly that Communion under both kinds in celebrations with large numbers of communicants entails various practical problems, in which cases it should not be offered.[41] But it stipulates that "the option of administering Communion by intinction always remains. If this modality is employed, however, hosts should be used which are neither too thin nor too small, and the communicant should receive the Sacrament from the Priest only on the tongue."[42]

---

[40] United States Conference of Catholic Bishops, *Norms for the Distribution and Reception of Holy Communion Under Both Kinds in the Dioceses of the United States of America* (Washington, DC: USCCB, 2002), §24 (p. 13). Intinction is also put forward as an option sometimes to be preferred in the document *Sacramentali Communione*, §6 (Extending the Practice of Communion Under Both Kinds), issued in 1970 by the Sacred Congregation for Divine Worship: "Otherwise the preference should be for the rite of communion under both kinds by intinction: it is more likely to obviate the practical difficulties and to ensure the reverence due the Sacrament more effectively. Intinction makes access to Communion under both kinds easier and safer for the faithful of all ages and conditions; at the same time it preserves the truth present in the more complete sign" (*Documents on the Liturgy, 1963–1979: Conciliar, Papal, and Curial Texts*, ed. Thomas C. O'Brien [Collegeville, MN: Liturgical Press, 1982], 666).

[41] Congregation for Divine Worship and the Discipline of the Sacraments, *Redemptionis Sacramentum*, §102:

The chalice should not be administered to lay members of Christ's faithful where there is such a large number of communicants that it is difficult to gauge the amount of wine for the Eucharist and there is a danger that "more than a reasonable quantity of the Blood of Christ remains to be consumed at the end of the celebration." The same is true wherever access to the chalice would be difficult to arrange, or where such a large amount of wine would be required that its certain provenance and quality could only be known with difficulty, or wherever there is not an adequate number of sacred ministers or extraordinary ministers of Holy Communion with proper formation, or where a notable part of the people continues to prefer not to approach the chalice for various reasons, so that the sign of unity would in some sense be negated.

[42] Ibid., §103.

Communion in the Hand according to the Instruction *Memoriale Domini*

The fittingness of the practice of Communion on the tongue compared with Communion in the hand is discussed in the Instruction *Memoriale Domini*, on the Manner of Distributing Holy Communion, from the Congregation for Divine Worship under Pope Paul VI.[43] The Instruction gives a good summary of the evolution of the practice of receiving Communion. It acknowledges the ancient practice of Communion in the hand while emphasizing the reverence with which Communion was thus distributed and received:

> It is quite true that ancient usage at times allowed the faithful to receive this divine food in the hand and to put it in their own mouth. It is also true that in the earliest years they could take the blessed sacrament away with them from the place of worship, principally in order that they might use it as viaticum in case they had to face danger for the sake of professing their faith.
>
> But it is also true that the laws of the Church and the writings of the Fathers give ample witness to a supreme reverence and utmost caution toward the eucharist. "No one . . . eats that flesh who has not first adored it"[44]; everyone receiving it is warned: ". . . Receive it with care that nothing of it be lost to you"[45]; "For it is the body of Christ."[46]

The Instruction then goes on to speak about the spread of the practice of Communion on the tongue, spurred by the growth of Eucharistic doctrine and devotion:[47]

---

[43] Sacred Congregation for Divine Worship, Instruction on the Manner of Distributing Holy Communion, *Memoriale Domini* (1969) (*AAS* 61 [1969]: 541–45; O'Brien, *Documents on the Liturgy*, 643–46).

[44] Augustine, *Ennarationes in Psalmos* 98.9 (PL, 37:1264).

[45] Cyril of Jerusalem, *Mystagogic Catecheses* 5.21 (PG, 33:1126).

[46] Sacred Congregation for Divine Worship, *Memoriale Domini* (O'Brien, *Documents on the Liturgy*, 644). The quotation is from Hippolytus, *Apostolic Tradition*, no. 37, ed. Bernard Botte (Paris: Cerf, 1963), 84.

[47] For this development around the ninth century, see Jungmann, *The Mass of the Roman Rite*, 2:381–82.

With the passage of time as the truth of the eucharistic mystery, its power, and Christ's presence in it were more deeply understood, the usage adopted was that the minister himself placed the particle of the consecrated bread on the tongue of the communicant. This measure was prompted by a keen sense both of reverence toward the sacrament and of the humility with which it should be received.[48]

The Instruction gives several reasons in favor of continuing the mode of receiving Communion on the tongue. The most important reason is that Communion on the tongue better expresses the reverence due to the Bread of Life, its distinction from ordinary food that we give to ourselves, and the humility of the recipient in the face of a gift from above. This should help reinforce faith in Christ's mysterious presence in the sacrament and aid the faithful to receive with a better disposition:

> In view of the overall contemporary situation of the Church, this manner of distributing communion must be retained. Not only is it based on a practice handed down over many centuries, but above all it signifies the faithful's reverence for the eucharist. Such a practice in no way takes away from the personal dignity of those coming to so great a sacrament and it is a part of the preparation that is a prerequisite for the fruitful reception of the Lord's body.[49] The reverence involved is a sign of sharing not "in ordinary bread and wine"[50] but in the Lord's body and blood.[51]

Two other reasons given in favor of the traditional practice are that it safeguards against profanation of the sacrament by making profanation or theft of the Sacred Host more difficult and by reducing the danger of fragments being lost and the consequent erosion of faith in the real presence:

---

[48] Sacred Congregation for Divine Worship, *Memoriale Domini* (O'Brien, *Documents on the Liturgy*, 644).

[49] See Augustine, *On the Psalms* 98.9 (PL, 37:1264–65).

[50] See Justin Martyr, *Apologia* 1.66 (PG, 6:427).

[51] Sacred Congregation for Divine Worship, *Memoriale Domini* (O'Brien, *Documents on the Liturgy*, 644–45).

Further, this way of distributing communion, which must now be regarded as the normal practice, more effectively, ensures that communion is distributed with the required reverence, decorum, and dignity; that there is less danger of disrespect for the eucharistic elements, in which "in a unique way Christ is present, whole and entire, God and man, substantially and continuously";[52] finally, that the caution is exercised which the Church has always counseled regarding the particles of the consecrated bread: "What you might permit to fall, think of as being the loss of a part of your own body."[53]

However, after declaring that Communion on the tongue is for these reasons the more fitting manner of receiving the Eucharist and thus should be retained, this Instruction also acknowledges that the Church is concerned to adapt her norms to the needs of the faithful, and therefore Paul VI decided to submit the question to the bishops of the Latin rite, permitting them to choose to allow Communion in the hand as long as three dangers are avoided: "the possibility of a lessening of reverence toward the august sacrament of the altar, its profanation, and the watering down of the true doctrine of the eucharist."[54] The last point refers to the danger of the weakening of the awareness of the real presence of Christ whole and entire in every fragment of the consecrated host.

Redemptionis Sacramentum, §92 addresses the issue of Communion in the hand. It states that a person always has the option to receive on the tongue, but to receive in the hand, a person must be in an area where there is the permission of the Bishops' Conference and the Apostolic See, and special care should be taken to prevent theft and profanation:

Although each of the faithful always has the right to receive Holy Communion on the tongue, at his choice, if any communicant should wish to receive the Sacrament in the hand, in areas where the Bishops' Conference with the *recognitio* of the Apostolic See has given permission, the sacred host is to

---

[52] Sacred Congregation of Rites, *Eucharisticum Mysterium*, §9.

[53] Sacred Congregation for Divine Worship, *Memoriale Domini* (O'Brien, *Documents on the Liturgy*, 645). The citation is from St. Cyril of Jerusalem, *Mystagogic Catecheses* 5.21 (PG, 33:1126).

[54] Ibid.

be administered to him or her. However, special care should
be taken to ensure that the host is consumed by the communicant in the presence of the minister, so that no one goes away
carrying the Eucharistic species in his hand. If there is a risk
of profanation, then Holy Communion should not be given in
the hand to the faithful.

Reception of Communion according to the General Instruction of the Roman Missal

The *General Instruction of the Roman Missal* gives the following
instruction on reception of Holy Communion:

> The Priest then takes the paten or ciborium and approaches
> the communicants, who usually come up in procession.
>
> It is not permitted for the faithful to take the consecrated
> Bread or the sacred chalice by themselves and, still less, to
> hand them on from one to another among themselves. The
> norm established for the Dioceses of the United States of
> America is that Holy Communion is to be received standing,
> unless an individual member of the faithful wishes to receive
> Communion while kneeling.[55]
>
> When receiving Holy Communion, the communicant
> bows his or her head before the Sacrament as a gesture of
> reverence and receives the Body of the Lord from the minister.
> The consecrated host may be received either on the tongue or
> in the hand, at the discretion of each communicant. When
> Holy Communion is received under both kinds, the sign of
> reverence is also made before receiving the Precious Blood.[56]

The reason the faithful cannot administer Communion to themselves is that the sensible sign of receiving Communion from a minister
manifests that salvation comes from Jesus Christ and not from ourselves.[57] It is fitting that the bread from heaven be received from a

---

[55] See Congregation for Divine Worship and the Discipline of the Sacraments,
Redemptionis Sacramentum, §91.

[56] *GIRM*, §160 (*RM*, 50).

[57] See Taft, *Beyond East and West*, 134–35: "The general rule in communion rites
right up through the Middle Ages, in both East and West, was that communion
is not just *taken*, not even by the clergy, but *given* and *received*. For communion

minister distinct from ourselves who represents Christ giving Himself to us. The ordinary minister, for this reason, is the bishop, priest, or deacon (CIC, can. 910, §1).

Extraordinary Ministers of Holy Communion

In cases of necessity, extraordinary ministers may be used for the administration of Communion. However, it is always preferable to have Communion administered by priests and deacons if reasonably possible because they alone, through the character of Holy Orders, have received a sacramental consecration so as to act in the person of Christ the Head and administer the Eucharist. The extraordinary minister of Holy Communion is defined by CIC, canon 910, §2, as "an acolyte or another member of the Christian faithful designated according to the norm of can. 230, §3," which states that extraordinary ministers of the distribution of Holy Communion are to be used to supply this properly clerical task only "when the need of the Church warrants it and ministers are lacking." Thus if there are sufficient priests to distribute Communion in a reasonable amount of time, extraordinary ministers should not be used.[58]

Extraordinary ministers are not to approach the altar until the priest has already communicated, so as not to confuse their roles with those of the priest or deacon, and they are to receive the vessel containing the sacred species from the hands of the priest.[59]

---

is at once a ministry and a gift and a sharing, and as such is *administered* to the communicant through the hands of another."

[58] See also Congregation for Divine Worship and the Discipline of the Sacraments, *Redemptionis Sacramentum*, §88: "It is the Priest celebrant's responsibility to minister Communion, perhaps assisted by other Priests or Deacons; and he should not resume the Mass until after the Communion of the faithful is concluded. Only when there is a necessity may extraordinary ministers assist the Priest celebrant in accordance with the norm of law."

[59] See *GIRM*, §162:

In the distribution of Communion the Priest may be assisted by other Priests who happen to be present. If such Priests are not present and there is a truly large number of communicants, the Priest may call upon extraordinary ministers to assist him, that is, duly instituted acolytes or even other faithful who have been duly deputed for this purpose. In case of necessity, the Priest may depute suitable faithful for this single occasion. These ministers should not approach the altar before the Priest has received Communion, and they are always to receive from

THANKSGIVING AFTER COMMUNION

Together with frequent Communion, the practice of thanksgiving after Communion is an indispensable aid for gathering the fruit that God wishes to impart to us. Given that Christ's humanity remains in us after Communion until the sacred species is digested, it is extremely fitting that Jesus receive a particular adoration during this time after Communion in which the communicant is, in effect, a holy tabernacle. In *Mediator Dei*, §126, Pius XII strongly recommends this practice:

> Why then, Venerable Brethren, should we not approve of those who, when they receive holy communion, remain on in closest familiarity with their divine Redeemer even after the congregation has been officially dismissed, and that not only for the consolation of conversing with Him, but also to render Him due thanks and praise and especially to ask help to defend their souls against anything that may lessen the efficacy of the sacrament and to do everything in their power to cooperate with the action of Christ who is so intimately present. We exhort them to do so in a special manner by carrying out their resolutions, by exercising the Christian virtues, as also by applying to their own necessities the riches they have received with royal Liberality. The author of that golden book *The Imitation of Christ* certainly speaks in accordance with the letter and the spirit of the liturgy, when he gives the following advice to the person who approaches the altar, "Remain on in secret and take delight in your God; for He is yours whom the whole world cannot take away from you."

Making an act of thanksgiving after Communion helps to complete the interior gift of self to God, which is the very heart of active participation in the sacrifice. Communion enables the faithful to offer themselves back to God not merely through their own power, but as they have been enriched by receiving Christ. After Holy Communion,

---

the hands of the Priest Celebrant the vessel containing the species of the Most Holy Eucharist for distribution to the faithful. (*RM*, 50)

See USCCB, *Norms for the Distribution and Reception of Holy Communion Under Both Kinds in the Dioceses of the United States of America*, §40 (p. 19).

the gift of oneself back to God includes Jesus Christ, for He has been received in the most intimate way.

St. John of the Cross, although he is not directly speaking about Holy Communion, but rather about the state of mystical matrimony with God, gives a magnificent description of what the soul can do after Holy Communion:

> Since God gives himself with a free and gracious will, so too the soul (possessing a will more generous and free the more it is united with God) gives to God, God himself in God; and this is a *true and complete gift of the soul to God*. It is conscious there that God is indeed its own and that it possesses him by inheritance, with the right of ownership, as his adopted child through the grace of his gift of himself. Having him for its own, it can give him and communicate him to whomever it wishes. Thus it gives him to its Beloved, who is the very God who gave himself to it. By this donation it repays God for all it owes him, since it willingly gives as much as it receives from him.[60]

Perfect spousal love creates a union of wills. This means that the soul is not content with receiving Jesus, but, impelled by love, seeks to imitate God's giving and thus to return the gift received through self-giving love. But what can the soul give in return? Since the soul has received nothing less than God Himself indwelling, she can return God to God by giving herself, as she has been enriched, entirely to God through love.

---

[60] John of the Cross, *The Living Flame of Love*, stanza 3, no. 78, in *Collected Works of St. John of the Cross*, trans. Kieran Kavanaugh and Otilio Rodriguez, rev. ed. (Washington, DC: ICS, 1991), 706 (my italics). See also John of the Cross, *Living Flame*, stanza 3, no. 80: "This is the soul's deep satisfaction and happiness: To see that it gives God more than it is worth in itself; and this it does with that very divine light and divine heat that are given to it. It does this in heaven by means of the light of glory and in this life by means of a highly illumined faith" (ibid., 707).

STUDY QUESTIONS

1. (a) What does St. Ambrose say about frequent Communion? (b) What do the Council of Trent and the *Catechism of the Council of Trent* say about frequent Communion?
2. What are the conditions for frequent or daily Communion given by Pius X?
3. What are the criteria for the reception of Holy Communion by children?
4. (a) Why is it possible for the faithful to receive Communion under only one species? (b) Why is it good to receive Communion under both kinds? (c) Why might it be advisable for Communion to be received only under the species of bread? (d) Why or when might intinction be considered the best method for distributing Communion? In what document does the Congregation for Divine Worship under Pope Paul VI speak of Communion in the hand? For what reasons does it recommend Communion on the tongue? What are the conditions it establishes for Communion in the hand?
5. Who are the ordinary ministers of Holy Communion? When can extraordinary ministers be used? When do extraordinary ministers approach the altar during Mass? Can they themselves take the vessels off of the altar to distribute Communion?
6. What is the special value of time spent in thanksgiving after Holy Communion?

SUGGESTIONS FOR FURTHER READING

Pius X. Decree on Frequent and Daily Reception of Holy Communion *Sacra Tridentina Synodus*. December 20, 1905.

Sacred Congregation of the Discipline of the Sacraments. Decree *Quam Singulari*. August 8, 1910.

✠

CHAPTER SIXTEEN

Eucharistic Adoration

EUCHARISTIC ADORATION AND THE THREE ENDS OF THE EUCHARIST

Since Christ is truly present in the Eucharist in His sacred humanity hypostatically united with the divine nature, the Eucharist should receive the adoration of *latria* that is given exclusively to God. Adoration of Christ in the Blessed Sacrament is a natural consequence of the Church's faith in the real substantial presence of Christ in the Eucharist.

Adoration corresponds most directly to the first of the three principal purposes for which Christ instituted the Eucharist, which is that Christ wished to perpetuate His adorable human presence among us after ascending definitively into heaven. The Eucharist is the solution to this problem. The divinity of Christ is omnipresent, but, after His Ascension, His humanity is substantially present only in heaven and in the Eucharist. Since the Son of God became man for us and has devised a marvelous way to remain with us in the Eucharist in the substantial presence of His humanity, it follows that adoration of and intimate encounter with Christ in the Blessed Sacrament is not an afterthought, but rather an essential aspect of the Eucharist. As Israel adored the special presence of God (the *shekhinah*) in the Ark of the Covenant and in the Holy of Holies in the Temple, how could the Church not fittingly adore the substantial presence of Christ, who makes Himself present with much greater generosity in every tabernacle?

Adoration is also intimately related to the other two ends of the Eucharist. Christ is adored in the Eucharist as the sacrificial Victim of Calvary whose body was given for us and whose blood was "poured out for many for the forgiveness of sins" (Matt 26:28). His presence

cannot be separated from His sacrificial self-gift. Eucharistic adoration enables us to spend time intimately thanking Him for His
sacrificial gift expressed in His Eucharistic words: "This is my body
which is given for you" (Luke 22:19). In the Eucharist we encounter
Him as the Victim of merciful love, and it is the nature of love that it
calls for a return in kind.[1]

At the same time, Christ is present in the tabernacle as the living
Bread from heaven, the "medicine of immortality," the "desire of the
everlasting hills,"[2] the perfect rest that fulfills every natural and supernatural desire. Eucharistic adoration helps us to nurture our desire so
that we grow in hunger and thirst for the Bridegroom who feeds His
Bride on His own Flesh and Blood so that she may share ever more
in His divinity.

Adoration also aids the faithful to be inserted more deeply into
the communion of the Mystical Body. As the practice of pilgrimage to
Jerusalem for the great festivals helped to consolidate the religious and
social unity of Israel, so Eucharistic adoration brings the faithful of
the New Covenant throughout the Catholic world together to adore
the same Lord present in every tabernacle. No geographical boundary
limits the unity of worship of the one Lord and His one Sacrifice. Furthermore, adoration of the Lord who has given Himself for the flock
helps nurture the faithful in cultivating the attitude of self-gift, which
is the heart of Catholic social doctrine.

The growth of Eucharistic adoration over the past two millennia
is a beautiful example of the organic development of doctrine and
of Christian life and worship. Like Mary, who kept the words of the
Lord in her heart and meditated on them day and night, the Church
has reflected over the centuries on her greatest treasure and the fitting
homage to give to it. The second millennium has witnessed the constant growth of the personal prayer of the faithful before the Blessed
Sacrament. Key figures in this development include St. Francis of
Assisi; St. Juliana of Cornillon, who received revelations concerning
the institution of the feast of Corpus Christi;[3] St. Thomas Aquinas,
who wrote the liturgy for Corpus Christi;[4] St. Louis de Montfort;

---

[1] See Thérèse of Lisieux, *Story of a Soul*, 194–200, 277.
[2] Gen 49:26; Litany of the Sacred Heart.
[3] See Benedict XVI, General Audience, November 17, 2010, on St. Juliana of
     Cornillon.
[4] See Paul Murray, *Aquinas at Prayer: The Bible, Mysticism and Poetry* (London:
     Bloomsbury, 2013), 167–259.

St. Alphonsus Liguori; St. Julian Peter Eymard; and many other saints.[5]

Objections to Eucharistic Adoration and a Response by Joseph Ratzinger

Joseph Ratzinger has a beautiful chapter on Eucharistic adoration in *The Spirit of the Liturgy* in which he addresses the objection that Eucharistic adoration is a late development in the life of the Church and the fruit of a decadence of her Eucharistic faith. He poses the objection as follows:

> The Church of the first millennium knew nothing of tabernacles. Instead, first the shrine of the Word, and then even more so the altar, served as sacred "tent." Approached by steps, it was sheltered, and its sacredness underscored, by a "ciborium," or marble baldacchino, with burning lamps hanging from it. A curtain was hung between the columns of the ciborium. The tabernacle as sacred tent, as place of the *Shekinah*, the presence of the living Lord, developed only in the second millennium. It was the fruit of passionate theological struggles and their resulting clarifications, in which the permanent presence of Christ in the consecrated Host emerged with greater clarity.
>
> Now here we run up against the decadence theory, the canonization of the early days and romanticism about the first century. Transubstantiation (the substantial change of the bread and wine), the adoration of the Lord in the Blessed Sacrament, eucharistic devotions with monstrance and processions—all these things, it is alleged, are medieval errors, errors from which we must once and for all take our leave. "The Eucharistic Gifts are for eating, not for looking at"— these and similar slogans are all too familiar.[6]

---

[5] For the history of Eucharistic adoration, see Benedict J. Groeschel and James Monti, *In the Presence of Our Lord: The History, Theology, and Psychology of Eucharistic Devotion* (Huntington, IN: *Our Sunday Visitor*, 1997).

[6] Joseph Ratzinger, *The Spirit of the Liturgy*, 85 (*TL*, 52).

Ratzinger responds to this objection by stressing the notion of doctrinal development. We have seen how the Berengarian heresy in the eleventh century was a great stimulus both to theological reflection on the Eucharist and to the developing practice of Eucharistic devotion:

> "He is here, He Himself, the whole of Himself, and He remains here." This realization came upon the Middle Ages with a wholly new intensity. It was caused in part by the deepening of theological reflection, but still more important was the new experience of the saints, especially in the Franciscan movement and in the new evangelization undertaken by the Order of Preachers. What happens in the Middle Ages is not a misunderstanding due to losing sight of what is central, but a new dimension of the reality of Christianity opening up through the experience of the saints, supported and illuminated by the reflection of the theologians. At the same time, this new development is in complete continuity with what had always been believed hitherto. Let me say it again: This deepened awareness of faith is impelled by the knowledge that in the consecrated species He is there and remains there. When a man experiences this with every fiber of his heart and mind and senses, the consequence is inescapable: "We must make a proper place for this Presence."[7]

This development brings to absolute fulfillment the typology of the worship of the presence of the Lord in the Ark of the Covenant. How could we not adore Christ, the new Temple of the New Covenant, who has willed to dwell in the tabernacle, the beating heart of all our temples? Ratzinger writes:

> And so little by little the tabernacle takes shape, and more and more, always in a spontaneous way, it takes the place previously occupied by the now-disappeared "Ark of the Covenant." In fact, the tabernacle is the complete fulfillment of what the Ark of the Covenant represented. It is the place of the "Holy of Holies." It is the tent of God, His throne. Here He is among us. His presence (*Shekinah*) really does now dwell

---

[7]   Ibid., 89 (*TL*, 54–55).

among us—in the humblest parish church no less than in the grandest cathedral. Even though the definitive Temple will only come to be when the world has become the New Jerusalem, still what the Temple in Jerusalem pointed to is here present in a supreme way. The New Jerusalem is anticipated in the humble species of bread.[8]

Ratzinger then addresses the objection made by Luther,[9] as well as twentieth-century theologians, that Jesus instituted the Eucharist for eating and not for adoring:

So let no one say, "The Eucharist is for eating, not looking at." It is not "ordinary bread," as the most ancient traditions constantly emphasize. Eating it—as we have just said—is a spiritual process, involving the whole man. "Eating" it means worshipping it. Eating it means letting it come into me, so that my "I" is transformed and opens up into the great "we," so that we become "one" in Him (cf. Gal 3:16). Thus adoration is not opposed to Communion, nor is it merely added to it. No, Communion only reaches its true depths when it is supported and surrounded by adoration. The Eucharistic Presence in the tabernacle does not set another view of the Eucharist alongside or against the Eucharistic celebration, but simply signifies its complete fulfillment. For this Presence has the effect, of course, of keeping the Eucharist forever in church. The church never becomes a lifeless space but is always filled with the presence of the Lord, which comes out of the celebration, leads us into it, and always makes us participants in the cosmic Eucharist. What man of faith has not experienced this? A church without the Eucharistic Presence is somehow dead, even when it invites people to pray. But a church in which the eternal light is burning before the tabernacle is always alive, is always something more than a building made of stones. In this place the Lord is always waiting for me, calling me, wanting to make me "eucharistic." In this way, He prepares me for the Eucharist, sets me in motion toward His return.

---

[8] Ibid., 89–90 (*TL*, 55–56).
[9] Martin Luther, *The Misuse of the Mass* (*LW*, 36:172–73).

The changes in the Middle Ages brought losses, but they also provided a wonderful spiritual deepening. They unfolded the magnitude of the mystery instituted at the Last Supper and enabled it to be experienced with a new fullness. How many saints . . . were nourished and led to the Lord by this experience! We must not lose this richness. If the presence of the Lord is to touch us in a concrete way, the tabernacle must also find its proper place in the architecture of our church buildings.[10]

MAGISTERIAL TEXTS ON EUCHARISTIC ADORATION

The post-conciliar Magisterium has a very rich teaching on the fundamental importance of Eucharistic adoration in the life of the Church.

Paul VI

In his encyclical *Mysterium Fidei* (1965), Paul VI speaks of the dignity of the Christian faithful who have God incarnate so close to them in every tabernacle that they can visit Him and converse intimately at all times. Moses exulted in the Lord's presence to Israel: "For what great nation is there that has a god so near to it as the Lord our God is to us, whenever we call upon him?" (Deut 4:7). But the New Israel has received a better Indwelling Presence of the Lord who died for us:

> No one can fail to see that the divine Eucharist bestows an incomparable dignity upon the Christian people. For it is not just while the Sacrifice is being offered and the Sacrament is being confected, but also after the Sacrifice has been offered and the Sacrament confected—while the Eucharist is reserved in churches or oratories—that Christ is truly Emmanuel, which means "God with us." For He is in the midst of us day and night; He dwells in us with the fullness of grace and of truth.[11]

---

[10] Ratzinger, *The Spirit of the Liturgy*, 90–91.
[11] Paul VI, *Mysterium Fidei*, §67.

The Eucharist reserved in the Church makes every parish a spiritual center greater than any other place on earth. Every other holy place, even the Temple of Jerusalem when it still stood in all its splendor, is but a shadow or figure of the substantial presence of Christ under the Eucharistic veils, Christ who is "the invisible Head of the Church, the Redeemer of the world, the center of all hearts, 'by whom all things are and by whom we exist.'"[12]

Paul VI also points out that the best means of fostering the social love that is the kingly task of the faithful in the world is through Eucharistic adoration of the Lord who is love.[13] He exhorts the faithful to visit the Blessed Sacrament daily, and he urges that it be reserved "with great reverence in a prominent place. Such visits are a sign of gratitude, an expression of love and an acknowledgment of the Lord's presence."[14]

In the Credo of the People of God of 1968, at the close of the Year of Faith, Paul VI makes reference to the "sweet duty" of adoring Christ present in the tabernacle, the "living heart" of our churches:

> The unique and indivisible existence of the Lord glorious in heaven is not multiplied, but is rendered present by the sacrament in the many places on earth where Mass is celebrated. And this existence remains present, after the sacrifice, in the Blessed Sacrament which is, in the tabernacle, the living heart of each of our churches. And it is our very sweet duty to honor and adore in the blessed Host which our eyes see, the Incarnate Word whom they cannot see, and who, without leaving heaven, is made present before us.[15]

St. John Paul II

St. John Paul II spoke on numerous occasions of the great importance of Eucharistic devotion in the life of the faithful and especially

---

[12] Ibid., §68.

[13] Ibid., §69: "Hence it is that devotion to the divine Eucharist exerts a great influence upon the soul in the direction of fostering a 'social' love, in which we put the common good ahead of private good, take up the cause of the community, the parish, the universal Church, and extend our charity to the whole world because we know that there are members of Christ everywhere."

[14] Ibid., §66.

[15] Paul VI, *Solemni Hac Liturgia*, §26.

of priests, and he was exemplary in putting this into practice. In his Apostolic Letter *Dominicae Cenae*, §§2–3, he speaks at length about Eucharistic adoration. He begins by saying that the priest is responsible for the Eucharist, and thus has been entrusted to bring it to the whole Church. Priests therefore must be exemplary in bearing witness to Eucharistic devotion,[16] which is "like a life-giving current that links our ministerial or hierarchical priesthood to the common priesthood of the faithful, and presents it in its vertical dimension and with its central value."[17]

He also emphasizes that Eucharistic devotion has a Trinitarian focus. On the altar during the Eucharistic consecration and in the tabernacle there is the humanity of the Son of God, who gave Himself for the glory of His Father, through the Holy Spirit. Christ is present as the Victim who has reconciled us with the Father and won for us the gift of His Spirit. We adore Christ present in this way, both within Mass and outside of it, to try "to repay that love immolated even to the death on the cross: it is our 'Eucharist,' that is to say our giving Him thanks, our praise of Him for having redeemed us by His death and made us sharers in immortal life through His resurrection."[18]

> This worship is directed towards God the Father through Jesus Christ in the Holy Spirit. In the first place towards the Father, who, as St. John's Gospel says, "loved the world so much that he gave his only Son, so that everyone who believes in him may not be lost but may have eternal life." It is also directed, in the Holy Spirit, to the incarnate Son, in the economy of salvation, especially at that moment of supreme dedication and total abandonment of Himself. . . . This worship, given therefore to the Trinity of the Father and of the Son and of the Holy Spirit, above all accompanies and permeates the celebration of the Eucharistic Liturgy. But it must fill our churches also outside the timetable of Masses.

---

[16] John Paul II, *Dominicae Cenae*, §2: "Thus we bishops and priests are entrusted with the great 'mystery of Faith,' and while it is also given to the whole People of God, to all believers in Christ, yet to us has been entrusted the Eucharist also 'for' others, who expect from us a particular witness of veneration and love towards this sacrament, so that they too may be able to be built up and vivified 'to offer spiritual sacrifices.'"

[17] Ibid.

[18] Ibid., §3.

Indeed, since the Eucharistic Mystery was instituted out of love, and makes Christ sacramentally present, it is worthy of thanksgiving and worship. And this worship must be prominent in all our encounters with the Blessed Sacrament, both when we visit our churches and when the sacred species are taken to the sick and administered to them.[19]

Because the Eucharist builds up the Church, John Paul II says that the deepening of Eucharistic worship and adoration will be the test of the renewal of the Church that was the aim of the Second Vatican Council:

The encouragement and the deepening of eucharistic worship are proofs of that authentic renewal which the council set itself as an aim and of which they are the central point. . . . The Church and the world have a great need of eucharistic worship. Jesus waits for us in this sacrament of love. Let us be generous with our time in going to meet Him in adoration and in contemplation that is full of faith and ready to make reparation for the great faults and crimes of the world. May our adoration never cease.[20]

He therefore encourages the forms of Eucharistic devotion traditional in the life of the Church.[21]

John Paul II returns to the subject of Eucharistic adoration in *Ecclesia de Eucharistia*. After lamenting that "in some places the practice of Eucharistic adoration has been almost completely aban-

---

[19] Ibid.
[20] Ibid.
[21] Ibid.:

> Adoration of Christ in this sacrament of love must also find expression in various forms of eucharistic devotion: personal prayer before the Blessed Sacrament, Hours of Adoration, periods of exposition—short, prolonged and annual (Forty Hours)—eucharistic benediction, eucharistic processions, eucharistic congresses. A particular mention should be made at this point of the Solemnity of the Body and Blood of Christ as an act of public worship rendered to Christ present in the Eucharist, a feast instituted by my predecessor Urban IV in memory of the institution of this great Mystery. All this therefore corresponds to the general principles and particular norms already long in existence but newly formulated during or after the Second Vatican Council.

doned,"[22] he explains its great importance in aiding the faithful to contemplate the face of Christ in prayer, clearly speaking from his own experience:

> It is pleasant to spend time with him, to lie close to his breast like the Beloved Disciple (cf. John 13:25) and to feel the infinite love present in his heart. If in our time Christians must be distinguished above all by the "art of prayer," how can we not feel a renewed need to spend time in spiritual converse, in silent adoration, in heartfelt love before Christ present in the Most Holy Sacrament? How often, dear brothers and sisters, have I experienced this, and drawn from it strength, consolation and support!

This practice, repeatedly praised and recommended by the Magisterium,[23] is supported by the example of many saints. Particularly outstanding in this regard was Saint Alphonsus Liguori, who wrote: "Of all devotions, that of adoring Jesus in the Blessed Sacrament is the greatest after the sacraments, the one dearest to God and the one most helpful to us."[24] The Eucharist is a priceless treasure: by not only celebrating it but also by praying before it outside of Mass we are enabled to make contact with the very wellspring of grace. A Christian community desirous of contemplating the face of Christ in the spirit which I proposed in the Apostolic Letters *Novo Millennio Ineunte* and *Rosarium Virginis Mariae* cannot fail also to develop this aspect of Eucharistic worship, which prolongs and increases the fruits of our communion in the body and blood of the Lord.[25]

---

[22] John Paul II, *EE*, §10.

[23] See Paul VI, *Mysterium Fidei*, §66: "In the course of the day the faithful should not omit visiting the Blessed Sacrament, which in accordance with liturgical law must be reserved in churches with great reverence in a prominent place. Such visits are a sign of gratitude, an expression of love and an acknowledgment of the Lord's presence" (*AAS* 57 [1965]: 771).

[24] From Alphonsus Liguori's *Visite al SS. Sacramento e a Maria Santissima* (Visits to the Most Blessed Sacrament and to the Blessed Virgin Mary: For Each Day of the Month).

[25] John Paul II, *EE*, §25 (italics original).

Benedict XVI, *Sacramentum Caritatis*

Pope Benedict XVI returned to the theme of Eucharistic adoration in his 2007 post-synodal apostolic exhortation *Sacramentum Caritatis*, §§66–69, in which he further develops the response that he had given in *The Spirit of the Liturgy* to objections against the practice of Eucharistic adoration:

> During the early phases of the reform, the inherent relationship between Mass and adoration of the Blessed Sacrament was not always perceived with sufficient clarity. For example, an objection that was widespread at the time argued that the eucharistic bread was given to us not to be looked at, but to be eaten. In the light of the Church's experience of prayer, however, this was seen to be a false dichotomy. As Saint Augustine put it: *"nemo autem illam carnem manducat, nisi prius adoraverit; peccemus non adorando—no one eats that flesh without first adoring it; we should sin were we not to adore it."*[26] In the Eucharist, the Son of God comes to meet us and desires to become one with us; eucharistic adoration is simply the natural consequence of the eucharistic celebration, which is itself the Church's supreme act of adoration. Receiving the Eucharist means adoring him whom we receive. Only in this way do we become one with him, and are given, as it were, a foretaste of the beauty of the heavenly liturgy. The act of adoration outside Mass prolongs and intensifies all that takes place during the liturgical celebration itself. Indeed, "only in adoration can a profound and genuine reception mature. And it is precisely this personal encounter with the Lord that then strengthens the social mission contained in the Eucharist, which seeks to break down not only the walls that separate the Lord and ourselves, but also and especially the walls that separate us from one another."

Eucharistic adoration is intrinsic to the Mass, and naturally continues outside the Mass to draw more fruit from the Gift received and to make space for the faithful to give themselves back to the Lord. We would sin, as St. Augustine says, if we did not adore Him who has made

---

[26] Augustine, *Enarrationes in Psalmos* 98.9 (PL, 37:1264).

Himself present, given Himself *for* us in sacrifice, given Himself *to* us in Communion, and continues to abide *with* us until He comes again.

Benedict then calls for more catechesis on the importance of Eucharistic adoration, and recommends that churches and oratories be set aside to offer perpetual adoration.[27] He also mentions that adoration is not just a personal devotion, but one that of its very nature leads to a greater appreciation of the communion of the Church. Through adoration of the sacramental Body, we are nourished in love for the Mystical Body. For this reason it is fitting that there also be times of collective Eucharistic adoration in the parish.[28]

Pope Francis on Adoration

Pope Francis has encouraged Eucharistic adoration on various occasions. In a letter to the Eucharistic Congress held in Genoa, he wrote:

---

[27] Benedict XVI, *Sacramentum Caritatis*, §67:

> With the Synod Assembly, therefore, I heartily recommend to the Church's pastors and to the People of God the practice of eucharistic adoration, both individually and in community. Great benefit would ensue from a suitable catechesis explaining the importance of this act of worship, which enables the faithful to experience the liturgical celebration more fully and more fruitfully. Wherever possible, it would be appropriate, especially in densely populated areas, to set aside specific churches or oratories for perpetual adoration. I also recommend that, in their catechetical training, and especially in their preparation for First Holy Communion, children be taught the meaning and the beauty of spending time with Jesus, and helped to cultivate a sense of awe before his presence in the Eucharist.

[28] Benedict XVI, *Sacramentum Caritatis*, §68:

> The personal relationship which the individual believer establishes with Jesus present in the Eucharist constantly points beyond itself to the whole communion of the Church and nourishes a fuller sense of membership in the Body of Christ. For this reason, besides encouraging individual believers to make time for personal prayer before the Sacrament of the Altar, I feel obliged to urge parishes and other church groups to set aside times for collective adoration. Naturally, already existing forms of eucharistic piety retain their full value. I am thinking, for example, of processions with the Blessed Sacrament, especially the traditional procession on the Solemnity of Corpus Christi, the Forty Hours devotion, local, national and international Eucharistic Congresses, and other similar initiatives. If suitably updated and adapted to local circumstances, these forms of devotion are still worthy of being practised today.

I want to encourage everyone to visit—if possible, every day—especially amid life's difficulties, the Blessed Sacrament of the infinite love of Christ and His mercy, preserved in our churches, and often abandoned, to speak filially with Him, to listen to Him in silence, and to peacefully entrust yourself to Him.[29]

In his homily at the Casa Santa Marta on October 20, 2016, Pope Francis spoke of the necessity of prayer to come to know Jesus Christ. But even "prayer on its own is not enough." There must be worship and silent adoration:

We cannot know the Lord without this habit of worship, to worship in silence, adoration. If I am not mistaken, I believe that this prayer of adoration is the least known by us, it's the one that we do least. Allow me to say this, waste time in front of the Lord, in front of the mystery of Jesus Christ. Worship him. There in silence, the silence of adoration. He is the Saviour and I worship Him.[30]

THE TABERNACLE

To help foster Eucharistic devotion, attention must be given to the architectural prominence of the tabernacle and its relationship with the altar. The altar, as the place of sacrifice and the symbol of its acceptance, should be the heart of every church.[31] After the altar,

---

[29] Francis, Message of July 7, 2016 to the Eucharistic Congress in Genoa, accessed July 7, 2017, http://en.radiovaticana.va/news/2016/07/07/pope_sends_message_for_italy%E2%80%99s_upcoming_eucharistic_congress/1242541.

[30] Francis, Homily of October 20, 2016, accessed July 7, 2017, http://en.radiovaticana.va/news/2016/10/20/pope_catechism_is_not_enough_to_know_jesus_we_need_prayer/1266534.

[31] See William Durand of Mende, *The Rationale Divinorum Officiorum*, trans. Timothy M. Thibodeau (New York: Columbia University Press, 2007), 1:14: "The arrangement of the materials of the church can be likened to the human body. The chancel, that is the place where the altar is, represents the head; the cross, from either side, represents the arms or the hands, while the remaining part extending to the west is seen as the rest of the body. The sacrifice of the altar signifies the offerings of the heart." See also Titus Burckhardt, *Chartres and the Birth of the Cathedral*, trans. William Stoddart, rev. ed. (Bloomington,

to which it is intrinsically linked,[32] the tabernacle with the Blessed Sacrament also pertains to the heart of the church and must be architecturally manifested as such. As Pius XII emphasizes, "it is one and the same Lord who is immolated on the altar and honored in the tabernacle, and who pours out his blessings from the tabernacle."[33] Containing the substantial presence of Jesus Christ, the tabernacle is the reality of which the Ark of the Covenant in the Holy of Holies in the Temple was the glorious type or figure. Every tabernacle is not only the heart of the church building but also contains the head and heart of the Mystical Body; it is the dwelling of the Bridegroom with His Bride.

The position and artistic worthiness of the tabernacle must reflect the sublime fact of the real presence.[34] If so much care was taken to create a suitable form and setting for the Ark of the Covenant[35] placed in the Holy of Holies in the Temple in Jerusalem, no less attention should be given to the place of the Blessed Sacrament, which is the holiest place in creation, this side of heaven. Pope Benedict stresses that the "correct positioning of the tabernacle contributes to the recognition of Christ's real presence in the Blessed Sacrament. Therefore, the place where the eucharistic species are reserved, marked by a sanc-

---

IN: World Wisdom, 2010), 114: "The altar is for the cathedral what the heart is for the body. For, through the presence of God in the sacrifice of the mass, the cathedral changes from a lifeless heap of stone into a living organism."

[32] See Pius XII, "The Liturgical Movement," Address to the International Congress on Pastoral Liturgy, Assisi, Italy, September 22, 1956: "We might say: 'Is the tabernacle, where dwells the Lord Who has come down amongst His people, greater than altar and sacrifice?' The altar is more important than the tabernacle, because on it is offered the Lord's sacrifice. No doubt the tabernacle holds the 'Sacramentum permanens,' but it is not an 'altare permanens,' for the Lord offers Himself in sacrifice only on the altar during the celebration of Holy Mass, not after or outside the Mass" (*The Liturgy Documents: Foundational Documents on the Origins and Implementation of Sacrosanctum Concilium*, vol. 3 [Chicago: Liturgy Training Publications, 2013], 261).

[33] Ibid.

[34] See Paul VI, *Mysterium Fidei*, §66; Sacred Congregation for the Sacraments and Divine Worship, Instruction Concerning Worship of the Eucharistic Mystery, *Inaestimabile Donum* (1980), §24: "The tabernacle in which the Eucharist is kept can be located on an altar, or away from it, in a spot in the church which is very prominent, truly noble, and duly decorated, or in a chapel suitable for private prayer and for adoration by the faithful."

[35] See Exod 35–37; 1 Kings 6:19–28; 2 Chron 3:8–14.

tuary lamp, should be readily visible to everyone entering the church."[36] The *General Instruction for the Roman Missal* addresses the issue of the position of the tabernacle in §§314–15. The tabernacle should be reserved in the church in a place that fulfills five fundamental criteria: it should be "truly noble, prominent, conspicuous, worthily decorated, and suitable for prayer."[37] There are two ways to fulfill these criteria: the tabernacle should be either in the sanctuary, or in a chapel "suitable for private adoration and prayer of the faithful." If the Sacrament is placed in a chapel, that chapel must be "organically connected to the church and readily noticeable by the Christian faithful."[38] If the Blessed Sacrament is reserved in the sanctuary, it must be in "an appropriate form and place." It should not be positioned on the altar currently in use, but can appropriately be placed on an "old altar no longer used for celebration."

Benedict XVI, in *Sacramentum Caritatis*, §69, gives some additional instructions on the position of the tabernacle in the sanctuary. If the church formerly had the tabernacle on the high altar that is still in place, it is most fitting for the tabernacle to remain (or be returned) there, taking care not to place the celebrant's chair in front of it. In a new church, if it is not possible to have a Blessed Sacrament chapel close to the sanctuary, then it is preferable that the tabernacle should be in the sanctuary itself, "in a sufficiently elevated place, at the center of the apse area, or in another place where it will be equally conspicuous." Final judgment is reserved for the diocesan bishop.

Study Questions

1. How would you respond to someone who says, "The Eucharist is for eating, not looking at?"
2. Explain this statement of Benedict XVI: "An intrinsic connection exists between [Eucharistic] celebration and adoration" (*Angelus*, June 10, 2007).
3. How can Eucharistic adoration be explained in the context of the three reasons why Jesus instituted the Eucharist? In what way does Eucharistic adoration have a sacrificial and ecclesial dimension?

---

[36] Benedict XVI, *Sacramentum Caritatis*, §69.
[37] *GIRM*, 314 (*RM*, 71).
[38] Ibid., 315 (*RM*, 72).

4. What criteria should be considered in the placement of the tabernacle in the church?

5. Explain the connection between Eucharistic adoration and devotion to the Sacred Heart of Jesus.[39]

Suggestions for Further Reading

Alphonsus de Liguori. "Visits to the Blessed Sacrament and to the Blessed Virgin." In *The Holy Eucharist*. St. Louis, MO: Redemptorist Fathers, 1934. First published in 1745. Pp. 109–208.

Benedict XVI. Post-Synodal Apostolic Exhortation on the Eucharist as the Source and Summit of the Church's Life and Mission *Sacramentum Caritatis*. February 22, 2007. §§66–69.

Groeschel, Benedict J., and James Monti. *In the Presence of Our Lord: The History, Theology, and Psychology of Eucharistic Devotion*. Huntington, IN: *Our Sunday Visitor*, 1997.

Guernsey, Daniel P., ed. *Adoration: Eucharistic Texts and Prayers Throughout Church History*. San Francisco: Ignatius Press, 1999.

John Paul II. Apostolic Letter on the Mystery and Worship of the Eucharist, *Dominicae Cenae*. February 24, 1980. §§2–3.

———. Encyclical Letter *Ecclesia de Eucharistia*. April 17, 2003. §25.

Paul VI. Encyclical Letter on the Eucharist *Mysterium Fidei*. September 3, 1965. §§56–70.

Ratzinger, Joseph. *The Spirit of the Liturgy*. Translated by John Saward. San Francisco: Ignatius Press, 2000 (*TL*, 52–56; See also *TL*, 295–98). Pp. 85–91.

Reid, Alcuin, ed. *From Eucharistic Adoration to Evangelization*. London: Burns & Oates, 2012.

---

[39] See the Conclusion below.

✠

Conclusion

In the course of this work we have seen that Christ instituted the Eucharist, the sacrament of charity, for three principal ends: to abide with His Church in His sacred humanity until the end of time, to give to the Church His perfect sacrifice of Calvary so that it can be offered in every place and time, and to unite Himself most perfectly to us through giving us His Body and Blood to be our spiritual nourishment. We have also seen that these three ends of the Eucharist—presence, sacrifice, and communion—are so intimately related that the sacrifice and communion presuppose the presence and communion presupposes the sacrifice. Without Christ's real presence in the Eucharist, the Mass could not be a sacrifice essentially one with Calvary, nor could Christ Himself be our spiritual nourishment. And without the sacrifice, there could be no communion in the fruit of the sacrifice through which, by receiving His Body and Blood offered for us, we come to share progressively in His divinity and build up His Mystical Body. All three ends of the Eucharist give us a foretaste of the life of heaven, a life of intimate presence, mutual self-gift, and perfect communion. All three embody the love of the Sacred Heart for us, a love surpassing all knowledge.

THE EUCHARIST AND THE SACRED HEART

There is an intimate relationship between adoration of Christ in the Eucharist and devotion to the Sacred Heart of Jesus. The Eucharist is the sacrament of love, and devotion to the Sacred Heart is centered on adoration of the divine and human love of Christ, symbolized by

His physical heart.[1] Eucharistic adoration is animated by the desire to return Christ's love poured out for us in the gift of the Eucharist. Our devotion to the Sacred Heart is likewise ordered to making reparation for the indifference of mankind to the superabundant love of Christ.

Eucharistic adoration is directed to the love of the heart of Jesus in three ways. First of all, Christ's Sacred Heart is present in the consecrated host to be adored and loved. Second, the Eucharist is the supreme offering of Our Lord's Sacred Heart to His Father on our behalf. In adoring the Eucharist, we adore the sacrificial love of the Lamb. Third, by remaining in the Eucharist, Jesus bequeathed His Heart to His Bride, the Church, to be received by her in Holy Communion, and to be encountered by her in Eucharistic adoration so that our hearts may be conformed ever more to His. It is no accident that the miraculous flesh of the Eucharistic miracle of Lanciano was determined to be flesh of the wall of the heart.[2]

The love of the Sacred Heart of Christ was burning for us throughout His entire earthly life, starting with the moment of His Incarnation. However, this love was most especially manifested in the institution of the Eucharist during the Last Supper and in His Passion, sacramentally made present in the Eucharist. Pius XII calls attention to this in his encyclical on Devotion to the Sacred Heart, *Haurietis Aquas* (1956):

> But who can worthily depict those beatings of the divine Heart, the signs of His infinite love, of those moments when He granted men His greatest gifts: Himself in the Sacrament of the Eucharist, His most holy Mother, and the office of the priesthood shared with us? Even before He ate the Last Supper with His disciples, Christ Our Lord, since He knew He was about to institute the sacrament of His body and blood by the shedding of which the new covenant was to be consecrated, felt His heart roused by strong emotions, which He revealed to the Apostles in these words: "With desire have I desired to

---

[1] See Pius XII, Encyclical Letter on Devotion to the Sacred Heart, *Haurietis Aquas* (1956), §22: "His Heart, more than all the other members of his body, is the natural sign and symbol of his boundless love for the human race. 'There is in the Sacred Heart . . . the symbol and express image of the infinite love of Jesus Christ that moves us to love in return'" (DS, 3922).

[2] See Odoardo Linoli, "Studio anatomo-istologico sul 'cuore' del Miracolo Eucaristico di Lanciano (VIII sec.)," *L'Osservatore Romano*, April 23, 1982, 5.

eat this Pasch with you before I suffer" (Lk 22:15). And these
emotions were doubtless even stronger when "taking bread,
He gave thanks, and broke, and gave to them, saying, 'This
is My body which is given for you . . .'" (Lk 22:19–20). It can
therefore be declared that the divine Eucharist, both the sacrament which He gives to men and the sacrifice in which He
unceasingly offers Himself "from the rising of the sun till the
going down thereof" (Mal 1:11), and likewise the priesthood,
are indeed gifts of the Sacred Heart of Jesus.[3]

The Eucharist manifests all the infinite love of Christ's Sacred
Heart first because it allows Him to continue to be present with each
of us as His beloved. Secondly, it contains and sacramentally perpetuates His sacrifice of Calvary so that we can participate in the
offering, and applies the riches it purchased for us. Third, it enables us
to receive that very Heart of Christ and the Blood that flowed from it
when it was pierced with a lance.

Although formal devotion to the Sacred Heart dates from the seventeenth century, the Fathers not infrequently speak about the love
of the heart of Jesus with reference to the piercing of His side on the
Cross, which they connect with the gifts of Baptism and the Eucharist.
The Liturgy of the Hours for Good Friday has a baptismal catechesis
to the neophytes by St. John Chrysostom in which he connects the
Heart of Jesus pierced in death, the blood that flowed from His side,
the Eucharist that sacramentally perpetuates that sacrifice and feeds
us with that blood, and the Church that is continually built up by the
gift of the Eucharist:

> Beloved, do not pass over this mystery without thought; it has
> yet another hidden meaning, which I will explain to you. I said
> that water and blood symbolised baptism and the holy Eucha-
> rist. From these two sacraments the Church is born: from
> baptism, "the cleansing water that gives rebirth and renewal
> through the Holy Spirit," and from the holy Eucharist. Since
> the symbols of baptism and the Eucharist flowed from his
> side, it was from his side that Christ fashioned the Church,
> as he had fashioned Eve from the side of Adam. Moses gives
> a hint of this when he tells the story of the first man and

---

[3] Pius XII, *Haurietis Aquas*, §§69–71.

makes him exclaim: "Bone from my bones and flesh from my flesh!" As God then took a rib from Adam's side to fashion a woman, so Christ has given us blood and water from his side to fashion the Church. God took the rib when Adam was in a deep sleep, and in the same way Christ gave us the blood and the water after his own death.

Do you understand, then, how Christ has united his bride to himself and what food he gives us all to eat? By one and the same food we are both brought into being and nourished. As a woman nourishes her child with her own blood and milk, so does Christ unceasingly nourish with his own blood those to whom he himself has given life.[4]

As Eve was created from Adam's rib as he slept, so the Church, Christ's Bride, is born from His pierced side as He slept in death. Christ willed to symbolize the Eucharist by the Blood that flowed from His Heart just after He died on the Cross. This typology points out the connection of the Eucharist both to Christ's Heart, as its supreme gift, and to the creation of His Bride, the Church. Christ builds up the Church by feeding her with His own Blood that He shed for her, to communicate to her His own life. In another homily on this same text of John 19:34, Chrysostom writes:

> It was not accidentally or by chance that these streams came forth, but because the Church has been established from both of these. Her members know this, since they have come to birth by water and are nourished by Flesh and Blood. The Mysteries have their source from there, so that when you approach the awesome chalice you may come as if you were about to drink from His very side.[5]

When we receive Communion we should remember that we are receiving it from the fountain opened up from the pierced side of Christ. It is fitting that the supernatural life of the Church comes to her from Christ's pierced side as He slept in death and poured out His

---

[4] John Chrysostom, *Baptismal Catechesis* 3.17–19, in *Liturgy of the Hours*, Good Friday, Office of Readings, 2nd Reading.

[5] John Chrysostom, Homily 85 (on John 19:16–20:9) (Goggin, *Commentary on Saint John*, 435).

Blood for His Bride. Eucharistic adoration is the effort of the Bride to contemplate the unfathomable love of the Heart of Christ shown in His perpetual presence with her and in the gift of His life for her in sacrifice and to her in Communion.

In his encyclical on the Eucharist, *Ecclesia de Eucharistia*, St. John Paul II speaks of his goal to "rekindle this Eucharistic 'amazement'"[6] before the greatness of the mystery. I hope that the present book may also contribute to bringing forth an amazement before the greatness of the gift that Jesus bequeathed to His Church on the night before He suffered and died. It is "the Church's treasure, the heart of the world, the pledge of the fulfillment for which each man and woman, even unconsciously, yearns."[7] As St. Thomas says, "In this sacrament is recapitulated the whole mystery of our salvation."[8]

---

[6] John Paul II, *EE*, §6.

[7] Ibid., §59.

[8] *ST* III, q. 83, a. 4.

✱
Bibliography

MAGISTERIAL TEXTS

Conciliar Documents

Council of Trent. Decree Concerning the Most Holy Sacrament of the Eucharist. Session 13, October 11, 1551.
———. Doctrine of Communion under Both Kinds and the Communion of Little Children. Session 21, July 16, 1562.
———. Doctrine Concerning the Sacrifice of the Mass. Session 22, September 17, 1562.
———. Decree Concerning the Sacrament of Orders. Session 23, July 15, 1563.
———. Decree Concerning Purgatory. Session 25, December 4, 1563.
Second Vatican Council. Constitution on the Sacred Liturgy, *Sacrosanctum Concilium*. December 4, 1963.
———. Dogmatic Constitution on the Church, *Lumen Gentium*. November 21, 1964.
———. Decree on the Ministry and Life of Priests, *Presbyterorum Ordinis*. December 7, 1965.

Papal Documents

Leo XIII. Encyclical on the Holy Eucharist, *Mirae Caritatis*. May 18, 1902.
Pius X. Instruction on Sacred Music, *Tra le Sollecitudini*. November 22, 1903.
———. Decree on Frequent and Daily Reception of Holy Communion, *Sacra Tridentina*. December 20, 1905.
Pius XII. Encyclical on the Sacred Liturgy, *Mediator Dei*. November 20, 1947.
———. Address to Cardinals, Archbishops and Bishops Gathered in Rome for Ceremonies in Honor of Our Lady, Nov. 2, 1954. In *Acta Apostolicae Sedis*. Vol. 46 (1954). English translation in *The Pope Speaks* 1 (1954).

———. Allocution to the International Congress of Pastoral Liturgy at Assisi, September 22, 1956. In *Acta Apostolicae Sedis* 48 (1956). English translation in *The Pope Speaks* 3, no. 3 (Winter 1956–1957).

Paul VI. Encyclical on the Eucharist, *Mysterium Fidei*. September 3, 1965.

———. Apostolic Letter on the Credo of the People of God, *Solemni hac Liturgia*. June 30, 1968.

John Paul II. Apostolic Letter on the Mystery and Worship of the Eucharist, *Dominicae Cenae*. February 24, 1980.

———. Apostolic Exhortation on the Role of the Christian Family in the Modern World, *Familiaris Consortio*. November 22, 1981.

———. Apostolic Letter on the Dignity and Vocation of Women on the Occasion of the Marian Year, *Mulieris Dignitatem*, August 15, 1988.

———. *Letters to My Brother Priests, 1979–1999*. Princeton, NJ: Scepter, 2000.

———. Encyclical Letter at the Close of the Great Jubilee of the Year 2000, *Novo Millennio Ineunte*. January 6, 2001.

———. Encyclical Letter on the Eucharist in Its Relationship to the Church, *Ecclesia de Eucharistia*. April 17, 2003.

———. Apostolic Letter for the Year of the Eucharist, *Mane Nobiscum Domine*. October 7, 2004.

Benedict XVI. Post-Synodal Apostolic Exhortation on the Eucharist as the Source and Summit of the Church's Life and Mission, *Sacramentum Caritatis*. February 22, 2007.

Pope Francis. Post-Synodal Apostolic Exhortation on Love in the Family, *Amoris Laetitia*. March 19, 2016.

Other Magisterial Texts and Collections

Sacred Congregation of the Discipline of the Sacraments. Decree *Quam Singulari*. August 8, 1910.

Missale Romanum: Ex Decreto SS. Concilii Tridentini Restitutum Summorum Pontificum Cura Recognitum. Vatican City: Typis Polyglottis Vaticanis, 1962.

Sacred Congregation of Rites. Instruction on Eucharistic Worship, *Eucharisticum Mysterium*. May 25, 1967.

Congregation for Divine Worship. Instruction on the Manner of Distributing Holy Communion, *Memoriale Domini*. May 29, 1969.

International Commission on English in the Liturgy. *Documents on the Liturgy, 1963–1979: Conciliar, Papal, and Curial Texts*. Edited and translated by Thomas C. O'Brien. Collegeville, MN: Liturgical Press, 1982.

Catechism of the Catholic Church. 2nd ed. Washington, DC: United States Catholic Conference, 2000.

Sacred Congregation for the Sacraments and Divine Worship. Instruction Concerning Worship of the Eucharistic Mystery, *Inaestimabile Donum.* April 17, 1980.

Congregation for the Doctrine of the Faith. Instruction on Certain Questions Concerning the Ministers of the Eucharist, *Sacerdotium Ministeriale.* August 6, 1983.

Kaczynski, Reiner, ed. *Enchiridion Documentorum Instaurationis Liturgicae.* 2 vols. Rome: CLV-Edizioni Liturgiche, 1990.

Congregation for the Clergy. Instruction on Certain Questions Regarding the Collaboration of the Non-Ordained Faithful in the Sacred Ministry of Priest. August 15, 1997.

Congregation for Divine Worship and the Discipline of the Sacraments. Fifth Instruction on Vernacular Translation of the Roman Liturgy, *Liturgiam Authenticam.* Washington, DC: United States Conference of Catholic Bishops, 2001.

Pontifical Council for Promoting Christian Unity. "Guidelines for Admission to the Eucharist between the Chaldean Church and the Assyrian Church of the East." July 20, 2001.

United States Conference of Catholic Bishops. *Norms for the Distribution and Reception of Holy Communion under Both Kinds in the Dioceses of the United States of America.* Washington, DC: United States Conference of Catholic Bishops, 2002.

Congregation for Divine Worship and the Discipline of the Sacraments. Instruction on Certain Matters to Be Observed or to Be Avoided Regarding the Most Holy Eucharist, *Redemptionis Sacramentum.* March 25, 2004.

——. *Compendium Eucharisticum.* Vatican City: Libreria Editrice Vaticana, 2009.

Roman Missal. 3rd typical edition. Washington, DC: United States Conference of Catholic Bishops, 2011.

Congregation for the Doctrine of the Faith. *On the Pastoral Care of the Divorced and Remarried.* Washington DC: United States Council of Catholic Bishops, 2012.

Denzinger, Heinrich. *Enchiridion Symbolorum: Compendium of Creeds, Definitions, and Declarations on Matters of Faith and Morals.* 43rd edition. Edited by Peter Hünermann. English edition edited by Robert Fastiggi and Anne Englund Nash. San Francisco: Ignatius Press, 2012.s

Patristic Sources

Ambrose. *De Mysteriis* and *De Sacramentis*. In *Saint Ambrose: Theological and Dogmatic Works*. Translated by R. J. Deferrari. Fathers of the Church 44. Washington, DC: Catholic University of America Press, 1963.

Augustine. *The City of God.* Translated by Henry Bettenson. New York: Penguin Books, 1972.

———. *The City of God: Books VIII–XVI*. Translated by G. G. Walsh and G. Monahan. Fathers of the Church 14. Washington, DC: Catholic University of America Press, 1952.

———. *Commentary on the Lord's Sermon on the Mount with Seventeen Related Sermons*. Fathers of the Church 11. Washington, DC: Catholic University of America Press, 1951.

———. *Confessions.* Translated by V. J. Bourke. Fathers of the Church 21. Washington, DC: Catholic University of America Press, 1953.

———. *Expositions of the Psalms*. Vol. 2, *Psalms 33–50*. Translated by Maria Boulding. Vol. 16 of Works of Saint Augustine, pt. III (Homilies). Hyde Park, NY: New City Press, 2000.

———. *Expositions of the Psalms*. Vol. 3, *Psalms 73–98*. Translated by Maria Boulding. Vol. 18 of Works of Saint Augustine, pt. III (Homilies). Hyde Park, NY: New City Press, 2002.

———. *Faith, Hope and Charity*. Edited by Johannes Quasten and Joseph C. Plumpe. Translated by L. A. Arand. Ancient Christian Writers 3. New York: The Newman Press, 1947.

———. *Newly Discovered Sermons*. Translated by Edmund Hill. Vol. 11 of Works of Saint Augustine, pt. III (Homilies). Hyde Park, NY: New City Press, 1997.

———. *Sermons (148–183) on the New Testament*. Translated by Edmund Hill. Vol. 5 of Works of Saints Augustine, pt. III (Homilies). New Rochelle, NY: New City Press, 1992.

———. *Sermons (184–229Z) on the Liturgical Seasons*. Translated by Edmund Hill. Vol. 6 of Works of Saint Augustine, pt. III (Homilies). New Rochelle, NY: New City Press, 1993.

———. *Sermons (230–272B) on the Liturgical Seasons*. Translated by Edmund Hill. Vol. 7 of Works of Saint Augustine, pt. III. New Rochelle, NY: New City Press, 1993.

———. *Sermons on the Liturgical Seasons.* Translated by Mary Sarah Muldowney. Fathers of the Church 38. Washington, DC: Catholic University of America Press, 1959.

————. *Tractates on the Gospel of John, 11–27.* Translated by J. W. Rettig. Fathers of the Church 79. Washington, DC: Catholic University of America Press, 1988.

————. *Tractates on the Gospel of John, 55–111.* Translated by J. W. Retting. Fathers of the Church 90. Washington, DC: Catholic University of America Press, 1994.

————. *Tractates on the Gospel of John, 112–24; Tractates on the First Epistle of John.* Translated by J. W. Rettig. Fathers of the Church 92. Washington, DC: Catholic University of America Press, 1995.

Cyril of Alexandria. *Commentary on John.* Edited by Joel C. Elowsky. Translated by David R. Maxwell. 2 vols. Ancient Christian Texts. Downers Grove, IL: InterVarsity Press, 2013–2015.

————. *Letters 1–50.* Translated by J. I. McEnerney. Fathers of the Church 76. Washington, DC: Catholic University of America Press, 1987.

Cyril of Jerusalem. *Lectures on the Christian Sacraments.* Edited by F. L. Cross. Crestwood, NY: St. Vladimir's Seminary Press, 1977.

Cyprian. *Saint Cyprian: Letters (1–81).* Translated by R. B. Donna. Fathers of the Church 51. Washington, DC: Catholic University of America Press, 1964

Gregory the Great. *Dialogues.* Translated by O. J. Zimmerman. Fathers of the Church 39. Washington, DC: Catholic University of America Press, 1959.

Hippolytus, *The Apostolic Tradition of Hippolytus.* Translated by Burton Scott Easton. Ann Arbor, MI: Archon Books, 1962.

Holmes, Michael, trans. *The Apostolic Fathers: Greek Texts and English Translations.* 3rd edition. Grand Rapids, MI: Baker Academic, 2007.

Irenaeus. *Against Heresies.* Translated by Alexander Roberts and William Rambaut. In *The Ante-Nicene Fathers* 1. Peabody, MA: Hendrickson, 1994.

Isidore of Seville. *De Ecclesiasticis Officiis.* Translated by T. L. Knoebel. Ancient Christian Writers 61. New York: The Newman Press, 2008.

————. *The Etymologies of Isidore of Seville.* Translated by Stephen A. Barney. Cambridge: Cambridge University Press, 2006.

John Chrysostom. *Commentary on Saint John the Apostle and Evangelist: Homilies 1–47.* Translated by T. A. Goggin. Fathers of the Church 33. Washington, DC: Catholic University of America Press, 1957.

————. *Commentary on Saint John the Apostle and Evangelist: Homilies 48–88.* Translated by T. A. Goggin. Fathers of the Church 41. Washington, DC: Catholic University of America Press, 1959.

————. *Six Books on the Priesthood.* Translated by Graham Neville. Crestwood, NY: St. Vladimir's Seminary Press, 1964.

————. *Baptismal Instructions.* Translated by Paul Harkins. Westminster, MD: The Newman Press, 1963.

John Damascene. *On the Orthodox Faith.* Translated by F. H. Chase Jr. In *Writings: Saint John of Damascus,* Fathers of the Church 37. Washington, DC: Catholic University of America Press, 1958.

Johnson, Lawrence J. *Worship in the Early Church: An Anthology of Historical Sources.* 4 vols. Collegeville, MN: Liturgical Press, 2009.

Justin Martyr. *The First Apology, The Second Apology, Dialogue with Trypho, Exhortation to the Greeks, Discourse to the Greeks, The Monarchy or The Rule of God.* Translated by T. B. Falls. Fathers of the Church 6. Washington, DC: Catholic University of America Press, 1948.

Leo the Great. *Sermons.* Translated by J. P. Freeland and A. J. Conway. Fathers of the Church 93. Washington, DC: Catholic University of America Press, 1996.

Proclus, *Proclus, Bishop of Constantinople: Homilies on the Life of Christ.* Translated by Jan Harm Barkhuizen. Brisbane, AU: Centre for Early Christian Studies, Australian Catholic University, 2001.

Medieval Sources

Albertus Magnus. *De Sacrificio Missae.* In *Opera Omnia,* vol. 38. Edited by Augustus Borgnet. Paris: Vivès, 1899.

Alger of Liège. *De Sacramentis Corporis et Sanguinis Dominici.* In *Patrologiae Cursus Completus: Series Latina,* vol. 180. Edited by J. P. Migne. Paris: Garnier and J. P. Migne, 1844–1865.

Aquinas, Thomas. *Catena Aurea.* Translated by John Henry Newman. 4 vols. Oxford: John Henry Parker, 1841–1845. Reprint, London: Saint Austin Press, 1997.

————. *Commentary on the Gospel of St. John: Chapters 13–21.* Translated by Fabian Larcher and James A. Weisheipl. Washington, DC: Catholic University of America Press, 2010.

————. *Commentary on the Epistle to the Hebrews.* Translated by Chrysostom Baer. South Bend, IN: St. Augustine's Press, 2006.

————. *Commentary on the Letter of Saint Paul to the Romans.* Translated by Fabian Larcher. Lander, WY: Aquinas Institute for the Study of Sacred Doctrine, 2012.

————. *Commentary on the Letters of Saint Paul to the Corinthians.* Translated by Fabian Larcher, B. Mortensen, and Daniel Keating. Lander, WY: Aquinas Institute for the Study of Sacred Doctrine, 2012.

———. *Officium de Festo Corporis Christi, ad Mandatum Urbani Papae IV Dictum Festum Instituentis.* In *Opuscula Theologica.* Vol. 2 of *De Re Spirituali.* Edited by Raimondo Spiazzi. Turin: Marietti, 1972.

———. *On the Power of God* [*Questiones Disputatae de Potentia Dei*]. Translated by the English Dominican Fathers. Westminster, MD: Newman Press, 1952.

———. *Sancti Thomae Aquinatis Opera Omnia.* Leonine edition. Rome, 1882–.

———. *Scriptum Super Libros Sententiarum Magistri Petri Lombardi Episcopi Parisiensis.* Edited by M. F. Moos Mandonnet. 4 vols. Paris: P. Lethielleux, 1929–1947.

———. *Summa Contra Gentiles.* Translated by Anton Pegis, James Anderson, Vernon Bourke, and Charles O'Neil. 4 vols. Notre Dame, IN: University of Notre Dame Press, 1975.

———. *Summa Theologica of St. Thomas Aquinas.* 2nd ed. Translated by Dominican Fathers of the English Province. London: Burns, Oates, & Washbourne, 1920–1932.

———. *Truth* [*De Veritate*]. Translated by Robert W. Schmidt. 3 vols. Chicago: Henry Regnery, 1954.

Berengarius, *De Sacra Coena adversus Lanfrancum Liber Posterior.* Edited by A. F. and F. Th. Vischer. Berlin: Sumptibus haude et Spener, 1834.

Gerbert of Aurillac. *De Corpore et Sanguine Domini.* In *Patrologiae Cursus Completus. Series Latina,* vol. 139. Edited by J. P. Migne. Paris: Garnier and J. P. Migne, 1844–1865.

Guitmund of Aversa. *On the Truth of the Body and Blood of Christ in the Eucharist.* Translated by Mark G. Vaillancourt. In The Fathers of the Church, Mediaeval Continuation, vol. 10. Washington, DC: Catholic University of America Press, 2009.

Haymo of Halberstadt, *De Corpore et Sanguine Domini.* In *Patrologiae Cursus Completus,* vol. 118. *Series Latina.* Edited by J. P. Migne. Paris: Garnier and J. P. Migne 1844–1865.

Hugh of St. Victor. *On the Sacraments of the Christian Faith.* Translated by Roy J. Deferrari. Cambridge, MA: Mediaeval Academy of America, 1951.

———. "Questions inédites de Hugues de St.-Victor." Edited by Odon Lottin. *Recherches de théologie ancienne et médiévale* 26 (1959); 27 (1960).

Lanfranc of Canterbury. *On the Body and Blood of the Lord.* Translated by Mark G. Vaillancourt. In Fathers of the Church, Mediaeval Continuation, vol. 10. Washington, DC: Catholic University of America Press, 2009.

Midrash Rabbah. Edited by Harry Freedman. 10 vols. London: Soncino Press, 1961.

Paschasius Radbertus. *De Corpore et Sanguine Domini: Cum Appendice Epistola ad Fredugardum.* Edited by Bedae Paulus. *Corpus Christianorum, Continuatio Mediaevalis* 16. Turnhout, BE: Brepols, 1969.

Peter Lombard. *The Sentences, Book 4: On the Doctrine of Signs.* Translated by Giulio Silano. Mediaeval Sources in Translation 48. Toronto: Pontifical Institute of Mediaeval Studies, 2010.

Ratramnus. *De Corpore et Sanguine Domine: texte établi d'après les manuscrits et notice bibliographique.* Edited by J. N. Bakhuizen van den Brink. Amsterdam: North-Holland Publishing, 1954.

———. *The Book of Ratramn the Priest and Monk of Corbey, Commonly Called Bertram, on the Body and Blood of the Lord.* Oxford: John Henry Parker, 1838.

REFORMATION AND RENAISSANCE SOURCES

Caietanus de Vio, Thomas Cardinal. Commentary on *Summa Theologiae* III. In *Sancti Thomae Aquinatis Opera omnia,* vol. 12. Leonine edition. Rome, 1906.

———. *Thomas de Vio Cajetanus, Opuscula Omnia.* Reprinted. Zürich: Georg Olms, 1995.

Calvin, John. *Institutes of the Christian Religion.* Translated by Henry Beveridge. Peabody, MA: Hendrickson, 2008.

The Book of Concord: The Confessions of the Evangelical Lutheran Church. Translated and edited by Theodore G. Tappert, Jaroslav Pelikan, Robert H. Fischer, and Arthur C. Piepkorn. Philadelphia, PA: Mühlenberg Press, 1959.

Creeds of the Churches: A Reader in Christian Doctrine from the Bible to the Present. Edited by John H. Leith. Revised edition. Richmond, VA: John Knox Press, 1973.

Luther, Martin. *Luther's Works.* Edited by Jaroslav Pelikan and Helmut Lehmann. 55 vols. Philadelphia, PA, and St Loius, MO: Fortress Press and Concordia, 1955–1986.

Zwingli, Huldrych. *Writings.* 2 vols. Translated by E. J. Furcha (vol. 1) and H. Wayne Pipkin (vol. 2). Allison Park, PA: Pickwick Publications, 1984.

———. *Zwingli and Bullinger: Selected Translations.* Translated by G.W. Bromiley. Library of Christian Classics 24. Philadelphia, PA: Westminster Press, 1953.

SECONDARY SOURCES

Adams, Marilyn Mccord. *Some Later Medieval Theories of the Eucharist: Thomas Aquinas, Giles of Rome, Duns Scotus, and William Ockham.* Oxford: Oxford University Press, 2010.

Albright, Matthew J. "Sacrifice as the Key to Understanding the Difference and Relationship Between the Priesthood of the Baptized and of the Ordained." *Antiphon* 19, no. 3 (2015).

Allen, Michael. "Sacraments in the Reformed and Anglican Reformation." In Boersma and Levering, eds., *The Oxford Handbook of Sacramental Theology.*

Alonso, Manuel. *El Sacrificio Eucarístico de la Última Cena del Señor según el Concilio Tridentino.* Madrid, ES: Editorial Razón y Fe, 1929.

Althaus, Paul. *The Theology of Martin Luther.* Translated by Robert C. Schultz. Philadelphia, PA: Fortress Press, 1966.

Anscombe, G. E. M. "On Transubstantiation." In *Ethics, Religion and Politics: The Collected Philosophical Papers of G. E. M. Anscombe.* Vol. 3. Oxford: Blackwell, 1981.

Aquilina, Mike. *The Mass of the Early Christians.* 2nd ed. Huntington, IN: Our Sunday Visitor, 2007.

Arinze, Francis, Francis George, Jorge Medina, and George Pell. *Reflections: Active Participation and the Liturgy.* Chicago: Hillenbrand Books, 2005.

Audet, Jean-Paul. *La Didachè: Instructions des Apôtres.* Paris: J. Gabalda, 1958.

Auer, Johann, and Joseph Ratzinger. *A General Doctrine of the Sacraments and the Mystery of the Eucharist.* Vol. 6 of *Dogmatic Theology.* Edited by Hugh M. Riley. Translated by Erasmo Leiva Merikakis. Washington, DC: Catholic University of America Press, 1995.

Aulén, Gustaf. *Eucharist and Sacrifice.* Philadelphia, PA: Mühlenberg Press, 1958.

Barber, Michael. *Coming Soon: Unlocking the Book of Revelation and Applying Its Lessons Today.* Steubenville, OH: Emmaus Road, 2005.

Barrett, C. K. *The Gospel according to St. John.* 2nd ed. Philadelphia, PA: Westminster, 1978.

Barth, Karl. "Luther's Doctrine of the Eucharist: Its Basis and Purpose." In *Theology and Church: Shorter Writings 1920–1928.* Translated by Louise Pettibone Smith. London: SCM Press, 1962.

Beckwith, Roger T., and Martin J. Selman, eds. *Sacrifice in the Bible.* Grand Rapids, MA: Baker Book House, 1995.

Belmonte, Charles. *Understanding the Mass: Its Relevance to Daily Life.* Princeton, NJ: Scepter, 1989.

Benoit, Pierre. *Jesus and the Gospel.* Translated by Benet Weatherhead. Vol. 1. New York: Herder and Herder, 1973.

Berger, David. "'Forma huius sacramenti sunt verba Salvatoris'—Die Form des Sakramentes der Eucharistie," *Divinitas,* n.s., special edition (2004).

———. *Thomas Aquinas and the Liturgy.* Naples, FL: Sapientia Press of Ave Maria University, 2004.

Berman, Joshua. *The Temple: Its Symbolism and Meaning Then and Now.* Northvale, NJ: Jason Aronson, 1995.

Billot, Ludovicus. *De Ecclesiae Sacramentis: Commentarius in Tertiam Partem S. Thomae.* Vol. 1. 7th ed. Rome: Apud Aedes Universitatis Gregorianae, 1931.

Billy, Dennis Joseph. *The Beauty of the Eucharist: Voices from the Church Fathers.* Hyde Park, NY: New City Press, 2010.

———. "Pope Benedict XVI on the Eucharist." *Emmanuel* 119, no. 3 (2013): 127–35.

Blankenhorn, Bernard. "The Instrumental Causality of the Sacraments: Thomas Aquinas and Louis-Marie Chauvet," *Nova et Vetera* (English) 4 (2006): 255–94.

Blinzler, Joseph. *The Trial of Jesus.* Translated by Isabel and Florence McHugh. Westminster, MD: The Newman Press, 1959.

Boersma, Hans, and Matthew Levering, eds. *The Oxford Handbook of Sacramental Theology.* New York: Oxford University Press, 2015.

Boissard, Guy. "Le sens chrétien du sacrifice." *Nova et Vetera* (French) 81 (2006): 35–50.

Botte, Bernard. *La Tradition apostolique de saint Hippolyte: Essai de reconstitution.* 5th edition. Münster: Aschendorff, 1989.

Bouyer, Louis. *The Christian Mystery: From Pagan Myth to Christian Mysticism.* Translated by Illtyd Trethowan. Petersham, MA: Saint Bede's, 1990.

———. *Dictionnaire Théologique.* Paris: Desclée, 1990.

———. *Eucharist: Theology and Spirituality of the Eucharistic Prayer.* Translated by Charles Underhill Quinn. Notre Dame, IN: University of Notre Dame Press, 1968.

———. *Rite and Man: Natural Sacredness and Christian Liturgy.* Translated by Joseph Costelloe. Notre Dame, IN: University of Notre Dame Press, 1963.

———. *The Word, Church and Sacraments in Protestantism and Catholicism.* Translated by A. V. Littledale. San Francisco: Ignatius Press, 2004.

Bradshaw, Paul F. "Did Jesus Institute the Eucharist at the Last Supper?" In *Issues in Eucharistic Praying in East and West: Essays in Liturgical and Theological Analysis,* edited by Maxwell Johnson, 1–19. Collegeville, MN: Liturgical Press, 2010.

———, ed. *Essays on Early Eastern Eucharistic Prayers*. Collegeville, MN: Liturgical Press, 1997.

——— and Maxwell E. Johnson. *The Eucharistic Liturgies: Their Evolution and Interpretation*. Collegeville, MN: Liturgical Press, 2012.

———. *The Origins of Feasts, Fasts, and Seasons in Early Christianity*. Collegeville, MN: Liturgical Press, 2011.

———, Maxwell E. Johnson, and L. Edward Phillips. *The Apostolic Tradition: A Commentary*. Minneapolis, MN: Augsburg Fortress, 2002.

Brock, Stephen L. "St. Thomas and the Eucharistic Conversion." *The Thomist* 65, no. 4 (2001): 529–65.

Brown, Christopher M. "Artifacts, Substances, and Transubstantiation: Solving a Puzzle for Aquinas's Views." *The Thomist* 71 (2007): 89–112.

Brown, Raymond, S.S. *The Gospel according to John*. 2 vols. Garden City, NY: Doubleday, 1970.

Brummond, Michael F. "The Thomistic Notion of the Non-Local Presence of Christ in the Eucharist: Its Meaning and Place in Catholic Tradition." *Antiphon* 17, no. 3 (2013): 247–75.

Bultmann, Rudolf. *The Gospel of John: A Commentary*. Translated by G. R. Beasley-Murray. Oxford: Basil Blackwell, 1971.

Burke, Raymond Cardinal. *Divine Love Made Flesh: The Holy Eucharist as the Sacrament of Charity*. San Diego: Catholic Action for Faith & Family, 2012.

Burkhardt, Titus. *Chartres and the Birth of the Cathedral: Revised*. Translated by William Stoddart. Bloomington, IN: World Wisdom, 2010.

Buttiglione, Rocco. "*Amoris Laetitia*: Risposte ai critici." *Lateranum* 83, no. 1 (2017): 191–240.

———. "The Joy of Love and the Consternation of Theologians: Thoughts on Pope Francis' Apostolic Exhortation *Amoris Laetitia*." *L'Osservatore Romano*, July 19, 2016, accessed June 14, 2017, http://www.osservatoreromano.va/en/news/joy-love-and-consternation-theologians.

Cabié, Robert. *The Eucharist*. Translated by Matthew O'Connell. Collegeville, MN: Liturgical Press, 1986.

Calkins, Arthur Burton. "Mary's Presence in the Mass: The Teaching of Pope John Paul II." *Antiphon* 10, no. 2 (2006): 132–58.

Cantalamessa, Raniero. *The Eucharist: Our Sanctification*. Translated by Frances Lonergan Villa. Collegeville, MN: Liturgical Press, 1995.

———. *This Is My Body: Eucharistic Reflections Inspired by* Adoro Te Devote *and* Ave Verum. Boston: Pauline Books & Media, 2005.

Carroll, Thomas K., and Thomas Halton. *Liturgical Practice in the Fathers*. Wilmington, DE: Michael Glazier, 1988.

Casel, Odo. *The Mystery of Christian Worship*. Edited by Burkhard Neunheuser. New York: Crossroad, 1999.

Cavalletti, Sofia. "Memorial and Typology in Jewish and Christian Liturgy." *Letter & Spirit* 1 (2005): 69–86.

Cessario, Romanus, O.P. "'Circa res . . . aliquid fit' (*Summa theologiae* II–II, q. 85, a. 3, ad 3): Aquinas on New Law Sacrifice. *Nova et Vetera* (English) 4, no. 2 (2006): 295–312.

———. "Sacramental Causality: Da capo!" *Nova et Vetera* (English) 11, no. 2 (2013): 307–16.

Chapman, M. E. "Sacrament and Sacrifice in the Theology of the Mass according to Luther, 1513–1526." *One in Christ* 28 (1992): 248–66.

Chauvet, Louis-Marie. *The Sacraments: The Word of God at the Mercy of the Body*. Collegeville, MN: Liturgical Press, 2001.

———. "'Sacrifice': An Ambiguous Concept in Christianity." In *The Ambivalence of Sacrifice*, edited by Luiz Carlos Susin, Diego Irarrázaval, and Daniel Franklin Pilario, 13–23. London: SCM Press, 2013.

———. *Symbol and Sacrament: A Sacramental Reinterpretation of Christian Existence*. Collegeville, MN: Liturgical Press, 1995.

Chilton, Bruce. *The Temple of Jesus: His Sacrificial Program within a Cultural History of Sacrifice*. University Park: Pennsylvania State University Press, 1992.

Chupungco, Anscar J., ed. *Handbook for Liturgical Studies*. Vol. 3, *The Eucharist*. Collegeville, MN: Liturgical Press, 1999.

Clark, Francis, S.J. *Eucharistic Sacrifice and the Reformation*. Westminster, MD: The Newman Press, 1960.

Colish, Marcia L. *Peter Lombard*. 2 vols. Leiden: Brill, 1994.

Coolman, Boyd Taylor. "The Christo-Pneumatic-Ecclesial Character of Twelfth-Century Sacramental Theology." In Boersma and Levering, eds., *The Oxford Handbook of Sacramental Theology*, 201–17.

Corbon, Jean. *The Wellspring of Worship*. San Francisco: Ignatius Press, 2005.

Cullen, Christopher M., S.J., and Joseph W. Koterski, S.J. "The New IGMR and Mass *Versus Populum*." *Homiletic and Pastoral Review*, June 2001, 51–54.

Cummings, Owen. F. "Eucharistic Prayer of Addai and Mari." *Emmanuel* 119, no. 3 (2013): 222–32.

———. "Justin and the Eucharist." *Emmanuel* 118, no. 4 (2012): 306–17.

Custer, Jack. "The Eucharist as Thanksgiving Sacrifice." *Antiphon* 12 (2008): 46–65.

Daly, Robert J., S.J. *Christian Sacrifice: The Judeo-Christian Background before Origen*. Washington, DC: Catholic University of America Press, 1978.

———. "Eucharistic Origins: From the New Testament to the Liturgies of the Golden Age." *Theological Studies*, 66 (2005): 3–22.

———. *The Origins of the Christian Doctrine of Sacrifice*. Philadelphia, PA: Fortress Press, 1978.

———. "Robert Bellarmine and Post-Tridentine Eucharistic Theology." *Theological Studies* 61 (2000): 239–260.

———. *Sacrifice Unveiled: The True Meaning of Christian Sacrifice*. London: Continuum and T. & T. Clark, 2009.

———. "Sacrifice Unveiled or Sacrifice Revisited: Trinitarian and Liturgical Perspectives." *Theological Studies* 64 (2003): 24–42.

Daly, Robert J., Gary Macy, and Jill Raitt. "The Ecumenical Significance of Eucharistic Conversion." *Theological Studies* 77 (2016): 8–31.

Daniélou, Jean, S.J. *The Bible and the Liturgy*. Notre Dame, IN: University of Notre Dame Press, 1956.

———. *From Shadows to Reality: Studies in the Biblical Typology of the Fathers*. Translated by Dom Wulstan Hibberd (Westminster, MD: The Newman Press, 1960.

Davis, Charles. "Understanding the Real Presence." In *The Word in History: The St. Xavier Symposium*, 154–78. New York: Sheed and Ward, 1966.

Davis, Thomas J. *This Is My Body: The Presence of Christ in Reformation Thought*. Grand Rapids, MI: Baker Academic, 2008.

De Aldama, Joseph A., Severino Gonzalez, Francis A. P. Sola, and Joseph F. Sagües. *Sacrae Theologiae Summa*. Vol. 4A, *On the Sacraments in General: On Baptism, Confirmation, Eucharist, Penance and Anointing*. 3rd ed. Translated by Kenneth Baker. Ramsey, NJ: Keep the Faith, 2015.

De Baciocchi, J. "Présence eucharistique et transsubstantiation." *Irénikon* 32 (1959): 139–61.

Deighan, Gerard, ed. *Celebrating the Eucharist: Sacrifice and Communion: Proceedings of the Fifth Fota International Liturgical Conference, 2012*. Wells, UK: Smenos Publications, 2014.

De la Taille, Maurice, S.J. *The Mystery of Faith*. Vol. 1, *The Sacrifice of Our Lord*. New York: Sheed & Ward, 1940.

———. *The Mystery of Faith*. Vol. 2, *The Sacrifice of the Church*. New York: Sheed & Ward, 1950.

De La Vega, Roberto. *Eucharist through the Centuries*. Hamden, CT: Circle, 1988.

De Margerie, Bertrand. *Remarried Divorcees and Eucharistic Communion*. Boston: Daughters of St. Paul, 1980.

Derville, Guillaume. *Eucharistic Concelebration: From Symbol to Reality*. Montreal: Wilson & Lafleur, 2011.

Di Nola, Gerardo. *Monumenta Eucharistica: La testimonianza dei Padri della Chiesa*. 2 volumes. Rome: Dehoniane, 1994–1997.

Dodaro, Robert, ed. *Remaining in the Truth of Christ: Marriage and Communion in the Catholic Church*. San Francisco: Ignatius Press, 2014.

Doronzo, Emmanuel, O.M.I. *Tractatus Dogmaticus de Eucharistia*. 2 vols. Milwaukee, WI: Bruce, 1947–1948.

Dougherty, Joseph. *From Altar-Throne to Table: The Campaign for Frequent Holy Communion in the Catholic Church*. Lanham, MD: Scarecrow Press, 2010.

Doval, Alexis James. *Cyril of Jerusalem, Mystagogue: The Authorship of the Mystagogic Catecheses*. Washington, DC: Catholic University of America Press, 2001.

Dowd, Edward F. *A Conspectus of Modern Catholic Thought on the Essence of the Eucharistic Sacrifice*. Washington, DC: Catholic University of America, 1937.

Driscoll, Jeremy, O.S.B. "Worship in the Spirit of Logos: Romans 12:1–2 and the Source and Summit of Christian Life." *Letter & Spirit* 5 (2009): 77–101.

Dulles, Avery, S.J. "The Death of Jesus as Sacrifice." *Josephinum Journal of Theology* 3 (1996): 4–17.

Dummett, Michael. "The Intelligibility of Eucharistic Doctrine." In *The Rationality of Religious Belief*, edited by W. J. Abraham and S. W. Holzer, 231– 61. Oxford: Clarendon Press, 1987.

Durrwell, F.-X. *The Eucharist: Presence of Christ*. Denville, NJ: Dimension Books, 1974.

Edersheim, Alfred. *The Temple: Its Ministry and Services*. Peabody, MA: Hendrickson, 1994.

Elavanal, Thomas. "The Pneumatology of the Anaphora of Addai and Mari Especially in Its Epiclesis." In *Studies on the Anaphora of Addai and Mari*, edited by Bosco Puthur, 146–67. Kochi, India: L.R.C. Publications, 2004.

Elliott, Peter. "Ars Celebrandi in the Sacred Liturgy." In *The Sacred Liturgy: Source and Summit of the Life and Mission of the Church— The Proceedings of the International Conference on the Sacred Liturgy, Sacra Liturgia 2013*, edited by Alcuin Reid, 69–85. San Francisco: Ignatius Press, 2014.

Emery, Gilles. "La fruit ecclésial de l'eucharistie chez saint Thomas d'Aquin." *Nova et Vetera* (French) 72, no. 4 (1997): 25–40.

Emminghaus, Johannes H. *The Eucharist: Essence, Form, Celebration*. Translated by Linda Maloney and revised and edited by Theodor Maas-Ewerd. Collegeville, MN: Liturgical Press, 1997.

Ernst, Joseph. *Die Lehre des hl. Paschasius Radbertus von der Eucharistie: Mit besonderer berücksichtigung der Stellung des hl. Rhabanus Maurus und des Ratramnus zu derselben.* Freiburg in Breisbau: Herder, 1896.

Espinel, José Luis. *La Eucaristía del Nuevo Testamento.* Salamanca, ES: Editorial San Esteban, 1980.

Eymard, Peter Julian. *Holy Communion.* Cleveland, OH: Emmanuel, 1940.

———. *The Real Presence: Eucharistic Meditations.* Cleveland, OH: Emmanuel, 1938.

Fagerberg, David W. "Divine Liturgy, Divine Love." *Letter & Spirit* 3 (2007): 95–112.

———. "Liturgy and Divinization." In *Called to Be the Children of God: The Catholic Theology of Human Deification*, edited by David Vincent Meconi and Carl Olson, 274–83. San Francisco: Ignatius Press, 2016.

———. *Consecrating the World: On Mundane Liturgical Theology.* Kettering, OH: Angelico Press, 2016.

———. *On Liturgical Asceticism.* Washington, DC: Catholic University of America Press, 2013.

———. *Theologia Prima: What Is Liturgical Theology?* 2nd ed. Chicago: Hillenbrand Books, 2004.

———. *What Is Liturgical Theology?: A Study in Methodology.* Collegeville, MN: Liturgical Press, 1992.

Fahey, John F. *The Eucharistic Teaching of Ratramn of Corbie.* Mundelein, IL: Saint Mary of the Lake Seminary, 1951.

Fandal, Damian. *The Essence of the Eucharistic Sacrifice.* River Forest, IL: Aquinas Library, 1960.

Farkasfalvy, Denis. "The Eucharistic Provenance of New Testament Texts." In *Rediscovering the Eucharist: Ecumenical Considerations*, edited by Roch A. Kereszty, 27–51. New York: Paulist Press, 2003.

Feingold, Lawrence. *Faith Comes from What Is Heard: An Introduction to Fundamental Theology.* Steubenville, OH: Emmaus Academic, 2016.

———. "God's Movement of the Soul through Operative and Cooperative Grace." In *Thomism and Predestination: Principles and Disputations*, edited by Steven A. Long, Roger W. Nutt, and Thomas Joseph White, 166–91. Washington, DC: Catholic University of America Press, 2017.

———. *The Mystery of Israel and the Church.* Vol. 1, *Figure and Fulfillment.* St. Louis, MO: Miriam Press, 2010.

———. *The Mystery of Israel and the Church.* Vol. 2, *Things New and Old.* St. Louis, MO: Miriam Press, 2010.

———. *The Mystery of Israel and the Church.* Vol. 3, *The Messianic Kingdom of Israel.* St. Louis, MO: Miriam Press, 2010.

———. "Vision of God in Christ: 'Who Loved Me and Gave Himself for Me.'" In *Love and Friendship: Maritain and the Tradition*, edited by Montague Brown, 218–32. Washington, DC: Catholic University of America Press, 2013

Ferreres, Juan B. *The Decree on Daily Communion: A Historical Sketch and Commentary*. Translated by H. Jimenez. St. Louis, MO: B. Herder, 1909.

Filip, Štěpán Martin, O.P. "Imago Repræsentativa Passionis Christi: St. Thomas Aquinas on the Essence of the Sacrifice of the Mass." *Nova et Vetera* (English) 7 (2009): 405–38.

Fisher, Eugene J., ed. *The Jewish Roots of Christian Liturgy*. New York: Paulist Press, 1990.

Flynn, Vinny. *Seven Secrets of the Eucharist*. Stockbridge, MA: MercySong, 2006.

Forrest, Michael D. *The Clean Oblation*. St. Paul, MN: Radio Replies Press, 1945.

Franzelin, Ioannis Bapt. *Tractatus de ss. Eucharistiae Sacramento et Sacrificio*. Rome: Ex Typographia Polyglotta, 1887.

Frenay, Adolph Dominic, O.P. *The Spirituality of the Mass in the Light of Thomistic Theology*. St. Louis: B. Herder, 1953.

Galadza, Peter. "Liturgy and Heaven in the Eastern Rites." *Antiphon* 10, no. 3 (2006): 239–60.

Galot, Jean. "Le parole eucaristiche di Gesù." *Civiltà Cattolica* 144, no. 2 (1993): 16–28.

Gamber, Klaus. "Die Eucharistia der Didache." *Ephemerides Liturgicae* 101 (1987): 3–32.

———. *The Reform of the Roman Liturgy: Its Problems and Background*. Translated by Klaus D. Grimm. Fort Collins, CO: Roman Catholic Books, n.d.

Garrigou-Lagrange, Reginald, O.P. "An Christus non Solum Virtualiter sed Actualiter Offerat Missas quae Quotidie Celebrantur?" *Angelicum* 19 (1942): 105–18.

———. *De Eucharistia et Paenitentia*. Turin: Marietti, 1948.

Gaudoin-Parker, Michael L., ed. *The Real Presence Through the Ages: Jesus Adored in the Sacrament of the Altar*. New York: Alba House, 1993.

Geiselmann, Josef. *Die Eucharistielehre der Vorscholastik*. Paderborn: F. Schönigh, 1926.

———. *Die Abendmahlslehre an der Wende der christlichen Spätantike zum Frühmittelalter: Isidor von Sevilla und das Sakrament der Eucharistie*. München: Max Hueber, 1933.

Gelston, A. *The Eucharistic Prayer of Addai and Mari*. Oxford: Clarendon Press, 1992.

Gerrish, Brian. *Grace and Gratitude: The Eucharistic Theology of John Calvin.* Minneapolis, MN: Fortress Press, 1993.

Gherardini, Brunero. "Le parole della Consacrazione eucaristica." *Divinitas,* n.s., numero speciale (2004): 141–69.

Ghysens, G. "Présence réelle et transsubstantiation dans les définitions de l'Eglise catholique." *Irénikon* 32 (1959): 420–435.

Giraudo, Cesare, S.J., ed. *The Anaphoral Genesis of the Institution Narrative in Light of the Anaphora of Addai and Mari: Acts of the International Liturgy Congress, Rome, 25–26 October 2011.* Rome: Edizioni Orientalia Christiana, 2013.

———. "L'anafora di Addai e Mari: banco di prova per la sistematica dell'Eucaristia." In *The Anaphoral Genesis of the Institution Narrative,* 209–33.

———. *Eucaristia per la chiesa: prospettive teologiche sull'eucaristia a partire dalla "lex orandi."* Rome: Gregorian University Press, 1989.

———. "The Eucharist as Re-presentation." *Religious Studies Bulletin* 4 (1984): 154–59.

———. "L'eucaristia: premio per i sani o medicina per i malati? Nuovi orizzonti di teologia a partire dalle anafore d'Oriente e d'Occidente." *La Civiltà Cattolica* 166 (September 26, 2015): 480–93.

———. "La genesi anaforica del racconto istituzionale alla luce dell'anafora di Addai e Mari: tra storia delle forme e liturgia comparata." In *The Anaphoral Genesis of the Institution Narrative,* 425–53.

———. *In unum corpus: trattato mistagogico sull'eucaristia.* Milan, IT: San Paolo, 2007.

———. *"In persona Christi—In persona Ecclesiae.* Formule eucaristiche alla luce della lex orandi," *Rassegna di teologia* 51 (2010): 181–95.

———. *La struttura letteraria della preghiera eucaristica: saggio sulla genesi letteraria di una forma : toda veterotestamentaria, beraka giudaica, anafora cristiana.* Rome : Biblical Institute Press, 1981.

Goering, Joseph. "The Invention of Transubstantiation." *Traditio* 46 (1991): 147–70.

Gorevan, Patrick. *"O Sacrum Convivium*—St Thomas on the Eucharist." *New Blackfriars* 90 (2009): 659–64.

Girard, René. *The One by Whom Scandal Comes.* Translated by Malcolm B. Debevoise. East Lansing: Michigan State University Press, 2014.

Granados, José. "The Liturgy: Presence of a New Body, Source of a Fulfilled Time." *Communio* 39, no. 4 (2012): 529–53.

Grisez, Germain. "An Alternative Theology of Jesus' Substantial Presence in the Eucharist." *Irish Theological Quarterly* 65 (2000): 111–31.

Groeschel, Benedict J., C.F.R, and James Monti. *In the Presence of Our Lord: The History, Theology, and Psychology of Eucharistic Devotion.* Huntington, IN: Our Sunday Visitor, 1997.

Guernsey, Daniel P., ed. *Adoration: Eucharistic Texts and Prayers throughout Church History.* San Francisco: Ignatius Press, 1999.

Gutwenger, E. "Substanz und Akzidenz in der Eucharistielehre." *Zeitschrift für katholische Theologie* 83 (1961): 257–306.

Gy, Pierre-Marie. "Avancées du traité de l'eucharistie de St. Thomas dans la Somme par rapport aux Sentences." *Revue des sciences philosophiques et théologiques* 77 (1993): 219–28.

Haffner, Paul. *The Sacramental Mystery.* Leominster, UK: Gracewing, 2008.

Hahn, Scott. *The Lamb's Supper: The Mass as Heaven on Earth.* New York: Doubleday, 1999.

——. "Temple, Sign, and Sacrament: Towards a New Perspective on the Gospel of John." *Letter & Spirit* 4 (2008): 107–43`.

Hamman, André. *The Mass: Ancient Liturgies and Patristic Texts.* New York: Alba House, 1967.

Haring, N. "Berengar's Definitions of *Sacramentum* and Their Influence on Medieval Sacramentology." *Mediaeval Studies* 10 (1948): 109–46.

Hauke, Manfred. "Shed for Many: An Accurate Rendering of the *Pro Multis* in the Formula of Consecration." *Antiphon* 14, no. 2 (2010): 169–229.

Healy, Mary. *The Gospel of Mark.* Grand Rapids, MI: Baker Academic, 2008.

Healy, Nicholas J. Jr. "The Eucharist as the Form of Christian Life." *Communio* 39, no. 4 (2012): 587–93.

Hemming, Laurence Paul. "After Heidegger: Transubstantiation." *Heythrop Journal* 41 (2000): 170–86.

Heringer, Dominik. *Die Anaphora der Apostel Addai und Mari: Ausdrucksform einer eucharistischen Ekklesiologie.* Göttingen: Vandenhoeck & Ruprecht, 2013.

Hirsh, Emil G. "Sacrifice." In *Jewish Encyclopedia.* Edited by Cyrus Adler and Isidore Singer. New York: Ktav Publishing House, 1964)

Hödl, Ludwig. "Sacramentum und res: Zeichen und Bezeichnetes. Eine begriffsgeschichtliche Arbeit zum frühscholastischen Eucharistietraktat." *Scholastik* 38 (1963): 161–82.

Hoffman, Adolph. "De Sacrificio Missae Juxta S. Thomam." *Angelicum* 15 (1938): 261–85.

Hoffman, Lawrence A., and David Arnow, eds. *My People's Haggadah: Traditional Texts, Modern Commentaries.* Woodstock, VT: Jewish Lights, 2008.

Hugon, Eduardo. *Tractatus Dogmatici.* Vol. 4, *De Sacramentis in Communi; de Eucharistia; de Novissimis.* Paris: Lethielleux, 1920.

Humbrecht, Thierry-Dominique, O.P. "L'eucharistie, 'représentation' du sacrifice du Christ, selon saint Thomas." *Revue Thomiste* 98 (1998): 355–86.

Hütter, Reinhard. "Transubstantiation Revisited: *Sacra Doctrina*, Dogma and Metaphysics." In *Ressourcement Thomism: Sacred Doctrine, the Sacraments, and the Moral Life*, edited by Reinhard Hütter and Matthew Levering, 21–79. Washington, DC: Catholic University of America Press, 2010.

Ibáñez, Ángel García. *L'Eucaristia, Dono e Mistero: Trattato storico-dogmatico sul mistero eucaristico*. Rome: Edizioni Università della Santa Croce, 2008.

Iserloh, Erwin. "Die Wert der Messe in der Diskussion der Theologen vom Mittelalter bis zum 16. Jahrhundert." *Zeitschrift für katholische Theologie* 83 (1961): 44–79.

Jammo, Sarhad. "The Anaphora of the Apostles Addai and Mari: A Study of Structure and Historical Background." In *Studies on the Anaphora of Addai and Mari*, edited by Bosco Puthur, 1–34. Kochi, India: L.R.C. Publications, 2004.

———. "The Chaldean Liturgy." In *Emmanuel: The Book of Public Prayer, Selected from the Yearly Cycle of the Hudhra, with the Volume of Kahnayta, Which Is the Book of the Rites of All the Sacraments, as Celebrated in the Chaldean Church of the East*, i–cii. San Diego: Chaldean Catholic Diocese of St. Peter the Apostle, 2013.

———. "The Mesopotamian Anaphora of Addai & Mari: The Organic Dialectic Between Its Apostolic Core and Euchological Growth." In Giraudo, *The Anaphoral Genesis of the Institution Narrative*, 387–424.

Jaubert, Annie. *The Date of the Last Supper*. Staten Island, NY: Alba House, 1965.

Jensen, Robin M. "Recovering Ancient Ecclesiology: The Place of the Altar and the Orientation of Prayer in the Early Latin Church." *Worship* 89, no. 2 (2015): 99–124.

Jenson, Philip J. "The Levitical Sacrificial System." In *Sacrifice in the Bible*, edited by Roger T. Beckwith and Martin J. Selman, 25–40. Grand Rapids, MI: Baker Book House, 1995.

Jeremias, Joachim. *The Eucharistic Words of Jesus*. Translated by Norman Perrin from the 3rd German edition. Philadelphia, PA: Fortress Press, 1977.

Johnson, Maxwell E., ed. *Issues in Eucharistic Praying in East and West: Essays in Liturgical and Theological Analysis*. Collegeville, MN: Liturgical Press, 2010.

Johnson, Maxwell E., and L. Edward Phillips, eds. *Studia Liturgica Diversa: Studies in Church Music and Liturgy: Essays in Honor of Paul F. Bradshaw*. Portland, OR: The Pastoral Press, 2004.

Jones, Cheslyn, Geoffrey Wainwright, Edward Yarnold, and Paul Bradshaw, eds. *The Study of Liturgy*. Revised edition. New York: Oxford University Press, 1992.

Jorissen, Hans. *Die Entfaltung der Transsubstantiationslehre bis zum Beginn der Hochscholastik*. Münster: Aschendorffsche Verlagsbuchhandlung, 1965.

Joseph de Sainte-Marie, OCD. "L'Eucharistie, sacrament et sacrifice du Christ et de l'Eglise: Développements des perspectives thomistes," *Divinitas* 18 (1974): 237–49.

———. *The Holy Eucharist: The World's Salvation; Studies on the Holy Sacrifice of the Mass, Its Celebration and Its Concelebration*. Leominster, UK: Gracewing, 2015.

Journet, Charles. *The Mass: The Presence of the Sacrifice of the Cross*. Translated by Victor Szczurek. South Bend, IN: St. Augustine's Press, 2008.

———. "Transubstantiation." *The Thomist* 38 (1974): 734–46.

Joy, John. "Love and Self-Gift: Sacrifice in St. Augustine's *City of God*." *Antiphon* 11, no. 2 (2007): 78–85.

Jüngel, Eberhard. *Justification: The Heart of the Christian Faith; A Theological Study with an Ecumenical Purpose*. Translated by Jeffrey F. Cayzer. Edinburgh: T & T Clark, 2001.

Jungmann, Josef A., S.J. *The Early Liturgy to the Time of Gregory the Great*. Translated by Francis A. Brunner. Notre Dame, IN: University of Notre Dame Press, 1959.

———. *The Eucharistic Prayer: A Study of the Canon Missae*. Translated by Robert Batley. Notre Dame, IN: Fides, 1963.

———. *The Mass: An Historical, Theological, and Pastoral Survey*. Translated by Julian Fernandes and edited by Mary E. Evans. Collegeville, MN: Liturgical Press, 1976.

———. *The Mass of the Roman Rite: Its Origins and Development*. 2 vols. Translated by Francis A. Brunner. New York: Benziger Brothers, 1951–1955.

Kampowski, Stephan, and Juan José Pérez-Soba, eds. *The Gospel of the Family: Going Beyond Cardinal Kasper's Proposal in the Debate on Marriage, Civil Re-Marriage and Communion in the Church*. San Francisco: Ignatius Press, 2014.

Keating, Daniel. *Deification and Grace*. Naples, FL: Sapientia Press of Ave Maria University, 2007.

———. "Deification in the Greek Fathers." In *Called to Be the Children of God: The Catholic Theology of Human Deification*, edited by Meconi, David Vincent, and Carl Olson, 40–58. San Francisco: Ignatius Press, 2016.

Keener, Craig S. *The Gospel of John: A Commentary*. Peabody, MA: Hendrickson, 2003.

Keller, Paul Jerome. "Is Spiritual Communion for Everyone?" *Nova et Vetera* (English) 12, no. 3 (2014): 631–55.

Kelly, B. "The Eucharist: Sacrifice or Meal?" *Irish Theological Quarterly* 35 (1968): 298–306.

Kereszty, Roch A., O. Cist. "Real Presence, Manifold Presence: Christ and the Church's Eucharist." *Antiphon* 6, no. 3 (2001): 23–36.

———. *Wedding Feast of the Lamb: Eucharistic Theology from a Historical, Biblical, and Systematic Perspective.* Chicago: Hillenbrand Books, 2004.

Kereszty, Roch A., ed. *Rediscovering the Eucharist: Ecumenical Considerations.* New York: Paulist Press, 2003.

Kilmartin, Edward J., S.J. *The Eucharist in the West: History and Theology.* Edited by Robert J. Daly. Collegeville, MN: Liturgical Press, 1998.

King, R. F. "The Origin and Evolution of a Sacramental Formula: *Sacramentum Tantum, Res et Sacramentum, Res Tantum,*" *The Thomist* 31 (1967): 21–82.

Klawans, Jonathan. *Purity, Sacrifice, and the Temple.* Oxford University Press, 2006.

Kleiner, Joseph. "Théologie de la concélébration: Réponse a quelques objections." *Esprit et vie* 89 (1979): 671–80.

———. "Théologie de la concélébration." *Esprit et vie* 90 (1980): 548–54.

Kodell, Jerome, O.S.B. *The Eucharist in the New Testament.* Collegeville, MN: Liturgical Press, 1988.

Kwasniewski, Peter A. "Doing and Speaking in the Person of Christ: Eucharistic Form in the Anaphora of Addai and Mari." *Nova et Vetera* (English) 4, no. 2 (2006): 313–80.

———. "Aquinas on Eucharistic Ecstasy: From Self-Alienation to Gift of Self." *Nova et Vetera* (English) 6, no. 1 (2008): 157–204.

La Femina, Anthony A. *Eucharist and Covenant in John's Last Supper Account.* New Hope, KY: New Hope Publications, 2011.

Lagrange, Marie-Joseph. *The Gospel of Jesus Christ.* London: Burns, Oates & Washbourne, 1947.

Landgraf, Artur Michael. *Dogmengeschichte der Frühscholastik.* 4 vols. Regensburg: Friedrich Pustet, 1952–.

Lane, Thomas. "The Jewish Temple Is Transfigured in Christ and the Temple Liturgies Are Transfigured in the Sacraments." *Antiphon* 19, no. 1 (2015): 14–28.

Lang, David P. *Why Matter Matters: Philosophical and Scriptural Reflections on the Sacraments.* Huntington, IN: Our Sunday Visitor, 2002.

Lang, Uwe Michael. "Augustine's Conception of Sacrifice in *City of God*, Book X, and the Eucharistic Sacrifice." *Antiphon* 19, no. 1 (2015): 29–51.

———. "The Crisis of Sacred Art and the Sources for Its Renewal in the Thought of Pope Benedict XVI." *Antiphon* 12, no. 3 (2008): 218–39.

———. "Eucharist without Institution Narrative? The 'Anaphora of Addai and Mari' Revisited." *Divinitas*, n.s., numero speciale (2004): 227–60.

———. *Signs of the Holy One: Liturgy, Ritual, and the Expression of the Sacred.* San Francisco: Ignatius Press, 2015.

———. *Turning towards the Lord: Orientation in Liturgical Prayer.* San Francisco: Ignatius Press, 2004.

———. The *Voice of the Church at Prayer: Reflections on Liturgy and Language.* San Francisco: Ignatius Press, 2012.

———. "What Makes Architecture Sacred?" *Logos* 17, no. 4 (2014): 44–64.

———, ed. *Die Anaphora von Addai und Mari: Studien zu Eucharistie und Einsetzungsworten.* Bonn: Verlag Nova & Vetera, 2007.

———, ed. *The Genius of the Roman Rite: Historical, Theological, and Pastoral Perspectives on Catholic Liturgy.* Chicago : Hillenbrand Books, 2010.

Langevin, Dominic M., O.P. *From Passion to Paschal Mystery: A Recent Magisterial Development concerning the Christological Foundation of the Sacraments.* Fribourg, CH: Academic Press, 2015.

Lemma, Keith. "Louis Bouyer's Defense of Religion and the Sacred: Sacrifice and the Primacy of Divine Gift in Christian Liturgy." *Antiphon* 12, no. 1 (2008): 2–24.

Léon-Dufour, Xavier. *Sharing the Eucharistic Bread: The Witness of the New Testament.* Translated by Matthew J. O'Connell. New York: Paulist Press, 1987.

Lepin, Marius. *L'idée du sacrifice de la Messe d'après les théologiens depuis l'origine jusqu'à nos jours.* Paris: Gabriel Beauchesne, 1926.

Leppin, Volker. "Martin Luther." In *A Companion to the Eucharist in the Reformation.* Edited by Lee Palmer Wandel. Leiden/Boston: Brill.

Levering, Matthew. "Aquinas on the Liturgy of the Eucharist." In *Aquinas on Doctrine: A Critical Introduction*, edited by Thomas Weinandy, Daniel Keating, and John Yocum, 183–98. London: T & T Clark, 2004.

———. *Christ's Fulfillment of Torah and Temple: Salvation according to Thomas Aquinas.* Notre Dame, IN: University of Notre Dame Press, 2002.

———. *Engaging the Doctrine of the Holy Spirit: Love and Gift in the Trinity and the Church.* Grand Rapids, MI: Baker Academic, 2016.

———. "John Paul II and Aquinas on the Eucharist." In *John Paul II & St. Thomas Aquinas*, edited by Michael Dauphinais and Matthew Levering, 209–31. Naples, FL: Sapientia Press of Ave Maria University, 2006.

———. "A Note on Joseph Ratzinger and Contemporary Theology of the Priesthood." *Nova et Vetera* (English) 5, no. 2 (2007): 271–84.

———. *Sacrifice and Community: Jewish Offering and Christian Eucharist.* Malden, MA: Blackwell, 2005.

Levering, Matthew, and Michael Dauphinais, eds. *Rediscovering Aquinas and the Sacraments: Studies in Sacramental Theology.* Chicago: Hillenbrand Books, 2009.

Levy, Ian Christopher, Gary Macy, and Kristen Van Ausdall, eds. *A Companion to the Eucharist in the Middle Ages.* Leiden/Boston: Brill, 2012.

Lewis, Keith D. "'Unica Oblatio Christi': Eucharistic Sacrifice and the First Zürich Disputation." *Renaissance and Reformation*, n.s., 17, no. 3 (1993): 19–42.

Lienhard, Joseph, S.J. "*Sacramentum* and the Eucharist in St. Augustine." *The Thomist* 77 (2013): 173–92.

Long, Steven A. "The Efficacy Of God's Sacramental Presence." *Nova et Vetera* (English) 7, no. 4 (2009): 869–76.

Lottin, Odon. *Psychologie et morale aux XIIe et XIIIe siècles.* Vol. 5. Gembloux, BE: J. Duculot, 1959.

Lubac, Henri de. *Corpus Mysticum: The Eucharist and the Church in the Middle Ages.* Translated by Gemma Simmonds. Notre Dame, IN: University of Notre Dame Press, 2007.

Lutherans and Catholics in Dialogue III: The Eucharist as Sacrifice. Washington, DC: U.S.A. National Committee of the Lutheran World Federation and the Bishops' Commission for Ecumenical Affairs, 1968.

Lynch, Reginald M., O.P. "Cajetan's Harp: Sacraments and the Life of Grace in Light of Perfective Instrumentality." *The Thomist* 78 (2014): 65–106.

———. "The Sacraments as Causes of Sanctification." *Nova et Vetera* (English) 12, no. 3 (2014): 791–836.

Macdonald, Allen J. *Berengar and the Reform of Sacramental Doctrine.* London: Longmans, Green, 1930.

Macomber, William F. "The Maronite and Chaldean Versions of the Anaphora of the Apostles." *Orientalia Christiana Periodica* 37 (1971): 55–84.

———. "The Oldest Known Text of the Anaphora of the Apostles *Addai and Mari,*" *Orientalia Christiana Periodica* 32 (1966): 335–71.

———. "The Ancient Form of the Anaphora of the Apostles." In *East of Byzantium: Syria and Armenia in the formative Period*, edited by N. G. Garsoïan, Y. G. Mathews, and R. W. Thomson, 73–88. Washington, DC: Dumbarton Oaks, 1982.

Macy, Gary. *The Theologies of the Eucharist in the Early Scholastic Period: A Study of the Salvific Function of the Sacrament according to the Theologians c.1080–c.1220.* New York: Oxford University Press, 1984.

Madeleine Grace, C.V.I. "Looking Again at Looking Eastward: *Ad orientem* Worship and Liturgical Renewal." *Antiphon* 14, no. 3 (2010): 285–300.

Malone, Richard. "Eucharist: Sacrifice According to the Logos." *Antiphon* 13, no. 1 (2009): 65–83.

Manelli, Stefano M., F.F.I. *Jesus Our Eucharistic Love: Eucharistic Life Exemplified by the Saints.* New Bedford, MA: Franciscan Friars of the Immaculate, 1996.

Manns, Frédéric. *Jewish Prayer in the Time of Jesus.* Jerusalem: Franciscan Printing Press, 1994.

Maritain, Jacques. *Untrammeled Approaches.* Translated by Bernard Doering. Vol. 20 of *Collected Works.* Notre Dame, IN: Univ. Notre Dame Press, 1997.

Marr, Ryan J. "René Girard and the Holy Sacrifice of the Mass: Re-Assessing the Twentieth Century Liturgical reform." *Antiphon* 20, no. 3 (2016): 191–12.

Marshall, Bruce D. "Debt, Punishment, and Payment: A Meditation on the Cross, in Light of St. Anselm," *Nova et Vetera* (English) 9 (2011): 163–81.

———. "The Eucharistic Presence of Christ." In *What Does It Mean to "Do This"?* edited by J. J. Buckley and M. Root, 209–31. Eugene, OR: Cascade Books, 2014.

———. "Identity, Being, and Eucharist." *The Saint Anselm Journal* 9, no. 2 (2014): 1–22.

———. "What Is the Eucharist? A Dogmatic Outline." In Boersma and Levering, eds., *The Oxford Handbook of Sacramental Theology,* 500–16.

———. "The Whole Mystery of Our Salvation: St. Thomas on the Eucharist as Sacrifice." In *Sacraments in Aquinas,* edited by Michael Dauphinais and Matthew Levering, 39–64. Chicago: Hillenbrand Books, 2009.

Martelet, Gustave. *The Risen Christ and the Eucharistic World.* Translated by René Hague. New York: Seabury Press, 1976.

Martimort, Aimé Georges, et al., eds. *The Church at Prayer: An Introduction to the Liturgy.* Vol. 2, *The Eucharist.* Collegeville, MN: Liturgical Press, 1986.

Martin, Francis, and William M. Wright IV. *The Gospel of John.* Grand Rapids, MI: Baker Academic, 2015.

Massa, James. "Building Communion on the Lord's Day: An Appraisal of John Paul II's *Dies Domini.*" *Antiphon* 8, no. 3 (2003): 13–20.

Masterson, Robert Reginald. "Sacramental Graces: Modes of Sanctifying Grace." *The Thomist* 18 (1955): 311–72.

Masure, Eugène. *The Christian Sacrifice.* Translated with a preface by Illtyd Trethowan. London: Burns and Oates, 1944.

———. *The Sacrifice of the Mystical Body.* London: Burns & Oates, 1954.

Matthiesen, Michon M. "De la Taille's *Mysterium Fidei*: Eucharistic Sacrifice and Nouvelle Théologie." *New Blackfriars* 94 (2013): 518–39.

———. *Sacrifice as Gift: Eucharist, Grace, and Contemplative Prayer in Maurice de la Taille.* Washington, DC: Catholic University of America Press, 2013.

Matthijs, Mannes M. *De Aeternitate Sacerdotii Christi et de Unitate Sacrificii Crucis et Altaris.* Rome: Pontificia Studiorum Universitas a S.Thoma Aq. in Urbe, 1963.

Mattox, Mickey L. "Sacraments in the Lutheran Reformation." In Boersma and Levering, eds., *The Oxford Handbook of Sacramental Theology*, 269–82.

Mazza, Enrico. "Che cos'è l'anafora eucaristica?" *Divinitas*, n.s., numero speciale (2004): 37–56.

———. *The Eucharistic Prayers of the Roman Rite.* New York: Pueblo, 1986.

———. *The Origins of the Eucharistic Prayer.* Collegeville, MN: Liturgical Press, 1995.

———. "La preghiera eucaristica come sacrificio: La testimonianza delle antiche anafore sulla concezione sacrificale dell'eucaristia." *Protest* 62 (2007): 263–90.

———. "Sul Canone della messa citato nel *De sacramentis* di Ambrogio." *Ecclesia Orans* 27 (2010): 271–93.

McCue, James F. "The Doctrine of Transubstantiation from Berengar through Trent: The Point at Issue." *Harvard Theological Review* 61 (1968): 385–430.

McDonnell, Kilian. *John Calvin, the Church, and the Eucharist.* Princeton, N.J.: Princeton University Press, 1967.

McGowan, Jean Carroll. *Concelebration: Sign of the Unity of the Church.* New York: Herder and Herder, 1964.

McGuckian, Michael, S.J. *The Holy Sacrifice of the Mass: A Search for an Acceptable Notion of Sacrifice.* Chicago: Hillenbrand Books, 2005.

McKenna, John H. *Eucharist and Holy Spirit: The Eucharistic Epiclesis in 20th Century Theology.* Alcuin Club Collections 57. Great Wakering, UK: Mayhew-McCrimmon, 1975.

———. *The Eucharistic Epiclesis: A Detailed History from the Patristic to the Modern Era.* 2nd ed. Chicago: Hillenbrand Books, 2009.

———. "Eucharistic Presence: An Invitation to Dialogue." *Theological Studies* 60 (June 1999): 294–317.

McNamara, Martin, ed. *Targum and Testament Revisited: Aramaic Paraphrases of the Hebrew Bible: A Light on the New Testament.* 2nd ed. Grand Rapids, MI: Eerdmans, 2010.

McPartlan, Paul. "The Eucharist as the Basis for Ecclesiology." *Antiphon* 6, no. 2 (2001): 12–19.

————. *The Eucharist Makes the Church: Henri De Lubac and John Zizioulas in Dialogue*. Fairfax, VA: Eastern Christian Publications, 2006.

Meconi, David Vincent. *The One Christ: St. Augustine's Theology of Deification*. Washington, DC: Catholic University of America Press, 2013.

Meconi, David Vincent, and Carl Olson, editors. *Called to Be the Children of God: The Catholic Theology of Human Deification*. San Francisco: Ignatius Press, 2016.

Megivern, James. *Concomitance and Communion: A Study in Eucharistic Doctrine and Practice*. Fribourg, CH: University Press, 1963.

Meier, John P. *A Marginal Jew: Rethinking the Historical Jesus*. Vol. 1. New York: Doubleday, 1991.

Meinert, John. "*Alimentum Pacis*: The Eucharist and Peace in St. Thomas Aquinas." *Nova et Vetera* (English) 14, no. 4 (2016): 871–90.

Merton, Thomas. *The Living Bread*. New York: Farrar, Straus & Cudahy, 1956.

Metzger, Marcel. "Nouvelles perspectives pour la prétendue 'Tradition apostolique.'" *Ecclesia Orans* 5 (1988): 241–59.

————. "Enquêtes autour de la prétendue 'Tradition apostolique.'" *Ecclesia Orans* 9 (1992): 7–36.

————. "Apropos des règlements ecclésiastiques et de la prétendue Tradition apostolique." *Revue des sciences religieuses* 66 (1992): 249–61.

————. "La prière eucharistique de la prétendue Tradition apostolique." In *Prex Eucharistica*. Vol. 3, pt. 1, *Studia: Ecclesia antiqua et occidentalis*, edited by A. Gerhards et al., Spicilegium Friburgense 42, 263–80. Fribourg, CH: University Press, 2005).

Minns, Denis, and Paul Parvis. *Justin, Philosopher and Martyr: Apologies*. Oxford: Oxford University Press, 2009.

Miralles, Antonio. *Ecclesia et sacramenta: raccolta di studi*. Edited by Rafael Díaz Dorronsoro and Ángel García Ibáñez. Siena, IT: Cantagalli, 2011.

————. *Los sacramentos cristianos: curso de sacramentaria fundamental*. Madrid, ES: Ediciones Palabra, 2006. Also available in Italian: *I sacramenti cristiani: trattato generale*. 2nd ed. Rome: Apollinare studi, 2008.

Moloney, Raymond. *The Eucharist*. Collegeville, MN: Liturgical Press, 1995.

Montclos, Jean de. *Lanfranc et Bérenger: La controverse eucharistique du XIe Siècle*. Leuven, BE: Spicilegium sacrum Lovaniense, 1971.

Mosebach, Martin. *The Heresy of Formlessness: The Roman Liturgy and Its Enemy*. Translated by Graham Harrison. San Francisco: Ignatius Press, 2006.

Mudd, Joseph C. *Eucharist as Meaning: Critical Metaphysics and Contemporary Sacramental Theology*. Collegeville, MN: Liturgical Press, 2014.

Muksuris, Stylianos. "A Brief Overview of the Structure and Theology of the Liturgy of the Apostles Addai and Mari." *Greek Orthodox Theological Review* 43 (1998): 59–83.

Murray, Paul. *Aquinas at Prayer: The Bible, Mysticism and Poetry.* London: Bloomsbury, 2013.

Mussone, Davide. *L'Eucaristia nel Codice di Diritto Canonico: Commento ai cann. 897–958.* Vatican City: Libreria Editrice Vaticana, 2002.

Nash, Thomas J. *The Biblical Roots of the Mass.* Manchester, NH: Sophia Institute Press, 2015.

Navarro Girón, María Angeles. *La carne de Cristo: El misterio eucaristico a la luz de la controversia entre Pascasio Radberto, Ratramno, Rabano Mauro y Godescalco.* Madrid, ES: UPCM, 1989.

Neunheuser, Burkhard. *L'eucharistie: au Moyen Âge et à l'époque moderne.* Translated by A. Liefooghe. Paris: Éditions du Cerf, 1966.

Nicolas, Marie-Joseph. *What Is the Eucharist?* Twentieth Century Encyclopedia of Catholicism 52. New York: Hawthorn Books, 1960.

Nicholas, Richard A. *The Eucharist as the Center of Theology: A Comparative Study.* New York: Peter Lang, 2005.

Nichols, Aidan. *The Holy Eucharist: From the New Testament to Pope John Paul II.* Eugene, OR: Wipf & Stock, 1991.

———. "The Holy Oblation: On the Primacy of Eucharistic Sacrifice." *Dowside Review* 122 (2004):259–72.

———. *Looking at the Liturgy: A Critical View of Its Contemporary Form.* San Francisco: Ignatius Press, 1996.

Nichols, Terrence. "Transubstantiation and Eucharistic Presence." *Pro Ecclesia* 11 (2002): 57–75.

Niederwimmer, Kurt. *The Didache: A Commentary.* Translated by Linda Maloney. Minneapolis, MN: Fortress Press, 1998.

Nocent, Adrien. "Christian Sunday." In *The Jewish Roots of Christian Liturgy,* edited by Eugene J. Fisher, 130–41. New York: Paulist Press, 1990.

Nutt, Roger. "The Application of Christ's One Oblation: Charles Journet on the Mass, the Real Presence, and the Sacrifice of the Cross." *Nova et Vetera* (English) 8, no. 3 (2010): 665–81.

———. "Faith, Metaphysics, and the Contemplation of Christ's Corporeal Presence in the Eucharist: Translation of St. Thomas Aquinas' Seventh Quodlibetal Dispute, Q. 4, A. 1 with an Introductory Essay," *Antiphon* 15, no. 2 (2011): 151–71.

———. *General Principles of Sacramental Theology.* Washington, DC: Catholic University of America Press, 2017.

O'Carroll, Michael. *Corpus Christi: An Encyclopedia of the Eucharist*. Wilmington, DE: Michael Glazier, 1988.

O'Connor, James T. *The Hidden Manna*. San Francisco: Ignatius Press, 1988.

O'Donoghue, Neil Xavier. "'Partakers of the Same Sacrifice.'" *Antiphon* 16, no. 2 (2012): 130–43.

Oesterley, William Oscar Emil. *The Jewish Background of the Christian Liturgy*. Gloucester, MA: P. Smith, 1965.

O'Neill, Colman E., O.P. *Meeting Christ in the Sacraments*. New York: Alba House, 1991.

———. *New Approaches to the Eucharist*. New York: Alba House, 1967.

———. *Sacramental Realism: A General Theory of the Sacraments*. Wilmington, DE: Michael Glazier, 1983.

O'Reilly, Kevin E., O.P. "The Eucharist and the Politics of Love According to Thomas Aquinas." *Heythrop Journal* 56 (2015): 399–410.

Parsch, Pius. *The Liturgy of the Mass*. 3rd ed. Translated by H. E. Winstone. St. Louis, MO: B. Herder, 1957.

Pelikan, Jaroslav. *The Christian Tradition: A History of the Development of Doctrine*. Chicago: University of Chicago Press, 1978.

Phelan, Owen M. "Horizontal and Vertical Theologies: 'Sacraments' in the Works of Paschasius Radbertus and Ratramnus of Corbie." *Harvard Theological Review* 103, no. 3 (2010): 271–89.

Piolanti, Antonio. "L'Eucaristia." In *Il Protestantesimo ieri e oggi*, edited by Antonio Piolanti, 1090–26. Rome: Libreria Editrice Religiosa F. Ferrari, 1958.

———. *The Holy Eucharist*. Translated by Luigi Penzo. New York: Desclee, 1961.

———. *Il Mistero Eucaristico*. Vatican City: Libreria Editrice Vaticana, 1983.

Pitre, Brant. *Jesus and the Jewish Roots of the Eucharist: Unlocking the Secrets of the Last Supper*. New York: Doubleday Religion, 2011.

———. *Jesus and the Last Supper*. Grand Rapids, MI: Eerdmans, 2015.

———. "The Last Supper and the Quest for Jesus." *Letter & Spirit* 9 (2014): 77–103.

Plested, Marcus. *Orthodox Readings of Aquinas*. Oxford: Oxford University Press, 2012.

Pohle, Joseph. *The Sacraments: A Dogmatic Treatise*. Vol. 2, *The Holy Eucharist*. 2nd revised ed. Edited by Arthur Preuss. St. Louis, MO: B. Herder, 1917.

Pomplun, Trent. "Post-Tridentine Sacramental Theology." In Boersma and Levering, eds., *The Oxford Handbook of Sacramental Theology*, 348–61.

Pourrat, P. *Theology of the Sacraments: A Study in Positive Theology*. St. Louis, MO: B. Herder, 1910.

Power, David N. *The Eucharistic Mystery: Revitalizing the Tradition*. New York: Crossroad, 1993.

———. *The Sacrifice We Offer: The Tridentine Dogma and Its Reinterpretation*. New York: Crossroad, 1987.

Powers, Joseph M. *Eucharistic Theology*. New York: Herder and Herder, 1967.

Pratzner, Ferdinand. *Messe und Kreuzesopfer: die Krise der sakramentalen Idee bei Luther und in der mittelalterlichen Scholastik*. Vienna, AT: Wien Herder, 1970.

Prosinger, Franz. *Das Blut des Bundes vergossen für viele? Zur Übersetzung und Interpretation des hyper pollōn in Mk 14,24*. Siegburg: Franz Schmitt, 2007.

Pruss, Alexander. "The Eucharist: Real Presence and Real Absence." In *The Oxford Handbook of Philosophical Theology*, edited by T. Flint and M. Rea, 512–40. Oxford: Oxford University Press, 2009.

Puthur, Bosco, ed. *Studies on the Anaphora of Addai and Mari*. Kochi, India: L.R.C. Publications, 2004.

Quasten, Johannes. *Patrology*. 4 vol. Westminster, MD: The Newman Press, 1950–1986.

Radding, Charles M., and Francis Newton. *Theology, Rhetoric, and Politics in the Eucharistic Controversy, 1078–1079: Alberic of Monte Cassino against Berengar of Tours*. New York: Columbia University Press, 2003.

Raes, Alfons. "Le récit de l'Institution eucharistique dans l'anaphore chaldéene et malabare des Apôtres." *Orientalia Christiana Periodica* 10 (1944): 216–26.

Rahner, Karl, S.J. "Multiplication of Masses." *Orate fratres* 24 (1950): 553–62.

Rahner, Karl, S.J., and Angelus Häussling. *The Celebration of the Eucharist*. Translated by W. J. O'Hara. New York: Herder and Herder, 1968.

Ranjith, Malcolm. "Towards an *Ars Celebrandi* in the Liturgy." *Antiphon* 13, no. 1 (2009): 7–17.

Ratzinger, Joseph. *Behold The Pierced One: An Approach to a Spiritual Christology*. Translated by Graham Harrison. San Francisco: Ignatius Press, 1986.

———. *Called to Communion: Understanding the Church Today*. Translated by Adrian Walker. San Francisco: Ignatius Press, 1996.

———. *Feast of Faith: Approaches to a Theology of the Liturgy*. Translated by Graham Harrison. San Francisco: Ignatius Press, 1986.

———. *God Is Near Us: The Eucharist, The Heart of Life*. Edited by Stephan Otto Horn and Vinzenz Pfnür. Translated by Henry Taylor and edited by Stephan Ott Horn and Vinzenz Pfnür. San Francisco: Ignatius Press, 2003.

———. *Jesus of Nazareth: The Infancy Narratives*. Translated by Philip J. Whitmore. New York: Image, 2012.

———. *Jesus of Nazareth: Holy Week, from the Entrance into Jerusalem to the Res-urrection.* Translated by Adrian J. Walker. San Francisco: Ignatius Press, 2011.

———. *A New Song for the Lord: Faith in Christ and Liturgy Today.* Translated by Martha M. Matesich. New York: Crossroad, 1997.

———. "Das Problem der Transsubstantiation und die Frage nach dem Sinn der Eucharistie." *Theologische Quartalschrift* 147 (1967): 129–58.

———. *The Spirit of the Liturgy.* Translated by John Saward. San Francisco: Ignatius Press, 2000.

———. "*The Spirit of the Liturgy* or Fidelity to the Council: Response to Father Gy." *Antiphon* 11, no. 1 (2007): 98–102.

———. "The Theology of the Liturgy." Translated by Margaret McHugh and John Parsons in *Looking Again at the Question of the Liturgy with Cardinal Ratzinger: Proceedings of the July 2001 Fontgombault Liturgical Conference,* edited by Alcuin Reid, 18–31. Farnborough, UK: Saint Michael's Abbey Press, 2003.

———. *Theology of the Liturgy: The Sacramental Foundation of Christian Exist-ence.* Vol. 11 in *Collected Works.* Translated by John Saward, Kenneth Baker, Henry Taylor, et al. and edited by Michael Miller San Francisco: Ignatius Press, 2014.

Reid, Alcuin, O.S.B. *The Organic Development of the Liturgy: The Principles of Liturgical Reform and Their Relation to the Twentieth-Century Liturgi-cal Movement Prior to the Second Vatican Council.* San Francisco: Ignatius Press, 2005.

———, editor. *From Eucharistic Adoration to Evangelization.* London: Burns & Oates, 2012.

———. *Liturgy in the Twenty-First Century: Contemporary Issues and Perspec-tives.* New York: Bloomsbury T&T Clark, 2016.

———. *The Sacred Liturgy: Source and Summit of the Life and Mission of the Church. The Proceedings of the International Conference on the Sacred Liturgy, Sacra Liturgia 2013, Pontifical University of the Holy Cross, Rome, 25–28 June 2013.* Edited by Alcuin Reid. San Francisco: Ignatius Press, 2014.

———. *T&T Clark Companion to Liturgy.* New York: Bloomsbury T&T Clark, 2016.

Robinson, Jonathan. *The Mass and Modernity: Walking to Heaven Backward.* San Francisco: Ignatius Press, 2005.

Rodríguez Luño, Ángel. "Can Epikeia Be Used in the Pastoral Care of the Divorced and Remarried Faithful?" In Congregation for the Doctrine of the Faith, *On the Pastoral Care of the Divorced and Remarried,* 49–59.

Washington DC: Libreria Editrice Vaticana, United States Council of Catholic Bishops, 2012.

Rogers, Elizabeth Frances. *Peter Lombard and the Sacramental System*. New York: Columbia University, 1917.

Rosemann, Philipp W. *Peter Lombard*. Oxford: Oxford University Press, 2004.

Rossetti, Stephen J., ed. *Born of the Eucharist: A Spirituality for Priests*. Notre Dame, IN: Ave Maria Press, 2009.

Roza, Devin. *Fulfilled in Christ: The Sacraments: a Guide to Symbols and Types in the Bible and Tradition*. Steubenville, OH: Emmaus Academic, 2015.

Rubin, M. *Corpus Christi: The Eucharist in Late Medieval Culture*. Cambridge: Cambridge University Press, 1991.

Russo, Nicholas V. "The Validity of the Anaphora of Addai and Mari: Crituqe of the Critiques." In *Issues in Eucharistic Praying in East and West: Essays in Liturgical and Theological Analysis*, edited by Maxwell Johnson, 21–62. Collegeville, MN: Liturgical Press, 2010.

Sandt, H. W. M. van de, and David Flusser. *The Didache: Its Jewish Sources and Its Place in Early Judaism and Christianity*. Assen, NL: Royal Van Gorcum; Minneapolis, MN, 2002.

Santogrossi, Ansgar. "Anaphoras without Institution Narrative: Historical and Dogmatic Considerations." *Nova et Vetera* (English) 10, no. 1 (2012): 27–59.

Sasse, Hermann. *This Is My Body: Luther's Contention for the Real Presence in the Sacrament of the Altar*. Minneapolis, MN: Augsburg, 1959.

Saward, John. "The Cosmic Liturgy and the Way of the Lamb: Retrieving the Tradition of Spiritual Exegesis of the Mass." *Antiphon* 7, no. 1 (2002): 18–28.

Schechter, Solomon. *Aspects of Rabbinic Theology: Major Concepts of the Talmud*. New York: Schocken Books, 1961.

Scheeben, Matthias Joseph. *The Mysteries of Christianity*. Translated by Cyril Vollert. St. Louis: B. Herder, 1951.

Schenk, R., O.P. "Verum sacrificium as the Fullness and Limit of Eucharistic Sacrifice in the Sacramental Theology of Thomas Aquinas." In *Ressourcement Thomism: Sacred Doctrine, the Sacraments, and the Moral Life*, edited by Reinhard Hütter and Matthew Levering, 169–207. Washington, DC: Catholic University of America Press, 2010.

Schillebeeckx, Eward, O.P. *The Eucharist*. Translated by N. D. Smith. New York: Sheed and Ward, 1968.

Schleck, Charles A. "St. Thomas on the Nature of Sacramental Grace." *The Thomist* 18 (1955): 1–30. Concluded in The Thomist 18, no. 2 (1995): 242–78.

Schmemann, Alexander. *The Eucharist.* Translated by Paul Kachur. Crestwood, NY: St. Vladimir's Seminary Press, 1987.

———. *For the Life of the World.* Crestwood, NY: St. Vladimir's Seminary Press, 1973.

Schneider, Athanasius. *Dominus est—It is the Lord!* Translated by Nicholas L. Gregoris. Pine Beach, NJ: Newman House, 2008.

Schönborn, Christoph Cardinal. "Presentation at Release of *Amoris Laetitia.*" *Origins* 46, no. 2 (May 12, 2016): 20–24.

———. *The Source of Life.* Translated by Brian McNeil. New York: Crossroad, 2007.

———. *God Sent His Son: A Contemporary Christology.* San Francisco: Ignatius Press, 2010.

Schoonenberg, Piet. "Presence and Eucharistic Presence." *Cross Currents* 17 (1967): 39–54.

———. "Christus' tegenwoordigheid voor ons." *Verbum* 31 (1964): 393–415.

Schnackenburg, Rudolf. *The Gospel according to St. John.* Translated by David Smith and C. A. Kon. 3 vols. New York: Crossroad, 1982.

Schulz, Hans Joachim. *The Byzantine Liturgy: Symbolic Structure and Faith Expression.* Translated by Matthew J. O'Connell. New York: Pueblo, 1986.

Seasoltz, R. Kevin. *The New Liturgy: A Documentation, 1903–1965.* New York: Herder and Herder, 1966.

Sedlmayr, Petrus. "Die Lehre des hl. Thomas von den accidentia sine subject remanentia—untersucht auf ihren Einklang mit der aristotelischen Philosophie." *Divus Thomas* (Foreign) 12 (1934): 315–326.

Seidl, Horst. "Zum Substanzbegriff der katholischen Transsubstantiationslehre: Erkenntnistheoretische und metaphysische Erörterungen." *Forum Katholische Theologie* 11 (1995): 1–16.

Semes, Steven. "Living Stones? The Formative Power of Architecture in the Church." *Antiphon* 7, no. 3 (2002): 8–13.

Serra, Dominic E. "The Roman Canon: The Theological Significance of Its Structure and Syntax." *Ecclesia Orans* 20 (2003): 99–128.

Sheedy, Charles E. *The Eucharistic Controversy of the Eleventh Century Against the Background of Pre-Scholastic Theology.* Washington DC: Catholic University of America Press, 1947.

Sievers, Joseph. "'Where Two or Three …': The Rabbinic Concept of Shekhinah and Matthew 18:20." In *The Jewish Roots of Christian Liturgy*, edited by Eugene J. Fisher, 47–64. New York: Paulist Press, 1990.

Slenczka, Notger. *Realpräsenz und Ontologie: Untersuchung der ontologischen Grundlagen der Transsignifikationslehre.* Göttingen: Vandenhoeck & Ruprecht, 1993.

Smith, Thomas Gorden. "Discernment, Decorum, Auctoritas: Keys to Rean-
imating Catholic Architecture." In *T&T Clark Companion to Liturgy*,
edited by Alcuin Reid, 425–54. New York: Bloomsbury T&T Clark, 2016.

Smyth, Matthieu. "The Anaphora of the So-Called Apostolic Tradition and
the Roman Eucharistic Prayer." In *Issues in Eucharistic Praying in East
and West: Essays in Liturgical and Theological Analysis*, edited by Maxwell
Johnson, 71–98. Collegeville, MN: Liturgical Press, 2010.

Solovey, Meletius Michael, O.S.B.M. *The Byzantine Divine Liturgy: History
and Commentary.* Translated by Demetrius Emil Wysochansky. Washington, DC: Catholic University of America Press, 1970.

Somerville, R. "The Case Against Berengar of Tours—A New Text." *Studi
Gregoriani* 9 (1972): 55–75.

———. "The Councils of Gregory VII." *Studi Gregoriani* 13 (1989): 33–53.

Spacil, Theophilus, S.J. *Doctrina Theologiae Orientis Separati De SS. Eucharistia.*
2 vols. Rome: Pontificium Institutum Orientalium Studiorum, 1929.

Spadaro, Antonio. "The Demands of Love: A Conversation with Cardinal
Schönborn about 'The Joy of Love.'" *America* 215, no. 4 (August 15, 2016):
23–27.

Spezzano, Daria E. *The Glory of God's Grace: Deification according to St. Thomas
Aquinas.* Ave Maria, FL: Sapientia Press of Ave Maria University, 2015.

Spicq, Ceslas. "*Trogein* : Est-il synonyme de *phagein* et d'*esthien* dans le
Nouveau Testament?" *New Testament Studies* 26 (1979–1980): 414–19.

Spinks, Bryan D. *Do This in Remembrance of Me: The Eucharist from the Early
Church to the Present Day.* London: SCM Press, 2013.

———. *Worship: Prayers from the East.* Washington DC: Pastoral Press, 1994.

Stephenson, Anthony A. "Two Views of the Mass: Medieval Linguistic Ambi-
guities." *Theological Studies* 22 (1961): 588–609.

Stone, Darwell. *A History of the Doctrine of the Holy Eucharist.* 2 vols. London:
Longmans, Green, 1909.

Stroik, Duncan. *The Church Building as a Sacred Place: Beauty, Transcendence,
and the Eternal.* Chicago: Hillenbrand Books, 2012.

Surmanski, Sr. Albert Marie, O.P. "Adoring and Eating: Reception of the
Eucharist in the Theology of Albert the Great." *Antiphon* 20, no. 3 (2016):
213–240.

Swetnam, James, S.J. *Hebrews: An Interpretation.* Rome: Gregorian and Biblica
Press, 2016.

———. "A Liturgical Approach to Hebrews 13." *Letter & Spirit* 2 (2006):
159–73.

Taft, Robert F. *Beyond East and West: Problems in Liturgical Understanding.* 2nd
ed. Rome: Edizioni Orientalia Christiana, Pontifical Oriental Institute,
1997.

———. "'Communion' from the Tabernacle—A Liturgico-Theological Oxymoron." *Worship* 88 (2014): 2–22.

———. "The Frequency of the Celebration of the Eucharist Throughout History." In *Between Memory and Hope: Readings on the Liturgical Year*, edited by Maxwell E. Johnson, 77–98. Collegeville, MN: Liturgical Press, 2000.

———. "Mass Without the Consecration? The Historic Agreement on the Eucharist between the Catholic Church and the Assyrian Church of the East." *Worship* 77 (2003): 482–509.

Talley, Thomas J. "The Literary Structure of the Eucharistic Prayer." *Worship* 58 (1984): 404–20.

Thompson, Michael. *Clothed with Christ: The Example and Teaching of Jesus in Romans 12.1–15.13* (Sheffield, UK: JSOT Press, 1991).

Thurian, Max. *The One Bread*. Translated by Theodore DuBois. New York: Sheed and Ward, 1969.

Tirot, Paul. "La concélébration et la tradition de l'Église." *Ephemerides Liturgicae* 101 (1987): 33–59.

Torrell, Jean-Pierre O.P. *A Priestly People: Baptismal Priesthood and Priestly Ministry*. Translated by Peter Heinegg. New York: Paulist Press, 2013.

Treanor, Oliver. "Apostolicity and the Eucharist." *Communio* 39, no. 4 (2012): 569–86.

Turrell James F. "Anglican Theologies of the Eucharist." In *A Companion to the Eucharist in the Reformation*, edited by Lee Palmer Wandel, 139–58. Leiden/Boston: Brill, 2014.

Tuzik, Robert L. *Lift up Your Hearts: A Pastoral, Theological, and Historical Survey of the Third Typical Edition of* The Roman Missal. Chicago: Archdiocese of Chicago: Liturgy Training Publications, 2011.

Vaillancourt, Mark G. "The Eucharistic Realism of St. Augustine: Did Paschasius Radbertus Get Him Right? An Examination of Recent Scholarship on the Sermons of St. Augustine." In *Papers presented at the Sixteenth International Conference on Patristic Studies held in Oxford* 2011 (Studia Patristica 70), vol. 18, St Augustine and his opponents, edited by Markus Vinzent, 569–76. Leuven, BE: Peeters, 2013.

———. "Guitmund of Aversa and Aquinas's Eucharistic Theology." *The Thomist* 68, no. 4 (2004): 577–600.

———. "Sacramental Theology from Gottschalk to Lanfranc." In Boersma and Levering, eds., *The Oxford Handbook of Sacramental Theology*, 187–200.

Van Zeller, Hubert. *The Mass in Other Words: A Presentation for Beginners*. Springfield, IL: Templegate, 1965.

Vogel, Cyrille. *Medieval Liturgy: An Introduction to the Sources*. Washington, DC: Pastoral Press, 1986.

Vonier, Anscar. *A Key to the Doctrine of the Eucharist*. Bethesda, MD: Zaccheus, 2003.

Von Balthasar, Hans Urs. "Eucharist: Gift of Love." *Communio* 43, no. 1 (2016): 139–53.

Von Cochem, Martin. *The Incredible Catholic Mass: An Explanation of the Mass*. Rockford, IL: TAN, 1997.

Von Hildebrand, Dietrich. *Liturgy and Personality*. Manchester, NH: Sophia Institute, 1986.

Vyner, Owen. "Friendship with the Fairest of the Children of Men: Relating the Ars celebrandi to Actuosa participatio." *Antiphon* 14, no. 3 (2010): 261–72.

Wahlberg, Mats. "Communion for the Divorced and Remarried: Why Revisionists in Moral Theology Should Reject Kasper's Proposal." *Nova et Vetera* (English) 13, no. 3 (2015): 765–85.

Wandel, Lee Palmer, ed. *A Companion to the Eucharist in the Reformation*. Leiden/Boston: Brill, 2014.

Washburn, Christian D. "The Value of Offering Sacrifice for the Dead in the Thought of the Fathers of the Church." *Antiphon* 16, no. 3 (2012): 154–78.

Wawrykow, Joseph. "The Heritage of the Late Empire: Influential Theology." In *A Companion to the Eucharist in the Middle Ages*, edited by I. Christopher Levy, G. Macy, and K. Van Ausdahl, 59–91. Leiden: Brill, 2012.

———. "The Sacraments in Thirteenth-Century Theology." In Boersma and Levering, eds., *The Oxford Handbook of Sacramental Theology*, 218–33.

Welch, Lawrence J. *Christology and Eucharist in the Early Thought of Cyril of Alexandria*. Lanham, MD: Catholic Scholars Press, 1994.

Wengier, Francis J. *The Eucharist-Sacrament*. Milwaukee, WI: Bruce, 1955.

White, Thomas J. *Exodus*. Grand Rapids, MI: Brazos Press, 2016.

Williamson, Peter. *Revelation*. Grand Rapids, MI: Baker Academic, 2015.

Willis, G. G. *Essays in Early Roman Liturgy*. London: SPCK, 1964.

Wilson, Stephen B. "The Anaphora of the Apostles Addai and Mari." In *Essays on Early Eastern Eucharistic Prayers*, edited by Paul F. Bradshaw, 19–37. Collegeville, MN: Liturgical Press, 1997.

Winkler, Gabriele. "A New Witness to the Missing Institution Narrative." *Studia Liturgica Diversa: Studies in Church Music and Liturgy: Essays in Honor of Paul F. Bradshaw*, edited by Maxwell Johnson and L. Edward Phillips, 117–28. Portland, OR: The Pastoral Press, 2004.

Wolterstorff, Nicholas. "John Calvin." In *A Companion to the Eucharist in the Reformation*, edited by Lee Palmer Wandel, 97–113. Leiden/Boston: Brill, 2014.

Wood, Jacob W. *Speaking the Love of God: An Introduction to the Sacraments.* Steubenville, OH: Emmaus Academic, 2016.

Wuerl, Donald Cardinal. "*Amoris Laetitia*: The Recent Synods and the Church's Ancient Teaching on Family." *Origins* 46, no. 2 (May 12, 2016): 24–28.

Wuerl, Donald Cardinal, and Mike Aquilina. *The Mass: The Glory, the Mystery, the Tradition.* New York: Doubleday, 2013.

Wyschogrod, Michael. *The Body of Faith: Judaism as Corporeal Election.* New York: Seabury Press, 1983.

Yarnold, Edward, S.J. "Anaphoras without Institution Narratives?" *Studia Patristica* 30 (1997): 395–410.

———. *The Awe-Inspiring Rites of Initiation: The Origins of the RCIA.* Collegeville, MN: The Liturgical Press, 1994.

Yerkes, Royden Keith. *Sacrifice in Greek and Roman Religions and Early Judaism.* London: Adam and Charles Black, 1953.

Young, Robin Darling. "The Eucharist as Sacrifice according to Clement of Alexandria." In *Rediscovering the Eucharist: Ecumenical Considerations,* edited by Roch A. Kereszty, 63–91. New York: Paulist Press, 2003.

Zheltov, Michael. "The Anaphora and the Thanksgiving Prayer from the Barcelona Papyrus: An Underestimated Testimony to the Anaphoral History in the Fourth Century." *Vigiliae Christianae* 62 (2008): 467–504.

———. "The Moment of Eucharistic Consecration in Byzantine Thought." In *Issues in Eucharistic Praying in East and West: Essays in Liturgical and Theological Analysis,* edited by Maxwell Johnson, 263–306. Collegeville, MN: Liturgical Press, 2010.

Zirkel, Patricia McCormick. "The Ninth-Century Eucharistic Controversy: a Context for the Beginnings of the Eucharistic Doctrine in the West," *Worship* 68 (January 1994): 2–23.

Zizoulas, John D. *Eucharist, Bishop, Church: The Unity of the Church in the Divine Eucharist and the Bishop During the First Three Centuries.* Translated by Elizabeth Theokritoff. Brookline, MA: Holy Cross Orthodox Press, 2001.

Index of Subjects and Names

A

Aaron, 41–42, 52, 58, 63, 64, 108n87, 110, 407

Abel, 45, 46, 48, 48n17, 122, 157, 368, 417, 418, 456

Abraham, 12, 13, 45–48, 157, 368, 417, 418

active participation, 425–33, 438, 448, 583

actual grace, 494–96

Adam, 19, 26, 45, 334, 422, 605–6

adoration, Eucharistic, 14n19, 61–62, 65, 160, 262n6, 294, 305, 307, 311n56, 311–12, 448n79, 550, 583, 587–601

Adoro te devote, 17–18, 276, 334n29, 469

Alan of Lille, 249

Alger of Liège, 183n12, 244–45, 247, 253, 255, 256n63, 258, 341–42

Allen, Michael, 304n34

Alphonsus Liguori (saint), 529–30, 589, 596

Althaus, Paul, 78n9, 295n8, 297n16, 299n20, 300n22

Ambrose (saint), 153–57, 177, 197, 201, 201n59, 203, 342n52, 345, 448n79, 501, 507, 562–64, 585

Amoris Laetitia (Pope Francis), 551–55

anamnesis, 145n44, 145–46, 146n49, 208, 216n97, 339, 372, 416, 419

Anaphora of Addai and Mari, 25, 25n41, 110n94, 125, 147nn51–52, 151n65, 212–23, 228, 490–91, 522

Anglican orders, 190n25

Anglican views, 304n34, 306–7, 310–311

annihilation, 248, 267–68, 294, 358

Anointing of the Sick, sacrament of, 5n5, 33–34, 36, 204, 495, 557, 558, 573

Apostolic Tradition, 132n9, 144–47, 176, 211n83, 578n46

Aquinas, Thomas (saint)
charity, Eucharist as sacrament of, 5–6, 13–14, 502, 516
on Communion under both kinds, 285, 574
on concelebration, 474n66
on concomitance, 282–86
Corpus Christi, liturgy of, 21n31, 61, 90n28, 257, 499n30, 509, 588
on divinization as effect of the Eucharist, 10n12, 21nn30–31, 183, 498–99
on eastward orientation in prayer, 440n63
ecclesial communion as fruit of the Eucharist, 8n9, 501–2, 536
on effects of Communion, 10n12, 285n53, 498–502, 504–5, 516

on Eucharist as greatest of the sacraments, 32–35, 607

on Eucharist as sacrifice and sacrament, 35, 343, 381, 487

on eschatological effect of the Eucharist, 522–26

on faith and reason, 16, 236, 259–60, 271–72

faith in the Eucharist, merit of, 17–18, 276

figures of the Eucharist, 39n1, 45, 89, 345–47, 349n71

fittingness of the Eucharist, 3–6, 13–14, 89, 192nn30–31, 194–97, 285n53

fittingness of Incarnation, 11, 18–19, 21nn30–31

fittingness of the sacraments, 3–5, 381

on forgiveness of venial sins through Communion, 506–8

on form of the Eucharist, 200, 203–5, 262–63, 268, 308

on the fruits of the Mass, 348–50, 466n42, 467–68

on gifts of the Holy Spirit, 496, 506

on instrumental causality in sacraments, 185–86, 188, 349–50, 391n43

on the Last Supper as Passover meal, 89–90, 99–101

on mode of substance and quantity, 279–82, 286–88, 291, 301

on the Passion, 333, 343–44, 348–50, 367, 391n43

on Passover as type of the Eucharist, 55–56n39, 346n64

on redemption, 18–19, 183, 197, 285n53, 333

on sacramental grace, 492–94, 497

on sacramental representation of the Passion, 192, 344–48, 389

on sacrifice, 50n27, 325–33, 358, 372, 487

on the sacrifice of the Mass, 111n95, 343–51, 355, 360–61, 380n18

on satisfactory power of the Mass, 467–68

on spiritual communion, 526–28

on substance and accidents, 260, 270–73

on substantial conversion, 261–68, 277–78

on three levels of the sacraments, 39n1, 183, 257

on transubstantiation, xxxi, 261–91, 308

on unworthy Communion, 535–39

architecture, ecclesial, 437–38, 589–92

Arnauld, Antoine, 313n64, 567

ars celebrandi, 432–33

Ascension and the Eucharist, 78, 300, 365, 371–72

Athanasius (saint), 149–50, 524

atonement, 18–19, 45, 49, 51–52, 54, 109–10, 117, 328n17, 330–33, 379n13, 437n55, 458

Audet, Jean-Paul, 129n1

Augustine (saint), 100, 252, 307, 323n2, 345, 524n92, 535, 538, 562–64, 578n44, 579n49

on the Bread of Life Discourse, 79–80

on indivisibility of Christ's presence in the Eucharist, 79–80, 252

on Communion, 5, 23, 508,
524n92
on divinization as effect of the
Eucharist, 5, 21, 23
on eastward orientation in prayer,
440–41
on ecclesial effect of the Eucharist,
157–62, 177, 181, 193, 490n10,
501, 535
on identity of Priest and Victim,
160, 334, 344n57
on the Incarnation, 16, 21, 22n32
on the Mass as sacrifice of propitiation, 161–62, 460–61
on participation of the faithful in
the sacrifice, 161–62, 411–12,
418, 487
on the real presence, 158–61
on sacraments, 179–81, 191, 205
on sacrifice, 325, 386, 406
on sacrifice of Calvary, 334
on worship of Christ in the Eucharist, 159–60, 597–98

B

Balthasar, Hans Urs von, 488
Bandinelli, Roland, 249
banquet, 9–10, 76, 118, 383–86,
393–98, 402–3, 434, 489, 517,
534, 568, 576
Baptism, sacrament of, 5n5, 135,
187–88, 189n23, 203, 253n57,
540n11, 570–71n28, 605
by desire, 526–34
character of, 423, 426, 497
compared with the Eucharist,
31–34, 35n59, 36, 378, 457, 469
giving eternal life, 525
giving the Holy Spirit, 515

incorporation into Christ and the
Church, 36, 66, 512, 525
matter and form of, 191–93
ordered to the Eucharist, 33–34,
64, 66, 525
sacramental grace of, 491, 493–95,
502
as spiritual birth, 3–4, 23–24, 491,
535
Barber, Michael, 123n118
Barrett, C. K., 91n32
Bellarmine, Robert (saint), 355–57,
424
Benedict XVI, xxviii, xxix, 7, 28n46,
94, 305n38, 371, 393n49, 472,
588n3
on *ars celebrandi*, 432–33
on Communion for the civilly
divorced and remarried, 550–51,
554n37
on Essene calendar hypothesis,
97–98
on Eucharistic adoration, 597–98
on participation of the faithful in
the Mass, 411–13, 420–21
on position of the tabernacle,
600–1
on typology of paschal lamb, 56–57
Benoit, Pierre, 91n32, 93n39, 98n56,
103n71, 107nn84–85, 114n105,
224n117
Berengarius, 76n5, 183n12, 233,
237–47, 250, 254–55, 257–59,
261–62, 270, 272, 274, 278,
300n24, 302–4, 314, 316
Berger, David, 213n91, 224n119
Berman, Joshua, 40n4, 49nn20–23,
50nn24–25, 54n34, 385n31,
487n1
Billot, Louis, 360

Blinzler, Joseph, 95n45, 98n56

Bossuet, Jacques-Bénigne, 210, 472n55

Botte, Bernard, 144n42, 219n106, 221

Bouyer, Louis, 131n7, 132n10, 132n13, 205, 218, 219n106, 221n109, 224n117, 385n31, 438n56, 439, 441n65, 473n59

Bradshaw, Paul, 144n42, 222n113, 399–402

bread, fittingness for the Eucharist, 77, 81, 192–96, 523n85, 524

Bread of Life Discourse, xxx, 67, 71–82, 108, 116, 127, 236, 522

bread of the Presence, xxx, 63–65, 69, 385n30

Brent, Allen, 144n42

Bridegroom, xxx, 6, 14, 22–23, 27–28, 380, 387, 430, 502, 517, 588, 600

Brock, Stephen, 288n59

Brown, Raymond, 91n34, 92nn35–36, 92n38, 95n45

Brummond, Michael, 281n46

Bultmann, Rudolf, 77, 92n35

Burke, Raymond, 542n15, 543n16

Buttiglione, Rocco, 553n35, 555n38, 555n40

C

Cabasilas, Nicolas, 528

Cabié, Robert, 224n121, 419n26

Cajetan, Thomas de Vio, 351–53, 355, 494n21

Calkins, Arthur B., 29n48

Calvin, John, 237n16, 313–14, 375n2
    on "private" Masses, 472
    on the real presence and transub-
        stantiation, 303–7
    on the sacrifice of the Mass, 384,

388–93

Capernaism, 79, 236, 244, 250, 300

Casel, Odo, 324n5, 360

Casti Connubii (Pius XI), 495n23

Catechism of the Catholic Church, xxixn6, 20, 81n15, 103, 146n49, 208, 316n71, 368–69, 393n47, 427n41, 457nn15–16, 462–63n33, 492n15, 494n20, 535n8, 537, 546, 549n24, 552–53, 554n36, 555n39

Catechism of the Council of Trent, 32, 35n59, 113n104, 190, 197–98, 207–8, 566–67, 585

Catherine of Siena (saint), 539–40n11

Chaput, Charles, 555n40

charity
    of Christ, xxix, 18, 20, 333, 454
    as condition for Communion, 535–36, 553
    Eucharist as sacrament of, xxix–xxx, 5–10, 13–15, 32, 603
    fraternal, 131, 548–49, 551, 593n13
    and the Indwelling, 316, 510–16
    nourished through Communion, xxxi, 4, 20, 24, 28, 61, 180, 182, 184, 190, 193, 366, 491–92, 495–520, 526, 530, 568, 571
    divinization through, 20–21, 390
    and spiritual communion, 528–31
    as spiritual sacrifice, 324, 407, 409, 414, 422, 428–29, 456–57, 464
    and unity of the Church, 157–58, 161, 182, 184, 366, 412

Chilton, Bruce, 49n20

Christifideles Laici (John Paul II), 427n41

Chrysologus, Peter (saint), 410–11

Chrysostom, John (saint), 56n40,

95n46, 101n63, 163–68, 177,
202, 340, 342n52, 350–51,
500–1, 504n38, 508, 515,
516n68, 534n5, 537, 539, 562,
605–6

Church
Bride of Christ, 6–8, 11, 22–23,
27–28, 33, 55, 127, 191, 335–36,
380, 430, 471, 535, 588, 600, 604,
606–7

built up by the Eucharist, xxxi, 36,
147, 158, 180, 184, 209, 603, 605

Eucharist as soul or heart of,
xxviiin5, 10, 17n23, 36, 71, 226,
380, 600

Mystical Body, 8, 11, 20, 23, 27,
36–37, 134, 157–58, 184, 208–9,
234, 255n63, 319, 335n31, 336,
363, 379–80, 420, 429, 463,
470–71, 517, 520–22, 526, 536,
588, 598, 600

offers the Sacrifice with Christ,
335n31, 336, 379–80, 386, 398,
420, 429, 454–55n10

power with regard to the sacraments, 199, 215, 219, 574–76

unity of built up by the Eucharist,
6, 8, 10, 44, 119, 129, 134–35,
152, 157–58, 174, 180–82, 184,
193, 197, 208–9, 256, 316, 364,
366, 412, 502, 516–22, 526, 532,
556

circumscriptive presence, 240, 301n25

City of God, 16, 325, 386, 406, 411,
418, 487, 521

Clark, Francis, 343n53, 355n87,
376n3 376n5, 467n43

Code of Canon Law, 108n88, 189n23,
192, 195–96, 198, 225n124,
398n60, 481–82, 551, 556n42,

557, 569–70, 573, 575, 582
Canon 915, 542–43
Canon 916, 10, 457n17, 540–42

common (or royal) priesthood, 126,
405–48, 604
Benedict XVI on, 411–13
in the Eucharistic liturgy, 415–23
in Israel, 407–8
John Paul II on, 421–22, 423n36
Vatican II on, 414–15, 425–30
Mary as model of, 422–23
and ministerial priesthood, 414–15,
438
Pius XII, *Mediator Dei*, on 415n16,
423–25, 429, 448
spiritual sacrifices of the, 409–13,
420, 422, 466

Communion,
for children, 569–73, 598n27
dispositions for, 533–73
and divinization of man, 20–26, 36,
198, 498–99
for divorced and remarried, 544–55
Benedict XVI, *Sacramentum
Caritatis* on, 550–51
Catechism of the Catholic Church
on, 546, 549n24
Congregation for the Doctrine
of the Faith on, 546, 549–50
Francis, *Amoris Laetitia* on,
551–55
John Paul II, *Familiaris Consortio* on, 544–50
effects of, 8–10, 23–25, 142–43,
151, 153, 157–58, 170–72, 198,
487–532, 603
extraordinary ministers of, 576–77,
582, 585
fittingness of, 3–29, 523–24, 561

forgiveness of venial sins through,
    506–9
frequency of, 561–69
in the hand, 578–81, 585
Holy Spirit, giving, 28–29, 491,
    514–16
and Indwelling of the Trinity,
    510–16
and Mary, 31
nuptials of the Lamb with His
    Church, 27–28
reception of, 561–85
resurrection as effect of, 522–26
and sacrifice, 7–10, 20, 32, 35,
    487–90
spiritual, 31, 422n34, 526–32, 541,
    554n37, 566
as spiritual nourishment, xxviii,
    xxxi, 3–5, 9, 24, 27–28, 31, 39,
    53–54, 58–62, 68–69, 71–72, 81,
    141–43, 180, 190, 192, 238, 269,
    273n30, 285, 304, 323, 356–57,
    366, 370, 394, 398, 402, 490, 498,
    500–1, 515–16, 524, 533, 535,
    561, 571, 603
as Viaticum, 61n46, 540, 573, 578
under both species, 285, 310,
    574–77
and unity of the Church, 515–22
unworthy, 534–43
concelebration, 199, 472–83, 555–56
concomitance, 244, 252–53, 282–86,
    291, 309–10, 312, 575–76, 580
condescension, divine, 12–15
Confirmation, sacrament of, 6n5,
    219n105
    by desire, 526
    character of, 497
    compared with the Eucharist,
        33–34, 35n59, 36, 502n35

giving the Holy Spirit, 28, 515
    sacramental grace of, 494–95
    giving spiritual maturity, 4, 36
conjoined instrument (Christ as),
    170, 188–90, 228, 349–50, 499
consolation, effect of Communion,
    14, 90n28, 509–10, 526, 583, 596
consubstantiation, 262–65, 291, 294,
    296–97, 300, 303, 309
contrition, 324, 326, 457, 462, 495,
    498, 507, 530–31, 539–40n11,
    541
Coolman, Boyd Taylor, 257n68,
    262n5
Corbett, John, 531n101
co-redemption, 421n31
corpus mysticum, 520–522
Cranmer, Thomas, 388n36
Cyprian (saint), 147–49, 193–94,
    197–98, 339n44, 562
Cyril of Alexandria (saint), 80, 82n16,
    170–72, 177, 326, 517–18
Cyril of Jerusalem (saint), 24–25, 65,
    150–52, 177, 456, 459–60, 578,
    580

D

Daly, Robert, 329n19, 337nn34–35,
    410n6
Damascene, John (saint), 24n37,
    174–75, 211n86, 265n14, 440,
    504, 516
Daniélou, Jean, 71n1
Davis, Charles, 314n65
Day of Atonement, 45, 49, 51, 109
de Aldama, Joseph, 494n22
de Baciocchi, J., 314n65
de La Soujeole, Benoît-Dominique,
    531n101

de la Taille, Maurice, 69n61, 325n7, 360, 364n115, 365n118, 371n128, 420n30, 475n68, 488

de Lubac, Henri, 520

de Lugo, John, 357

Derville, Guillaume, 473n59

Didache, 129–32, 139, 143, 176, 193n33, 222, 339nn41–42, 399, 533

Dies Domini (John Paul II), 435–36

divinization, 20–25, 36, 152, 198, 330n23, 498

Dix, Gregory, 144n42

docility to the Holy Spirit, 496–97, 506, 552

Dominicae Cenae (John Paul II), xxvii, 395n53, 421–22, 434n49, 594

domus ecclesiae, 437–38

Doronzo, Emmanuel, 9n10, 355n87, 359n99, 359n101

Dougherty, Joseph, 569n25

Doval, Alexis James, 150n61

Dowd, Edward, 355n87

Driscoll, Jeremy, 410n6

E

east, orientation in prayer, 439–43

Ecclesia de Eucharistia (John Paul II), xxvii–xxix, 28–29, 108n88, 227, 336n32, 363–64, 370–71, 385, 512–15, 519, 528, 536–37, 543, 556–58, 595–96, 607. *See* John Paul II

  on the Resurrection and the Eucharist, 37, 523n86, 524

  on the sacrifice of the Mass, 354n84, 367n120, 384n29, 391n42, 398–99, 466n41, 468n48, 489–90, 534n4

  on Mary and the sacrifice of the Mass, 29–31, 422n34, 423n36

ecclesial communion, as condition for Communion, 533–34, 540–43, 555–58

ecclesial unity, 6, 8, 316, 318, 498, 501–502, 515–20, 526, 535–36

Edersheim, Alfred, 49n20

Elavanal, Thomas, 147n51, 522n83

Elliott, Peter, 432n45

epiclesis, 141n36, 145–46, 147nn51–52, 151, 167, 206, 207n74, 208–11, 211–12n86, 217–18, 219n106, 228, 338–39, 419–20, 458, 463n33, 490–91, 497, 506, 514–15, 518–19, 521n79, 522

Ephrem (saint), 28–29, 515

eschatological orientation of Eucharist, 442, 522–26

Essene calendar hypothesis, 93, 96–99

Eucharisticum Mysterium, 482n83, 580n52

evil, 11n14, 18, 140, 142n38, 509n52, 538, 543, 554n36, 555n39

exaggerated realism. *See* Capernaism

existentialism, 314

exitus-reditus, 436

Exodus, 66, 71–72, 91, 105, 109, 127

ex opere operato, 454, 458, 462, 463n33, 464n37, 475, 491

Extreme Unction, sacrament of, 5n5, 33–34. *See* Anointing of the Sick

Eymard, Peter Julian (saint), 14n19, 589

F

Fagerberg, David, 29n50, 346n67, 365n116

Fahey, John, 236n11

faith, 72–73, 80, 82n16, 89, 120, 141,
  175, 205, 324, 347, 407, 579,
  584n60
  disposition for Communion,
    490–91, 515, 533, 536, 556–58,
    566
  effect of Communion, 505–6, 512,
    569
  eucharistic presence through, 239,
    300–7, 310, 315
  participation in offering the
    Sacrifice through, 411, 429, 456,
    459, 468
  justification by, 350, 376–77, 411
  merit of, 11, 16–18, 27–29, 184,
    269–70
  in real presence, 149–50, 153,
    259–60, 271, 315n70, 579–80,
    590, 595, 600
  and reason, 3, 239–40, 243, 247,
    274, 308
  and spiritual communion, 526, 528,
    531, 566
Fandal, Damian, 350n75
Familiaris Consortio (John Paul II),
  544–50
Feingold, Lawrence, 3n1, 72n1, 75n4,
  95n47, 186n18, 277n37, 329n18,
  495n24
Filip, Štěpán Martin, 344n60
fittingness, arguments for the Eucharist, 3–29, 523–24
Florence, Council of, 192, 197,
  200n55, 206–8, 214–15
form (essential words) of the Eucharist, 199–208, 212–19, 226–28,
  262, 268, 284–85, 344, 364–65,
  394, 476, 523n85
Fourth Lateran Council, 250, 261,
  564, 571

Francis (pope), 551–55, 598–99
Francis (saint), 588
Franzelin, Johann Baptist, 357
frequent Communion, 561–69
fruits of the Mass, xxxi, 152, 183–84,
  235, 336, 342–45, 348–51, 361,
  371, 391–92, 419n26, 451–72,
  474–81
fruits of the Spirit, 519

G

Galot, Jean, 107nn85–86, 112–
  13n101, 115n107
Gamber, Klaus, 131n7, 441n65,
  442n66, 443n68
Garrigou-Lagrange, Réginald,
  209n77
Gaudium et Spes, 26, 554n36
Gelston, A., 213n91, 216nn97–99,
  220n107
General Instruction on the Roman
  Missal, 392n45, 433, 443–44,
  463n34, 575–76, 581, 582–
  83n59, 601
Gerrish, Brian, 303n31
Gherardini, Brunero, 213n91
gift of self, Eucharist as, xxviii–xxx,
  6–10, 14, 324, 328, 356, 358, 386,
  583, 588, 603
gifts of the Holy Spirit, 492, 494,
  496–97, 506, 526
Giraudo, Cesare, 91nn32–33, 94n44,
  110n92, 212n88, 213n91,
  222, 223nn114–15, 224n118,
  225n123, 339n40, 458n19,
  506n45, 521n79
Goering, Joseph, 249n47
Girard, René, 329n19
Gottschalk of Orbais, 236n9

grace
actual, 23, 34, 494–96
given through Communion, 9,
· 23–24, 32n55, 34, 35n59, 61, 67,
81, 116, 491, 498–505, 510, 512,
522–23, 526, 530
merited on Calvary, 12, 34, 187,
189–90, 457, 468, 500, 523
sacramental, xxxi, 3–5, 9, 10n12, 23,
179–184, 187–90, 491–98
sanctifying, xxxi, 4, 8–9, 11, 16,
20–21, 491–93, 502–3, 533–540
state of, 16, 24, 51n27, 458, 462,
490, 497, 511, 519, 522, 530, 532,
534–35, 540–45, 553n34, 563,
568, 572
Gregory Nazianzen (saint), 162, 362,
363n11
Gregory of Nyssa (saint), 24, 162–63,
202, 524
Gregory the Great (saint), 173–74
Grisez, Germain, 265n13, 272n30,
287n57, 287–88n59
Guitmund of Aversa, 76n5, 241–42,
244–51, 254–55n63, 256, 258,
263n7, 274n34, 280n43, 340–41
Gutwenger, E., 309n50

H
Hahn, Scott, 123n118
Hauke, Manfred, 112–13n101,
113n103
Haymo of Halberstadt, 236n9
Healy, Mary, 86n20, 88n25, 103n71,
111n100, 113n101m
heavenly liturgy present in Eucharist,
122–27, 160–59, 346n67, 519,
597
Heringer, Dominik, 213n91, 216n97
High Priest, Jesus as, xxviii, 41, 148,

161, 165–66, 169, 225–26, 234,
334, 336–37, 340, 346, 348, 354,
360n103, 361, 372n130, 379n12,
409, 411, 414, 425, 428, 445, 458,
462, 466, 477–80
Hilary of Poitiers (saint), 152–53,
176, 521, 537
Hincmar of Reims, 236n9
Hirsh, Emil, 54n36
Hödl, Ludwig, 181n10
Holy Orders, sacrament of, 5n5,
31–32, 189, 225–27, 414, 495,
497, 582
Holy Spirit
docility to, 496–97, 506, 552
gifts of, 492–94, 496–97, 506, 526
given in Communion, 28–29, 491,
514–16
Indwelling of, 512–15, 526
invoked in epiclesis, 146–47, 151,
166–68, 174–75, 208–10, 217,
338–39, 490–91, 497, 514,
521n79, 522
offering Sacrifice through, 166–68,
378, 386, 419–20, 438, 594
realizing conformity with Christ,
492n15, 528
realizing the Incarnation, 76n5,
80n14, 139n29, 146, 175, 338
realizing Eucharistic conversion, xxviii, 10n13, 34, 151,
168, 174–75, 208–10, 211n86,
243n31, 251, 337–38, 426, 476
unity of the Church through, 515,
518–19, 556
hope, 5n5, 11, 16, 18, 27, 393, 435,
456, 495, 505–506, 531, 536, 548
Eucharist as pledge of, 14, 68, 143,
147n52, 164, 210, 301, 491, 522
in communion of saints, 124, 525

increased through the Eucharist,
504, 505, 525

of Israel, 54, 71n1, 78, 116, 347

as spiritual offering, 324, 407,
421n31, 429–30, 432, 456

Hugh of St. Victor, 180–81, 252,
255–57

Humbrecht, Thierry-Dominique,
344n60

humility, 11, 14–16, 528, 563, 579

I

Ibáñez, Ángel García, 107n86,
119n109, 121n111, 201n58,
211n85, 309n50, 314n66,
355n87, 360n106, 361n109,
467n43

identity of priest and victim. See
Victim

identity of Calvary and the Mass. See
Victim

Ignatius of Antioch (saint), 68,
133–35, 140–41, 153, 176, 473,
522

Ignatius of Loyola (saint), 565

Imitation of Christ, 583

Inaestimabile Donum, 600n34

Incarnation,

and atoning sacrifice, 11, 18–19, 48,
332–34

and the Eucharist, xxvii, xxx,
10–31, 37, 38, 68, 80n14, 138–39,
174–75, 209, 262n5, 290, 392,
498–99, 513, 604

divine interchange, 20–23

fittingness of, 10–29, 38

prefigured in the shekhinah, 40–44

indivisibility of Christ's presence in
the Eucharist, 79–80, 252–53,

280, 286–88, 310, 312, 318, 518,
575–76, 580, 593

Indwelling of the Trinity, effect of
Communion, 8, 510–16, 526

Innocent III, 182, 250, 424, 474n64,
506

institution narrative, 82, 85, 128, 131,
138, 145–46, 191, 339, 381–82,
401, 401n66, 416, 419, 458

as form of the sacrament, 201–25

lacking in the Anaphora of Addai
and Mari, 212–23

sacrificial connotations of, 106–17

instrumental causes, sacraments as.
See sacraments

intercommunion, 555–58

Irenaeus (saint), 21n31, 140–43,
153, 165, 191, 413n12, 499n30,
524n87

Isaac, 12, 45, 47–48

Isaiah, 71n1

Isidore of Seville, (saint), 327n13,
328, 461, 563

Israel

common priesthood in, 259, 407–8

and Eucharist, 41, 55

hope of, 78

and indwelling of God, 12–13,
40–45

messianic kingdom of, 71–72

prefiguring the Eucharist, 39, 46

sacrificial worship of, 49–57,
63–65, 76, 101

J

Jacob, 12, 43n6, 45, 49

Jammo, Sarhad, 25n42, 110n94,
213n91, 220n108, 221n110

Jansenism, 313, 567

Jaubert, Annie, 97, 98n57
Jensen, Robin, 441n65
Jenson, Philip, 49n20
Jeremias, Joachim, 82, 86n20, 91n30,
    91n33, 92n35, 92n38, 93n39,
    93n40, 93n41, 96n49, 97n50,
    98n56, 105n76, 106n81, 106n83,
    107n85, 111n92, 112n96,
    113n101, 113n102, 205n68,
    224n117, 401n66
Jerusalem, 69, 86–88, 102–3, 116,
    120–22, 124, 160, 439, 588
    New, 23, 27, 61, 122, 439, 519, 591
John the Baptist (saint), 22, 98
John of the Cross (saint), 584
John Paul II (saint), 37, 215n96,
    225n125
    on common priesthood of the
        faithful, 421–22, 423n36,
        427n41
    on Communion for the civilly
        divorced and remarried, 544–50
    on Eucharistic adoration, 593–96
    on gift of the Eucharist, xxvii– xxix,
        393, 607
    on heavenly liturgy present in
        Eucharist, 519
    on Holy Spirit given in the Eucha-
        rist, 28–29
    on intercommunion, 556
    on Marian dimension of the
        Eucharist, 29–31
    on nuptial dimension of the
        Eucharist, 27–28n46
    on paschal mystery present in the
        Eucharist, 391, 523n86
    on priestly minister, 227
    on presence of the Resurrection
        in the Eucharist, 37, 370–71,
        523n86, 524
    on sacrificial dimension of the
        Eucharist, 108n88, 336–37,
        354n84, 363–64, 367n120,
        384n29, 385, 395n53, 398–99,
        434n49, 466n41, 468n48, 534n4
    on spiritual communion, 528
    on Sunday, 435–36
    on union with Christ in Commun-
        ion, 512–13
    on unity of Eucharistic sacrifice
        and banquet, 489–90
    on unworthy Communion, 536–37,
        543
Joseph de Sainte-Marie, 474n65,
    475n67
Josephus, 52n31, 88n26, 102n68
Journet, Charles, 104, 279n41,
    290n63, 352n82, 355n87,
    356n92, 361, 389n41, 468, 488
Judaism, 12–13, 54–55, 131n7,
    137n26, 223n115, 328, 487–88
Judas, 88, 91, 163, 537–39
Jungmann, Joseph, 106n82, 130n4,
    131n6, 132n8, 211n85, 218n102,
    219n106, 224n117, 368n123,
    379n12, 382n22, 393–94,
    395n53, 416n18, 416n21,
    417–18, 418n23, 421n31,
    422n33, 437n55, 439n58,
    473n62, 474n64, 562n8, 578n47
Justin Martyr (saint), 224, 339n41,
    395n54, 436, 533, 579n50

K

Karlstadt, Andreas, 295–96, 300
Keating, Daniel, 20n29, 22n33
Keener, Craig, 90n29, 93n39, 96n48,
    98n56
Keller, Paul Jerome, 531n101

Kereszty, Roch, 66n56, 139n28,
269n21, 315n69
Kilmartin, Edward J., 152n69,
153n71, 180n7, 202n59, 337n34,
340n48, 360n106, 396n55,
397–98, 467n43
King, R. F., 179n1
Kleiner, Joseph, 476n70
Kwasniewski, Peter, 205n68, 209n77,
213n91, 218n104, 475n69,
505n41, 505n42

L

La Femina, Anthony, 83n18
Lagrange, Marie-Joseph, 114n105
Lamb of God, 27, 55–56, 96–98, 104,
162–63, 363
Lanfranc, 239n19, 239n23, 244,
244n32, 244n35, 245–46,
255nn63–64, 270,
Lang, Uwe Michael, 213n91,
219n106, 325n6, 411n8, 442n66,
444nn71–72
Langevin, Dominic, 37n61, 370n126
Last Supper, 121–22, 175, 455, 512,
537
    as Passover meal, 89–106
    fittingness for institution of the
    Eucharist, 9, 89–90
    institution of the Eucharist, 109,
    111, 130n5, 148, 160, 190, 192,
    194–95, 201–3, 260, 275, 360,
    371, 399–401, 592, 604
    synopsis, 83–86
leisure, mass as true, 436
Leo the Great (saint), 26, 46, 89,
172–73, 299n21, 503
Leo XIII, xxviiin5, 190n25, 360, 504,
524–25
Leppin, Volker, 297n16

Lessius, Leonardus, 357
Levering, Matthew, 47n15, 272n28,
282n48, 385n31, 396n54,
396n56, 398n61
Lewis, Keith, 388n36
Lienhard, Joseph, 157n79
Lombard, Peter, 32n55, 61n46,
179n2, 18182, 187, 188n21,
193n32, 193n34, 203, 240,
247n43, 257, 262n4, 263n11,
267n17, 290n64, 304, 342, 344,
361, 364, 492n16
love. *See* charity
    spousal, xxx, 7–8, 27n46, 584
    "to the end," xxix–xxx, 20,
    27–28n46, 84, 92, 334, 505
Lumen Gentium, 30n52, 392n45,
414–15, 423, 426–27, 448,
502n11
Luther, Martin, 241, 257, 443, 591
    on consubstantiation, 261–62, 293,
    296
    on justification through faith,
    376–77
    on minister of the Eucharist,
    225–27
    on "private" Masses, 471
    on the real presence, 293–303,
    305–6
    rejection of transubstantiation,
    293–97
    on the sacrifice of the Mass, 351,
    353, 368, 375–87, 394n51,
    400n65, 403, 430, 458, 469–70
    on ubiquitism, 297–99, 301n25,
    302
Lynch, Reginald, 184n15

M

Macomber, William, 213n90, 219n106

manna, xxx, 39n1, 41, 58–62, 69, 73, 75, 78, 81, 237, 251, 561, 567

Manns, Frédéric, 105n78

Maritain, Jacques, 369–70n124

marriage. See Matrimony
  indissolubility, 545, 547, 549, 554n37
  irregular situations, 547–55

Marshall, Bruce, 195n38

Martelet, Gustave, 37n61, 370n126

Mary, 15, 29–31, 46, 74, 152, 159, 234, 237, 243n31, 278, 502, 588
  co-offering the Sacrifice, 30–31, 422–23

Massa, James, 435n51

Masterson, Robert, 494n19

Masure, Eugène, 8n8, 107n84, 184n14, 363n114, 364n115, 391n44

matrimony, mystical, 27, 127, 498, 584

Matrimony, sacrament of, 5n5, 33, 36, 189n23, 191, 495, 497, 544, 551

Matthiesen, Michon, 360n102, 524n88

Matthijs, Mannes, 350n75

Mattox, Mickey, 294n5

McDonnell, Kilian, 303n31

McGuckian, Michael, 358n98

McKenna, John, 167n101, 202n61

McNamara, Martin, 40n3

Meconi, David, 20n29, 22n32

mediation, 47, 188–89, 331–32, 369, 372, 381, 398, 403, 405, 430

Mediator Dei (Pius XII). See Pius XII

medicine of immortality, 68, 72, 75, 134, 140, 296, 522, 523n86, 588

Megivern, James, 239n21, 252n56, 254n62

Meier, John P., 95n45, 98n59

Meinert, John, 519n75

Melchior Cano, 367–68

Melchizedek, 39n1, 45, 48, 62, 354, 417–18

Melito of Sardis, 45–46

memorial, 9, 20, 56, 63, 66, 87, 90n28, 108–10, 140, 146, 183, 341, 344–45, 363, 392, 397, 419, 422n34, 459, 462, 466n41

Memoriale Domini (Paul VI), 578–80

Messiah, 23, 48, 58, 62, 71–73, 114, 116, 332, 435

Midrash Rabbah, 54n36, 123n116

minister
  of Communion, 542–43, 557–58, 572–73, 576–77, 579–82, 585
  of the Eucharist, 175, 188, 200, 203–4, 225–28, 336, 422, 432–33, 471n52, 558
  holiness of, 462, 463n33
  as instrumental cause, 188–92, 463n33, 467n43

Mirae Caritatis (Leo XIII), xxviii–xxixn5, 504, 524–25

Miralles, Antonio, 493n19, 497n29

mode of quantity, 79n11, 279–82, 286–88, 351

mode of substance, 79n11, 279–82, 286–88, 291, 295, 301, 351

Moloney, Raymond, 106n83, 109n90, 110n92

Monica (saint), 460

Montclos, Jean de, 244n32

Moses, 40–43, 49, 55, 57–59, 63, 72–73, 77, 109, 114, 122, 154n73, 155, 160, 173, 385, 440, 592, 605

Mount Sinai, 40, 57, 63, 114, 116, 122, 407

Muksuris, Stylianos, 213n92

Mulieris Dignitatem (John Paul II), 27n46

multiplication of the loaves, 71–72

Murray, Paul, 588n4

Mussone, Davide, 541n12

Mysterium Fidei (Paul VI), 313, 315, 316n71, 317, 472, 592, 596n23, 600n34

mystery, Eucharist as, 36, 57, 60, 74, 82n16, 150, 152–53, 163, 173–74, 179, 182–83, 198, 209, 240, 246, 259–60, 290, 316, 318–19, 346, 347, 364, 371, 390–91, 393, 468, 521, 592, 607

Mystical Body. *See* Church

N

Nash, Thomas, 80n34, 81n15

natural law, sacrifice as, 329–32, 372

New Covenant

  Eucharist as, 36–37, 111, 114–16, 381–82

  Eucharist as manna of, 60, 75

  Eucharist as Passover of, 104–5, 111

  Eucharist as sacrifice of, 48, 53, 55, 58, 123, 143, 165, 169, 335–37, 347–48, 382, 401, 417

  Eucharist as theophany of, 122

  Jesus as High Priest of. *See* High Priest

  Jesus as mediator of, 116, 122

  Jesus as Temple of, 600

  Jesus as Victim of, 114

  as nuptial union, 27–28

  in relation with Old, 89, 96, 103, 347, 408–9, 588

  sealed by Blood of Christ, 58, 114–16, 143–44, 382, 430, 604

New Evangelization, 430–32, 434

Newman, John Henry, 176

Nicolas, Marie-Joseph, 105n77, 273n32, 280n45, 326n8, 350n77, 358n97, 367n119, 370n124, 421n31, 452n3, 462n32

Niederwimmer, Kurt, 129n1, 132n11

Noah, 45, 47

nuptial dimension of the Eucharist, 11, 23, 27–28, 32, 127, 503, 607

nuptials of the Lamb, 23, 27–28, 127

Nutt, Roger, 18–19n26, 190n24, 282n48, 314–15n68, 348n69, 361n108, 389, 391n44, 495n24

O

oblation, 327–28, 355n88, 357–58, 360. *See* sacrifice

  interior, 324–27, 345, 360, 365–66, 389, 405–6, 409–13, 416, 420–25, 466–67

O'Connor, James, 137n25, 141n36, 233n1, 239n22, 244n33, 367n119

Oesterley, William O. E., 95n45

Old Covenant, 40–41, 57–58, 64, 68, 89, 96, 103–4, 114, 122, 143, 160, 164–65, 169, 236–37, 345–47, 382n23, 408–9, 437n55, 527, 588

Old Testament, 13, 22, 39–69, 71n1, 80, 100, 108–10, 115, 120, 123, 143, 223n115, 237, 332, 345–48, 382, 385, 395, 417

O'Neill, Colman, 254n62, 316n71, 317n72, 371n129, 379n13, 398n59, 452n2, 454n9, 464n37, 471n53 orientation of eucharistic liturgy, 438–449

original sin. *See* sin

Orth, Stefan, 394n51

P

parousia, 132n13, 440–42

Paschal Mystery, 66, 110n94, 146, 339, 346, 367, 396
present in the Eucharist, xxvii, 14, 27n46, 37, 38, 217, 367–73, 391, 495, 498, 520

Paschasius Radbertus, 235–238, 257, 279–79n40, 342n52, 517

Passover,
Christ as, xxviii, 45, 97–98, 103, 111, 118–19, 173
and Last Supper, 82–106, 195–96
figure of the Eucharist, xxx, 49, 51–57, 66, 69, 71, 94, 97–98, 103–4, 109, 346n64, 395, 487

Paul VI, 199, 200n54, 219n105, 313, 315–16, 319n75, 472, 600n34
on Communion in the hand, 578–80
on Eucharistic adoration, 592–93, 596n23
on transsignification, 317–18

Pell, George, 544n18

Penance, sacrament of, 5n5, 32–34, 36, 187, 191, 457, 491, 495, 498, 526, 530–31, 534, 537, 540–42, 545–46, 553, 557, 558, 563n10, 571–73

Pentecost, 49, 51, 120–21, 513

Piolanti, Antonio, 295n6, 304n34

Pitre, Brant, 62n47, 63n48, 65, 72n3, 86n20, 88n24, 91n32, 93, 95n45, 98n56, 98nn58–59, 101n64, 101n66, 102n67, 103n70,

105n75, 105n79, 111n100, 120n110

Pius V (saint), 313n63

Pius VII, 207n74

Pius X (saint), 30n52, 561, 567–73, 585

Pius XI, 495n23

Pius XII,
on concelebration, 477–81
on Eucharistic adoration, 600
on the fruits of the Mass, 37n62, 326n11, 392–93, 452–56, 471
on participation of the faithful in offering the Sacrifice, 415n16, 422–25, 429, 448
on Sacred Heart, Eucharist as gift of, 604–5
on the Sacrifice of the Mass, 360n103, 361–63, 379n12, 389n38
on spiritual communion, 528
on thanksgiving after Communion, 583

Piolanti, Antonio, 295n6, 304n34, 475n67

Pomplun, Trent, 356n89

Pourrat, P., 191n28

Power, David, 395–96, 398

Presbyterorum Ordinis, xxviii, 34, 392n45, 426, 473n61, 482

priesthood. *See* minister
acting *in persona Christi*, xxxi, 36, 141, 165–67, 183, 189, 206, 214, 217–18, 225–27, 332, 336, 361–62, 414–16, 424, 438, 441, 462, 467n43, 470, 472–73, 476–81, 582
of Christ, xxviii, 41, 62, 148, 161, 165–66, 169, 226, 234, 334, 336–37, 340, 346, 348–50. *See*

High Priest

common. *See* common priesthood

in New Covenant, 36, 109, 123, 169–70, 332, 354

in Old Covenant, 41, 47–58, 123, 331–32, 407–8

in natural religion and natural law, 323–32, 406–7

ministerial, 165–68, 336, 352, 361, 363, 406–9, 414–15, 422, 438, 441–42, 447–48n79, 466, 604–5

ministerial and common compared, 225, 414–15, 438, 441–42, 466, 594

ordered to the Eucharist, xxviii–xxixn5, 336

and sacrifice, 46–49, 225, 329, 331–32, 405–7

unity of under the bishop, 134–35, 473, 481–82

private Masses, 470–72

Proclus, 19n27

propitiatory effect of the Mass, 151–52, 365, 456–63, 467, 469–70

Prosinger, Franz, 113n101

Q

Quam singulari (Pius X), 570, 571n30, 572

Quasten, Johannes, 148n55, 163n92–93, 166–67n100, 167n101, 168n103, 202n61

R

Rabanus Mauro, 236n9

Raes, Alfons, 219n106

Rahner, Karl, 472n57, 477, 477–78n72

Ranjith, Malcolm, 432n46

Ratramnus, 236–38

Ratzinger, Joseph, 5n4, 43–44, 48n18, 54n37, 98n55, 103n72, 294n4, 314n65, 330–31n23, 400–1n65, 437n55, 438n57, 471, 543, 546n20, 555n39

on ecclesial dimension of Eucharist, 521–22

on Eucharistic adoration, 589–592

on institution narrative, 217–18, 227

on orientation, 439, 442–44, 447

on participation of the faithful in the Sacrifice, 418, 428n42

on resurrection and the Eucharist, 523n86

on the sacrifice of the Mass, 368, 376n4, 377, 382n24, 393n47, 394n51, 400–1n65, 488

on Sunday, 434, 435n51

real presence, xxx–xxxi, 13, 118–19, 207n74, 313

and Berengarian controversy, 233, 239, 242, 257, 262

cessation of, 288–89

and effects of Communion, 8–10, 23–25, 142, 151, 153, 157–58, 170–72, 498–99, 503, 520–21

according to the Fathers, 133–34, 137–38, 140–41, 149–56, 161, 163–64, 168, 170–77, 180n7, 265n14

figures of, 39–40, 44, 53

fostering faith in, 579–80, 589, 593, 600

in mode of substance, 280, 295–99, 301, 316, 580

not contradictory, 273–74

Protestant views of, 207n74, 293, 295–307, 376

as *res et sacramentum*, 147n51, 183, 190, 209, 235, 365

and sacrifice of the Mass, 351, 365, 376, 383, 389n41, 390–91, 476, 603

through substantial conversion, 263–65, 267, 271

and transsignification theories, 314–20

Trent on, 273–74, 308–12

redemption,

Eucharist as sacrament of, 7, 19, 28n46, 36–37, 39, 81, 148, 183, 197, 226, 285n53, 338n36, 345, 366, 367n120, 371, 391–92, 395n54, 435, 452–54, 456n14, 460, 465, 468, 471

hope of, 11, 54, 66, 328

participation in, 334, 336, 379–80, 420–23, 430

through Christ's sacrifice, 7, 18–19, 22, 48, 333, 353, 372n130, 377, 379, 392

Redemptionis Sacramentum, 572, 573n34, 577, 580, 581n55, 582n58

Reid, Alcuin, 447n77

religion as a virtue, 323–24, 329,

reparation, 18, 54, 324, 324–25n5, 334, 462n32, 495, 595, 604

res et sacramentum, 39n1, 55n39, 147n51, 158, 179–84, 190, 209, 228, 235, 238, 254–57, 304, 317–18, 364–66, 497, 503, 514

res tantum, 39n1, 55n39, 147n51, 158, 179–84, 190, 197, 209, 235, 254n63, 257, 304, 364–66, 514, 536

resurrection,

commemorated in the Mass, 9, 146, 157, 170, 216–17, 419

as effect of Communion, 37, 67, 142–43, 147n52, 490–91, 522–26

manifesting the Father's acceptance of the Sacrifice, 399, 417

type of the Christian life, 255n65, 256

type of our resurrection, 22, 594

made present in the Eucharist, 37, 57, 117, 253, 256, 282–84, 365, 369–73, 471

as new creation, 137n26, 435–36

and Sunday Mass, 137n26, 434–36

Roman Canon, 48, 113, 123, 144n42, 145n46, 156, 211, 223n116, 246, 339n43, 368, 372, 416, 418, 423, 455, 456n12, 462, 466, 468, 490, 518n73

royal priesthood. *See* common priesthood

Russo, Nicholas, 203n62, 211n84, 213n91, 221n110, 224n119

S

Sacra Tridentina Synodus (Pius X), 561, 567, 568n18–21, 572

sacramental grace. *See* grace

sacramental sign, xxx, 5, 13, 31, 50, 58, 62, 65, 81, 122, 124, 179–83, 188–91, 198–99, 215, 235, 238, 242, 254–55, 273n30, 285, 289, 315–17, 355, 364–66, 389, 394, 501, 503, 524–25

sacraments,

Eucharist as greatest, 31–38, 380n18

fittingness of, 3–5, 31–34, 36, 380

as instrumental causes, 33, 184–90, 209, 228, 289, 339–50, 452, 479, 497, 514

three levels of, 179–84, 364–66

Sacramentum Caritatis (Benedict XVI), 28n46, 371, 472

on ars celebrandi, 432–33

on Communion for the civilly divorced and remarried, 550–51, 554n37

Eucharistic adoration, 597–98

on participation of the faithful in the Mass, 411–13

on position of the tabernacle, 600–1

typology of paschal lamb, 56–57

sacramentum tantum, 39n1, 55n39, 179–83, 254–57, 364–66, 503

Sacred Heart, Eucharist as gift of, 603–7

sacrifice

as act of the virtue of religion, 50–51n27, 324–31

of Calvary, 50, 53, 332–35, 337, 390–91

of Calvary made present in the Mass, 53, 106–7, 110–12, 148–49, 161,165, 169, 332, 340–56, 359–68, 388–93, 451–54, 456–57, 459, 462, 465, 468, 470, 477, 489, 500, 603, 605

as figures of Calvary, 45–58, 107, 331

of the Mass, 53, 335–404

in the Mosaic Law, 49–58, 63–65, 335

and natural law, 329–31

participation of the faithful in, 405–33

of the patriarchs, 46–48,

propitiatory effect, 151–52, 365, 456–63, 467, 469–70

of praise, 123, 454–55, 468

and priesthood, 331–32

of thanksgiving, 47, 455

Sacrosanctum Concilium, 9, 124, 354n84, 379n12, 392n45, 425–26, 442n66, 443, 447, 481, 575, 600n32

Santogrossi, Ansgar, 131n8, 206n71, 210n81, 213n91, 224n119

Sarah, Robert, 442n66, 447

Schechter, Solomon, 40n3

Scheeben, Matthias Joseph, 10n13, 17n23, 19n28, 24n36, 25n43, 79n12, 80n14, 270n25, 280n44, 290n65, 335n31, 357, 357nn94–95, 370n127, 513n62, 514, 521n80

Schillebeeckx, Edward, 309n50, 314n65, 315

Schleck, Charles A., 493n19

Schmemann, Alexander, 430–31

Schmitz, Rudolf Michael, 475n67

Schnackenburg, Rudolf, 92nn36–37, 102n68

Schönborn, Christoph, 13n17, 106n82, 386n33, 420, 544n18, 553n35

Schoonenberg, Piet, 314nn65–66

Scotus (Bl. Duns), 467n43

Sharar (Maronite Eucharistic Prayer), 211n83, 219–20, 419, 458, 462

Sheedy, Charles, 239n21, 239n23, 240n24, 241nn27–28, 245n37, 247n44, 253n58, 254n63, 255n66

Sheen, Fulton, 331n24

shekhinah, xxx, 40–44, 53, 69, 587

Sievers, Joseph, 40n3

sin,

Communion as remedy for,
490–91, 506–9, 515, 522, 526,
532, 563–64, 568, 572

forgiveness of, won by Christ, 7–8,
11–12, 18–19, 31, 37, 50, 98,
107–8, 110–13, 115–16, 123,
133, 158, 333–34, 352, 365, 377,
409, 454, 587

Mass offered for forgiveness of,
151–52, 162, 174, 217, 342, 353,
375n2, 414, 451–52, 456–63,
467, 469–70

mortal, 81, 506–8, 565, 569, 572

original, 5n5, 40, 67, 75, 470, 491

and reception of Holy Communion, 129–30, 490, 510, 533–39,
552–55, 563–65, 572

sacraments as remedy for, 5n5, 36,
187–88, 495

sacrifice offered for, 334

venial, 5n5, 457n15, 506–8, 510,
526, 532, 563, 568–69

sin offerings, 49–52, 54–55, 76

Slenczka, Notger, 314n67

Smyth, Matthieu, 132n11, 144n42

Solomon, 43, 52–53, 160

Solovey, Meletius Michael, 533n3

Somerville, R., 243n31

Spacil, Theophilus, 206n71

Spadaro, Antonio, 553n35

Spezzano, Daria, 5–6n5, 20n29,
503n37

Spinks, Bryan, 144n42, 144n43,
221n110, 222n112

Spicq, Ceslas, 77n6

spiritual communion, 31, 422n34,
526–32, 541, 554n37, 566

spiritual nourishment. See
Communion

spiritual sacrifices, 324–27, 365–66,
409–13, 420–21, 466

Sukkoth, 49, 51

Sunday Mass, 121, 130, 131n8,
136–37, 329, 428, 434–37, 572

Swetnam, James, 123n114

T

Taft, Robert, 203n62, 210, 211,
212n87, 212n88, 213n91,
213n93, 221n110, 222n113,
569n25, 581n57

Temple, 12, 46, 49–54, 63–65, 69, 86,
88, 92–94, 96–99, 104–105, 107,
111, 120–21, 144, 256, 335, 385,
395, 437–39, 443, 561

Christ as new, 44, 338n36, 443,
590

of the heart, 44, 511

type of Christ present in the
Eucharist, xxx, 40–44, 69, 160,
587, 591, 593, 600

Teresa of Avila (saint), 529

thanksgiving

after Communion, 569, 583–84

Mass as sacrifice of, 54, 106, 123,
136–37, 139, 396–97, 425, 436,
454–55, 459, 462–63, 465

prayer of, 106, 125, 130–32,
145–46, 216, 224n122, 394

purpose of sacrifice, 47, 50n26, 54,
326, 332, 387, 425, 436, 462–63,
465

Theodore of Mopsuestia, 102n66,
168–70, 299n19

theophany, 122

theological virtues, 494, 503–5

Thirty-Nine Articles of the Church
of England, 306–7

Thomas Aquinas. See Aquinas

Thurian, Max, 107n85

Tirot, Paul, 473n62, 476n70, 477n71

Tolkien, J.R.R., 510, 569

transsignification, 314–20

transubstantiation, xxx–xxxi, 74, 183
  accidents of bread and wine
    remain, 268–73
  Aquinas on, 259–91
  change in Christ, does not cause,
    273, 287–88n59, 290–91
  creation, comparison with, 276–78
  development of the doctrine of,
    238–39, 243–44, 249–50, 257,
    259
  effected by divine omnipotence,
    268, 274–77
  effected by the power of the Holy
    Spirit, 151, 168, 174–75, 208–10,
    211n86, 243n31, 251, 337–38,
    426, 476
  effected by the words of Christ,
    204, 218n102, 226–27, 414
  implicit in the Fathers, 129, 139,
    140–41, 167
  Luther on, 293–300
  miraculous, 268–69, 275–77
  mystery of, 60, 273–76, 282, 290
  natural change, comparison with,
    276–78
  Paul VI on, 317–19
  presence of Christ whole and
    entire, 79, 244, 250–52, 273n32,
    279–88, 310, 312, 316, 318, 357,
    580
  rejection of, 241, 293–97, 298n18,
    300, 303, 306–7, 313, 589
  sacramental mode, Christ present
    in, 278–91
  and sacrifice of the Mass, 336, 351,

362–63, 366, 389–90, 459, 474,
    476, 479
  substance and accidents, distinc-
    tion of, 259–61
  substantial conversion, 261–68
  Trent, Council of, on, 308–12
  twentieth-century challenges to,
    314–20, 589

Treanor, Oliver, 337n36, 556n41

Trinitarian dimension of the Eucharist, 337–39, 386, 438, 511–16,
  528, 556, 594

tree of life, 67–68, 75, 134, 235

Trent, Council of
  on the Church's power with regard
    to the sacraments, 199, 215n95,
    219n105
  on the consecration, 207
  on Communion, 529, 537, 541–42,
    561, 566–67, 572, 574–76
  on concomitance, 284–85, 309–10
  on Eucharistic adoration, 311–12
  on the priesthood, 226
  on the real substantial presence,
    273–74, 308–12, 340n48
  on the sacrifice of the Mass, 37n62,
    353–55, 361–63, 388, 451–52,
    454, 458–59, 471n52, 479
  on transubstantiation, 308–9, 312,
    317

typology prefiguring the Eucharist,
  39–69, 95, 99, 590

U

ubiquitism, 297–99, 301n25, 302–3,
  319

unbloody sacrifice, 157, 170, 336, 346,
  352–53, 355–56, 360n103, 361,
  363, 379n12, 388, 451, 458

unleavened bread, 50–51, 56n39, 66,
66n57, 83–84, 86, 86n21, 87,
90n29, 99, 100, 100n60, 101,
105, 118, 195–96, 196n39
unworthy Communion, 118, 534–43,
563n10

V

Vaillancourt, Mark G., 76n5, 234n3,
236nn9–11, 239n19, 241n28,
242n30, 244n32, 244nn32–33,
244nn35–36, 245n38, 246n39,
246n41, 247n42, 248n45,
249n46, 251nn52–53, 252nn54–
55, 255n64, 258, 263n7, 270n23,
274n34, 278n40, 280n42,
341n49
Van Zeller, Hubert, 332n26
Vázquez, Gabriel, 359
Viaticum, 61n46, 540, 573, 578
Victim, Christ as, xxxi, 7, 8, 14, 19,
30n52, 31, 37, 50, 58, 105, 107–8,
114, 157, 170, 173, 184, 251, 336,
352, 365, 370–71, 379n12, 384,
398, 403, 414, 460, 465, 489,
587–88, 594
identical with the Priest, xxvii,
55, 160–61, 163, 165, 334, 336,
344n57, 346n66
co-offered by the faithful, 414–29,
436, 448, 466–68
one in every Mass and on Calvary,
251, 340, 343, 345–48, 349n71,
352–56, 359–63, 365n116,
366–68, 388–91, 459, 476–77,
500
reception of in Communion, 500,
509, 534n5, 535
Vonier, Anscar, 361
Vyner, Owen, 433n46

W

Washburn, Christian, 460n23
Welch, Lawrence, 172n112
Westminster Confession, 305,
306n39, 311n56
White, Thomas J., 495n24
William of Champeaux, 252–53
Williamson, Peter, 123n118
Willis, G. G., 223n116, 224n122
Wilson, Stephen, 221n110
wine,
fittingness for the Eucharist, 9,
24–25, 62, 64–66, 75, 76n5,
107n84, 192–94, 196n42,
523n85, 524–25
mixed with water, 136, 147–49,
196–98
at Passover, 87, 105–6
reception under species of, 571n28,
574–77
sign of ecclesial unity, 525–26
sign of spiritual inebriation,
193–94, 509
Winkler, Gabrielle, 221n110
words of institution, 105n76, 106–17,
123, 128, 141, 144, 148, 153, 162,
167, 172, 203–18, 246, 263n7,
302, 305, 377n8, 383, 385. *See*
institution narrative
Wycliffe, John, 257, 294, 295n7, 375
Wyschogrod, Michael, 12

Y

Yarnold, Edward, 150n61, 211–
12n86, 222n113, 224n119
Yerkes, Royden Keith, 40n20, 328n17,
385n31
Yom Kippur, 49, 51. *See* Day of
Atonement

Z

zebach tôdâ, 54, 123

Zheltov, Michael, 145n44, 202n60,
     203n63, 206n71, 211n83

Zwingli, Huldrych, 78, 241, 296–305,
     314, 351, 388

Scripture Index

Genesis

1, 86

1:1–2:4, 436

1:3–5, 436

1:11, 175

3:22–24, 67

4:3–5, 46

8:20–21, 47

12:1, 12

14:17–20, 62

15:17, 114n105

22:8, 48

22:14, 48

22:16–18, 47n16

49:26, 501, 588n2

Exodus

10:25, 109

12, 56n39

12:1–14, 45n9, 46n11

12:1–28, 56

12:3–15, 87

12:6, 104n74

12:8, 56n39

12:14, 109

12:15–19, 195

12:18, 90n29

12:43–51, 56

15:23–25, 154n73

16:4–35, 58

19:5–6, 407

19:6, 409, 409n4

20:24, 109n91

24:5–8, 57n42, 114n106

24:8, 57, 114, 382

24:16–17, 40n2

25:8, 41

25:21–22, 42

25:30, 63

29:12, 111n99

29:35–41, 109

29:40, 63

29:42–46, 42

35–37, 600n35

40:34–38, 42

49:26, 501

Leviticus

1–7, 51

2:2, 109n91, 110n93

2:9, 110n93

2:16, 110n93

3:2, 50n25

3:17, 77n8

4:7, 111n99

4:18, 111n99

4:25, 111n99

4:30, 111n99

4:34, 111n99

5:12, 110n93

7:12–15, 123n115

7:15–16, 50n26

7:26–27, 77n8

9:9, 111n99

9:22, 109n89

10:12–14, 108n87

10:14, 108

16, 51n30

16:11, 349n71

16:21–22, 52

16:24, 109

17:11, 49

17:11–12, 328n17

23, 51

23:8, 101

23:25, 109

24:5–9, 63, 385n30

24:7, 109n91

24:16–17, 40n2

Numbers

6:24–27, 54n35

9:10, 100

15:5–7, 64n50

15:11–14, 109n89

18:1–8, 561n2

18:12, 108

28:4–7, 63, 64n50

28:9, 51n28

28:11, 51

28:19–24, 51n29

28–29, 51

35:34, 42

Deuteronomy

7:6, 12

4:7, 43, 592

8:3, 60

8:16, 60n43

12:10–14, 53n32

12:26–27, 50n26, 86n22, 111n99

16:2–3, 101

16:5–6, 53n32

16:5–7, 86n23

17:13, 103

18:15–19, 72n2

33:10, 49n19

Judges

13:16, 109n89

1 Samuel

15:22, 55n38

21:4–6, 64, 385n30

1 Kings

6:19–28, 600n35

8:10–13, 40n3, 43n5,

13, 408n3

2 Kings

5:17, 109n89

2 Chronicles

3:8–14, 600n35

7:1–2, 43

7:5, 52

Psalms

22:5, 218n102

31:10, 30n52

33, 160

34:8, 61, 68

40:4–6, 55n38

42:1–2, 68

50, 55n38

50:19, 325n8, 409n5

51:17, 55n38

67:34, 440n63

78:25, 61

83:3, 324n4

103:5, 508

103:15, 196n42

110:4, 62

115–118, 106
116, 106
116:12–13, xxvii, 455
116:12–17, 106
116:13, 66
118, 106
134:6, 174
148:5, 155

Song of Songs
5:1, 509

Wisdom
1:13–14, 358n98
16:20, 39n1
16:20–21, 60

Sirach
24:8, 43n6
35:6–7, 110n93
38:11, 110n93
45:16, 110

Isaiah
1:11, 55n38
1:11–15, 408
6:6, 504
11:2–3, 506
25:6–7, 76n5
25:6–8, 75
42:6, 115n108, 116
49:8–9, 116
53:7, 46n10
53:10, 107
53:11–12, 112, 112n101
53:12, 107n85
55:1–3, 68
64:1, 68

Jeremiah
2:27, 448n79
31:31–33, 115

Ezekiel
16:8–14, 22n34
37, 76, 78
37:12–14, 76, 78
43:25, 109n89
44:15, 49n39
44:23, 49n39

Hosea
2:19–20, 22

Amos
5:21, 55n38

Zechariah
3:8, 440n61
6:12, 440n63
9:9–12, 115

Malachi
1:10–14, 130
1:11, 53n33, 130, 139, 160, 339, 391,
    401, 451, 605
4:2, 440n61

Matthew
5:23–24, 130n2
6:9, 441n64
8:11, 399
9:15, 23
11:30, 549
12:1–6, 64
12:3–6, 385n30
18:3–5, 570
18:20, 40n3

20:28, 107

22:8–9, 23

24:27, 440, 440n63

24:28, 13

26:17, 86n21, 90n29, 100, 195, 537

26:17–19, 83, 86n20

26:20–23, 84

26:23, 91

26:26, 117, 138, 143, 146, 150, 155,
     156, 157, 160, 168, 168n103,
     175, 224n118, 240, 246, 262,
     262n6, 263, 264n11, 267, 268,
     275, 284, 296, 298n18, 300

26:26–30, 85

26:27, 172, 172n112

26:27–28, 111n98

26:28, 9n11, 19, 108n108, 112,
     112n101, 113n102, 114,
     123, 138, 146, 150, 157, 168,
     168n103, 175, 224n118, 246,
     284, 386, 398, 490, 500, 587

26:29, 85, 196, 196n42

26:30, 85, 106n81

28:19, 191

Mark

2:19, 151n63

2:25–26, 64n52

4:25, 503

10:2–12, 550

10:13–16, 570

14:12, 86, 86n20, 90n29, 98, 100,
     105n75, 195

14:12–16, 83–84

14:13–17, 88

14:14, 86n20

14:16, 86n20

14:17, 84

14:20, 91

14:22, 117, 138, 143, 146, 150,
     155, 156, 157, 160, 168, 175,
     224n118, 240, 246, 262, 262n6,
     263, 264n11, 267, 268, 275, 284,
     296, 298n18, 300

14:24, 108n88, 111n98, 112n101,
     114, 123, 138, 146, 150, 157,
     168, 175, 224n118, 246, 284

14:25, 85

14:26, 106n81

Luke

1:34–35, 175

1:45, 29n51

1:78, 440n61

2:22, 30

2:34–35, 30

6:1–5, 64n52

11:3, 563

12:1, 66n57

12:41, 112n101

13:9, 399

22:6, 105n75

22:7, 86n20, 86n21, 90n29, 195

22:7–8, 98

22:7–13, 84

22:8, 86n20

22:11, 86n20

22:13, 86n20

22:15, 86n20, 99, 104, 105n75, 605

22:17, 130n5

22:19, 106–108, 117, 138, 143, 150,
     155, 156, 157, 160, 168, 175,
     224n118, 207, 240, 246, 262,
     262n6, 263, 264n11, 267, 268,
     275, 296, 298n18, 300, 499, 588

22:19–20, 28n46, 86, 105n76, 172,
     605

22:20, 9, 36, 105n76, 108n88,
     111n97, 113–115, 138, 150, 157,

168, 175, 224n118, 246, 381, 398,

22:39, 86

24:29, 120

24:30–31, 120

24:35, 120

John

1:14, 43, 43n6

1:16, 21

1:17, 10n12, 499

1:29, 98

2:19–21, 44

3, 73

3:13, 74

3:16, 19, 45

3:29, 22

4, 73

4:10–14, 23

4:15, 73

6, xxx, 71–79

6:4, 71

6:14–15, 72

6:26–27, 72

6:28–29, 73

6:31, 73

6:32–35, 73

6:35, 37, 371

6:39–40, 74

6:41–53, 504n38, 532

6:42, 74

6:46, 75

6:48, 37, 371

6:48–51, 59, 75

6:50, 508

6:50–51, 67

6:51, 76, 108, 161, 171, 183, 365n117, 371, 398, 403

6:53, 81, 82n16, 171, 180n7

6:53–57, 77

6:54, 4n2, 77, 116, 522, 563n10

6:55, 77, 180n7, 193

6:55–56, 153

6:56, 156, 501, 524n92

6:56–57, 512

6:57, 13, 513

6:58, 499

6:62–63, 78

6:63, 78–81

6:68, 80

10:15, 108n88, 398

10:17–18, 108n88, 398

11:47–53, 173n114

11:52, 112n101

13, 91

13:1, xxix, 20, 28n46, 90n29, 92, 92n35, 334

13:21–30, 84, 91, 91n32

13:23, 91

13:25, 91, 596

13:26, 91

13:34, 520

14–16, 512

14:6, 501

14:15–17, 512

14:20, 512

14:23, 512

14:26, 496n27

15:4, 513

15:13, xxix

15:14, 513

17:21, 517

17:21–23, 520

18:28, 92, 95n46, 96, 99, 100n61, 101, 101n63

19:14, 92, 101, 102, 102n67, 102n68

19:25–26, 422

19:31, 102, 102n68

19:34, 180n7, 350, 500, 606

19:42, 102

Acts

1:11, 435, 440n62
2:42, 121
2:42–46, 120
2:46, 561
3:13–26, 132n11
4:27–30, 132n11
10:4, 110
12:12, 121
20:7–8, 121, 436n52
20:35, 387

Romans

1:18–32, 410n6
5:5, 496n26
5:12, 112n101
5:15, 112n101
6:3, 391n43
6:9, 341
8:15, 515n67
8:29, 413
8:32, 48
12:1, 340, 410n6, 410–12, 418, 424, 427n41
12:1–2, 410n6

1 Corinthians

4:1, 199
5:6–8, 66n57, 118–119
5:7, 196
6:13–20, 44
10:2, 527
10:16, 163
10:16–21, 118–119
10:17, 8, 193, 518
10:18, 487
10:31, 413
11, 131, 163, 401n66
11:23, 353, 401
11:23–25, 86

11:23–32, 117–18
11:23–24, 117
11:24, 108, 138, 143, 146, 150, 155–157, 160, 162, 167, 168, 172, 175, 224n118, 240, 246, 262, 262n6, 263, 264n11, 267, 268, 275, 296, 298n18, 300
11:24–25, 207
11:25, 111n97, 114, 115, 175, 381
11:26, 118, 156, 175, 383
11:26–30, 534
11:27, 563n10
11:27–29, 547
11:27–31, 118
11:28, 537, 542
11:29, 401n65, 541, 563n10, 566
16:1–2, 121, 436n52
16:22, 399, 401n65

2 Corinthians

5:14, 505
5:14–15, 112n101
5:17, 435
5:20, 537
11:2, 23

Galatians

2:19–20, 429
2:20, 58, 114, 333, 505, 512
3:16, 591
5:6, 536
5:22–23, 519

Ephesians

1:7, 180n7
5:2, 45, 343
5:25–27, 7
5:26, 191
5:32, 33, 36

Philippians

2:4–8, 13
2:5, 425n38
2:8, 398
3:12, 412
4:18, 410

Colossians

1:15, 436
1:18, 436
2:17, 160
3:3, 503

1 Thessalonians

4:13–17, 435

Titus

2:11, 112n101
3:5, 4n2

Hebrews

4:12, 174
4:15, 334
5:1, 50n27, 329n20, 332, 406
7, 62
7:25, 372
8–10, 169
9:2–7, 41
9:7, 52
9:8, 347
9:11–12, 372n130
9:15, 523n85
9:20, 123n113
9:22, 331n24, 328n16
9:24–26, 165, 340
9:25, 388
9:26, 388
9:28, 123
10, 345
10:1, 160, 169n106, 236n8, 347

10:1–4, 331
10:1–7, 55
10:10, 123n113
10:12, 372n130
10:14, 349n71, 367
10:29, 123
11:1, 16
12, 126
12:18–28, 122
13:7–21, 123
13:8, 389
13:10, 123
13:15, 123
13:15–16, 409
13:20, 123

1 Peter

1:18–20, 57
2:4–5, 426
2:5, 409n5, 424, 427
2:9, 409, 426
3:20–21, 527

2 Peter

1:4, 20, 26n44, 61n44, 151, 184, 502,
    536

1 John

2:2, 112n101

Revelation

1:5–6, 409
2:7, 67n59
4, 124
4:1–2, 124
4:6–11, 125
4–5, 123–127
5:6–10, 126
5:6–14, 125
5:9–10, 409

5:11–14, 126
7:10, 519
17:15, 197n46, 198
19:1–9, 126
21:2, 23
21:5, 435
22:2, 67n59
22:20, 399